Planning Activities for Child Care

A Curriculum Guide For Early Childhood Education

by

Caroline Spang Rosser

Director
Workshop on Wheels
Central Missouri State University
Warrensburg, Missouri

Publisher
THE GOODHEART-WILLCOX COMPANY, INC.
Tinley Park, Illinois

Library of Congress Catalog Card Number 2001032611

International Standard Book Number 1-56637-846-X

1 2 3 4 5 6 7 8 9 10   01   06 05 04 03 02 01

Library of Congress Cataloging-in-Publication Data

Rosser, Caroline Spang.
Planning activities for child care: a curriculum guide for early childhood education/by Caroline Spang Rosser.
    p. cm.
  Includes bibliographical references and index.
  ISBN 1-56637-846-X
    1. Early childhood education—United States—Curricula.
2. Curriculum planning—United States. 3. Child development—United States. I. Title.
LB1139.25R67   2001
372.19'0973—dc21   2001032611

Credits

Reviewers:

Janie Hott Humphries, Ed.D.
Coordinator of Early Childhood Education
College of Human Ecology
Louisiana Tech University
Ruston, Louisiana

Penny S. Seeber
Director
Greenville Technical College Child
    Development Center
Greenville, South Carolina

Illustrator:

Paulette Hackman Wilkinson
Commercial Artist and Interior Designer
Mexico, Missouri

Cover Images:

©2001 Art Rosser

About the Author

Caroline Spang Rosser has 30 years' experience in the early childhood/child care field. Currently, she is director of the Central Missouri State University Workshop on Wheels Child Care Resource and Referral, which offers instructional workshops, on-site technical assistance for child care providers, and referrals to parents seeking child care. This program has been awarded the Missouri Outstanding Postsecondary Vocational Program. In connection with her work at Workshop on Wheels, Caroline and her staff provide over 350 child care in-service training workshops each year. She teaches child care and child development courses for Central Missouri State University's extended campus, writes grants to fund child care in-service training, and edits a monthly child care newsletter for 3,400 child care providers. She has written several articles and given numerous presentations on child care curriculum and child care management.

Caroline is a member of the National and Missouri Associations for the Education of Young Children, Missouri Association for School-Age Care, the American and Missouri Associations for Career and Technical Education, Missouri Family and Consumer Sciences Association, and Phi Delta Kappa. She has served the Missouri Board for Accreditation of Early Childhood Programs as treasurer, vice president, and president. Caroline was awarded the Missouri Department of Elementary and Secondary Education 2001 Distinguished Service Award in Early Childhood. *Planning Activities for Child Care: A Curriculum Guide for Early Childhood Education* was awarded the Early Childhood News Directors' Award in 1996.

ACKNOWLEDGMENTS

Many individuals have contributed to the development of *Planning Activities for Child Care: A Curriculum Guide for Early Childhood Education.* I am indebted to Dr. Cynthia Arendt, Director, Family and Consumer Sciences, Missouri Department of Elementary and Secondary Education; and to the Department of Human Environmental Sciences, Central Missouri State University, for their joint support and encouragement.

This curriculum guide was developed to meet the needs of the providers of home- and center-based child care. These needs were identified through a needs-assessment questionnaire unitized by Central Missouri State's Workshop on Wheels Child Care Resource and Referral. A special thanks is extended to all the child care providers and directors who took the time to share their suggestions.

The following consultants provided guidance and instructional expertise in developing and testing this material:

Pegi Stamps
Education Specialist
KCMC Child Development Corporation
Kansas City, Missouri

Dr. Sherri Griffin
Professor, Early Childhood Education
Central Methodist College
Fayette, Missouri

Clare Terry
Research Associate, Macomb Projects
Western Illinois University
Macomb, Illinois

Donna Conn
Director, KIDS Program
Dickinson, North Dakota

The input of the Workshop on Wheels Advisory Council was invaluable and appreciated more than words can express. The members of the Advisory Council included

Janice Ksara
Missouri Central Region Child Care
Licensing Supervisor
Springfield, Missouri

Janet Richter
Warrensburg, Missouri

Sandra Slaughter
Director
Pinocchio Child Care Center
Camdenton, Missouri

Suggestions from the following people were extremely helpful in planning the curriculum units: Marilyn Schlosser, Coordinator, Workshop on Wheels, Southeast Missouri State University, Cape Girardeau; Jeanne Edwards, Director, Education on Wheels, St. Louis Community College at Florissant Valley; Dr. Peggy Miller, Professor, Early Childhood, Northwest Missouri State University, Maryville; and Debbie Landgraf and Linda Gosche, Center for Child Studies, Southeast Missouri State University, Cape Girardeau.

Sally McCray Hackman and Paulette Hackman Wilkinson helped me with every phase of this project and to them I owe my sanity. A special thanks goes to April Hall, who has helped a great deal with the revision of this book.

Last, but not least, a special thanks to my husband, Art, who has supported and encouraged me to complete this project with the hope that all children in child care facilities will have happy days filled with many different and interesting learning experiences; and to Kirsten and Art who, years ago, enjoyed many of these activities. I'd like to add a special thanks for Sophie Grace, our new granddaughter, who is already helping us read her baby books. I'm sure she will enjoy many of these activities very soon.

CONTENTS

INTRODUCTION
CONTENTS

INTRODUCTION

You have a very important position–caring for children! It can be rewarding, exciting, fun, and challenging. However, it can also be tiring, frustrating, and stressful. To become a successful child care provider, you must thoroughly understand the following three areas:

1. The development of young children.
2. Early childhood curriculum.
3. Planning for the needs of young children.

THE DEVELOPMENT OF YOUNG CHILDREN

To understand the development of young children, you need to observe and become aware of most children's abilities at two, three, four, or five years of age; realize how most children grow and develop in a gradual, step-by-step manner; and see how different each child is from other children the same age.

Development refers to the gradual changes that take place as the result of growth, and it needs to be considered as you plan for the children in your care. Development includes four areas:

- Small and Large Muscle Development.
- Social-Emotional Development.
- Language Development.
- Cognitive (Thinking) Development.

Small muscle (fine motor) development incorporates the hand and finger skills involved in painting, cutting with scissors, and drawing with crayons and markers. Large muscle development involves the development of skills such as running, pedaling a tricycle, lifting blocks, and pushing a wagon.

Social-emotional development includes the skills children develop to help them feel good about themselves and to interact with others. Social skills, such as dressing themselves, toileting, and sharing with others, also fit into this category.

Language development involves communication and is very important in the social development of children. It incorporates expressive language (what is said to others) and receptive language (what is heard and understood).

Cognitive (thinking) development involves the growth of intellectual skills, such as language, imagination, mathematical concepts, and problem-solving. Skills in this area include knowing the difference between large and small; counting; one-to-one correspondence; matching colors; and listening to stories.

Each child is unique and develops at a different rate. However, children achieve developmental tasks in a certain order. For example, children generally grow from the head down (cephalocaudal development). When you observe infants and toddlers, you will see that they first gain control of their head (lift it off a shoulder); then their arms (lifting themselves off the bed); and finally their legs (creeping around the coffee table). Children also develop from the center of the body (spinal cord) outwards (proximodistal development). You will observe that children's arms and legs develop before their hands and feet.

As you plan for children, you need to keep this development in mind. Large muscle activities are needed before small muscle activities, because large muscle growth, necessary for such skills as running, hopping, and throwing, is needed before small muscle skills, such as drawing, cutting, and writing, can be achieved successfully.

Developmental Characteristics of Two-Year-Olds

Two-year-old children tend to be very busy and learn best through their senses: sight, hearing, touch, taste, and smell. They are very curious and will explore almost everything. They are very daring and may frighten you with their exploratory natures.

Therefore, they need constant supervision. Their attention spans are very short–two to five minutes–unless something really interests them. Then they may want to be involved for longer periods of time.

Two-year-olds like activities that involve running, jumping, and climbing, which help develop their large muscles. Give them plenty of opportunities to perform these activities. They also should be given opportunities to develop eye-hand coordination and small muscle skills through activities such as using crayons, markers, and paint, tearing paper, and using scissors. At this point, they will begin to choose right- or left-handedness.

Two-year-olds are affectionate and offer hugs and kisses. They also enjoy parallel play (playing beside other children but not with them). They may have difficulty leaving their families.

Two-year-olds frequently use the word "no." They may say no to questions such as "Would you like an ice cream cone?" as they jump up and down waiting for you to scoop one for them. You can save a great deal of aggravation by phrasing your comments as statements, so that "no" is not an alternative. For example, say "It is time for lunch." instead of asking if they are ready for lunch.

The two-year-olds' language involves joining two to three words together in a phrase. They frequently ask questions beginning with "what" or "where." Two-year-olds often understand many more words (receptive language) than they can speak (expressive language) and as a result they may become frustrated when they are not understood. Stuttering may occur between 2 1/2 and 3 1/2 years of age, because the child's mind works faster than his or her tongue. Stuttering may cause you anxiety. However, children usually out-grow it as they develop.

Two-year-olds enjoy dramatic play. Give them opportunities to role-play adult roles, such as mommy, daddy, child care provider, and community helpers.

Developmental Characteristics of Three-Year-Olds

Three-year-olds are able to pedal tricycles, have more control than two-year-olds when running and jumping, and hop on one foot. They may enjoy kicking balls and climbing on playground equipment. They can also control crayons and markers better than two-year-olds and make horizontal, vertical, and circular marks. They are becoming accomplished at using scissors.

Three-year-olds are becoming more independent than two-year-olds and are generally friendly, affectionate, and eager to please. They are more involved in associative play (playing with other children but choosing what they want to do). Three-year-olds often have "best" friends whom they hold hands with as they walk. However, that "best" friend may fall out of favor twenty minutes later. Three-year-olds like to help with chores especially if the chores involve using water.

Three-year-olds enjoy listening to age-appropriate stories and like to look at the same books over and over again. However, their attention spans are still quite short. They talk in sentences of three or more words. Strangers may be able to understand their language, although there may still be some speaking errors. Their vocabulary has grown to 900-1,000 words. Three-year-olds can usually follow two to three related directions.

Three-year-olds enjoy fingerplays and singing simple songs. They can count to three and match the corresponding number of objects. They can match six colors. They also enjoy dramatic play and get more involved in role-playing. They like to imagine and may have an imaginary friend.

Developmental Characteristics of Four-Year-Olds

Four-year-olds can walk up and down stairs alternating feet, hop on one foot, and ride tricycles while negotiating curves and avoiding obstacles. They can use scissors to cut on a curved line. They can copy circles and squares and draw people with five body parts. They can put together large, multiple-piece puzzles.

Four-year-olds are enthusiastic, noisy, and outgoing and are developing independence. Four-year-olds often "bend" the truth, make up stories, and tattle. They are becoming more aware of authority than younger children and are beginning to develop a conscience. Making mistakes is very difficult for them. They have special friends and are becoming involved in cooperative play (play that is planned and organized by a group of children).

Four-year-olds may tend to try your patience with silly talk and jokes. They often resort to profanity when frustrated. They may be interested in printing their names and copying letters they have seen in their environments. You should help them on an individual basis. Four-year-olds should not be expected to do "writing" in a group setting.

Four-year-olds enjoy dramatic play and become very involved in establishing roles for one another. They enjoy dressing up and will often incorporate dramatic play and building with blocks.

Developmental Characteristics of Five-Year-Olds

Five-year-old children enjoy their lives, homes, families, and communities. They are happy, serene, and more secure than younger children. They enjoy where they are and what they are doing. They consider their primary caregivers–their mothers, fathers, or guardians–the center of their worlds, and they quote their teachers as absolute authorities. Five-year-olds like to please adults. They play reasonably well with other children and have developed a sense of fairness. When they are angry, they are beginning to express themselves verbally, rather than physically.

Five-year-olds can walk forward, backward, and sideways on balance beams. They enjoy climbing fences and trees. Five-year-olds can generally descend stairs, while alternating their feet. They can catch a ball with both hands. They enjoy jumping rope. Five-year-olds generally have chosen handedness. However, they may still reverse numbers and letters when writing. Tying shoelaces is a challenge.

Five-year-olds love to be read to and like new words. They use descriptive language when telling stories and enjoy telling original stories. They ask many questions and never seem to stop talking. They are becoming more interested in time and often know what happens when the hands of the clock are in certain positions. They can rote count from one to twenty. Five-year-olds are beginning to understand the concepts of positions such as first, middle, and last. They can recognize their names and many can write their first names. Their attention span is expanding but is still quite short. They may have difficulty distinguishing between reality and fantasy.

As you work with two-, three-, four-, and five-year-olds, you must keep in mind that the developmental characteristics discussed are only averages. These "averages" have been established by observing millions of children. Some children achieve these developmental tasks at an early age, while others achieve them at a later age. Each child has his or her own time clock, so you must be aware of "individual" differences in development, as well as "chronological" (age) differences. You must plan for these differences when planning the activities for the children in the group.

The following chart lists the developmental skills the "average" child will have at two, three, four, and five years of age. It also suggests activities that you might use to enhance that skill. Remember to consider the "individual abilities" of each child as you plan.

THE DEVELOPMENT AND GUIDANCE OF YOUNG CHILDREN

TWO-YEAR-OLDS

Small and Large Muscle Development

Because two-year-olds usually can:

- Run forward well.

- Walk on tiptoe.

- Jump in place, using both feet.

Provide these activities:

- Have the children run to the swings.
- Have the children run from the playground to the building.

- Show the children a picture of a ballet dancer and let each pretend to be one, dancing on his or her tiptoes.
- Have the children pretend to be birds on a limb, walking on their tiptoes.

- Put masking tape on the floor in the shape of a box and have the children jump into the box.
- Have the children jump to the sandbox.

- Snip with scissors.

- Tear pieces of paper.
- Have the children pick up cotton balls with ice tongs or meat tongs.
- Put ten spring clamp clothespins in a pan. Have the children pinch them open and attach them to the edge of the pan.
- Have the children roll playdough into hot dog shapes and snip them into pieces.
- Give the children long strips of paper to cut into tiny pieces.

Social-Emotional Development

Because two-year-olds usually can:

- Play near other children.

- Play house.

- Participate in simple group activities.

- Identify gender (boy/girl)

Provide these activities:

- Set up stacking toys and puzzles, near the children to encourage play.
- Put two to three push/pull toys on the pavement near the children.

- Place pots and pans on the play range for the children.
- Provide a broom for the children.
- Let the children help you wash off the tables.

- Sing songs, such as "Mary Had a Little Lamb," with the children.

- Have all the boys hop to the table.
- Have all the girls run to the slide.

Language Development

Because two-year-olds usually can:

- Join vocabulary together in two-word phrases.

- Enjoy listening to stories and request them to be repeated.

Provide these activities:

- Give the children opportunities to talk many times during the day.
- Ask the children open-ended questions that begin with "Who," "What," "Why," "Where," and "How."
- Share ideas with the children at lunchtime.

- Read stories to the children individually and in groups.
- Tape-record a story for the children to listen to during self-selected times.
- Place felt board figures on a shelf so the children can repeat a story for a friend.
- Write a story with illustrations on a large sheet of newsprint, so the children can see them and retell the story.

Cognitive (Thinking) Development

Because two-year-olds usually can:

- Stack rings on pegs in order of size.

- Have a limited attention span.

- Imitate adult actions.

Provide these activities:

- Place stacking toys where the children can use them.
- Give the children different size boxes that will stack inside one another.

- Read simple, two- to five-minute time span stories to the children.
- Repeat fingerplays and poetry with children.

- Put hats, purses, briefcases, and shoes in the dramatic play area, so the children can pretend.
- Place mirrors where children can see themselves.

THREE-YEAR-OLDS

Small and Large Muscle Development

Because three-year-olds usually can:

- Balance on one foot.

- Hop on one foot.

- Broad jump.

- Copy circles, vertical lines, and crosses.

Provide these activities:

- Show the children a picture of a flamingo. Have the children stand on one foot.
- Put a flat rock on the floor and tell the children to pretend that it is in the middle of a pond. Then, tell them to stand on it on one foot. If they lose their balance, have them pretend that their feet will get wet.

- Place carpet squares on the floor between two lines of tape. Have the children pretend that the area between the tape is a river as they hop across it on one foot.
- Have the children hop on one foot on the sidewalk while avoiding the cracks. Then have them switch feet and hop on the other foot.
- Have the children pretend they are frogs hopping after each other on the playground.

- Place two ropes on the ground, and have the children broad jump from one rope to the other or from one hoop into another. Widen the gap between the ropes as they progress.
- Play red rover. Call the children to jump from one side of the room to the other.

- Fill a box lid with two inches of cornmeal and let the children make circles, vertical lines, and crosses.
- Have the children finger-paint in a cookie sheet or on waxed paper with two tablespoons of chocolate pudding.
- Put shaving cream on a table and let the children make big circles and lines in the shaving cream.

- Cut with scissors

- Have the children pick up cotton balls with tweezers.
- Let the children cut fringe on a paper bag vest.
- Give the children opportunities to cut paper streamers.

Social-Emotional Development

Because three-year-olds usually can:

- Join in play with others and begin to interact.

- Dress themselves.

- Enjoy dramatic play.

- Make choices.

- Enjoy helping.

Provide these activities:

- Set up the dramatic play area with four places at the table for children to play.
- Set up chairs for the children to play car, train, or bus. Put a steering wheel in front of one chair.

- Put dress-up clothes with buttons, zippers, and buckles in the play area, so the children can practice.
- Place zipper, button, and snap boards in the manipulatives area for the children to use.

- Put different hats and dress-up clothes in the dramatic play area for the children to use.
- Place small hoes, rakes, shovels, buckets, pots, and plastic flowers in the sandbox for the children to manipulate.
- Empty food containers for shopping and food preparation.
- Set up chairs in rows for the children to play bus or train. Put a steering wheel in front of one chair.

- Set up the room with several learning centers, so the children can make activity choices.
- Let children choose food at snacktime (cheese or peanut butter crackers, a banana, or an apple).

- Show the children how to clean up after snacktime (throw napkins in the trash, place cups on a tray).
- Let the children set the table and wash the table after snacktime.
- Make a game out of clean-up time. Sing "Hector is a helper" or "Sandy is a helper" as you work.

Language Development

Because three-year-olds usually can:

- Name pictures.

Provide these activities:

- Place pictures based on the theme around the room at the children's eye level. Talk with the children about the pictures.
- Talk about the pictures in books with one or two children.

- Understand 900-1,000 words.

- Talk about new words with the children. Use pictures if you think the vocabulary is new to the children. For example, wolf, giraffe, ostrich might be new words.
- Encourage the children to demonstrate "under" the table and "beside" the table with their bodies. Have them put their hands on "top" of their heads and "under" their bottoms or "beside" their feet.

- Follow directions.

- Have the children follow the directions, "Crawl under the table" or "Walk around the chair."

- Sing simple songs.

- Sing songs such as "Old King Cole," "Old MacDonald," and "The Farmer in the Dell," several times a day.
- Help the children make up songs of their own.
- Use musical recordings.

- Carry out a series of two to three related directions.

- Several times a day give the children short, specific directions to follow. For example, "Put your napkin in the trash and your glass on the tray" or "Put the truck on the shelf and come to the circle."
- Play Simon says with the children. Simon says, "Put your hand on your head."

- Talk in sentences of three or more words.

- Give the children opportunities to talk about what they did at home, with whom they play, and about their pets.
- Ask the children open-ended questions that begin with "Who," "What," "Why," "Where," "When," and "How" to help them expand their language.
- Listen to the children and enjoy their conversations.
- Write down what they say about their drawings if they want you to.

Cognitive (Thinking) Development

Because three-year-olds usually can:

- Count up to three and choose three objects.

Provide these activities:

- Have the children choose three animal cookies at snacktime.
- Have the children place napkins, cups, and plates on the table for each child.
- Let the children choose three flowers to pick from the garden.

- Recognize and match four to six colors. Emphasize red, yellow, blue, and green and follow with purple, brown, black, and orange.

- Divide a pizza round cardboard into six pie-shaped pieces and color each a different color. Have the children match six colored clothespins to the appropriate colored piece on the pizza round.
- Put out six colored boxes and matching beanbags. Have the children throw the beanbags into the appropriate boxes (yellow beanbag/yellow box).
- Put eight to ten different-colored objects in a bag. Let the children pull them out and name the color.

- Enjoy repetitive stories.

- Read stories such as *Brown Bear, Brown Bear, What Do You See?* by B. Martin Jr. or sing songs such as "Wheels on the Bus."

FOUR-YEAR-OLDS

Small and Large Muscle Development

Because four-year-olds usually can:

- Hop on one foot.

Provide these activities:

- Draw a hopscotch square on the sidewalk for the children. Let them make up their own rules.
- Ask the children to hop to the snack table or to the playground. Then have them switch feet and hop back on the other foot.
- Lay color squares on the floor. Have the children throw a beanbag to a color square and hop to it, or have them choose a color card and hop to that color square.

- Copy circles, squares, and crosses.

- Put a bucket upside down in the sandbox to make a circle shape. Talk with the children about the shape. Let the children make large shapes in the sand with a wooden dowel rod.
- Dampen the sand and discuss the differences between wet and dry sand as the children draw shapes in the sand. Have square and round containers for the children to use in the sand.

- Cut on a line.

- Draw lines on the bottom of paper bag vests for the children to cut fringe.
- Have each child draw a picture and cut it out.
- Draw circles around catalog pictures with a black marker and let the children cut around the circles.

- Walk up stairs alone, alternating feet.

- Use a portable step unit in an obstacle course or regularly go up and down stairs.
- Encourage the children to play on the climbing equipment.

Social-Emotional Development

Because four-year-olds usually can:

- Button clothing.

Provide these activities:

- Place dress-up clothes with buttons in the dramatic play area for the children to use.
- Choose doll clothes that button for the children to use.

- Play interactive games.

- Play games, such as "Duck, Duck, Goose" or "The Farmer in the Dell," with groups of children.

- Engage in cooperative play.

- Add materials, such as trucks, people, and animal figures, to the block area to encourage cooperative play among the children.
- Add prop boxes of materials to the dramatic play area, so the children can role-play in a hospital, store, or office.

- Imagine and may have imaginary playmates.

- Read *Where the Wild Things Are* by M. Sendak and let the children dance like the "wild things."
- Listen to the children's imaginary stories.
- Have one child be a story starter in a group and have the other children add to the story.

Language Development

Because four-year-olds usually can:

Provide these activities:

- Comprehend words and are very interested in them.

- Label the different areas of the room, such as art, blocks, and food, with pictures, objects, and words, so the children begin to classify and return objects to the proper place during clean-up time.
- Label the different areas of the room, such as shelving.
- Write new words from the curriculum theme, such as cat, dog, kennel, bird, and cage, and put a picture representing the word next to it, so the children can "read" the chart.
- Label the children's artwork and block creations if they want you to.

- Comprehend prepositions

- Get a large cardboard box and cut a door and window in the box or create a house using cardboard, chairs, or hollow blocks. Talk with the children about going *into* the house, *out* of the house, *through* the door, *beside* the house, and *over* the house.
- Go for a walk with the children. Walk *around* the slide, *under* the tree, and *over* the tire in the yard.
- Make an obstacle course that gives the children an opportunity to crawl *under* the jungle gym, *into* the swing, *out* of the house, and *over* the tires. Talk about the children's movements as they make them.

- Match animal sounds to animals.

- Make a tape recording of familiar animal sounds, such as cows, horses, dogs, and cats. Put toy figures out that represent the animals in the area. See if the children can match the sounds and animals.
- Read books about animals. Let the children imitate the animal sounds.
- Sing "Old Mac Donald."

- Relate experiences.

- Write down the children's description of their art work on the papers or on separate pieces of paper.
- Make books of the children's drawings and stories or cut out magazine pictures with the children's descriptions. Place these materials in resealable plastic bags and fasten the bags together.
- Put index cards on block constructions with each child's description of his or her project written on the card.
- Take pictures of block constructions and put them on the bulletin board along with the children's descriptions.
- Write stories about field trips and classroom guests.

- Follow three unrelated commands in proper order.

- When using the obstacle path on the playground, tell the children to, "Walk to the starting line, climb over the jungle gym, and then crawl through the tunnel."
- At snacktime, tell the children to, "Come to the table, sit down on the chair, and put your napkin in your lap."

- Join sentences together.

- Ask the children open-ended questions that begin with "Who," "What," "Why," "Where," "When," and "How" to encourage them to talk with you. Be sure that you listen and respond to their conversations.
- Talk about what happens next in a story.

Cognitive (Thinking) Development

Because four-year-olds usually can:

- Pick the longer of two lines.

Provide these activities:

- Cut pieces of bright-colored ribbon and talk with the children about which is longer.
- Cut straws into three or four different lengths. Compare lengths with the children and ask them to put them in order.

- Count to four or more.

- Set up a beanbag toss game. Let the children choose four beanbags. Count them as they throw them.
- Have the children hop and count their hops.
- Point to and count the number of children at snacktime or at the table.
- Have the children count four pretzels from the bowl.
- Let the children cut four slices of banana.
- Vote about group decisions. Have the children count the votes and decide which choice received the most votes. Then make a graph that shows the votes for each choice. Each square can be one vote.

- Recognize and name six colors. Emphasize red, yellow, blue, and green and follow with purple, brown, black, and orange.

- Discuss colors of objects throughout the day. For example, green tree, red light, and yellow banana.
- Sort colored objects into groups with the children and discuss the similarities and differences of each group.

FIVE-YEAR-OLDS

Small and Large Muscle Development

Because five-year-olds usually can:

- Walk a straight line.

- Descend stairs, while alternating feet.

- Attempt to jump rope.

- Choose handedness.

- Write numerals and letters.

Provide these activities:

- Put masking tape on the floor in a straight line and let the children follow one another up and down the line.
- Draw a chalk line on the pavement and let the children walk up and down it. Provide a basket for them to carry for extra fun.

- Let the children climb and descend stairs.
- Use climbing equipment or climb steps on a slide.

- Place jump ropes on the pavement for the children to use.

- Set out crayons, markers, scissors, and paint-brushes for the children to use.
- Place an old typewriter in the writing center, so the children can use both hands.
- Set out children's golf clubs for the children to practice hitting golf balls.
- Play bowling with balls and empty 2-liter plastic bottles.

- Put out sandpaper letters and numbers for the children to use.
- Fill a cookie sheet with cornmeal for the children to write numerals and letters. Guide their fingers around the numeral or letter in the proper manner used for writing.
- Encourage the children to use chalk at the chalk-board to write.
- Put wooden dowels in the sandbox, so the children can write messages.
- Add an old typewriter to aid in numeral and letter exploration.
- Add a calculator with a printer to the math area.

Social-Emotional Development

Because five-year-olds usually can:

- Show caring behavior regarding their homes, streets, neighborhoods, and communities.

- Play reasonably well with other children.

- Dress and undress without help.

Provide these activities:

- Let each child care for a pet in the room, wash tables, and clean up after lunch.
- Have the children help you make "Feed the Cat" bags by decorating paper bags to look like cats. Then let the children use the bags to clean up the playground.
- Let a child be a special friend to a new child by showing him or her around the child care home or center.

- Have the children play cooperative games, such as a sack relay or hide-and-seek.
- Set up the block area and dramatic play area to encourage group play.

- Provide dress-up clothes, so the children can practice buttoning, unbuttoning, snapping, lacing, and tying.
- Give the children enough time to be successful at dressing themselves.

Language Development

Because five-year-olds usually can:

- Tell original stories.

- Ask the meanings of words.

- Ask what words spell.

Provide these activities:

- Let the children tell stories about their weekend activities, pets, and families.
- Put a tape recorder in the library area for the children to tape-record their stories. Other children can then listen to the tape recordings of the stories.
- Write a child's story on a large sheet of newsprint as he or she tells it to you.

- Make charts illustrating the words the children question.
- Read poems and stories that use the words the children question.
- Use the words that the children question in daily discussions.

- Label storage areas, so the children become aware of how different words are spelled.
- Label specific items the children are interested in using, such as a chair, table, or door.
- Make self-sealing plastic bag picture books based on the theme in the child care center or home. For example, a pet book might have pictures of dogs, cats, horses, and birds labeled with their names.

Cognitive (Thinking) Development

Because five-year-olds usually can:

- Recognize their first names.

- Rote count from one to twenty.

- Write numerals one through five.

- Carry out commands involving forward, backward, inside, and outside.

- Understand first, middle, and last positions.

Provide these activities:

- Make name tags for each child's cubby.
- Put each child's name on a mailbox made from a shoe box in the writing center. Do this when the child is watching you.
- Encourage the children to write their names on their projects.
- Choose helpers by using name cards.

- Count the number of children at the lunch table.
- Count the napkins.
- Count the cookies on the plate.
- Count the fish in the aquarium.
- Count the swings on the playground.

- Provide crayons, markers, pencils, and paper for writing numerals.
- Put shaving cream on a table and let the children practice writing numerals.

- Make up an obstacle path that gives the children the opportunity to physically carry out commands.

- Have the children alternate their positions in line at the water fountain, so each child can be first, middle, and last during the week.
- Make masking tape streets on a table or on the floor. Put out small cars and trucks and ask the children to line up three cars. Talk about which vehicle is first, middle, or last.

DEVELOP A CHILD CARE PHILOSOPHY

You must have a philosophy for your child care program. It should be a simple, easy-to-read written statement that reflects what you believe is best for children and their families and explains why you are providing your program.

To develop your philosophy, you will first need to determine *why* you are working with children, *what* they will gain from the experience, and *how* you plan to offer the experiences in your program. Then you will need to think about how children grow and develop, determine their needs, and decide how you can meet these needs. As you do this, you need to be realistic because you cannot provide for all the children's needs.

As you write your child care philosophy, remember that there is no right or wrong way to write it. It is simply a tool to help guide you as you develop a curriculum, choose a staff, and purchase materials and equipment. It is a marketing tool that will help you explain your program and your beliefs regarding the care of children.

[1]CURRICULUM FOR YOUNG CHILDREN

Once you have established a philosophy for your child care program, you are ready to plan the curriculum. Early childhood curriculum is what happens throughout the day in your child care home or center. It includes all the experiences you provide to help the children grow from the smiling "Hello!" in the morning to the cheery "See you tomorrow!" in the afternoon or evening.

Quality early childhood curriculum includes choosing activities, materials, and resources that are interesting to the children and appropriate to their age and development. Good early childhood curriculum takes careful planning to include activities that help children grow in the four developmental skill areas: small and large muscle, social-emotional, language, or cognitive (thinking). Selecting an activity because it looks like a "cute" idea is not an appropriate method of planning activities for children.

As you plan the activities for each day, you should ask yourself:
- *Why* am I doing this particular activity? *Why* is it important in the curriculum? *Why* did I choose this piece of equipment for three-year-olds?

- *What* can I do to make this activity appropriate for two-, three-, four-, and five-year-olds? *What* materials are needed to carry out this activity?
- *How* will I carry out the program? *How* can I plan activities so that I can help children grow and mature?

Early childhood curriculum, as mentioned above, includes every part of the children's day. It includes experiences in the areas of art, music, dramatic play, science, woodworking, and language. It includes the self-help skills that the children learn as they begin to dress, feed, and clean-up after themselves.

Children can learn these skills through play. Play gives them the opportunity to explore, discover, and enjoy materials, ideas, and people. Understanding what children learn as they play in each of the curriculum areas mentioned above is essential if you wish to plan an early childhood program that emphasizes the growth of the "whole" child.

The following charts show what children learn in the different curriculum areas and what you can do to help them learn. The curriculum areas are as follows:
- Group Activities.
- Art Experiences.
- Block Area.
- Dramatic Play Area.
- Food Experiences.
- Library Area.
- Manipulative Activities.
- Math Area.
- Music and Creative Movement.
- Sand Play.
- Science Area.
- Water Play.
- Woodworking Experiences.
- Writing Area.
- Indoor or Outdoor Large Muscles Activities.

You might find it helpful to enlarge these charts and place them in the appropriate curriculum areas in your child care home or center. They may be helpful in training new child care providers. As experienced child care providers execute the various activities, they can refer back to these charts to focus in on the learning that takes place in each area. They might also be a good parent education tool for you to use when explaining what children learn as they "play."

1 Permission granted to adapt materials by: Griffin, S. 1984. *Child-care Provider Instructor's Materials.* Columbia, MO: University of Missouri Instructional Materials Laboratory

WHAT DO CHILDREN LEARN?

During Group Activities

Children learn to:

- Enjoy being with their friends.

- Listen to fingerplays, stories, and songs.

- Position themselves in a circle for group time.

- Communicate with others.

- Listen to one another.

- Gain self-confidence.

You can help by:

- Enjoying the children.

- Planning activities that are appropriate for the children.

- Placing individual mats in a circle on the floor.
- Creating a circle on the floor using colored tape.

- Giving the children opportunities to talk about their families, friends, and pets.

- Encouraging the children to listen to others and ask questions.

- Listening to the children, so they realize that you feel that they are important.
- Giving the children opportunities to talk, such as at snacktime, group time, or one-on-one with you.

From Art Experiences

Children learn to:

- Explore different art media, such as crayons, paint, markers, glue, collage materials, chalk, and paper.

- Express their own ideas in their own ways.

- Respect their own creativity.

- Build self-esteem.

- Use large and small muscles.

- Develop independence

- Question, explore, and experiment.

You can help by:

- Providing and rotating a variety of art media.

- Letting the children choose what they want to do.
- Letting the children experiment with the art media.

- Emphasizing process (how it is done) not the product (what it looks like).
- Not providing coloring books, dittos, or teacher-made models.

- Showing interest.
- Respecting the children's work (write the child's name, the date, and his or her comments on the work or help the child write it himself or herself).
- Displaying photos of the children and their artwork.

- Providing paintbrushes, clay, playdough, large sheets of paper, and scissors for the children to use.

- Providing adequate time and space.

- Discussing lines and colors.

In the Block Area

Children learn to:

- Play cooperatively.

- Use their creativity.

- Classify blocks by their size, shape, order, and function.
- Stack and balance blocks.
- Experiment.
- Label.
- Develop eye-hand coordination.
- Learn how much space blocks take and how much space their bodies take.

You can help by:

- Clearly defining the rules regarding the block area.
- Encouraging the children to work freely within the rules.
- Providing props, such as cars, traffic signs, and figures of people, to promote interest.
- Encouraging the children.
- Praising the children.
- Taking pictures of block structures and displaying them.
- Arranging and labeling blocks, so they are easy to use and store.
- Providing space for the children to use the blocks.
- Displaying pictures pertaining to a theme.
- Labeling shelves for block storage.
- Making verbal suggestions for building.
- Protecting construction projects.

In the Dramatic Play Area

Children learn to:

- Cooperate and play together.

- Role-play different roles in the home and the community.
- Take care of play materials.

- Talk and laugh with friends.

You can help by:

- Discussing the use and care of materials.
- Establishing the number of children who can play safely in the area.
- Avoiding sex stereotyping in your comments and suggestions.
- Labeling shelves.
- Keeping the area clean and orderly.
- Discussing the use and care of materials.
- Providing easy access to materials.
- Rotating materials in play area often.

From Food Experiences

Children learn to:

- Measure and mix ingredients.

- Observe changes in texture, color, and consistency of ingredients.
- Smell and taste the ingredients.

You can help by:

- Providing hands-on opportunities for the children to pour, measure, mix, and knead.
- Emphasizing the process of the food activity and not the product.
- Providing spoons for tasting.

- Follow directions.

- Become aware of good nutrition.

- Try new foods.

- Developing nonreader recipe cards that illustrate the steps used in the food activity.

- Offering different foods for the children to try.

- Incorporating multicultural recipes.

In the Library Area

Children learn to:

- Enjoy reading books.

- Listen to rhymes and poetry.

- Care for books.

- Increase ideas.

- Enjoy talking.

- Arrange stories on a felt board.

- Tell a story using a puppet.

You can help by:

- Providing a special, out-of-the-way area that encourages the children to enjoy books.
- Providing a carpeted area and soft seating.
- Including books made by the children or class.

- Speaking clearly and correctly when reciting rhymes and poetry.

- Showing the children how to care for books.

- Encouraging the children to share both ideas and information.
- Encouraging the children to tell stories.

- Talking with and listening to each child at least once a day.

- Providing a felt board, felt board figures, puppets, puppet stage, tapes, tape recorder, records, recorder player, filmstrips, and movies.

- Providing puppets to enrich your curriculum themes.

From Manipulative Activities

Children learn to:

- Use small muscles.

- Develop eye-hand coordination.

- Compare differences in size, shape, and color.

- Question, explore, and experiment.

- Learn new words.

- Develop independence.

You can help by:

- Providing lacing cards, pegboards, puzzles, and shape blocks for the children to use.

- Encouraging the children to experiment with the above mentioned materials.

- Checking to see that all pieces are available.

- Watching to see that an activity or material is age-appropriate.
- Asking the children questions that encourage exploration and experimentation.

- Introducing each new activity and problem solve with the children on how to use the materials.
- Writing words on the picture labels for the storage shelves.

- Encouraging the children to experiment with materials (within reason).

In the Math Area

Children learn to:

- Classify by size and shape.

- Measure and weigh.

- Experiment with materials.

- Balance objects of different weights.

- Determine one-to-one correspondence.

- Match numerals with the correct number of objects.

- Identify parts and whole.

- Count objects.

- Learn new vocabulary.

You can help by:

- Providing blocks and other objects of various sizes.

- Making a height and weight chart.
- Preparing food using 1 cup, 1/2 cup, teaspoons, and tablespoons.
- Providing rulers and tape measures.

- Providing a variety of products for the children to measure and weigh.

- Placing a balance scale and objects to experiment with in the area.

- Developing materials for the felt board.

- Making sandpaper numerals.

- Making puzzles available.

- Emphasizing math concepts through fingerplays, poetry, and stories.

- Using vocabulary such as taller, shorter, smaller, larger, square, and circle.

From Music and Creative Movement

Children learn to:

- Enjoy music.

- Coordinate large muscles.
- Exhibit creativity.

- Learn new vocabulary.

- Move and dance to rhythm.

- Sing songs.

You can help by:

- Having materials ready before the children arrive.
- Planning and utilizing music throughout the day.
- Providing the children with simple instruments, such as shakers, drums, rhythm sticks, and tambourines.

- Encouraging the children to march to music.

- Letting the children make their own musical instruments, using items such as sticks, blocks, and pan lids.

- Having words on cards.
- Writing songs on charts.
- Reading books with illustrated songs, such as "Wheels on the Bus" and "The Farmer in the Dell."

- Using props, such as bells, balloons, streamers, hoops, and scarves, for movement.

- Using music during waiting and transition times.

During Sand Play

Children learn to:

- Use large and small muscles.

- Build self-esteem.

- Question, explore, and experiment.

- Use their imaginations.

- Pour from one container to another.

- Develop independence.

- Involve senses.

- Talk and laugh with friends.

You can help by:

- Putting shovels, rakes, large buckets, and other containers in the area.

- Talking with the children.

- Varying the materials used in the sand area (shovels, trucks, spoons, funnels, water buckets, sieves).

- Permitting the children to experiment with above mentioned materials.

- Emphasizing the process not the product.

- Defining rules with the children. (Remember that safety is important!)

- Putting water in the sand area.

- Providing adequate time and space.

In the Science Area

Children learn to:

- Discover objects in the world around them.

- Become aware of and enjoy the beauty of the world.

- Ask "why" and become curious.

- Explore.

- Experiment with materials.

- Discover differences and similarities in color, shape, and size of objects.

You can help by:

- Repeating experiences–children learn through repetition. For example, use magnifying glasses several times a year.

- Encouraging the children to observe. Might go for walks at different times of the year and talk about what you see.

- Answering questions simply and honestly.

- Using hands-on experiences, such as letting the children discover that water is wet, cold, or warm.

- Providing a variety of materials, such as magnifying glasses, funnels, and water containers.

- Providing a variety of experiences using objects varying in color, shape, and size.

From Water Play

Children learn to:

- Explore and experiment.

- Enjoy the sensory contact with water.

- Pour from one container to another.

You can help by:

- Permitting the children to experiment with water.

- Discussing wet, dry, warm, and cold.

- Rotating materials such as cups, pitchers, spoons, basters, sponges, and funnels.

- Measure.

- Interact with friends in a safe manner.

- Become independent.

- Providing liquid measuring cups.
- Using new vocabulary such as empty, full, heavy, and light.

- Defining rules with the children. (Remember that safety is important!)
- Determining the number of children who can play safely in the water area.

- Helping the children learn to clean up spills.

From Woodworking Experiences

Children learn to:

- Use large and small muscles.
- Develop eye-hand coordination.

- Release frustration and aggression.

- Solve problems.

- Use their imaginations.

- Learn new vocabulary.

- Use tools safely.

- Care for tools and equipment.

You can help by:

- Providing child-sized tools, such as hammers, saws, screwdrivers, rulers, pencils, nails, and sandpaper.

- Making the woodworking area available for children who are feeling frustrated or aggressive.

- Letting the children explore and experiment with the materials.

- Not expecting the children to make a product.

- Discussing the tools and materials you provide.

- Defining rules with the children. (Remember that safety is important!)
- Demonstrating safe use of tools.

- Discussing and demonstrating the care of tools with the children.

In the Writing Area

Children learn to:

- Use large and small muscles.

- Identify numerals and letters.

- Build self-esteem.

You can help by:

- Providing paper, pencils, markers, and crayons.
- Keeping a supply of used envelopes and stamps available.
- Supplying a chalkboard and chalk.

- Providing rubber stamps and stamp pads for the children to make letters, numerals, and designs.
- Adding an old typewriter to the area.
- Supplying a magnetic board and magnetic letters.
- Making sandpaper numerals and letters for the children to explore.

- Respecting the children's work.
- Praising the children's efforts.
- Answering the children's questions about letters and words.

- Question, explore, and experiment.

- Express their own ideas.

- Develop independence.

- Encouraging the children to write words as they hear them.
- Making picture lists of words the children ask you to spell.
- Writing positive notes to each child at his or her correct developmental level.
- Adding children's dictionaries to the area.
- Labeling parts and areas of the child care home or center.
- Supplying writing materials to expand the theme in your child care home or center. For instance, pads of paper for taking orders or giving tickets, large index cards and craft sticks to make signs, or old magazines to find pictures to add to books.
- Adding staplers, tape, and glue sticks.
- Showing interest in their writing.
- Avoiding the urge to correct their spelling.
- Letting the children choose what they want to write.
- Asking open-ended questions that help the children expand their ideas.
- Making shoe box mailboxes, so the children can write to one another.
- Providing both adequate time and space for writing activities.
- Making the writing center a choice during learning center time.

From Indoor or Outdoor Large Muscle Activities

Children learn to:

- Use large muscles.

- Interact with other children.

- Enjoy being outdoors.

- Balance on one foot.

You can help by:

- Planning activities involving running, throwing, hopping, pedaling, and climbing.

- Setting up activities that involve several children, such as parachute games and games with balls.

- Demonstrating that you enjoy being outdoors.

- Placing balance beams in the area.

EQUIPPING THE LEARNING CENTERS

A child care setting should have four to eight learning centers for children to choose from during self-selected activity times. These centers should be based on the curriculum areas discussed above. The learning centers in a child care home or center should be colorful and enticing. They should "hook" the children and say "come over here to play and learn."

Simple signs using pictures and words can help the children recognize the different learning center areas, as in Figure 1. The learning centers can be divided by making masking tape borders on the floor, using bookcases to enclose corners, tying plastic soft drink holders together to form open walls, or hanging banners from the ceiling.

Materials and resources should be placed in each of the learning centers to help the children grow in the four developmental skill areas: small and large muscle, social-emotional, language, and cognitive (thinking). The materials and equipment should be organized and labeled, so the children can identify where these items belong. Materials should be rotated throughout the year to provide added interest for the children.

A throw rug can become a learning center (manipulative) if you place two or three lacing cards shaped like fire trucks or police cars on it for the children to lace. A cookie sheet on a table can become a finger paint center (art) by placing a sheet of waxed paper on the inside of the tray for the children to paint on. A plastic milk crate can hold the people figures and the small vehicles needed to enhance the block area when you talk about the fire station or the police station.

The basic materials and equipment needed to set up learning centers in your child care home or center can be very expensive. However, if you set up a budget and shop wisely, you will be able to acquire the materials you need inexpensively. You can purchase materials and equipment at garage sales and auctions if you search for items that are developmentally appropriate for the age of the children and follow the toy and equipment safety guidelines. Inexpensive materials and equipment are suggested throughout this curriculum guide.

Figure 1. A child care center with identified learning centers encourages children to experiment, explore, and learn.

Suggestions for equipping each of the different learning centers are as follows:

ART

Supplies and equipment:

Blunt scissors
Clay
Collage materials
Construction paper
Crayons
Drying rack
Easel
Finger paint
Glue
Manila paper
Markers

Newsprint
Paintbrushes
Paste
Paste brushes
Playdough
Scrap paper and wallpaper
Smocks
Tape
Tempera paint
Watercolor paint

Helpful hints:

1. Provide plenty of blank sheets of paper for the children to use. They need opportunities to develop their creativity, experiment with art media, and develop a sense of "I Can Do It!" without basing their work on adult models, such as ditto sheets or coloring books.
2. Put a small amount of liquid detergent in the tempera paint when you mix it. If paint is spilled on a child's clothing, it will wash out much easier than if the detergent is not there.
3. If you have carpeting in your child care home or center, put a plastic tablecloth under the easel to avoid spots and stains.
4. All art activities should be done at the art table or easel. Be consistent with this rule.
5. Children should use scissors only when they are sitting at the art table. When the scissors are not being used, they should be kept in a rack or container.
6. If a child is having difficulty using scissors, you may need to help strengthen his or her pincer muscles by supplying paper to tear or spring clamp clothespins to attach to the top of a can. When the child's muscles are strong enough, he or she should be able to successfully cut rolled playdough with scissors.

BLOCKS

Supplies and equipment:

Cardboard blocks
Cardboard boxes
Farm animal figures
Large unit blocks
Milk carton blocks
People figures representing families and
    community helpers

Plastic supermarket supplies
Pull toys
Shelf labels with shapes of each type of block
Signs
Small vehicles
Vehicles to haul blocks and other supplies
Zoo animal figures

Helpful hints:

1. To prevent injuries, first determine how high the children can safely stack blocks (perhaps no higher than their shoulders or heads).
2. Place the block area in a corner protected by the block storage cabinets. This placement will keep the children's block structures from being destroyed, which will happen if the block area is in a traffic area.
3. Put pictures of buildings, houses, and other structures pertaining to the theme at the children's eye level in the block area. Talk with the children about these pictures and ask questions such as "How do you think this roof was made?" or "What kind of blocks would you need to construct that bridge?"

DRAMATIC PLAY

Supplies and equipment:

Broom
Cabinet (child-sized)
Doll bed
Doll clothes
Dolls (multicultural)
Dress-up clothes
Dust pan
Full-length mirror
Hooks or clothes tree to hang clothing
Iron (child-sized)
Ironing board (child-sized)
Mop

Pans
Place mats
Plastic dishes
Pots
Range (child-sized)
Refrigerator (child-sized)
Rocking chair (child-sized)
Sink (child-sized)
Table and chair set (child-sized)
Tea set
Telephone

Helpful hints:

1. The dress-up clothing will be used more often when places to hang and store them are provided. Use a clothes tree cut down to child-size or put hooks on the back of a storage cabinet. Store jewelry in plastic see-through containers. Organize the shoes on an old shoe rack.

2. Create shapes by drawing around plates, cups, pots, pans, and food preparation utensils. Cover these shapes with self-adhesive plastic and attach them in the appropriate places in the child-sized cabinet. Show the children where each item belongs, so they can return it to its proper place when they are finished using it. A flatware divider will help organize the eating utensils. As the children put items away, they will learn to classify by size and shape, which is a necessary skill when they later begin to distinguish between the different numbers and letters.

3. Prepare prop boxes to add variety to the dramatic play area. (Prop boxes contain materials and equipment that foster playing a certain role.) For instance, a "Community Helper" prop box focusing on fire fighters might include an old vacuum hose for the fire fighter; a fire fighter's hat and boots; pictures of fire fighters at work; and books, poems, and fingerplays about fire fighters.

4. Use large range, dishwasher, washer, dryer, or refrigerator boxes from an appliance dealer to create fire trucks, police cars, ambulances, fast-food restaurant drive-in windows, fix-it shops, and cardboard furniture and appliances, as in Figure 2. An X-Acto® knife (used by you only), markers, and paint can transform a box to any of these dramatic play resources. Small boxes can be stacked inside the range, refrigerator, cabinet, and sink for storage. A small plastic tub can be placed in the sink. You can also use chairs, cardboards, and large hollow blocks to create the dramatic play resources listed above.

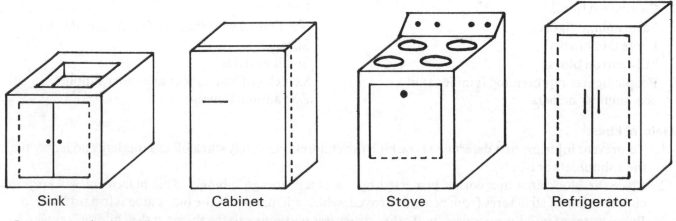

Sink   Cabinet   Stove   Refrigerator

Do not cut on the dotted lines of the cardboard appliances. They are to be folded after you cut the doors, and they should be reinforced with duct tape.

Figure 2. Dramatic play appliances can be created with large cardboard boxes and imagination.

FOOD

Supplies and equipment:

Basic foodstuffs
Cake pans
Cookie sheets
Eating utensils
Knives
Measuring cups
Measuring spoons

Mixing bowls
Mixing spoons
Pans
Plastic tasting spoons
Pots
Rotary egg beater

Helpful hints:

1. Wash your hands and have the children wash their hands before food preparation begins.
2. Make sure that the food preparation is a hands-on activity for the children. Plan the activity so that the children have opportunities to measure, pour, and stir.
3. Have plastic spoons and paper cups available for tasting. As each child uses a spoon to taste, put it in a waste container, so it is not reused.
4. Talk about textures, colors, smells, and tastes as you prepare the food.
5. Keep pot and pan handles turned to the back of the range at all times, so the children cannot pull pots or pans over on top of themselves.
6. If you work with preschool children, you should do any stirring that is required on the range. School-age children should be carefully supervised.

LIBRARY

Supplies and equipment:

Assorted books
Beanbag chair
Bookshelf and/or plastic milk crates
Chalk
Chalkboard
Felt board
Felt board figures
Markers

Paper
Pencils
Pillows
Puppets
Puppet stage
Rocker
Tape recorder
Typewriter

Helpful hints:

1. Show children how to open and care for books. Talk about how books are the children's friends and that they must be cared for, so everyone can enjoy them.
2. Be a good role model. Hold books like they are very special to you. Let the children observe you reading. Talk with the children about all the different items you read–magazines, cookbooks, newspapers, curriculum books, and children's books.
3. Several times during the day, sit and read to two or three children. Sit on the floor or in a beanbag chair near the children and position your body so you can see the entire room. Supervise the children in the other learning centers as you give special time to children in the library area. You might put an adult-sized rocking chair in the library area and hold one or two children as you read.
4. Read a book once or twice before you read it to the children. This will help you become familiar with the story line ahead of time.
5. Have puppets representing characters in the books for children to use or develop a felt board story from a book, such as *Corduroy* by D. Freeman or *Goldilocks and the Three Bears.*
6. Make a felt board by cutting a piece of plywood or heavy cardboard to eighteen by twenty-four inches or twenty-four by thirty-six inches. Staple felt to the plywood or glue and tape it to the cardboard. Store the felt board in a plastic bag to keep it clean and usable.

7. As you plan to purchase additional materials for your child care home or center, determine which stories you read frequently and purchase those story puzzles to add to your library or manipulatives areas.
8. Two-year-old children enjoy books about themselves and their families, picture books, books with simple sentences, realistic stories about animals and toys they are able to identify, spiral bound books that lie flat, and books that are easy to hold and use.
9. Three-year-old children enjoy books with repetition in them; realistic stories about families, neighbors and children; talking animal and machine books; and books they can hold themselves.
10. Four-year-old children enjoy books with realistic stories, pretend stories about real things, ridiculous situations, and funny words; books about children their own age; counting books; and informative books (how and why books).
11. Five-year-old children enjoy counting books; alphabet books; books about real boys and girls, families, and going to school; and books with nonsense verse. They still have difficulty telling fantasy from reality, and they still engage in magical thinking. Therefore, it may be best to steer clear of books that may feed fears. Five-year-olds need books that encourage them to want to read. These books can have fewer pictures and more words. Some five-year-olds will be ready for easy-to-read books that they can read themselves.

MANIPULATIVES

Supplies and equipment:

Board games
Bristle blocks
Color blocks
Cylinder boards
Dolls to dress
Lacing cards
Lacing, zipping, and buttoning forms
Legos® plastic building blocks
Lincoln Logs® building blocks

Lotto cards
Parquetry blocks
Pegboards
Puzzles
Nesting boxes
Sequence puzzles
Shape blocks
Small figures
Stringing beads

Helpful hints:

1. If you work with children under three years of age, check all of the small pieces in this area with a choke tube to make sure that they are not too small. Choke tubes are available from early childhood supply companies.
2. Make a "needle" for the lacing cards or stringing beads by cutting a piece of thick yarn and winding masking tightly around the yarn about one and one-half inches from the end. This taped end will make it easier for the children to put the yarn through the lacing card or beads. It is also much safer than a real needle.
3. If you are making lacing cards, punch two holes at each space with a hole punch for children under three years of age. Place the holes further apart for younger children. Punch one hole at each space for children over three years of age.
4. Make a feely box by covering a box and lid with colorful gift wrap or self-adhesive plastic. Cut an opening in the box large enough for a child's hand to fit. You can cut a circle, square, triangle, and rectangle on the four sides to make this box a sensory experience too.
5. Make a feely bag by cutting a rectangular shape piece of fabric, folding it in half, and sewing up the two long sides. Hem the top, leaving a slot in the hem to pull a drawstring through. The child can put his or her hand through the drawstring opening to feel the objects. A feely bag can also be made from an old pillow case.

MATH

Supplies and equipment:

Alarm clock
Balance scale
Beads
Cash register
Cuisenaire Rods™
Egg timer
Felt board
Felt board objects to count and match
Height chart
Large and small objects for counting
Magnetic board
Magnetic numbers
Markers
Object and number puzzles
Paper
Pencils
Play money
Rulers
Sandpaper numbers
Scales
Shape blocks
Shape puzzles
Small blocks
Tape measure

Helpful hints:

1. Math can be taught throughout the day. For example, have the children put a napkin beside each glass, take two cookies, or count the children at the easel. You can also measure and weigh each child and record his or her height and weight on a chart. Then have students compare–is Beth taller than Sue? Is Sam shorter than Marvin? Repeat this activity several times during the year, so the children can compare their own growth.
2. Let the children match felt board squares, rectangles, triangles, and circles.
3. Make circles, squares, triangles, and rectangles on the floor with masking tape. Have the children jump into a square, sit in a circle, hop from one triangle to another, or jump inside the rectangle.

MUSIC AND CREATIVE MOVEMENT

Supplies and equipment:

Cassette tapes
Compact disc player
Compact discs
Costumes
Earphones
Homemade instruments
Puppets
Rhythm instruments
Tape recorder
Scarves for dancing
Selection of songs
Streamers for dancing

Helpful hints:

1. Use music to transition (change) the children from one activity to another throughout the day. For example, sing "Joey is a helper" and "Melinda is a helper" as you clean up the block center. Sing the "Wheels on the Bus" as you pretend to be buses on the way to the playground. Sit down on the floor and sing "Row, Row, Row Your Boat" as you wait for the last four parents to pick up their children. Have two children sit across from each other touching toes, holding hands, and swaying back and forth to the music.
2. Play soft, quiet music for the children to settle down for a nap.
3. Play rock and roll, country, classical, jazz, and children's music, so the children can hear many different types of music.
4. Provide a tape recorder and earphones so that children can listen to music when they choose.

SAND

Supplies and equipment:

Buckets
Containers
Dowel rods for writing or drawing
Funnels
Measuring cups
Measuring spoons

Pitchers
Sandbox (outdoor)
Sand table or tub (indoors)
Shovels
Strainers

Helpful hints:

1. Decide how many children can play in the sand area safely.
2. Do not allow sand to be thrown. If a child cannot follow this rule, redirect him or her to another activity area of the room or playground.
3. Speak positively in this learning center. "Keep the sand low." "Keep the sand in the sandbox."
4. Use the indoor sand table or tub for sensory experiences. You might use rice, cornmeal, potting soil, cedar shavings, feathers, cotton balls, shaving cream, and beans or corn with four-year-olds and five-year-olds who are not as likely to push these materials up their noses or in their ears.
5. Place a plastic tablecloth under the sand table or sand tub to catch the sand that falls out as the children play.

SCIENCE

Supplies and equipment:

Balance scale
Children's collections of nuts, seeds, leaves, shells,
    flowers, rocks, or insects
Conservation posters
Magnifying glasses

Measuring cups
Measuring spoons
Pets
Pet cages
Science books

Helpful hints:

1. Science takes place both indoors and outdoors. Be sure to plan hands-on experiences in both areas.
2. Let the children start collections–nuts, seeds, leaves, shells, flowers, rocks, or insects. Set up displays on the science table. Provide magnifying glasses for the children to use to examine the collected items.
3. Magnifying glasses make it exciting to look at hands, hair, and pores in the skin. Provide books and posters that describe the human body. Children love to look at what is inside.
4. Involve children in the weather in a concrete way. Talk about the weather as you come in and out of your child care home or center. Instead of placing a construction paper sun on a weather chart on a sunny day or a snow person on the chart when it snows, let the children experience the weather through their senses. Let them feel the cold snow; touch and smell the wet rain; see the bright, yellow sun and feel its heat; and feel the wind in their hair.

WATER PLAY

Supplies and equipment:

Basters
Funnels
Measuring cups
Measuring spoons
Pitchers
Plastic containers
Sponges

Strainers
Swimming pool
Water
Water hose
Water table or tub
Water toys

Helpful hints:

1. Decide how many children can play in the water play area safely.
2. Water should stay in the water table or tub. If a child cannot follow this rule, redirect him or her to another activity area of the room.
3. If you have a swimming pool available, supervise this water play carefully. At least one person on the premises should have cardiopulmonary resuscitation (CPR) training in case of an emergency.

WOODWORKING

Supplies and equipment:

Balsa wood
Bolts (large)
Cleanouts (plumbing)
End caps (plastic plumbing)
Elbows (plastic plumbing)
Hammers (10 oz.)
Level
Nails (large head)
Nuts (large)
Pegboard
Pine wood
Pipe (plastic plumbing)
Ruler

Safety goggles
Saws
Screwdrivers
Screws
Tape measure
T-shaped plumbing connectors
Vise
Workbench
For two-year-olds and young three-year-olds:
Golf tees
Large roofing nails
Styrofoam® plastic foam blocks
Wooden hammer

Helpful hints:

1. Establish how many children can play safely in the woodworking area. Then provide that number of safety goggles for the area. When they are all being used, the area is full.
2. Place the workbench in a corner against the wall. This placement will make it more difficult for observers to get in the way of hammers and saws.
3. Place pegboard above the workbench. Outline the tools on the pegboard, so that they can be returned when the children are finished with them.
4. Always show the children how to use tools correctly before making them available.
5. The woodworking area offers many opportunities for problem-solving, experimenting, and creativity. The process is more important than the project, so do not expect the children to make specific projects.

Supplies and Equipment:

Card stock
Chairs
Chalk
Chalkboard
Computer
Construction paper
Cookie sheet with cornmeal
Crayons
Glue sticks
Hole punch (different shapes)
Index cards
Loose paper
Magnetic board

Markers
Pads of paper
Pencils
Poster board
Printing calculator
Scissors
Shoe box mailbox for each child
Stamps
Stapler
Table
Tape
Typewriter

Helpful hints:

1. Put out plenty of paper and writing tools for the children. Change the materials to reflect the theme in your child care home or center.
2. Make writing materials part of all your learning centers. For instance, the children can write journals in the science area, take messages in the offices in the dramatic play area, and make road signs in the block area. Be flexible with the materials and encourage interest in writing.
3. Children's writing in the early childhood years begins with scribbles and develops into letters and numerals identified by adults. Encourage each child to write at his or her own developmental level.
4. Do not require young children to sit in a group to write. Let them choose writing as an individual experience from the planned learning centers.

PLANNING FOR THE NEEDS OF YOUNG CHILDREN

After you have equipped your child care home or center, you are ready to start planning for a quality early childhood program.

The Daily Schedule

When you plan a daily schedule for your early childhood program, you need to remember to take the children's needs into account. Like adults, children learn through experience. As you plan different experiences, remember that children need routines that include quiet and active periods; small group, large group, and individual activities; rest times; and nutritional breaks (snacks and lunch).

Having a well-planned schedule gives structure to the day. However, you also need to be flexible and willing to adapt your plans to the needs and interests of the children, as in Figure 3.

When you begin to plan your daily schedule, the following suggestions may be helpful:

- Plan enough flexible arrival time to let you greet each child.
- Plan for large blocks of time in the schedule that include routine and transition (change) to the next activity.
- Provide 45 to 60 minutes of play at the learning centers in both the morning and afternoon. Let the children select the learning centers at which they want to play. This selection will give them the opportunity to make choices and decisions.

SAMPLE DAILY SCHEDULE

7:00 - 8:15 Arrival Breakfast Free Play	**10:30 - 11:30** Outdoor Play
	11:30 - 12:15 Bathroom (Wash up for lunch.) Lunchtime
8:15 - 8:30 Group Time (Planning for choices in the learning centers. Introduce new learning center choices.)	**12:15 - 12:45** Bathroom (Brush teeth.) Settle down for nap
8:30 - 9:30 Learning Centers (Self-selected activity time. Children will be playing in one of the thirteen possible learning center areas, such as dramatic play, blocks, library, or art.)	**12:45 - 2:30** Rest or Nap Time Quiet play for those who do not nap.
	2:30 - 3:30 Bathroom (After nap.) Outdoor Play
9:30 - 10:00 Clean-up Bathroom (Wash up for snack.) Snacktime	**3:30 - 5:00** Bathroom (Wash up for snack.) Snacks Learning Centers (Self-selected activity time.) Clean-up
10:00 - 10:30 Group Time (Story, puppets, creative movement.)	
Transition (Change) and Dress for Outdoor Play	**5:00 - 5:30** Group Sharing Time (Activities such as discussing the day's activities, reading a story together, or using puppets.) Departure

Figure 3. This sample daily schedule provides for both structure and flexibility.

- Provide opportunities for individual, small group, and large group activities each day.
- Tailor your schedule to the ages and developmental levels of the children in the group.
- Allow flexibility in your schedule for the unexpected, such as a pet brought to the facility or the announcement of a child's new baby sister. These experiences keep interest high and can be great incidental teaching experiences.
- If the weather permits, provide 45 to 60 minutes of outdoor play in the morning and in the afternoon. In case the weather is adverse, be prepared for indoor large muscle activity, such as creative movement, dance, or exercise.
- Plan lunch and snack to be social times. Sit with the children and join them in conversation. This time is good for learning about the children and their families.
- Offer foods and use recipes that help children begin to understand our multicultural world.
- Although, bathroom times are listed on the sample schedule, try to let children use the bathroom whenever they need to or in small groups. Lining up a large group of children wastes time. However, if your facility does not allow children to move freely to and from a bathroom, plan activities, such as songs or fingerplays, so time spent waiting in line is not wasted.

When children are familiar with the daily routine, they feel secure because they know what to expect. Planning the day will also make you feel secure and more prepared.

Planning the Curriculum

Many methods are used to plan early childhood curriculum. One is the process-centered approach, which describes learning as an interactive process. In this method, the children are actively involved in their environment. Most activities are planned to be hands-on activities. All four areas of child development are considered when planning these activities. It's important to prepare the environment in a way that allows children to choose how to use the time, space, equipment, and materials available to them.

To help children experience the most from their child care environment, you can use themes to plan class activities. Themes can serve as the core of the curriculum, tying activities together throughout a set time, such as a week or month. (Examples are *spring, farm animals,* and *my family*.) Themes make planning easier for you and help you teach children some of the concepts you feel are important. However, be sure not to overuse the theme by planning every activity around it.

Themes for two-year-olds should center around them, their families, toys, and moving objects. For three- and four-year-olds, themes about pets, friends, and the community can be added. Themes can be expanded for five-year-olds to include the world around them.

To help you preplan for a theme, photocopy and use the brainstorming web in Figure 4. Post the web in a visible place (cabinet door, bulletin board, counter) two to three weeks before you will start planning. Write the theme title in the web's center. Ask colleagues and others for activities and experiences related to the theme. What have they done as children, successfully used in their child care home or center, or seen in workshops and resource books? Ask children what they know about the theme and what they want to learn. Write each idea in its category on the web. Add ideas until it is time to plan. By then, you should have enough ideas to plan for your group based on the theme.

The Weekly Lesson Plan

After you have identified the activities you want to include for your theme, you are ready to write your weekly lesson. This plan displays the activities and experiences you will use for each curriculum area, day of the week, and time of the day. A lesson plan helps you think through your plans and serves as a guide for the week. The completed sample in Figure 5 includes activities from this curriculum guide (followed by page number) and other activities, some of which are meant to enhance the developmental skills of specific children in the group.

Make enough photocopies of the blank lesson plan forms in Figure 6 to last all year. Then, using the sample lesson plan (Figure 5) as a guide, create one week's lesson plan. Choose the activities you plan to use. Look at the activity pages and decide which ones

(Continued on page 44)

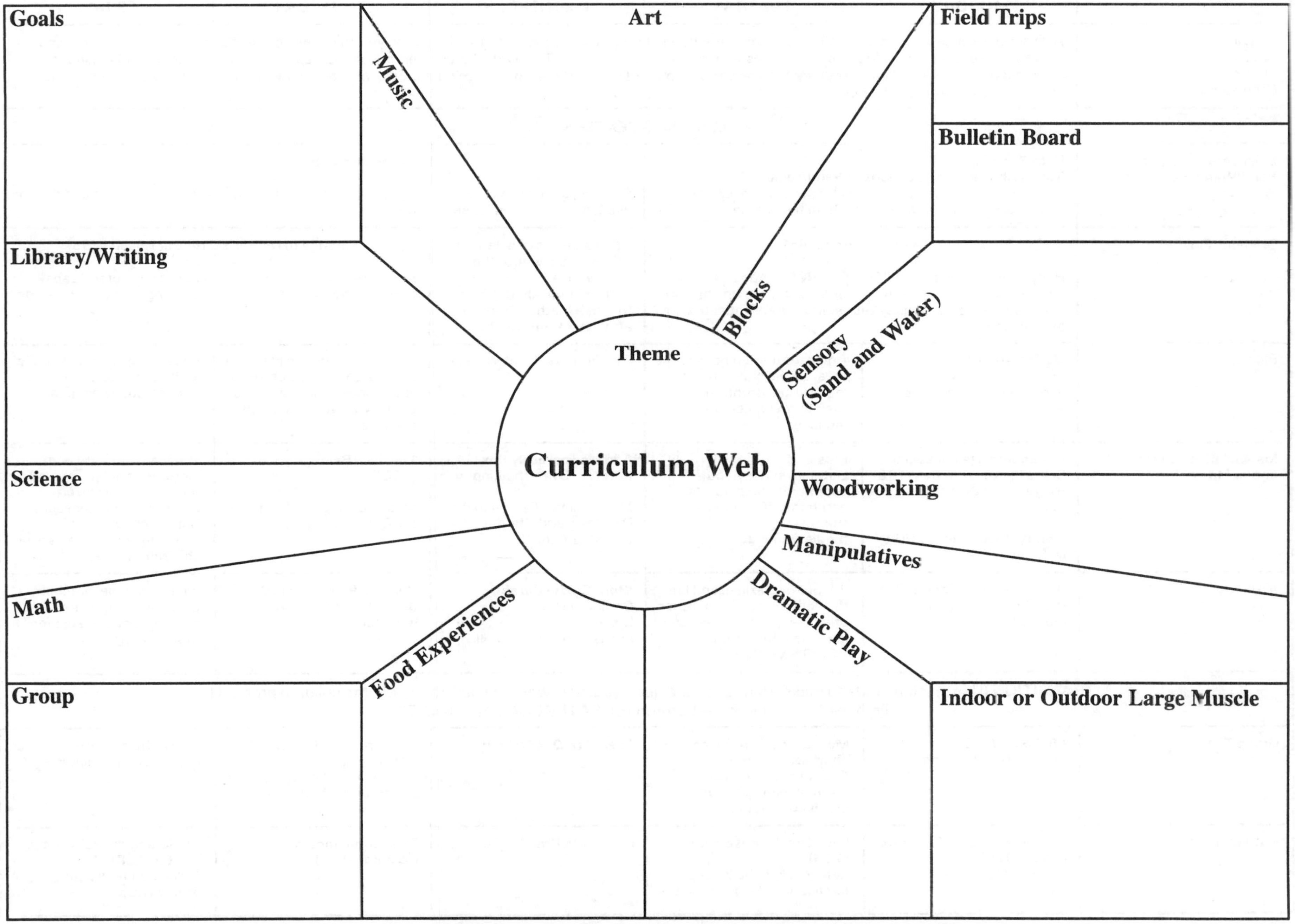
Goals
Art
Field Trips
Music
Bulletin Board
Library/Writing
Blocks
Theme
Sensory (Sand and Water)
Curriculum Web
Science
Woodworking
Manipulatives
Math
Food Experiences
Dramatic Play
Group
Indoor or Outdoor Large Muscle

Figure 4. Jot down notes on this curriculum web before you begin planning for a new theme.

Sample Weekly Lesson Plan Theme: Community Helpers

	MONDAY	TUESDAY	WEDNESDAY	THURSDAY	FRIDAY
Arrival Breakfast Free Play Group time	Arrival time varies in child care. Children may have free play throughout the center or home, or you may set up specific choices. During this time, plan for the day and introduce new materials and new learning centers. Talk with the children about their special interests. As they talk use a tape recorder (Kristen, Jami—language), two-year-olds may stay in a group for five minutes. Five-year-olds may last for ten to fifteen minutes in an "interesting" group session.				
	LEARNING CENTERS				
Science/Math and/or Sand/Water Play and/or Woodworking	**Rock Samples** (119) **Steam Shovel in the Sandbox or Sand Table** (117) Put these centers adjacent to each other, so you can talk about sand and rocks and from where they come.			**Woodworking Shop** (125) Science, sand, and wood working activities can be introduced on separate days and then be available to children for several days.	
Dramatic Play		**Dentist's Office** (96) Hang up signs saying "DENTIST OFFICE." Add a reception desk, chairs, magazines, play money, child's lawn chair for a dental chair, and a white dress shirt for the dentist to wear as a lab coat.	Hang pictures of a dentist office on the wall at the children's eye level. Talk with children about "how to brush teeth." Practice after snack and lunch.	**Change to Doctor's Office or Hospital** (95) Add cots, doctors' bags, and nurses' and doctors' caps. Continue by caring for patients—serving meals on trays, etc.	
Blocks	**Our Town** (88) (Sandy, Cindy, Miguel, Jami—large muscle, social emotional)	Add cardboard blocks to the area, so the children can make large structures in their town (Jake—small muscle)	**Fire Fighters' Ladders** (87)	Extended dramatic play into block area. Hang pictures of ambulances and fire trucks on the wall at the children's eye level.	Encourage children to build ambulances to carry patients to the hospital.
Manipulatives/Library and/or Music	**Community Helper Lacing Cards** (110) **& Puzzles** (109) (Miguel, Sarah—small muscle) Library: Read *Dandelion* by D. Freeman	Music Listen to songs about community helpers. Use earphones if you have them. (Eddie—language)	Add **Medical Feely Box** (111) (Kirsten, Sam—thinking) Music: Sing "Farmer in the Dell" and add "farmer takes a doctor."	**This Tool Belongs To...** (108) Music: Continue "Farmer in the Dell" with revisions.	Make posterboard with pictures of people at work on one side. Make an appropriate hat for each. Use Velcro™ strips on the board and on the hat, so the children can match.
Art/Food	**Busy Baker Playdough** (81) (Sandy, Sarah—small muscle)	Put out magazines and let the children cut out pictures of houses, and offices, and glue them to a mural about "Our Town."	**Stop, Go, Be Careful Cookies** (101) Discuss Eat as a snack with milk.	**Chicken Rice Soup** (102) Serve as lunch in the hospital.	Put out collage materials, glue, paper, markers, crayons, and scissors for the children to use.
	TRANSITION (Use masking tape to make a ladder on the floor leading toward the bathroom. Let the children pretend to climb the fire ladder to the bathroom.), **BATHROOM, AND SNACK**				
Group Time	*My Dentist* (68) (all children—thinking)	Make a good grooming chart after reading *Dandelion*. List brushing teeth, washing hands, brushing hair, etc.	*I Can Be a Doctor* (70)	*Five Little Fire Fighters* (71) Give five children fire hats made from construction paper for the fingerplay.	*Police Officers* (65) (Eddie, Jami—language)
Outdoor Play	**Steam Shovel the Sandbox or Sand Table** (117) (Sandy, Miguel—large muscle)	**Let's Dig the Basement** (118) Refer back to the Blocks and talk about making real houses.	Parachute Crawl (130)	**The Ambulance is Coming!** (129)	I'm Taking the Baby to the Doctor (128) Talk about how police officers help.

Figure 5. This sample weekly lesson plan uses the Community Helpers theme.

Sample Weekly Lesson Plan   Theme: Community Helpers

	MONDAY	TUESDAY	WEDNESDAY	THURSDAY	FRIDAY
Bathroom Lunch/Snack Nap	Lunch or snack should be a social time. It should be relaxed and fun for both the children and you. You should sit with the children. Help the children learn to use utensils. They must be taught, since is it not an inborn trait. This is a time to incidentally teach manners to children as they grow. You are the best role model. This is also a time to talk about foods, textures, colors, and heat. It is a time for you and the children to share your interests. (All children—social-emotional)				
Indoor or Outdoor Large muscle	Set up an obstacle path for the children. Have them crawl through a box, crawl over a tire, walk on a rope or balance beam, climb a jungle gym, swing on the swings, and hop to the door—cut cut arrows or footprints and place on the ground to direct them. (Jami, Brent, Miguel—large muscle)			Set up streets with STOP signs or stop lights. Have a police officer direct traffic. Put a "POLICE" sign on a tricycle. Put an "AMBULANCE" sign on wagon to take the baby to the hospital.	
LEARNING CENTERS					
Science/Math and/or Sand/Water Play and/or Woodworking		CONTINUE FROM THE MORNING Add **Nuts and Bolts** (124) to the Woodworking center (Sarah, Sam—small muscle) Add water to the sand table to let the children experiment with building with wet and dry sand.			
Dramatic Play		CONTINUE FROM THE MORNING			(If the children's interest diminishes, add a few new resources such as toys, paper, markers or different dress-up clothes to the area.) (Miguel, Jake—social-emotional)
Blocks	(Cindy, Jake—large muscle)	CONTINUE FROM THE MORNING			
Art/Food	Continue playing with playdough. Talk about shapes—round, square, rectangle. Have cookie cutters to use. (Miguel, Sandy—small muscle)	Continue mural from the morning. Put out crayons, and markers, so the children can add to the magazine cutouts.		Easel painting should be available for two to four children at a time. Change the paint colors and types of paper. (Sarah, Miguel, Jake—small muscle, social-emotional)	
Manipulatives/Library and/or Music		CONTINUE FROM THE MORNING			
CLEAN-UP, TRANSITION (Let the children pretend to carry a fire hose and put out a fire on the way to the bathroom.), **BATHROOM, AND SNACK**					
Group (music, stories, felt board, puppets, games, and transition) evaluation and dismissal.	Find poem "The Dentist" by R. Fyleman from *The Fairy Queen.* Put it on a chart with a picture of a dentist's office and talk about it.	Talk about the good grooming chart you made after reading *Dandelion* by D. Freeman. Let children role-play the good grooming habits.	Use the medical feely box in your group time. Put it back in manipulatives.	*Fire Engines* (72)	**A Trip to the Police Station** (73) (all children—thinking, language)

Figure 5. Continued.

Sample Weekly Lesson Plan   Theme:

	MONDAY	TUESDAY	WEDNESDAY	THURSDAY	FRIDAY
Arrival Breakfast Free Play Group time					
LEARNING CENTERS					
Science/Math and/or Sand/Water Play and/or Woodworking					
Dramatic Play					
Blocks					
Manipulatives/Library and/or Music					
Art/Food					
TRANSITION, BATHROOM, AND SNACK					
Group Time					
Outdoor Play					

Figure 6. These blank lesson plans can be used to plan your weekly curriculum plan.

Sample Weekly Lesson Plan   Theme: _____

	MONDAY	TUESDAY	WEDNESDAY	THURSDAY	FRIDAY
Bathroom Lunch/Snack Nap					
Indoor/Outdoor Large Muscle					
LEARNING CENTERS					
Science/Math and/or Sand/Water Play and/or Woodworking					
Dramatic Play					
Blocks					
Art/Food					
Manipulatives/Library and/or Music					
CLEAN-UP, TRANSITION, BATHROOM, AND SNACK					
Group (music, stories, felt board, puppets, games, and transition) evaluation and dismissal					

Figure 6. Continued.

will be most appropriate for working with groups of two-, three-, four-, or five-year-old children. If you work with a mixed-age group, you can adapt the activities to make them more relevant for the developmental level of the children by providing appropriate materials and resources.

After you have chosen the activities, write the title of each activity and its page number in the appropriate place on the forms. Then, add any other activities you wish to use. Remember to plan some activities that do not apply to the theme. Overemphasis on the theme will make the day monotonous.

Finally, plan to meet the developmental needs of individual children. For instance, if Jami and Miguel need to work on large muscle skills, plan an obstacle path that includes the large muscle activities they need. Then, on the lesson form, write the names of the individual children next to the activities that will emphasize the developmental skills they need.

Assessing Your Plans

At the end of each day, assess your plans by answering the following questions about each activity:
- Was the activity appropriate for the children?
- Was the activity too difficult or too easy?
- How could I change the activity to make it more appropriate for the developmental level of the children?
- Did the activity hold the interest of the children?
- Was sex-role stereotyping avoided in the activity?
- What materials could I add to the learning center or change in the learning center to make the activity developmentally appropriate for each child?
- Did I have enough materials or equipment?
- Did I allow enough time for the children to choose, complete, and clean up after the activity?
- Was the activity fun for the children?

After you have assessed the individual activities, evaluate the entire day by answering the following questions:
- Did the children have an interesting, enjoyable day in my child care home or center?
- Did I talk with each child at least once during the day?
- Did I touch each child in a positive manner (a hug, kiss, pat on the shoulder, or a few minutes on my lap)?
- Was my guidance consistent? (If the rule was important enough to make on Monday, did I enforce it on Friday afternoon when I was tired?)
- Did I read to the children during the day?
- Did I encourage both boys and girls to play in all the learning center areas?

- Were soft places to sit, such as sofa, rocking chair, beanbag chairs, pillows, available to the children?
- Did I help the children share their day with their families?

Communicating with Families

Planning and assessing your daily plans are essential components of quality child care. Helping families stay informed and involved in the daily life of their children is also important and contributes to the success of your child care program.

A family bulletin board placed by the door is a good way to communicate with families. The weekly lesson plan and menu, articles on parenting, meeting dates, and samples of all the children's work can be posted on the bulletin board. Occasional telephone calls, family dinner nights, and conferences are other options for keeping in touch with families.

Sending home letters is another excellent way to communicate. You can tell families about your philosophy of teaching young children, Figure 7. You can discuss early childhood curriculum issues, Figure 8. You can let families know what activities their children are doing in your program, Figure 9. When addressing letters to parents, make sure you use the correct last name for each parent. Children sometimes do not have the same last name as their parents.

Getting to know each family is very important and will help you and the family become partners in the care of the child. You should make an effort to greet each parent when the child is dropped off in the morning and to talk to the parent when he or she picks up the child in the evening.

As you continue planning for children, keep in mind that children need love and that you are in partnership with families in the most important job in the world–caring for children!

USING THE CURRICULUM UNITS

Each of the following curriculum units has been developed around a theme. These themes are:
- Community Helpers.
- Friends.
- Me, I'm Special.
- Nursery Rhymes.
- Pets.
- Transportation.

The activities described in each curriculum unit are further divided into three areas:
- Group Activities.
- Learning Center Activities.
- Indoor or Outdoor Large Muscle Activities.

Dear _____:

Many of you have talked with me about how to guide your child's behavior. I would like to share some of the techniques I have found that work best:

- Make a few simple rules to keep your child safe and healthy. For example, "Walk in the house." "Wash your hands before eating." "Play in the yard or on the sidewalk."
- Be consistent–if you say "no" to a cookie before dinner today, say "no" tomorrow even if you are busy.
- Get down to your child's eye level to talk with him or her.
- Talk to him or her in a quiet voice. Yelling is usually ineffective.
- At this age, children usually have very short attention spans. Therefore, do not expect them to sit for long periods of time. Children can normally sit quietly for the same number of minutes as they are old unless they are particularly interested in an activity or story. Misbehavior is often the result of unrealistic expectations.
- Children need routines. Try to establish an evening and a morning routine. This routine may be difficult if you work all day. However, the children will be happier and calmer and so will you.
- Directing young children to a new activity from what they are doing is the simplest way to change negative behavior.

Most of all, love and enjoy your child. Try to remember that he or she will only be a child once. Take the time to enjoy the world through his or her eyes–he or she has such a fresh point of view.

Mr. Eric

Mr. Eric
Best There Is to Offer Child Care Center

Figure 7. Guiding children's behavior is often a concern to families.

Group Activities

Group activities include the entire group of children. These activities include storytelling, puppet stories, felt board stories, games, music, or creative movement. While these activities are directed by you, they are planned so that the children are actively involved through language, creative movement, observation, or participation.

The following tips will help to enhance group activities:

- Plan activities that are developmentally appropriate. For instance, two-, three-, and four-year-olds and even five-year-olds should not be expected to sit still for long periods of time.
- Sit on the floor or a small chair at the children's level when you are reading to them. Looking up at

(Continued on page 47)

Dear _____:

You will notice that I plan activities encouraging the children to become involved with materials, other children, and the environment, while using their senses of sight, touch, taste, smell, and hearing.

For instance, on Monday afternoon, we are going to visit The Tasty Bakery. The children will watch the baker bake bread and mix cookies. I have made arrangements for the children to help the baker cut out the cookies and put them on the trays to bake. They will be able to watch the cookies bake through the glass oven doors, and of course, they will get to eat the cookies with a glass of milk. Can you imagine the wonderful aroma?

On Tuesday morning, we will talk about our trip to The Tasty Bakery. I will write down what the children remember about the trip and make a story chart. During learning center time, perhaps, some of the children will draw a picture about our trip to The Tasty Bakery.

That afternoon, we will make our own cookies. I will have a recipe chart ready. The children will measure the ingredients, mix the dough, and spoon it onto the cookie sheets. We will bake the cookies and have them ready to share with you at pickup time Tuesday evening. The children will have the tables set and be waiting for you to attend their cookie party.

Think about all that your child is learning and all of the developmental skills that will have been enhanced:

- Small and large muscle development–walking to the bakery, mixing the cookie dough, cutting the cookies, drawing pictures, and pouring milk.
- Social-emotional development–talking with his or her friends, talking with the baker whom he or she did not know, planning a party for you, pouring milk for himself or herself, and washing his or her hands before cooking or serving cookies.
- Language development–talking with the baker, listening to the baker, and telling you about his or her trip when you come to the cookie party.
- Cognitive (thinking) development–discovering where bread and cookies are baked, learning to bake cookies, "reading" a recipe chart, asking the baker questions, and telling me what to write on our story chart

As I've said before, "Play is the best way for children to learn." Isn't it wonderful to know that they are learning so much while they are having an exciting, interesting day in child care? Won't you join us for our cookie party on Tuesday evening?

Ms. Jeannette

Ms. Jeannette
Best There Is to Offer Child Care Center

Figure 8. Families are often interested in learning about your child care philosophy in terms of different activities.

people can make the children's necks hurt and they cannot see the pictures in the book.

- Hold books so that each picture can be shown to each child.
- Read books before you attempt to read them with the children.
- Have children pretend to be the "Eency, Weency Spider" or "Jack and Jill." The songs will be enjoyed and remembered for a longer period of time.
- Children will understand the concepts "slow" and "fast" quicker if they can dance with streamers to "slow" and "fast" music.

Learning Center Activities

A good child care environment offers children many choices and hands-on experiences. Children learn best when they involve their senses–sight, taste, touch, smell, and hearing–in the exploration and discovery of concepts in their environments.

In your child care home or center, you should plan four to eight activities for the children to choose from during the self-selected activity time each morning and afternoon. If children have been in an environment where all the activities have been directed by a child care provider, they often have difficulty making

Dear Mom and Dad:

Look at all the bright colors I used in my painting today. I made some big circles and my lines went from the top to the bottom of the paper. I found out that thin paint likes to drip when I paint at the easel.
Isn't it neat that I learned this all by myself?

Love,

Art

Art
(Staple Art's painting to the letter.)

Figure 9. Families are always interested in knowing the value of their children's activities.

choices. You should start with two or three learning centers each day for the first week or two if you have not used learning centers before. Then slowly add more learning centers until you feel comfortable with four to eight learning centers a day. By slowly adding more learning centers, the children can adapt to an environment where they are in control and can choose their own activities.

Even though the children choose their activities in the learning centers, you still play a very active role. You need to move from one group of children to another observing them as they play and learn. This movement helps you become aware of the developmental level of each child. For example, you will see that three-year-old Jonathan is unable to hold the scissors to cut a straight line or that five-year-old Latoya is having difficulty sharing. Then you can make notes to plan activities to help Jonathan develop his small muscle skills and encourage Latoya to develop her social-emotional skills.

As you move from group to group, you can also add to the children's play by adding resources such as a sheet to the dramatic play area to make a sail for a boat or markers and paper to the block area, so the children can make signs for their streets. Oftentimes the children will ask you to participate in a play situation by being a baby or dog.

You can also help children as they play by asking open-ended questions. This questioning extends their learning and helps them think of alternative ways to solve problems. For example, ask "Why is the baby crying?" "What could you do to help the baby feel better?" "What does a dog like to eat?" or "Where do you think the dog would go if it could get out of the yard?"

Before you use the learning centers, you will need to introduce each one to the children and let them know how many children can play in each area. You will also need to show them what they can do in each area and how they should take care of the materials and equipment.

Indoor or Outdoor Large Muscle Activities

Indoor or outdoor large muscle activities are planned for a large, open, indoor area or for the outside playground. These activities give children opportunities to develop large muscle skills, such as running, jumping, climbing, pushing and pulling, and throwing and catching. Opportunities to pedal tricycles, swing on swings, crawl through tunnels, climb and hang from climbing equipment, and slide down play equipment are pinpointed.

Social-emotional, language, and cognitive (thinking) skills are also enhanced in indoor or outdoor large muscle activities. Group activities and games are planned to encourage the children to begin playing and working together.

Understanding the Activity Pages

For each of the three types of activities discussed above, suggested activities are described in this curriculum guide. The descriptions are designed to help you become more aware of the importance of your role as a child care provider in the growth and development of the children in your care.

The top portion of each page contains the title of the activity and indicates if the activity is a group activity, learning center activity, or indoor or outdoor large muscle activity. This information will help you as you write your weekly plan.

The remainder of the activity page is divided into five instructional sections. Each of the sections has a picture of a child care provider asking you questions that will help you plan and implement the activity for the children. These questions are as follows:

- What do I do? (This details what you need to do before the children arrive.)
- Why do I have children do this? (This explains how the activity helps enhance one of the developmental skills discussed earlier in this introduction.)
- What do I need? (This is a list of materials you will need.)
- What might I see children doing? (This gives you examples of what you might observe the children doing during the activity.)
- What might we talk about? (These are open-ended questions that can be used to encourage the children to think and problem solve as they participate in the activity.)

Figure 10 shows how activity pages appear in this curriculum guide. Information describing each of the five sections of the activity page is given in Figure 11. Refer to this sample activity page to help you understand the various sections.

BUSY BAKER PLAYDOUGH
Learning Center (art)

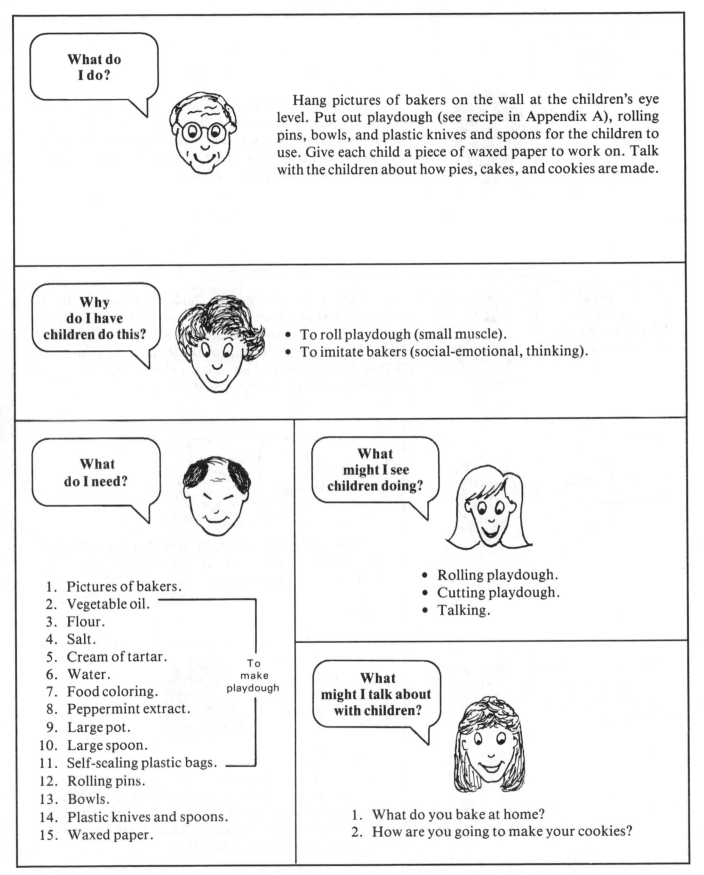

What do I do?

Hang pictures of bakers on the wall at the children's eye level. Put out playdough (see recipe in Appendix A), rolling pins, bowls, and plastic knives and spoons for the children to use. Give each child a piece of waxed paper to work on. Talk with the children about how pies, cakes, and cookies are made.

Why do I have children do this?

- To roll playdough (small muscle).
- To imitate bakers (social-emotional, thinking).

What do I need?

1. Pictures of bakers.
2. Vegetable oil.
3. Flour.
4. Salt.
5. Cream of tartar.
6. Water.
7. Food coloring.
8. Peppermint extract.
9. Large pot.
10. Large spoon.
11. Self-sealing plastic bags.
12. Rolling pins.
13. Bowls.
14. Plastic knives and spoons.
15. Waxed paper.

To make playdough

What might I see children doing?

- Rolling playdough.
- Cutting playdough.
- Talking.

What might I talk about with children?

1. What do you bake at home?
2. How are you going to make your cookies?

Figure 10. This sample activity is from the Community Helpers unit.

This section gives the title of the activity and describes how it may be used–as a group activity, a learning center activity, or an indoor or outdoor large muscle activity.

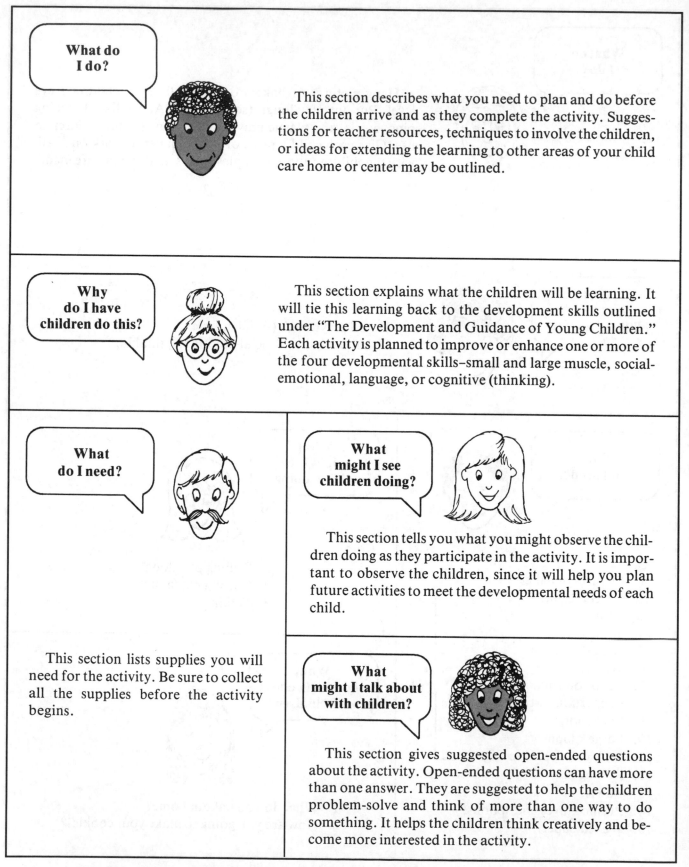

What do I do?

This section describes what you need to plan and do before the children arrive and as they complete the activity. Suggestions for teacher resources, techniques to involve the children, or ideas for extending the learning to other areas of your child care home or center may be outlined.

Why do I have children do this?

This section explains what the children will be learning. It will tie this learning back to the development skills outlined under "The Development and Guidance of Young Children." Each activity is planned to improve or enhance one or more of the four developmental skills–small and large muscle, social-emotional, language, or cognitive (thinking).

What do I need?

This section lists supplies you will need for the activity. Be sure to collect all the supplies before the activity begins.

What might I see children doing?

This section tells you what you might observe the children doing as they participate in the activity. It is important to observe the children, since it will help you plan future activities to meet the developmental needs of each child.

What might I talk about with children?

This section gives suggested open-ended questions about the activity. Open-ended questions can have more than one answer. They are suggested to help the children problem-solve and think of more than one way to do something. It helps the children think creatively and become more interested in the activity.

Figure 11. Each section of this activity page describes the child care provider's responsibility.

SELECTED BIBLIOGRAPHY OF RESOURCE MATERIALS FOR CHILD CARE PROVIDERS

The following resource materials have information and activities that will be helpful in your child care homes or centers. As you choose materials, please be selective, consider the developmental growth of the children you work with, and plan your program to meet their needs.

CHILD DEVELOPMENT

Allen, K. E., and Marotz, L. R.1994. *Developmental Profiles: Birth to Six.* New York, NY: Delmar Publishers Inc.

Ames, L. B., Ilg, F. I.., and Haber, C. C. 1983. *Your One-Year-Old: The Fun-Loving Fussy 12 to 24 Month Old.* New York, NY: Delta Publishing Co.

Ames, L. B., and Ilg, F. L. 1980. *Your Two-Year-Old: Terrible or Tender.* New York, NY: Delta Publishing Co.

Ames, L. B., and Ilg, F. L. 1980. *Your Three-Year-Old: Friend or Enemy.* New York, NY: Delta Publishing Co.

Ames, L. B., and Ilg, F. L. 1989. *Your Four-Year-Old: Wild and Wonderful.* New York, NY: Delta Publishing Co.

Ames, L. B., and Ilg, F. L. 1981. *Your Five-Year-Old: Sunny and Serene.* New York, NY: Delta Publishing Co.

Ames, L. B., and Ilg, F. L. 1981. *Your Six-Year-Old: Loving and Defiant.* New York, NY: Delta Publishing Co.

Ames, L. B., and Haber, C. C. 1987. *Your Seven-Year-Old: Life in a Minor Key.* New York, NY: Delta Publishing Co.

Brisbane, H. E. 1997. *The Developing Child: Understanding Children and Parenting.* Mission Hills, CA: Glencoe Publishing Company.

Decker, C. A. 1995. *Children: The Early Years.* Tinley Park, IL: The Goodheart-Willcox Company, Inc.

[1]Domblewski, C. 1990. *Child Development—Roles, Responsibilities, Resources.* Needham, MA: Prentice Hall.

Elkind, D. 1988. *Hurried Child: Growing Up Too Fast Too Soon.* Reading, MA: Addison-Wesley Publishing Co., Inc.

Marhoefer, P. E., and Vadnais, L. A. *1992. Caring for the Developing Child.* Albany, NY: Delmar Publishers Inc.

Miller, K. 1985. *Ages and Stages.* Marshfield, MA: TelShare Publishing Co., Inc.

Segal, M. 1991. *Your Child at Play: Birth to One Year.* New York, NY: Newmarket Press.

Segal, M., and Adcock, D. 1991. *Your Child at Play: One to Two Years.* New York, NY: Newmarket Press.

White, B. L. 1995. *The New First Three Years of Life: The Completely Revised and Updated Edition of the Parenting Classic.* New York, NY: Prentice Hall.

HEALTH, SAFETY, AND NUTRITION

[1]Ackerman, C. 1981. *Cooking with Kids.* Reston, VA: Acropolis Books.

Comer, D. 1987. *Developing Safety Skills with the Young Child.* Albany, NY: Delmar Publishers Inc.

Faggella, K.1985. *Concept Cookery.* Weston, MA: First Teacher Press.

Johson, B., and Plemons, B. 1990. *Cup Cooking: Individual Child Portion Picture Recipes.* Lake Alfred, FL: Early Educator's Press.

Marotz, L., Rush, J., and Cross, M. 1997. *Health, Safety and Nutrition for the Young Child.* Albany, NY: Delmar Publishers Inc.

CURRICULUM

Adcock, D., and Segal, M. 1993. *Play Together Grow Together: A Cooperative Curriculum for Teachers of Young Children.* White Plains, NY: Mailman Family Press.

[1]Bailey, R. A., and Burton, E. C. 1989. *The Dynamic Infant: Activities to Enhance Infant and Toddler Development.* St. Paul, MN: Redleaf Press.

Beaty, J. J. 1992. *Preschool: Appropriate Practices.* Orlando, FL: Holt, Rinehart and Winston, Inc.

Beaty, J. J. 1995. *Skills for Preschool Teachers.* Columbus, OH: Macmillan.

Beckman, C., Simmons, R., and Thomas, N. 1982. *Channels to Children: Early Childhood Activity Guide for Holidays and Seasons.* Colorado Springs, CO: Channels to Children.

Borba, M., and Borba, C. 1984. *Self-Esteem: A Classroom Affair, Vol. 1.* San Francisco, CA: Harper San Francisco.

Borba, M., and Borba, C. 1985. *Self-Esteem: A Classroom Affair, Vol. 2.* San Francisco, CA: Harper San Francisco.

Bos, B. 1983. *Before the Basics: Creating Conversations with Children.* Roseville, CA: Turn-the-Page Press, Inc.

Bos, B. 1978. *Don't Move the Muffin Tins: A Hands-Off Guide to Art for the Young Child.* Roseville, CA: Turn-the-Page Press, Inc.

Brashears, D. 1985. *Dribble Drabble: Art Experiences for Young Children.* Orinda, CA: Deya Brashears.

Bredekamp, S., and Copple, C. (eds.). *1997. Developmentally Appropriate Practice in Early Child Programs.* Washington, DC: National Association for the Education of Young Children.

Brokering, L. 1990. *Resources for Dramatic Play.* Belmont, CA: Fearon Teacher Aids.

Coletta, A., and Coletta, K. 1986. *Year' Round Activities for Two-Year-Old Children.* West Nyack, NY: The Center for Applied Research in Education Inc.

Coletta, A., and Coletta, K. 1986. *Year' Round Activities for Three-Year-Old Children.* West Nyack, NY: The Center for Applied Research in Education Inc.

Coletta, A., and Coletta, K. 1986. *Year' Round Activities for Four-Year-Old Children.* West Nyack, NY: The Center for Applied Research in Education Inc.

[1]Cromwall, L., and Hibner, D. 1979. *Explore and Create: Activities for Young Children: Art, Games, Cooking, Science, and Math.* Livonia, MI: Partner Press.

Cryer, D., Harms, T., and Bourland, B. 1987. *Active Learning for Ones.* Reading, MA: Addison-Wesley Publishing Company.

Cryer, D., Harms, T., and Bourland, B. 1988. *Active Learning for Twos.* Reading, MA: Addison-Wesley Publishing Company.

Cryer, D., Harms, T., and Bourland, B. 1988. *Active Learning for Threes.* Reading, MA: Addison-Wesley Publishing Company.

Curtis, D., and Carter, M. 1996. *Reflecting Children's Lives: A Handbook for Planning Child-Centered Curriculum.* St. Paul, MN: Redleaf Press.

Davidson, J. 1996. *Emergent Literacy and Dramatic Play in Early Education.* Albany, NY: Delmar Publishers Inc.

Dodge, D. T., Goldhammer, M., and Colker, L. J. 1992. *The Creative Curriculum for Early Childhood.* Washington, DC: Teaching Strategies.

Eliason, C. F., and Jenkins, L. T. 1993. *A Practical Cuide to Early Childhood Curriculum (2nd ed.).* St. Louis: C. V. Mosby Company.

Gestwicki, C. 1995. *Developmentally Appropriate Practice: Curriculum and Development in Early Education.* Albany, NY: Delmar Publishers Inc.

Gregson, B. 1982. *The Incredible Indoor Games Book: One Hundred and Sixty Group Projects, Games, and Activities.* Belmont, CA: Fearon Teacher Aids.

Gregson, B. 1984. *Outrageous Outdoor Games.* Belmont, CA: Fearon Teacher Aids.

[1]Hamilton, D. S., and Flemming, B. M. 1990. *Resources for Creative Teaching in Early Childhood Education (2nd ed.).* New York, NY: Harcourt Brace Jovanovich, Publishers.

Hendrick, J. 1993. *Total Learning: Developmental Curriculum for the Young Child.* New York, NY: Macmillian.

Herr, J. 1998. *Working with Young Children.* Tinley Park, IL: The Goodheart-Willcox Company, Inc.

Houle, G. B. 1987. *Learning Centers for Young Children.* West Greenwich, RI: Consortium Publishing.

Jones, E., and Nimmo, J. 1994. *Emergent Curriculum.* Washington, DC: National Association for the Education of Young Children.

Kohl, M. A. 1989. *Mudworks: Creative Clay, Dough and Modeling Experiences.* Bellingham, WA: Bright Ring Publishing.

Maxim, G. 1994. *The Sourcebook: Activities for Infants and Young Children (2nd ed.).* Columbus, OH: Merrill Publishing Company.

Miller, K. 1989. *The Outside Play and Learning Book: Activities for Young Children.* Mt. Rainier, MD: Gryphon House.

Miller, K. 1990. *Things to Do with Toddlers and Twos.* Marshfield, MA: TelShare Publishing Co., Inc.

Raines, S. C., and Canady, R. J. 1989. *Story S-T-R-E-T-C-H-E-R-S: Activities to Expand Children's Favorite Books.* Mt. Rainier, MD: Gryphon House.

Rogers, F., and Head, B. 1993. *Mister Rogers' Plan and Playbook.* New York, NY: Berkley Publishing Group.

Rockwell, R. E., Sherwood, E., and Williams, R. 1983. *Hug a Tree and Other Things to Do Outdoors with Young Children.* Mt. Rainier, MD: Gryphon House.

Schickedanz, J. 1986. *More Than the ABC's.* Washington, DC: National Association for the Education of Young Children.

Warren, J. 1986. 1-2-3 *Games: No-Lose Group Games for Young Children.* Everett, WA: Warren Publishing House.

Warren, J. (Ed.). 1983. *Piggyback Songs.* Everett, WA: Warren Publishing House.

Warren, J. (Ed.). 1985. *Piggyback Songs for Infants and Toddlers.* Everett, WA: Warren Publishing House.

Warren, J. (Ed.). 1988. *Holiday Piggyback Songs.* Tulsa, OK: Warren Publishing House.

Weissman, J. 1986. *Great Big Book of Rhythm-Rhythm Activities: Songs and Games to Develop Skills in Children.* Overland Park, KS: Miss Jackie Music Co.

Wilmes, L., and Wilmes, D. 1984. *Felt Board Fun.* Elgin, IL: Building Blocks.

[1]Wilson, L. C. 1990. *Infants and Toddlers: Curriculum and Teaching,* 2E. Albany, NY: Delmar Publishers Inc.

MUSICAL RECORDINGS

Cramer, P. T. *Dynamic Dinosaurs.* Oklahoma City, OK: Melody House Publishing Company.

Glazer, T. *Children's Greatest Hits (Vols. 1-2).* Scarborough, NY: Tom Glazer Sings Music, Inc.

Glazer, T. *Let's Sing Fingerplays.* Scarborough, NY: Tom Glazer Sings Music, Inc.

Jenkins, E. *I Know the Colors in the Rainbow.* Cambridge, MA: Rounder Records.

Jenkins, E. *This-A-Way, That-A-Way.* Cambridge, MA: Rounder Records.

Jenkins, E. *You'll Sing a Song and I'll Sing a Song.* Cambridge, MA: Rounder Records.

Macmillan Educational Company. *Macmillan Sing and Learn Program.* Hicksville, NY: Author.

Millang, S., and Scelsa, G. *On the Move with Greg and Steve.* Los Angeles, CA: Creative Youngheart Records.

Millang, S., and Scelsa, G. *We All Live Together (Vols. 1-4).* Los Angeles, CA: Creative Youngheart Records.

Palmer, H., and Palmer, M. *Witches' Brew: Pot Full of Songs for Oral Language Development.* Freeport, NY: Educational Activities, Inc.

Palmer, H. *Creative Movement and Rhythmic Exploration.* Freeport, NY: Educational Activities, Inc.

Palmer, H. *Easy Does It: Activity Songs for Basic Motor Skill Development.* Freeport, NY: Educational Activities, Inc.

Palmer, H. *Feelin' Free: A Personalized Approach to Vocabulary and Language Development.* Freeport, NY: Educational Activities, Inc.

Palmer, H. *Folk Song Carnival.* Freeport, NY: Educational Activities, Inc.

Palmer, H. *Getting to Know Myself.* Freeport, NY: Educational Activities, Inc.

Palmer, H. *Holiday Songs and Rhythms.* Freeport, NY: Educational Activities, Inc.

Palmer, H. *Homemade Band.* Freeport, NY: Educational Activities, Inc.

Palmer, H. *Ideas, Thoughts and Feelings.* Freeport, NY: Educational Activities, Inc.

Palmer, H. *Learning Basic Skills Through Music (Vols. 1-5).* Freeport, NY: Educational Activities, Inc.

Palmer, H. *Learning with Circles and Sticks.* Freeport, NY: Educational Activities, Inc.

Palmer, H. *Math Readiness: Vocabulary and Concepts.* Freeport, NY: Educational Activities, Inc.

Palmer, H. *Mod Marches.* Freeport, NY: Educational Activities, Inc.

Palmer, H. *Modern Tunes for Rhymes and Instruments.* Freeport, NY: Educational Activities, Inc.

Palmer, H. *Movin'.* Freeport, NY: Educational Activities, Inc.

Palmer, H. *Patriotic and Morning Time Songs.* Freeport, NY: Educational Activities, Inc.

Palmer, H. *Pretend.* Freeport, NY: Educational Activities, Inc.

Palmer, H. *Sally the Swinging Snake.* Freeport, NY: Educational Activities, Inc.

Palmer, H. *Simplified Folk Songs.* Freeport, NY: Educational Activities, Inc.

Palmer, H. *Turn on the Music.* Freeport, NY: Educational Activities, Inc.

Palmer, H. *Walter the Waltzing Worm.* Freeport, NY: Educational Activities, Inc.

Palmer, M., and Palmer, H. *Tickly Toddle: Songs for Very Young Children.* Freeport, NY: Educational Activities, Inc.

Poelker, K. *Amazing Musical Moments: In Song, Movement, Imagery, and Dance.* Wheeling, IL: Look At Me Records, Inc.

Poelker, K. *Kathy Poelker Sings.* Wheeling, IL: Look At Me Records, Inc.

Poelker, K. *Look at the Holidays.* Wheeling, IL: Look At Me Records, Inc.

Poelker, K. *Look at Me.* Wheeling, IL: Look At Me Records, Inc.

Poelker, K. *Look at My World.* Wheeling, IL: Look At Me Records, Inc.

Raffi. *Baby Beluga and Rise and Shine.* Norcroft, GA: MCA-Yuni Distributing.

Raffi. *Singable Songs for the Very Young.* Norcroft, GA: MCA-Yuni Distributing.

Raffi. *More Singable Songs.* Norcroft, GA: MCA-Yuni Distributing.

Sharon, Lois, and Bram. *Mainly Mother Goose.* Marietta, GA: PGD Records.

Sharon, Lois, and Bram. *One Elephant.* Marietta, GA: PGD Records.

Sharon, Lois, and Bram. *Smorgasboard.* Marietta, GA: PGD Records.

Stewart, G. L. *Bean Bag Activities and Coordination Skills for Early Childhood and Adaptable for Special Education.* Long Branch, NJ: Kimbo Educational.

Weissman, J. *Lollipops and Spaghetti.* Overland Park, KS: Miss Jackie.

Weissman, J. *Miss Jackie Says: Hello Rhythm.* Overland Park, KS: Miss Jackie.

Weissman, *J. Miss Jackie and her Friends Sing about . . . Peanut Butter, Tarzan and Roosters.* Overland Park, KS: Miss Jackie.

Weissman, J. *Sniggles, Squirrels, and Chicken Pox (Vols. 1-2).* Overland Park, KS: Miss Jackie.

Weimer, T. *Animal Friends for Sale.* Pittsburg, PA: Pearce Evetts Productions.

Weimer, T. *Folk Songs for Children.* Pittsburg, PA: Pearce Evetts Productions.

White, D. *Action Songs for Indoor Days.* Tom Thumb Records.

POETRY AND FINGERPLAYS

[1]Aldis, D. 1927. *Everything and Anything.* New York, NY: The Putnam Publishing Group.

[1]Allen, M. L. 1939. *A Pocket Full of Poems.* New York, NY: Harper & Row Publishers.

[1]Arbuthnot, M. H. 1968. *Time for Poetry.* Glenview, IL: ScottForesman and Company.

[1]Browne, J. 1991. *Sing Me a Story: Action Songs to Sing and Play.* New York, NY: Crown Publishing Co.

[1]Chute, M. 1957. *Around and About.* New York, NY: E. P. Dutton & Co., Inc.

[1]Chute, M. 1974. *Rhymes about Us.* New York, NY: E. P. Dutton & Co., Inc.

[1]Coatsworth, E. 1966. *Sparrow Bush.* New York, NY: W. W. Norton and Company, Inc.

[1]Cole, J. 1984. *A New Treasury of Children's Poetry.* New York, NY: Doubleday and Company, Inc.

Cromwell, L., and Hibner, D. 1983. *Finger Frolics: Fingerplays for Young Children.* Livonia, MI: Partner Press.

[1]De Regniers, B. S. 1988. *The Way I Feel . . . Sometimes.* New York, NY: Clarion Books.

[1]De Regniers, B. S. 1986. *A Week in the Life of Best Friends: And Other Poems of Friendship.* New York, NY: Atheneum Children's Books.

[1]De Regniers, B. S., Moore, E., White, M. M., and Carr, J. (Eds.).1991. *Sing a Song of Popcorn: Every Child's Book of Poems.* New York, NY: Scholastic, Inc.

[1]Duncan, L. 1982. *From Spring to Spring: Poems and Photographs.* Louisville, KY: Westminster John Knox Press.

[1]Field, R. 1930. *Pointed People.* New York, NY: Macmillan Publishing Company.

[1]Fisher, A. 1973. *My Cat Has Eyes of Sapphire Blue.* New York, NY: Thomas Y. Crowell Company.

[1]Fisher, A. 1983. *Rabbits, Rabbits.* New York, NY: HarperCollins Children's Books.

Flint Public Library. (Eds.). 1988. *Ring a Ring O'Roses: Finger Plays for Pre-school Children.* Flint, MI: Author.

Frank, J. (Ed.). 1982. *Poems to Read to the Very Young.* New York, NY: Random House, Inc.

[1]Fukikawa, G. 1976. *Oh, What a Busy Day.* New York, NY: The Putnam Publishing Group.

[1]Fyleman, R. 1923. *The Fairy Queen.* New York, NY: Doubleday & Company, Inc.

[1]Fyleman, R. 1932. *Fifty-one New Nursery Rhymes.* New York, NY: Doubleday & Company, Inc.

[1]Geismer, B. P., and Suter, A. B. (Eds.). 1945. *Very Young Verses.* Boston: Houghton Mifflin Company.

Harrison, M., and Stuart-Clark, C. (Eds.). 1988. *The Oxford Treasury of Children's Poems.* Oxford, AT: Oxford University Press.

[1]Hoberman, M. A. 1959. *Hello and Goodby.* Boston, MA: Little, Brown and Company.

[1]Hopkins, L. B. (Ed.). 1983. *A Dog's Life.* San Diego, CA: Harcourt Brace Jovanovich, Publishers.

Hopkins, L. B. (Ed.). 1986. *Best Friends.* New York, NY: HarperCollins Children's Books.

[1]Hopkins, L. B. (Ed.). 1980. *Elves, Fairies and Gnomes.* New York, NY: Alfred A. Knopf, Inc.

[1]Hopkins, L. B. (Ed.). 1981. *I Am the Cat*. New York, NY: Harcourt Brace Jovanovich, Publishers.

Hopkins, L. B. (Ed.). 1986. *Surprises*. New York, NY: HarperCollins Children's Books.

[1]Huck, C., Jenkins, W. A., and Pyle, W. J. (Eds.). 1971. *The World's So Big*. Glenview, IL: ScottForesman and Company.

[1]Hughes, R. (Ed.). 1958. *Let's Enjoy Poetry*. Boston, MA: Houghton Mifflin Company.

[1]Jacobs, L. 1964. *Just Around the Corner*. New York, NY: Holt, Rinehart and Winston, Inc.

[1]Krauss, R. 1976. *Somebody Spilled the Sky*. New York, NY: William Morrow and Company.

[1]Livingston, M. C. 1965. *The Moon and a Start and Other Poems*. San Diego, CA: Harcourt Brace Jovanovich, Publishers.

[1]Livingston, M. C. 1974. *The Way Things Are, and Other Poems*. New York, NY: Macmillan Publishing Company.

Lobel, A. 1988. *Whiskers and Rhymes*. New York, NY: William Morrow and Co., Inc.

[1]McCord, D. 1986. *All Small*. Boston, MA: Little, Brown and Co.

McCord, D. 1986. *One at a Time*. Boston, MA: Little, Brown and Co.

[1]Mitchell, L. S. 1937. *Another Here and Now Story Book*. New York, NY: E. P. Dutton and Company.

[1]Merriam, E. 1981. *A Word or Two with You*. New York, NY: Atheneum.

[1]Nave, Y. 1990. *Goosebumps and Butterflies*. New York, NY: Orchard Books.

Prelutsky, J. 1980. *Rainy, Rainy Saturday*. New York, NY: Greenwillow Books.

[1]Ridlon, M. 1969. *That Was Summer*. Chicago, IL: Follett Publishing.

Roberts, L. 1986. *Mitt Magic: Fingerplays for Finger Puppets*. Mt. Rainier, MD: Gryphon House.

Rossetti, C. 1969. *Sing Song: A Nursery Rhyme Book*. New York, NY: Dover Publications, Inc.

Sky-Peck, K. (Ed.). 1993. *Who Has Seen the Wind? An Illustrated Collection, Museum of Fine Arts, Boston*. New York, NY: Rizzoli International Publications.

[1]Tippett, J. 1970. *Crickety Cricket! The Best Loved Poems of James Tippett*. New York, NY: Harper & Row Publishers.

Waters, F. (Ed.). 1990. *Whiskers and Paws*. Los Angeles, CA: Interlink Publishing Group, Inc.

Weimer, T. 1995. *Fingerplays and Action Chants: Animals, Vol. 1*. Pittsburgh, PA: Pearce-Evetts Publishing.

Weimer, T. 1995. *Fingerplays and Action Chants: Family and Friends, Vol. 2*. Pittsburgh, PA: Pearce-Evetts Publishing.

Wirth, M., and Stassevitch, V. 1983. *Musical Games, Fingerplays and Rhythmic Activities for Early Childhood*. New York, NY: Prentice Hall.

[1]Wolman, B. 1992. *Taking Turns: Poetry to Share*. New York, NY: Macmillan Publishing Co., Inc.

[1]Zolotow, C. 1967. *All that Sunlight*. New York, NY: Harper & Row Publishers.

Zolotow, C. 1987. *Everything Glistens and Everything Sings*. New York, NY: Harcourt Brace Jovanovich, Publishers.

---

[1]This book is no longer in print. You may, however, be able to find it at your local library.

JOURNALS

Day Care and Early Education
1 year $45.00
Human Sciences Press
233 Spring St.
New York, NY 10013-1578

Dimensions of Early Childhood
1 year $25.00
Southern Early Childhood Association
PO Box 5593
Little Rock, AR 72215

Early Childhood Today
1 year $19.95
Scholastic, Inc.
PO Box 54031
Boulder, CO 80322

Everyday TLC
1 year $17.95
PO Box 180
Wilmington, NC 28402

School Age NOTES
1 year $26.95
PO Box 40205
Nashville, TN 37204

Texas Child Care
1 year $10.00
Corporate Child Development Fund of Texas
PO Box 162881
Austin, TX 78716-2881

Young Children
1 year $50.00 for nonmember
The Journal of the National Association for the
Education of Young Children
NAEYC
1509 16th St., NW
Washington, DC 20036-1426

Child Care Information Exchange
1 year $38.00
Exchange Press, Inc.
17916 NE 103rd Court
Redmond, WA 98052-3243

Early Childhood News
Free
Advertising Sales Office
2 Lower Ragsdale Dr., Suite 125
Monterey, CA 93940

EARLY CHILDHOOD CATALOG

Curriculum Materials, Equipme
Books:

ABC School Supply, Inc.
3312 N. Berkley Lake Rd.
Duluth, GA 30096-9419

Angeles Group, Inc.
9 Capper Dr.
Dailey Industrial Park
Pacific, MO 63069

Bowlus School Supply
201 E. 5th St.
Pittsburg, KS 66762

Childcraft Education Corporation
PO Box 3239
Lancaster, PA 17604

Community Playthings
PO Box 901
Rifton, NY 12471

Constructive Playthings
13201 Arrington Rd.
Grandview, MO 64030

Environments, Inc.
PO Box 1348
Beaufort, SC 29901-1348

Kaplan School Supply
PO Box 609
Lewisville, NC 27023

Lakeshore Learning Materials
2695 E. Dominguez St.
PO Box 6261
Carson, CA 90749

School Specialty Supply, Inc.
3525 S. Ninth St.
Salina, KS 67402

RESOURCE BOOKS FOR TEACHERS AND CHILDREN

Building Blocks
38W567 Brindlewood
Elgin, IL 60123

Gryphon House, Inc.
Early Childhood Books
PO Box 207
Beltsville, MO 20704-0207

Redleaf Press
450 N. Syndicate, Suite 5
St. Paul, MN 55104-4125

School Age NOTES
P. O. Box 40205
Nashville, TN 37204

Unit 1

COMMUNITY HELPERS

CONTENTS

COMMUNITY HELPERS

"Community Helpers" includes activities to help the children recognize how their lives go much more smoothly when everyone in the community works together, or cooperates, than when people do not work together. The children will see that:

- Everyone in the community depends on one another.
- Each person in the community is important.
- Each person in the community has a specific and important job to do to help the community run smoothly.
- Cooperation makes everyone's life easier.
- Everyone can be a community helper.

A TRIP TO THE MAILBOX
Group, Field Trip

What do I do?

Let each child put a stamp on a letter to a friend, which you have already addressed. As the children put stamps on the envelopes, talk with them about why they are doing this. Then take a trip to a mailbox to mail the letters. Talk about the color of the mailbox. Talk about dropping the letters in the slot. Plan a trip to the post office if it is near the child care home or center. Have the mail carrier talk about what he or she does at work as he or she shows the children around the post office or mail truck.

Why do I have children do this?

- To see what the mail carrier does when he or she is at work (thinking).
- To talk about how letters get to their friends when they send them (language).
- To walk in their community (large muscle).

What do I need?

1. Envelopes.
2. Postage stamps.
3. Mailbox.
4. Post office.
5. Mail carrier.
6. Mail truck.

What might I see children doing?

- Walking.
- Talking.
- Mailing a letter.

What might I talk about with children?

1. How could you invite your Grandpa to dinner?
2. What could you say in a letter to Grandma or your friend Johnny?

A TRIP TO THE FIRE STATION
Group, Field Trip

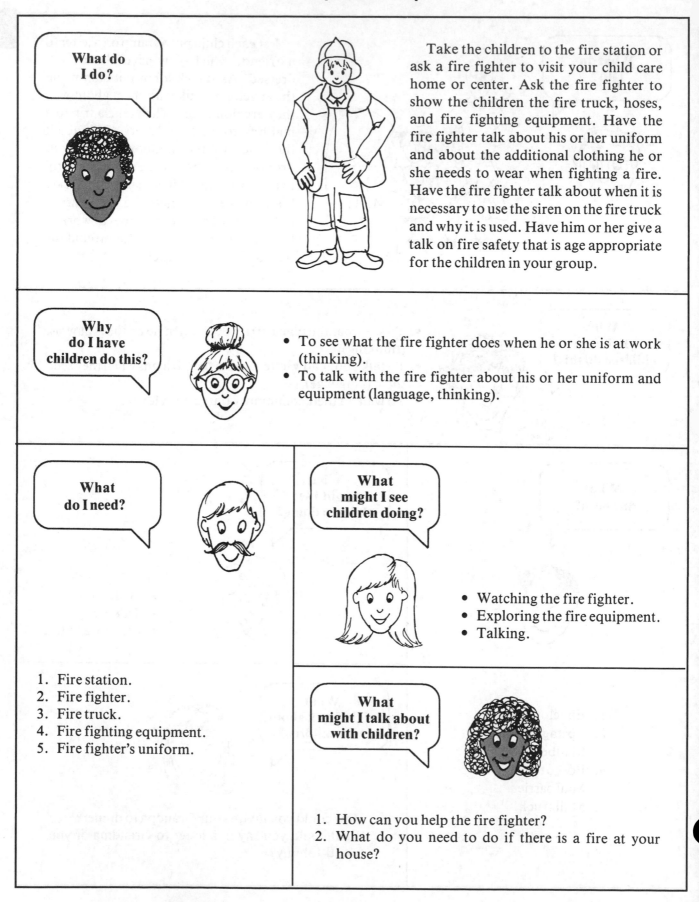

What do I do?

Take the children to the fire station or ask a fire fighter to visit your child care home or center. Ask the fire fighter to show the children the fire truck, hoses, and fire fighting equipment. Have the fire fighter talk about his or her uniform and about the additional clothing he or she needs to wear when fighting a fire. Have the fire fighter talk about when it is necessary to use the siren on the fire truck and why it is used. Have him or her give a talk on fire safety that is age appropriate for the children in your group.

Why do I have children do this?

- To see what the fire fighter does when he or she is at work (thinking).
- To talk with the fire fighter about his or her uniform and equipment (language, thinking).

What do I need?

1. Fire station.
2. Fire fighter.
3. Fire truck.
4. Fire fighting equipment.
5. Fire fighter's uniform.

What might I see children doing?

- Watching the fire fighter.
- Exploring the fire equipment.
- Talking.

What might I talk about with children?

1. How can you help the fire fighter?
2. What do you need to do if there is a fire at your house?

POLICE OFFICERS
Group, Learning Center (library)

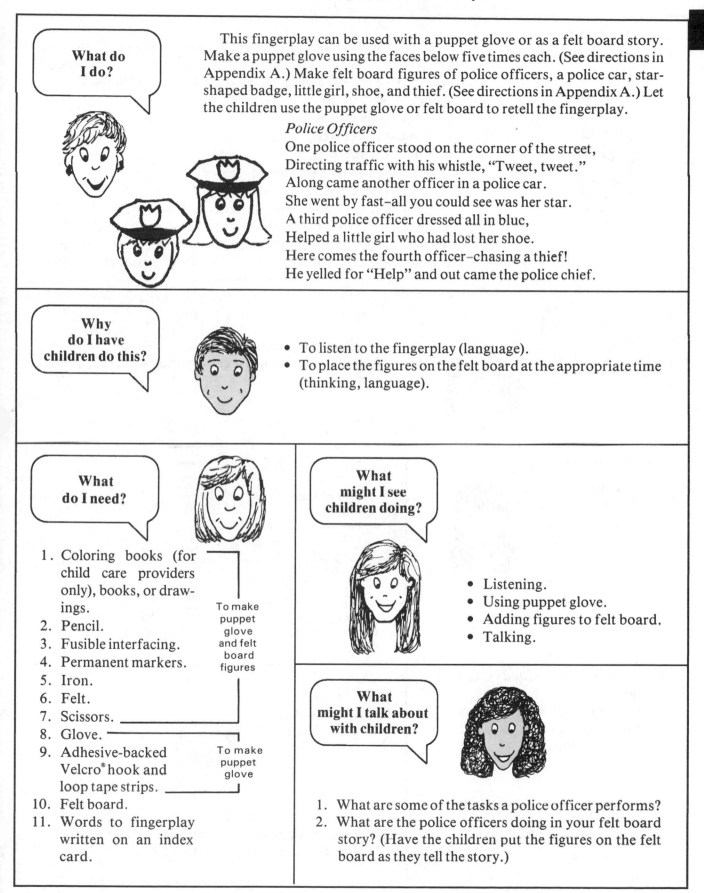

What do I do?

This fingerplay can be used with a puppet glove or as a felt board story. Make a puppet glove using the faces below five times each. (See directions in Appendix A.) Make felt board figures of police officers, a police car, star-shaped badge, little girl, shoe, and thief. (See directions in Appendix A.) Let the children use the puppet glove or felt board to retell the fingerplay.

Police Officers
One police officer stood on the corner of the street,
Directing traffic with his whistle, "Tweet, tweet."
Along came another officer in a police car.
She went by fast–all you could see was her star.
A third police officer dressed all in blue,
Helped a little girl who had lost her shoe.
Here comes the fourth officer–chasing a thief!
He yelled for "Help" and out came the police chief.

Why do I have children do this?

- To listen to the fingerplay (language).
- To place the figures on the felt board at the appropriate time (thinking, language).

What do I need?

1. Coloring books (for child care providers only), books, or drawings.
2. Pencil.
3. Fusible interfacing.
4. Permanent markers.
5. Iron.
6. Felt.
7. Scissors.
8. Glove.
9. Adhesive-backed Velcro® hook and loop tape strips.
10. Felt board.
11. Words to fingerplay written on an index card.

To make puppet glove and felt board figures

To make puppet glove

What might I see children doing?

- Listening.
- Using puppet glove.
- Adding figures to felt board.
- Talking.

What might I talk about with children?

1. What are some of the tasks a police officer performs?
2. What are the police officers doing in your felt board story? (Have the children put the figures on the felt board as they tell the story.)

"A TISKET, A TASKET"
Group

What do I do?

Have the children sit in a circle. Choose one child to be the mail carrier. As he or she moves around the circle carrying a "mailbag" with a large envelope inside, have the rest of the children sing "A Tisket, A Tasket."

"A Tisket, A Tasket"
A tisket, A tasket,
I have a mail basket,
I wrote a letter to my friend
And on the way I dropped it.

Have the mail carrier drop the letter in the lap of a child in the circle. Then have the child, who has just "received" the letter, chase the mail carrier once around the circle. This child is then the mail carrier. Repeat the game until all children have been the mail carrier.

Why do I have children do this?

- To run (large muscle).
- To choose a friend (social-emotional).
- To sing a song (language).

What do I need?

What might I see children doing?

- Singing.
- Choosing a friend.
- Running around the circle.

1. Words to song written on an index card.
2. Mailbag (mailbag, large purse, or paper bag with handles).
3. Large envelope.

What might I talk about with children?

1. How are letters delivered?
2. What do mail carriers do with our letters?
3. Why do we send letters to friends?

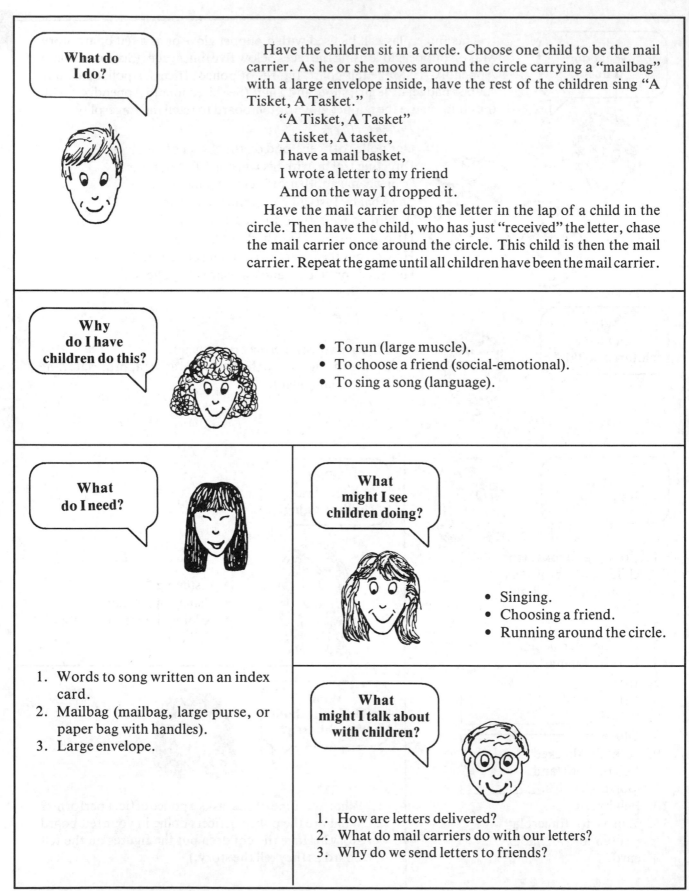

ANIMAL CRACKER SNACKS
Group

What do I do?

Fill a legal-sized envelope with animal crackers and mail one to each child. At snacktime, ask the children to check their mailboxes (the ones created in the dramatic play activity "The Post Office" on page 98), and bring their "mail" to snacktime. Serve the animal crackers with cheese and milk or juice.

Why do I have children do this?

- To receive mail (social-emotional).
- To share snacks (social-emotional).

What do I need?

1. Legal-sized envelopes (one for each child).
2. Animal crackers.

What might I see children doing?

- Talking.
- Checking mailboxes.
- Opening envelopes.
- Eating.

What might I talk about with children?

1. What kinds of items can you mail?
2. What have you received in the mail?

MY DENTIST
Group

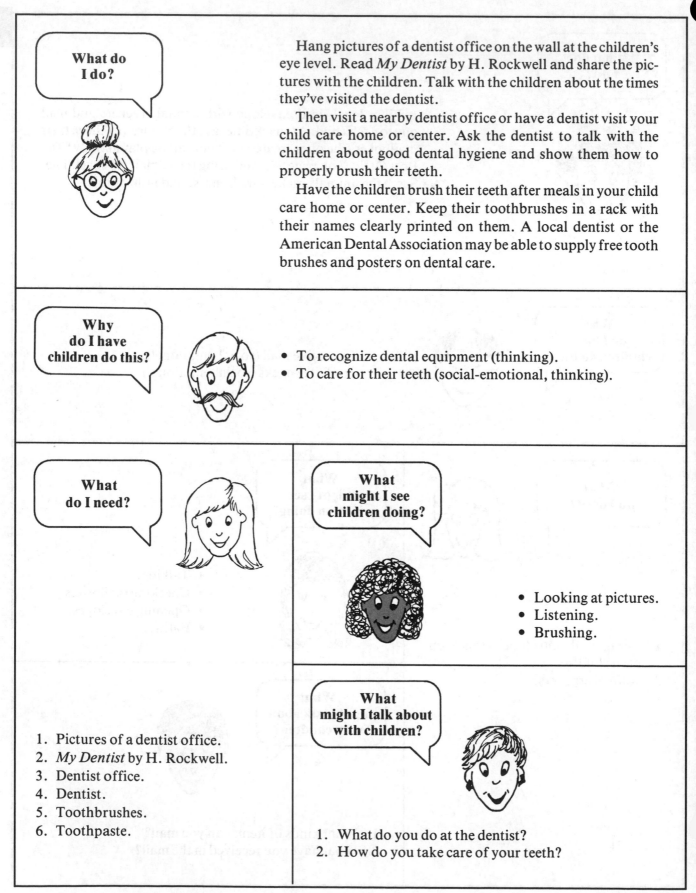

What do I do?

Hang pictures of a dentist office on the wall at the children's eye level. Read *My Dentist* by H. Rockwell and share the pictures with the children. Talk with the children about the times they've visited the dentist.

Then visit a nearby dentist office or have a dentist visit your child care home or center. Ask the dentist to talk with the children about good dental hygiene and show them how to properly brush their teeth.

Have the children brush their teeth after meals in your child care home or center. Keep their toothbrushes in a rack with their names clearly printed on them. A local dentist or the American Dental Association may be able to supply free tooth brushes and posters on dental care.

Why do I have children do this?

- To recognize dental equipment (thinking).
- To care for their teeth (social-emotional, thinking).

What do I need?

What might I see children doing?

- Looking at pictures.
- Listening.
- Brushing.

1. Pictures of a dentist office.
2. *My Dentist* by H. Rockwell.
3. Dentist office.
4. Dentist.
5. Toothbrushes.
6. Toothpaste.

What might I talk about with children?

1. What do you do at the dentist?
2. How do you take care of your teeth?

"FIVE LITTLE MONKEYS"
Group

Make a puppet glove using monkey figures. (See directions in Appendix A.) Then use the puppet glove to teach the children the following chant. Let the children repeat the chant using the puppet glove.

"Five Little Monkeys"

What do I do?

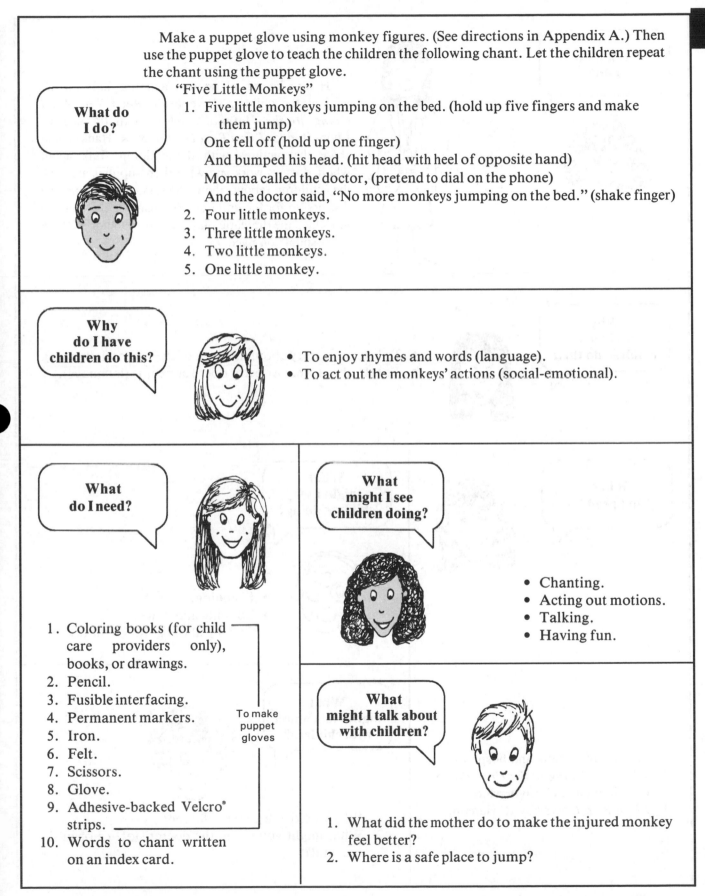

1. Five little monkeys jumping on the bed. (hold up five fingers and make them jump)
   One fell off (hold up one finger)
   And bumped his head. (hit head with heel of opposite hand)
   Momma called the doctor, (pretend to dial on the phone)
   And the doctor said, "No more monkeys jumping on the bed." (shake finger)
2. Four little monkeys.
3. Three little monkeys.
4. Two little monkeys.
5. One little monkey.

Why do I have children do this?

- To enjoy rhymes and words (language).
- To act out the monkeys' actions (social-emotional).

What do I need?

1. Coloring books (for child care providers only), books, or drawings.
2. Pencil.
3. Fusible interfacing.
4. Permanent markers.
5. Iron.
6. Felt.
7. Scissors.
8. Glove.
9. Adhesive-backed Velcro® strips.
10. Words to chant written on an index card.

To make puppet gloves

What might I see children doing?

- Chanting.
- Acting out motions.
- Talking.
- Having fun.

What might I talk about with children?

1. What did the mother do to make the injured monkey feel better?
2. Where is a safe place to jump?

I CAN BE A DOCTOR
Group

What do I do?

Hang pictures of doctors and hospitals on the wall at the children's eye level. Read *Why Am I Going to the Hospital?*, by C. Ciliotta and C. Livingston, or *I Can Be a Doctor*, by R. Hankin, and share the pictures with the children. Talk about where doctors work and what their supplies are. Ask the children about their doctors. Ask what the doctors do for the children. You can use the story to introduce the dramatic play activity "Doctor's Office or Hospital" on page 95.

Why do I have children do this?

- To listen to a story about the work of the doctor (language).
- To talk about what a doctor does for people (language).

What do I need?

1. Pictures of doctors and hospitals.
2. *Why Am I Going to the Hospital?* by C. Ciliotta and C. Livingston.
3. *I Can Be a Doctor* by R. Hankin.

What might I see children doing?

- Listening.
- Looking at pictures.
- Talking about going to the doctor.

What might I talk about with children?

1. Why would you go see a doctor?
2. What might you see in the doctor's office or in the hospital?

FIVE LITTLE FIRE FIGHTERS
Group

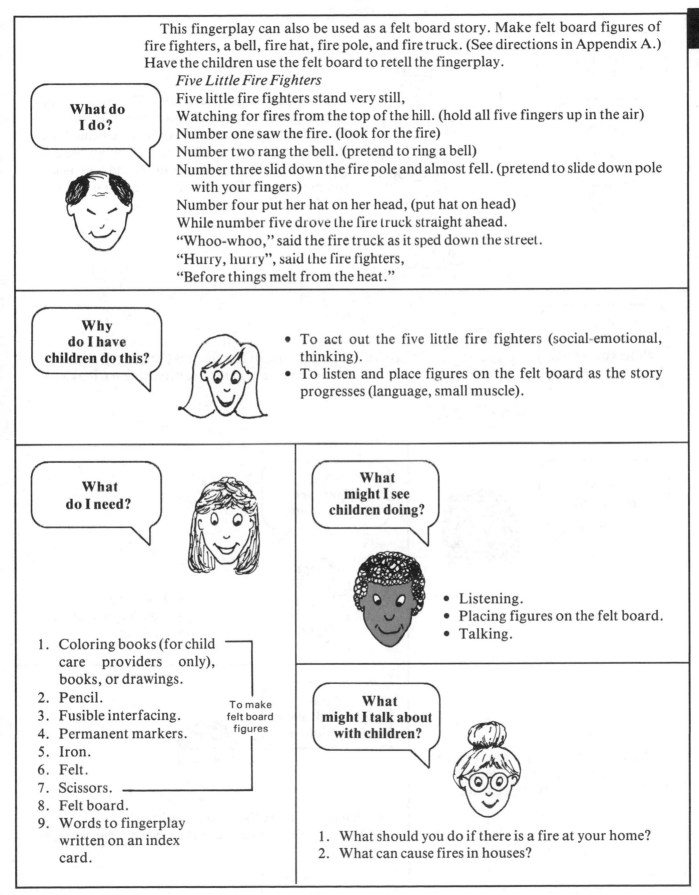

What do I do?

This fingerplay can also be used as a felt board story. Make felt board figures of fire fighters, a bell, fire hat, fire pole, and fire truck. (See directions in Appendix A.) Have the children use the felt board to retell the fingerplay.

Five Little Fire Fighters

Five little fire fighters stand very still,
Watching for fires from the top of the hill. (hold all five fingers up in the air)
Number one saw the fire. (look for the fire)
Number two rang the bell. (pretend to ring a bell)
Number three slid down the fire pole and almost fell. (pretend to slide down pole with your fingers)
Number four put her hat on her head, (put hat on head)
While number five drove the fire truck straight ahead.
"Whoo-whoo," said the fire truck as it sped down the street.
"Hurry, hurry", said the fire fighters,
"Before things melt from the heat."

Why do I have children do this?

- To act out the five little fire fighters (social-emotional, thinking).
- To listen and place figures on the felt board as the story progresses (language, small muscle).

What do I need?

1. Coloring books (for child care providers only), books, or drawings.
2. Pencil.
3. Fusible interfacing.
4. Permanent markers.
5. Iron.
6. Felt.
7. Scissors.
8. Felt board.
9. Words to fingerplay written on an index card.

To make felt board figures

What might I see children doing?

- Listening.
- Placing figures on the felt board.
- Talking.

What might I talk about with children?

1. What should you do if there is a fire at your home?
2. What can cause fires in houses?

FIRE ENGINES
Group

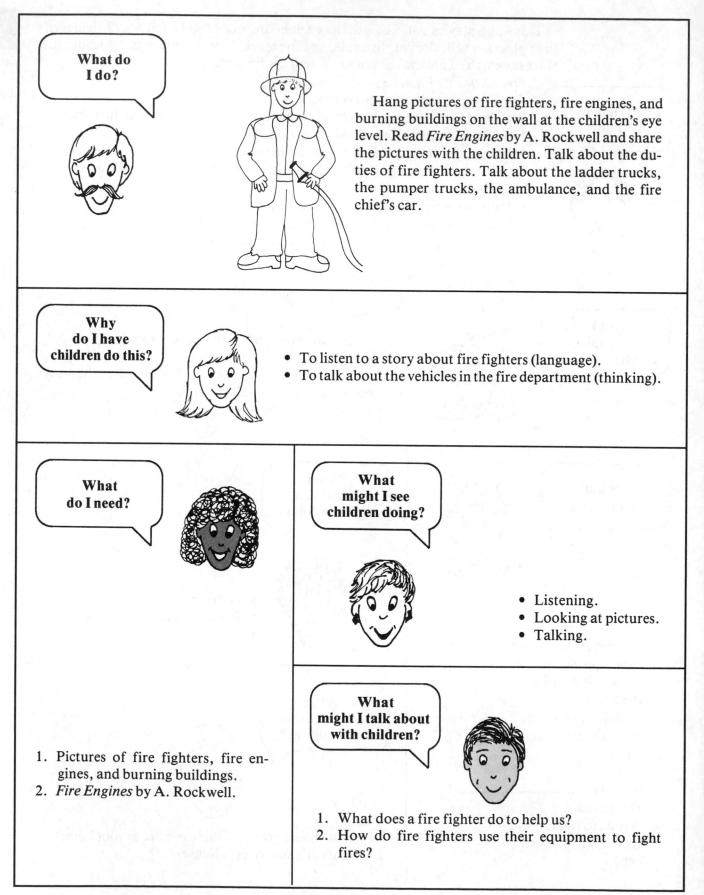

What do I do?

Hang pictures of fire fighters, fire engines, and burning buildings on the wall at the children's eye level. Read *Fire Engines* by A. Rockwell and share the pictures with the children. Talk about the duties of fire fighters. Talk about the ladder trucks, the pumper trucks, the ambulance, and the fire chief's car.

Why do I have children do this?

- To listen to a story about fire fighters (language).
- To talk about the vehicles in the fire department (thinking).

What do I need?

What might I see children doing?

- Listening.
- Looking at pictures.
- Talking.

1. Pictures of fire fighters, fire engines, and burning buildings.
2. *Fire Engines* by A. Rockwell.

What might I talk about with children?

1. What does a fire fighter do to help us?
2. How do fire fighters use their equipment to fight fires?

A TRIP TO THE POLICE STATION
Group, Field Trip

What do I do?

Take the children to the police station or ask a police officer to visit your child care home or center. Ask a police officer to show the children a police car, demonstrate the siren, and explain what it is used for. Have the police officer talk about his or her uniform, badge, and weapons. Have the police officer show the children basic traffic signs (STOP, YIELD, RAILROAD CROSSING) and discuss how they are used for the children's safety. Ask the police officer to tell the children about the tasks he or she performs on the job, such as directing traffic, helping at accidents, teaching safety, helping "lost" children, giving traffic tickets, and finding lawbreakers. Involve children by letting them pretend to direct traffic or give tickets.

Why do I have children do this?

- To recognize all the parts of the police officer's job (thinking).
- To list some of the police officer's equipment (language, thinking).

What do I need?

1. Police station.
2. Police officer.
3. Police car.
4. Police officer's uniform.
5. Traffic signs.

What might I see children doing?

- Sitting in a police car.
- Demonstrating how to use the siren.
- Listening.
- Pretending to direct traffic or give tickets.

What might I talk about with children?

1. How can you help the police officer?
2. If you lose your mommy or daddy, what should you tell the police officer so he or she could take you home?

FIRE DRILL
Group

What do I do?

Develop a fire exit plan for your child care home or center, mark all the exits, and post a copy of the plan for parents and staff. Go over the plan with the children and explain to them how important it is to move quickly during a fire drill.

Then have a fire drill. Turn on the fire alarm or smoke alarm, so that the children will be aware of how it sounds and what it means. (You may need to comfort the younger children, since the noise may frighten them.) Have the children line up at the door and quickly count them as you take them out of the building. When you have reached your designated checkpoint, count the children again.

Why do I have children do this?

- To identify the sounds of the alarm (thinking).
- To quickly exit the building in case of a fire (social-emotional, thinking).

What do I need?

1. A fire exit plan.
2. Copies of your fire exit plan.
3. Fire or smoke alarm.

What might I see children doing?

- Listening.
- Lining up at the door.
- Exiting quickly.
- Talking.

What might I talk about with children?

1. What is the best way to quickly leave your room in case of fire?
2. Where do you go when you have a fire drill at home?

I WANT TO BE A POLICE OFFICER
Group

What do I do?

Hang pictures of police officers at work on the wall at the children's eye level and talk with them about the pictures. Read *Officer Buckle and Gloria* by P. Rathman or *I Want to Be a Police Officer* by E. Baker and share the pictures with the children. Talk with the children about what police officers do at work, emphasizing how they help make people's lives safer. Talk about how some police officers direct traffic, others teach safety to children, and all help keep people from breaking the law.

Why do I have children do this?

- To learn what the police officers do at work (thinking).
- To talk about the police officer's work and equipment (language).

What do I need?

What might I see children doing?

- Looking at pictures.
- Listening.
- Talking.

1. Picture of police officers at work.
2. *Officer Buckle and Gloria* by P. Rathman.
3. *I Want to Be a Police Officer* by E. Baker.

What might I talk about with children?

1. What does a police officer do to help you?
2. Where does a police officer work?
3. Which safety tip is most important to you?

"LITTLE RED WAGON"
Group

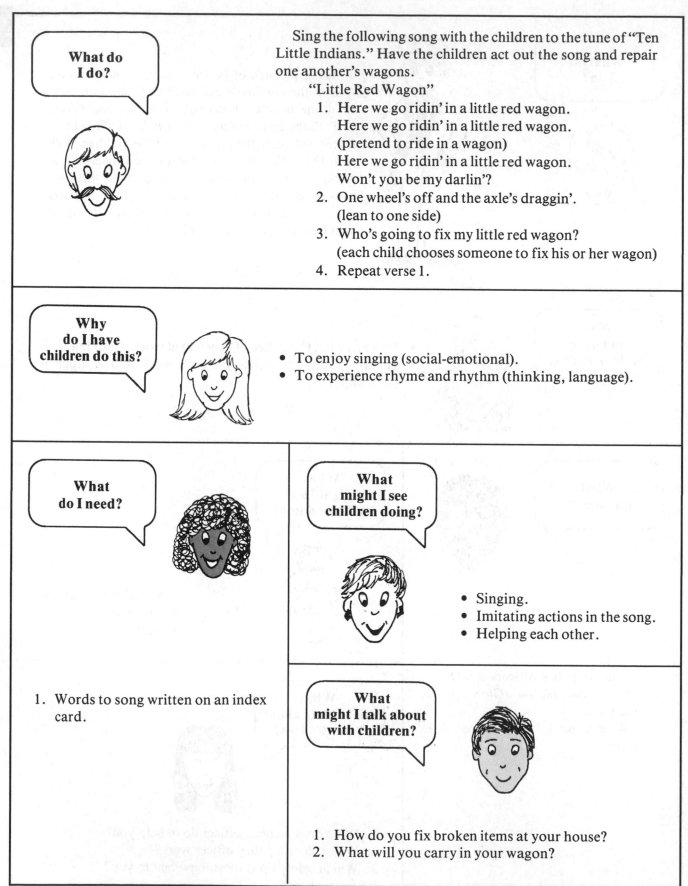

What do I do?

Sing the following song with the children to the tune of "Ten Little Indians." Have the children act out the song and repair one another's wagons.

"Little Red Wagon"
1. Here we go ridin' in a little red wagon.
   Here we go ridin' in a little red wagon.
   (pretend to ride in a wagon)
   Here we go ridin' in a little red wagon.
   Won't you be my darlin'?
2. One wheel's off and the axle's draggin'.
   (lean to one side)
3. Who's going to fix my little red wagon?
   (each child chooses someone to fix his or her wagon)
4. Repeat verse 1.

Why do I have children do this?

- To enjoy singing (social-emotional).
- To experience rhyme and rhythm (thinking, language).

What do I need?

1. Words to song written on an index card.

What might I see children doing?

- Singing.
- Imitating actions in the song.
- Helping each other.

What might I talk about with children?

1. How do you fix broken items at your house?
2. What will you carry in your wagon?

MIKE MULLIGAN AND HIS STEAM SHOVEL
Group

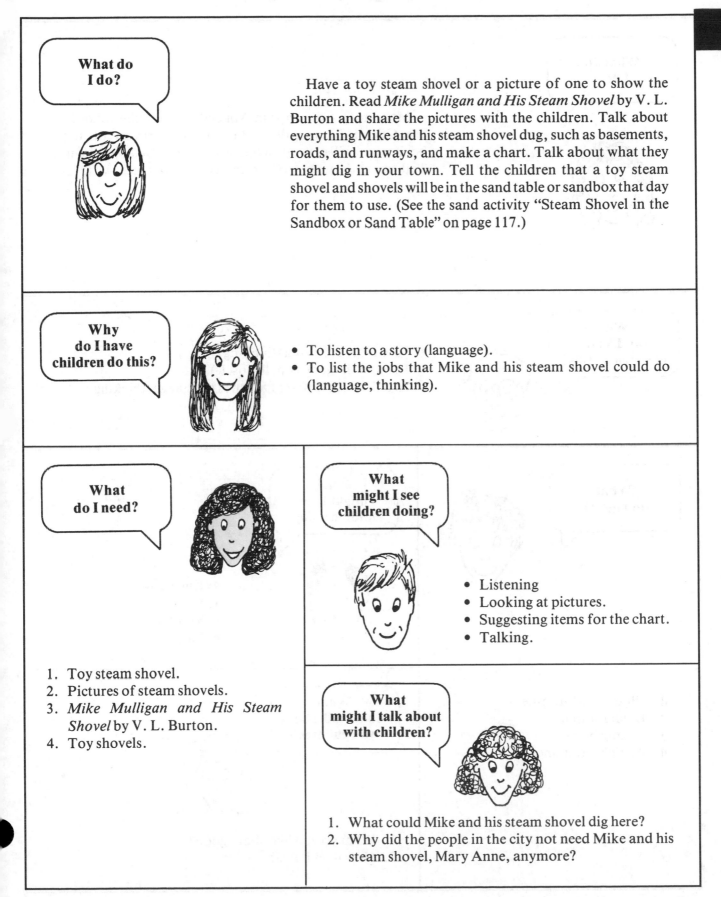

What do I do?

Have a toy steam shovel or a picture of one to show the children. Read *Mike Mulligan and His Steam Shovel* by V. L. Burton and share the pictures with the children. Talk about everything Mike and his steam shovel dug, such as basements, roads, and runways, and make a chart. Talk about what they might dig in your town. Tell the children that a toy steam shovel and shovels will be in the sand table or sandbox that day for them to use. (See the sand activity "Steam Shovel in the Sandbox or Sand Table" on page 117.)

Why do I have children do this?

- To listen to a story (language).
- To list the jobs that Mike and his steam shovel could do (language, thinking).

What do I need?

What might I see children doing?

- Listening
- Looking at pictures.
- Suggesting items for the chart.
- Talking.

1. Toy steam shovel.
2. Pictures of steam shovels.
3. *Mike Mulligan and His Steam Shovel* by V. L. Burton.
4. Toy shovels.

What might I talk about with children?

1. What could Mike and his steam shovel dig here?
2. Why did the people in the city not need Mike and his steam shovel, Mary Anne, anymore?

GOOP
Learning Center (art)

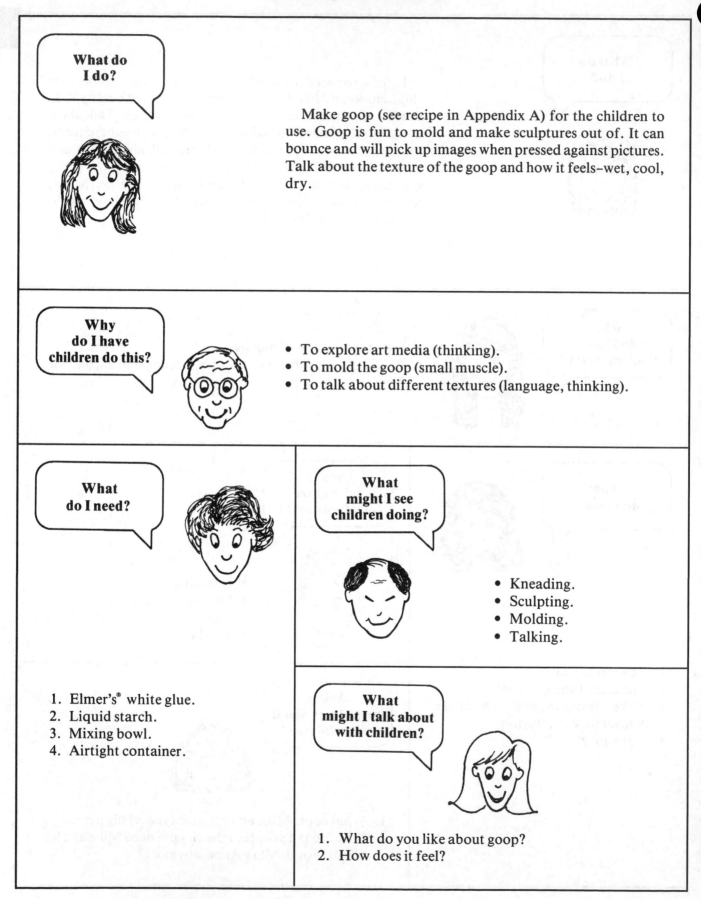

What do I do?

Make goop (see recipe in Appendix A) for the children to use. Goop is fun to mold and make sculptures out of. It can bounce and will pick up images when pressed against pictures. Talk about the texture of the goop and how it feels–wet, cool, dry.

Why do I have children do this?

- To explore art media (thinking).
- To mold the goop (small muscle).
- To talk about different textures (language, thinking).

What do I need?

What might I see children doing?

- Kneading.
- Sculpting.
- Molding.
- Talking.

1. Elmer's® white glue.
2. Liquid starch.
3. Mixing bowl.
4. Airtight container.

What might I talk about with children?

1. What do you like about goop?
2. How does it feel?

CAST SCULPTURES
Learning Center (art)

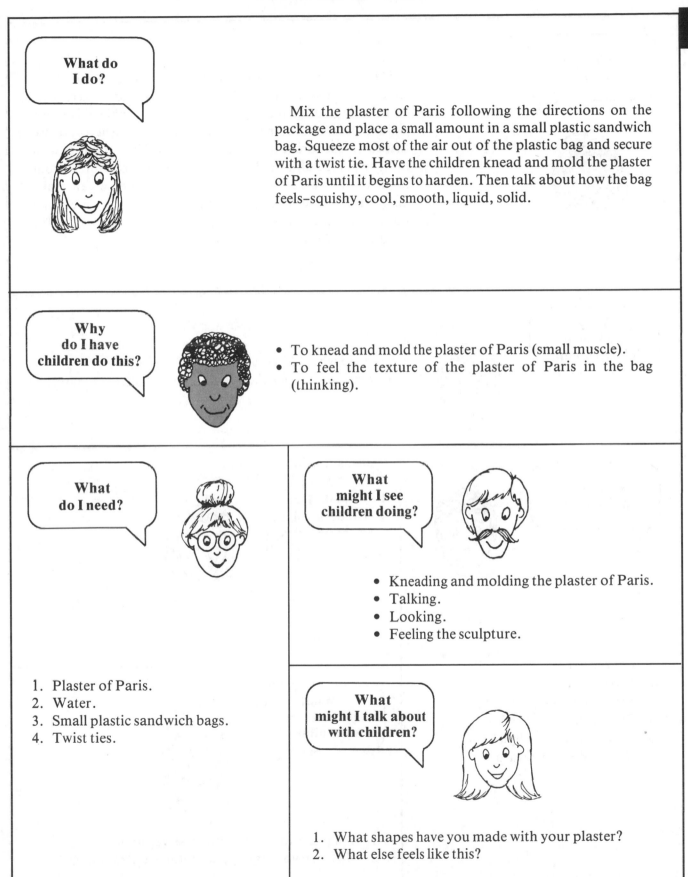

What do I do?

Mix the plaster of Paris following the directions on the package and place a small amount in a small plastic sandwich bag. Squeeze most of the air out of the plastic bag and secure with a twist tie. Have the children knead and mold the plaster of Paris until it begins to harden. Then talk about how the bag feels–squishy, cool, smooth, liquid, solid.

Why do I have children do this?

- To knead and mold the plaster of Paris (small muscle).
- To feel the texture of the plaster of Paris in the bag (thinking).

What do I need?

1. Plaster of Paris.
2. Water.
3. Small plastic sandwich bags.
4. Twist ties.

What might I see children doing?

- Kneading and molding the plaster of Paris.
- Talking.
- Looking.
- Feeling the sculpture.

What might I talk about with children?

1. What shapes have you made with your plaster?
2. What else feels like this?

VEGGIE BUILDING
Learning Center (art)

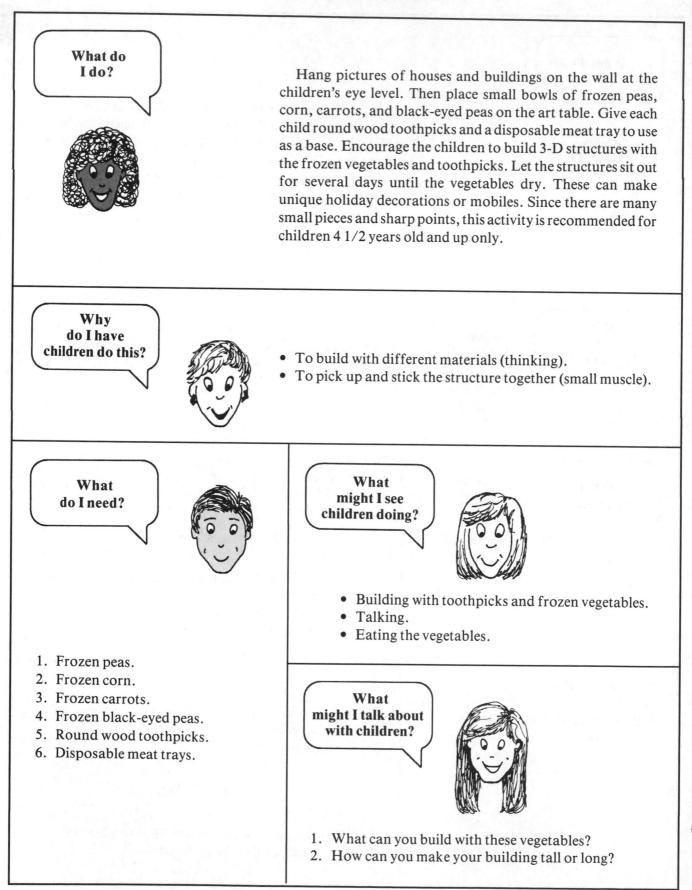

What do I do?

Hang pictures of houses and buildings on the wall at the children's eye level. Then place small bowls of frozen peas, corn, carrots, and black-eyed peas on the art table. Give each child round wood toothpicks and a disposable meat tray to use as a base. Encourage the children to build 3-D structures with the frozen vegetables and toothpicks. Let the structures sit out for several days until the vegetables dry. These can make unique holiday decorations or mobiles. Since there are many small pieces and sharp points, this activity is recommended for children 4 1/2 years old and up only.

Why do I have children do this?

- To build with different materials (thinking).
- To pick up and stick the structure together (small muscle).

What do I need?

1. Frozen peas.
2. Frozen corn.
3. Frozen carrots.
4. Frozen black-eyed peas.
5. Round wood toothpicks.
6. Disposable meat trays.

What might I see children doing?

- Building with toothpicks and frozen vegetables.
- Talking.
- Eating the vegetables.

What might I talk about with children?

1. What can you build with these vegetables?
2. How can you make your building tall or long?

BUSY BAKER PLAYDOUGH
(art)

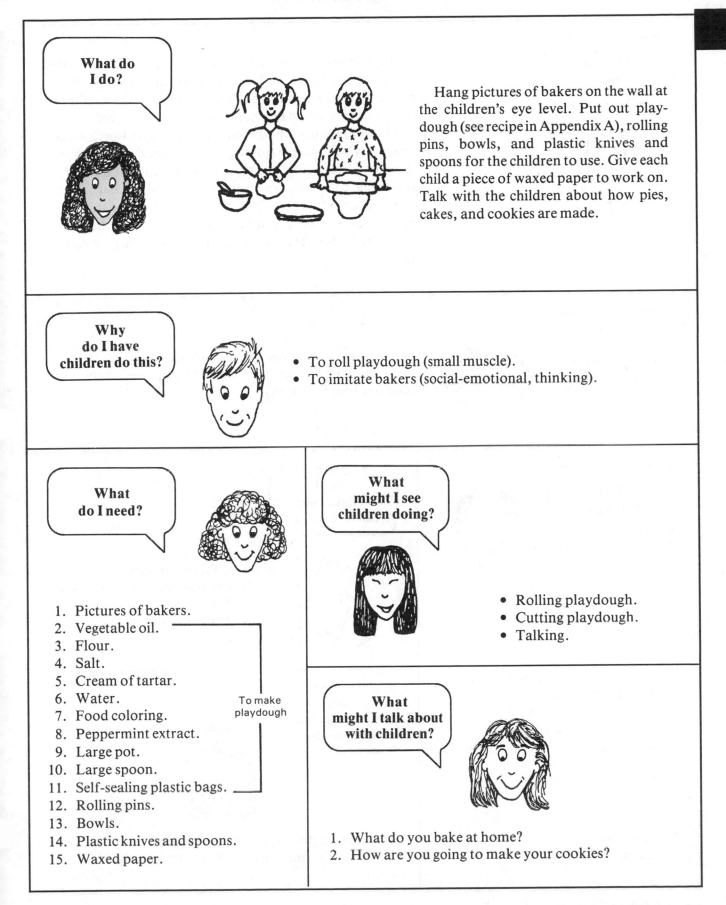

What do I do?

Hang pictures of bakers on the wall at the children's eye level. Put out playdough (see recipe in Appendix A), rolling pins, bowls, and plastic knives and spoons for the children to use. Give each child a piece of waxed paper to work on. Talk with the children about how pies, cakes, and cookies are made.

Why do I have children do this?

- To roll playdough (small muscle).
- To imitate bakers (social-emotional, thinking).

What do I need?

1. Pictures of bakers.
2. Vegetable oil.
3. Flour.
4. Salt.
5. Cream of tartar.
6. Water.
7. Food coloring.
8. Peppermint extract.
9. Large pot.
10. Large spoon.
11. Self-sealing plastic bags.
12. Rolling pins.
13. Bowls.
14. Plastic knives and spoons.
15. Waxed paper.

To make playdough

What might I see children doing?

- Rolling playdough.
- Cutting playdough.
- Talking.

What might I talk about with children?

1. What do you bake at home?
2. How are you going to make your cookies?

FIRE TRUCK SPONGES
Learning Center (art)

What do I do?

Hang pictures of fire trucks and fire fighters at work on the wall at the children's eye level. Talk about the shape of the tires, body, and windows on the fire truck. Line three disposable meat trays with damp paper towels and pour red, black, or white tempera paint into each tray. The paper towels create a blotter, which makes painting more successful. (Mix liquid detergent in the paint, so the paint will wash out of clothes easier.) Place the meat trays on the table and put out smocks for the children to wear. Then cut sponges into the shapes of circles, squares, triangles, and rectangles and place them near the meat trays for the children to paint with on large sheets of paper.

Why do I have children do this?

- To experiment with paint (small muscle).
- To talk about shapes, such as circles, squares, rectangles, and triangles (thinking).

What do I need?

1. Pictures of fire trucks and fire fighters at work.
2. Paper towels.
3. Disposable meat trays.
4. Red, black, and white tempera paint.
5. Liquid detergent.
6. Smocks.
7. Sponges.
8. Scissors.
9. Large sheets of paper.

What might I see children doing?

- Choosing paints.
- Experimenting with sponges.
- Talking about shapes.
- Talking about colors.
- Having fun.

What might I talk about with children?

1. What shapes do you see on this fire truck?
2. Where do you think that fire truck is going?

PAINTING AROUND YOUR COMMUNITY
Learning Center (art)

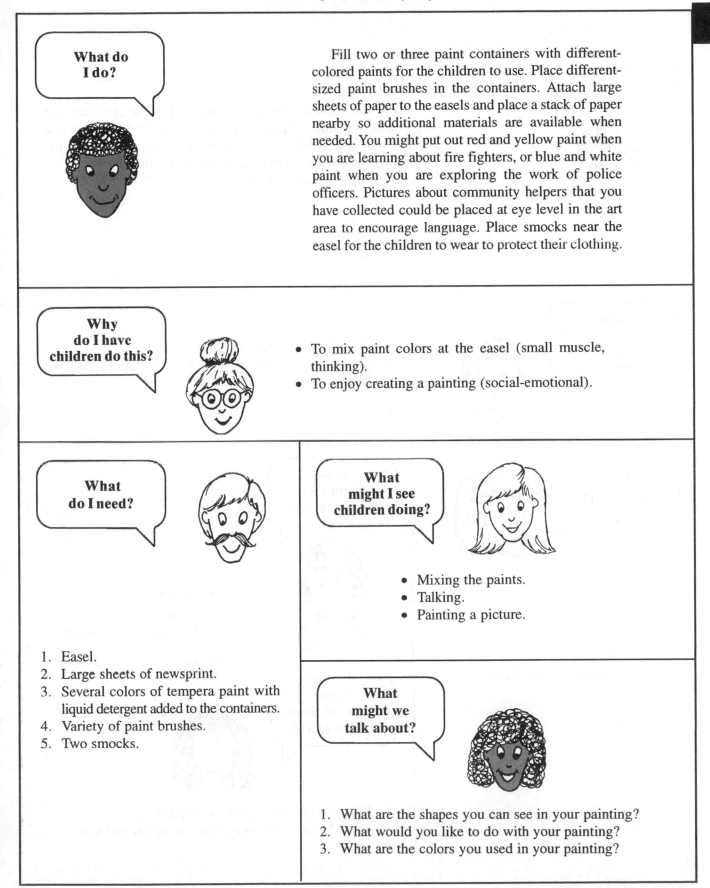

What do I do?

Fill two or three paint containers with different-colored paints for the children to use. Place different-sized paint brushes in the containers. Attach large sheets of paper to the easels and place a stack of paper nearby so additional materials are available when needed. You might put out red and yellow paint when you are learning about fire fighters, or blue and white paint when you are exploring the work of police officers. Pictures about community helpers that you have collected could be placed at eye level in the art area to encourage language. Place smocks near the easel for the children to wear to protect their clothing.

Why do I have children do this?

- To mix paint colors at the easel (small muscle, thinking).
- To enjoy creating a painting (social-emotional).

What do I need?

1. Easel.
2. Large sheets of newsprint.
3. Several colors of tempera paint with liquid detergent added to the containers.
4. Variety of paint brushes.
5. Two smocks.

What might I see children doing?

- Mixing the paints.
- Talking.
- Painting a picture.

What might we talk about?

1. What are the shapes you can see in your painting?
2. What would you like to do with your painting?
3. What are the colors you used in your painting?

HAIRSTYLE COLLAGE
Learning Center (art)

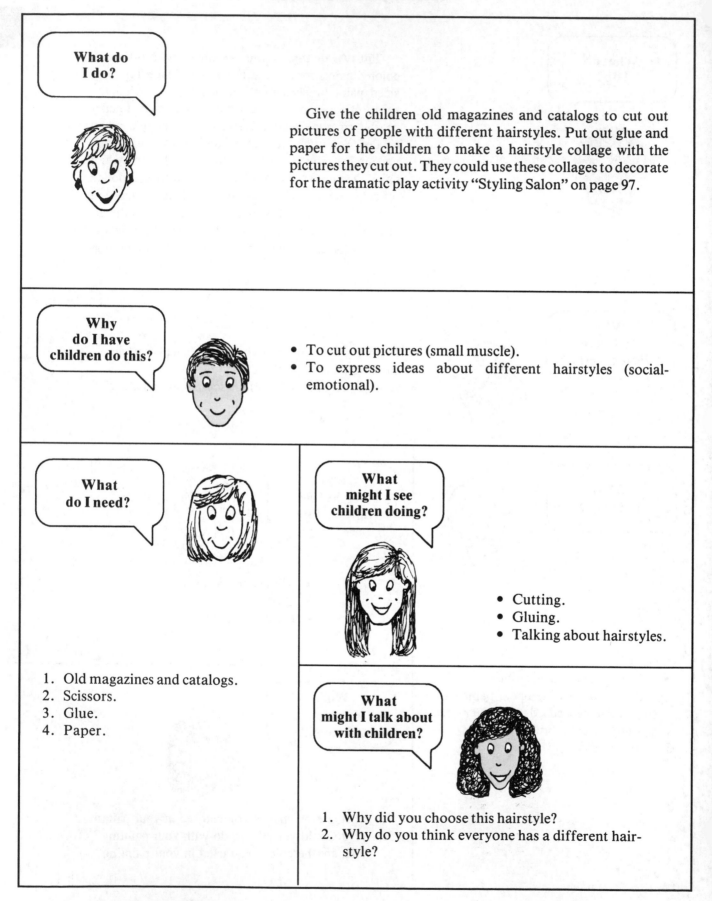

What do I do?

Give the children old magazines and catalogs to cut out pictures of people with different hairstyles. Put out glue and paper for the children to make a hairstyle collage with the pictures they cut out. They could use these collages to decorate for the dramatic play activity "Styling Salon" on page 97.

Why do I have children do this?

- To cut out pictures (small muscle).
- To express ideas about different hairstyles (social-emotional).

What do I need?

1. Old magazines and catalogs.
2. Scissors.
3. Glue.
4. Paper.

What might I see children doing?

- Cutting.
- Gluing.
- Talking about hairstyles.

What might I talk about with children?

1. Why did you choose this hairstyle?
2. Why do you think everyone has a different hairstyle?

SALON ART
Learning Center (art)

What do I do?

Line disposable meat trays with damp paper towels and pour tempera paint over the paper towels. This creates a blotter, which makes painting more successful. Have two or three different colored paints available for children to choose from. (Mix liquid detergent in the paint, so the paint will wash out of clothes easier.) Place objects from the list below near each of the meat trays and encourage the children to paint with them on large sheets of paper. Discuss textures, lines, designs, and color mixing with the children as they paint.

Why do I have children do this?

- To experiment with different objects in paint (small muscle, thinking).
- To talk about the designs and colors (thinking, language).

What do I need?

1. Paper towels.
2. Disposable meat trays.
3. Tempera paint.
4. Liquid detergent.
4. Large sheets of paper.
5. Shaving brushes.
6. Squirt bottles.
7. Curlers.
8. Brushes.
9. Combs.
10. Cotton swabs.
11. Cotton balls.
12. Hair pins.

What might I see children doing?

- Painting.
- Experimenting.
- Talking.

What might I talk about with children?

1. What other ways can these items be used?
2. What other items can make interesting designs?

PERSONAL POSTAGE STAMPS
Learning Center (art)

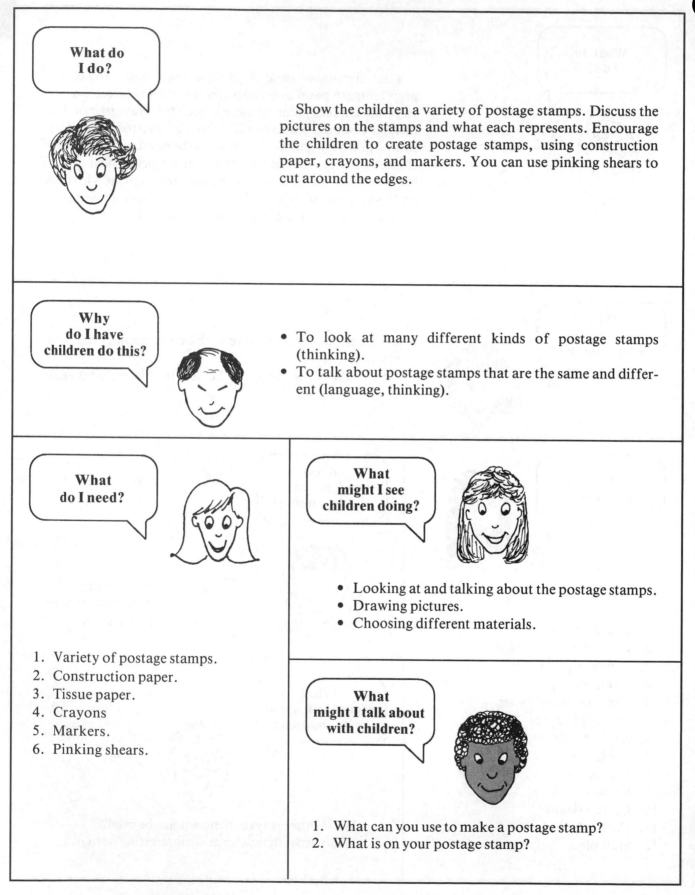

What do I do?

Show the children a variety of postage stamps. Discuss the pictures on the stamps and what each represents. Encourage the children to create postage stamps, using construction paper, crayons, and markers. You can use pinking shears to cut around the edges.

Why do I have children do this?

- To look at many different kinds of postage stamps (thinking).
- To talk about postage stamps that are the same and different (language, thinking).

What do I need?

1. Variety of postage stamps.
2. Construction paper.
3. Tissue paper.
4. Crayons
5. Markers.
6. Pinking shears.

What might I see children doing?

- Looking at and talking about the postage stamps.
- Drawing pictures.
- Choosing different materials.

What might I talk about with children?

1. What can you use to make a postage stamp?
2. What is on your postage stamp?

FIRE FIGHTERS' LADDERS
Learning Center (blocks)

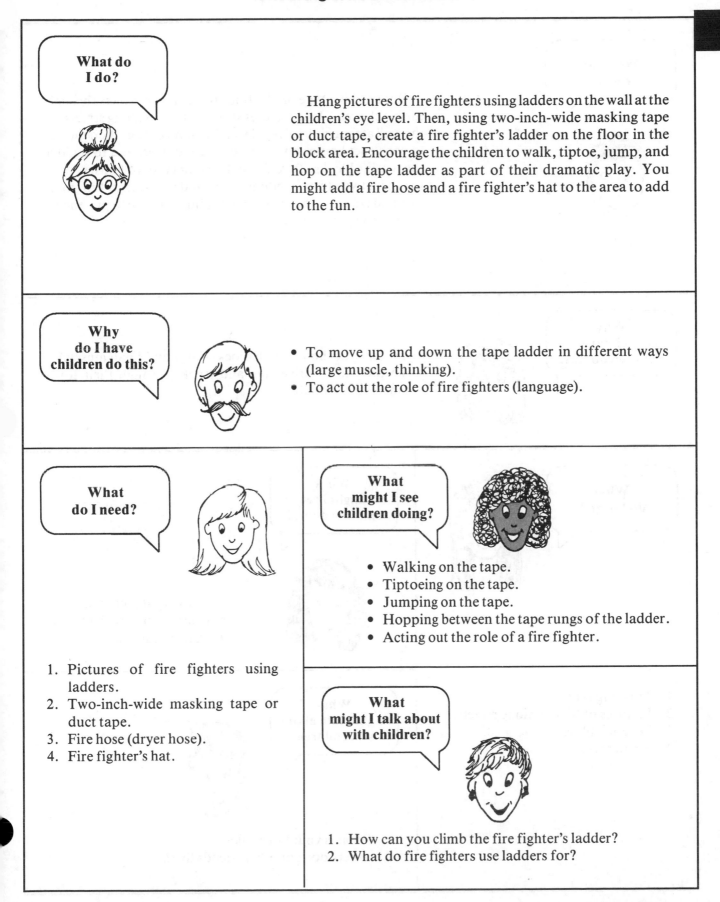

What do I do?

Hang pictures of fire fighters using ladders on the wall at the children's eye level. Then, using two-inch-wide masking tape or duct tape, create a fire fighter's ladder on the floor in the block area. Encourage the children to walk, tiptoe, jump, and hop on the tape ladder as part of their dramatic play. You might add a fire hose and a fire fighter's hat to the area to add to the fun.

Why do I have children do this?

- To move up and down the tape ladder in different ways (large muscle, thinking).
- To act out the role of fire fighters (language).

What do I need?

What might I see children doing?

- Walking on the tape.
- Tiptoeing on the tape.
- Jumping on the tape.
- Hopping between the tape rungs of the ladder.
- Acting out the role of a fire fighter.

1. Pictures of fire fighters using ladders.
2. Two-inch-wide masking tape or duct tape.
3. Fire hose (dryer hose).
4. Fire fighter's hat.

What might I talk about with children?

1. How can you climb the fire fighter's ladder?
2. What do fire fighters use ladders for?

OUR TOWN
Learning Center (blocks)

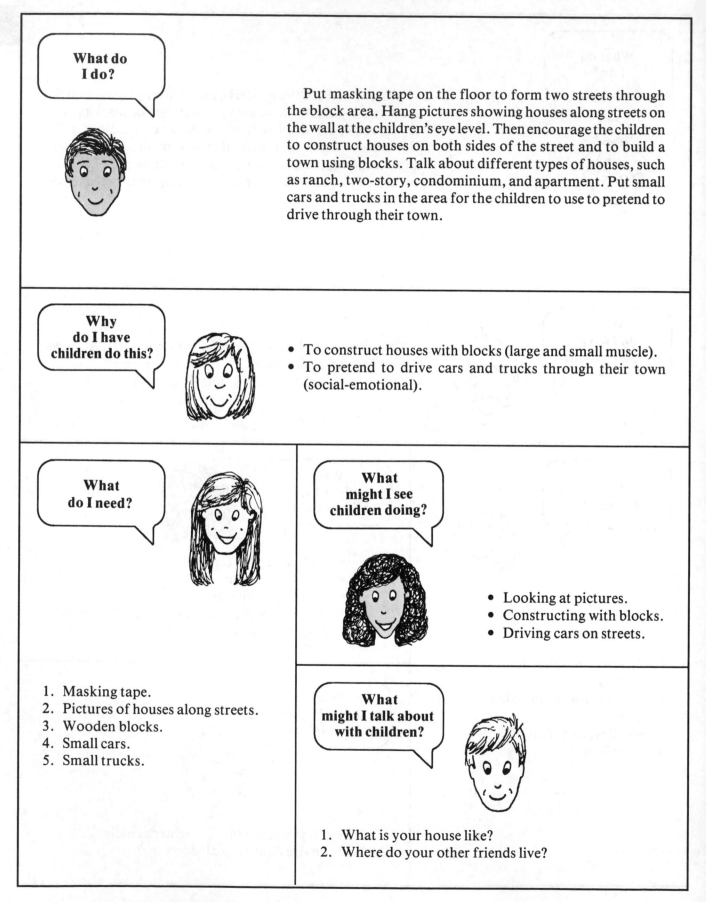

What do I do?

Put masking tape on the floor to form two streets through the block area. Hang pictures showing houses along streets on the wall at the children's eye level. Then encourage the children to construct houses on both sides of the street and to build a town using blocks. Talk about different types of houses, such as ranch, two-story, condominium, and apartment. Put small cars and trucks in the area for the children to use to pretend to drive through their town.

Why do I have children do this?

- To construct houses with blocks (large and small muscle).
- To pretend to drive cars and trucks through their town (social-emotional).

What do I need?

What might I see children doing?

- Looking at pictures.
- Constructing with blocks.
- Driving cars on streets.

1. Masking tape.
2. Pictures of houses along streets.
3. Wooden blocks.
4. Small cars.
5. Small trucks.

What might I talk about with children?

1. What is your house like?
2. Where do your other friends live?

WE NUMBER OUR HOUSES
Learning Center (blocks)

What do I do?

Hang pictures of houses with numerals on them on the wall at the children's eye level. Talk with the children about the numerals, or addresses, on their homes. Encourage the children to build houses in their block center town. Then cut numerals out of paper and have the children tape them to the houses. Talk about the reasons why the houses are numbered, such as so mail can be delivered, you can find a house, and you can give directions.

Why do I have children do this?

- To build with blocks (small and large muscle).
- To use numerals (thinking).

What do I need?

What might I see children doing?

- Looking at pictures
- Building houses.
- Taping numbers to houses.
- Having fun.

1. Pictures of houses with numerals on them.
2. Blocks.
3. Paper.
4. A pair of scissors.
5. Tape.

What might I talk about with children?

1. Where can the numerals be found on your houses?
2. How do you think you could number your block houses?

LET'S PLAY TEACHER
Learning Center (dramatic play)

What do I do?

Set up a child care center in the dramatic play area. Provide dress-up clothes, so the children can dress up like a teacher or parents who are dropping their children off at the center. Then set up the dramatic play area, so the children can pretend to go through the daily schedule. Place paper, crayons, markers, and scissors at a table in the dramatic play area. Put out several books and three to four mats on the floor for the children to sit on for group time. Put out a cot or two for nap time. Set out the felt board and some felt board figures, puppets, and other teaching materials the teacher can use when teaching. You may want to also plan a snacktime.

Why do I have children do this?

- To role-play being a teacher (social-emotional, thinking).
- To read to other children (language).

What do I need?

1. Dress-up clothes.
2. Paper.
3. Crayons.
4. Markers.
5. Scissors.
6. Books.
7. Floor mats.
8. Cots.
9. Felt board.
10. Felt board figures.
11. Puppets.
12. Snack food.

What might I see children doing?

- Dressing like teacher or parents.
- Reading to other children.
- Rubbing a child's back.
- Talking.

What might I talk about with children?

1. What does the teacher do each day?
2. What does the teacher do when he or she goes home?

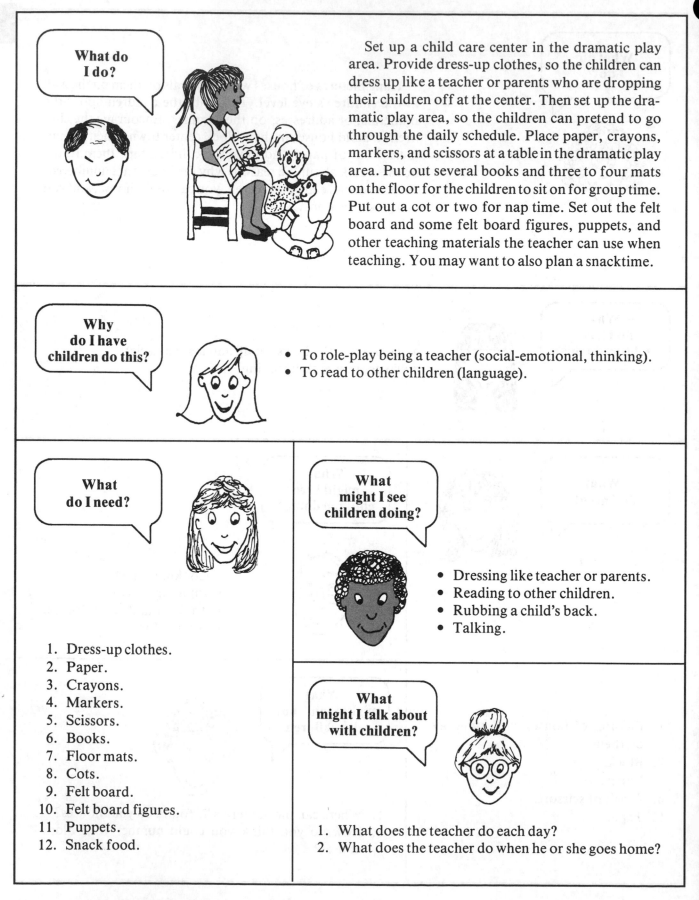

A NURSE IS A VERY IMPORTANT PERSON
Learning Center (dramatic play)

What do I do?

Provide a cot, "sick" doll (or another child to act as a patient), nurse's cap, play medical kit, and food tray for the children to use. Put a sheet and blanket on the cot, so the patient can be covered up. Make charts from paper stapled together or paper on a clipboard for the nurse to write on. Explain to the children that nurses always write down what they have done when caring for a patient. For example, he or she gave the patient a pill, took the patient's temperature, or listened to the patient's heart. Talk with the children about the fact that men can be nurses. If one of the fathers is a nurse, or you know a male nurse, ask him to visit your child care home or center and speak to the children.

Why do I have children do this?

- To care for others (social-emotional).
- To make the bed, take food and medicine to the patient, and help them in and out of bed (large muscle).

What do I need?

1. Cot.
2. Dolls.
3. Child patient.
4. Nurse's cap.
5. Play medical kit.
6. Food tray.
7. Water glass.
8. Sheet.
9. Blanket.
10. Paper.
11. Stapler.
12. Clipboard.

What might I see children doing?

- Putting on nurses' caps.
- Making beds.
- Helping patients into bed.
- Listening to patients' hearts.
- Writing on chart or clipboard.

What might I talk about with children?

1. How do you feel today?
2. How will you care for yourself when you get home?

FIX-IT-SHOP
Learning Center (dramatic play)

What do I do?

This activity is for children four years of age and up. Hang up a sign in the dramatic play area that says "FIX-IT-SHOP." Place broken or old objects, such as telephones, clocks, lawn mower engines, toasters, and hair dryers, on the table. (Be sure to remove any electrical cords, so the children cannot plug in a defective appliance.) Provide screwdrivers, glue, wrenches, hammers, nails, and screws for the children to use to fix the objects. Place paper, pencils, a play cash register, and play money on the table for the children to record what is broken and to accept payment for the repairs.

Why do I have children do this?

- To use tools, such as screwdrivers and wrenches (small muscle).
- To role-play the fix-it-person (social-emotional).

What do I need?

1. "FIX-IT SHOP" sign.
2. Broken or old objects–telephones, clocks, lawn mower engines, toasters, hair dryers.
3. Screwdrivers.
4. Glue.
5. Wrenches.
6. Hammers.
7. Nails.
8. Screws.
9. Paper.
10. Pencils.
11. Play cash register.
12. Play money.

What might I see children doing?

- Using screwdrivers.
- Taking apart appliances.
- Recording repairs.
- Giving change.
- Talking.

What might I talk about with children?

1. What do you think is wrong with this toaster?
2. How will you fix this lawn mower engine?

HELPING POLICE OFFICERS AND FIRE FIGHTERS
Learning Center (dramatic play)

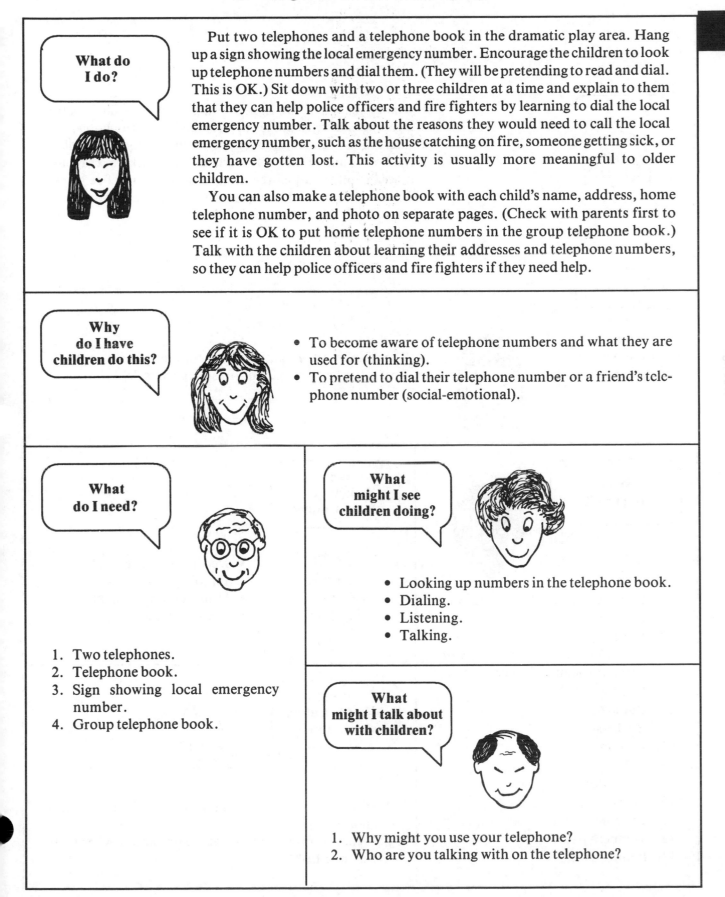

What do I do?

Put two telephones and a telephone book in the dramatic play area. Hang up a sign showing the local emergency number. Encourage the children to look up telephone numbers and dial them. (They will be pretending to read and dial. This is OK.) Sit down with two or three children at a time and explain to them that they can help police officers and fire fighters by learning to dial the local emergency number. Talk about the reasons they would need to call the local emergency number, such as the house catching on fire, someone getting sick, or they have gotten lost. This activity is usually more meaningful to older children.

You can also make a telephone book with each child's name, address, home telephone number, and photo on separate pages. (Check with parents first to see if it is OK to put home telephone numbers in the group telephone book.) Talk with the children about learning their addresses and telephone numbers, so they can help police officers and fire fighters if they need help.

Why do I have children do this?

- To become aware of telephone numbers and what they are used for (thinking).
- To pretend to dial their telephone number or a friend's telephone number (social-emotional).

What do I need?

1. Two telephones.
2. Telephone book.
3. Sign showing local emergency number.
4. Group telephone book.

What might I see children doing?

- Looking up numbers in the telephone book.
- Dialing.
- Listening.
- Talking.

What might I talk about with children?

1. Why might you use your telephone?
2. Who are you talking with on the telephone?

FIRE FIGHTERS AT WORK
Learning Center (dramatic play, blocks)

What do I do?

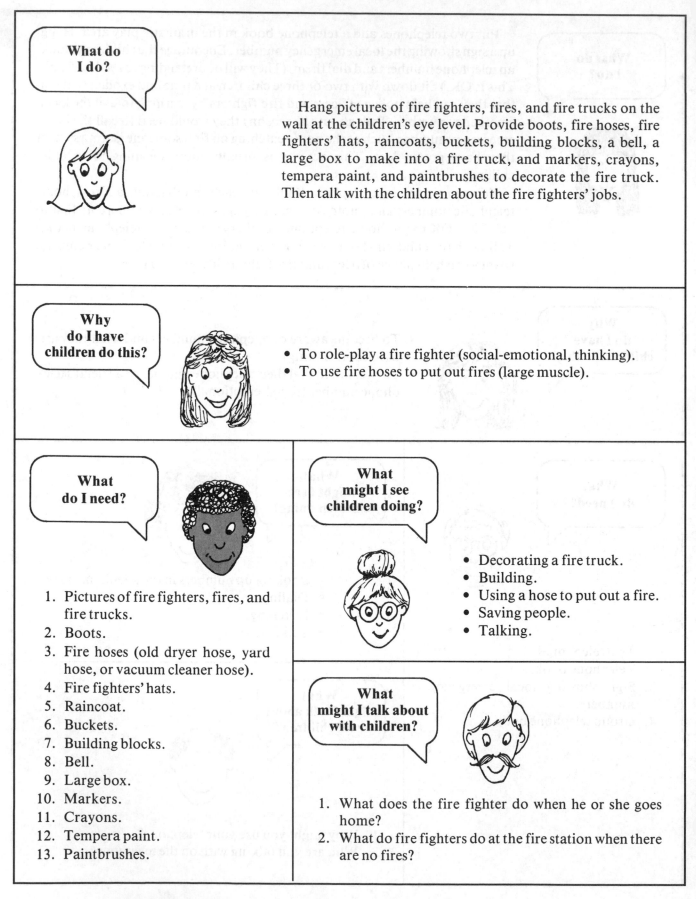

Hang pictures of fire fighters, fires, and fire trucks on the wall at the children's eye level. Provide boots, fire hoses, fire fighters' hats, raincoats, buckets, building blocks, a bell, a large box to make into a fire truck, and markers, crayons, tempera paint, and paintbrushes to decorate the fire truck. Then talk with the children about the fire fighters' jobs.

Why do I have children do this?

• To role-play a fire fighter (social-emotional, thinking).
• To use fire hoses to put out fires (large muscle).

What do I need?

1. Pictures of fire fighters, fires, and fire trucks.
2. Boots.
3. Fire hoses (old dryer hose, yard hose, or vacuum cleaner hose).
4. Fire fighters' hats.
5. Raincoat.
6. Buckets.
7. Building blocks.
8. Bell.
9. Large box.
10. Markers.
11. Crayons.
12. Tempera paint.
13. Paintbrushes.

What might I see children doing?

• Decorating a fire truck.
• Building.
• Using a hose to put out a fire.
• Saving people.
• Talking.

What might I talk about with children?

1. What does the fire fighter do when he or she goes home?
2. What do fire fighters do at the fire station when there are no fires?

DOCTOR'S OFFICE OR HOSPITAL
Learning Center (dramatic play)

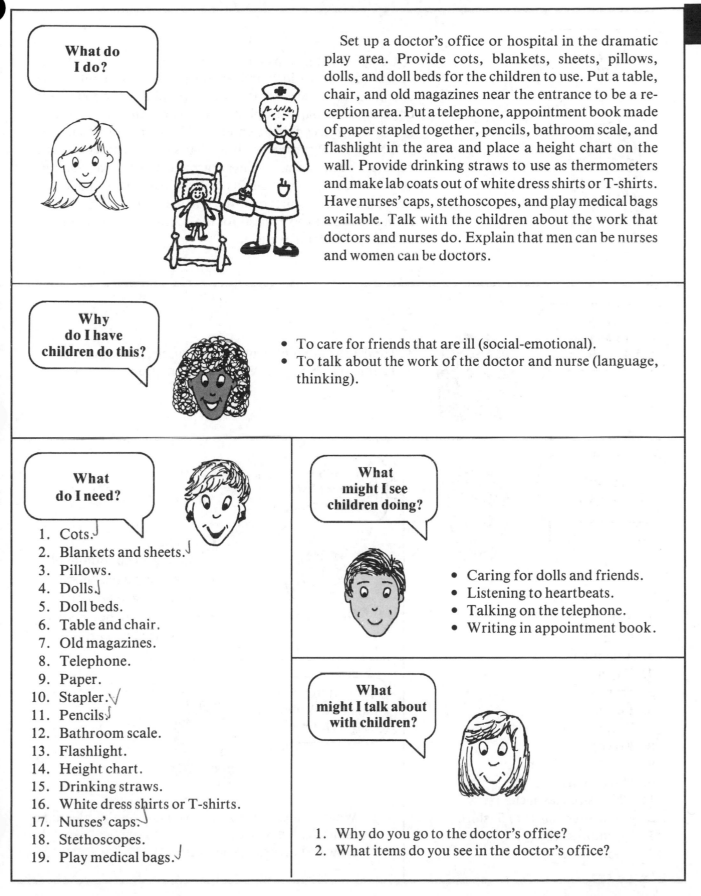

What do I do?

Set up a doctor's office or hospital in the dramatic play area. Provide cots, blankets, sheets, pillows, dolls, and doll beds for the children to use. Put a table, chair, and old magazines near the entrance to be a reception area. Put a telephone, appointment book made of paper stapled together, pencils, bathroom scale, and flashlight in the area and place a height chart on the wall. Provide drinking straws to use as thermometers and make lab coats out of white dress shirts or T-shirts. Have nurses' caps, stethoscopes, and play medical bags available. Talk with the children about the work that doctors and nurses do. Explain that men can be nurses and women can be doctors.

Why do I have children do this?

- To care for friends that are ill (social-emotional).
- To talk about the work of the doctor and nurse (language, thinking).

What do I need?

1. Cots.
2. Blankets and sheets.
3. Pillows.
4. Dolls.
5. Doll beds.
6. Table and chair.
7. Old magazines.
8. Telephone.
9. Paper.
10. Stapler.
11. Pencils.
12. Bathroom scale.
13. Flashlight.
14. Height chart.
15. Drinking straws.
16. White dress shirts or T-shirts.
17. Nurses' caps.
18. Stethoscopes.
19. Play medical bags.

What might I see children doing?

- Caring for dolls and friends.
- Listening to heartbeats.
- Talking on the telephone.
- Writing in appointment book.

What might I talk about with children?

1. Why do you go to the doctor's office?
2. What items do you see in the doctor's office?

DENTIST'S OFFICE
Learning Center (dramatic play)

What do I do?

Complete the group activity *"My Dentist"* on page 68. Set up a dentist's office in your dramatic play area. Put out a table and chair as a receptionist's desk, telephone, appointment book made of paper stapled together, pencils, play money, and box of prizes for the children. Hang up a sign that says "DENTIST." Place two to three chairs near the receptionist's desk and some old magazines for patients who are waiting. Use child-sized lawn chairs as dental chairs. Make lab coats out of white dress shirts or T-shirts and provide a set of plastic teeth and a large toothbrush for the dentist to teach his or her patient good dental hygiene.

Why do I have children do this?

- To write up appointments (small muscle, thinking).
- To role-play being a dentist (social-emotional).

What do I need?

1. Table.
2. Chairs.
3. Telephone.
4. Paper.
5. Stapler.
6. Pencil.
7. Play money.
8. Box of prizes.
9. "DENTIST" sign.
10. Old magazines.
11. Child-sized lawn chairs.
12. White dress shirts or T-shirts.
13. Toothbrushes.
14. Toothpaste.

What might I see children doing?

- Talking.
- Making an appointment.
- Talking on a telephone.
- Pretending to be patients.
- Pretending to be a dentist.
- Looking at magazines.

What might I talk about with children?

1. What would you say when you answer the telephone in the dentist office?
2. How do you brush your teeth?

STYLING SALON
Learning Center (dramatic play)

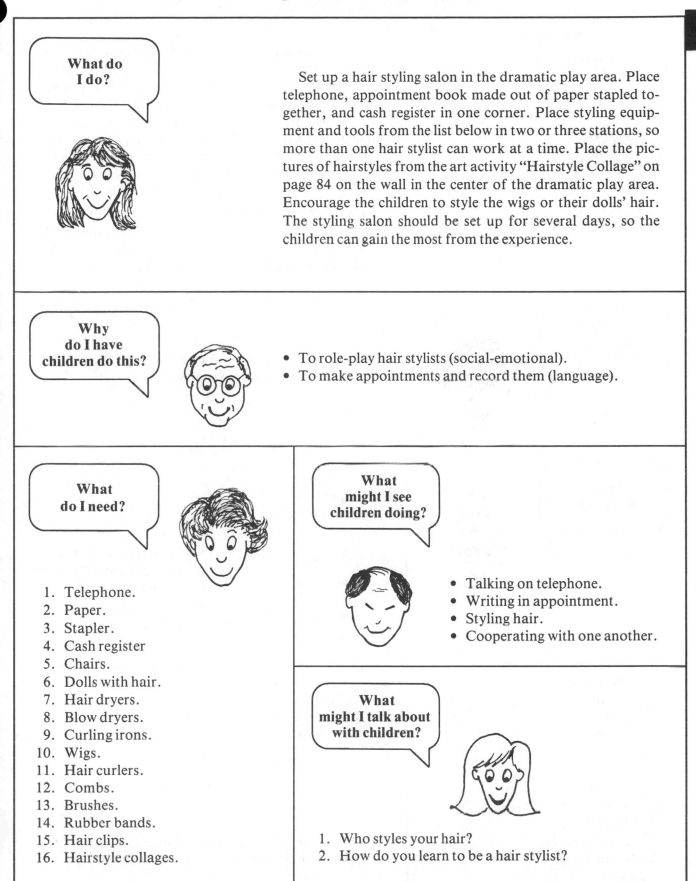

What do I do?

Set up a hair styling salon in the dramatic play area. Place telephone, appointment book made out of paper stapled together, and cash register in one corner. Place styling equipment and tools from the list below in two or three stations, so more than one hair stylist can work at a time. Place the pictures of hairstyles from the art activity "Hairstyle Collage" on page 84 on the wall in the center of the dramatic play area. Encourage the children to style the wigs or their dolls' hair. The styling salon should be set up for several days, so the children can gain the most from the experience.

Why do I have children do this?

- To role-play hair stylists (social-emotional).
- To make appointments and record them (language).

What do I need?

1. Telephone.
2. Paper.
3. Stapler.
4. Cash register
5. Chairs.
6. Dolls with hair.
7. Hair dryers.
8. Blow dryers.
9. Curling irons.
10. Wigs.
11. Hair curlers.
12. Combs.
13. Brushes.
14. Rubber bands.
15. Hair clips.
16. Hairstyle collages.

What might I see children doing?

- Talking on telephone.
- Writing in appointment.
- Styling hair.
- Cooperating with one another.

What might I talk about with children?

1. Who styles your hair?
2. How do you learn to be a hair stylist?

THE POST OFFICE
Learning Center (dramatic play)

What do I do?

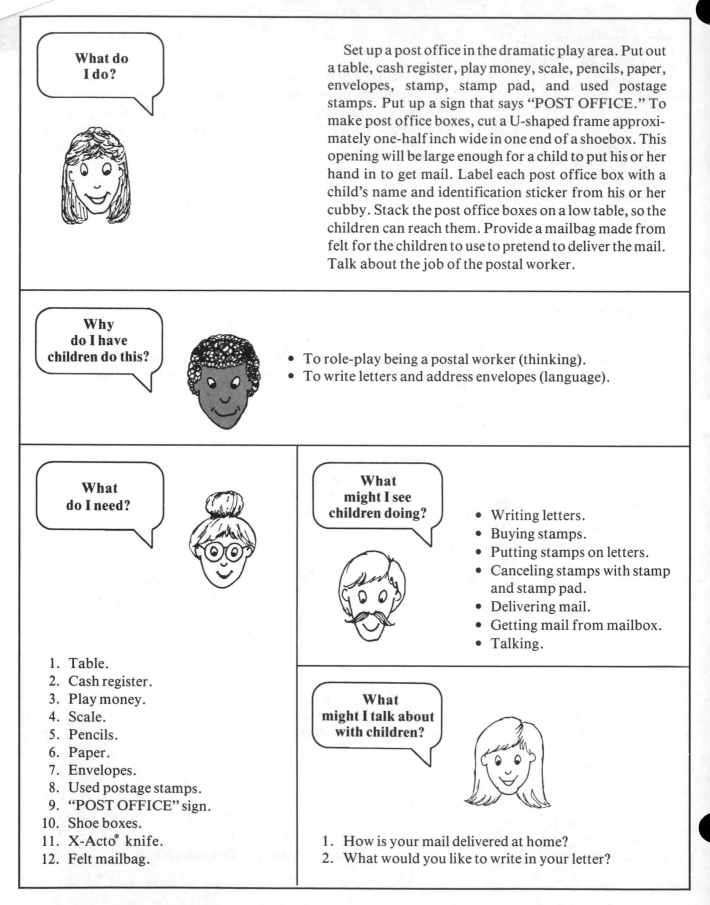

Set up a post office in the dramatic play area. Put out a table, cash register, play money, scale, pencils, paper, envelopes, stamp, stamp pad, and used postage stamps. Put up a sign that says "POST OFFICE." To make post office boxes, cut a U-shaped frame approximately one-half inch wide in one end of a shoebox. This opening will be large enough for a child to put his or her hand in to get mail. Label each post office box with a child's name and identification sticker from his or her cubby. Stack the post office boxes on a low table, so the children can reach them. Provide a mailbag made from felt for the children to use to pretend to deliver the mail. Talk about the job of the postal worker.

Why do I have children do this?

- To role-play being a postal worker (thinking).
- To write letters and address envelopes (language).

What do I need?

What might I see children doing?

- Writing letters.
- Buying stamps.
- Putting stamps on letters.
- Canceling stamps with stamp and stamp pad.
- Delivering mail.
- Getting mail from mailbox.
- Talking.

1. Table.
2. Cash register.
3. Play money.
4. Scale.
5. Pencils.
6. Paper.
7. Envelopes.
8. Used postage stamps.
9. "POST OFFICE" sign.
10. Shoe boxes.
11. X-Acto® knife.
12. Felt mailbag.

What might I talk about with children?

1. How is your mail delivered at home?
2. What would you like to write in your letter?

WE'LL WRAP IT!
Learning Center (dramatic play)

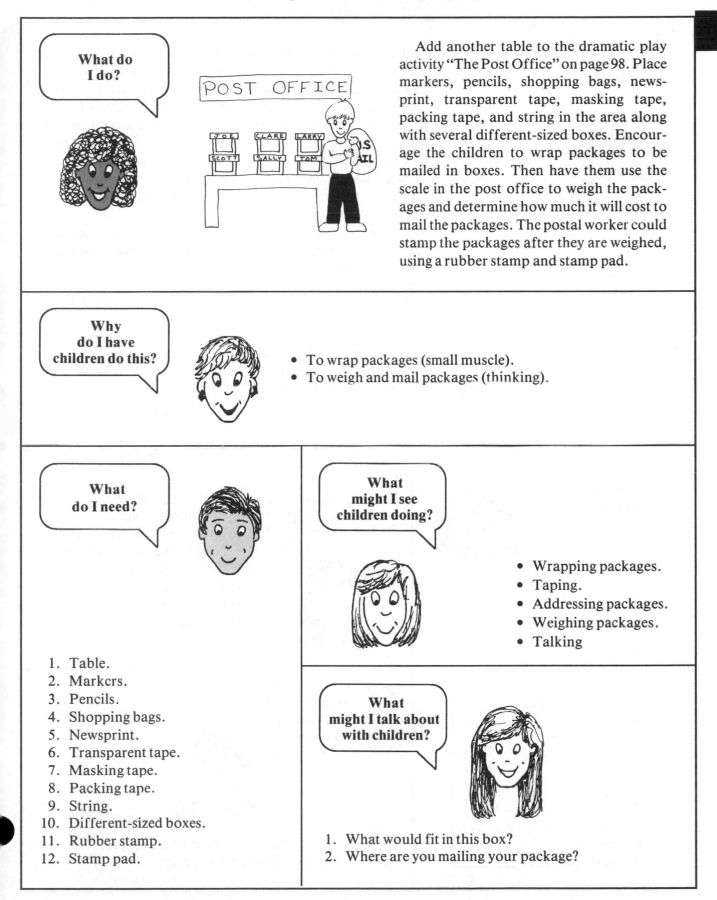

What do I do?

Add another table to the dramatic play activity "The Post Office" on page 98. Place markers, pencils, shopping bags, newsprint, transparent tape, masking tape, packing tape, and string in the area along with several different-sized boxes. Encourage the children to wrap packages to be mailed in boxes. Then have them use the scale in the post office to weigh the packages and determine how much it will cost to mail the packages. The postal worker could stamp the packages after they are weighed, using a rubber stamp and stamp pad.

Why do I have children do this?

- To wrap packages (small muscle).
- To weigh and mail packages (thinking).

What do I need?

1. Table.
2. Markers.
3. Pencils.
4. Shopping bags.
5. Newsprint.
6. Transparent tape.
7. Masking tape.
8. Packing tape.
9. String.
10. Different-sized boxes.
11. Rubber stamp.
12. Stamp pad.

What might I see children doing?

- Wrapping packages.
- Taping.
- Addressing packages.
- Weighing packages.
- Talking

What might I talk about with children?

1. What would fit in this box?
2. Where are you mailing your package?

BUSY BAKER PIES
Learning Center (food)

What do I do?

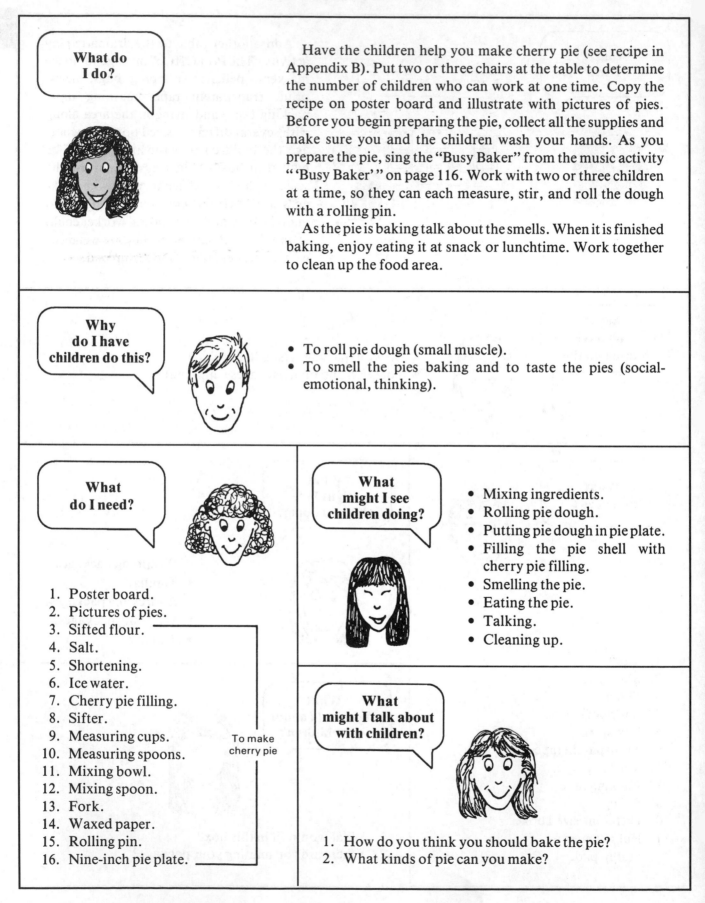

Have the children help you make cherry pie (see recipe in Appendix B). Put two or three chairs at the table to determine the number of children who can work at one time. Copy the recipe on poster board and illustrate with pictures of pies. Before you begin preparing the pie, collect all the supplies and make sure you and the children wash your hands. As you prepare the pie, sing the "Busy Baker" from the music activity "'Busy Baker'" on page 116. Work with two or three children at a time, so they can each measure, stir, and roll the dough with a rolling pin.

As the pie is baking talk about the smells. When it is finished baking, enjoy eating it at snack or lunchtime. Work together to clean up the food area.

Why do I have children do this?

- To roll pie dough (small muscle).
- To smell the pies baking and to taste the pies (social-emotional, thinking).

What do I need?

1. Poster board.
2. Pictures of pies.
3. Sifted flour.
4. Salt.
5. Shortening.
6. Ice water.
7. Cherry pie filling.
8. Sifter.
9. Measuring cups.
10. Measuring spoons.
11. Mixing bowl.
12. Mixing spoon.
13. Fork.
14. Waxed paper.
15. Rolling pin.
16. Nine-inch pie plate.

To make cherry pie

What might I see children doing?

- Mixing ingredients.
- Rolling pie dough.
- Putting pie dough in pie plate.
- Filling the pie shell with cherry pie filling.
- Smelling the pie.
- Eating the pie.
- Talking.
- Cleaning up.

What might I talk about with children?

1. How do you think you should bake the pie?
2. What kinds of pie can you make?

STOP, GO, BE CAREFUL COOKIES
Learning Center (food)

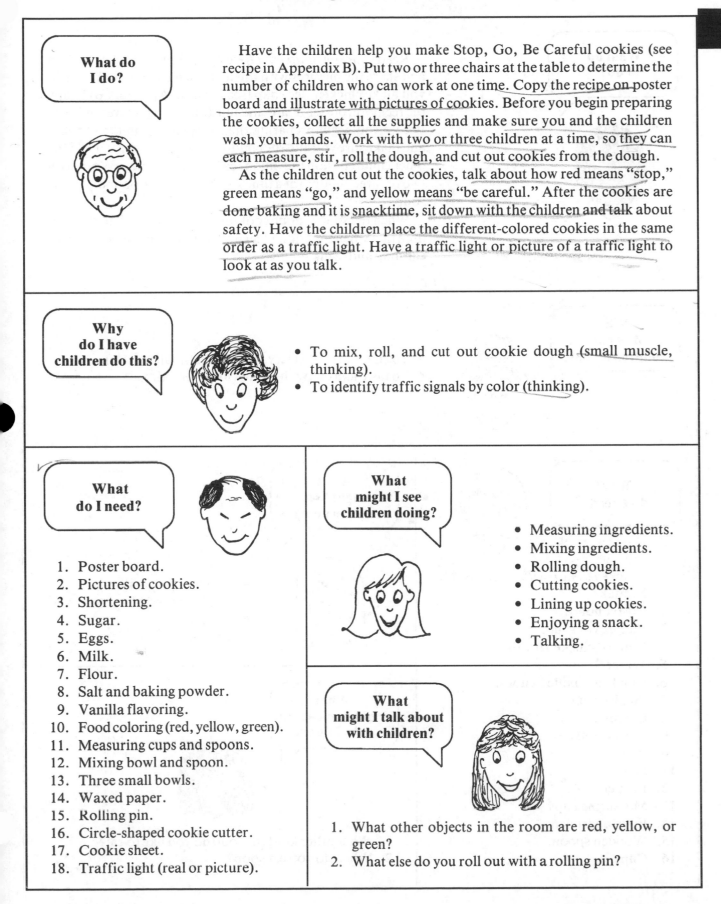

What do I do?

Have the children help you make Stop, Go, Be Careful cookies (see recipe in Appendix B). Put two or three chairs at the table to determine the number of children who can work at one time. Copy the recipe on poster board and illustrate with pictures of cookies. Before you begin preparing the cookies, collect all the supplies and make sure you and the children wash your hands. Work with two or three children at a time, so they can each measure, stir, roll the dough, and cut out cookies from the dough.

As the children cut out the cookies, talk about how red means "stop," green means "go," and yellow means "be careful." After the cookies are done baking and it is snacktime, sit down with the children and talk about safety. Have the children place the different-colored cookies in the same order as a traffic light. Have a traffic light or picture of a traffic light to look at as you talk.

Why do I have children do this?

- To mix, roll, and cut out cookie dough (small muscle, thinking).
- To identify traffic signals by color (thinking).

What do I need?

1. Poster board.
2. Pictures of cookies.
3. Shortening.
4. Sugar.
5. Eggs.
6. Milk.
7. Flour.
8. Salt and baking powder.
9. Vanilla flavoring.
10. Food coloring (red, yellow, green).
11. Measuring cups and spoons.
12. Mixing bowl and spoon.
13. Three small bowls.
14. Waxed paper.
15. Rolling pin.
16. Circle-shaped cookie cutter.
17. Cookie sheet.
18. Traffic light (real or picture).

What might I see children doing?

- Measuring ingredients.
- Mixing ingredients.
- Rolling dough.
- Cutting cookies.
- Lining up cookies.
- Enjoying a snack.
- Talking.

What might I talk about with children?

1. What other objects in the room are red, yellow, or green?
2. What else do you roll out with a rolling pin?

CHICKEN RICE SOUP
Learning Center (food)

What do I do?

Read *Chicken Soup with Rice* by M. Sendak to the children and share the pictures with them. Then have the children help you make chicken rice soup (see recipe in Appendix B). Copy the recipe on poster board and illustrate with pictures of soup. Before you begin preparing the soup, collect all the supplies and make sure you and the children wash your hands. Help the older children chop the onion, carrots, and celery. Work with two or three children at a time, so they can each pour or stir the soup.

When the soup is done cooking, serve in cups. Tell the children that when they don't feel well, the doctor may tell them to eat soup and drink liquids.

Why do I have children do this?

- To chop carrots, celery, and onion (small muscle).
- To taste and enjoy the soup (social-emotional).

What do I need?

1. *Chicken Soup with Rice* by M. Sendak.
2. Poster board.
3. Pictures of soup.
4. Canned chicken broth.
5. Water.
6. Chicken bouillon cubes.
7. Small onion.
8. Carrots.
9. Celery stalks.
10. Rice.
11. Salt.
12. Pepper.
13. Measuring cups.
14. Four-quart pan.
15. Wooden spoon.
16. Cups.

What might I see children doing?

- Chopping vegetables.
- Stirring vegetables into broth.
- Tasting.
- Talking.

What might I talk about with children?

1. What other kinds of soup do you like to eat?
2. When do you eat soup?

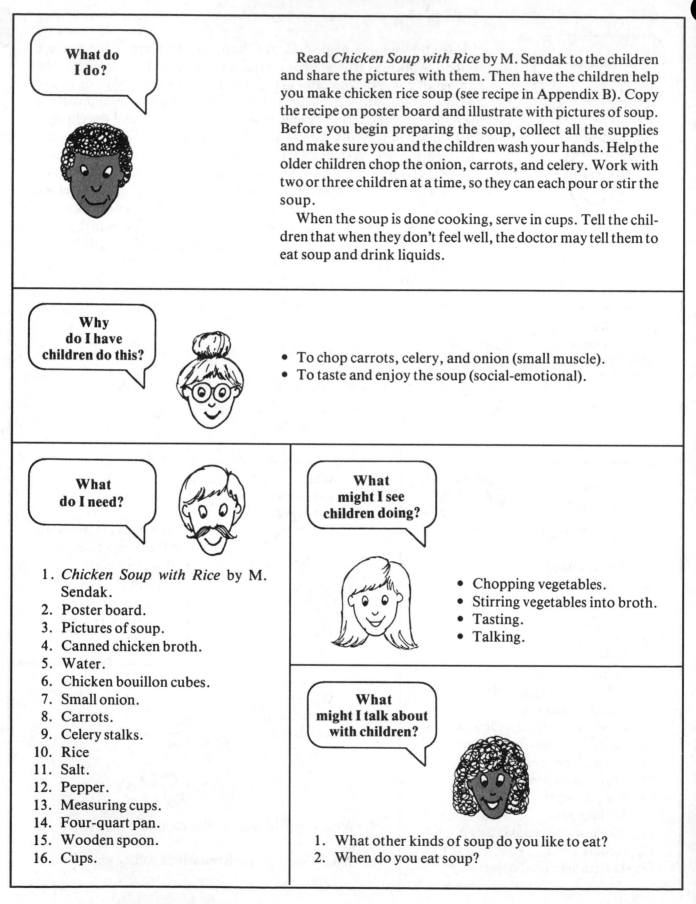

DANDELION
Learning Center (library)

What do I do?

Read *Dandelion* by D. Freeman to two or three children at a time. Talk with them about how Dandelion felt when he got his hair cut, and how they feel when they get their hair cut. Talk about how Dandelion felt when Jennifer did not recognize him and wouldn't let him in. Have the children help you make a chart that they can follow for a week to remember good grooming.

Why do I have children do this?

- To remember to take a bath, brush teeth, and brush hair (thinking).
- To talk about taking care of themselves (language).

What do I need?

1. *Dandelion* by D. Freeman.
2. Chart paper.
3. Marker.

What might I see children doing?

- Listening.
- Talking.
- Sharing ideas for the chart.

What might I talk about with children?

1. Why do you take a bath?
2. What do you use when you brush your teeth?

YOU CAN BE ANYTHING–JUST LIKE MOM AND DAD
Learning Center (library)

What do I do?

Collect a variety of books about people in nontraditional occupations, such as *My Daddy Is a Nurse* by M. Wandro and J. Blank or *Mothers Can Do Everything* by J. Lasker. Take time to sit and read these books to two or three children at a time. Discuss what the children's mothers, fathers, aunts, uncles, and neighbors do for a living. Make felt board figures based on the books–a female taxi driver, lawyer, dentist, or zookeeper and a male nurse, children's librarian, telephone operator, ballet dancer, or weaver. (See directions in Appendix A.) Let the children put these figures on the felt board as you discuss the books. Invite parents and friends who have nontraditional occupations to speak to the children.

Why do I have children do this?

- To discuss occupations that they might consider when they grow up (language, thinking).
- To share ideas with other children (social-emotional, language).

What do I need?

1. *My Daddy Is a Nurse* by M. Wandro and J. Blank.
2. *Mothers Can Do Everything* by J. Lasker.
3. Coloring books (for child care providers only), books, or drawings.
4. Pencil.
5. Fusible interfacing.
6. Permanent markers.
7. Iron.
8. Felt.
9. Scissors.
10. Felt board.

To make felt board figures

What might I see children doing?

- Listening.
- Talking.
- Manipulating felt board figures.

What might I talk about with children?

1. What would you like to do when you grow up?
2. What can you do outside or inside?

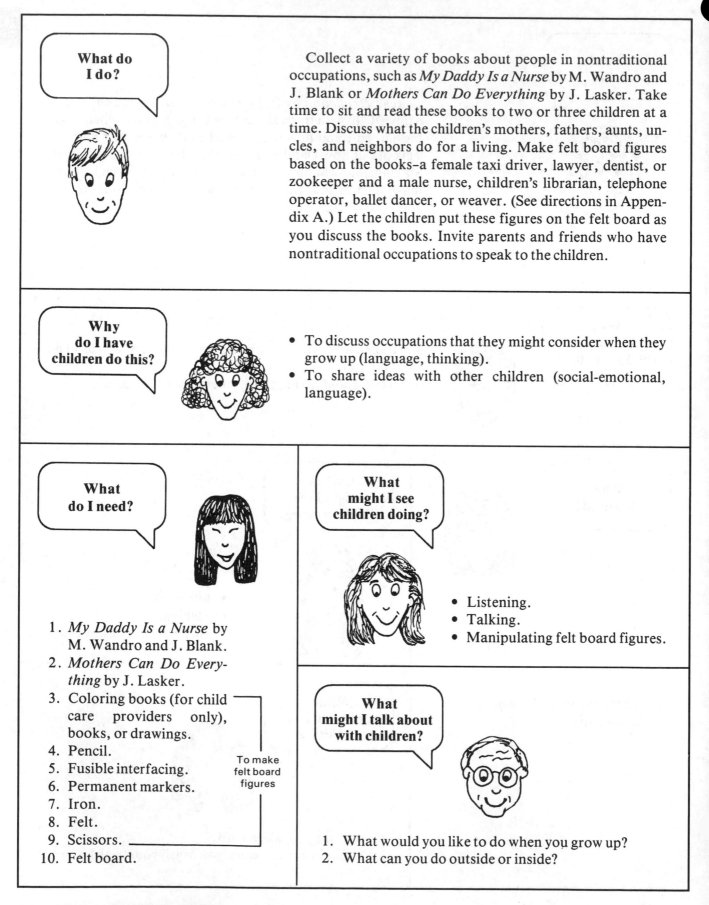

BUILD ME A HOUSE
Learning Center (manipulatives)

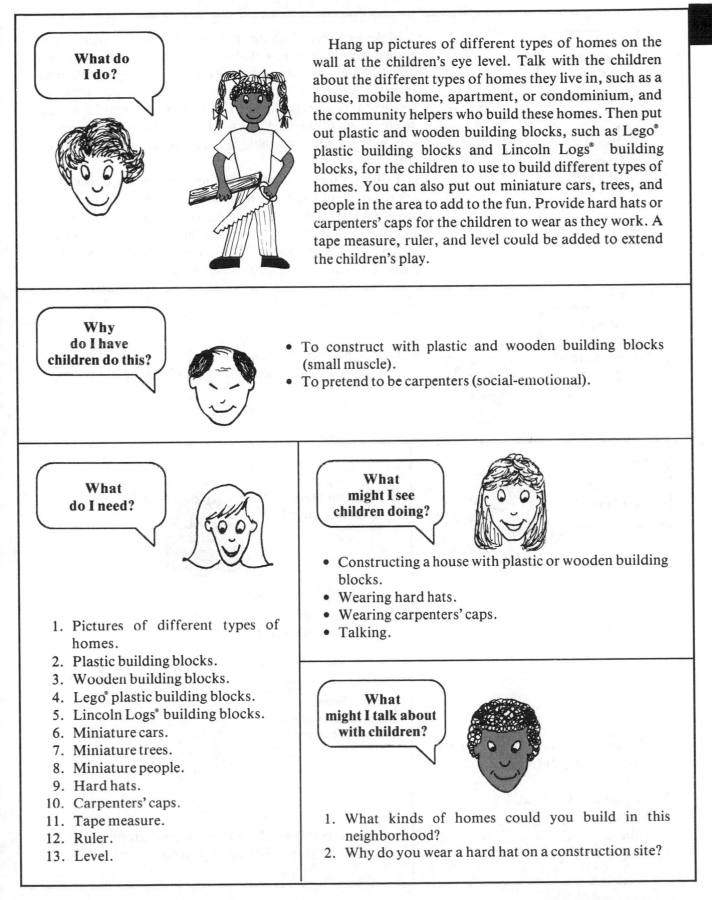

What do I do?

Hang up pictures of different types of homes on the wall at the children's eye level. Talk with the children about the different types of homes they live in, such as a house, mobile home, apartment, or condominium, and the community helpers who build these homes. Then put out plastic and wooden building blocks, such as Lego® plastic building blocks and Lincoln Logs® building blocks, for the children to use to build different types of homes. You can also put out miniature cars, trees, and people in the area to add to the fun. Provide hard hats or carpenters' caps for the children to wear as they work. A tape measure, ruler, and level could be added to extend the children's play.

Why do I have children do this?

- To construct with plastic and wooden building blocks (small muscle).
- To pretend to be carpenters (social-emotional).

What do I need?

1. Pictures of different types of homes.
2. Plastic building blocks.
3. Wooden building blocks.
4. Lego® plastic building blocks.
5. Lincoln Logs® building blocks.
6. Miniature cars.
7. Miniature trees.
8. Miniature people.
9. Hard hats.
10. Carpenters' caps.
11. Tape measure.
12. Ruler.
13. Level.

What might I see children doing?

- Constructing a house with plastic or wooden building blocks.
- Wearing hard hats.
- Wearing carpenters' caps.
- Talking.

What might I talk about with children?

1. What kinds of homes could you build in this neighborhood?
2. Why do you wear a hard hat on a construction site?

MATCH MY HOUSE
Learning Center (manipulatives)

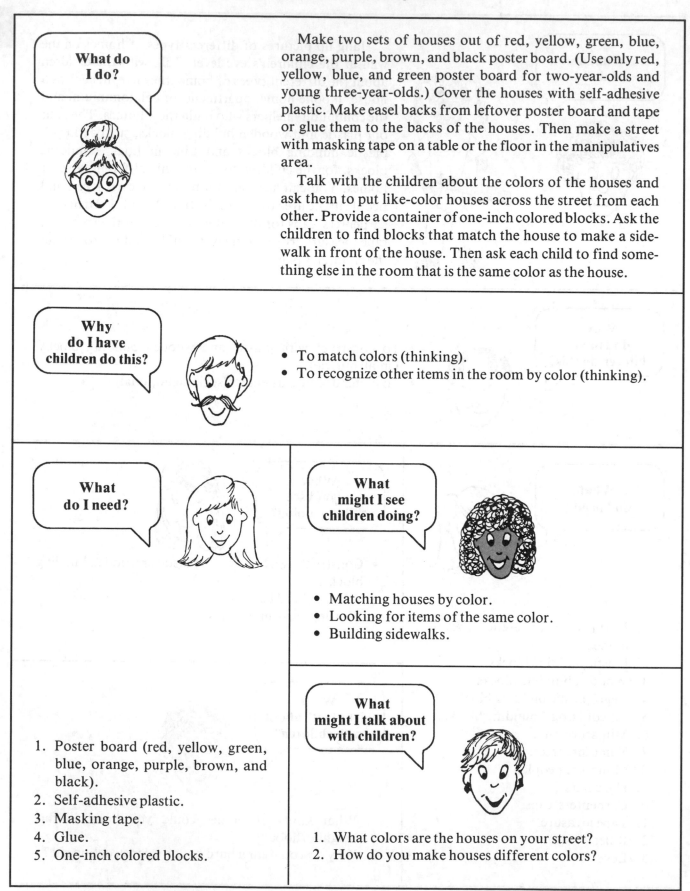

What do I do?

Make two sets of houses out of red, yellow, green, blue, orange, purple, brown, and black poster board. (Use only red, yellow, blue, and green poster board for two-year-olds and young three-year-olds.) Cover the houses with self-adhesive plastic. Make easel backs from leftover poster board and tape or glue them to the backs of the houses. Then make a street with masking tape on a table or the floor in the manipulatives area.

Talk with the children about the colors of the houses and ask them to put like-color houses across the street from each other. Provide a container of one-inch colored blocks. Ask the children to find blocks that match the house to make a sidewalk in front of the house. Then ask each child to find something else in the room that is the same color as the house.

Why do I have children do this?

- To match colors (thinking).
- To recognize other items in the room by color (thinking).

What do I need?

What might I see children doing?

- Matching houses by color.
- Looking for items of the same color.
- Building sidewalks.

What might I talk about with children?

1. Poster board (red, yellow, green, blue, orange, purple, brown, and black).
2. Self-adhesive plastic.
3. Masking tape.
4. Glue.
5. One-inch colored blocks.

1. What colors are the houses on your street?
2. How do you make houses different colors?

BAKING NUMBER COOKIES
Learning Center (manipulatives, dramatic play)

What do I do?

Make one to 10 poster board cookie sheets depending on the age of the children (two-year-olds–two sheets, three-year-olds–three sheets, four-year-olds–four sheets, and five-year-olds–five or more sheets). Number the cookie sheets with the numbers 1, 2, 3, or 4, illustrate with drawings of the same number of cookies, and cover with self-adhesive plastic. Then make 3 dozen poster board cookies covered with self-adhesive plastic or 3 dozen playdough cookies. (See recipe for playdough in Appendix A.) Have the children place the correct number of cookies on the cookie sheets. Children will match to the cookies drawn on the tray before they will to the numerals.

The children can also use the cookies and cookie sheets when they play in the dramatic play area. They could bake the cookies and serve them to their "family" or "friends."

Why do I have children do this?

- To match cookies on tray (thinking).
- To pretend to bake cookies (social-emotional).

What do I need?

1. Poster board.
2. Markers.
3. Self-adhesive plastic.
4. Vegetable oil.
5. Flour.
6. Salt.
7. Cream of tartar.
8. Water.
9. Food coloring.
10. Peppermint extract.
11. Pot.
12. Large spoon.
13. Self-sealing plastic bags.

To make playdough

What might I see children doing?

- Matching cookies.
- Placing cookie sheets in play oven.
- Serving cookies.
- Talking to friends.

What might I talk about with children?

1. What do you like to drink with cookies?
2. What kinds of cookies do you make at home?

THIS TOOL BELONGS TO . . .
Learning Center (manipulatives)

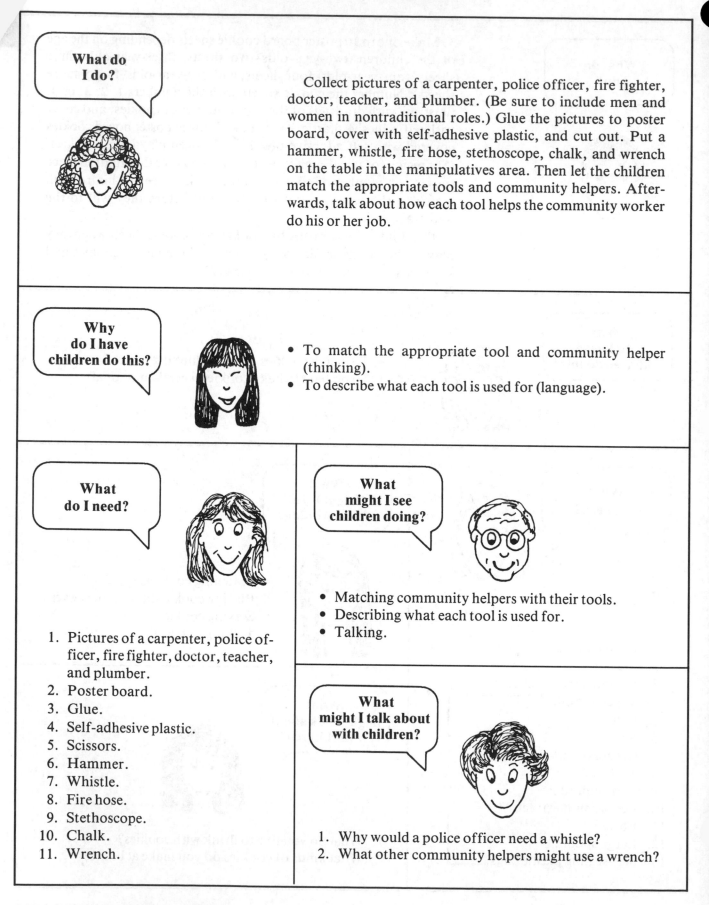

What do I do?

Collect pictures of a carpenter, police officer, fire fighter, doctor, teacher, and plumber. (Be sure to include men and women in nontraditional roles.) Glue the pictures to poster board, cover with self-adhesive plastic, and cut out. Put a hammer, whistle, fire hose, stethoscope, chalk, and wrench on the table in the manipulatives area. Then let the children match the appropriate tools and community helpers. Afterwards, talk about how each tool helps the community worker do his or her job.

Why do I have children do this?

- To match the appropriate tool and community helper (thinking).
- To describe what each tool is used for (language).

What do I need?

1. Pictures of a carpenter, police officer, fire fighter, doctor, teacher, and plumber.
2. Poster board.
3. Glue.
4. Self-adhesive plastic.
5. Scissors.
6. Hammer.
7. Whistle.
8. Fire hose.
9. Stethoscope.
10. Chalk.
11. Wrench.

What might I see children doing?

- Matching community helpers with their tools.
- Describing what each tool is used for.
- Talking.

What might I talk about with children?

1. Why would a police officer need a whistle?
2. What other community helpers might use a wrench?

COMMUNITY HELPER PUZZLES
Learning Center (manipulatives)

What do I do?

Put out several puzzles with varying numbers of pieces that show different community helpers. Puzzles can be purchased from early childhood curriculum materials catalogs or you can make them yourself. (See directions in Appendix A.) Sit down and talk with the children about the puzzles. Talk with them about the various community helpers and what they do. Encourage the children to put the puzzles together. Talk about the shapes and colors to do more incidental teaching in those areas. Encourage the children to place puzzles back on the shelves when they are finished.

Why do I have children do this?

- To put puzzles together (small muscle).
- To talk about what the community helper does in the community (language).

What do I need?

1. Puzzles of community helpers.
2. Wood or heavy cardboard.
3. Pictures of community helpers.
4. Glue.
5. Band saw or X-Acto® knife.
6. Sandpaper.
7. Lacquer, varnish, or clear acrylic finish.
8. Self-adhesive plastic.

To make puzzle

What might I see children doing?

- Choosing puzzles.
- Putting puzzles together.
- Returning the puzzles to the shelves.
- Talking.

What might I talk about with children?

1. What do you think you would do if you spent the day with the fire fighter at work?
2. What do you think a police officer does when he or she is at work?

COMMUNITY HELPER LACING CARDS
Learning Center (manipulatives)

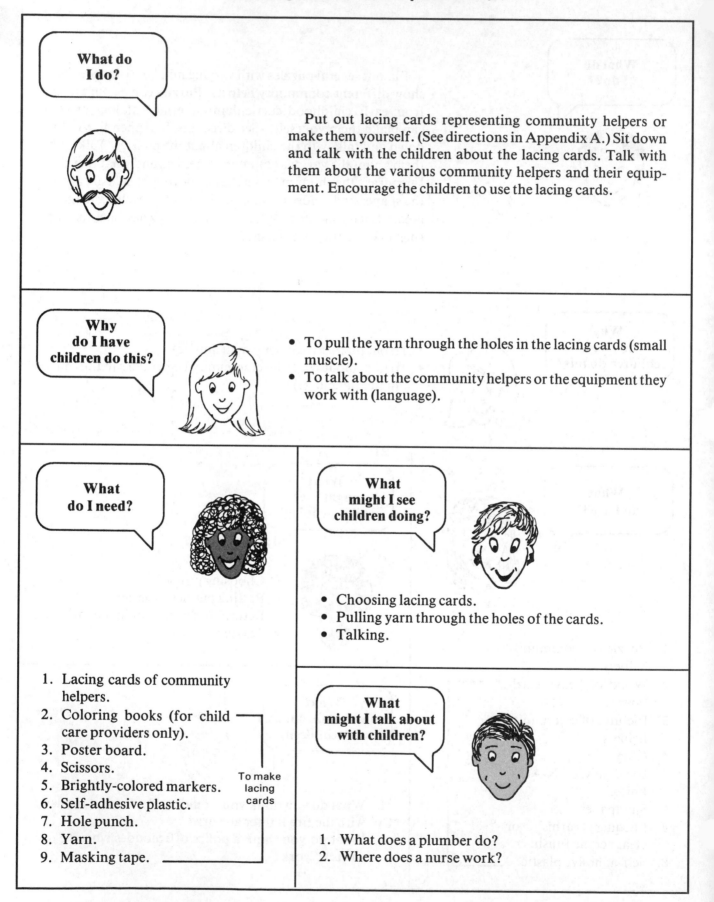

What do I do?

Put out lacing cards representing community helpers or make them yourself. (See directions in Appendix A.) Sit down and talk with the children about the lacing cards. Talk with them about the various community helpers and their equipment. Encourage the children to use the lacing cards.

Why do I have children do this?

- To pull the yarn through the holes in the lacing cards (small muscle).
- To talk about the community helpers or the equipment they work with (language).

What do I need?

1. Lacing cards of community helpers.
2. Coloring books (for child care providers only).
3. Poster board.
4. Scissors.
5. Brightly-colored markers.
6. Self-adhesive plastic.
7. Hole punch.
8. Yarn.
9. Masking tape.

To make lacing cards

What might I see children doing?

- Choosing lacing cards.
- Pulling yarn through the holes of the cards.
- Talking.

What might I talk about with children?

1. What does a plumber do?
2. Where does a nurse work?

MEDICAL FEELY BOX
Learning Center (manipulatives, library)

What do I do?

Place three to five medical items from the list below in a feely box. As a child shows an interest in the activity, ask him or her to reach in the box and describe the object he or she is touching without looking at it or taking it out of the box. Encourage the child to use size and shape words. If he or she has trouble, suggest descriptive words, such as hard, soft, smooth, rough, heavy, and light. After the child has described the object, encourage him or her to take the object out of the feely box and look at it. Ask the child if the object was what he or she thought it was when he or she felt it. Ask the child if he or she has seen this object before and what is it used for.

Why do I have children do this?

- To identify objects by touch (thinking).
- To describe objects without looking at them (language).

What do I need?

What might I see children doing?

- Feeling.
- Describing objects.
- Talking.

1. Feely box.
2. Plastic syringe with needle removed.
3. Stethoscope.
4. Cotton ball.
5. Adhesive bandage.
6. Tongue depressor.
7. Elastic bandage.
8. Gauze.
9. Surgical mask.

What might I talk about with children?

1. What do you think a doctor or nurse might use this object for?
2. What do you think doctors and nurses do when they leave the hospital?

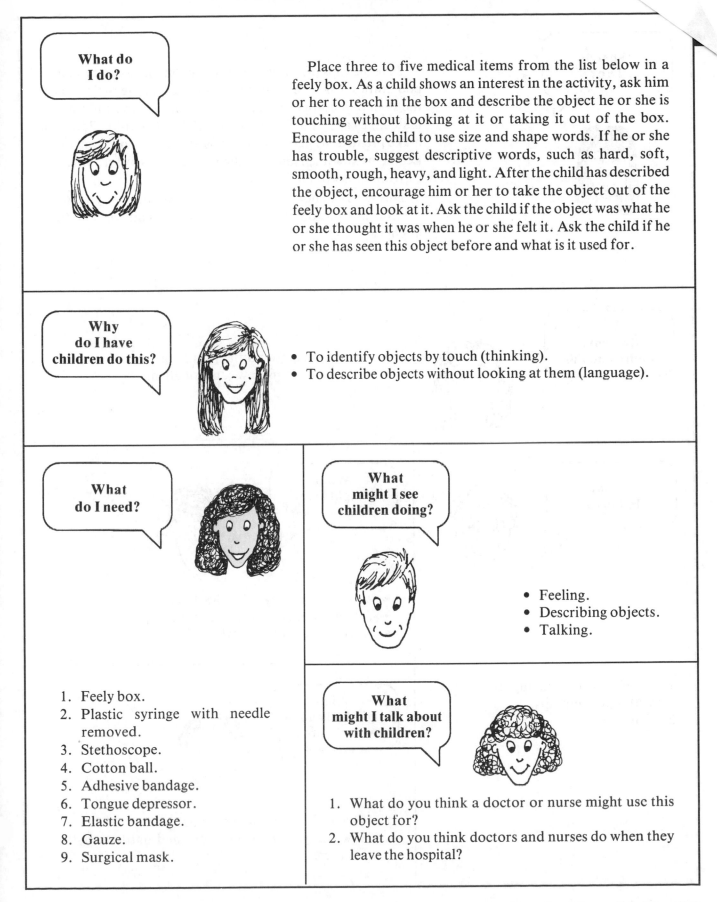

SHAMPOO BOTTLE MATCH
Learning Center (manipulatives)

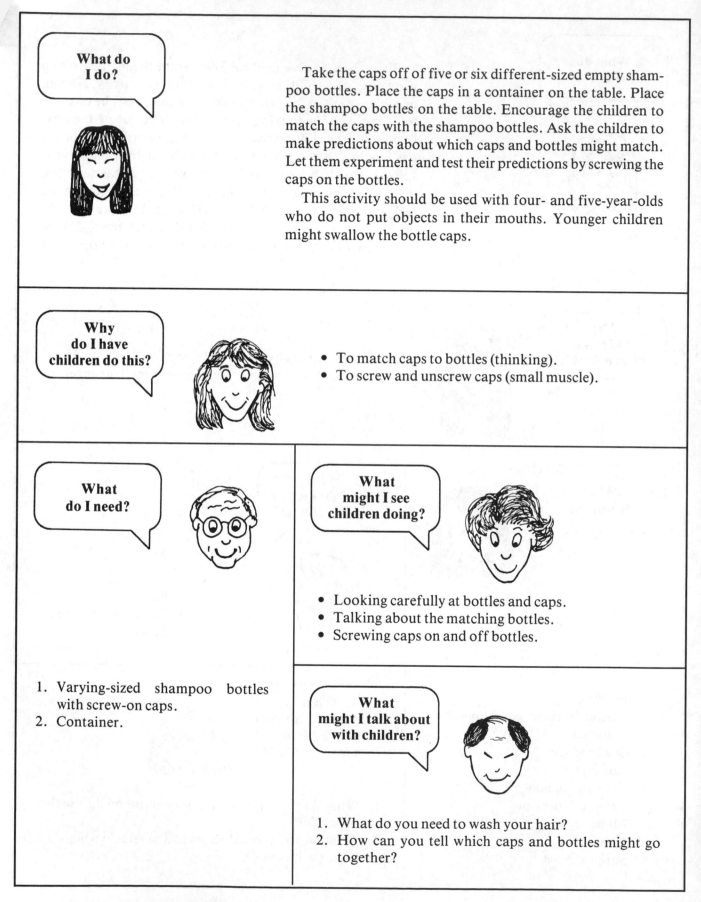

What do I do?

Take the caps off of five or six different-sized empty shampoo bottles. Place the caps in a container on the table. Place the shampoo bottles on the table. Encourage the children to match the caps with the shampoo bottles. Ask the children to make predictions about which caps and bottles might match. Let them experiment and test their predictions by screwing the caps on the bottles.

This activity should be used with four- and five-year-olds who do not put objects in their mouths. Younger children might swallow the bottle caps.

Why do I have children do this?

- To match caps to bottles (thinking).
- To screw and unscrew caps (small muscle).

What do I need?

1. Varying-sized shampoo bottles with screw-on caps.
2. Container.

What might I see children doing?

- Looking carefully at bottles and caps.
- Talking about the matching bottles.
- Screwing caps on and off bottles.

What might I talk about with children?

1. What do you need to wash your hair?
2. How can you tell which caps and bottles might go together?

STAMP LOTTO
Learning Center (manipulatives)

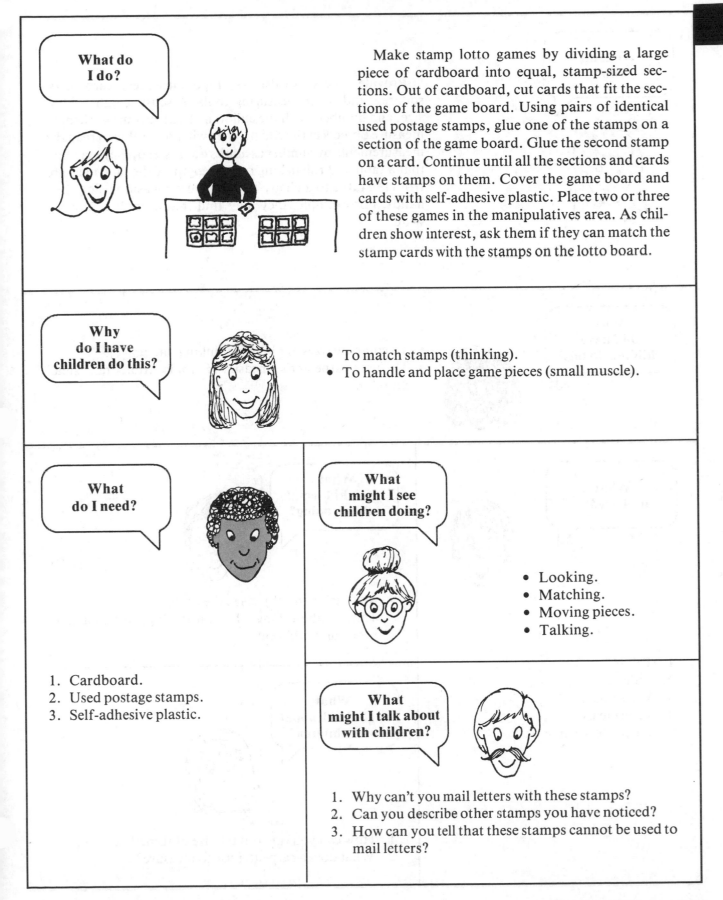

What do I do?

Make stamp lotto games by dividing a large piece of cardboard into equal, stamp-sized sections. Out of cardboard, cut cards that fit the sections of the game board. Using pairs of identical used postage stamps, glue one of the stamps on a section of the game board. Glue the second stamp on a card. Continue until all the sections and cards have stamps on them. Cover the game board and cards with self-adhesive plastic. Place two or three of these games in the manipulatives area. As children show interest, ask them if they can match the stamp cards with the stamps on the lotto board.

Why do I have children do this?

- To match stamps (thinking).
- To handle and place game pieces (small muscle).

What do I need?

1. Cardboard.
2. Used postage stamps.
3. Self-adhesive plastic.

What might I see children doing?

- Looking.
- Matching.
- Moving pieces.
- Talking.

What might I talk about with children?

1. Why can't you mail letters with these stamps?
2. Can you describe other stamps you have noticed?
3. How can you tell that these stamps cannot be used to mail letters?

MEASURING TOOLS
Learning Center (math, science)

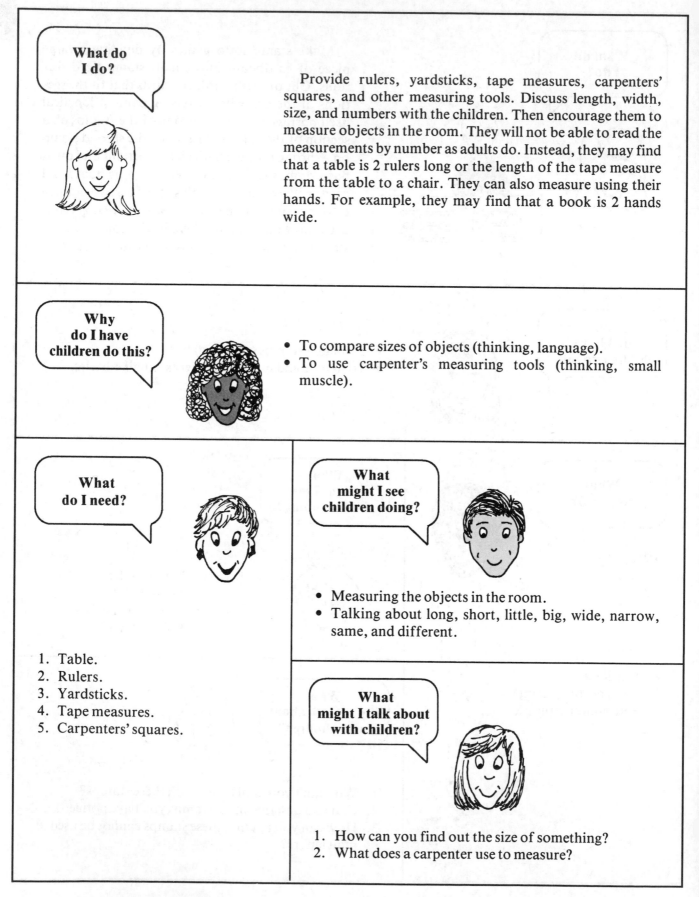

What do I do?

Provide rulers, yardsticks, tape measures, carpenters' squares, and other measuring tools. Discuss length, width, size, and numbers with the children. Then encourage them to measure objects in the room. They will not be able to read the measurements by number as adults do. Instead, they may find that a table is 2 rulers long or the length of the tape measure from the table to a chair. They can also measure using their hands. For example, they may find that a book is 2 hands wide.

Why do I have children do this?

- To compare sizes of objects (thinking, language).
- To use carpenter's measuring tools (thinking, small muscle).

What do I need?

1. Table.
2. Rulers.
3. Yardsticks.
4. Tape measures.
5. Carpenters' squares.

What might I see children doing?

- Measuring the objects in the room.
- Talking about long, short, little, big, wide, narrow, same, and different.

What might I talk about with children?

1. How can you find out the size of something?
2. What does a carpenter use to measure?

COUNTING COOKIES FROM THE BAKERY
Learning Center (math, snacktime)

What do I do?

After you have talked about bakers and completed the food activity "Stop, Go, Be Careful Cookies" on page 101, have each child take cookies. Base the number of cookies each child takes on the development of the child. For example, two-year-olds can take one or two cookies, and five-year-olds can take five or more cookies. Then have one child hand out a napkin to each child at the table. Have another child pass a glass of milk to each child at the table.

Why do I have children do this?

- To count 1, 2, 3, 4, and 5 objects (thinking).
- To serve one another (social-emotional).

What do I need?

1. Cookies.
2. Napkins.
3. Glasses.
4. Milk.

What might I see children doing?

- Counting 1, 2, 3, 4, or 5.
- Handing out napkins to each child.
- Passing out glasses of milk to each child.
- Talking.

What might I talk about with children?

1. How could you make cookies?
2. What are some other items you can count?

"BUSY BAKER"
Learning Center (music)

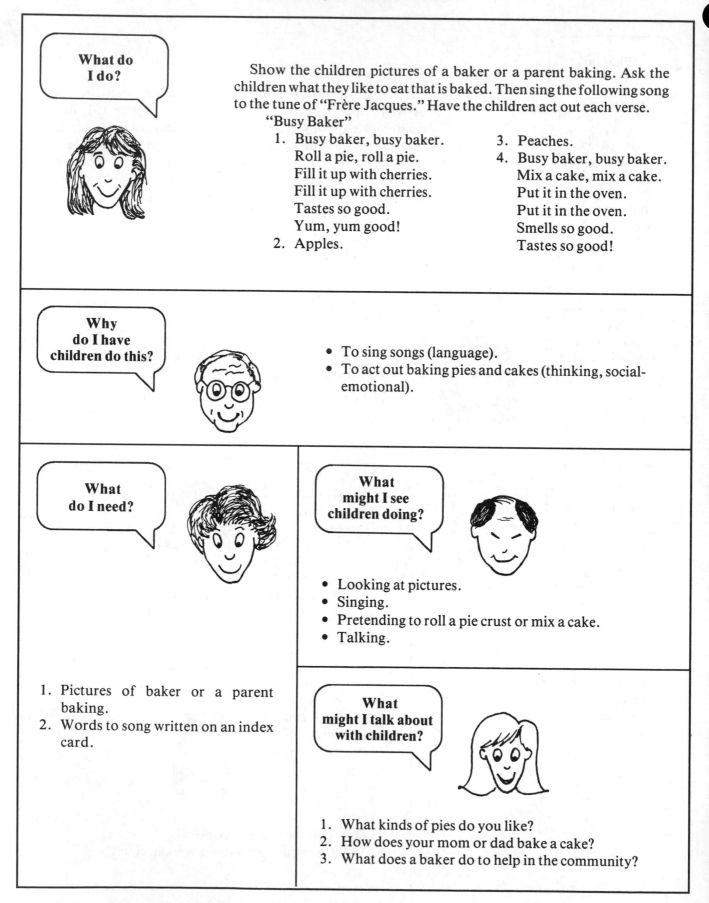

What do I do?

Show the children pictures of a baker or a parent baking. Ask the children what they like to eat that is baked. Then sing the following song to the tune of "Frère Jacques." Have the children act out each verse.

"Busy Baker"

1. Busy baker, busy baker.
   Roll a pie, roll a pie.
   Fill it up with cherries.
   Fill it up with cherries.
   Tastes so good.
   Yum, yum good!
2. Apples.
3. Peaches.
4. Busy baker, busy baker.
   Mix a cake, mix a cake.
   Put it in the oven.
   Put it in the oven.
   Smells so good.
   Tastes so good!

Why do I have children do this?

- To sing songs (language).
- To act out baking pies and cakes (thinking, social-emotional).

What do I need?

1. Pictures of baker or a parent baking.
2. Words to song written on an index card.

What might I see children doing?

- Looking at pictures.
- Singing.
- Pretending to roll a pie crust or mix a cake.
- Talking.

What might I talk about with children?

1. What kinds of pies do you like?
2. How does your mom or dad bake a cake?
3. What does a baker do to help in the community?

STEAM SHOVEL IN THE SANDBOX OR SAND TABLE
Learning Center (sand), Indoor or Outdoor Large Muscle

What do I do?

Complete the group activity "*Mike Mulligan and His Steam Shovel*" on page 77. Talk with children about everything Mike Mulligan and his steam shovel could dig. Place toy steam shovels, dump trucks, and shovels in the sand table or sandbox. Encourage the children to dig roads, airport runways, tunnels, and basements. You might add cars, trucks, and wooden houses to the area after they work for awhile or on the second day you use the area. Talk with the children about full shovels, half-full shovels, and empty shovels. Talk about big and little holes.

Why do I have children do this?

- To dig in the sand (small and large muscle).
- To use new words, such as full, empty, big, and little (thinking).

What do I need?

1. Sand table or sandbox.
2. Toy steam shovels.
3. Toy dump trucks.
4. Toy shovels.

What might I see children doing?

- Using steam shovels.
- Digging.
- Filling dump trucks.
- Talking.
- Enjoying sand.

What might I talk about with children?

1. What are you going to dig with the steam shovel?
2. How do you dig a basement?

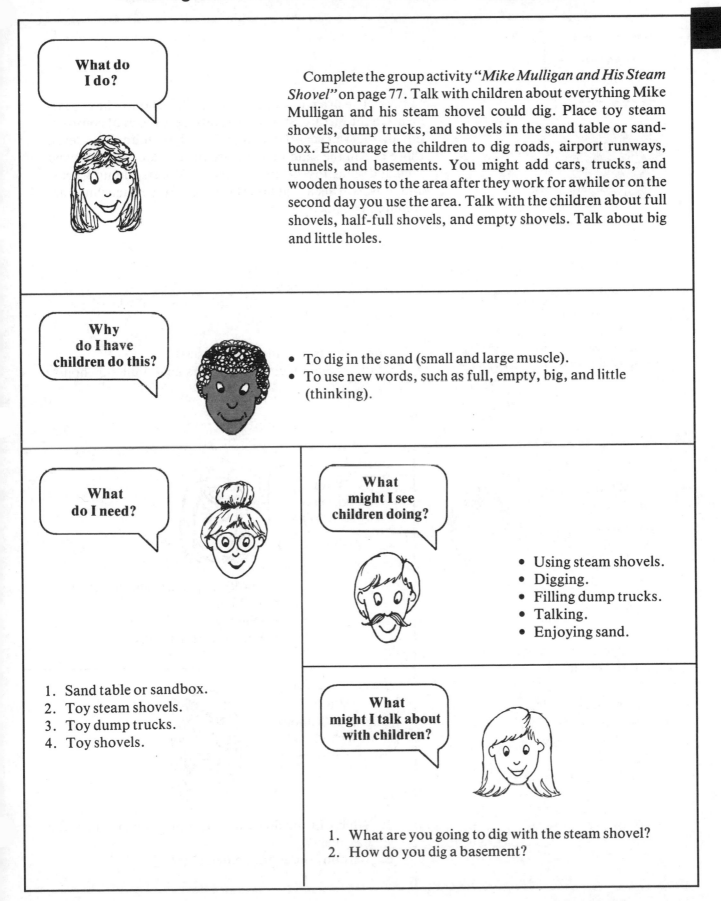

LET'S DIG THE BASEMENT
Learning Center (sand), Indoor or Outdoor Large Muscle

What do I do?

If you live in a part of the country where houses have basements, hang pictures showing the different stages of construction on the wall near the sand table at the children's eye level. Place dirt in the sand table or use the outdoor sandbox and then add some toy steam shovels, bulldozers, dump trucks, and shovels. Talk about how the drivers of these machines are community helpers.

Why do I have children do this?

- To dig in dirt (small and large muscle).
- To talk about digging basements and building houses (language).

What do I need?

1. Pictures of different stages of construction.
2. Dirt.
3. Toy steam shovels.
4. Toy bulldozers.
5. Toy dump trucks.
6. Toy shovels.
7. Sand table or sandbox.

What might I see children doing?

- Looking at construction pictures.
- Talking.
- Digging.
- Putting dirt in trucks.

What might I talk about with children?

1. What will you do with the dirt that you dig out of the basement?
2. Why do houses have basements?

ROCK SAMPLES
Learning Center (science)

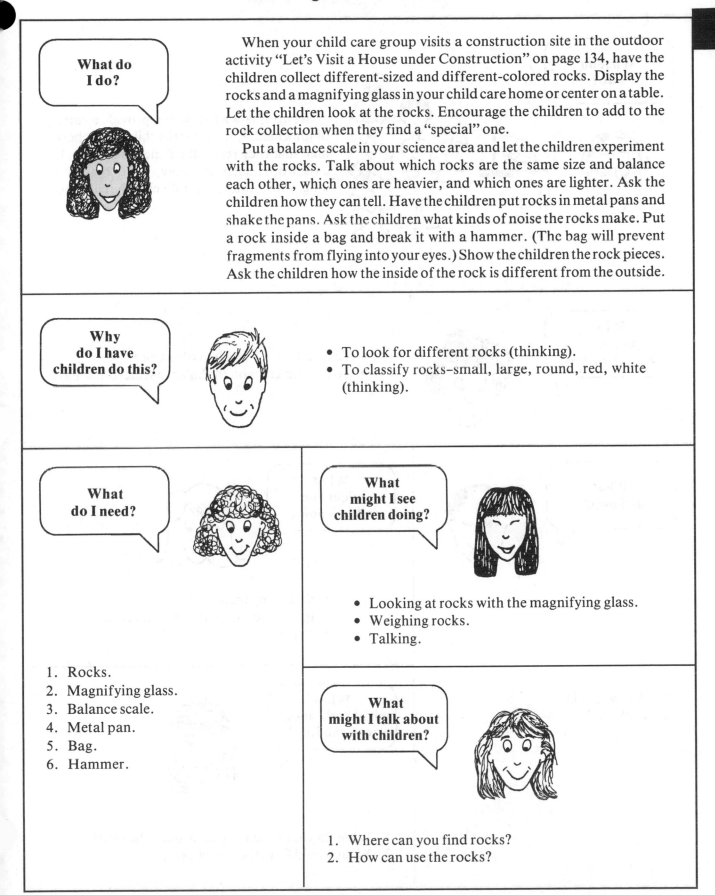

What do I do?

When your child care group visits a construction site in the outdoor activity "Let's Visit a House under Construction" on page 134, have the children collect different-sized and different-colored rocks. Display the rocks and a magnifying glass in your child care home or center on a table. Let the children look at the rocks. Encourage the children to add to the rock collection when they find a "special" one.

Put a balance scale in your science area and let the children experiment with the rocks. Talk about which rocks are the same size and balance each other, which ones are heavier, and which ones are lighter. Ask the children how they can tell. Have the children put rocks in metal pans and shake the pans. Ask the children what kinds of noise the rocks make. Put a rock inside a bag and break it with a hammer. (The bag will prevent fragments from flying into your eyes.) Show the children the rock pieces. Ask the children how the inside of the rock is different from the outside.

Why do I have children do this?

- To look for different rocks (thinking).
- To classify rocks–small, large, round, red, white (thinking).

What do I need?

1. Rocks.
2. Magnifying glass.
3. Balance scale.
4. Metal pan.
5. Bag.
6. Hammer.

What might I see children doing?

- Looking at rocks with the magnifying glass.
- Weighing rocks.
- Talking.

What might I talk about with children?

1. Where can you find rocks?
2. How can use the rocks?

HOW HEAVY IS YOUR MAIL?
Learning Center (science)

What do I do?

Set up a balance scale and provide a variety of junk mail. Encourage the children to choose mail that they feel will balance the scale. Discuss words such as heavy, light, big, little, long, short, thick, and thin with the children.

Why do I have children do this?

- To match mail by weight (thinking).
- To experiment with the balance scale (thinking).

What do I need?

1. Balance scale.
2. Junk mail.

What might I see children doing?

- Balancing mail.
- Experimenting with balance scale.
- Talking.

What might I talk about with children?

1. What do your parents send through the mail?
2. What would fit in these packages?

PUTTING OUT FIRES
Learning Center (water play)

What do I do?

Place a large bucket of water at one end of a balance beam and an empty bucket at the other end. When a bell is sounded or the children who are watching make the sound of a bell or siren, have a child dip a small bucket into the water and carry the bucket to the opposite end of the beam. Then he or she should pour the water into the empty bucket and walk backwards or turn and walk back to the beginning. Let each child try this activity. Two- and three-year-olds can carry the water in a bucket while walking on the ground instead of on the balance beam.

Why do I have children do this?

- To walk on the balance beam (large muscle).
- To respond to a signal, bell, or siren (thinking).

What do I need?

What might I see children doing?

- Making sounds of bells or sirens.
- Walking on the balance beam.
- Talking.
- Having fun.

1. Balance beam.
2. Large bucket of water.
3. Small bucket.

What might I talk about with children?

1. How can you get to the end of the beam?
2. What can you do to put out a fire?

SHAMPOO BUBBLES
Learning Center (water play)

What do I do?

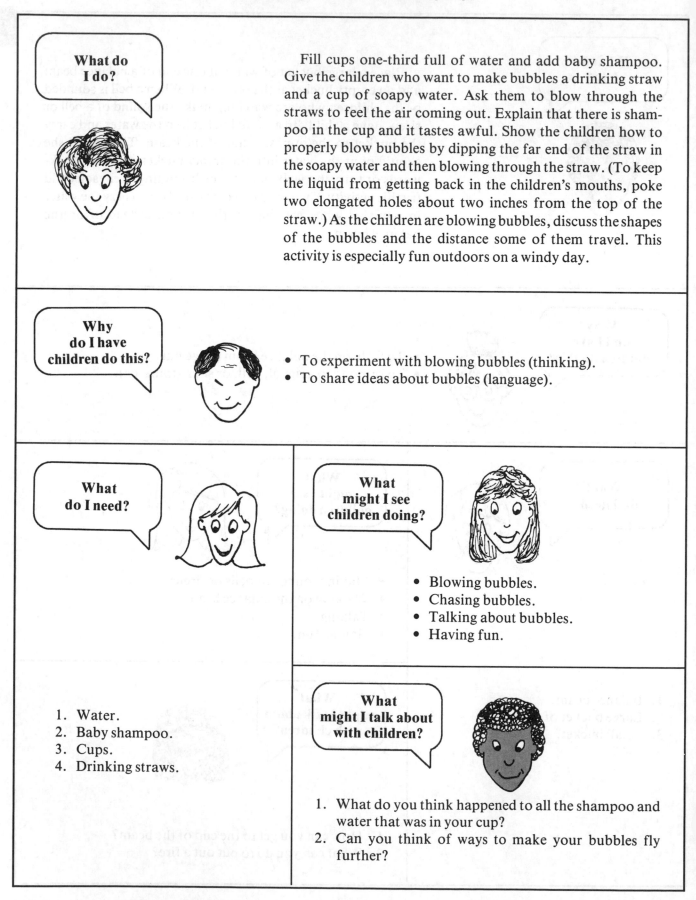

Fill cups one-third full of water and add baby shampoo. Give the children who want to make bubbles a drinking straw and a cup of soapy water. Ask them to blow through the straws to feel the air coming out. Explain that there is shampoo in the cup and it tastes awful. Show the children how to properly blow bubbles by dipping the far end of the straw in the soapy water and then blowing through the straw. (To keep the liquid from getting back in the children's mouths, poke two elongated holes about two inches from the top of the straw.) As the children are blowing bubbles, discuss the shapes of the bubbles and the distance some of them travel. This activity is especially fun outdoors on a windy day.

Why do I have children do this?

- To experiment with blowing bubbles (thinking).
- To share ideas about bubbles (language).

What do I need?

1. Water.
2. Baby shampoo.
3. Cups.
4. Drinking straws.

What might I see children doing?

- Blowing bubbles.
- Chasing bubbles.
- Talking about bubbles.
- Having fun.

What might I talk about with children?

1. What do you think happened to all the shampoo and water that was in your cup?
2. Can you think of ways to make your bubbles fly further?

PLUMBER, PLUMBER, FIX MY PIPES
Learning Center (woodworking, science)

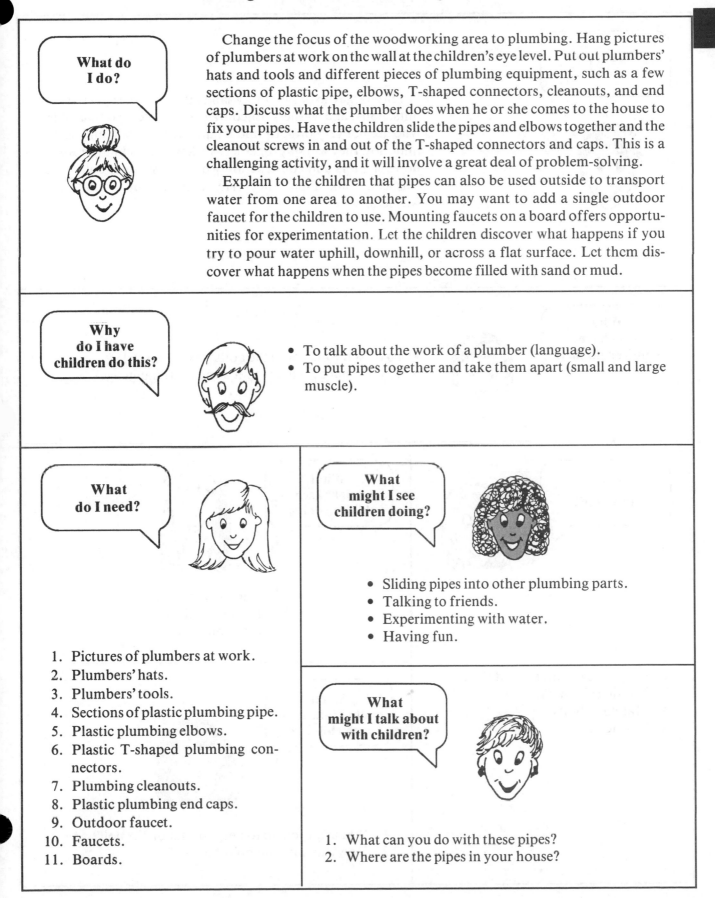

What do I do?

Change the focus of the woodworking area to plumbing. Hang pictures of plumbers at work on the wall at the children's eye level. Put out plumbers' hats and tools and different pieces of plumbing equipment, such as a few sections of plastic pipe, elbows, T-shaped connectors, cleanouts, and end caps. Discuss what the plumber does when he or she comes to the house to fix your pipes. Have the children slide the pipes and elbows together and the cleanout screws in and out of the T-shaped connectors and caps. This is a challenging activity, and it will involve a great deal of problem-solving.

Explain to the children that pipes can also be used outside to transport water from one area to another. You may want to add a single outdoor faucet for the children to use. Mounting faucets on a board offers opportunities for experimentation. Let the children discover what happens if you try to pour water uphill, downhill, or across a flat surface. Let them discover what happens when the pipes become filled with sand or mud.

Why do I have children do this?

- To talk about the work of a plumber (language).
- To put pipes together and take them apart (small and large muscle).

What do I need?

1. Pictures of plumbers at work.
2. Plumbers' hats.
3. Plumbers' tools.
4. Sections of plastic plumbing pipe.
5. Plastic plumbing elbows.
6. Plastic T-shaped plumbing connectors.
7. Plumbing cleanouts.
8. Plastic plumbing end caps.
9. Outdoor faucet.
10. Faucets.
11. Boards.

What might I see children doing?

- Sliding pipes into other plumbing parts.
- Talking to friends.
- Experimenting with water.
- Having fun.

What might I talk about with children?

1. What can you do with these pipes?
2. Where are the pipes in your house?

NUTS AND BOLTS
Learning Center (woodworking)

What do I do?

Fill a large tub or the empty sand table with varying sizes of nuts, bolts, and washers. Encourage four- and five-year-olds, who are not very oral, to find a nut that fits a bolt and determine how they will stay together. Talk with the children about how repairers and construction workers use nuts, bolts, and washers. Talk about the many uses of nuts, bolts, and washers.

Why do I have children do this?

- To twist the nuts onto the bolts (small muscle).
- To talk about the uses of nuts and bolts (language).

What do I need?

1. Large tub or empty sand table.
2. Varying size nuts.
3. Matching bolts.
4. Washers.

What might I see children doing?

- Matching nuts and bolts.
- Sorting nuts and bolts.
- Twisting and turning nuts.

What might I talk about with children?

1. What can you do to keep the nut on the bolt?
2. How can nuts and bolts be used?

THE WOODWORKING SHOP
Learning Center (woodworking)

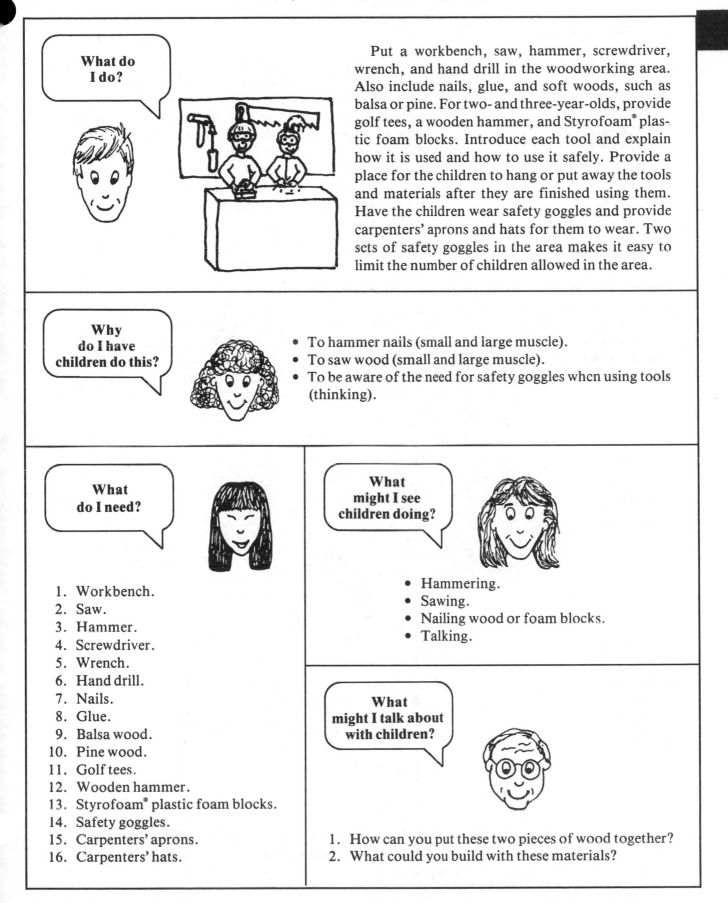

What do I do?

Put a workbench, saw, hammer, screwdriver, wrench, and hand drill in the woodworking area. Also include nails, glue, and soft woods, such as balsa or pine. For two- and three-year-olds, provide golf tees, a wooden hammer, and Styrofoam® plastic foam blocks. Introduce each tool and explain how it is used and how to use it safely. Provide a place for the children to hang or put away the tools and materials after they are finished using them. Have the children wear safety goggles and provide carpenters' aprons and hats for them to wear. Two sets of safety goggles in the area makes it easy to limit the number of children allowed in the area.

Why do I have children do this?

- To hammer nails (small and large muscle).
- To saw wood (small and large muscle).
- To be aware of the need for safety goggles when using tools (thinking).

What do I need?

1. Workbench.
2. Saw.
3. Hammer.
4. Screwdriver.
5. Wrench.
6. Hand drill.
7. Nails.
8. Glue.
9. Balsa wood.
10. Pine wood.
11. Golf tees.
12. Wooden hammer.
13. Styrofoam® plastic foam blocks.
14. Safety goggles.
15. Carpenters' aprons.
16. Carpenters' hats.

What might I see children doing?

- Hammering.
- Sawing.
- Nailing wood or foam blocks.
- Talking.

What might I talk about with children?

1. How can you put these two pieces of wood together?
2. What could you build with these materials?

OUR NEWSPAPER
Learning Center (writing)

What do I do?

Place copies of newspapers in the writing area. Place large sheets of newsprint, pencils, markers, and crayons near an old typewriter. Put out pieces of yarn to tie newspapers when they are rolled for delivery. Talk with the children about the different ways newspapers are delivered to people, such as by a child on a bicycle or an adult in a car. Talk about how newspapers are placed next to the door, placed in a box next to the mailbox, or thrown into the yard or onto the porch. Add newspaper tubes made from gift wrap tubes next to the children's shoe box mailboxes. Talk about why people like to get the newspaper and what they can learn when they read the newspaper.

Why do I have children do this?

- To write a newspaper (small muscle, language).
- To talk about newspapers (language).
- To role-play delivering the newspaper (small and large muscle, social-emotional).

What do I need?

1. Newspapers.
2. Large sheets of newsprint.
3. Pencils.
4. Markers.
5. Crayons.
6. Old typewriter.
7. Yarn.
8. Gift wrap tubes.

What might I see children doing?

- Writing a newspaper.
- Typing on the typewriter.
- Rolling and tying newspapers.
- Delivering newspapers.
- Talking.
- Reading the newspaper.

What might I talk about with children?

1. Where can you buy a newspaper?
2. Who reads the newspaper at your house?

WRITING TRAFFIC TICKETS
Learning Center (writing)

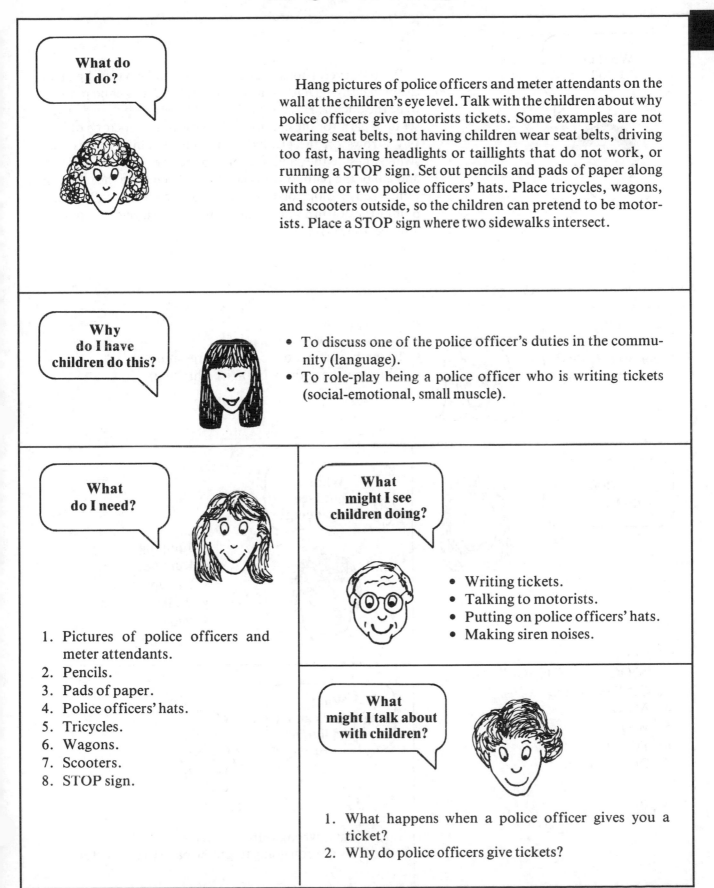

What do I do?

Hang pictures of police officers and meter attendants on the wall at the children's eye level. Talk with the children about why police officers give motorists tickets. Some examples are not wearing seat belts, not having children wear seat belts, driving too fast, having headlights or taillights that do not work, or running a STOP sign. Set out pencils and pads of paper along with one or two police officers' hats. Place tricycles, wagons, and scooters outside, so the children can pretend to be motorists. Place a STOP sign where two sidewalks intersect.

Why do I have children do this?

- To discuss one of the police officer's duties in the community (language).
- To role-play being a police officer who is writing tickets (social-emotional, small muscle).

What do I need?

1. Pictures of police officers and meter attendants.
2. Pencils.
3. Pads of paper.
4. Police officers' hats.
5. Tricycles.
6. Wagons.
7. Scooters.
8. STOP sign.

What might I see children doing?

- Writing tickets.
- Talking to motorists.
- Putting on police officers' hats.
- Making siren noises.

What might I talk about with children?

1. What happens when a police officer gives you a ticket?
2. Why do police officers give tickets?

I'M TAKING THE BABY TO THE DOCTOR
Outdoor Large Muscle

What do I do?

Put out several dolls. At the swings or under a tree, hang up a sign that says "DOCTOR'S OFFICE" and let a child pretend to be the doctor. Have a cardboard box be a baby's bed. Then set up a path for the children to follow to the doctor's office. Lay arrows on the ground that take the children past the swings, beside the sandbox, or around the slide. Be creative and adapt the path to your play yard. Then have the children jump, run, gallop, or walk their way down the path, while pulling the doll in a wagon, carrying it on a tricycle, or pushing it in the doll carriage.

Why do I have children do this?

- To jump, run, gallop, or walk (large muscle).
- To follow the path to the office (thinking).

What do I need?

1. Dolls.
2. "DOCTOR'S OFFICE" sign.
3. Cardboard box.
4. Arrows.
5. Wagon.
6. Tricycle.
7. Doll carriage.

What might I see children doing?

- Jumping.
- Running.
- Galloping.
- Walking.
- Pedaling a tricycle.
- Laughing.

What might I talk about with children?

1. What is wrong with your baby?
2. How are you going to get the baby to the doctor?

THE AMBULANCE IS COMING!
Outdoor Large Muscle

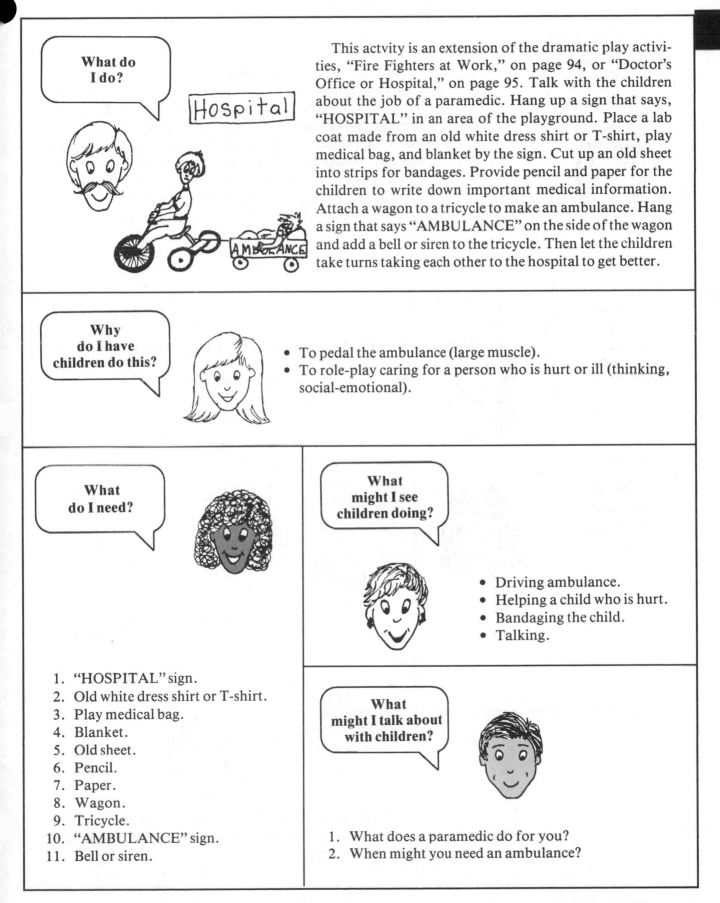

What do I do?

Hospital

This actvity is an extension of the dramatic play activities, "Fire Fighters at Work," on page 94, or "Doctor's Office or Hospital," on page 95. Talk with the children about the job of a paramedic. Hang up a sign that says, "HOSPITAL" in an area of the playground. Place a lab coat made from an old white dress shirt or T-shirt, play medical bag, and blanket by the sign. Cut up an old sheet into strips for bandages. Provide pencil and paper for the children to write down important medical information. Attach a wagon to a tricycle to make an ambulance. Hang a sign that says "AMBULANCE" on the side of the wagon and add a bell or siren to the tricycle. Then let the children take turns taking each other to the hospital to get better.

AMBULANCE

Why do I have children do this?

- To pedal the ambulance (large muscle).
- To role-play caring for a person who is hurt or ill (thinking, social-emotional).

What do I need?

What might I see children doing?

- Driving ambulance.
- Helping a child who is hurt.
- Bandaging the child.
- Talking.

1. "HOSPITAL" sign.
2. Old white dress shirt or T-shirt.
3. Play medical bag.
4. Blanket.
5. Old sheet.
6. Pencil.
7. Paper.
8. Wagon.
9. Tricycle.
10. "AMBULANCE" sign.
11. Bell or siren.

What might I talk about with children?

1. What does a paramedic do for you?
2. When might you need an ambulance?

PARACHUTE CRAWL
Outdoor Large Muscle

What do I do?

Have the children sit around a parachute from the early childhood catalogs or a queen- or king-sized bed sheet. Talk with them about the dangers of fire and smoke. Explain to them the importance of staying close to the ground and moving quickly if they are ever caught in a fire. Have the parachute represent smoke and hold it low to the ground. Then have the children practice crawling underneath it. Afterwards, have them suggest different ways to move under the "smoke." Explain to the children how to stop, drop, and roll if they catch on fire.

Why do I have children do this?

- To introduce the idea of staying low during a fire (thinking).
- To crawl at a low level (large muscle).

What do I need?

1. Parachute or queen- or king-sized bed sheet.

What might I see children doing?

- Listening.
- Talking about fires.
- Crawling under the parachute.

What might I talk about with children?

1. What would you do if you were in a fire?
2. How can you get from one side of the parachute to the other?

CLIMB THE FIRE LADDER
Outdoor Large Muscle

What do I do?

Draw one or more fire ladders on the sidewalk using chalk. Have the children use it to practice climbing up on tiptoe, tossing a ball from one end to the other, tossing a ball to have it land inside a square, hopping on both feet from one square to another, and hopping up it on one foot. Then fill squirt bottles or empty liquid detergent squirt bottles with water and have the children pretend to put out fires as they climb the ladder. Have them see how far they can squirt the water. You can also have the children use the ladder on the slide to pretend to be fire fighters climbing ladders. Explain to children that they should use both hands when they climb a real ladder.

Why do I have children do this?

- To hop on one foot and two feet (large muscle).
- To squirt out pretend fires with water in a squirt bottle (small muscle, large muscle).

What do I need?

What might I see children doing?

- Walking on tiptoe.
- Hopping.
- Putting out fires with squirt bottles.

1. Chalk.
2. Ball.
3. Squirt bottles or empty liquid detergent squirt bottles.

What might I talk about with children?

1. What are some other ways you could climb this ladder?
2. What should you do if your house catches on fire?

I CAN DIRECT TRAFFIC
Outdoor Large Muscle

What do I do?

Talk about traffic safety with the children. Explain that police officers can give tickets to people who do not follow the safety rules. Then set up streets on the sidewalk or in the play yard. Make a traffic light by covering a one-half gallon milk carton with dark paper. Cut out red, yellow, and green circles out of construction paper and glue in order on the covered carton. Place the traffic light on the top of a dowel rod or broom handle that you can stick into the ground. Put out tricycles, bicycles, scooters, and doll carriages for the children to ride and push. Put out a police officer's hat and whistle and pad of paper and pencil to write tickets. Let the children take turns being the police officer, drivers, or pedestrians.

Why do I have children do this?

- To pedal or push vehicles (large muscle).
- To recognize traffic signs and signals (thinking).

What do I need?

1. One-half gallon milk carton.
2. Dark paper.
3. Red, yellow, and green construction paper.
4. Glue.
5. Dowel rod or broom handle.
6. Tricycles.
7. Bicycles.
8. Scooters.
9. Doll carriages
10. Police officer's hat.
11. Whistle.
12. Pad of paper.
13. Pencil.

What might I see children doing?

- Pedaling tricycles.
- Pushing doll carriages.
- Pretending to be a police officer.
- Giving tickets.
- Getting tickets.
- Talking.

What might I talk about with children?

1. Why do some people get traffic tickets?
2. What does a police officer do to help us?

PAINT THE HOUSE
Outdoor Large Muscle

What do I do?

Put out several paint buckets full of water and different-sized paintbrushes. Make sure that the children are dressed for water play. Then sit down with them at the side of the building and talk about how the painter is a community helper, since houses and buildings need to be painted. Let the children experiment with the brushes and paint the house with water. You can also talk about evaporation and what happens to the water on hot, sunny days.

Why do I have children do this?

- To paint with different brushes (small muscle).
- To have fun playing in water (social-emotional).

What do I need?

1. Paint buckets.
2. Water.
3. Different-sized paintbrushes.

What might I see children doing?

- Painting with water.
- Feeling water.
- Splashing in water.
- Laughing and having fun.

What might I talk about with children?

1. How could you paint the top of this house?
2. What have you painted at your house?

LET'S VISIT A HOUSE UNDER CONSTRUCTION
Outdoor Large Muscle, Field Trip

What do I do?

If a house is being built in your child care home or center's neighborhood, first obtain permission and then visit it several times while it is under construction. You should visit the site before taking the children, so you can guide their learning. Discuss with the children what they are seeing–the basement being dug, foundation being poured, frame being constructed, roofing and siding being applied, fireplaces being built, windows and doors being put in, and interior being finished. Each time you visit the construction site, have the children draw a picture of it to put into a house book they create. You can use this activity to introduce a lesson about carpenters, utility workers, or other building-related community helpers.

Why do I have children do this?

- To see the stages of house building (thinking).
- To talk about the work that carpenters, plumbers, roofers, and other construction people do (language).

What do I need?

1. Construction site.
2. Paper.
3. Markers.
4. Crayons.

What might I see children doing?

- Looking at men and women working.
- Talking about the house.
- Drawing pictures.

What might I talk about with children?

1. What do you think they will do next on the house?
2. Tell me what you would do if you lived in this house?

BIBLIOGRAPHY

COMMUNITY HELPERS

[2]Allard, H. 1985. *Miss Nelson Is Missing!* Boston, MA: Houghton Mifflin Co.
A mystery occurs when the class of Room 207 loses its teacher to Miss Viola Swamp.

[2,3]Arnold, C. 1982. *Who Keeps Us Safe?* New York, NY: Franklin Watts.
Discusses how police, firefighters, and other emergency personnel aid their community.

[3]Baker, E. 1969. *I Want to Be a Taxi Driver.* Chicago, IL: Children's Press.
Easy-to-read text describes the work of a taxi driver.

[3]Baker, E. 1973. *I Want to Be a Lawyer.* Chicago, IL: Children's Press.
Easy-to-read text describes a lawyer's job and training.

[3]Baker, E. 1978. *I Want to Be a Police Officer.* Chicago, IL: Children's Press.
Ramon's uncle explains the work of police officers to Ramon and his friends. The
    author uses simple, bold text, and colorful pictures to illustrate the police offi-
    cer's role and equipment.

Barton, B. 1988. *I Want to Be an Astronaut.* New York, NY: HarperCollins
    Children's Books.
Large pictures are used to describe what it would be like to be an astronaut.

Berenstain, S., and Berenstain, J. 1981. *The Berenstain Bears Go to the Doctor.*
    New York, NY: Random House.
Dr. Grizzly gives the Berenstain cubs a regular checkup.

[3]Buchheimer, N. 1967. *I Know a Teacher.* New York, NY: G.P. Putnam's Sons.
The reader spends a day at school with David, who is in the first grade.

Burton, V.L. 1939. *Mike Mulligan and His Steam Shovel.* Boston, MA: Houghton
    Mifflin Co.
Mike Mulligan and his steam shovel, Mary Anne, prove the shovel is not too old to
    build the new town hall.

Burton, V.L. 1973. *Katy and the Big Snow.* Boston, MA: Houghton Mifflin Co.
Katy the snowplow uncovers the city of Geoppolis from a thick blanket of snow.

Carrick, C. 1988. *Left Behind.* New York, NY: Clarion Books.
Christopher gets lost on the subway during an excursion to the aquarium with his
    class. He gets help from a police officer.

[3]Chlad, D. 1982. *When There Is a Fire Go Outside*. Chicago, IL: Children's Press.
Safety is a must during fires. Read how firefighters help during a fire.

Ciliotta, C., and Livingston, C. 1981. *Why Am I Going to the Hospital?* New York, NY: Carol Communications, Inc.
Answers questions children have about going to the hospital. It very honestly discusses hospital routines, the role of doctors and nurses, and what children can expect when they go to the hospital.

[2]Cole, J. 1987. *The Magic School Bus Inside the Earth*. New York, NY: Scholastic Inc.
Ms. Frizzle's class explores "Inside the Earth" on an imaginary school bus and learns a great deal about rocks, soil, and layers of earth.

Freeman, D. 1964. *Dandelion*. New York, NY: Viking Children's Books.
A lion decides to dress up for his friend's come-as-you-are party and is turned away because he is not recognized. He decides it is best to be yourself.

[3]Florian, D. 1983. *People Working*. New York, NY: HarperCollins Children's Books.
Briefly describes where and how people work in the community.

Gibbons, G. 1987. *Fire! Fire!* New York, NY: HarperCollins Children's Books.
This book covers the procedures that take place in firefighting and how volunteers respond and operate in the country.

[2]Gibbons, G. 1989. *Marge's Diner*. New York, NY: HarperCollins Children's Books.
Describes a day at Marge's Diner, detailing the responsibilities of those who work there.

Good, M. 1993. *Reuben and the Fire*. Intercourse, PA: Good Books Publishing.
This book captures the simplicity of life in an Amish community. It describes some of the grown-up responsibilities of those who work there.

Goodall, J. 1999. *Dr. White*. New York, NY: North-South Books.
Features Dr. White, a small, white dog who's been given credit for saving the lives of dozens of children in a London hospital.

[3]Hankin, R. 1985. *I Can Be a Doctor*. Chicago, IL: Children's Press.
Photographs and simple text tell about becoming a doctor, different kinds of doctors, and doctor's responsibilities.

[3]Hankin, R. 1985. *I Can Be a Fire Fighter*. Chicago, IL: Children's Press.
Photographs and simple text introduce the important work of firefighters as they rescue people, fight fires, give medical care, and give safety talks.

[1,3]Kightley, R. 1988. *The Postman*. New York, NY: Macmillan Children's Book Group.
Brightly colored pictures with delightful look-and-discover details and a simple rhyming text make this a wonderful learning book. As the postman moves on his rounds through the busy town, he sees many aspects of its life, from the teachers at the local school to children in the swimming pool.

Lasker, J. 1972. *Mothers Can Do Anything*. Morton Grove, IL: Albert Whitman and Company.
This books discusses all the jobs mothers can do and emphasizes nontraditional roles, such as building construction, road construction, and power and light utilities jobs.

[2,3]Marino, B.P. 1979. *Eric Needs Stitches*. New York, NY: HarperCollins Children's Books.
Although he is afraid, Eric goes to the hospital emergency room to get stitches in his knee after a bad fall. He learns what the emergency room is all about.

[3]Matthias, C. 1984. *I Can Be a Police Officer*. Chicago, IL: Children's Press.
Simple text and illustrations describe some of the duties of a police officer.

Muntean, M. 1983. *Bicycle Bear*. New York, NY: Parents Magazine Press.
Items are never too big or too small—Bicycle Bear delivers them all.

Numeroff, L. 1998. *What Daddies Do Best/What Mommies Do Best*. New York, NY: Simon and Schuster.
This book celebrates the best community helpers—Mommy and Daddy—and describes all the things parents do for children.

[3]Oxenbury, H. 1983. *The Checkup*. New York, NY: Dial Books.
This story is about a young boy's trip to the doctor.

Rathmann, P. 1995. *Officer Buckle and Gloria*. New York: G.P. Putnam's Sons.
Napville's new police dog really makes things interesting when she joins Officer Buckle on his safety tour. Learn how they become a great team teaching safety.

Rey, M., and Shalleck, A.J. 1985. *Curious George at the Fire Station*. Boston, MA: Houghton Mifflin Company.
Curious George spends the day exploring the fire station.

[3]Rockwell, A. 1985. *The Emergency Room*. New York, NY: Macmillan Children's Book Group.
Explores the equipment and procedures of a hospital emergency room by describing what one patient sees while being treated for a sprained ankle.

[1]Rockwell, A. 1986. *Fire Engines*. New York, NY: Dutton Children's Books.
A Dalmatian puppy describes the parts of a fire engine and how firefighters use them to fight fires. This is a colorful picture book.

[3]Rockwell, A., and Rockwell, H. 1981. *My Barber*. New York, NY: Macmillan Publishing Company.
A young boy and his father visit their barber.

Rockwell, H. 1973. *My Doctor*. New York, NY: Macmillan Children's Book Group.
Simple text and illustrations describe a visit to the doctor.

Rockwell, H. 1975. *My Dentist*. New York, NY: Greenwillow Books.
Tells about a visit to the dentist and the equipment in his office. Simple text and good illustrations.

[2,3]Roth, H. 1988. *Let's Look All Around the Town*. New York, NY: The Putnam Publishing Group.
Child takes a trip visiting the community. The child flips up doors and looks behind them to see the grocer, police officer, airplane, and fire truck.

Sendak, M. 1962. *Chicken Soup with Rice*. New York, NY: HarperCollins Children's Books.
Talks about chicken soup with rice during each month of the year.

Simon, N. 1995. *Fire Fighters*. New York: Simon & Schuster.
Explains the routines and procedures for fighting fires. Trusty Dalmatians help children understand the seriousness of the situation, from the first alarm, through rescues and danger, to the cleanup chores.

[2]Smith, B. 1981. *A Day in the Life of a Fire Fighter*. Mahwah, NJ: Troll Associates.
Wonderful photographs help paint a detailed picture of a day in the life of a firefighter. The text is easy to read but rather lengthy.

[3]Stanek, M. 1968. *Community Friends*. Westchester, IL: Benefic Press.

Simple text and colorful drawings tell about our community helpers including police officers, doctors, mail carriers, and librarians.

Steig, W. 1968. *Doctor De Soto*. New York, NY: Farrar, Straus, and Giroux, Inc.
Dr. De Soto and his wife devise a plan to rid a fox of toothaches forever.

[3]Wandro, M. and Blank, J. 1981. *My Daddy Is a Nurse*. Reading, MA: Addison-Wesley Publishing Company.
Describes the work of men with 10 occupations traditionally reserved for women: nurse, flight attendant, homemaker, dental hygienist, weaver, children's librarian, telephone operator, ballet dancer, office worker, and preschool teacher.

Weiss, L. 1986. *My Teacher Sleeps in School*. New York, NY: Viking Children's Books.
Helps children realize teachers have lives outside the school.

Winkleman, K. 1996. *Firehouse*. New York: Walker & Co.
Firehouses and firefighters are explored in this picture book. It helps children understand how firefighters divide up their work. It explains the differences in firehouses.

We have marked these books if we think they are definitely more applicable to one age. Many can be used by all ages with adaptations by the teacher.

[1]Books for one-year-olds, two-year-olds, and three-year-olds.

[2]Books for five-year-olds.

[3]This book is no longer in print. However, you may be able to find it at your local library.

Unit 2

FRIENDS

CONTENTS

FRIENDS

"Friends" consists of activities that help the children identify the people who are important to them and who are their friends. The children will see that:
- Friends can be relatives, neighbors, or even pets.
- Friends can be different ages, sizes, and colors.
- Friends can be made at home, school, or anywhere in the world.
- Friends are people they enjoy being with and who enjoy them.
- Friends are people with whom they can share happiness, sadness, and anger.
- Friends are people who know them very well and still like them.
- Friends are people who play with them.
- Friends help one another.
- Friends are kind to them, and they are kind to their friends.

TALK ABOUT FRIENDS
Group

What do I do?

Hang up pictures of children, adults, and pets on the wall at the children's eye level. Talk with the children about how these people and animals can be friendly. Ask questions to start the conversation:

- What kind of person is a friendly person?
- Who can be your friend?
- How can you be a special friend to others?
- How can you help someone who is not very friendly become friendly?

Write down the children's answers on chart paper. This will let the children know you think their ideas are important.

Why do I have children do this?

- To talk about friends (language).
- To write the children's ideas (language, social-emotional).

What do I need?

What might I see children doing?

- Looking at pictures.
- Listening.
- Sharing ideas.
- Watching the child care provider write down the answers.

1. Pictures of children, adults, and pets.
2. Chart paper.
3. Markers.

What might I talk about with children?

1. How can you tell that people are friends?
2. What do you like to do with your friends?

"NINE LITTLE FRIENDS"
Group

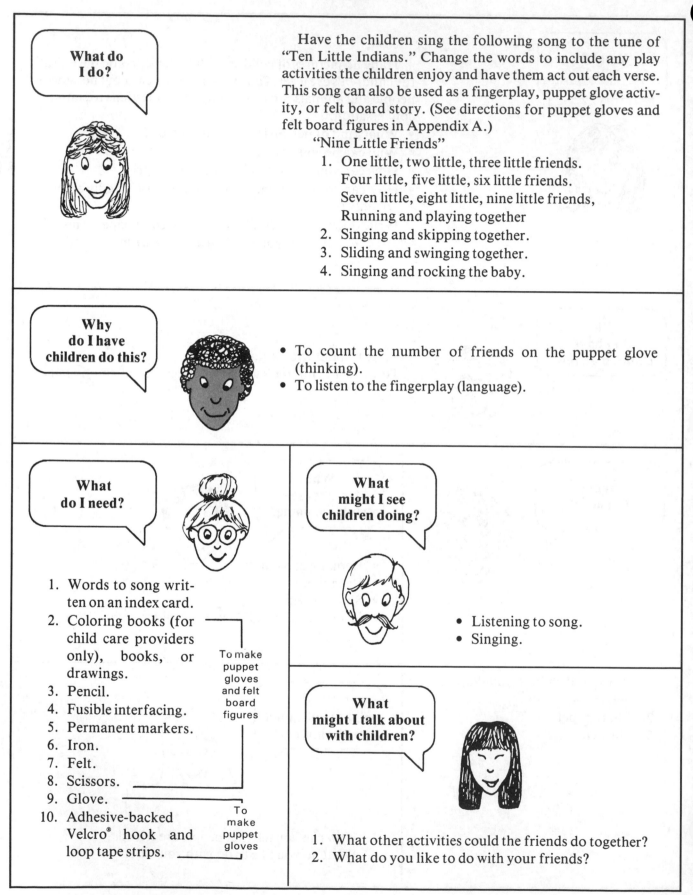

What do I do?

Have the children sing the following song to the tune of "Ten Little Indians." Change the words to include any play activities the children enjoy and have them act out each verse. This song can also be used as a fingerplay, puppet glove activity, or felt board story. (See directions for puppet gloves and felt board figures in Appendix A.)

"Nine Little Friends"

1. One little, two little, three little friends.
   Four little, five little, six little friends.
   Seven little, eight little, nine little friends,
   Running and playing together
2. Singing and skipping together.
3. Sliding and swinging together.
4. Singing and rocking the baby.

Why do I have children do this?

- To count the number of friends on the puppet glove (thinking).
- To listen to the fingerplay (language).

What do I need?

1. Words to song written on an index card.
2. Coloring books (for child care providers only), books, or drawings.
3. Pencil.
4. Fusible interfacing.
5. Permanent markers.
6. Iron.
7. Felt.
8. Scissors.
9. Glove.
10. Adhesive-backed Velcro® hook and loop tape strips.

To make puppet gloves and felt board figures

To make puppet gloves

What might I see children doing?

- Listening to song.
- Singing.

What might I talk about with children?

1. What other activities could the friends do together?
2. What do you like to do with your friends?

I LIKE YOU
Group

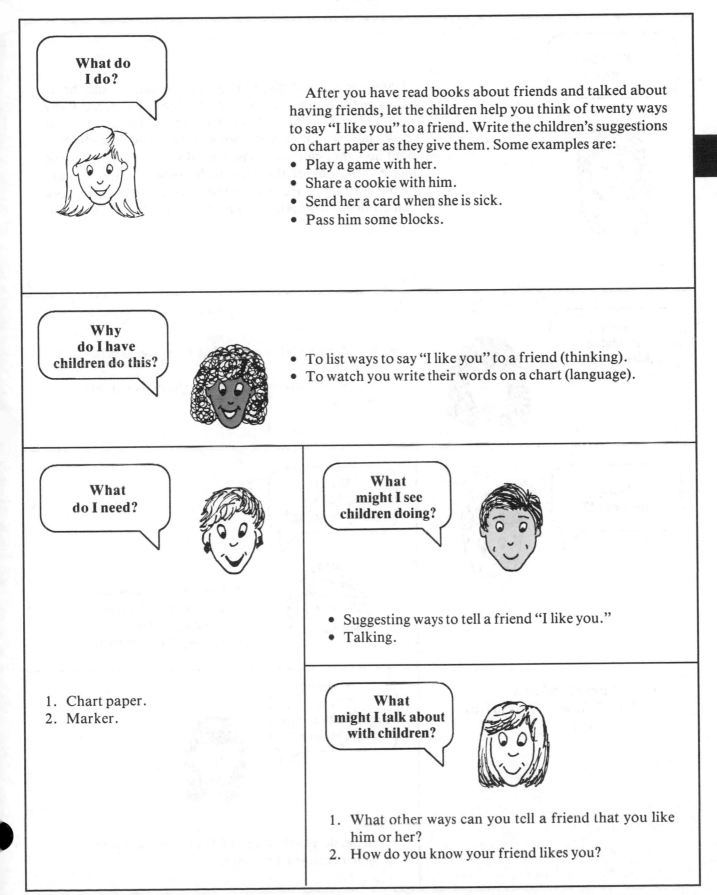

What do I do?

After you have read books about friends and talked about having friends, let the children help you think of twenty ways to say "I like you" to a friend. Write the children's suggestions on chart paper as they give them. Some examples are:

- Play a game with her.
- Share a cookie with him.
- Send her a card when she is sick.
- Pass him some blocks.

Why do I have children do this?

- To list ways to say "I like you" to a friend (thinking).
- To watch you write their words on a chart (language).

What do I need?

1. Chart paper.
2. Marker.

What might I see children doing?

- Suggesting ways to tell a friend "I like you."
- Talking.

What might I talk about with children?

1. What other ways can you tell a friend that you like him or her?
2. How do you know your friend likes you?

WILL I HAVE A FRIEND?
Group

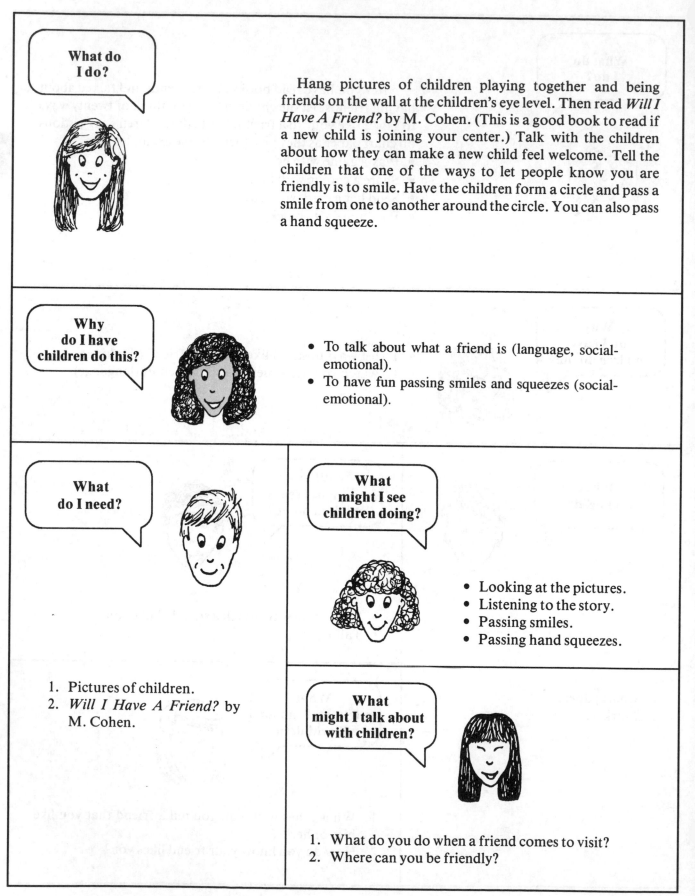

What do I do?

Hang pictures of children playing together and being friends on the wall at the children's eye level. Then read *Will I Have A Friend?* by M. Cohen. (This is a good book to read if a new child is joining your center.) Talk with the children about how they can make a new child feel welcome. Tell the children that one of the ways to let people know you are friendly is to smile. Have the children form a circle and pass a smile from one to another around the circle. You can also pass a hand squeeze.

Why do I have children do this?

- To talk about what a friend is (language, social-emotional).
- To have fun passing smiles and squeezes (social-emotional).

What do I need?

1. Pictures of children.
2. *Will I Have A Friend?* by M. Cohen.

What might I see children doing?

- Looking at the pictures.
- Listening to the story.
- Passing smiles.
- Passing hand squeezes.

What might I talk about with children?

1. What do you do when a friend comes to visit?
2. Where can you be friendly?

WILL I HAVE A FRIEND? MURAL
Group

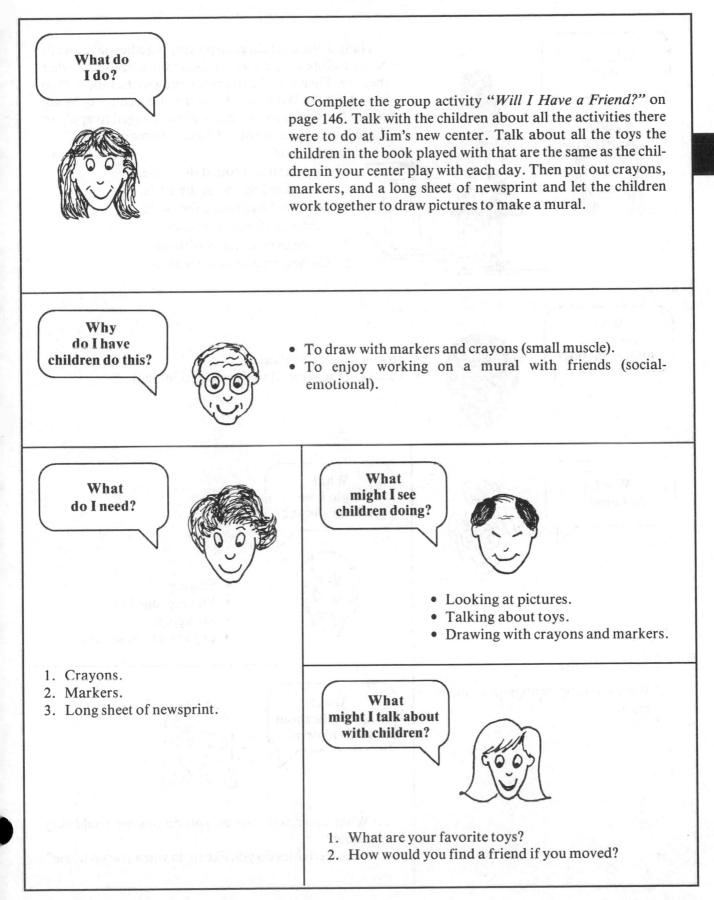

What do I do?

Complete the group activity *"Will I Have a Friend?"* on page 146. Talk with the children about all the activities there were to do at Jim's new center. Talk about all the toys the children in the book played with that are the same as the children in your center play with each day. Then put out crayons, markers, and a long sheet of newsprint and let the children work together to draw pictures to make a mural.

Why do I have children do this?

• To draw with markers and crayons (small muscle).
• To enjoy working on a mural with friends (social-emotional).

What do I need?

1. Crayons.
2. Markers.
3. Long sheet of newsprint.

What might I see children doing?

• Looking at pictures.
• Talking about toys.
• Drawing with crayons and markers.

What might I talk about with children?

1. What are your favorite toys?
2. How would you find a friend if you moved?

"BEST FRIENDS"
Group

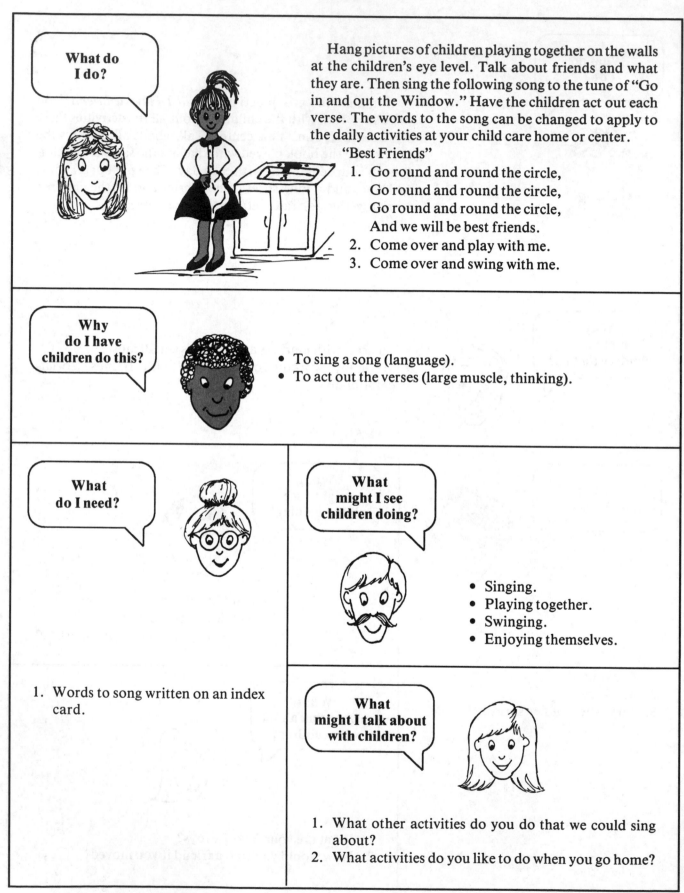

What do I do?

Hang pictures of children playing together on the walls at the children's eye level. Talk about friends and what they are. Then sing the following song to the tune of "Go in and out the Window." Have the children act out each verse. The words to the song can be changed to apply to the daily activities at your child care home or center.

"Best Friends"
1. Go round and round the circle,
   Go round and round the circle,
   Go round and round the circle,
   And we will be best friends.
2. Come over and play with me.
3. Come over and swing with me.

Why do I have children do this?

- To sing a song (language).
- To act out the verses (large muscle, thinking).

What do I need?

1. Words to song written on an index card.

What might I see children doing?

- Singing.
- Playing together.
- Swinging.
- Enjoying themselves.

What might I talk about with children?

1. What other activities do you do that we could sing about?
2. What activities do you like to do when you go home?

WE ARE BEST FRIENDS
Group

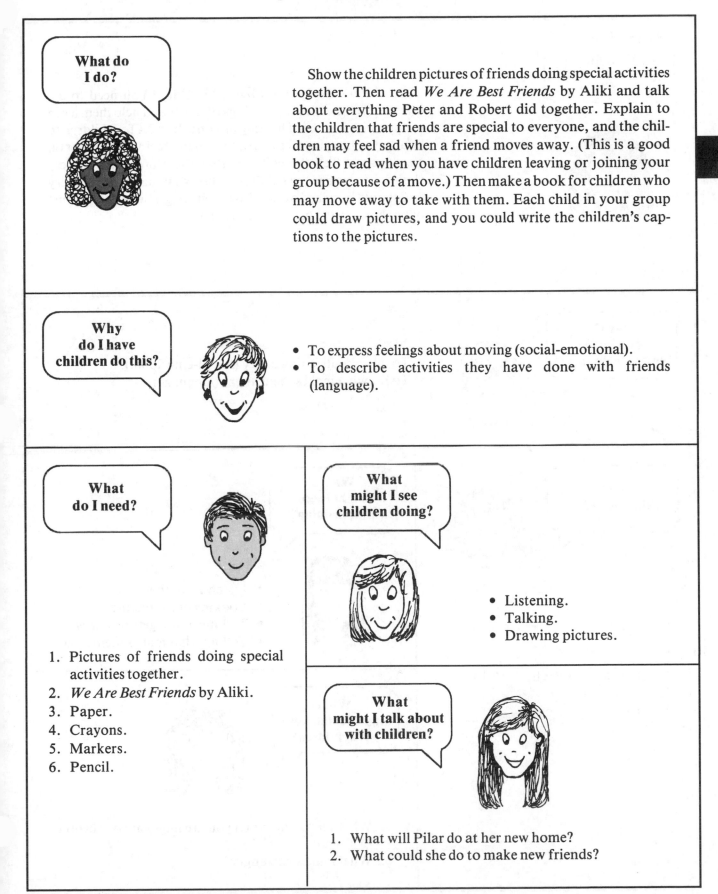

What do I do?

Show the children pictures of friends doing special activities together. Then read *We Are Best Friends* by Aliki and talk about everything Peter and Robert did together. Explain to the children that friends are special to everyone, and the children may feel sad when a friend moves away. (This is a good book to read when you have children leaving or joining your group because of a move.) Then make a book for children who may move away to take with them. Each child in your group could draw pictures, and you could write the children's captions to the pictures.

Why do I have children do this?

- To express feelings about moving (social-emotional).
- To describe activities they have done with friends (language).

What do I need?

1. Pictures of friends doing special activities together.
2. *We Are Best Friends* by Aliki.
3. Paper.
4. Crayons.
5. Markers.
6. Pencil.

What might I see children doing?

- Listening.
- Talking.
- Drawing pictures.

What might I talk about with children?

1. What will Pilar do at her new home?
2. What could she do to make new friends?

LET'S BE ENEMIES
Group

What do I do?

Read *Let's Be Enemies* by J. M. Udry. You need to acknowledge the children's feelings of anger and help them learn to cope with it without hurting anyone. It is OK for children to be angry. Then glue pictures of two chairs facing each other on chart paper. Tell the children that these are "talk-it-over" chairs. Encourage the children to list what makes them angry and should be talked over. Write their suggestions on the chart paper beneath the pictures of the chairs.

Why do I have children do this?

- To talk about getting angry (social-emotional).
- To list what makes them angry (language).

What do I need?

1. *Let's Be Enemies* by J. M. Udry.
2. Chart paper.
3. Pictures of two chairs.
4. Marker.

What might I see children doing?

- Listening to the story.
- Looking at the pictures.
- Talking about getting angry.
- Telling what makes them angry.

What might I talk about with children?

1. What do you do when you are angry at your brother or sister?
2. What makes you angry?

FRIENDS PARADE
Group

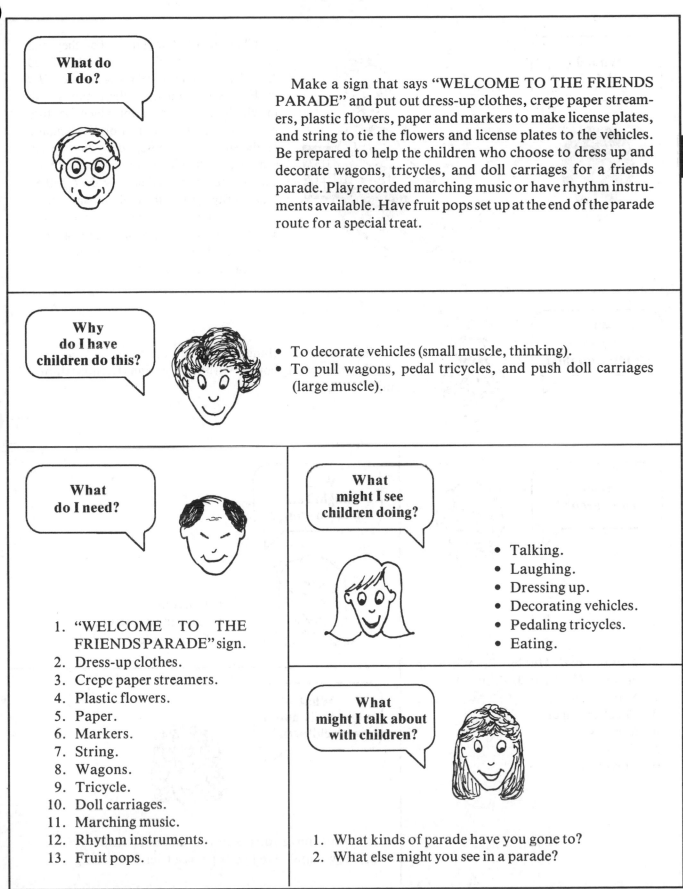

What do I do?

Make a sign that says "WELCOME TO THE FRIENDS PARADE" and put out dress-up clothes, crepe paper streamers, plastic flowers, paper and markers to make license plates, and string to tie the flowers and license plates to the vehicles. Be prepared to help the children who choose to dress up and decorate wagons, tricycles, and doll carriages for a friends parade. Play recorded marching music or have rhythm instruments available. Have fruit pops set up at the end of the parade route for a special treat.

Why do I have children do this?

- To decorate vehicles (small muscle, thinking).
- To pull wagons, pedal tricycles, and push doll carriages (large muscle).

What do I need?

1. "WELCOME TO THE FRIENDS PARADE" sign.
2. Dress-up clothes.
3. Crepe paper streamers.
4. Plastic flowers.
5. Paper.
6. Markers.
7. String.
8. Wagons.
9. Tricycle.
10. Doll carriages.
11. Marching music.
12. Rhythm instruments.
13. Fruit pops.

What might I see children doing?

- Talking.
- Laughing.
- Dressing up.
- Decorating vehicles.
- Pedaling tricycles.
- Eating.

What might I talk about with children?

1. What kinds of parade have you gone to?
2. What else might you see in a parade?

MARGIE AND ME
Group

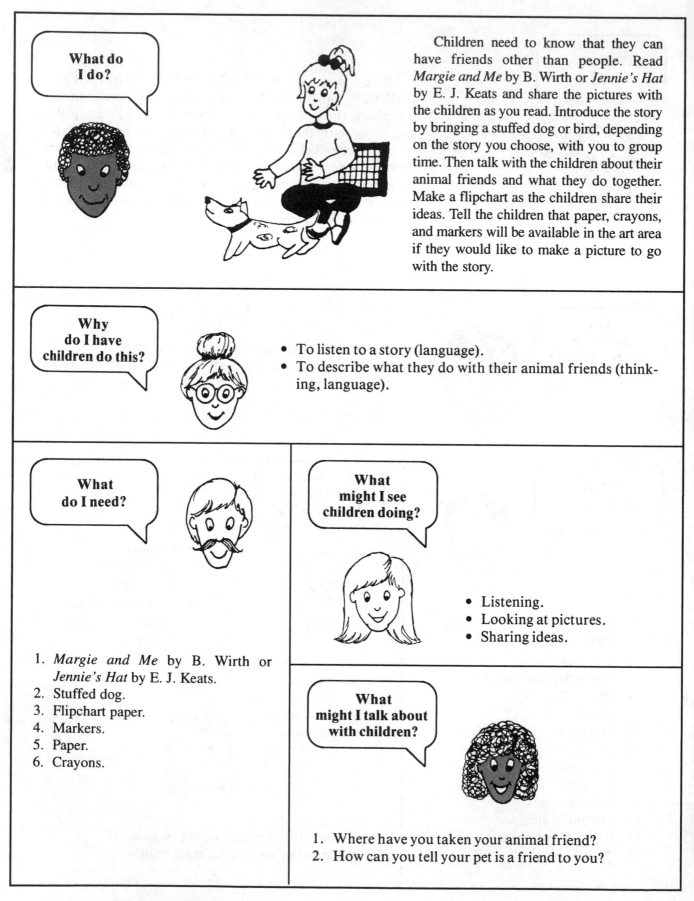

What do I do?

Children need to know that they can have friends other than people. Read *Margie and Me* by B. Wirth or *Jennie's Hat* by E. J. Keats and share the pictures with the children as you read. Introduce the story by bringing a stuffed dog or bird, depending on the story you choose, with you to group time. Then talk with the children about their animal friends and what they do together. Make a flipchart as the children share their ideas. Tell the children that paper, crayons, and markers will be available in the art area if they would like to make a picture to go with the story.

Why do I have children do this?

- To listen to a story (language).
- To describe what they do with their animal friends (thinking, language).

What do I need?

What might I see children doing?

- Listening.
- Looking at pictures.
- Sharing ideas.

1. *Margie and Me* by B. Wirth or *Jennie's Hat* by E. J. Keats.
2. Stuffed dog.
3. Flipchart paper.
4. Markers.
5. Paper.
6. Crayons.

What might I talk about with children?

1. Where have you taken your animal friend?
2. How can you tell your pet is a friend to you?

What do I do?

Hang pictures of children playing near city buildings on the walls at the children's eye level. Read *Apt. 3* by E. J. Keats and share the pictures with the children. Talk about how the blind man in the story plays the harmonica and his music tells how he feels–happy, sad, excited. Show the children what a harmonica looks like. Play the harmonica, or if you know someone who does, ask him or her to share his or her talent. If not, play a recording of harmonica music, so the children can hear harmonica music.

Why do I have children do this?

- To see how friends can help each other (social-emotional).
- To see that people in apartment buildings often see and hear others but do not meet them (social-emotional).

What do I need?

1. Pictures of children playing near city buildings.
2. *Apt. 3* by E. J. Keats.
3. Harmonica.
4. Recording of harmonica music.

What might I see children doing?

- Listening.
- Talking.
- Sharing ideas.

What might I talk about with children?

1. How do you meet a new person in your neighborhood?
2. How could Ben and Galen help their new friend who is blind?

LITTLE BLUE AND LITTLE YELLOW
Group

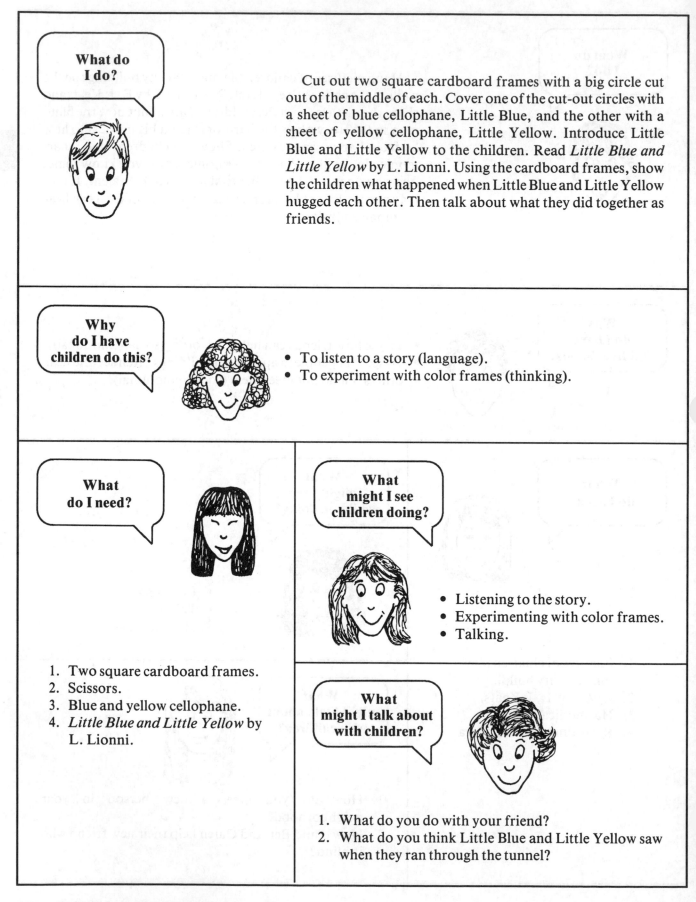

What do I do?

Cut out two square cardboard frames with a big circle cut out of the middle of each. Cover one of the cut-out circles with a sheet of blue cellophane, Little Blue, and the other with a sheet of yellow cellophane, Little Yellow. Introduce Little Blue and Little Yellow to the children. Read *Little Blue and Little Yellow* by L. Lionni. Using the cardboard frames, show the children what happened when Little Blue and Little Yellow hugged each other. Then talk about what they did together as friends.

Why do I have children do this?

- To listen to a story (language).
- To experiment with color frames (thinking).

What do I need?

1. Two square cardboard frames.
2. Scissors.
3. Blue and yellow cellophane.
4. *Little Blue and Little Yellow* by L. Lionni.

What might I see children doing?

- Listening to the story.
- Experimenting with color frames.
- Talking.

What might I talk about with children?

1. What do you do with your friend?
2. What do you think Little Blue and Little Yellow saw when they ran through the tunnel?

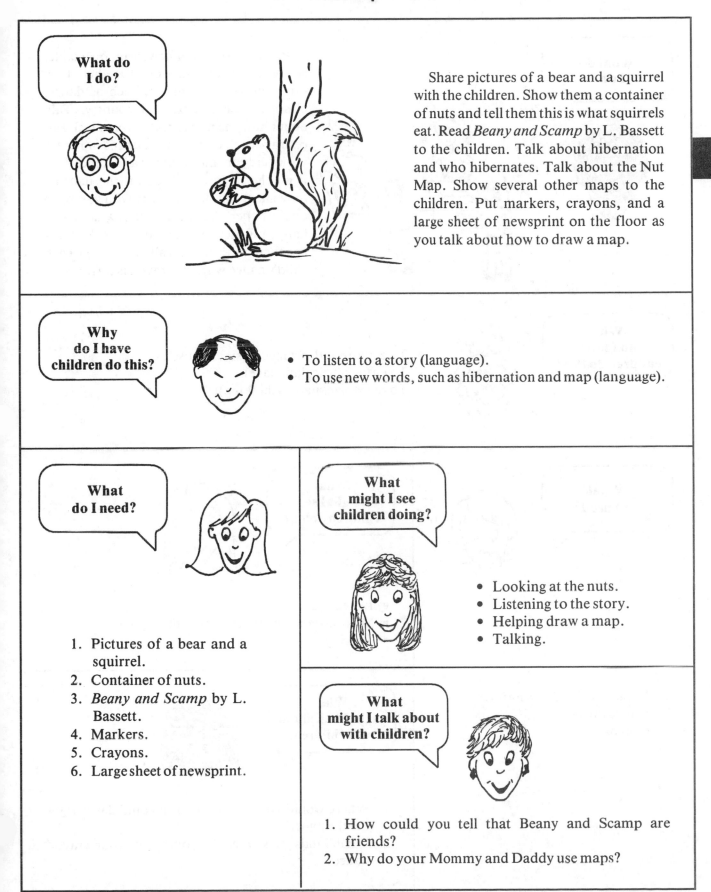

What do I do?

Share pictures of a bear and a squirrel with the children. Show them a container of nuts and tell them this is what squirrels eat. Read *Beany and Scamp* by L. Bassett to the children. Talk about hibernation and who hibernates. Talk about the Nut Map. Show several other maps to the children. Put markers, crayons, and a large sheet of newsprint on the floor as you talk about how to draw a map.

Why do I have children do this?

- To listen to a story (language).
- To use new words, such as hibernation and map (language).

What do I need?

1. Pictures of a bear and a squirrel.
2. Container of nuts.
3. *Beany and Scamp* by L. Bassett.
4. Markers.
5. Crayons.
6. Large sheet of newsprint.

What might I see children doing?

- Looking at the nuts.
- Listening to the story.
- Helping draw a map.
- Talking.

What might I talk about with children?

1. How could you tell that Beany and Scamp are friends?
2. Why do your Mommy and Daddy use maps?

DANCING WITH CRAYONS AND MY FRIENDS
Learning Center (art)

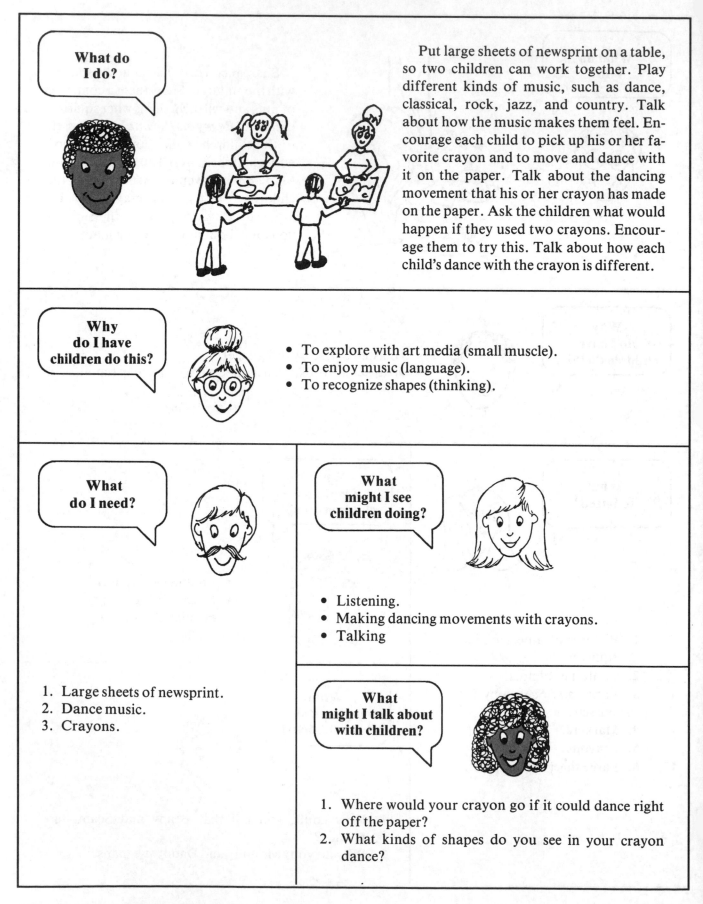

What do I do?

Put large sheets of newsprint on a table, so two children can work together. Play different kinds of music, such as dance, classical, rock, jazz, and country. Talk about how the music makes them feel. Encourage each child to pick up his or her favorite crayon and to move and dance with it on the paper. Talk about the dancing movement that his or her crayon has made on the paper. Ask the children what would happen if they used two crayons. Encourage them to try this. Talk about how each child's dance with the crayon is different.

Why do I have children do this?

- To explore with art media (small muscle).
- To enjoy music (language).
- To recognize shapes (thinking).

What do I need?

1. Large sheets of newsprint.
2. Dance music.
3. Crayons.

What might I see children doing?

- Listening.
- Making dancing movements with crayons.
- Talking

What might I talk about with children?

1. Where would your crayon go if it could dance right off the paper?
2. What kinds of shapes do you see in your crayon dance?

FRIENDS CAN PLAY WITH PLAYDOUGH
Learning Center (art)

What do I do?

Collect all of the supplies to make playdough (see recipe in Appendix A) before the children join you to work. Work with two or three children at a time, so they can each measure and mix the ingredients. When the playdough has cooled, form it into balls. Put several balls on waxed paper for the children to knead and explore.

Why do I have children do this?

- To measure ingredients and mix playdough (thinking, small muscle).
- To knead playdough (small muscle).

What do I need?

1. Vegetable oil.
2. Flour.
3. Salt.
4. Cream of tartar.
5. Water.
6. Food coloring.
7. Peppermint extract.

To make playdough

8. Measuring cups.
9. Measuring spoons.
10. Pot.
11. Large spoon.
12. Self-sealing plastic bags.

What might I see children doing?

- Measuring ingredients.
- Mixing ingredients.
- Kneading playdough.

What might I talk about with children?

1. What does the playdough smell like to you?
2. What does the playdough feel like?

FRIENDS PAINT ON THE FENCE
Learning Center (art, outdoor large muscle)

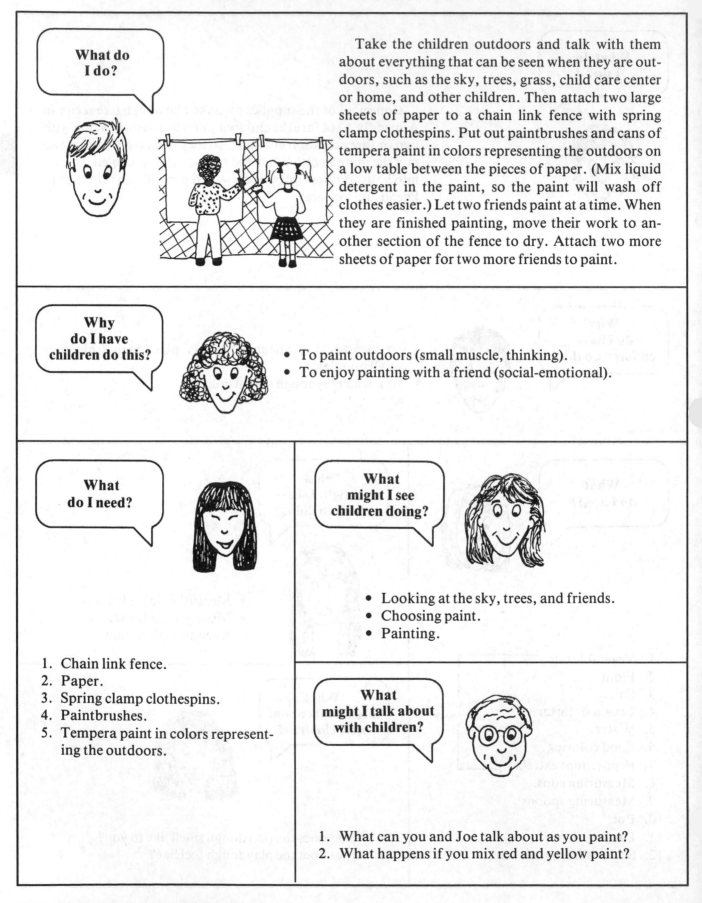

What do I do?

Take the children outdoors and talk with them about everything that can be seen when they are outdoors, such as the sky, trees, grass, child care center or home, and other children. Then attach two large sheets of paper to a chain link fence with spring clamp clothespins. Put out paintbrushes and cans of tempera paint in colors representing the outdoors on a low table between the pieces of paper. (Mix liquid detergent in the paint, so the paint will wash off clothes easier.) Let two friends paint at a time. When they are finished painting, move their work to another section of the fence to dry. Attach two more sheets of paper for two more friends to paint.

Why do I have children do this?

- To paint outdoors (small muscle, thinking).
- To enjoy painting with a friend (social-emotional).

What do I need?

1. Chain link fence.
2. Paper.
3. Spring clamp clothespins.
4. Paintbrushes.
5. Tempera paint in colors representing the outdoors.

What might I see children doing?

- Looking at the sky, trees, and friends.
- Choosing paint.
- Painting.

What might I talk about with children?

1. What can you and Joe talk about as you paint?
2. What happens if you mix red and yellow paint?

GOOP IS FOR FRIENDS
Learning Center (art)

What do I do?

Collect all of the supplies to make goop (see recipe in Appendix A) before the children join you to work. Work with two or three children at a time, so they can each mix and knead the goop. It is very simple to make and bounces and breaks off easily. After you have made the goop, have the children play with it with their friends. They can stretch, knead, and bounce the goop as they play.

Why do I have children do this?

- To experiment with another art medium (small muscle).
- To enjoy working with friends (social-emotional).

What do I need?

What might I see children doing?

- Feeling the goop.
- Stretching the goop.
- Kneading the goop.
- Bouncing the goop.
- Talking.

What might I talk about with children?

1. Elmer's® white glue.
2. Liquid starch.
3. Mixing bowl.
4. Airtight container.

1. What can you do with goop?
2. How does goop feel?

WE ARE BEST FRIENDS BOOK
Learning Center (art)

What do I do?

Complete the group activity *"We Are Best Friends"* on page 149. Put out crayons, markers, paper, scissors, glue, and other collage materials in your art area. Hang pictures of friends doing activities on the wall at the children's eye level. Talk with the children as they come to the art area about what they do with their best friends. Then let them experiment with and use the materials as they wish. If they would like to tell you about their pictures, write their comments on their papers. For example, "This is Joe. We play in the tree house."

Why do I have children do this?

- To explore with art media (small muscle).
- To tell a story for you to write (thinking).

What do I need?

What might I see children doing?

- Choosing colors.
- Drawing pictures.
- Talking about the pictures.
- Watching you write.

1. Crayons.
2. Markers.
3. Paper.
4. Scissors.
5. Glue.
6. Collage materials.
7. Pictures of friends doing activities.

What might I talk about with children?

1. Who are the people in your picture?
2. What do you and James like to do?

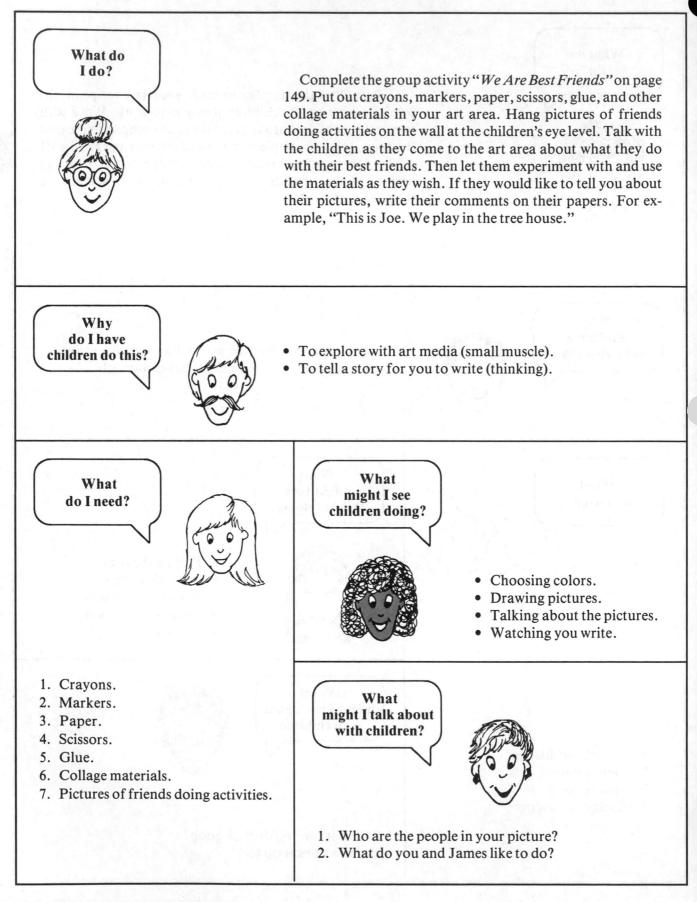

OUR TV SHOW
Learning Center (art)

What do I do?

Put out a long sheet of paper, markers, and crayons. Let each child draw a picture on a section of the paper. Talk with the children about their pictures and write their descriptions on the paper. Older children might want to illustrate a story, such as *The Three Billy Goats Gruff*.

Make a TV out of a cardboard box. Remove the back of the box and cut out a screen in the front with an X-Acto® knife. Cut two circles directly behind the screen on each side and insert two cardboard paper towel tubes. Roll the sheet of paper starting with the ending of the TV show onto the paper towel tube and tape the other end to the bottom tube. Then wind the paper from the top tube into the bottom tube to show the TV show. This TV can be used in the dramatic play activity "Slumber Party" on page 171.

Why do I have children do this?

- To experiment with art media (small muscle).
- To describe their drawings (language).
- To illustrate a story (language).

What do I need?

1. Long sheet of paper.
2. Markers.
3. Crayons.
4. Cardboard box.
5. X-Acto® knife.
6. Two cardboard paper towel tubes.
7. Masking tape.

What might I see children doing?

- Drawing.
- Talking about pictures.
- Helping put paper in the TV.
- Imagining.

What might I talk about with children?

1. What pictures could you make for the TV show?
2. What shows do you like on TV?

LITTLE BLUE AND LITTLE YELLOW PAINTING
Learning Center (art)

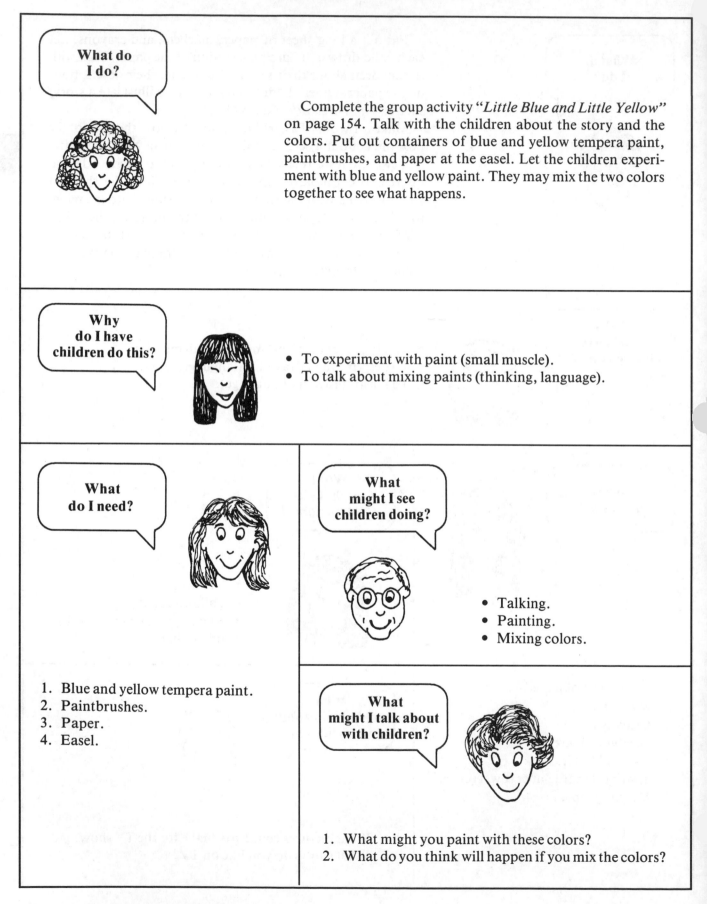

What do I do?

Complete the group activity *"Little Blue and Little Yellow"* on page 154. Talk with the children about the story and the colors. Put out containers of blue and yellow tempera paint, paintbrushes, and paper at the easel. Let the children experiment with blue and yellow paint. They may mix the two colors together to see what happens.

Why do I have children do this?

- To experiment with paint (small muscle).
- To talk about mixing paints (thinking, language).

What do I need?

1. Blue and yellow tempera paint.
2. Paintbrushes.
3. Paper.
4. Easel.

What might I see children doing?

- Talking.
- Painting.
- Mixing colors.

What might I talk about with children?

1. What might you paint with these colors?
2. What do you think will happen if you mix the colors?

FRIENDSHIP PICTURES
Learning Center (art)

What do I do?

Introduce the following two friendship symbols to the older children. Two index fingers hooked together is the sign language symbol for friendship, and a broken arrow is a Native American sign of peace. Talk with the children about their ideas of friends and friendship. Then put out glue, crayons, markers, collage materials, scissors, and paper for the children to enjoy.

Why do I have children do this?

- To learn different ways to communicate with symbols (language).
- To explore with art media (small muscle).

What do I need?

1. Picture of two index fingers hooked together.
2. Picture of a broken arrow.
3. Glue.
4. Crayons.
5. Markers.
6. Collage materials.
7. Scissors.
8. Paper.

What might I see children doing?

- Looking at the symbols.
- Using crayons and markers.
- Cutting.
- Gluing.

What might I talk about with children?

1. What are other ways you can use your hands to talk? ("V" for victory, wave for hello)
2. What colors have you used in your picture?

FOAM BLOCKS ARE QUIET FRIENDS
Learning Center (blocks)

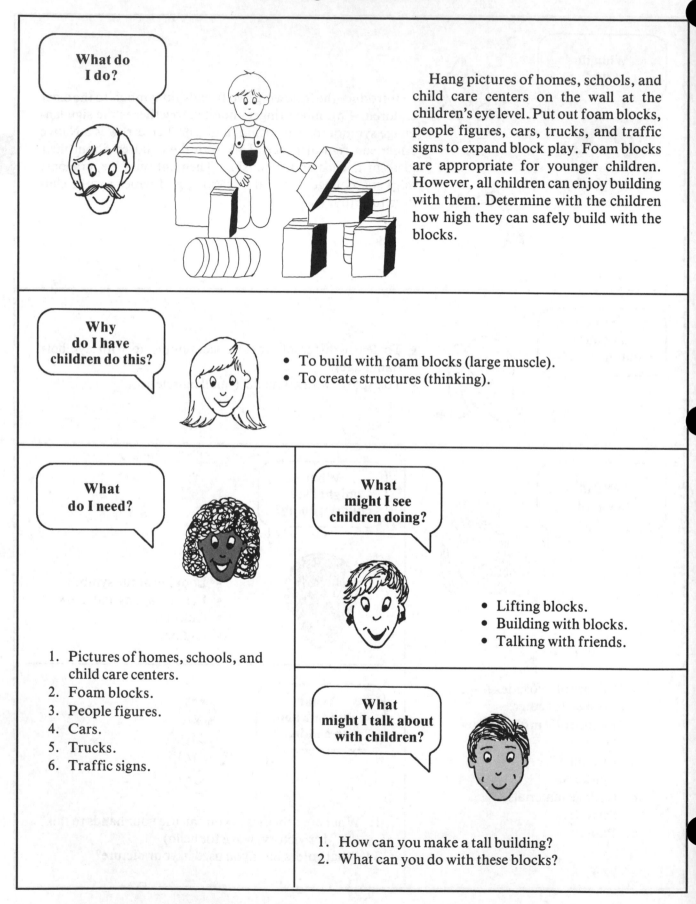

What do I do?

Hang pictures of homes, schools, and child care centers on the wall at the children's eye level. Put out foam blocks, people figures, cars, trucks, and traffic signs to expand block play. Foam blocks are appropriate for younger children. However, all children can enjoy building with them. Determine with the children how high they can safely build with the blocks.

Why do I have children do this?

- To build with foam blocks (large muscle).
- To create structures (thinking).

What do I need?

1. Pictures of homes, schools, and child care centers.
2. Foam blocks.
3. People figures.
4. Cars.
5. Trucks.
6. Traffic signs.

What might I see children doing?

- Lifting blocks.
- Building with blocks.
- Talking with friends.

What might I talk about with children?

1. How can you make a tall building?
2. What can you do with these blocks?

FRIENDS IN THE BLOCK AREA
Learning Center (blocks)

What do I do?

Hang pictures of children playing together on the wall at the children's eye level. Talk about how you can tell that the children in the pictures are friends. Place people figures, cars, a bus, and a wagon in the block area for the children to use in addition to the blocks. Then talk with the children about friendship as they build with blocks. For example, "Friends help each other by passing blocks." "John is a friend when he helps build the road." "These are friends riding in the car."

Why do I have children do this?

- To build with blocks (small and large muscle).
- To talk about friends and what they do (language).

What do I need?

1. Pictures of children playing together.
2. People figures.
3. Cars.
4. Bus.
5. Wagon.
6. Blocks.

What might I see children doing?

- Looking at pictures.
- Building with blocks.
- Putting friends (people figures) in the cars.
- Talking to friends.

What might I talk about with children?

1. Where would you like to go with your friend?
2. What do friends do together?

I'M HAVING A BIRTHDAY PARTY FOR MY FRIEND
Learning Center (dramatic play)

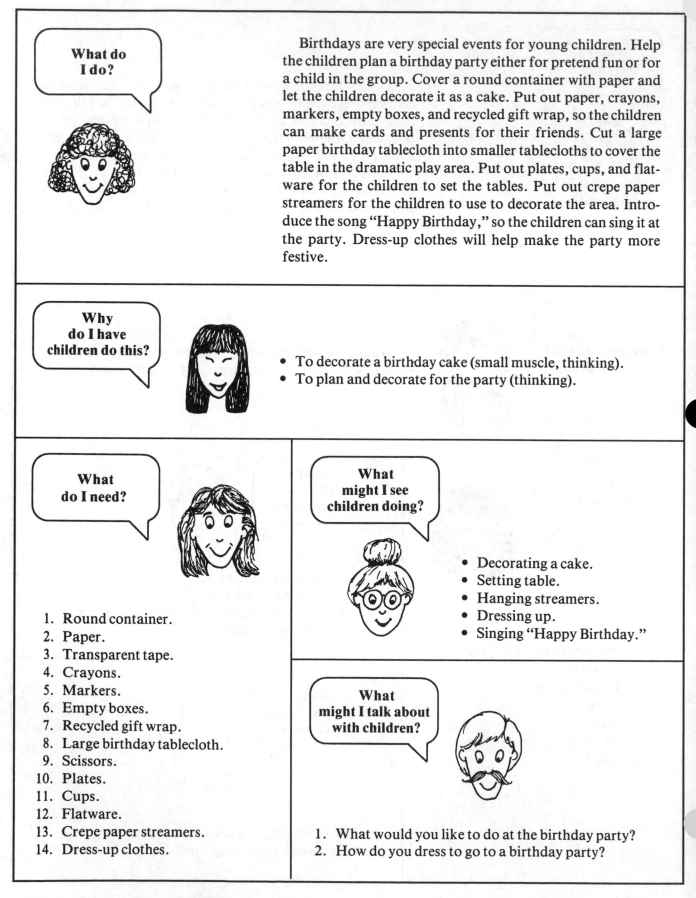

What do I do?

Birthdays are very special events for young children. Help the children plan a birthday party either for pretend fun or for a child in the group. Cover a round container with paper and let the children decorate it as a cake. Put out paper, crayons, markers, empty boxes, and recycled gift wrap, so the children can make cards and presents for their friends. Cut a large paper birthday tablecloth into smaller tablecloths to cover the table in the dramatic play area. Put out plates, cups, and flatware for the children to set the tables. Put out crepe paper streamers for the children to use to decorate the area. Introduce the song "Happy Birthday," so the children can sing it at the party. Dress-up clothes will help make the party more festive.

Why do I have children do this?

- To decorate a birthday cake (small muscle, thinking).
- To plan and decorate for the party (thinking).

What do I need?

1. Round container.
2. Paper.
3. Transparent tape.
4. Crayons.
5. Markers.
6. Empty boxes.
7. Recycled gift wrap.
8. Large birthday tablecloth.
9. Scissors.
10. Plates.
11. Cups.
12. Flatware.
13. Crepe paper streamers.
14. Dress-up clothes.

What might I see children doing?

- Decorating a cake.
- Setting table.
- Hanging streamers.
- Dressing up.
- Singing "Happy Birthday."

What might I talk about with children?

1. What would you like to do at the birthday party?
2. How do you dress to go to a birthday party?

TAKE A FRIEND TO A FAST-FOOD RESTAURANT
Learning Center (dramatic play)

What do I do?

Set up your dramatic play area as a fast-food restaurant. Ask a local fast-food restaurant to donate items such as sandwich boxes, French fry boxes, paper cups, napkins, and place mats to use for this activity. Have a play cash register and a pad of paper and a pencil for taking orders set up on a table. Make a sign representing a fast-food restaurant out of poster board and hang it up over the "serving counter." If you have play food, such as hamburgers or French fries, put them in the donated boxes to sell to the customers. Add a few cookie sheets for the children to carry the food. Put out a dish rag or a sponge for the attendant to clean tables and a broom for him or her to sweep the floors. Add a drive-in window by putting a cardboard box on the serving counter with a window cut out of it for vehicles to pull up to outside the restaurant.

Why do I have children do this?

- To pretend to work or eat in a fast-food restaurant with a friend (social-emotional).
- To take orders and give change (thinking).

What do I need?

1. Sandwich boxes.
2. French fry boxes.
3. Paper cups.
4. Napkins.
5. Place mats.
6. Play cash register.
7. Pad of paper.
8. Pencil.
9. Poster board.
10. Play food.
11. Cookie sheets.
12. Tables.
13. Dish rag.
14. Sponge.
15. Broom.
16. Cardboard box with a window cut out of it.
17. Toy vehicles.

What might I see children doing?

- Ordering food.
- Taking orders.
- Serving food.
- Cleaning tables.
- Sweeping floors.
- Pretending to eat.
- Talking.

What might I talk about with children?

1. Where do you like to go out to eat?
2. What are your favorite foods?

MY FRIENDS AND I GO ON A PICNIC
Learning Center (dramatic play, outdoor large muscle)

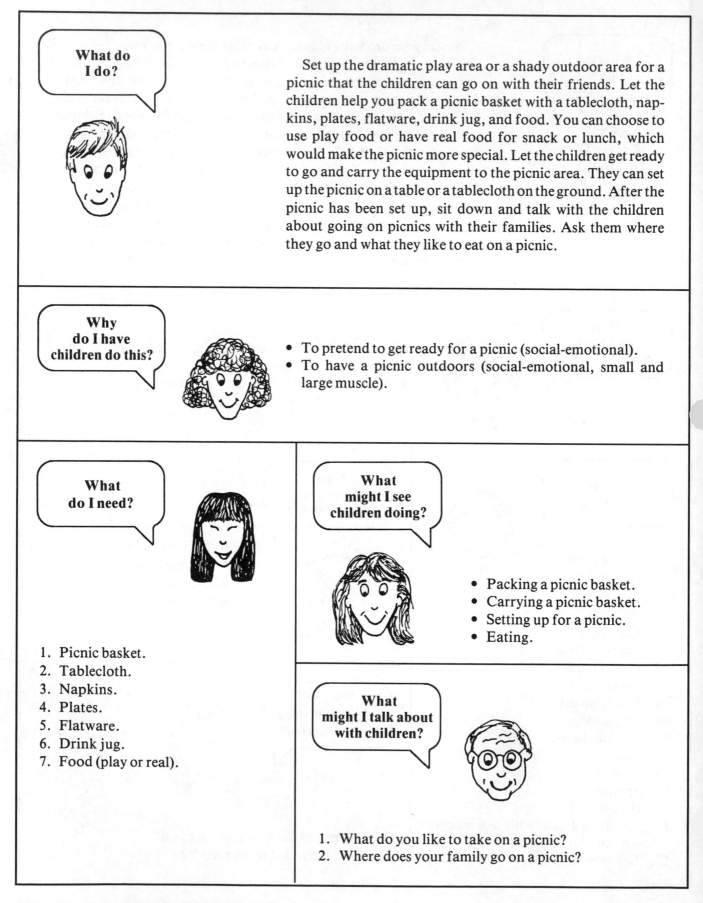

What do I do?

Set up the dramatic play area or a shady outdoor area for a picnic that the children can go on with their friends. Let the children help you pack a picnic basket with a tablecloth, napkins, plates, flatware, drink jug, and food. You can choose to use play food or have real food for snack or lunch, which would make the picnic more special. Let the children get ready to go and carry the equipment to the picnic area. They can set up the picnic on a table or a tablecloth on the ground. After the picnic has been set up, sit down and talk with the children about going on picnics with their families. Ask them where they go and what they like to eat on a picnic.

Why do I have children do this?

- To pretend to get ready for a picnic (social-emotional).
- To have a picnic outdoors (social-emotional, small and large muscle).

What do I need?

1. Picnic basket.
2. Tablecloth.
3. Napkins.
4. Plates.
5. Flatware.
6. Drink jug.
7. Food (play or real).

What might I see children doing?

- Packing a picnic basket.
- Carrying a picnic basket.
- Setting up for a picnic.
- Eating.

What might I talk about with children?

1. What do you like to take on a picnic?
2. Where does your family go on a picnic?

"THE TELEPHONE CALL"
Learning Center (dramatic play)

What do I do?

Hang a picture of a person talking on the telephone on the wall at the children's eye level. Read the poem "The Telephone Call" from *Rainy, Rainy Saturday* by J. Prelutsky to the children. Then talk with the children about the poem and calling friends on the telephone. Ask the children if they are allowed to make telephone calls at home. Put out play telephones for them to practice dialing and talking with friends. Make a telephone book with each child's home telephone number in it for the children to use. (Check with parents first to see if it is OK to put home telephone numbers in the group telephone book.) If there is an identifying picture or sticker on each child's cubby, use the same one next to the child's name in the group telephone book. This will help the children identify one another's telephone numbers. Add a blank page book near the telephone for the children to create their own telephone book.

Why do I have children do this?

- To dial numbers on the telephone (thinking, small muscle).
- To talk with a friend (language).

What do I need?

1. Picture of a person talking on the telephone.
2. *Rainy, Rainy Saturday* by J. Prelutsky.
3. Play telephones.
4. Paper stapled together to make class telephone book.
5. Stickers.
6. Blank page book.

What might I see children doing?

- Looking up telephone numbers.
- Dialing the telephone.
- Talking on the telephone.

What might I talk about with children?

1. What could you talk about if you called Yolanda or Scott?
2. What would you say if you called your Mommy?

FRIENDS LOVE THE MOVIES
Learning Center (dramatic play)

What do I do?

Talk with the children about going to a movie with a friend, buying tickets from a cashier, and being ushered to their seats. Set up the dramatic play area like a movie theater. Line up chairs into rows of seats. Turn a table into a ticket booth with paper for tickets, a play cash register, and play money. Make a sign that says "TICKETS FOR SALE." If you have a VCR, you can show a child-oriented movie, or you can borrow a film or filmstrip from your library to show to the children.

Why do I have children do this?

- To role-play going to a movie with a friend (social-emotional).
- To pretend to sell tickets (thinking, social-emotional).

What do I need?

1. Chairs.
2. Table.
3. Paper for tickets.
4. Play cash register.
5. Play money.
6. "TICKETS FOR SALE" sign.
7. VCR, film projector, or film-strip projector.
8. Child-oriented movie, film, or filmstrip.

What might I see children doing?

- Selling tickets.
- Making change.
- Ushering friends to their seats.

What might I talk about with children?

1. What are some movies you have seen?
2. How can you tell if a movie is real or not?

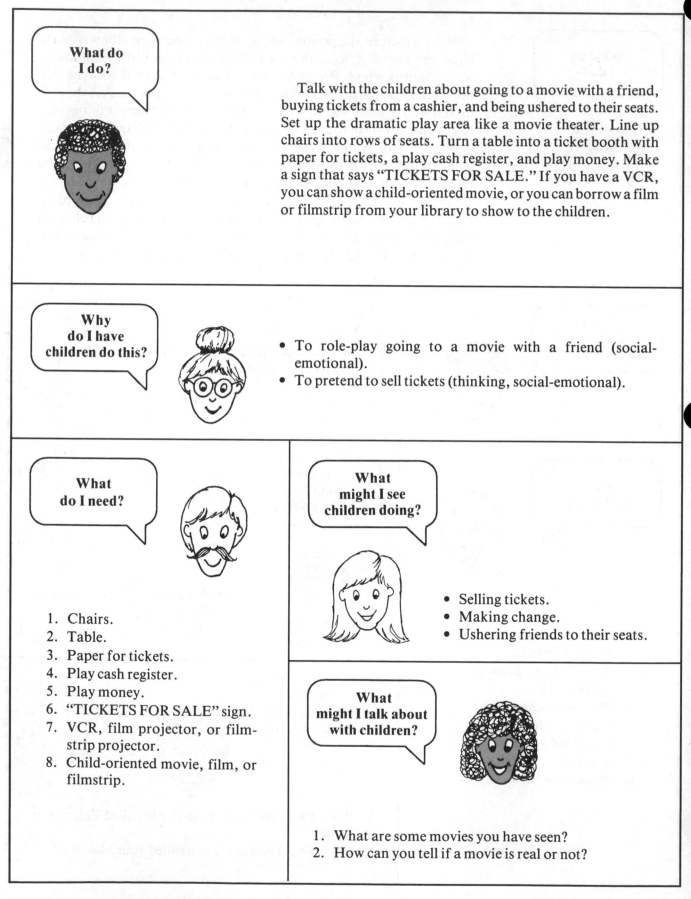

SLUMBER PARTY
Learning Center (dramatic play)

What do I do?

Set up a slumber party in the dramatic play area. Put out pillows and two or three cots or mats for the children to "sleep" on. Let the children wear clean pajamas to your center or home that day, so they will have something to "sleep" in. Put a radio and the TV from the art activity "Our TV Show" on page 161 in the dramatic play area, for them to listen to and watch. You can serve them snacks, such as pieces of fruit or a cookie and a glass of milk, in the dramatic play area as a special treat. As they play, talk with the children about slumber parties. Ask if they have ever stayed all night with a friend or had a friend stay over with them.

Why do I have children do this?

- To pretend that they are having a slumber party (social-emotional).
- To enjoy eating their snacks (social-emotional).

What do I need?

1. Pillows.
2. Cots or mats.
3. Radio.
4. Cardboard TV.
5. Snacks.

What might I see children doing?

- Talking.
- Pretending to sleep.
- Watching the TV.
- Eating.

What might I talk about with children?

1. What do you do at a slumber party?
2. Who would come to a slumber party?

AGGRESSION COOKIES . . . FOR FRIENDS TO MAKE WHEN THEY AREN'T FEELING FRIENDLY Learning Center (food)

What do I do?

If the children are grouchy, angry, or the weather is bad outside, have them help you make aggression cookies (see recipe in Appendix B). Copy the recipe on poster board and decorate with pictures of cookies. Before you begin preparing the cookies, collect all the supplies and make sure you and the children wash your hands. Mashing, kneading, and pounding the dough will help the children get rid of some of their anger or boredom. Tell them that the longer and harder they mix the dough, the better the cookies will taste. Work with two or three children at a time, so they can each mix, knead, and roll the dough.

Why do I have children do this?

- To measure ingredients (thinking).
- To mix, knead, and pound dough (small and large muscle).

What do I need?

1. Poster board.
2. Pictures of cookies.
3. Measuring cups.
4. Measuring spoons.
5. Oatmeal.
6. Brown sugar.
7. Flour.
8. Butter.
9. Baking powder.
10. Measuring cups.
11. Measuring spoons.
12. Large mixing bowl.
13. Waxed paper.
14. Cookie sheet.

What might I see children doing?

- Measuring ingredients.
- Mixing dough.
- Mashing dough.
- Pounding dough.
- Rolling dough into balls.
- Eating cookies.

What might I talk about with children?

1. What could you do to get rid of your anger?
2. What else might you put in cookies?

MAKING A SMOOTHIE FOR A FRIEND
Learning Center (food)

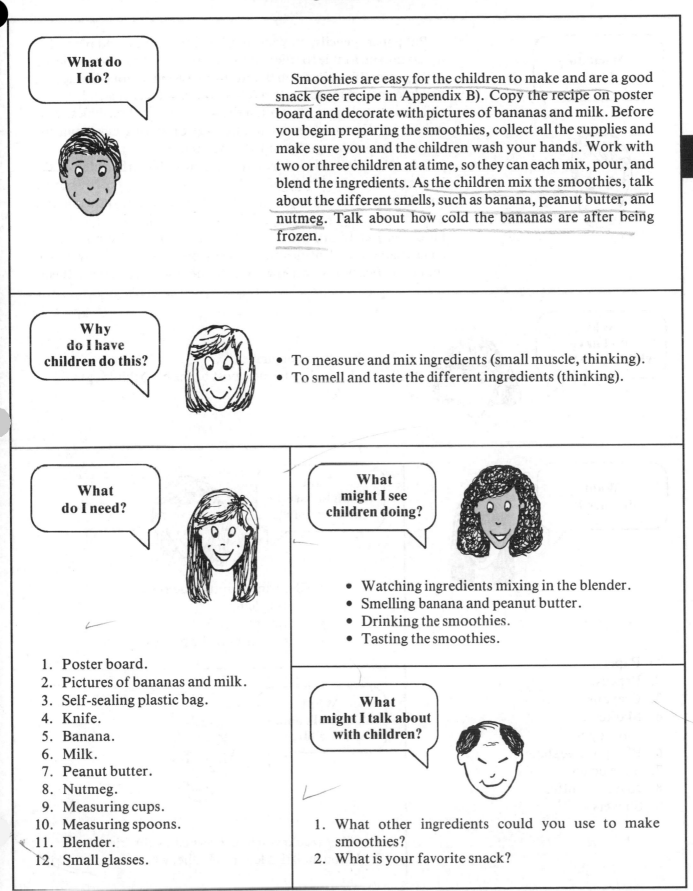

What do I do?

Smoothies are easy for the children to make and are a good snack (see recipe in Appendix B). Copy the recipe on poster board and decorate with pictures of bananas and milk. Before you begin preparing the smoothies, collect all the supplies and make sure you and the children wash your hands. Work with two or three children at a time, so they can each mix, pour, and blend the ingredients. As the children mix the smoothies, talk about the different smells, such as banana, peanut butter, and nutmeg. Talk about how cold the bananas are after being frozen.

Why do I have children do this?

- To measure and mix ingredients (small muscle, thinking).
- To smell and taste the different ingredients (thinking).

What do I need?

1. Poster board.
2. Pictures of bananas and milk.
3. Self-sealing plastic bag.
4. Knife.
5. Banana.
6. Milk.
7. Peanut butter.
8. Nutmeg.
9. Measuring cups.
10. Measuring spoons.
11. Blender.
12. Small glasses.

What might I see children doing?

- Watching ingredients mixing in the blender.
- Smelling banana and peanut butter.
- Drinking the smoothies.
- Tasting the smoothies.

What might I talk about with children?

1. What other ingredients could you use to make smoothies?
2. What is your favorite snack?

MAILING A LETTER TO A FRIEND
Learning Center (library)

What do I do?

Put paper, pencils, crayons, markers, envelopes, and play postage stamps on a table for the children to use to write letters to friends in the group. If a child from the group has recently moved away, the children may want to write a letter to him or her instead. When children write letters, they often draw pictures and scribbles. This writing is OK, since they are in this stage of writing development. Ask the children to read their letters to you.

After the children have written their letters, have them deliver the letters to their friends' post office boxes. To make post office boxes, cut a U-shaped frame approximately one-half inch wide in one end of a shoe box. This opening will be large enough for a child to put his or her hand in to get mail. Label each post office box with a child's name and identification sticker from his or her cubby. Stack the post office boxes on a low table, so the children can reach them.

Why do I have children do this?

- To write letters (language).
- To put letters in a friend's post office box (thinking).

What do I need?

1. Paper.
2. Pencils.
3. Crayons.
4. Markers.
5. Envelopes.
6. Play postage stamps.
7. Shoe boxes.
8. X-Acto® knife.
9. Stickers.

What might I see children doing?

- Choosing writing materials.
- Writing letters.
- Licking stamps.
- Putting letter in the post office box.

What might I talk about with children?

1. What would you like to write to your friend?
2. If you mail this letter to Eddie, where do you take it?

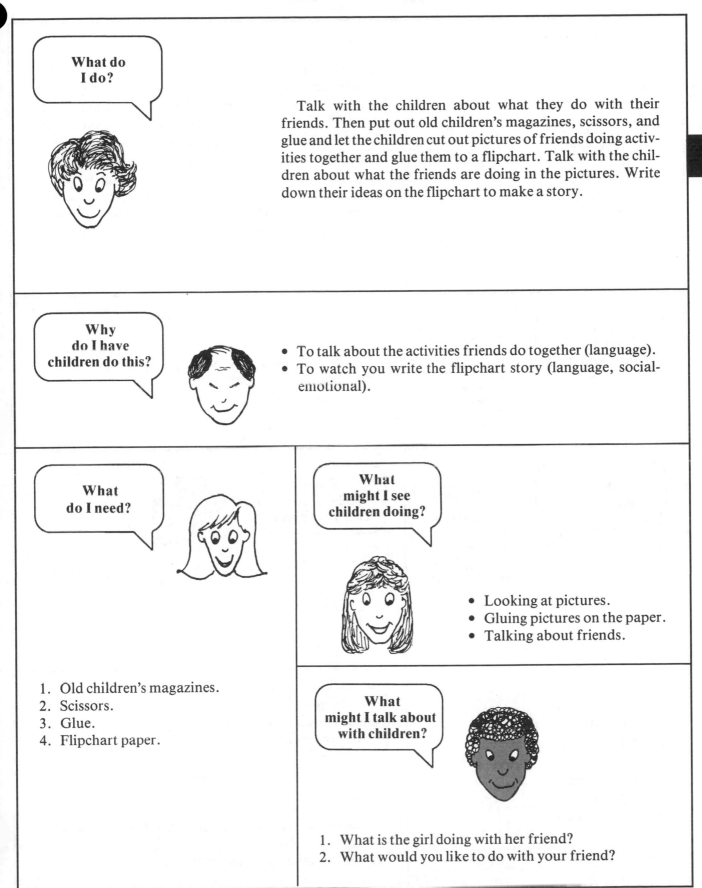

What do I do?

Talk with the children about what they do with their friends. Then put out old children's magazines, scissors, and glue and let the children cut out pictures of friends doing activities together and glue them to a flipchart. Talk with the children about what the friends are doing in the pictures. Write down their ideas on the flipchart to make a story.

Why do I have children do this?

- To talk about the activities friends do together (language).
- To watch you write the flipchart story (language, social-emotional).

What do I need?

What might I see children doing?

- Looking at pictures.
- Gluing pictures on the paper.
- Talking about friends.

1. Old children's magazines.
2. Scissors.
3. Glue.
4. Flipchart paper.

What might I talk about with children?

1. What is the girl doing with her friend?
2. What would you like to do with your friend?

ZIP, BUCKLE, BUTTON, AND SNAP
Learning Center (manipulatives)

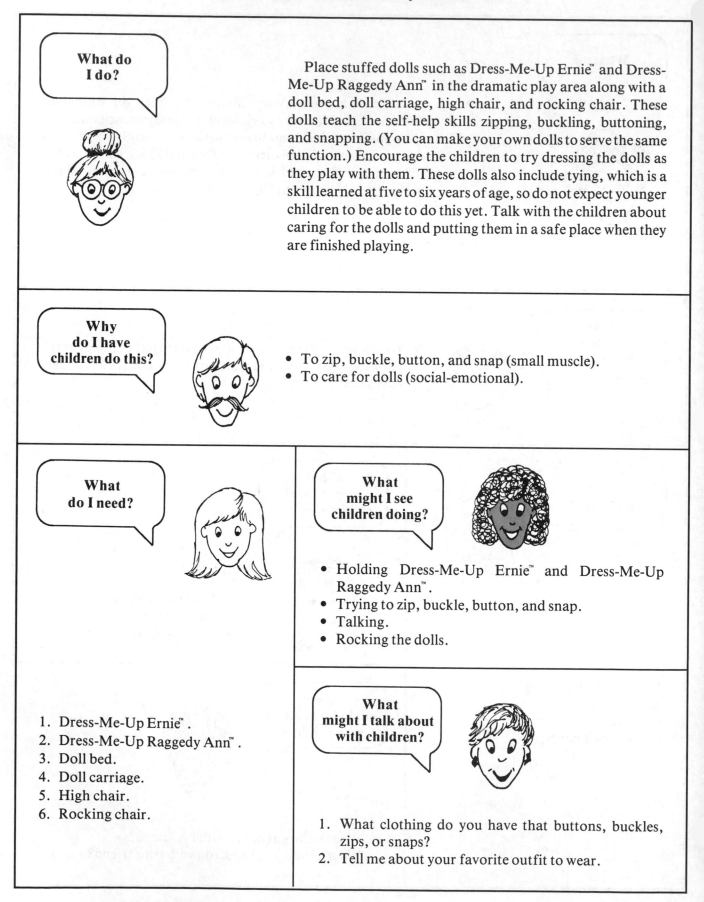

What do I do?

Place stuffed dolls such as Dress-Me-Up Ernie™ and Dress-Me-Up Raggedy Ann™ in the dramatic play area along with a doll bed, doll carriage, high chair, and rocking chair. These dolls teach the self-help skills zipping, buckling, buttoning, and snapping. (You can make your own dolls to serve the same function.) Encourage the children to try dressing the dolls as they play with them. These dolls also include tying, which is a skill learned at five to six years of age, so do not expect younger children to be able to do this yet. Talk with the children about caring for the dolls and putting them in a safe place when they are finished playing.

Why do I have children do this?

- To zip, buckle, button, and snap (small muscle).
- To care for dolls (social-emotional).

What do I need?

What might I see children doing?

- Holding Dress-Me-Up Ernie™ and Dress-Me-Up Raggedy Ann™.
- Trying to zip, buckle, button, and snap.
- Talking.
- Rocking the dolls.

1. Dress-Me-Up Ernie™.
2. Dress-Me-Up Raggedy Ann™.
3. Doll bed.
4. Doll carriage.
5. High chair.
6. Rocking chair.

What might I talk about with children?

1. What clothing do you have that buttons, buckles, zips, or snaps?
2. Tell me about your favorite outfit to wear.

FRIENDS AT PLAY MATCHING GAME
Learning Center (manipulatives)

What do I do?

Make matching games for the children. Cut two sets of six pictures of children playing out of child-oriented gift wrap for each matching game. Glue one set of pictures to library pockets or envelopes and glue the library pockets or envelopes to the inside of a file folder in two rows of three. Glue the other set to individual index cards. Then glue an envelope to the back of the file folder and put the index cards in it. Let the children match the two sets of pictures by sliding the index cards into the matching library pockets or envelopes. Talk with them about what the friends in the pictures are playing.

Why do I have children do this?

- To match sets of friends playing (thinking, small muscle).
- To identify what the friends are playing (thinking).

What do I need?

1. Child-oriented gift wrap.
2. Scissors.
3. Glue.
4. Library pockets or envelopes.
5. Index cards.
6. File folders.
7. Envelopes.

What might I see children doing?

- Looking at pictures.
- Matching pictures.
- Talking about friends in the pictures.

What might I talk about with children?

1. What games do you like to play?
2. What are the friends doing?

HELP YOUR FRIEND SORT THE POM-POMS
Learning Center (manipulatives)

What do I do?

Glue blue, red, green, yellow, black, brown, orange, and purple felt circles on the bottoms of the different sections of a muffin tin. Use only blue, red, green, and yellow felt circles for two-year-olds and young three-year-olds. On a table set with two chairs, place a container of the same colored pom-poms beside the muffin tin and let friends sort the pom-poms into the matching muffin tin sections. Talk with the children about the different colors in the room as they work. Ask them to find the green book, the red chair, or the black truck.

Why do I have children do this?

- To match colored pom-poms to colored felt circles in the muffin tin (thinking).
- To identify objects in the room by color (thinking).

What do I need?

1. Blue, red, green, yellow, black, brown, orange, and purple colored felt.
2. Muffin tin.
3. Glue.
4. Blue, red, green, yellow, black, brown, orange, and purple pom-poms.
5. Container.

What might I see children doing?

- Sorting pom-poms.
- Matching pom-poms to colored circles in the muffin tins.
- Talking.

What might I talk about with children?

1. What do you have to wear that is red?
2. What colors are you wearing today?

STRING A NECKLACE FOR YOUR FRIEND
Learning Center (manipulatives)

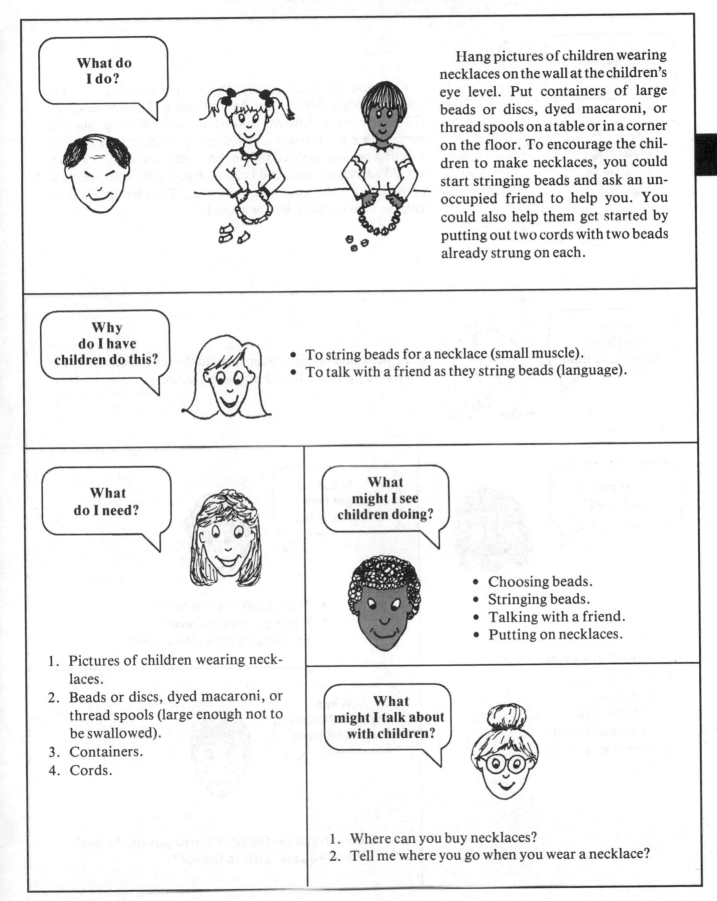

What do I do?

Hang pictures of children wearing necklaces on the wall at the children's eye level. Put containers of large beads or discs, dyed macaroni, or thread spools on a table or in a corner on the floor. To encourage the children to make necklaces, you could start stringing beads and ask an unoccupied friend to help you. You could also help them get started by putting out two cords with two beads already strung on each.

Why do I have children do this?

- To string beads for a necklace (small muscle).
- To talk with a friend as they string beads (language).

What do I need?

1. Pictures of children wearing necklaces.
2. Beads or discs, dyed macaroni, or thread spools (large enough not to be swallowed).
3. Containers.
4. Cords.

What might I see children doing?

- Choosing beads.
- Stringing beads.
- Talking with a friend.
- Putting on necklaces.

What might I talk about with children?

1. Where can you buy necklaces?
2. Tell me where you go when you wear a necklace?

WRAPPING COOKIES FOR A FRIEND
Learning Center (manipulatives)

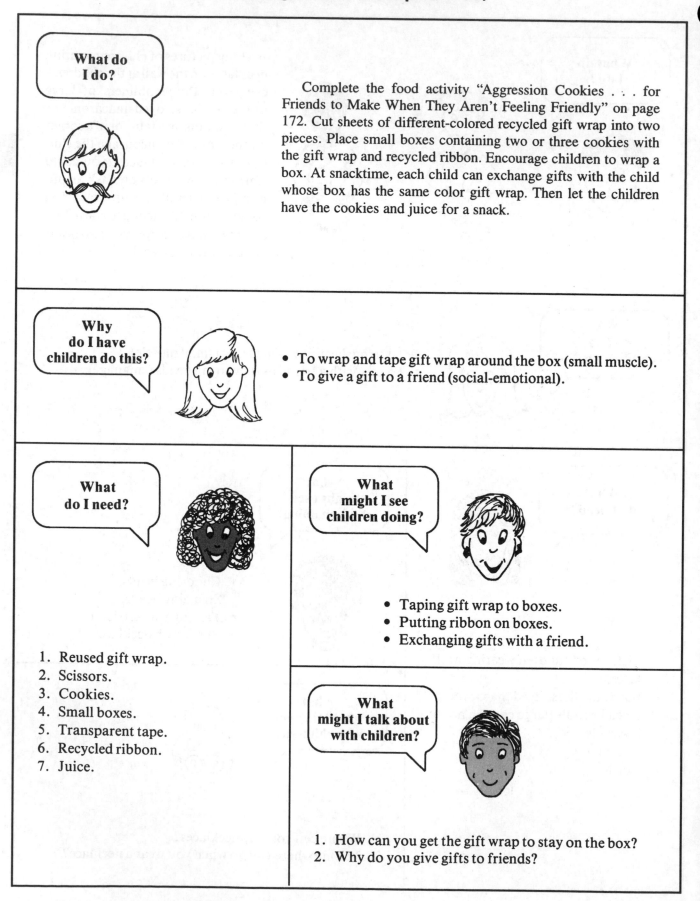

What do I do?

Complete the food activity "Aggression Cookies . . . for Friends to Make When They Aren't Feeling Friendly" on page 172. Cut sheets of different-colored recycled gift wrap into two pieces. Place small boxes containing two or three cookies with the gift wrap and recycled ribbon. Encourage children to wrap a box. At snacktime, each child can exchange gifts with the child whose box has the same color gift wrap. Then let the children have the cookies and juice for a snack.

Why do I have children do this?

- To wrap and tape gift wrap around the box (small muscle).
- To give a gift to a friend (social-emotional).

What do I need?

1. Reused gift wrap.
2. Scissors.
3. Cookies.
4. Small boxes.
5. Transparent tape.
6. Recycled ribbon.
7. Juice.

What might I see children doing?

- Taping gift wrap to boxes.
- Putting ribbon on boxes.
- Exchanging gifts with a friend.

What might I talk about with children?

1. How can you get the gift wrap to stay on the box?
2. Why do you give gifts to friends?

ONE FOR YOU AND ONE FOR ME
Learning Center (math)

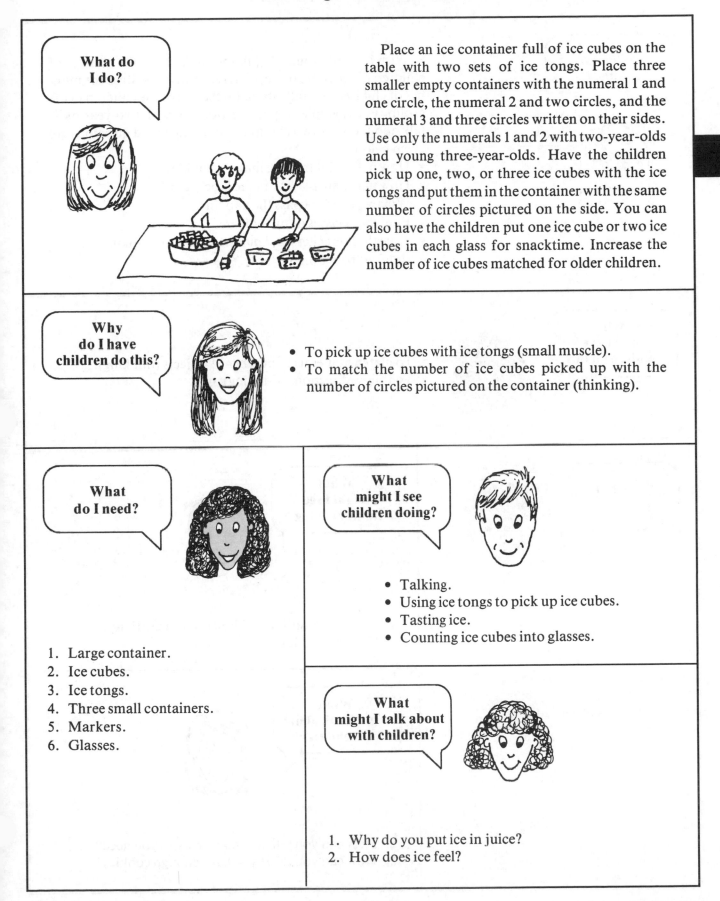

What do I do?

Place an ice container full of ice cubes on the table with two sets of ice tongs. Place three smaller empty containers with the numeral 1 and one circle, the numeral 2 and two circles, and the numeral 3 and three circles written on their sides. Use only the numerals 1 and 2 with two-year-olds and young three-year-olds. Have the children pick up one, two, or three ice cubes with the ice tongs and put them in the container with the same number of circles pictured on the side. You can also have the children put one ice cube or two ice cubes in each glass for snacktime. Increase the number of ice cubes matched for older children.

Why do I have children do this?

- To pick up ice cubes with ice tongs (small muscle).
- To match the number of ice cubes picked up with the number of circles pictured on the container (thinking).

What do I need?

1. Large container.
2. Ice cubes.
3. Ice tongs.
4. Three small containers.
5. Markers.
6. Glasses.

What might I see children doing?

- Talking.
- Using ice tongs to pick up ice cubes.
- Tasting ice.
- Counting ice cubes into glasses.

What might I talk about with children?

1. Why do you put ice in juice?
2. How does ice feel?

COUNTING MY FRIENDS
Learning Center (math)

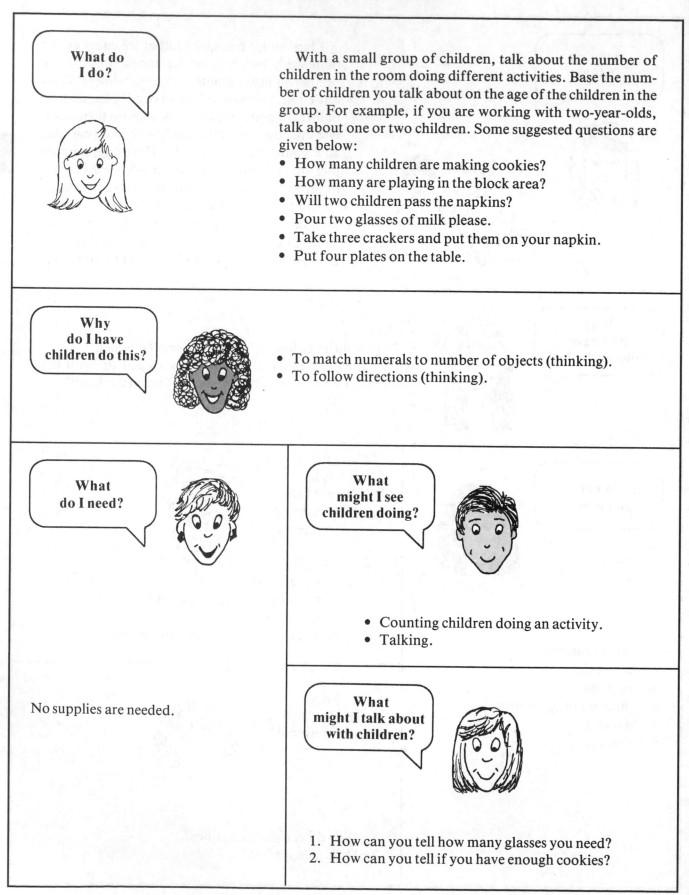

What do I do?

With a small group of children, talk about the number of children in the room doing different activities. Base the number of children you talk about on the age of the children in the group. For example, if you are working with two-year-olds, talk about one or two children. Some suggested questions are given below:

- How many children are making cookies?
- How many are playing in the block area?
- Will two children pass the napkins?
- Pour two glasses of milk please.
- Take three crackers and put them on your napkin.
- Put four plates on the table.

Why do I have children do this?

- To match numerals to number of objects (thinking).
- To follow directions (thinking).

What do I need?

No supplies are needed.

What might I see children doing?

- Counting children doing an activity.
- Talking.

What might I talk about with children?

1. How can you tell how many glasses you need?
2. How can you tell if you have enough cookies?

COMPARING FRIENDS
Learning Center (math)

What do I do?

Cut out three figures of girls, boys, dogs, and cats from felt. Make one figure large, one medium, and one small. Place the figures next to the felt board. Ask the children to put them in order of height–tall, taller, and tallest or short, shorter, and shortest. Leave these figures out where the children can find them to use. Use only the large and small figures with two-year-olds and young three-year-olds until they understand this concept. Then add the middle-sized figure and have them compare all three figures.

Why do I have children do this?

- To compare sizes of children and pets (thinking).
- To use new words, such as tallest and shortest (language).

What do I need?

1. Scissors.
2. Felt.
3. Felt board.
4. Self-sealing plastic bags to store figures.

What might I see children doing?

- Looking at felt figures.
- Placing figures in order of height.
- Talking.

What might I talk about with children?

1. Which children are the tallest in the group?
2. Which children are the shortest in the group?

"FRIENDS" FROM *ON THE MOVE WITH GREG AND STEVE*
Learning Center (music), Indoor or Outdoor Large Muscle, Group

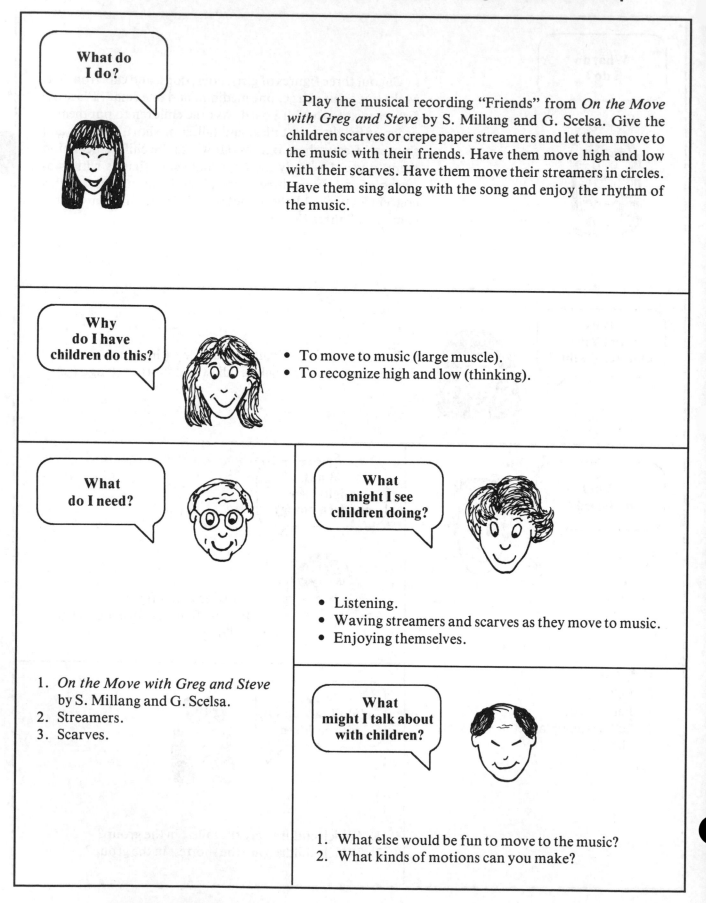

What do I do?

Play the musical recording "Friends" from *On the Move with Greg and Steve* by S. Millang and G. Scelsa. Give the children scarves or crepe paper streamers and let them move to the music with their friends. Have them move high and low with their scarves. Have them move their streamers in circles. Have them sing along with the song and enjoy the rhythm of the music.

Why do I have children do this?

- To move to music (large muscle).
- To recognize high and low (thinking).

What do I need?

1. *On the Move with Greg and Steve* by S. Millang and G. Scelsa.
2. Streamers.
3. Scarves.

What might I see children doing?

- Listening.
- Waving streamers and scarves as they move to music.
- Enjoying themselves.

What might I talk about with children?

1. What else would be fun to move to the music?
2. What kinds of motions can you make?

SCAMP'S NUTS
Learning Center (sand)

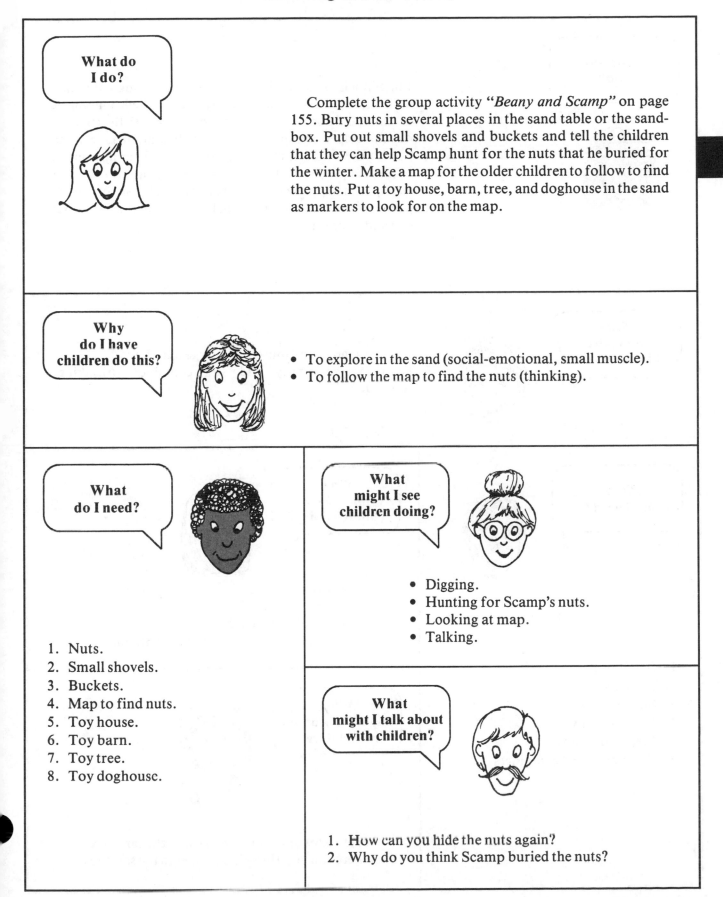

What do I do?

Complete the group activity *"Beany and Scamp"* on page 155. Bury nuts in several places in the sand table or the sandbox. Put out small shovels and buckets and tell the children that they can help Scamp hunt for the nuts that he buried for the winter. Make a map for the older children to follow to find the nuts. Put a toy house, barn, tree, and doghouse in the sand as markers to look for on the map.

Why do I have children do this?

- To explore in the sand (social-emotional, small muscle).
- To follow the map to find the nuts (thinking).

What do I need?

1. Nuts.
2. Small shovels.
3. Buckets.
4. Map to find nuts.
5. Toy house.
6. Toy barn.
7. Toy tree.
8. Toy doghouse.

What might I see children doing?

- Digging.
- Hunting for Scamp's nuts.
- Looking at map.
- Talking.

What might I talk about with children?

1. How can you hide the nuts again?
2. Why do you think Scamp buried the nuts?

PLAYING IN THE SANDBOX
Learning Center (sand)

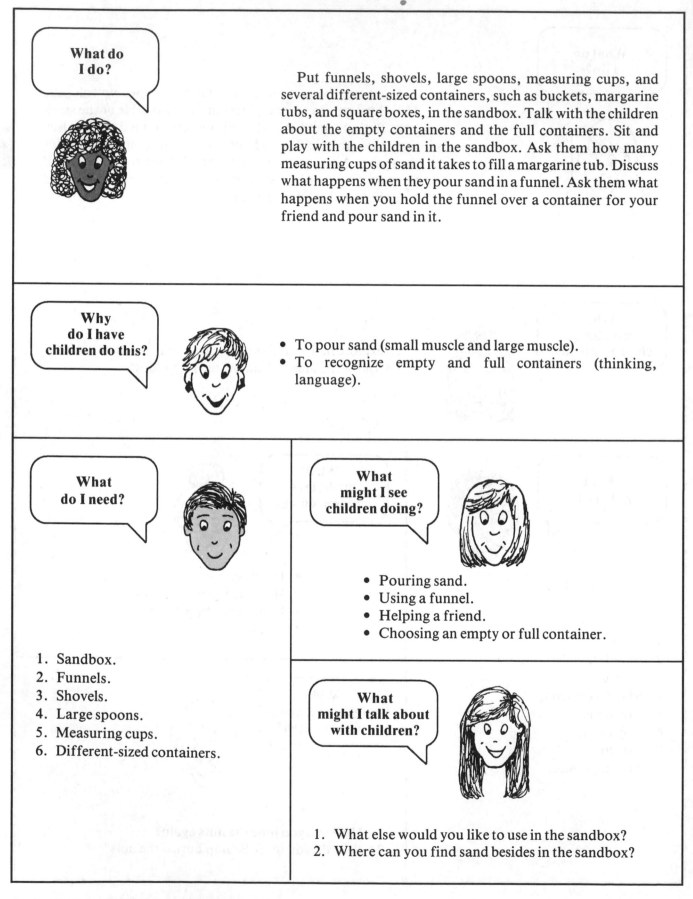

What do I do?

Put funnels, shovels, large spoons, measuring cups, and several different-sized containers, such as buckets, margarine tubs, and square boxes, in the sandbox. Talk with the children about the empty containers and the full containers. Sit and play with the children in the sandbox. Ask them how many measuring cups of sand it takes to fill a margarine tub. Discuss what happens when they pour sand in a funnel. Ask them what happens when you hold the funnel over a container for your friend and pour sand in it.

Why do I have children do this?

- To pour sand (small muscle and large muscle).
- To recognize empty and full containers (thinking, language).

What do I need?

1. Sandbox.
2. Funnels.
3. Shovels.
4. Large spoons.
5. Measuring cups.
6. Different-sized containers.

What might I see children doing?

- Pouring sand.
- Using a funnel.
- Helping a friend.
- Choosing an empty or full container.

What might I talk about with children?

1. What else would you like to use in the sandbox?
2. Where can you find sand besides in the sandbox?

MY FRIEND AND I LOOK FOR SIGNS OF THE SEASONS
Learning Center (science)

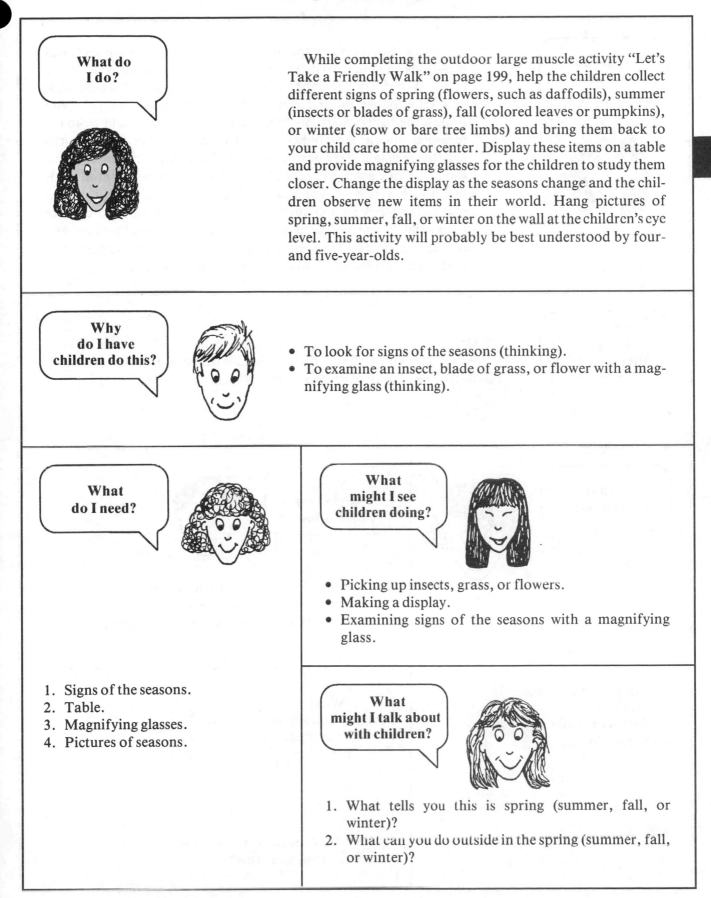

What do I do?

While completing the outdoor large muscle activity "Let's Take a Friendly Walk" on page 199, help the children collect different signs of spring (flowers, such as daffodils), summer (insects or blades of grass), fall (colored leaves or pumpkins), or winter (snow or bare tree limbs) and bring them back to your child care home or center. Display these items on a table and provide magnifying glasses for the children to study them closer. Change the display as the seasons change and the children observe new items in their world. Hang pictures of spring, summer, fall, or winter on the wall at the children's eye level. This activity will probably be best understood by four- and five-year-olds.

Why do I have children do this?

- To look for signs of the seasons (thinking).
- To examine an insect, blade of grass, or flower with a magnifying glass (thinking).

What do I need?

1. Signs of the seasons.
2. Table.
3. Magnifying glasses.
4. Pictures of seasons.

What might I see children doing?

- Picking up insects, grass, or flowers.
- Making a display.
- Examining signs of the seasons with a magnifying glass.

What might I talk about with children?

1. What tells you this is spring (summer, fall, or winter)?
2. What can you do outside in the spring (summer, fall, or winter)?

WEIGHING AND MEASURING A FRIEND
Learning Center (science, math)

What do I do?

Hang a long sheet of paper on the wall. Put a bathroom scale and measuring tape next to it. Have one child at a time come up to the paper. Write his or her name on the paper. Weigh the child on the scale and write the weight under his or her name. Have the child stand against the paper, mark his or her height, measure it, and write the measurement under his or her name. Tack a piece of brightly-colored yarn to the height mark or where the child's name is written. The yarn should be long enough to reach from the top of the child's head to his or her feet. While you are measuring a child, the other children can play in the block or dramatic play area. After all the children have been weighed and measured, have them gather around the paper and compare their sizes. Then have two children of different heights stand next to each other. Ask who is taller and who is shorter.

Why do I have children do this?

- To weigh on a bathroom scale (thinking).
- To compare heights (thinking).

What do I need?

1. Long sheet of paper.
2. Marker.
3. Bathroom scale.
4. Measuring tape.

What might I see children doing?

- Standing on a bathroom scale.
- Standing to be measured.
- Watching you write on the paper.
- Comparing heights.

What might I talk about with children?

1. Who is taller than you at home?
2. What helps you grow?

SOMETIMES FRIENDS LIKE TO PLAY IN MUD
Learning Center (water play)

What do I do?

Mud has rich colors and is cool and fun to mold. Let the children play in the mud with their friends. Place dirt in a large tub with enough water to make mud. Put toy shovels and different-sized containers, such as plastic bowls and margarine tubs, in the mud. Collect seeds, leaves, and twigs for the children to decorate mud pies and other mud creations. Place the tub of mud near a water source or keep a tub of clean water nearby for children to wash their hands. Give them paper towels to dry their hands. When the children are done playing in the mud, have them wash their hands with lots of soap and water. Give the children smocks or old dress shirts to wear to keep their clothes as clean as possible. This activity is a good one for summer when children are wearing shorts or swimsuits.

Why do I have children do this?

- To explore with mud (thinking, small muscle).
- To enjoy working with friends (social-emotional).

What do I need?

1. Large tub.
2. Dirt.
3. Water.
4. Toy shovels.
5. Different-sized containers.
6. Seeds, leaves, and twigs.
7. Tub of clean water.
8. Paper towels.
9. Smocks or old dress shirts.

What might I see children doing?

- Mixing dirt and water.
- Molding mud.
- Washing hands.
- Talking with friends.

What might I talk about with children?

1. Where do you usually find mud?
2. What does mud feel like to you?

FRIENDS POUND ON A TREE STUMP
Learning Center (woodworking, outdoor large muscle)

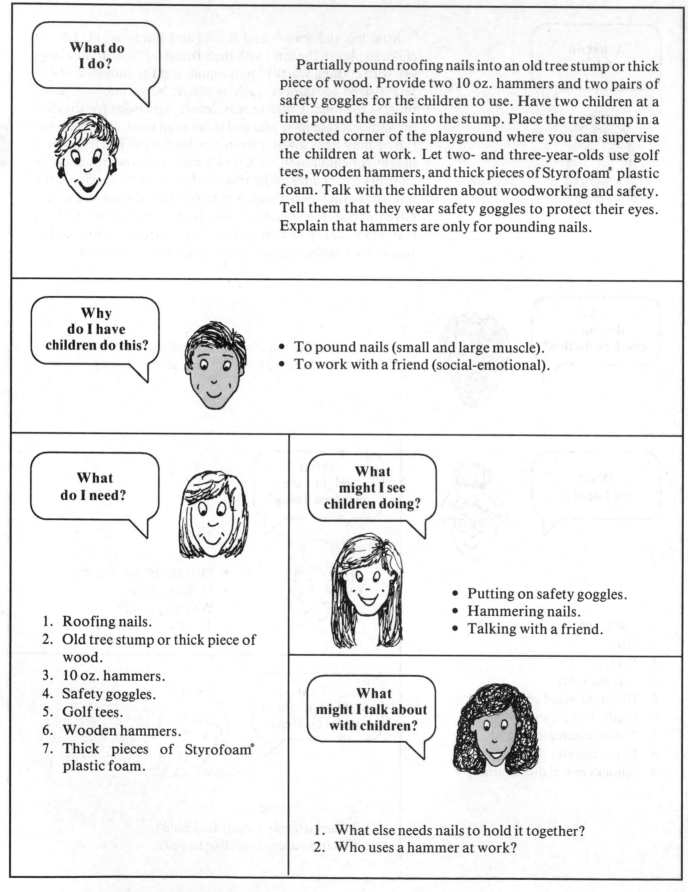

What do I do?

Partially pound roofing nails into an old tree stump or thick piece of wood. Provide two 10 oz. hammers and two pairs of safety goggles for the children to use. Have two children at a time pound the nails into the stump. Place the tree stump in a protected corner of the playground where you can supervise the children at work. Let two- and three-year-olds use golf tees, wooden hammers, and thick pieces of Styrofoam® plastic foam. Talk with the children about woodworking and safety. Tell them that they wear safety goggles to protect their eyes. Explain that hammers are only for pounding nails.

Why do I have children do this?

- To pound nails (small and large muscle).
- To work with a friend (social-emotional).

What do I need?

1. Roofing nails.
2. Old tree stump or thick piece of wood.
3. 10 oz. hammers.
4. Safety goggles.
5. Golf tees.
6. Wooden hammers.
7. Thick pieces of Styrofoam® plastic foam.

What might I see children doing?

- Putting on safety goggles.
- Hammering nails.
- Talking with a friend.

What might I talk about with children?

1. What else needs nails to hold it together?
2. Who uses a hammer at work?

PARTY INVITATIONS
Learning Center (writing)

What do I do?

Hang pictures of birthday parties on the wall at the children's eye level. Talk with the children about birthday parties and invitations. Put out brightly-colored paper, stickers, envelopes, glue, pencils, crayons, and markers. Let the children make invitations for the dramatic play activity "I'm Having a Birthday Party for My Friend" on page 166. The children can deliver the invitations by putting them in the children's shoe box mailboxes.

Why do I have children do this?

- To let them invite a friend to a birthday party (social-emotional).
- To experiment with writing materials (small muscle).

What do I need?

1. Pictures of birthday parties.
2. Brightly-colored paper.
3. Stickers.
4. Envelopes.
5. Glue.
6. Pencils.
7. Crayons.
8. Markers.

What might I see children doing?

- Choosing paper.
- Choosing markers or crayons.
- Writing invitations.
- Putting invitations in envelopes.
- Putting invitations in mailboxes.
- Talking to a friend.

What might I talk about with children?

1. What kinds of invitations have you gotten?
2. Why do you like to go to parties?

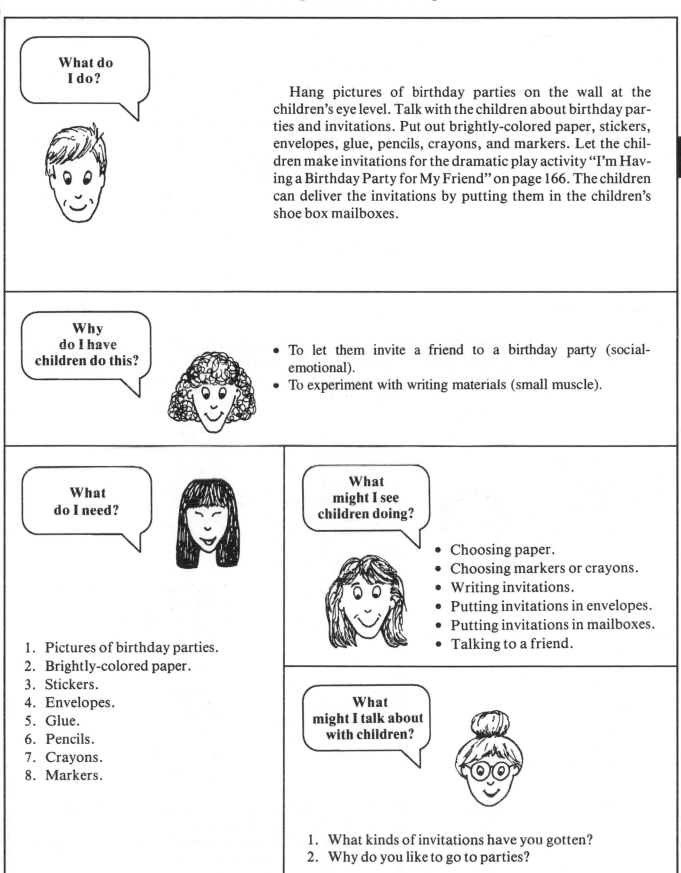

THANK YOU FOR INVITING ME
Learning Center (writing)

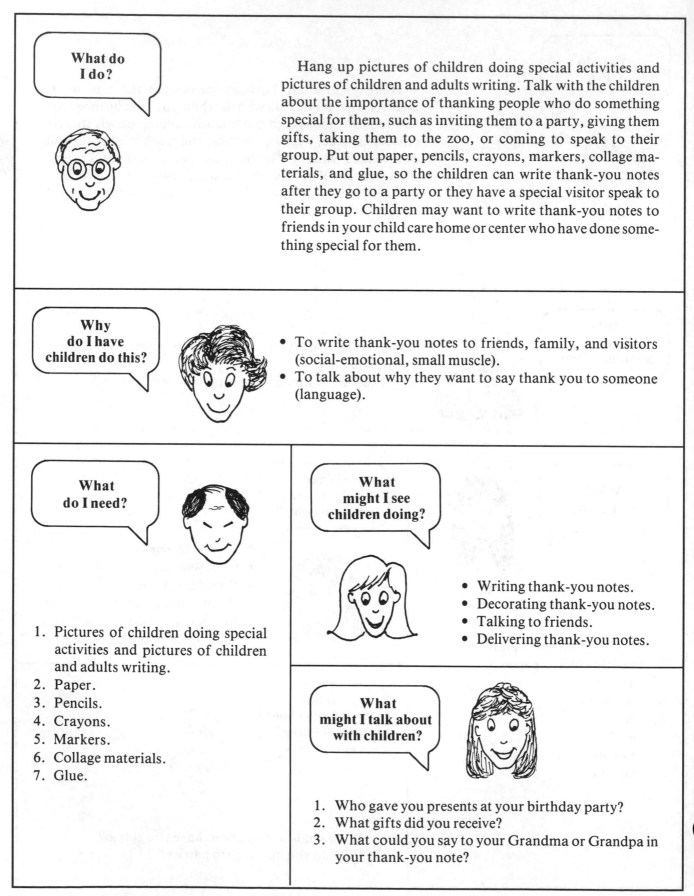

What do I do?

Hang up pictures of children doing special activities and pictures of children and adults writing. Talk with the children about the importance of thanking people who do something special for them, such as inviting them to a party, giving them gifts, taking them to the zoo, or coming to speak to their group. Put out paper, pencils, crayons, markers, collage materials, and glue, so the children can write thank-you notes after they go to a party or they have a special visitor speak to their group. Children may want to write thank-you notes to friends in your child care home or center who have done something special for them.

Why do I have children do this?

- To write thank-you notes to friends, family, and visitors (social-emotional, small muscle).
- To talk about why they want to say thank you to someone (language).

What do I need?

1. Pictures of children doing special activities and pictures of children and adults writing.
2. Paper.
3. Pencils.
4. Crayons.
5. Markers.
6. Collage materials.
7. Glue.

What might I see children doing?

- Writing thank-you notes.
- Decorating thank-you notes.
- Talking to friends.
- Delivering thank-you notes.

What might I talk about with children?

1. Who gave you presents at your birthday party?
2. What gifts did you receive?
3. What could you say to your Grandma or Grandpa in your thank-you note?

FRIEND TO FRIEND
Indoor or Outdoor Large Muscle

What do I do?

Sit in a circle and discuss how to play the game. Help each child find a friend to face him or her. Make sure that each pair of friends has a large amount of space around them, so they can move around freely. Then direct the children to "Touch your nose to your friend's wrist" or "Touch your hand to your friend's toe." These movements may cause the children to giggle. The children may switch friends halfway through the game. After you have given two or three directions, let a child be a "friend director." This child can use his or her imagination to make up new directions. This game works well with older four-year-olds and five-year-olds.

Why do I have children do this?

- To listen and follow directions (language, thinking).
- To have fun together (social-emotional).

What do I need?

No supplies are needed.

What might I see children doing?

- Finding a friend.
- Giggling.
- Talking.
- Listening.
- Following directions.

What might I talk about with children?

1. What other parts of your bodies could you use?
2. What other games do you like to play?

FRIENDLY SWITCH
Indoor or Outdoor Large Muscle

What do I do?

Help each child choose a friend as a partner. Play a musical recording with a lively beat and tell the partners to hold hands and jump, march, hop, or shake to the music. Stop the music periodically, so the children can switch partners if they wish. Let the children make up different actions to perform to the music.

Why do I have children do this?

- To jump, march, hop, or shake (large muscle).
- To listen to music and your directions (language).

What do I need?

What might I see children doing?

- Choosing a partner.
- Hopping to music.
- Talking.
- Enjoying music.

1. Musical recording of lively music.
2. Record player or tape player.

What might I talk about with children?

1. What could you do while the music plays?
2. Who are some of your friends at home?

IT IS A FUNNY HOUSE
Outdoor Large Muscle, Learning Center (dramatic play)

What do I do?

Hang a clothesline between two trees, your building and a tree, or two poles. Put a large blanket over the clothesline and pull out the sides to form an upside down "V." Secure the sides with large, smooth stones. Then put out tea cups and plates on a tablecloth on the ground or a small table inside the house. Sit on the ground or on small chairs with the children to have a tea party. Bring out some dress-up clothes, so the children can dress up as Mommy, Daddy, or a guest. Bring out a doll carriage, wagon, dolls, or stuffed toys and let the children play in the house.

Why do I have children do this?

- To crawl in and out of the house and have fun (large muscle).
- To enjoy an outdoor tea party with friends (social-emotional).

What do I need?

1. Clothesline.
2. Blanket.
3. Large smooth stones.
4. Tea cups and plates.
5. Tablecloth.
6. Small table.
7. Small chairs.
8. Dress-up clothes.
9. Doll carriage.
10. Wagon.
11. Dolls or stuffed toys.

What might I see children doing?

- Helping put up the house.
- Crawling in and out of the house.
- Enjoying the tea party.

What might I talk about with children?

1. What could you do to keep the house from falling down?
2. What other kinds of houses could you make?

SCULPTURE A FRIEND
Indoor or Outdoor Large Muscle

What do I do?

This is a good activity to use after you work with clay in the art area. Show the children a statue or picture of a statue. Then have them choose a friend and pretend that their friend is clay. Let them mold their friend into a sculpture by moving body parts. You will need to talk about molding with the children. They can put their friend's arm up in the air, tilt their friend's head sideways, or bend their friend's leg. After the children mold for one minute, say "freeze" and let everyone admire the sculptures. Then the friends can switch and let the other child be the sculptor. You can choose a friend to form into a sculpture and then mold you.

Why do I have children do this?

• To choose body parts to mold (thinking).
• To stand in the position that a friend molds them (small and large muscle).

What do I need?

No supplies are needed.

What might I see children doing?

• Raising arm.
• Bending body.
• Tilting head.
• Laughing.

What might I talk about with children?

1. Where would you see a sculpture?
2. What can we use to make a sculpture?

"RING AROUND THE ROSIE"
Indoor or Outdoor Large Muscle, Learning Center (music)

What do I do?

Help the children hold hands and make a circle. (Make a circle from a long length of rope to help young children form a circle.) Sing "Ring around the Rosie." At the end of the last line, have the children fall down. Choose one child to stand in the center of the circle during each verse and sing his or her name. Give each child a chance to stand in the center of the circle. This helps children get to know one another's names.

"Ring around the Rosie"

Ring around the Rosie.
A pocket full of posies.
Ashes to ashes,
We all fall down.

Ring around the (name of child in center of circle).
Holding hands together.
Singing and laughing,
We all fall down.

Why do I have children do this?

- To sing together (language).
- To move in a circle and fall down (large muscle).

What do I need?

1. Long length of rope.
2. Words to song written on an index card.

What might I see children doing?

- Making a circle.
- Holding hands.
- Singing.
- Standing in the middle of the circle.

What might I talk about with children?

1. How could you make the game different?
2. What other games do you like to play?

FOLLOW YOUR FRIEND
Indoor or Outdoor Large Muscle

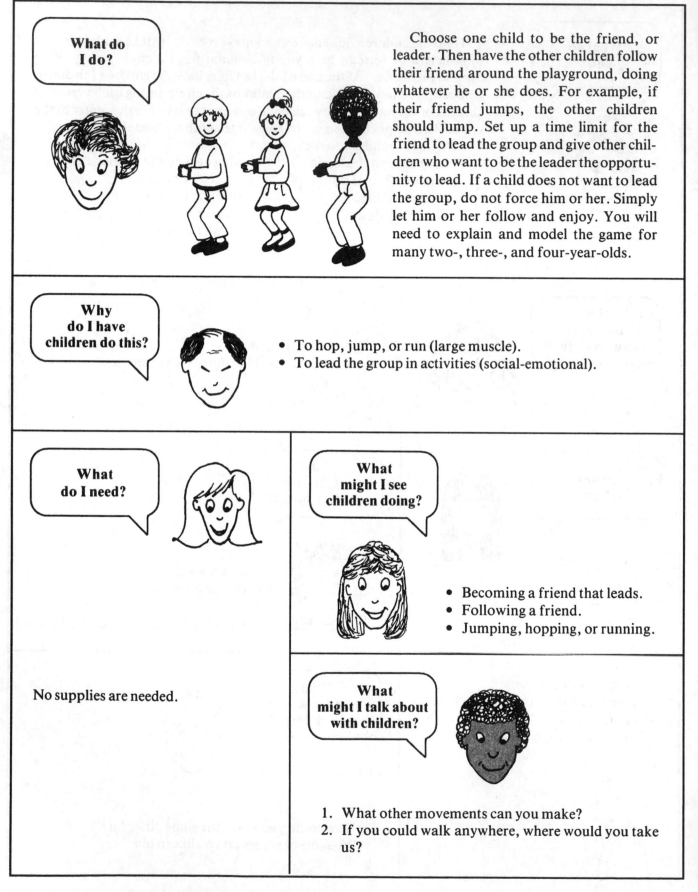

What do I do?

Choose one child to be the friend, or leader. Then have the other children follow their friend around the playground, doing whatever he or she does. For example, if their friend jumps, the other children should jump. Set up a time limit for the friend to lead the group and give other children who want to be the leader the opportunity to lead. If a child does not want to lead the group, do not force him or her. Simply let him or her follow and enjoy. You will need to explain and model the game for many two-, three-, and four-year-olds.

Why do I have children do this?

- To hop, jump, or run (large muscle).
- To lead the group in activities (social-emotional).

What do I need?

No supplies are needed.

What might I see children doing?

- Becoming a friend that leads.
- Following a friend.
- Jumping, hopping, or running.

What might I talk about with children?

1. What other movements can you make?
2. If you could walk anywhere, where would you take us?

LET'S TAKE A FRIENDLY WALK
Outdoor Large Muscle

What do I do?

Have the children choose a friend and take a walk with the children. As you take your walk, have the children look for different items. In the spring, help them look for buds on the trees, flowers blooming, and nests being built by the birds. In the summer, help them look for flowers, insects, and vegetables in gardens. In the fall, help them look for different-colored leaves and birds flying south. In winter, help them look for tracks in the snow, empty birds' nests, and trees without leaves. Make a set of binoculars for each child to use to look for items by taping two toilet paper rolls together and using a thick piece of yarn to make a neck strap. Teach children to be observant and to see their world. Walk your planned route ahead of time to locate items for the children to find.

Why do I have children do this?

- To walk outdoors (large muscle).
- To look for items, such as buds, birds, and insects (thinking).

What do I need?

1. Toilet paper rolls.
2. Tape.
3. Thick yarn.

What might I see children doing?

- Talking.
- Using binoculars.
- Looking for items, such as insects, birds, and buds.
- Walking together.

What might I talk about with children?

1. How do leaves get on the trees?
2. What can you grow from seeds?

FRIENDS LIKE TO DRAW OUTDOORS
Outdoor Large Muscle, Learning Center (art)

What do I do?

Take the children outdoors and let them choose a friend and find a special sidewalk square. If you are using a driveway or patio, you may need to use chalk to make squares for each set of friends. Give each pair of children colored chalk and let them draw pictures in their special sidewalk square. After they are finished drawing pictures, let them write their names in the corner or write their names for them. Talk about how artists sign their work. Show the children a painting or a picture of a painting that the artist has signed.

Why do I have children do this?

- To draw with chalk (small muscle).
- To draw with a friend (social-emotional).

What do I need?

1. Sidewalk, driveway, or patio.
2. Colored chalk.
3. Pictures with artists' signatures.

What might I see children doing?

- Choosing a friend to work with.
- Drawing with chalk.
- Signing their names.
- Talking.
- Looking at pictures.

What might I talk about with children?

1. How does the chalk sound when you use it on the sidewalk?
2. What is special about your picture?

MAKING A SNOW FRIEND
Outdoor Large Muscle

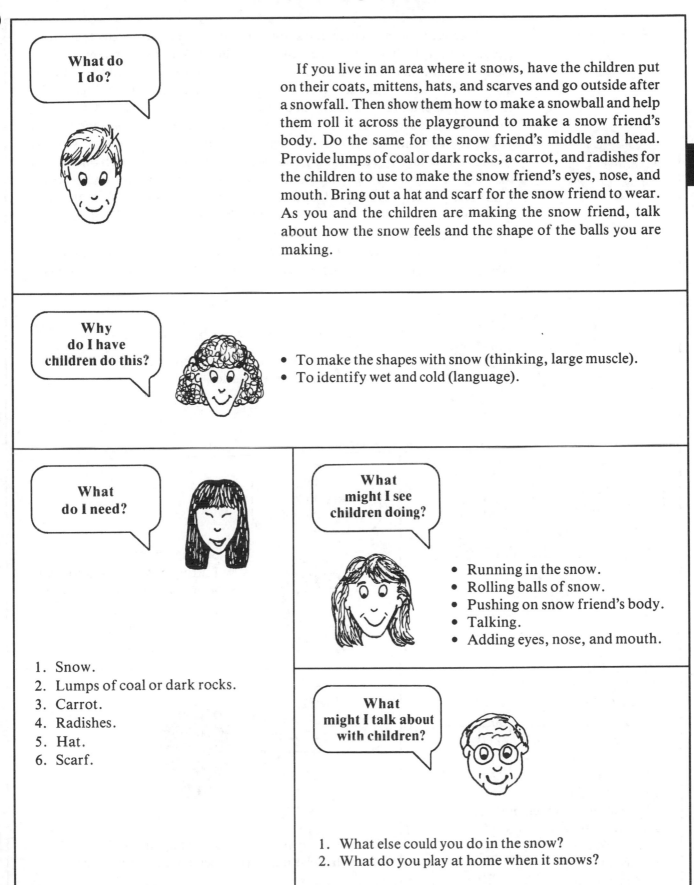

What do I do?

If you live in an area where it snows, have the children put on their coats, mittens, hats, and scarves and go outside after a snowfall. Then show them how to make a snowball and help them roll it across the playground to make a snow friend's body. Do the same for the snow friend's middle and head. Provide lumps of coal or dark rocks, a carrot, and radishes for the children to use to make the snow friend's eyes, nose, and mouth. Bring out a hat and scarf for the snow friend to wear. As you and the children are making the snow friend, talk about how the snow feels and the shape of the balls you are making.

Why do I have children do this?

- To make the shapes with snow (thinking, large muscle).
- To identify wet and cold (language).

What do I need?

1. Snow.
2. Lumps of coal or dark rocks.
3. Carrot.
4. Radishes.
5. Hat.
6. Scarf.

What might I see children doing?

- Running in the snow.
- Rolling balls of snow.
- Pushing on snow friend's body.
- Talking.
- Adding eyes, nose, and mouth.

What might I talk about with children?

1. What else could you do in the snow?
2. What do you play at home when it snows?

FRIENDS ENJOY CAMPING
Outdoor Large Muscle

What do I do?

This activity can last several days. Put up a tent or tepee and provide sleeping bags or blankets, backpacks, canteens, flashlights, empty sunscreen bottles, picnic basket with food, small grill, rocks, and wood for a pretend fire. Put out a few different items each day to make the activity different and exciting. Let the children pretend to be campers. You can make a tepee from eight 9-foot long tree limbs bound together at the top with rope or a piece of rawhide and fanned out at the bottom. Sew two queen-sized sheets together lengthwise. Lay the sheets on the floor and anchor a 7-foot piece of string with a pencil on one end to the center top of the sheets. Holding the string out straight, draw a half circle from one corner of the top edge to the other corner. Cut out this half circle. Hang the cut sheet around the tree limbs with the cut out half circle at the bottom. Safety pin the sides together, leaving an opening for the door. Let the children use markers to decorate the tepee with Native American symbols or pictures of the outdoors. Save the tepee supplies and use them for other units.

Why do I have children do this?

- To pretend to be campers (social-emotional).
- To set up camp (large muscle).

What do I need?

1. Tent.
2. Tree limbs.
3. Rope or rawhide.
4. Two queen-sized sheets.
5. Seven-foot piece of string.
6. Pencil.
7. Scissors.
8. Safety pins.
9. Markers.
10. Sleeping bags or blankets.
11. Backpacks.
12. Canteens.
13. Flashlights.
14. Empty sunscreen bottles.
15. Picnic basket with food.
16. Rocks.
17. Wood.

To make tepee

What might I see children doing?

- Setting up camp.
- Putting out picnic equipment.
- Pretending to cook on a grill.
- Putting on a backpack.
- Sleeping in tent or tepee.
- Enjoying camping.

What might I talk about with children?

1. Where have you camped with your family?
2. What else might you need on a camping trip?

BIBLIOGRAPHY

FRIENDS

[3]Alexander, M. 1989. *My Outrageous Friend Charlie*. New York, NY: Dial Books for Young Readers.
Jessie Mae admires her outrageous friend, Charlie, because he can do anything. However, when he gives her a Super Deluxe Triple Magic Kit for her birthday, she finds she can be outrageous, too.

Aliki. 1982. *We Are Best Friends*. New York, NY: Greenwillow Books.
When Robert's best friend, Peter, moves away, both are unhappy, but they learn they can make new friends and still remain best friends.

[3]Anglund, J.W. 1983. *A Friend Is Someone Who Likes You: Silver Anniversary Edition*. New York, NY: Harcourt Brace Jovanovich, Publishers.
This is an enchanting book for small children with easy-to-understand text and wonderful illustrations. It demonstrates some of the many happy surprises just waiting to be discovered in the world.

[3]Bassett, L. 1987. *Beany and Scamp*. New York, NY: The Putnam Publishing Group.
The story is about Beany Bear and his friend, Scamp Squirrel who search for Scamp's misplaced winter nut supply.

Baylor, B. 1992. *Guess Who My Favorite Person Is?* New York, NY: Macmillan Children's Book Group.
This book is about two friends and their game, tell-what-your-favorite-thing-is. The book offers a flowing text and lovely watercolor illustrations.

Carle, E. 1971. *Do You Want to Be My Friend?* New York, NY: HarperCollins Children's Books.
The only words in this book are "Do you want to be my friend?" A mouse is trying to find a friend. He asks many animals along the way until he finds another mouse.

Caseley, J. 1991. *Harry and Willy and Carrothead*. New York, NY: Greenwillow Books.
Harry was born without a left hand. He does everything other kids do and is very matter-of-fact. He knows how to be a good friend.

Cohn, J. 1987. *I Had a Friend Named Peter: Talking to Children About the Death of a Friend*. New York, NY: Morrow.
Betsy learns about the sudden death of her friend, Peter, and her parents help her cope with the news. In the introduction, a psychotherapist discusses guidelines on explaining death and funeral practices to children age five and up.

Cohen, M. 1967. *Will I Have a Friend?* New York, NY: Macmillan Children's Book Group.
Jim goes to a new center and asks his Daddy, "Will I have a friend?" Jim's experiences are described with warmth and the understanding of how a child feels.

Cohen, M. 1971. *Best Friends*. New York, NY: Macmillan Children's Book Group.
Jim experiences friendships at school. The author writes of Jim's experiences with empathy, simplicity, and warmth.

Cowen-Fletcher, J. 1994. *It Takes a Village*. New York, NY: Scholastic.
When Yemi's little brother wanders away at the market, she learns how important it is to belong to a close community, because the neighbors gather around to care for him. The story is based on an old African proverb.

[3]Dauer, R. 1977. *My Friend, Jasper Jones*. New York, NY: Parents Magazine Press.
A child has a make-believe friend who gets blamed for everything. However, the child must finally clean up after his friend.

[3]Delton, J. 1974. *Two Good Friends*. New York, NY: Crown Publishers, Inc.
This is a humorous book about the friendship between Duck and Bear.

[3]Dowling, P. 1990. *Meg and Jack's New Friends*. Boston, MA: Houghton Mifflin Company.
This books shows how children make friends in different ways by telling about Meg and Jack, who move to a new neighborhood.

Fleischman, S. 1988. *The Scarebird*. New York, NY: Greenwillow Books.
A lonely, old farmer realizes the value of human friendship when a young man comes to help him and his scarecrow with their farm.

Freeman, D. 1968. *Corduroy*. New York, NY: Viking Children's Books.
Corduroy is a teddy bear who needs a home. Lisa buys him, and they become best friends.

[1]Fujikawa, G. 1977. *Our Best Friends*. New York, NY: The Putnam Publishing Group.
A sturdy book that is good for toddlers. A little girl, her doll, and kitten wish for new friends and get their wish.

Grimm, J., and Grimm, W.K. 1988. *Snow White and Rose Red*. New York, NY: North-South Books.
A lonely widow and her two daughters lived in a lonely cottage. One day a knock on the door brought an unexpected new friend. Snow White and Rose Red become friends with an enchanted bear.

Hallinan, P.K. 1977. *That's What a Friend Is*. Chicago, IL: Children's Press.
Describes friendship in rhymed text with illustrations.

[2,3]Hasler, E. 1981. *Martin Is Our Friend*. Nashville, TN: Abingdon.
Martin is a child with a disability whose classmates make fun of him. However, Martin has a special friend. When he rescues her, the other children come around.

Heine, H. 1986. *Friends*. New York, NY: Macmillan Children's Book Group.
The book is illustrated with colorful watercolor paintings. It is a fun celebration of
    friendship between Charlie Rooster, Johnny Mouse, and Percy pig.

Henkes, H. 1986. *Jessica*. New York, NY: Greenwillow Books.
Ruthie had a special imaginary friend, Jessica, who did everything with her. Ruthie's
    parents hoped she'd find friends in kindergarten, and they get a surprise.

[2]Hoban, R. 1969. *Best Friends for Frances*. New York, NY: HarperCollins
    Children's Books.
Frances feels all sorts of emotions—jealousy, stubbornness, and insecurity—as she
    is confronted with predicaments of friendships.

Holabird, K. 1987. *Angelina and Alice*. New York, NY: Clarkson N. Potter Books.
Two mice, Angelina and Alice, are best friends, and they discover the importance of
    teamwork.

Hutchins, P. 1986. *The Doorbell Rang*. New York, NY: Greenwillow.
Ma has made a dozen delicious cookies. It should be enough for her two children
    but the doorbell rings and rings. Will she run out of cookies? The final visitor
    has the answer.

Keats, E.J. 1985. *Jennie's Hat*. New York, NY: HarperCollins Children's Books.
Jennie has a new spring hat. Her bird friends help her make it special by decorating
    it with flowers, leaves, and even a nest. Wonderful paintings and collages.

Keats, E.J. 1986. *Apt. 3*. New York, NY: Macmillan Children's Books Group.
Two brothers find a friend in Mr. Muntz, the blind man behind the door of Apt. 3.

[2]Kellogg, S. 1986. *Best Friends*. New York, NY: Dial Books for Young Readers.
Kathy feels lonely and betrayed when her best friend goes away for the summer and
    leaves her alone. Kathy, however, gets a new neighbor.

Komaiko, L. 2001. *Annie Bananie*. New York, NY: Harper Collins Publisher.
Annie Bananie is moving away—what will her friend do?

[2]Kraus, R. 1975. *Three Friends*. New York, NY: NAL/Dutton.
Milton (the panda), Herman (the octopus), and Leo (the tiger) become friends and
    go on several adventures. The illustrations tell the story of their adventures.

Lalli, J. 1996. *Make Someone Smile and 40 More Ways to Be a Peaceful Person*.
    Minneapolis, MN: Free Spirit Publishing Inc.
A photographic essay illustrating the many ways children (and big people) can
    become more peaceful persons.

Lamorisse, A. 1967. *Red Balloon*. New York, NY: Doubleday and Company, Inc.
A lyrical story about Pascal and his best friend, a balloon. Beautiful photos are used
    to illustrate this story. It is a classic tale of friendship.

Lionni, L. 1959. *Little Blue and Little Yellow*. New York, NY: Astor-Honor.
A story about the adventures of two dots, one blue and one yellow, who are best
    friends. The book also teaches about colors.

[3]Majewski, J. 1988. *A Friend for Oscar Mouse*. New York, NY: Dial Books for Young Readers.
Oscar Mouse loves to explore. He finds a hole in his house and crawls into the garden where he meets a new friend. They spend the day doing new things.

[2, 3]Mannheim, G. 1968. *The Two Friends*. New York, NY: Alfred A Knopf, Inc.
The multicultural story of two friends who meet at school.

McBratney, S. 2001. *I'll Always Be Your Friend*. New York, NY: Harper Collins Publisher.
As night descends, Baby shows his independence by saying, "I won't be your friend." Mama Fox says, "I'll always be your friend."

McKissack, P.C. 1989. *Nettie Jo's Friends*. New York, NY: Alfred A. Knopf, Inc.
Nettie Jo desperately needs a needle to sew a new dress for her doll, but the three animals she makes friends with during her search do not seem inclined to give her their assistance. However, Nettie Jo has a big surprise in the end.

[3]Millang, S., and Scelsa, G. 1983. *On the Move with Greg and Steve*. Los Angeles, CA: Creative Youngheart Records.
Music with a contemporary beat that invites children to move with rhythm and sing, feel, and grow.

[3]Nilsson, U. 1988. *Little Bunny and Her Friends*. San Francisco, CA: Chronicle Books.
This is a story of a group of friends who had difficulty choosing something they all liked to do until Little Bunny thought of a storybook.

Nickl, P. 1989. *The Story of the Kind Wolf*. New York, NY: North-South Books.
The animals in the forest find out about the kindness and wisdom of the wolf.

[3]Paige, R. 1988. *Some of My Best Friends Are Monsters*. New York, NY: Bradbury Press.
The narrator describes how helpful and friendly his best friends, monsters, can be.

Prelutsky, J. 1980. *Rainy, Rainy Saturday*. New York, NY: Greenwillow Books.
Collection of poetry for school-age children.

Reiser, L. 1993. *Margaret and Margarita/Margarita y Margaret*. New York, NY: Greenwillow.
Margaret and Margarita learn each other's language. With their help in this bilingual book, you may too.

[3]Rosner, R. 1987. *Arabba, Gah, Zee, Marissa and Me!* Morton Grove, IL: Albert Whitman and Company.
Two friends with vivid imaginations play at being spies, ballerinas, rock stars, pirates, and sisters, and have so much fun they never want to stop.

[3]Rylant, C. 1983. *Miss Maggie*. New York, NY: Dutton Children's Books.
The story of the friendship between a young boy and an elderly recluse.

Rylant, C. 1988. *All I See*. New York, NY: Orchard Books.
A beautifully illustrated book about Charlie and his painter friend.

[3]Schertle, A. 1988. *William and Grandpa*. New York, NY: Lothrop, Lee and Shepard Books.
William and Grandpa enjoy each other's friendship as they do the things Grandpa did when he was a little boy.

[3]Schick, E. 1969. *Making Friends*. The Macmillan Company.
Pictures tell the story of a boy's day with his mother and all the exciting friendships he makes.

[3]Schick, E. 1979. *Summer at the Sea*. New York, NY: Greenwillow Books.
A young girl remembers her summer at the sea and her special friend.

[3]Sharmat, M. 1975. *I'm Not Oscar's Friend Anymore*. New York, NY: E.P. Dutton, Inc.
Oscar's best friend tells all the reasons they aren't friends anymore. However, Oscar doesn't even remember they had a fight, and their relationship returns to normal.

[3]Spier, P. 1982. *Peter Spier's Rain*. New York, NY: Doubleday and Company, Inc.
Pictures tell the story of the activities a brother and sister do while it is raining.

Spier, P. 1988. *People*. Garden City, NY: Doubleday and Company, Inc.
This book is a wonderful introduction to the faces, homes, and customs of the people of the world. It also introduces the global village.

Steptoe, J. 1969. *Stevie*. New York, NY: HarperCollins Children's Books.
Robert's mother is going to care for Stevie during the week. Robert and Stevie learn how to be friends, as Robert overcomes his feelings of jealousy and rejection.

Tharlet, E. 1989. *Little Pig, Big Trouble*. Saxonville, MA: Picture Book Studio Ltd.
Little Pierre and Henri the pig are friends who enjoy each other's company and do everything together. However, Henri has a way of always getting into trouble.

Udry, J.M. 1961. *Let's Be Enemies*. New York, NY: HarperCollins Children's Books.
John and James are tiring of each other, and John is going to tell James that he is angry and not going to play anymore. However, everything works out fine.

Viorst, J. 1974. *Rosie and Michael*. New York, NY: Macmillan Children's Group Books.
Rosie and Michael play tricks on one another, but they are still friends.

Wahl, J. 1987. *Humphrey's Bear*. New York, NY: Henry Holt and Company.
Humphrey has wonderful adventures with his toy bear after they go to bed at night, just as his father did before him.

Weiss, N. 1983. *Maude and Sally*. New York, NY: Greenwillow Books.
Maude and Sally are best friends. However, one summer Sally goes to camp. Maude finds she can be best friends with Emmylou also. Later the girls figure out they can all be best friends.

Wells, R. 2000. *Timothy Goes To School*. New York, NY: Viking Books.
Timothy is very excited about starting school, but gets very discouraged and frustrated by Claude. He feels down until he meets a new friend named Violet.

Wilhelm, H. 1989. *I'll Always Love You*. New York, NY: Crown Publishers, Inc.
A boy and dog had always been together. Then, suddenly, the dog was old. A child's love for his aging and dying dog is movingly told in this tender and comforting yet realistic story.

Winthrop, E. 1977. *That's Mine*. New York, NY: Holiday.
Two friends quarrel over a block and learn the necessity of sharing.

[3]Wirth, B. 1983. *Margie and Me*. New York, NY: Four Winds Press.
The story is about a young girl's pet, Margie. The little girl is telling of her love for her pet and how to care for it.

Wittman, S. 1985. *Special Trade*. New York, NY: HarperCollins Children's Books.
Tells about a friendship between a little girl and an older neighbor.

[3]Zolotow, C. 1966. *If It Weren't for You*. New York, NY: HarperCollins Children's Books.
Brothers can be best friends, too.

Zolotow, C. 1968. *My Friend John*. New York, NY: HarperCollins Children's Books
A wonderful little book about John and his best friend. Even though John and his friend like different things, and do some things differently, they are best friends.

[1]Zolotow, C. 1972. *Hold My Hand*. New York, NY: HarperCollins Children's Books.
Two friends explore on a snowy day and find holding hands helps keep them warm.

[3]Zolotow, C. 1981. *The New Friend*. New York, NY: HarperCollins Children's Books.
A little girl speaks of losing a friend. The story deals with how the hurt and disappointment of a lost friend can be overcome.

[2,3]Zolotow, C. 1982. *The White Marble*. New York, NY: HarperCollins Children's Books.
A boy and girl build a special friendship. They find beauty and wonder in the park on a hot night.

Zolotow, C. 1984. *I Know a Lady*. New York, NY: Greenwillow Books.
Sally loves a kind old lady who lives in her neighborhood. This book shows best friends can be any age.

We have marked these books if we think they are definitely more applicable to one age. Many can be used by all ages with adaptations by the teacher.

[1]Books for one-year-olds, two-year-olds, and three-year-olds.

[2]Books for five-year-olds.

[3]This book is no longer in print. However, you may be able to find it at your local library.

Unit 3

_____ME, I'M SPECIAL_____

CONTENTS

ME, I'M SPECIAL

"Me, I'm Special" includes activities that help young children develop self-esteem. The development of self-esteem is important, because it defines how children see themselves and how they think other people see them–physically, intellectually, socially, and emotionally.

You play an important part in building children's self-esteem, or feelings of "Me, I'm Special," when you care for children, accept them as they are, and make them feel warm, comfortable, and secure. Planning child-oriented activities helps children realize that:

- Their bodies can move and perform in many different ways.
- No one else is exactly like them.
- They look different than anyone else unless they have an identical twin.
- They each have special feelings of happiness, sadness, anger, tiredness, and excitement that are OK.

KNOTS ON A COUNTING ROPE
Group

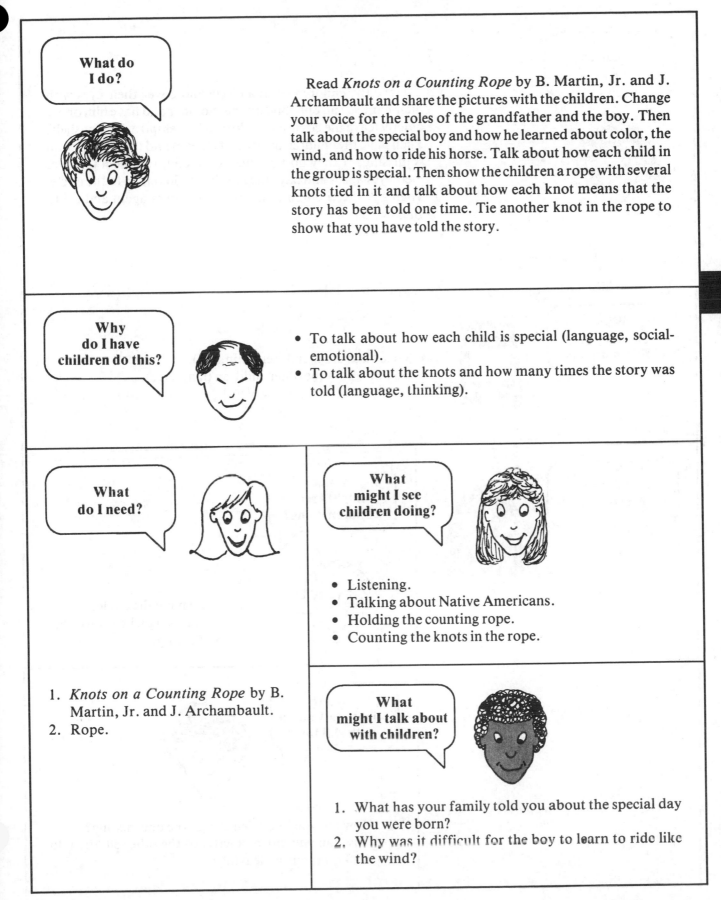

What do I do?

Read *Knots on a Counting Rope* by B. Martin, Jr. and J. Archambault and share the pictures with the children. Change your voice for the roles of the grandfather and the boy. Then talk about the special boy and how he learned about color, the wind, and how to ride his horse. Talk about how each child in the group is special. Then show the children a rope with several knots tied in it and talk about how each knot means that the story has been told one time. Tie another knot in the rope to show that you have told the story.

Why do I have children do this?

- To talk about how each child is special (language, social-emotional).
- To talk about the knots and how many times the story was told (language, thinking).

What do I need?

1. *Knots on a Counting Rope* by B. Martin, Jr. and J. Archambault.
2. Rope.

What might I see children doing?

- Listening.
- Talking about Native Americans.
- Holding the counting rope.
- Counting the knots in the rope.

What might I talk about with children?

1. What has your family told you about the special day you were born?
2. Why was it difficult for the boy to learn to ride like the wind?

WHO IS MISSING?
Group

What do I do?

Have the children sit in a circle and cover their eyes with their hands. Tap one child on the shoulder and have him or her quietly leave the circle and hide nearby behind a door or shelf. Then have the children uncover their eyes and try to guess who is missing. If they do not guess correctly, tell them to cover their eyes again and have the missing child return to the circle. Then ask the children to uncover their eyes again and try to guess who came back.

Why do I have children do this?

- To look at other children (thinking).
- To talk about the other children (language).

What do I need?

No supplies are needed.

What might I see children doing?

- Leaving the circle.
- Guessing who is missing.
- Talking.

What might I talk about with children?

1. How did you know Sarah was the one missing?
2. How can you move quietly, so the other children do not know you are leaving?

HERE ARE MY HANDS
Group

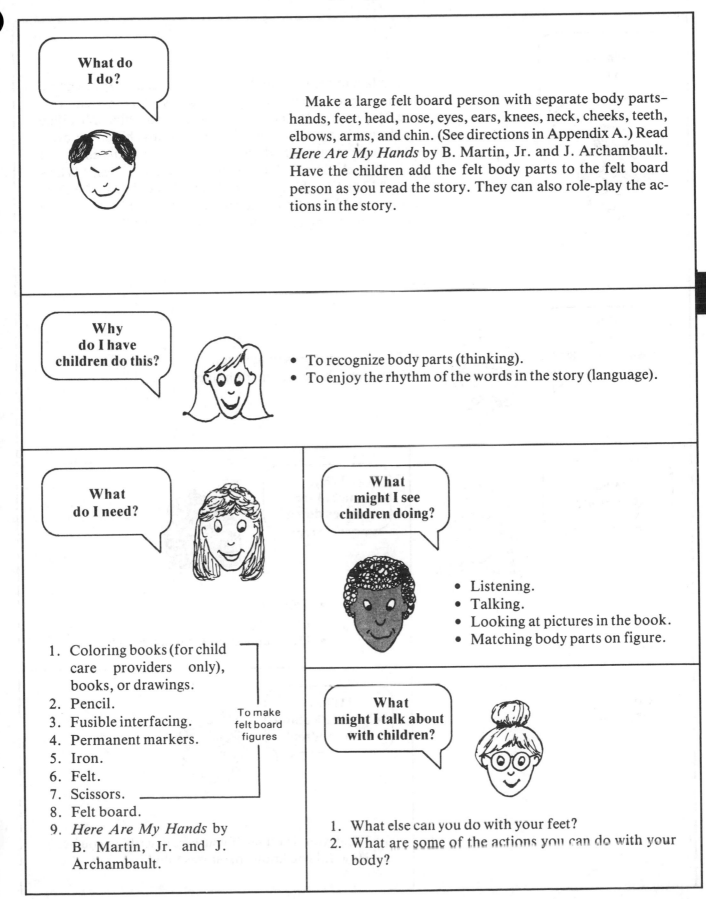

What do I do?

Make a large felt board person with separate body parts–hands, feet, head, nose, eyes, ears, knees, neck, cheeks, teeth, elbows, arms, and chin. (See directions in Appendix A.) Read *Here Are My Hands* by B. Martin, Jr. and J. Archambault. Have the children add the felt body parts to the felt board person as you read the story. They can also role-play the actions in the story.

Why do I have children do this?

- To recognize body parts (thinking).
- To enjoy the rhythm of the words in the story (language).

What do I need?

1. Coloring books (for child care providers only), books, or drawings.
2. Pencil.
3. Fusible interfacing.
4. Permanent markers.
5. Iron.
6. Felt.
7. Scissors.

To make felt board figures

8. Felt board.
9. *Here Are My Hands* by B. Martin, Jr. and J. Archambault.

What might I see children doing?

- Listening.
- Talking.
- Looking at pictures in the book.
- Matching body parts on figure.

What might I talk about with children?

1. What else can you do with your feet?
2. What are some of the actions you can do with your body?

KNOCK, KNOCK
Group

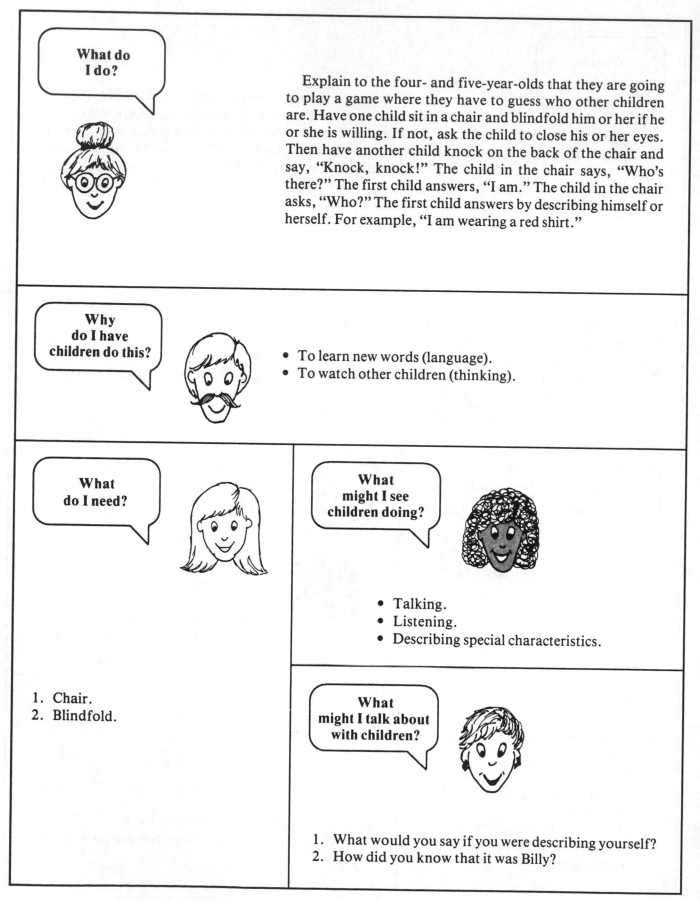

What do I do?

Explain to the four- and five-year-olds that they are going to play a game where they have to guess who other children are. Have one child sit in a chair and blindfold him or her if he or she is willing. If not, ask the child to close his or her eyes. Then have another child knock on the back of the chair and say, "Knock, knock!" The child in the chair says, "Who's there?" The first child answers, "I am." The child in the chair asks, "Who?" The first child answers by describing himself or herself. For example, "I am wearing a red shirt."

Why do I have children do this?

- To learn new words (language).
- To watch other children (thinking).

What do I need?

1. Chair.
2. Blindfold.

What might I see children doing?

- Talking.
- Listening.
- Describing special characteristics.

What might I talk about with children?

1. What would you say if you were describing yourself?
2. How did you know that it was Billy?

A SPECIAL BOX
Group

What do I do?

Make a Special Box by decorating a box with child-oriented gift wrap and gluing or taping a mirror in the bottom of the box. Ask four- and five-year-old children "Who do you think is the most special person in the world?" Tell them that you have a special box and when they look inside they will see who the most special person is. Let each child come up and look in the box. Then whisper to each child to keep the secret until everyone has looked. After all the children have had a chance to look, talk about what each child thinks is special about himself or herself. Write all the special traits on a large sheet of paper. As an art activity, have each child draw who he or she saw.

Why do I have children do this?

- To talk about themselves (language).
- To have fun keeping a secret (social-emotional).

What do I need?

1. Box.
2. Child-oriented gift wrap.
3. Mirror.
4. Glue or tape.
5. Large sheet of paper.
6. Marker.

What might I see children doing?

- Looking in the secret box.
- Giggling.
- Drawing a self-portrait.
- Having fun.

What might I talk about with children?

1. What is special about the person you saw in the box?
2. Who else could have been in this box?

I LOVE MY MOTHER
Group

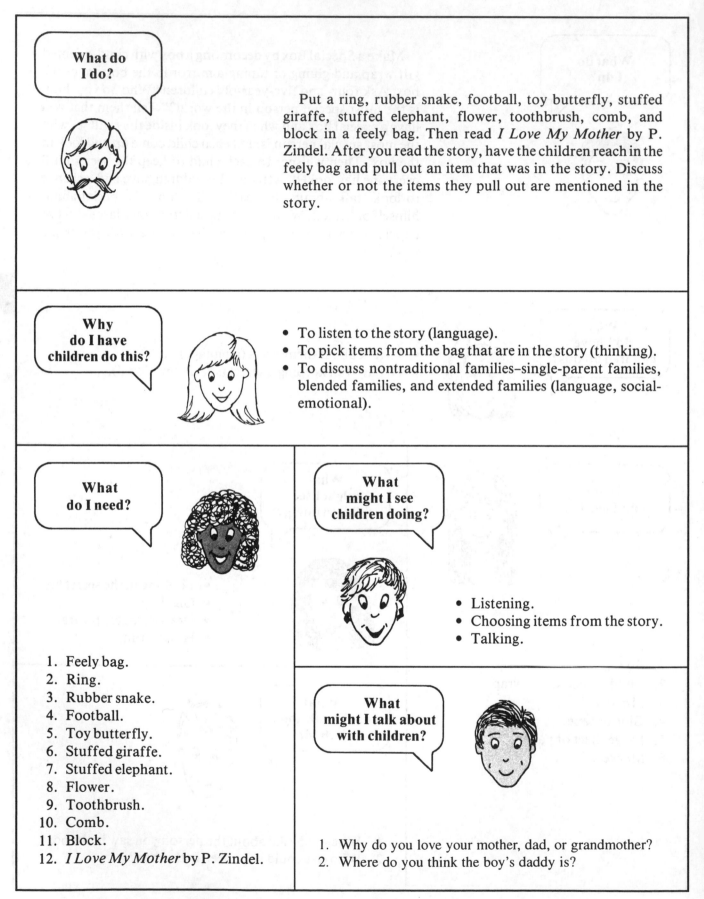

What do I do?

Put a ring, rubber snake, football, toy butterfly, stuffed giraffe, stuffed elephant, flower, toothbrush, comb, and block in a feely bag. Then read *I Love My Mother* by P. Zindel. After you read the story, have the children reach in the feely bag and pull out an item that was in the story. Discuss whether or not the items they pull out are mentioned in the story.

Why do I have children do this?

- To listen to the story (language).
- To pick items from the bag that are in the story (thinking).
- To discuss nontraditional families–single-parent families, blended families, and extended families (language, social-emotional).

What do I need?

1. Feely bag.
2. Ring.
3. Rubber snake.
4. Football.
5. Toy butterfly.
6. Stuffed giraffe.
7. Stuffed elephant.
8. Flower.
9. Toothbrush.
10. Comb.
11. Block.
12. *I Love My Mother* by P. Zindel.

What might I see children doing?

- Listening.
- Choosing items from the story.
- Talking.

What might I talk about with children?

1. Why do you love your mother, dad, or grandmother?
2. Where do you think the boy's daddy is?

PLAY WITH ME
Group

What do I do?

Read *Play with Me* by M. Ets and share the pictures with the children. Use a doll that looks like the little girl in the book to introduce the story. Discuss the little girl, why she wanted to play, and why the animals ran away.

Why do I have children do this?

• To understand that animals can be frightened by people (thinking).
• To share stories (social-emotional).

What do I need?

1. *Play with Me* by M. Ets.
2. Doll.

What might I see children doing?

• Listening.
• Looking at pictures.
• Sharing ideas.

What might I talk about with children?

1. What animals have you seen in the fields or woods?
2. Which animals would you choose to play with?

THIS IS WHAT I LIKE TO DO
Group

What do I do?

Give each four- or five-year-old child a large sheet of paper, an old magazine, and a pair of scissors. Then have the children cut out pictures that show what they like to do and glue the pictures to their papers. When the children are finished, have them tell the others about the pictures they selected.

Why do I have children do this?

- To share what they like (social-emotional, language).
- To cut out pictures (small muscles).

What do I need?

1. Large sheets of paper.
2. Old magazines.
3. Scissors.
4. Glue.

What might I see children doing?

- Cutting.
- Gluing.
- Talking about what they like to do.

What might I talk about with children?

1. What can you tell me about your picture?
2. What can I write about this picture?

BACKPACK SURPRISE
Group

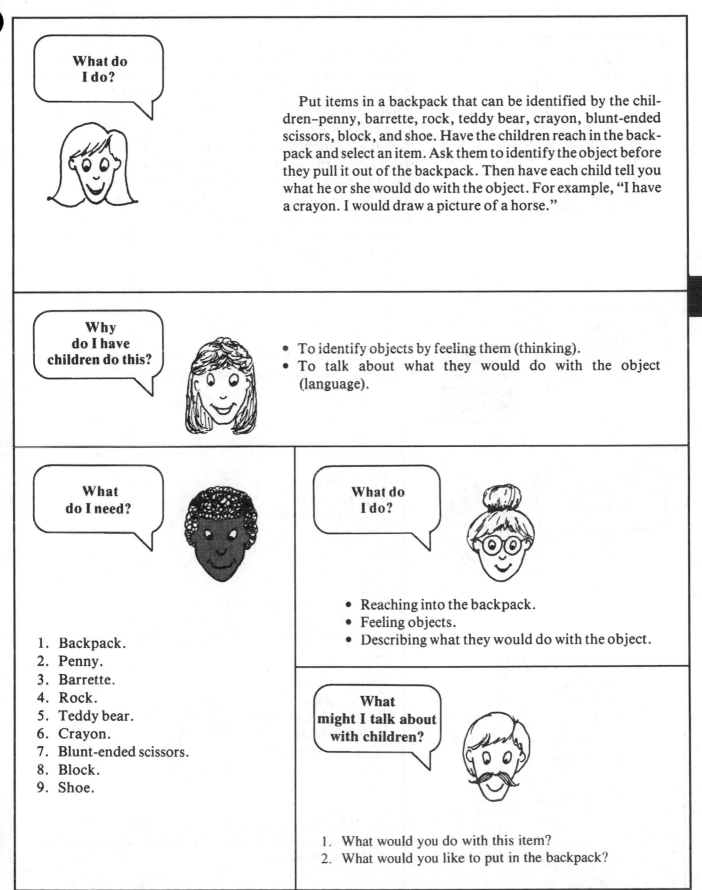

What do I do?

Put items in a backpack that can be identified by the children–penny, barrette, rock, teddy bear, crayon, blunt-ended scissors, block, and shoe. Have the children reach in the backpack and select an item. Ask them to identify the object before they pull it out of the backpack. Then have each child tell you what he or she would do with the object. For example, "I have a crayon. I would draw a picture of a horse."

Why do I have children do this?

- To identify objects by feeling them (thinking).
- To talk about what they would do with the object (language).

What do I need?

1. Backpack.
2. Penny.
3. Barrette.
4. Rock.
5. Teddy bear.
6. Crayon.
7. Blunt-ended scissors.
8. Block.
9. Shoe.

What do I do?

- Reaching into the backpack.
- Feeling objects.
- Describing what they would do with the object.

What might I talk about with children?

1. What would you do with this item?
2. What would you like to put in the backpack?

I CAN MOVE MY SHADOW
Group

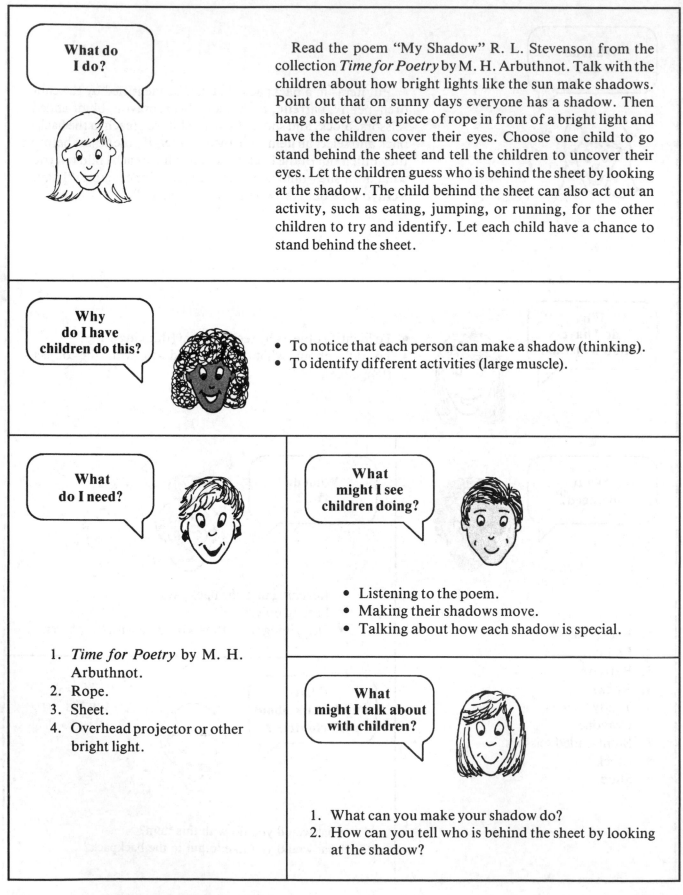

What do I do?

Read the poem "My Shadow" R. L. Stevenson from the collection *Time for Poetry* by M. H. Arbuthnot. Talk with the children about how bright lights like the sun make shadows. Point out that on sunny days everyone has a shadow. Then hang a sheet over a piece of rope in front of a bright light and have the children cover their eyes. Choose one child to go stand behind the sheet and tell the children to uncover their eyes. Let the children guess who is behind the sheet by looking at the shadow. The child behind the sheet can also act out an activity, such as eating, jumping, or running, for the other children to try and identify. Let each child have a chance to stand behind the sheet.

Why do I have children do this?

- To notice that each person can make a shadow (thinking).
- To identify different activities (large muscle).

What do I need?

1. *Time for Poetry* by M. H. Arbuthnot.
2. Rope.
3. Sheet.
4. Overhead projector or other bright light.

What might I see children doing?

- Listening to the poem.
- Making their shadows move.
- Talking about how each shadow is special.

What might I talk about with children?

1. What can you make your shadow do?
2. How can you tell who is behind the sheet by looking at the shadow?

JUST LIKE DADDY
Group, Learning Center (library)

What do I do?

Make felt board figures of a little bear, daddy bear, mommy bear, coat, bowl of cereal, boots, and fishing rod. (See direction in Appendix A.) Read *Just Like Daddy* by F. Asch to the children, while placing the figures on the felt board. Then discuss with the children what they do that their daddies or male role-models do. Place the book, felt board, and felt board figures in the library area, so the children can tell each other the story.

Why do I have children do this?

- To listen to the story (language).
- To discuss what they do that their daddies do (language, social-emotional).

What do I need?

What might I see children doing?

- Listening.
- Placing figures on the felt board.

1. Coloring books (for child care providers only), books, or drawings.
2. Pencil.
3. Fusible interfacing.
4. Permanent markers.
5. Iron.
6. Felt.
7. Scissors.
8. Felt board.
9. *Just Like Daddy* by F. Asch.

To make felt board figures

What might I talk about with children?

1. What can you do that your daddy does?
2. Where does your family go to have fun?

MATCH ME IN THE MORNING
Group, Learning Center (library, manipulatives)

What do I do?

Collect items that family members use to get ready in the morning–toothbrush, soap, comb, brush, and bladeless razor. Trace around each item on a piece of poster board. Put the items in a box. Color in the outlines of the items with markers and cover the poster board with self-adhesive plastic. Have the children match the objects with the pictures. Then let the children act out how each object is used.

Why do I have children do this?

• To match items with pictures (thinking).
• To talk about what family members do to get ready in the morning (language).

What do I need?

1. Toothbrush.
2. Soap.
3. Comb.
4. Brush.
5. Bladeless razor.
6. Poster board.
7. Pencil.
8. Markers.
9. Self-adhesive plastic.
10. Box.

What might I see children doing?

• Matching objects with pictures.
• Talking about what they do to get ready in the morning.
• Acting out how objects are used.

What might I talk about with children?

1. What do you do when you get up in the morning?
2. What other objects do you use to get ready in the morning?

THE SNOWY DAY
Group

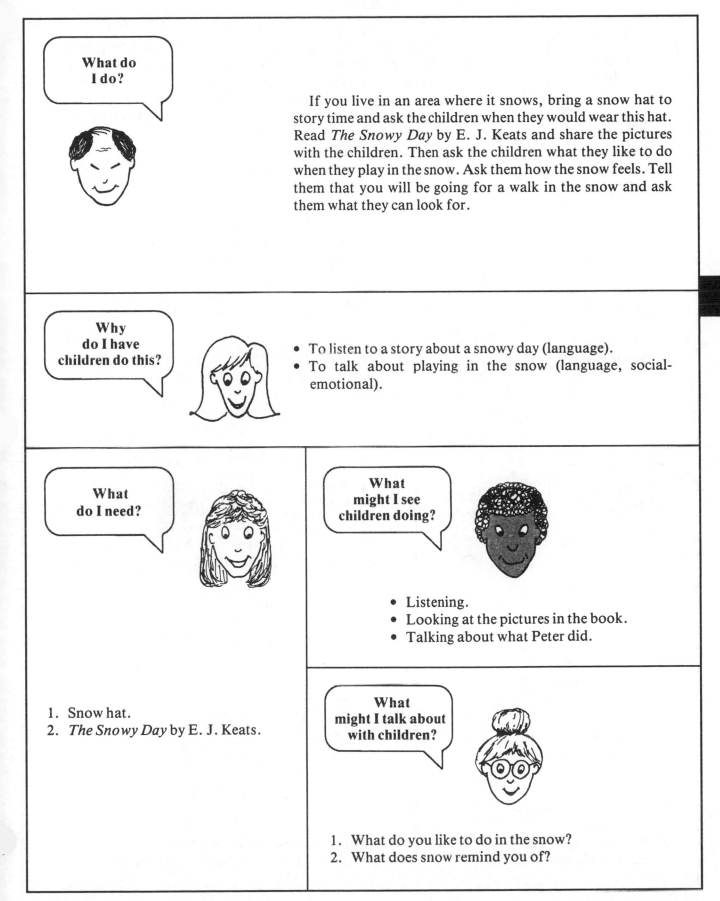

What do I do?

If you live in an area where it snows, bring a snow hat to story time and ask the children when they would wear this hat. Read *The Snowy Day* by E. J. Keats and share the pictures with the children. Then ask the children what they like to do when they play in the snow. Ask them how the snow feels. Tell them that you will be going for a walk in the snow and ask them what they can look for.

Why do I have children do this?

- To listen to a story about a snowy day (language).
- To talk about playing in the snow (language, social-emotional).

What do I need?

1. Snow hat.
2. *The Snowy Day* by E. J. Keats.

What might I see children doing?

- Listening.
- Looking at the pictures in the book.
- Talking about what Peter did.

What might I talk about with children?

1. What do you like to do in the snow?
2. What does snow remind you of?

"OH, I DROPPED MY NOSE"
Group, Learning Center (music)

What do I do?

Make felt board figures of a child, a nose on a face, a belly button on a tummy, eyes on a face, and a smile on a face. (See directions in Appendix.) Using the felt board, place the body part figures on the child figure as you teach the children the following chant. Let the children repeat the chant using the felt board.

"Oh, I Dropped My Nose"
1. Pick it up, pick it up.
   Oh, I dropped my nose.
   Pick it up, pick it up.
   And put it back on my face (sniff and smell).
2. Belly button, tummy (pat).
3. Eyes to face (wink and blink).
4. Smile (sing sadly), put on face (smile).

Why do I have children do this?

- To recognize body parts (thinking).
- To enjoy chanting (social-emotional).

What do I need?

1. Coloring books (for child care providers only), books, or drawings.
2. Pencil.
3. Fusible interfacing.
4. Permanent markers.
5. Iron.
6. Felt.
7. Scissors.
8. Felt board.
9. Words to chant written on an index card.

To make felt board figures

What might I see children doing?

- Chanting.
- Imitating motions in chant.
- Placing body parts on felt board.

What might I talk about with children?

1. What else could you chant about?
2. What body part is missing from the felt figure?

CLYDE MONSTER
Group, Learning Center (library)

What do I do?

Read *Clyde Monster* by R. Crowe and share the pictures with the children. Use a monster puppet to introduce the story. Talk about monsters hiding in the dark and emphasize that they are just pretend. Let the children take turns holding the monster puppet. Be aware that some young children are afraid of puppets.

Why do I have children do this?

- To listen to a story (language).
- To talk about their fears (language, social-emotional).

What do I need?

1. *Clyde Monster* by R. Crowe.
2. Monster puppet.

What might I see children doing?

- Listening.
- Sharing their fears.
- Enjoy holding the monster puppet.

What might I talk about with children?

1. Where did Clyde and his parents look for the people?
2. What makes you feel frightened?

"GOOD MORNING"
Group

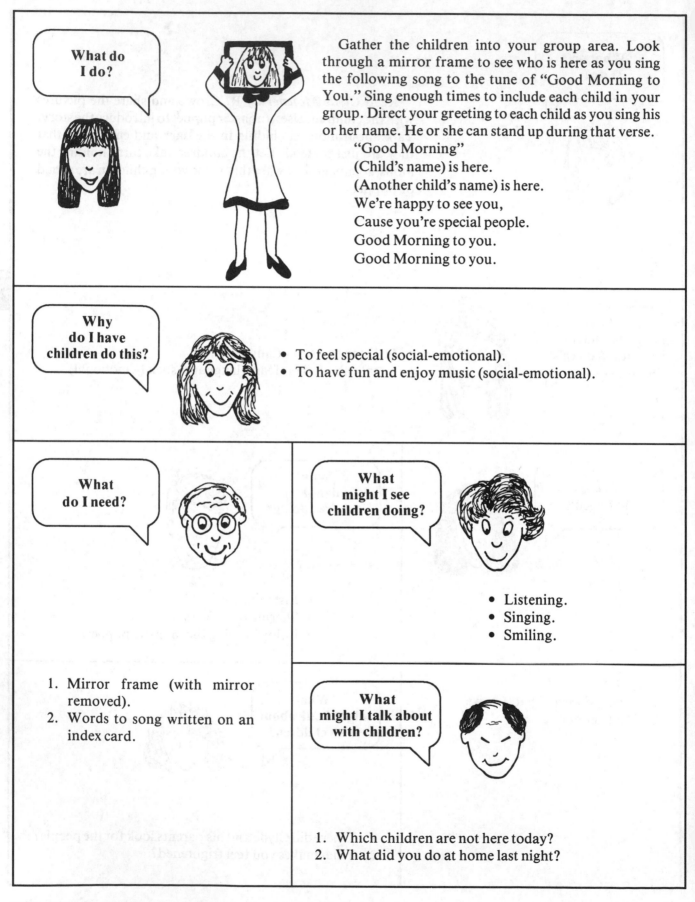

What do I do?

Gather the children into your group area. Look through a mirror frame to see who is here as you sing the following song to the tune of "Good Morning to You." Sing enough times to include each child in your group. Direct your greeting to each child as you sing his or her name. He or she can stand up during that verse.

"Good Morning"
(Child's name) is here.
(Another child's name) is here.
We're happy to see you,
Cause you're special people.
Good Morning to you.
Good Morning to you.

Why do I have children do this?

• To feel special (social-emotional).
• To have fun and enjoy music (social-emotional).

What do I need?

What might I see children doing?

• Listening.
• Singing.
• Smiling.

1. Mirror frame (with mirror removed).
2. Words to song written on an index card.

What might I talk about with children?

1. Which children are not here today?
2. What did you do at home last night?

SIMON SAYS
Group

What do I do?

Play Simon Says with the children. Tell the children to pretend that you are Simon, and they should follow your directions. For example, "Simon says touch your toes." Challenge the older children, by making the directions harder. For example, "Simon says touch your elbow." Tell the older children that they should follow the directions only if you say "Simon says." If they do not follow your directions, have them move to the center of the circle for two turns. Let the children take turns being Simon.

Why do I have children do this?

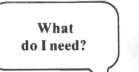

- To join with others in game playing (social-emotional).
- To follow one-step directions (thinking).

What do I need?

No supplies are needed.

What might I see children doing?

- Pointing to body parts.
- Listening.
- Laughing.
- Talking.

What might I talk about with children?

1. What else could Simon have you do?
2. How can you point to the back of your foot?

MY HANDS
Learning Center (art)

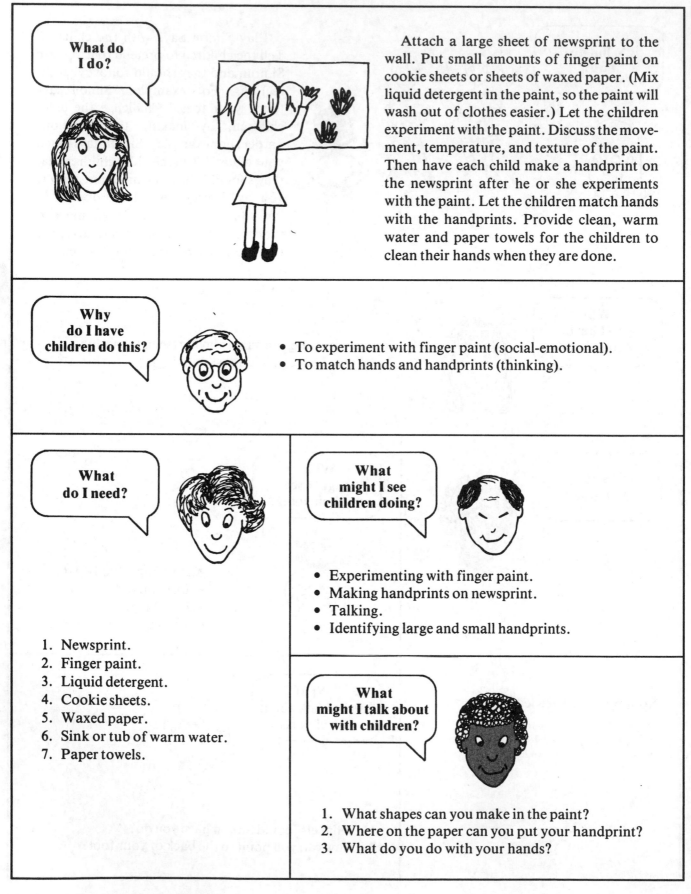

What do I do?

Attach a large sheet of newsprint to the wall. Put small amounts of finger paint on cookie sheets or sheets of waxed paper. (Mix liquid detergent in the paint, so the paint will wash out of clothes easier.) Let the children experiment with the paint. Discuss the movement, temperature, and texture of the paint. Then have each child make a handprint on the newsprint after he or she experiments with the paint. Let the children match hands with the handprints. Provide clean, warm water and paper towels for the children to clean their hands when they are done.

Why do I have children do this?

- To experiment with finger paint (social-emotional).
- To match hands and handprints (thinking).

What do I need?

1. Newsprint.
2. Finger paint.
3. Liquid detergent.
4. Cookie sheets.
5. Waxed paper.
6. Sink or tub of warm water.
7. Paper towels.

What might I see children doing?

- Experimenting with finger paint.
- Making handprints on newsprint.
- Talking.
- Identifying large and small handprints.

What might I talk about with children?

1. What shapes can you make in the paint?
2. Where on the paper can you put your handprint?
3. What do you do with your hands?

MY BODY
Learning Center (art)

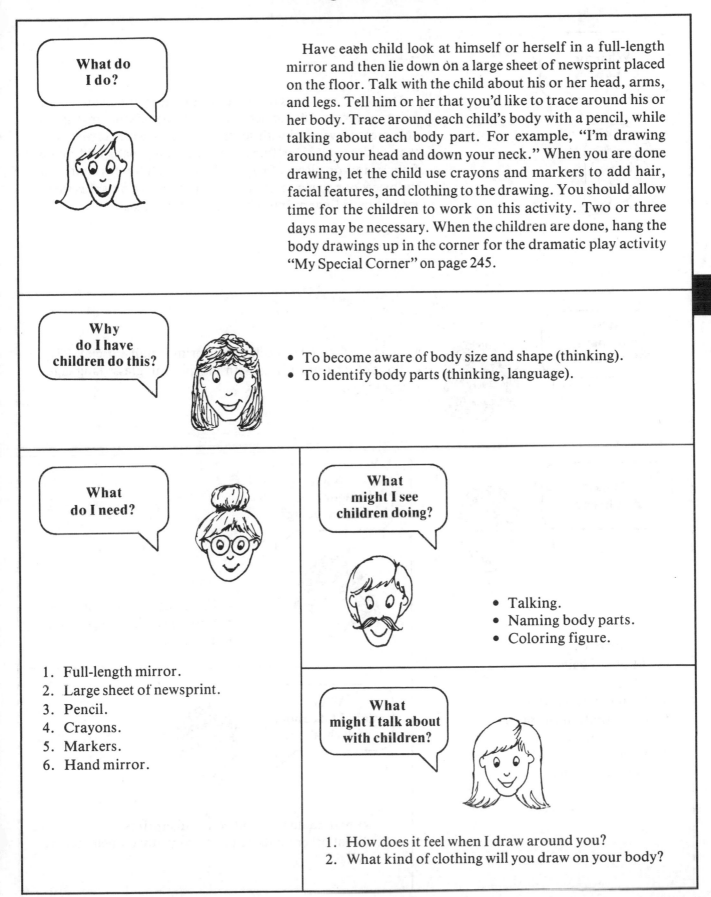

What do I do?

Have each child look at himself or herself in a full-length mirror and then lie down on a large sheet of newsprint placed on the floor. Talk with the child about his or her head, arms, and legs. Tell him or her that you'd like to trace around his or her body. Trace around each child's body with a pencil, while talking about each body part. For example, "I'm drawing around your head and down your neck." When you are done drawing, let the child use crayons and markers to add hair, facial features, and clothing to the drawing. You should allow time for the children to work on this activity. Two or three days may be necessary. When the children are done, hang the body drawings up in the corner for the dramatic play activity "My Special Corner" on page 245.

Why do I have children do this?

- To become aware of body size and shape (thinking).
- To identify body parts (thinking, language).

What do I need?

1. Full-length mirror.
2. Large sheet of newsprint.
3. Pencil.
4. Crayons.
5. Markers.
6. Hand mirror.

What might I see children doing?

- Talking.
- Naming body parts.
- Coloring figure.

What might I talk about with children?

1. How does it feel when I draw around you?
2. What kind of clothing will you draw on your body?

FINGERPRINTS
Learning Center (art)

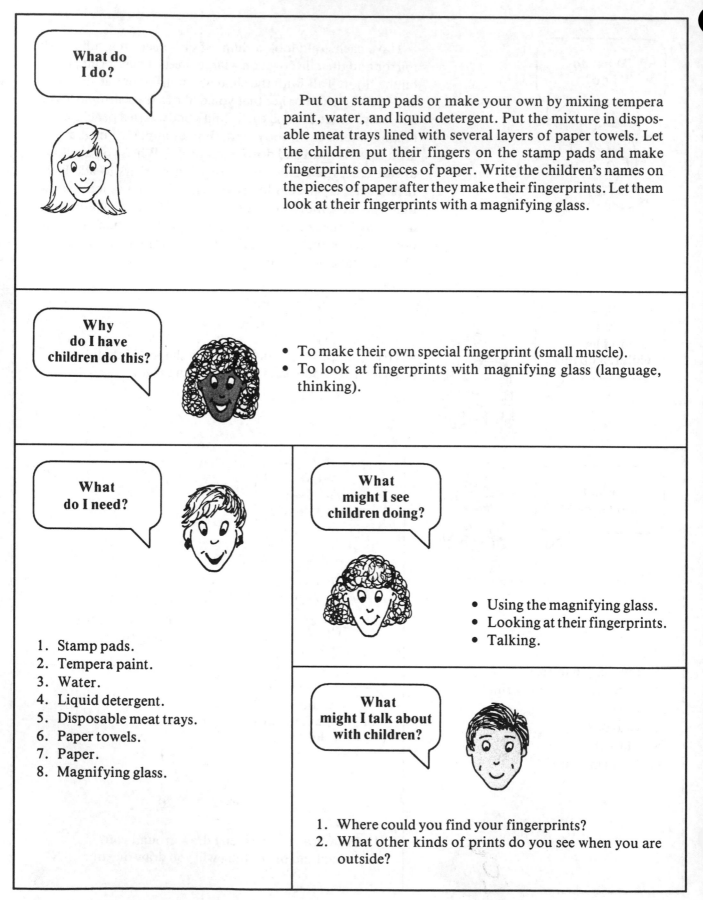

What do I do?

Put out stamp pads or make your own by mixing tempera paint, water, and liquid detergent. Put the mixture in disposable meat trays lined with several layers of paper towels. Let the children put their fingers on the stamp pads and make fingerprints on pieces of paper. Write the children's names on the pieces of paper after they make their fingerprints. Let them look at their fingerprints with a magnifying glass.

Why do I have children do this?

- To make their own special fingerprint (small muscle).
- To look at fingerprints with magnifying glass (language, thinking).

What do I need?

1. Stamp pads.
2. Tempera paint.
3. Water.
4. Liquid detergent.
5. Disposable meat trays.
6. Paper towels.
7. Paper.
8. Magnifying glass.

What might I see children doing?

- Using the magnifying glass.
- Looking at their fingerprints.
- Talking.

What might I talk about with children?

1. Where could you find your fingerprints?
2. What other kinds of prints do you see when you are outside?

ME PUPPETS
Learning Center (art)

What do I do?

Cut out two puppet-shaped felt pieces for each child. Glue or machine stitch two pieces together to make puppets. Be sure to leave the bottom open, so the children can put their hands inside. Put out yarn, felt, pom-poms, fabric, glue, and scissors and let the children decorate their own puppets. (You can make your own puppet too.) Then give the children the opportunity to role-play with the puppets.

Why do I have children do this?

- To explore with different art media (small muscle).
- To use the puppets to role-play (language, thinking).

What do I need?

1. Scissors.
2. Felt.
3. Glue.
4. Sewing machine.
5. Yarn.
6. Felt.
7. Pom-poms.
8. Fabric.

What might I see children doing?

- Cutting.
- Gluing.
- Decorating.
- Role-playing with puppets.
- Talking.

What might I talk about with children?

1. What can the puppet tell me about your family?
2. Where could you keep your puppet?

MY SPECIAL CAR
Learning Center (art), Indoor or Outdoor Large Muscle

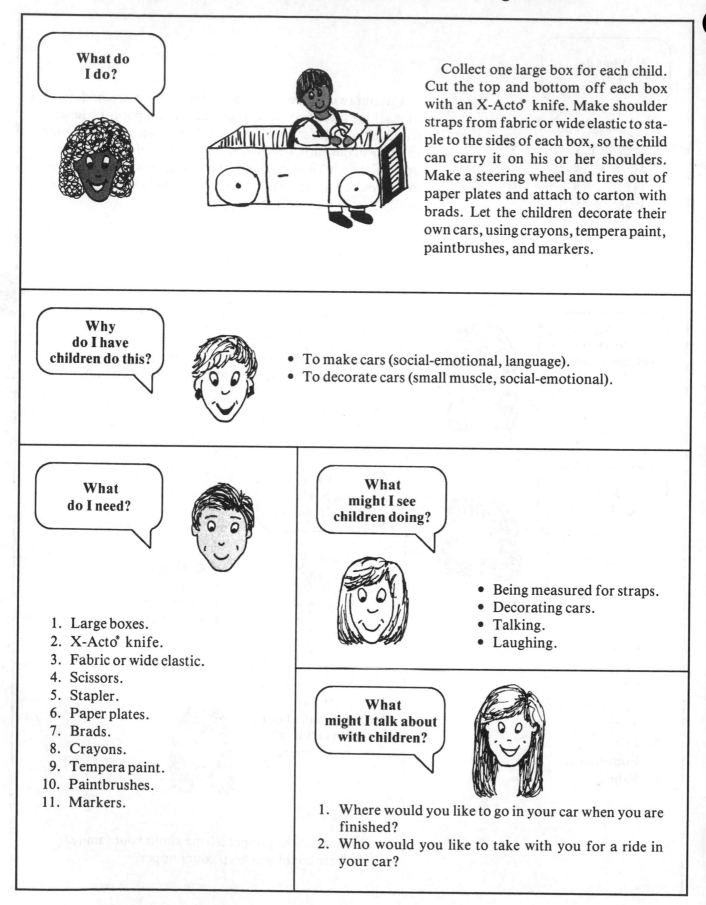

What do I do?

Collect one large box for each child. Cut the top and bottom off each box with an X-Acto® knife. Make shoulder straps from fabric or wide elastic to staple to the sides of each box, so the child can carry it on his or her shoulders. Make a steering wheel and tires out of paper plates and attach to carton with brads. Let the children decorate their own cars, using crayons, tempera paint, paintbrushes, and markers.

Why do I have children do this?

- To make cars (social-emotional, language).
- To decorate cars (small muscle, social-emotional).

What do I need?

1. Large boxes.
2. X-Acto® knife.
3. Fabric or wide elastic.
4. Scissors.
5. Stapler.
6. Paper plates.
7. Brads.
8. Crayons.
9. Tempera paint.
10. Paintbrushes.
11. Markers.

What might I see children doing?

- Being measured for straps.
- Decorating cars.
- Talking.
- Laughing.

What might I talk about with children?

1. Where would you like to go in your car when you are finished?
2. Who would you like to take with you for a ride in your car?

I LOVE MY MOMMY, I LOVE MY DADDY
Learning Center (art, library, manipulatives)

What do I do?

Hang two large sheets of newsprint on the wall at the children's eye level. Write the words "I Love My Mommy" and "I Love My Daddy" across the top of the sheets of newsprint. Put scissors, glue, and old magazines on the table. Have the children tear out or cut out pictures of what Mommy and Daddy do for them and give them. Let each child glue his or her pictures to the sheets of newsprint. Talk about what parents do for their children and what they give them to make them feel special, such as hugs, kisses, food, beds, and gifts. Write the children's responses on the newsprint.

Why do I have children do this?

- To tear (small muscle).
- To cut (small muscle).
- To glue (small muscle).
- To talk about families (language).
- To choose pictures (thinking).

What do I need?

1. Large sheets of newsprint.
2. Markers.
3. Scissors.
4. Glue.
5. Old magazines.

What might I see children doing?

- Looking for pictures.
- Cutting.
- Talking.
- Gluing.

What might I talk about with children?

1. What does your mother do for you?
2. What can you use to hold your picture on the paper?

ME FLAGS
Learning Center (art)

What do I do?

Complete the group activity "This Is What I Like to Do" on page 220. Show four- and five-year-olds flags people have for their homes. Tell the children that some people like to sail on boats and have flags on their boats. Some people live on ranches and have flags with their names on them. Tell the children that paper, crayons, markers, collage materials, scissors, and glue are available if they would like to make Me Flags. Expect each flag to be different.

Why do I have children do this?

• To experiment with art media (small muscle).
• To learn new words (language).

What do I need?

1. Pictures of flags for homes.
2. Paper.
3. Crayons.
4. Markers.
5. Collage materials.
6. Scissors.
7. Glue.

What might I see children doing?

• Talking.
• Coloring.
• Gluing.
• Cutting.

What might I talk about with children?

1. What will you do with your flag?
2. How could you make your flag, so it tells us something about you?

CLYDE MONSTER MURAL
Learning Center (art)

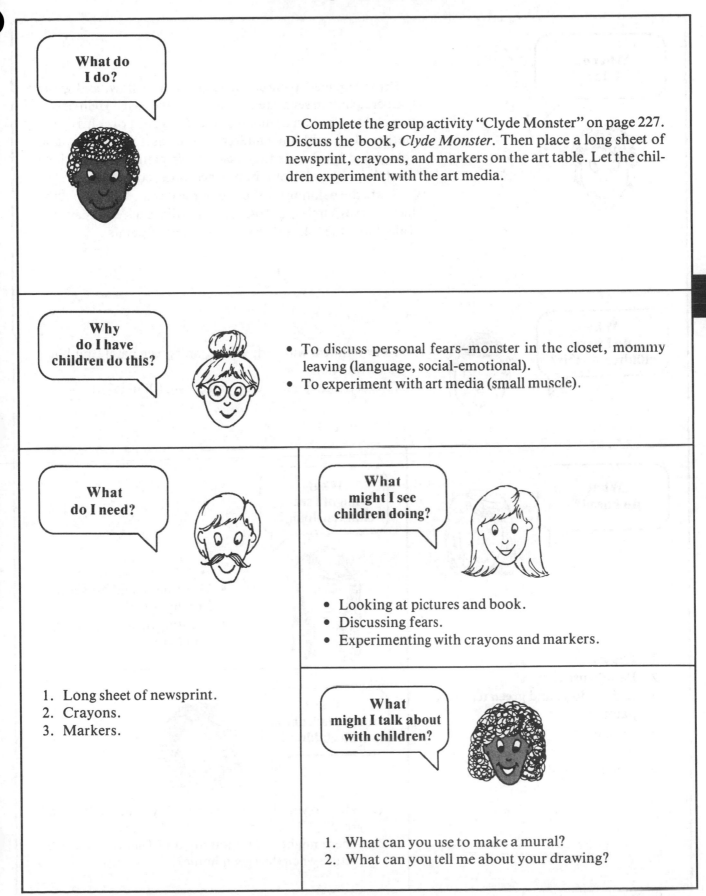

What do I do?

Complete the group activity "Clyde Monster" on page 227. Discuss the book, *Clyde Monster*. Then place a long sheet of newsprint, crayons, and markers on the art table. Let the children experiment with the art media.

Why do I have children do this?

- To discuss personal fears–monster in the closet, mommy leaving (language, social-emotional).
- To experiment with art media (small muscle).

What do I need?

1. Long sheet of newsprint.
2. Crayons.
3. Markers.

What might I see children doing?

- Looking at pictures and book.
- Discussing fears.
- Experimenting with crayons and markers.

What might I talk about with children?

1. What can you use to make a mural?
2. What can you tell me about your drawing?

MY PICTURES
Learning Center (art)

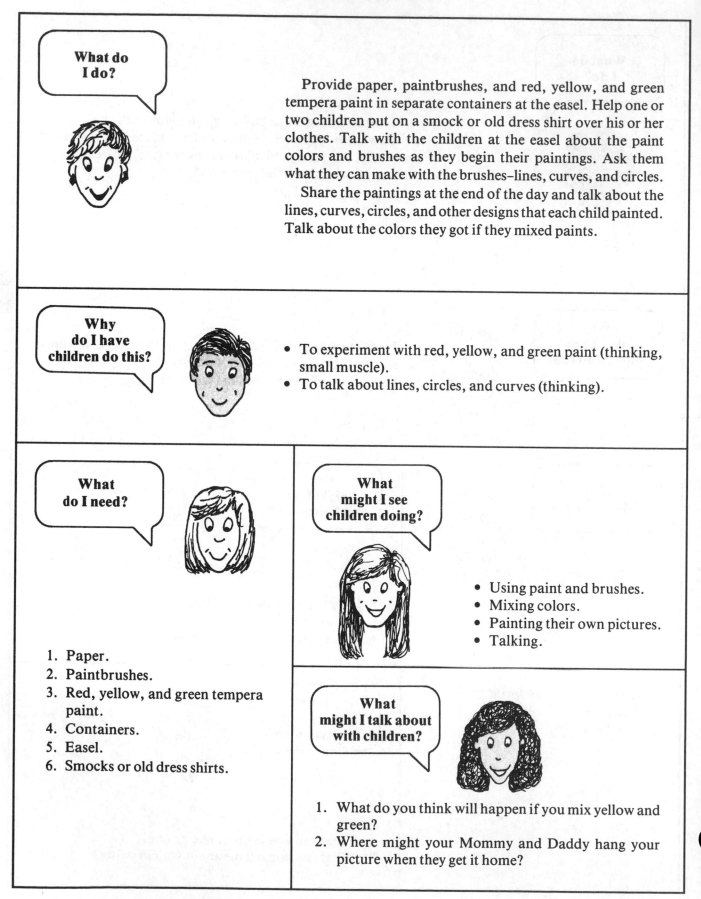

What do I do?

Provide paper, paintbrushes, and red, yellow, and green tempera paint in separate containers at the easel. Help one or two children put on a smock or old dress shirt over his or her clothes. Talk with the children at the easel about the paint colors and brushes as they begin their paintings. Ask them what they can make with the brushes–lines, curves, and circles.

Share the paintings at the end of the day and talk about the lines, curves, circles, and other designs that each child painted. Talk about the colors they got if they mixed paints.

Why do I have children do this?

- To experiment with red, yellow, and green paint (thinking, small muscle).
- To talk about lines, circles, and curves (thinking).

What do I need?

1. Paper.
2. Paintbrushes.
3. Red, yellow, and green tempera paint.
4. Containers.
5. Easel.
6. Smocks or old dress shirts.

What might I see children doing?

- Using paint and brushes.
- Mixing colors.
- Painting their own pictures.
- Talking.

What might I talk about with children?

1. What do you think will happen if you mix yellow and green?
2. Where might your Mommy and Daddy hang your picture when they get it home?

ME BOOK
Learning Center (art, library)

What do I do?

Place several books pertaining to "Me, I'm Special," such as *Here Are My Hands* by B. Martin, Jr. and J. Archambault, in the library area. In the art area, put out old magazines, self-sealing plastic bags, paper, markers, crayons, glue, and scissors. Talk with the children about making their own special book. Ask each child about his or her interests–what he or she likes to do or eat, family, pets, toys, and friends. Let each child draw related pictures on paper or cut out related pictures from a magazine. When the child is done, place two pictures back-to-back in each self-sealing plastic bag. Write the child's description on each picture. For example, "Ashley likes to paint" or "Max thinks reading books is fun." Then staple all the child's self-sealing plastic bags together along the permanently sealed side and cover the staples with plastic tape. Put the books in the library area to enjoy or use them in the dramatic play activity "My Special Corner" on page 245. These books may take several days to finish.

Why do I have children do this?

- To choose their favorite interests (thinking).
- To cut, draw, and glue (small muscle).

What do I need?

1. Books pertaining to "Me, I'm Special."
2. Old magazines.
3. Self-sealing plastic bags.
4. Paper.
5. Markers.
6. Crayons.
7. Glue.
8. Scissors.
9. Pencil.
10. Stapler.
11. Plastic tape.

What might I see children doing?

- Cutting.
- Gluing.
- Drawing.
- Telling you about his or her interests.
- Enjoying books.

What might I talk about with children?

1. What do you like to do for fun?
2. What kinds of food do you like?

HOW TALL AM I?
Learning Center (blocks, math)

What do I do?

Place large foam blocks or cardboard blocks in the block area. Hang pictures of different-sized buildings and children on the wall at the children's eye level. Talk about how high the blocks would be if they were as tall as the child. Help the children pile the blocks, so the children can see how tall they are. Then lay the blocks out lengthwise on the floor. Have the children lie down beside the blocks, so they can see how long they are.

Why do I have children do this?

- To stack blocks (large and small muscle).
- To compare their height with the blocks (thinking).

What do I need?

1. Large foam or cardboard blocks.
2. Pictures of different-sized buildings and children.

What might I see children doing?

- Stacking blocks.
- Comparing height.
- Talking.
- Looking at the pictures.

What might I talk about with children?

1. What are the tallest buildings in your town?
2. Which children in the group are shorter than you?

MOTHERS CAN DO ANYTHING
Learning Center (blocks, library)

What do I do?

Hang pictures of women doing construction work and constructing buildings on the wall at the children's eye level. Read *Mothers Can Do Anything* by J. Lasker to two or three children in the library area. Then talk about the pictures on the wall. Encourage girls to play in the block area. Put out construction hard hats for all the children to wear as they play.

Why do I have children do this?

- To try the block area (social-emotional).
- To build with blocks (large and small muscle).

What do I need?

1. Pictures of women doing construction work and constructing buildings.
2. *Mothers Can Do Anything* by J. Lasker.
3. Construction hard hats.
4. Blocks of different sizes.

What might I see children doing?

- Talking about the pictures.
- Building with blocks.
- Wearing the construction hard hats.

What might I talk about with children?

1. What kinds of buildings will you build?
2. What kinds of houses and buildings have you seen workers building?

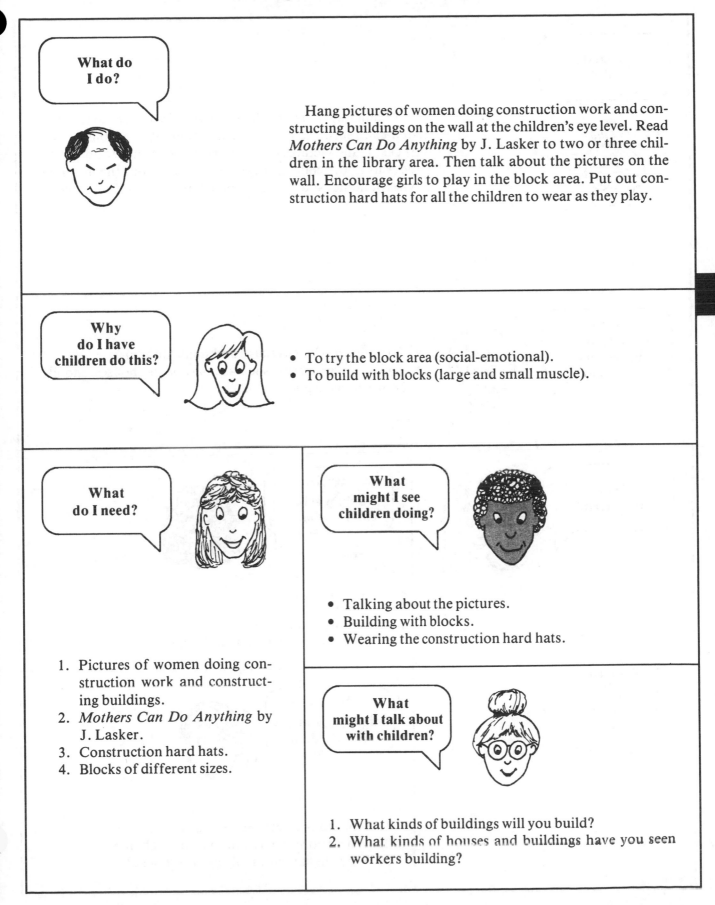

HOME BUILDING
Learning Center (blocks)

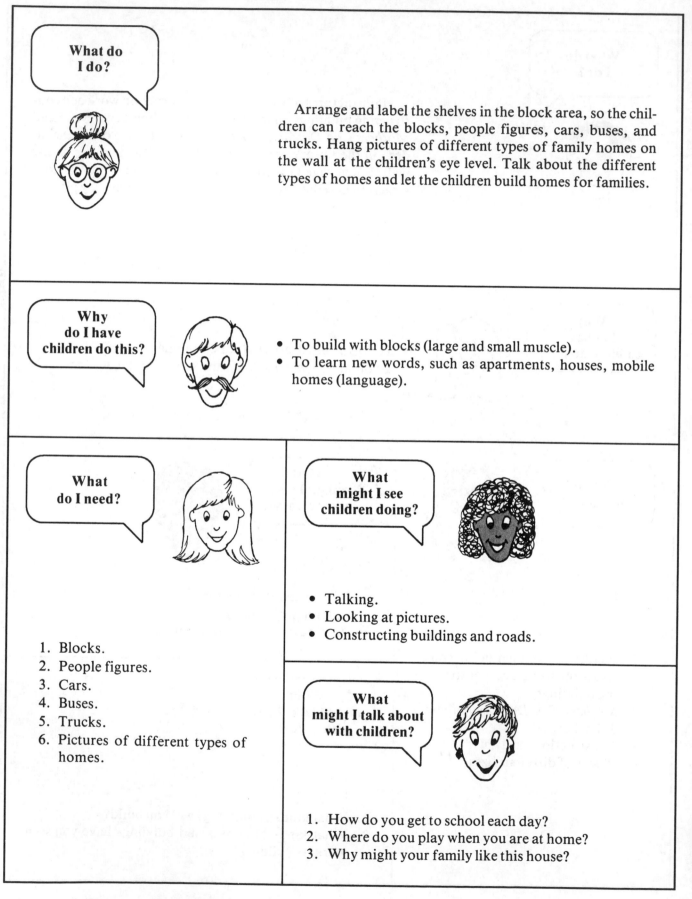

What do I do?

Arrange and label the shelves in the block area, so the children can reach the blocks, people figures, cars, buses, and trucks. Hang pictures of different types of family homes on the wall at the children's eye level. Talk about the different types of homes and let the children build homes for families.

Why do I have children do this?

- To build with blocks (large and small muscle).
- To learn new words, such as apartments, houses, mobile homes (language).

What do I need?

1. Blocks.
2. People figures.
3. Cars.
4. Buses.
5. Trucks.
6. Pictures of different types of homes.

What might I see children doing?

- Talking.
- Looking at pictures.
- Constructing buildings and roads.

What might I talk about with children?

1. How do you get to school each day?
2. Where do you play when you are at home?
3. Why might your family like this house?

MY NEIGHBORHOOD
Learning Center (blocks)

What do I do?

Add a small play house, cars, and people figures to the block area. Hang pictures of different types of neighborhoods, such as rural farmhouses, mobile home parks, suburban developments, and apartment complexes, on the wall at the children's eye level. Talk with the children about the different types of neighborhoods. Then encourage them to build a neighborhood in the block area. Have the children help you make signs for their structures. For example, "THIS IS JENNIFER'S HOME."

Why do I have children do this?

- To stack blocks (small and large muscle).
- To label their structures (language).
- To identify the style of their homes (thinking).

What do I need?

1. Blocks.
2. Small play house.
3. Small cars.
4. People figures.
5. Pictures of different types of neighborhoods.
6. Paper.
7. Markers.
8. Tape.

What might I see children doing?

- Building with blocks.
- Making signs.
- Labeling structures.
- Talking.

What might I talk about with children?

1. What kinds of places do you know of where people can live?
2. What can you tell me about your home?

CITY LIFE
Learning Center (blocks)

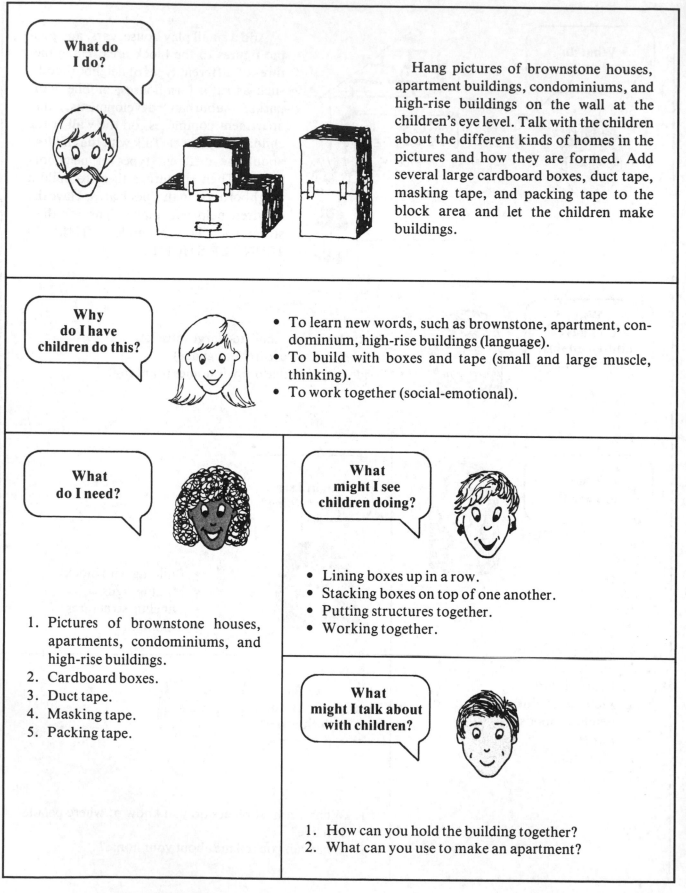

What do I do?

Hang pictures of brownstone houses, apartment buildings, condominiums, and high-rise buildings on the wall at the children's eye level. Talk with the children about the different kinds of homes in the pictures and how they are formed. Add several large cardboard boxes, duct tape, masking tape, and packing tape to the block area and let the children make buildings.

Why do I have children do this?

- To learn new words, such as brownstone, apartment, condominium, high-rise buildings (language).
- To build with boxes and tape (small and large muscle, thinking).
- To work together (social-emotional).

What do I need?

1. Pictures of brownstone houses, apartments, condominiums, and high-rise buildings.
2. Cardboard boxes.
3. Duct tape.
4. Masking tape.
5. Packing tape.

What might I see children doing?

- Lining boxes up in a row.
- Stacking boxes on top of one another.
- Putting structures together.
- Working together.

What might I talk about with children?

1. How can you hold the building together?
2. What can you use to make an apartment?

MY SPECIAL CORNER
Learning Center (dramatic play)

What do I do?

In one corner of the room, place a large appliance box with a door cut out of one side and window cut out on the opposite side. Let the children paint the box with tempera paint and paintbrushes. Then on one side of the box, make a photo gallery from photographs of the children at play that the parents have sent you. On another side of the box, hang up pictures the children have cut out of their favorite foods. On the final side of the box, hang up a height chart and place a scale in front of it. Hang a height and weight book and a pencil on the box, so you can record the children's height and weight several times a year. Put play makeup and a hand mirror in the box for them to use to decorate their faces. Place the books created in the art activity "Me Book" on page 239, inside the box for the children to read. Hang the body drawings from the art activity "My Body" on page 231, on the wall. Make masking tape streets on the floor leading to the box. The children can drive cars to and from the box.

Why do I have children do this?

- To measure their height (thinking).
- To identify themselves and their friends in the photos (thinking, social-emotional).

What do I need?

1. Large appliance box.
2. X-Acto® knife.
3. Tempera paint.
4. Paintbrushes.
5. Photographs of children at play.
6. Pictures of food.
7. Glue.
8. Height chart and scale.
9. Height and weight book.
10. Pencil.
11. Play makeup.
12. Hand mirror.
13. Books about the children.
14. Body drawings.
15. Masking tape.
16. Small cars.

What might I see children doing?

- Looking at books.
- Sitting in "My Special Corner."
- Talking.

What might I talk about with children?

1. What are you doing in this photograph?
2. What is your favorite food?

DRIVING MY SPECIAL CAR
Learning Center (dramatic play)

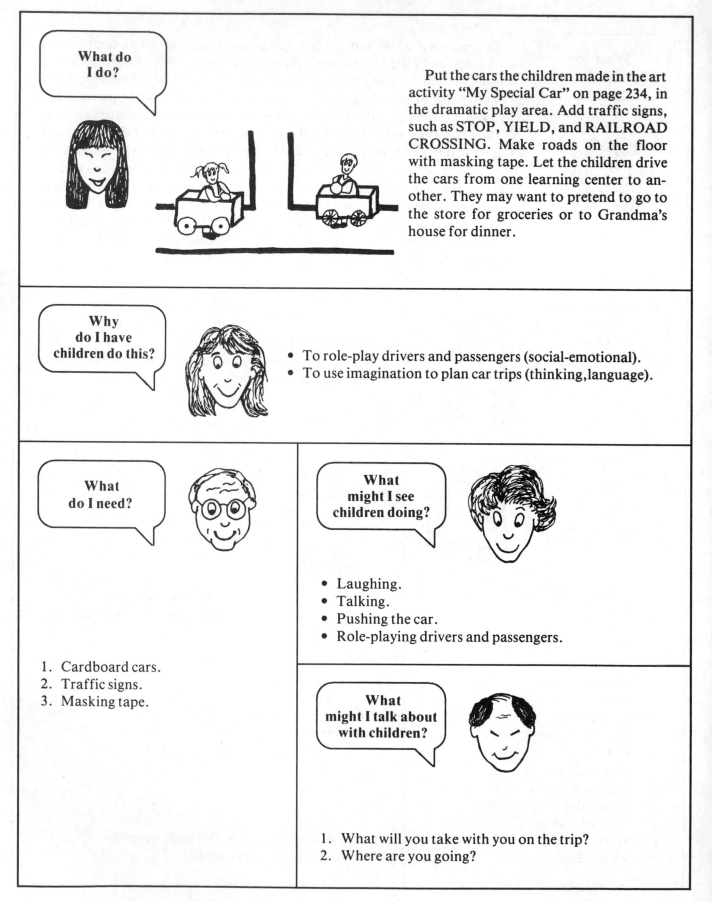

What do I do?

Put the cars the children made in the art activity "My Special Car" on page 234, in the dramatic play area. Add traffic signs, such as STOP, YIELD, and RAILROAD CROSSING. Make roads on the floor with masking tape. Let the children drive the cars from one learning center to another. They may want to pretend to go to the store for groceries or to Grandma's house for dinner.

Why do I have children do this?

- To role-play drivers and passengers (social-emotional).
- To use imagination to plan car trips (thinking, language).

What do I need?

1. Cardboard cars.
2. Traffic signs.
3. Masking tape.

What might I see children doing?

- Laughing.
- Talking.
- Pushing the car.
- Role-playing drivers and passengers.

What might I talk about with children?

1. What will you take with you on the trip?
2. Where are you going?

I PLAY JUST LIKE DADDY OR MOMMY
Learning Center (dramatic play)

What do I do?

To extend the group activity *"Just Like Daddy"* on page 223, put out dress-up clothes and shoes that zip, button, snap, and lace. Encourage the children to try the clothes on, fasten them up, and then role-play activities their parents do. Hang pictures of families and their activities on the walls at the children's eye level. Discuss them with the children.

Why do I have children do this?

- To improve self-help skills, such as dressing, zipping, and buttoning (social-emotional).
- To talk about families and family activities (language).

What do I need?

1. Dress-up clothes and shoes that zip, button, snap, and lace.
2. Pictures of families and their activities.

What might I see children doing?

- Buttoning dress-up clothes.
- Zipping dress-up clothes.
- Lacing shoes.
- Talking.

What might I talk about with children?

1. Where could you wear these big, black boots?
2. What clothing do you have at home that zips, buttons, snaps, or laces?

I CAN DO IT!
Learning Center (dramatic play)

What do I do?

Hang pictures of children dressing themselves on the wall at the children's eye level. Put dress-up clothes that have large buttons, zippers, and snaps in the dramatic play area. Add a mirror and encourage the children to dress up in the clothes.

Why do I have children do this?

- To zip, button, and snap clothing (small muscle).
- To enjoy dressing up (social-emotional).

What do I need?

What might I see children doing?

- Zipping clothes.
- Snapping clothes.
- Buttoning clothes.
- Laughing.
- Talking.

1. Pictures of children dressing themselves.
2. Dress-up clothes with large buttons, zippers, and snaps.
3. Full-length mirror.

What might I talk about with children?

1. How does your shirt stay closed?
2. What else can you find in the room that snaps?

ME PUPPET SHOW
Learning Center (dramatic play)

What do I do?

Put out the puppets from the art activity "Me Puppets" on page 233, and a card table with a tablecloth or blanket over the front of it in the dramatic play area. Use your Me Puppet to begin a puppet show. You might begin by having your puppet tell about what you did last weekend. Let the children join you and let them tell about their lives. As the children become involved, withdraw and let them stage their own shows.

Why do I have children do this?

- To role-play the activities in their lives (social-emotional, language).
- To cooperate with other children in putting on a puppet show of their own (social-emotional).

What do I need?

1. Me puppets.
2. Card table.
3. Tablecloth or blanket.

What might I see children doing?

- Role-playing.
- Talking.
- Cooperating.
- Listening.
- Laughing.

What might I talk about with children?

1. What could you tell us about your trip to the zoo?
2. Where did you go last weekend? Let the puppet tell us about it.

MY MORTAR MIX
Learning Center (food)

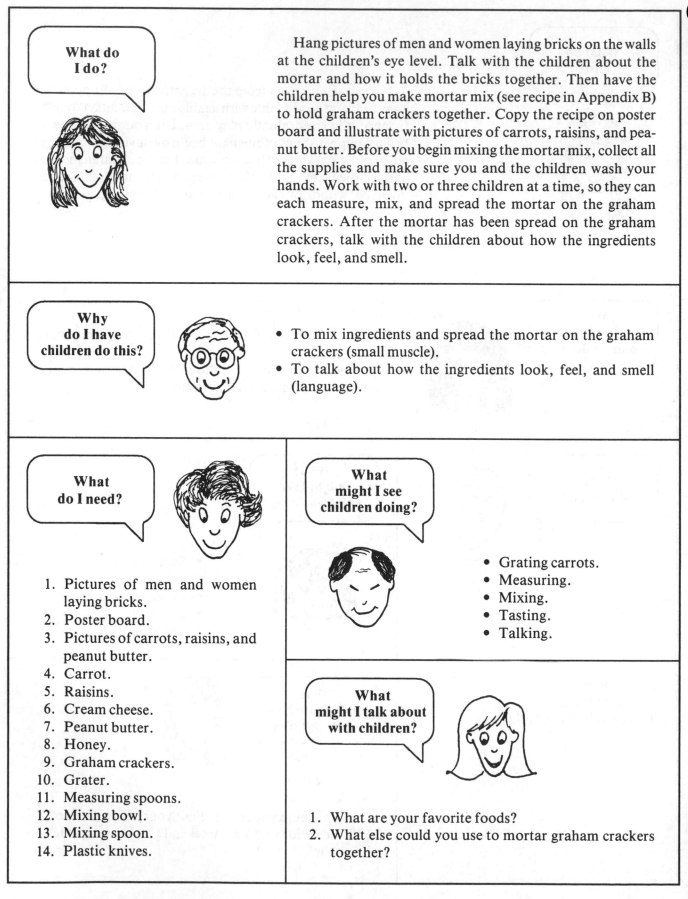

What do I do?

Hang pictures of men and women laying bricks on the walls at the children's eye level. Talk with the children about the mortar and how it holds the bricks together. Then have the children help you make mortar mix (see recipe in Appendix B) to hold graham crackers together. Copy the recipe on poster board and illustrate with pictures of carrots, raisins, and peanut butter. Before you begin mixing the mortar mix, collect all the supplies and make sure you and the children wash your hands. Work with two or three children at a time, so they can each measure, mix, and spread the mortar on the graham crackers. After the mortar has been spread on the graham crackers, talk with the children about how the ingredients look, feel, and smell.

Why do I have children do this?

- To mix ingredients and spread the mortar on the graham crackers (small muscle).
- To talk about how the ingredients look, feel, and smell (language).

What do I need?

1. Pictures of men and women laying bricks.
2. Poster board.
3. Pictures of carrots, raisins, and peanut butter.
4. Carrot.
5. Raisins.
6. Cream cheese.
7. Peanut butter.
8. Honey.
9. Graham crackers.
10. Grater.
11. Measuring spoons.
12. Mixing bowl.
13. Mixing spoon.
14. Plastic knives.

What might I see children doing?

- Grating carrots.
- Measuring.
- Mixing.
- Tasting.
- Talking.

What might I talk about with children?

1. What are your favorite foods?
2. What else could you use to mortar graham crackers together?

PEOPLE SANDWICHES
Learning Center (food)

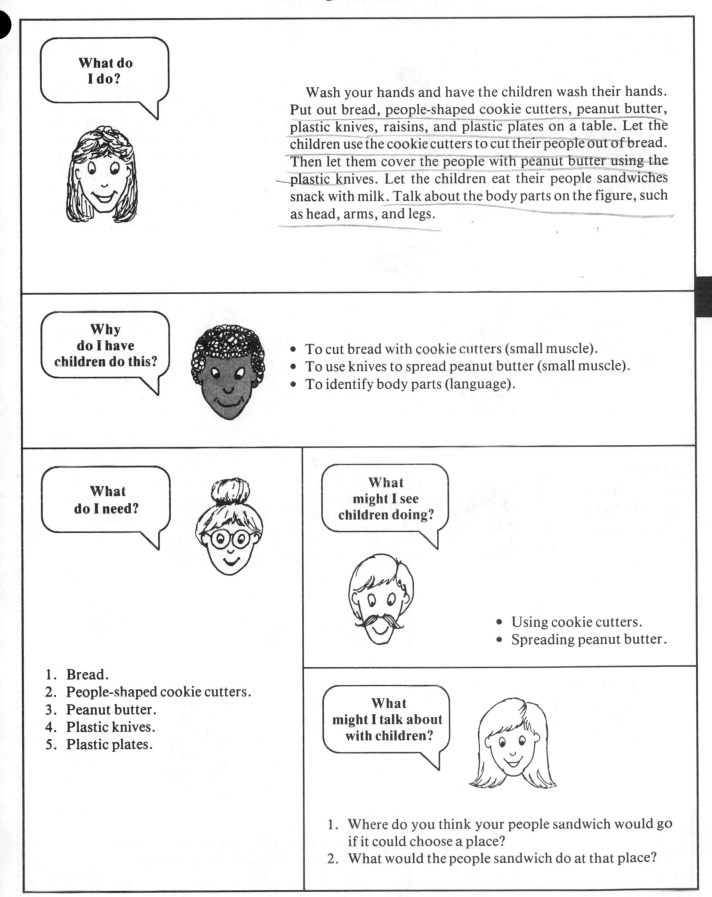

What do I do?

Wash your hands and have the children wash their hands. Put out bread, people-shaped cookie cutters, peanut butter, plastic knives, raisins, and plastic plates on a table. Let the children use the cookie cutters to cut their people out of bread. Then let them cover the people with peanut butter using the plastic knives. Let the children eat their people sandwiches snack with milk. Talk about the body parts on the figure, such as head, arms, and legs.

Why do I have children do this?

- To cut bread with cookie cutters (small muscle).
- To use knives to spread peanut butter (small muscle).
- To identify body parts (language).

What do I need?

1. Bread.
2. People-shaped cookie cutters.
3. Peanut butter.
4. Plastic knives.
5. Plastic plates.

What might I see children doing?

- Using cookie cutters.
- Spreading peanut butter.

What might I talk about with children?

1. Where do you think your people sandwich would go if it could choose a place?
2. What would the people sandwich do at that place?

MY FELT HOUSE BOXES
Learning Center (library, manipulatives)

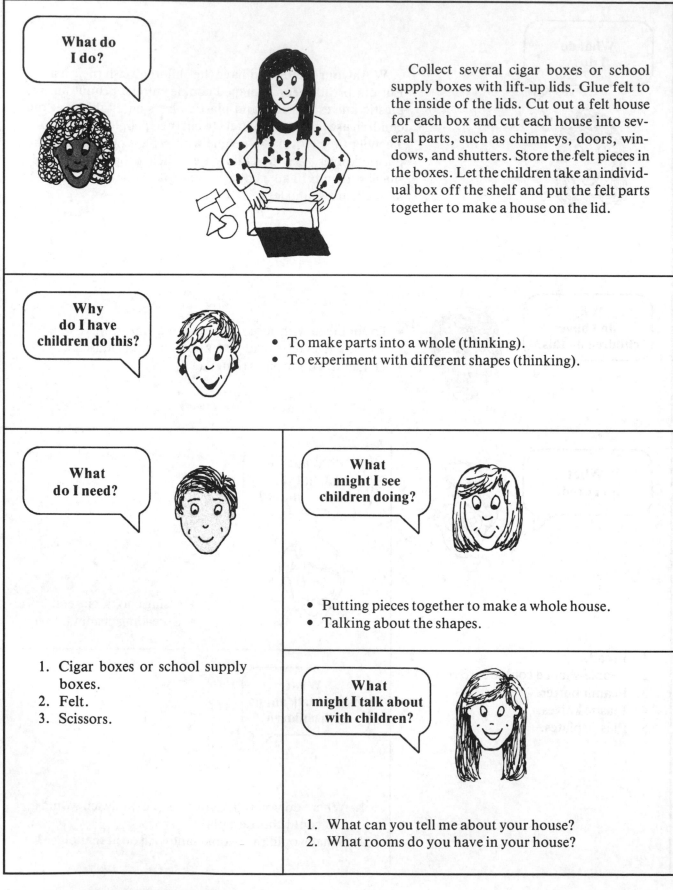

What do I do?

Collect several cigar boxes or school supply boxes with lift-up lids. Glue felt to the inside of the lids. Cut out a felt house for each box and cut each house into several parts, such as chimneys, doors, windows, and shutters. Store the felt pieces in the boxes. Let the children take an individual box off the shelf and put the felt parts together to make a house on the lid.

Why do I have children do this?

- To make parts into a whole (thinking).
- To experiment with different shapes (thinking).

What do I need?

What might I see children doing?

- Putting pieces together to make a whole house.
- Talking about the shapes.

1. Cigar boxes or school supply boxes.
2. Felt.
3. Scissors.

What might I talk about with children?

1. What can you tell me about your house?
2. What rooms do you have in your house?

HAPPY THOUGHTS BOX
Learning Center (library)

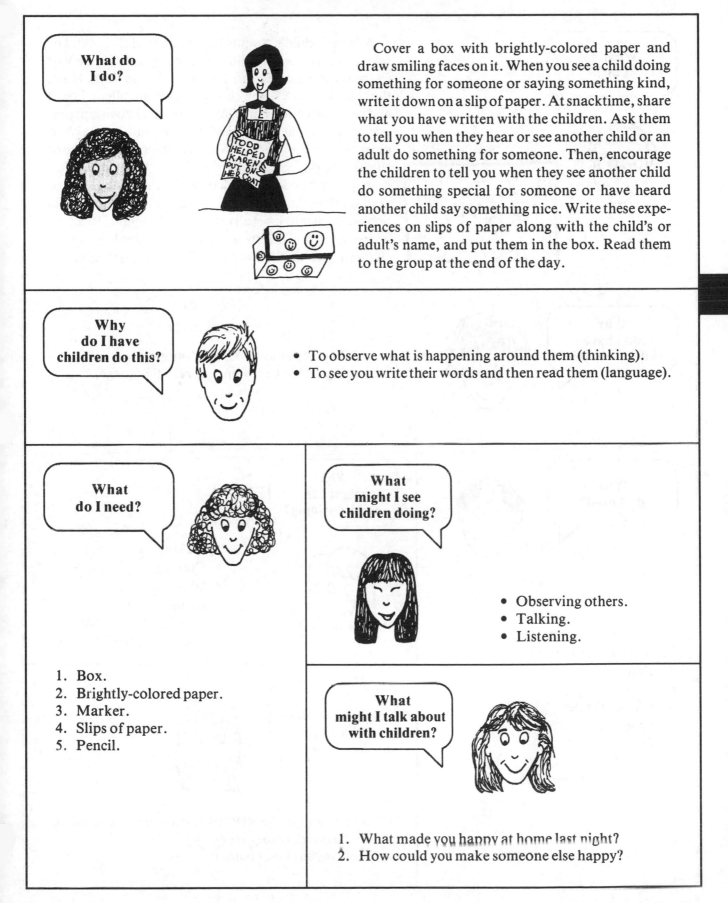

What do I do?

Cover a box with brightly-colored paper and draw smiling faces on it. When you see a child doing something for someone or saying something kind, write it down on a slip of paper. At snacktime, share what you have written with the children. Ask them to tell you when they hear or see another child or an adult do something for someone. Then, encourage the children to tell you when they see another child do something special for someone or have heard another child say something nice. Write these experiences on slips of paper along with the child's or adult's name, and put them in the box. Read them to the group at the end of the day.

Why do I have children do this?

- To observe what is happening around them (thinking).
- To see you write their words and then read them (language).

What do I need?

1. Box.
2. Brightly-colored paper.
3. Marker.
4. Slips of paper.
5. Pencil.

What might I see children doing?

- Observing others.
- Talking.
- Listening.

What might I talk about with children?

1. What made you happy at home last night?
2. How could you make someone else happy?

I'M A VIP
Learning Center (library)

What do I do?

Ask each child's parents for a picture of their child or take a picture of each child. Choose one child to be a VIP (Very Important Person) for two or three days. Hang the child's picture in the center of a small bulletin board and write the child's name in large letters. Provide paper, crayons, old magazines, and scissors and let the child draw or cut out pictures of his or her interests–what he or she likes to do, pets, or favorite foods. Write the child's description beside each picture. Invite the parents to send small items from home, such as pictures or special books. Be sure to label all personal belongings. Read the board several times to one child or a small group of children. Let the VIP choose the snack for one day.

Why do I have children do this?

- To share what they enjoy (social-emotional).
- To see writing and to hear someone read (language).

What do I need?

1. Pictures of the children.
2. Small bulletin board.
3. Paper.
4. Crayons.
5. Old magazines.
6. Scissors.
7. Glue.
8. Pencil.
9. Stapler or thumb tacks.

What might I see children doing?

- Talking.
- Cutting.
- Gluing.
- Using crayons.
- Reading with an adult.
- Looking at the VIP board.

What might I talk about with children?

1. When you are the VIP, what do you want to put up on the bulletin board?
2. What is your dog's name?

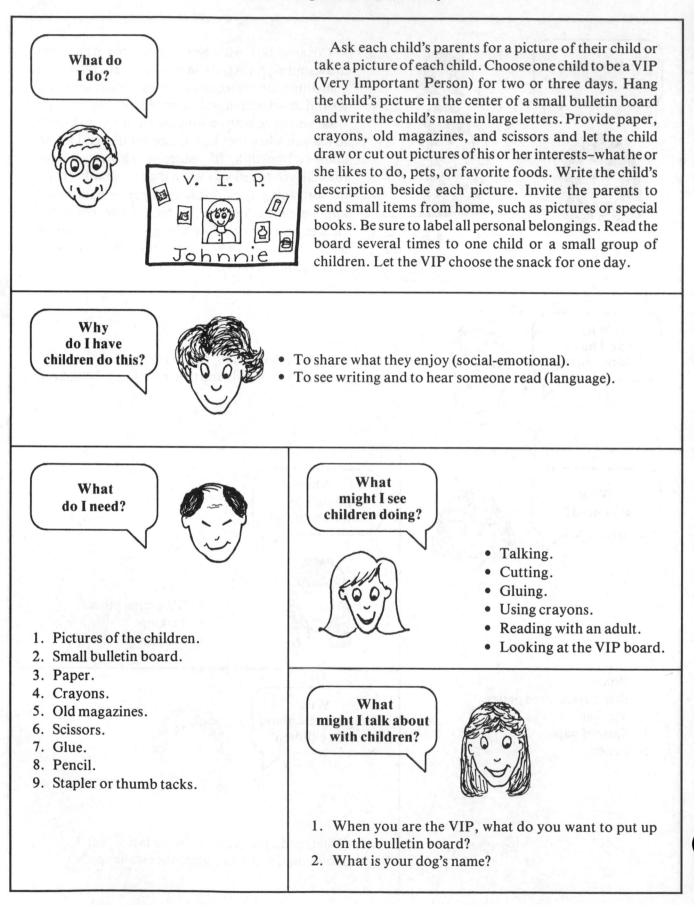

MY FAVORITE TOY SHOW
Learning Center (library)

What do I do?

Collect several boxes and stack them on a table to make a display case. Hang a sign above the table that says, "MY FAVORITE TOY SHOW." Ask the parents to let their child bring a favorite toy from home. Have the children put their toys in the display case. Write each child's name on an index card and place the card beside his or her toy. Let the children look at the different toys. Give each child a chance to talk about his or her favorite toy with the other children sometime during the day.

Why do I have children do this?

- To experience going to a special display of toys (social-emotional).
- To talk about and share special belongings (language).

What do I need?

1. Boxes.
2. "MY FAVORITE TOY SHOW" sign.
3. Index cards.

What might I see children doing?

- Talking.
- Listening.
- Looking at the toy show.

What might I talk about with children?

1. Where might you see other kinds of displays?
2. What else could you put in the display cases?

FAMILIES ARE IMPORTANT
Learning Center (library)

What do I do?

Hang pictures of families working and playing together on the wall at the children's eye level. You might want to ask for pictures from the children's families. Collect books, such as *I Love My Mother* by P. Zindel; *Boundless Grace* by M. Hoffman; *Owl Babies* by M. Waddell; *My Apron* by E. Carle; and *Grandmother and I, Grandfather and I* and *My Sister and I* by H. Buckley. Read these books to small groups of children over a period of two or three days. Then discuss the different activities they can do with different family members.

Why do I have children do this?

- To talk about special family members (language).
- To talk about the different activities they do with different family members (thinking, language).

What do I need?

1. Pictures of families working and playing together.
2. *I Love My Mother* by P. Zindel.
3. *Boundless Grace* by M. Hoffman.
4. *Owl Babies* by M. Waddell.
5. *My Apron* by E. Carle.
6. *Grandmother and I* by H. Buckley.
7. *Grandfather and I* by H. Buckley.
8. *My Sister and I* by H. Buckley.

What might I see children doing?

- Talking.
- Enjoying a story.
- Looking at pictures of their families.

What might I talk about with children?

1. What can you tell me about your family?
2. Who lives in your house?
3. What do you and your sister or brother fight about?

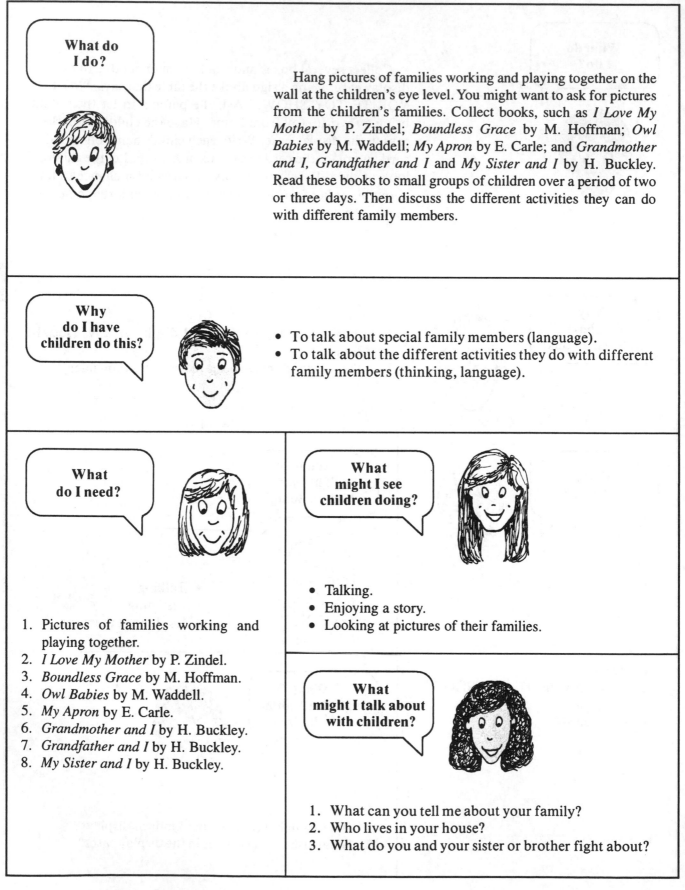

What do I do?

Put a tape recorder with a microphone in the library area and hang pictures of children talking on the wall at the children's eye level. Talk with a small group of children about their families, pets, friends, and what they do at home or the center. Let them speak into the microphone. Play back the tape, so they can listen to the voices. See if they can pick out their own voices.

Why do I have children do this?

- To give them an opportunity to use a tape recorder (thinking).
- To let them listen to one another's voices (language).

What do I need?

1. Tape recorder with microphone.
2. Pictures of children talking.

What might I see children doing?

- Talking.
- Listening.

What might I talk about with children?

1. Where do you use microphones?
2. How was your trip to Kansas City?

I CAN DRESS MYSELF
Learning Center (manipulatives)

What do I do?

Make several boy or girl cardboard or felt board figures. (See directions for felt board figures in Appendix A.) Then make several sets of felt or paper doll-type clothes for the figures by tracing clothing from coloring books and using an opaque projector to enlarge them to fit the figures. Let the children dress the figures for different types of weather—cold, warm, rainy, or sunny. Talk about how clothes keep you warm or help you stay cool. Let the children play with the figures.

Why do I have children do this?

- To put the appropriate clothing on the figures (small muscle, thinking).
- To talk about what they wear in different weather (language).

What do I need?

1. Cardboard figures.
2. Coloring books (for child care providers only), books, or drawings.
3. Pencil.
4. Fusible interfacing.
5. Permanent markers.
6. Iron.
7. Felt.
8. Scissors.
9. Opaque projector.

To make felt board figures

What might I see children doing?

- Dressing the figures.
- Talking about weather.
- Playing together.

What might I talk about with children?

1. What do you wear in hot weather?
2. What clothes are the hardest for you to put on by yourself?

COUNTING ROPE KNOTS
Learning Center (math)

What do I do?

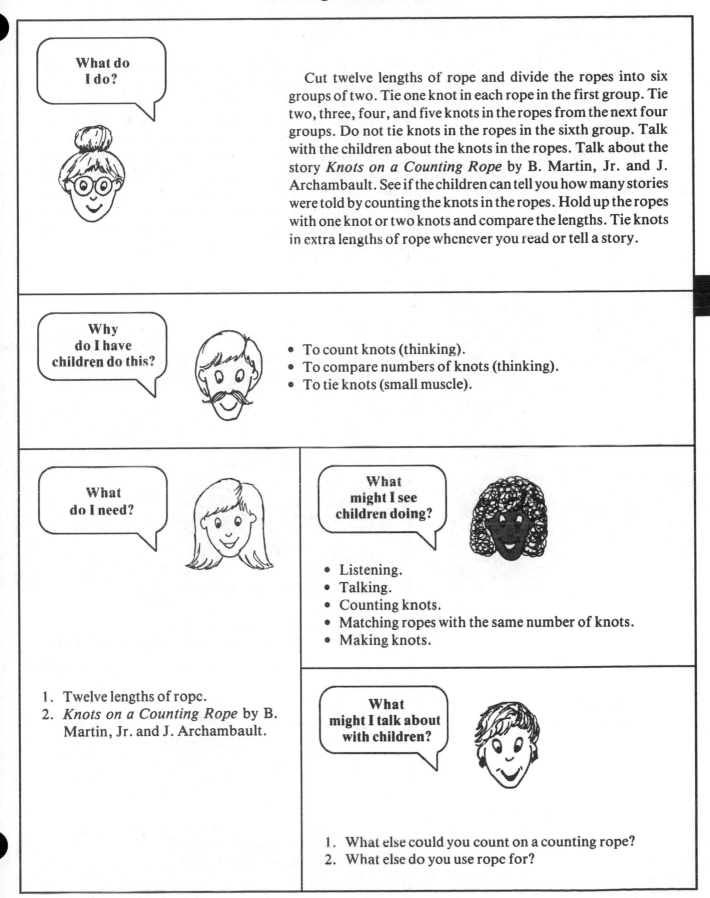

Cut twelve lengths of rope and divide the ropes into six groups of two. Tie one knot in each rope in the first group. Tie two, three, four, and five knots in the ropes from the next four groups. Do not tie knots in the ropes in the sixth group. Talk with the children about the knots in the ropes. Talk about the story *Knots on a Counting Rope* by B. Martin, Jr. and J. Archambault. See if the children can tell you how many stories were told by counting the knots in the ropes. Hold up the ropes with one knot or two knots and compare the lengths. Tie knots in extra lengths of rope whenever you read or tell a story.

Why do I have children do this?

- To count knots (thinking).
- To compare numbers of knots (thinking).
- To tie knots (small muscle).

What do I need?

1. Twelve lengths of rope.
2. *Knots on a Counting Rope* by B. Martin, Jr. and J. Archambault.

What might I see children doing?

- Listening.
- Talking.
- Counting knots.
- Matching ropes with the same number of knots.
- Making knots.

What might I talk about with children?

1. What else could you count on a counting rope?
2. What else do you use rope for?

COMPARISONS
Learning Center (math)

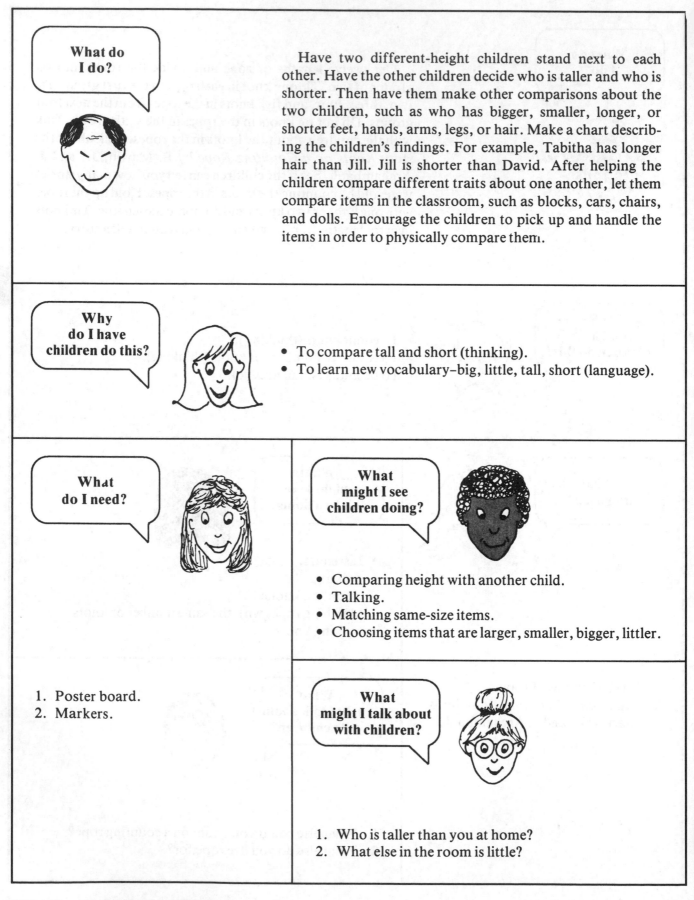

What do I do?

Have two different-height children stand next to each other. Have the other children decide who is taller and who is shorter. Then have them make other comparisons about the two children, such as who has bigger, smaller, longer, or shorter feet, hands, arms, legs, or hair. Make a chart describing the children's findings. For example, Tabitha has longer hair than Jill. Jill is shorter than David. After helping the children compare different traits about one another, let them compare items in the classroom, such as blocks, cars, chairs, and dolls. Encourage the children to pick up and handle the items in order to physically compare them.

Why do I have children do this?

- To compare tall and short (thinking).
- To learn new vocabulary—big, little, tall, short (language).

What do I need?

What might I see children doing?

- Comparing height with another child.
- Talking.
- Matching same-size items.
- Choosing items that are larger, smaller, bigger, littler.

1. Poster board.
2. Markers.

What might I talk about with children?

1. Who is taller than you at home?
2. What else in the room is little?

FUNNY PEOPLE
Learning Center (math)

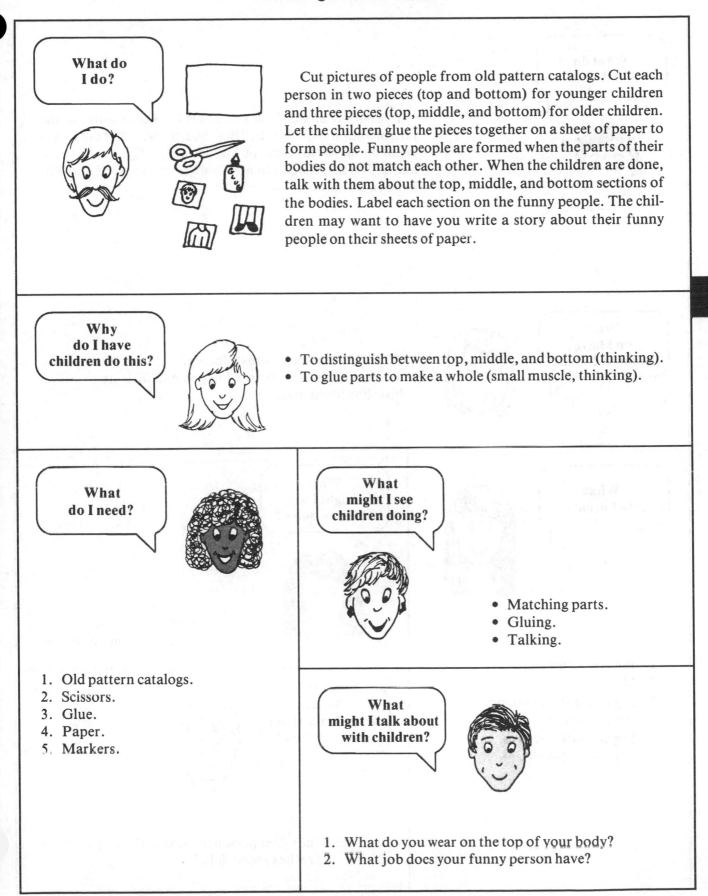

What do I do?

Cut pictures of people from old pattern catalogs. Cut each person in two pieces (top and bottom) for younger children and three pieces (top, middle, and bottom) for older children. Let the children glue the pieces together on a sheet of paper to form people. Funny people are formed when the parts of their bodies do not match each other. When the children are done, talk with them about the top, middle, and bottom sections of the bodies. Label each section on the funny people. The children may want to have you write a story about their funny people on their sheets of paper.

Why do I have children do this?

- To distinguish between top, middle, and bottom (thinking).
- To glue parts to make a whole (small muscle, thinking).

What do I need?

1. Old pattern catalogs.
2. Scissors.
3. Glue.
4. Paper.
5. Markers.

What might I see children doing?

- Matching parts.
- Gluing.
- Talking.

What might I talk about with children?

1. What do you wear on the top of your body?
2. What job does your funny person have?

THIS IS LITTLE, THIS IS BIG
Learning Center (math), Group

What do I do?

Put out big and little boxes. Label the boxes with big and little shapes and the words, "Big" and "Little." Put out a variety of big and little rubber or wooden people figures, pictures, and dolls. Have the children put big items in a big box and little items in a little box.

Why do I have children do this?

- To compare items by size (thinking).
- To match big items with a big box and little items with a little box (thinking).

What do I need?

1. Big and little boxes.
2. Markers.
3. Big and little rubber or wooden people figures.
4. Big and little pictures.
5. Big and little dolls.

What might I see children doing?

- Matching big and little.
- Comparing items by size.

What might I talk about with children?

1. Who is the tallest person in the room?
2. Where are the biggest dolls?

FEELING SONG
Learning Center (music)

What do I do?

Make up words to familiar tunes to help the children express how they feel or how you feel as you spend time together. For example, sing the following song to the tune of "Frère Jacques."

"Feeling Song"

I am happy. I am happy.
Yes, I am. Yes, I am.
I can play with Megan.
  I can play with Megan.
You can too! You can too!

I am angry! Oh, so angry!
I broke my truck.
  I broke my truck.

It can't be fixed. It can't be fixed.
And I am mad. Yes, I'm mad.

I am sad. Oh, so sad.
I could cry. I could cry.
Won't you hold me?
  Won't you hold me?
On your lap. On your lap.

Why do I have children do this?

- To sing about feelings (language, social-emotional).
- To solve problems (thinking).

What do I need?

No supplies are needed.

What might I see children doing?

- Crying.
- Laughing.
- Screaming.
- Singing.

What might I talk about with children?

1. What other feelings can we sing about?
2. How do you think we could fix this truck?

"MARY HAD A LITTLE LAMB"
Learning Center (music)

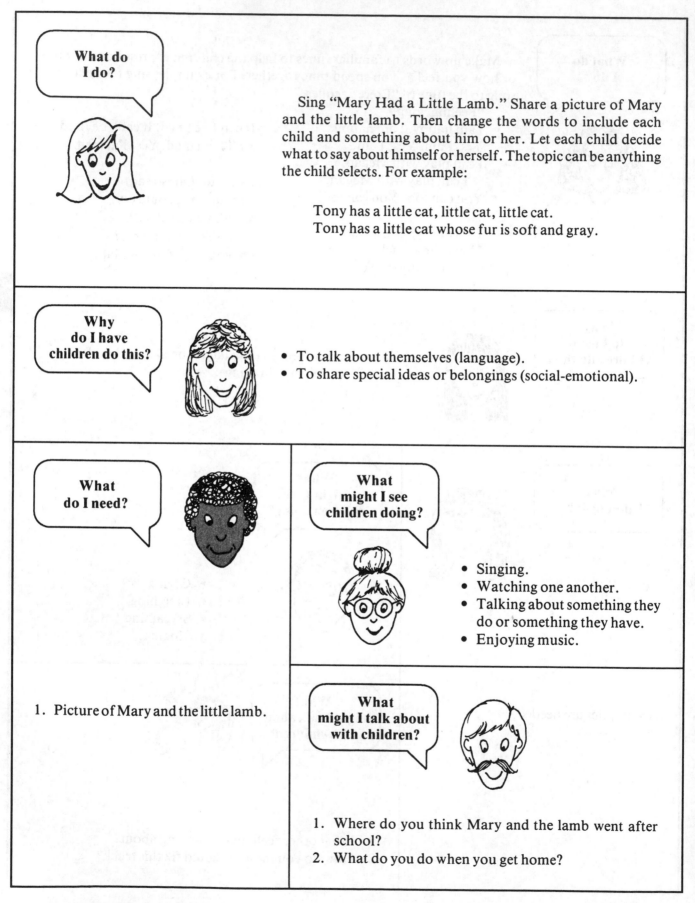

What do I do?

Sing "Mary Had a Little Lamb." Share a picture of Mary and the little lamb. Then change the words to include each child and something about him or her. Let each child decide what to say about himself or herself. The topic can be anything the child selects. For example:

Tony has a little cat, little cat, little cat.
Tony has a little cat whose fur is soft and gray.

Why do I have children do this?

- To talk about themselves (language).
- To share special ideas or belongings (social-emotional).

What do I need?

1. Picture of Mary and the little lamb.

What might I see children doing?

- Singing.
- Watching one another.
- Talking about something they do or something they have.
- Enjoying music.

What might I talk about with children?

1. Where do you think Mary and the lamb went after school?
2. What do you do when you get home?

FOOTPRINTS IN THE SAND
Learning Center (sand)

What do I do?

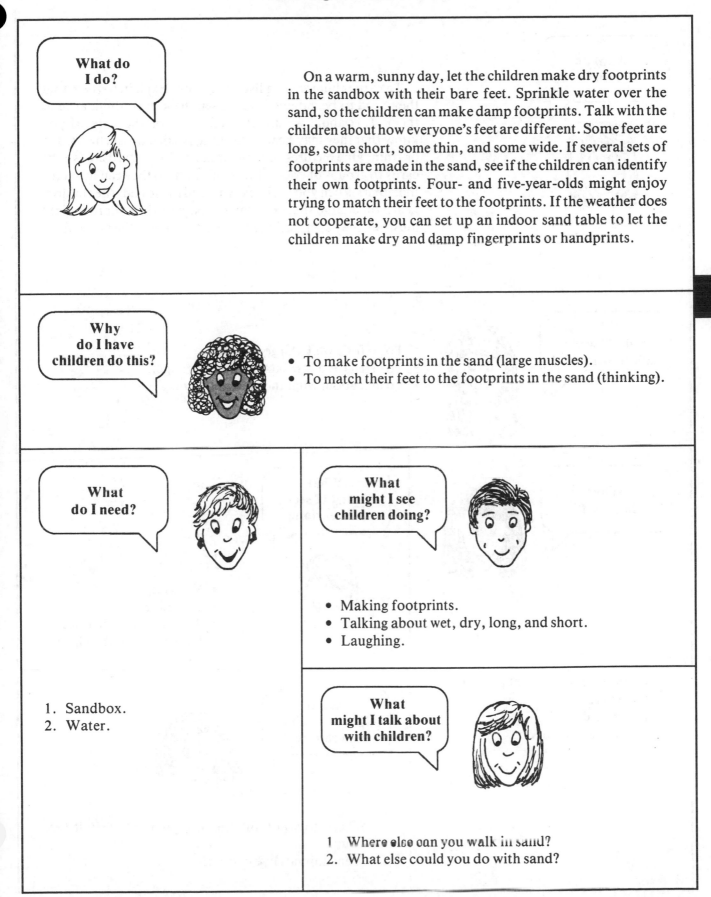

On a warm, sunny day, let the children make dry footprints in the sandbox with their bare feet. Sprinkle water over the sand, so the children can make damp footprints. Talk with the children about how everyone's feet are different. Some feet are long, some short, some thin, and some wide. If several sets of footprints are made in the sand, see if the children can identify their own footprints. Four- and five-year-olds might enjoy trying to match their feet to the footprints. If the weather does not cooperate, you can set up an indoor sand table to let the children make dry and damp fingerprints or handprints.

Why do I have children do this?

- To make footprints in the sand (large muscles).
- To match their feet to the footprints in the sand (thinking).

What do I need?

What might I see children doing?

- Making footprints.
- Talking about wet, dry, long, and short.
- Laughing.

1. Sandbox.
2. Water.

What might I talk about with children?

1. Where else can you walk in sand?
2. What else could you do with sand?

LISTENING WALK
Learning Center (science)

What do I do?

Take the children on a listening walk. Explain to them that they need to be a quiet, so they can hear everything around them. Talk about what they might hear on the walk. If you know that they may hear something particular, such as a dog or train, glue pictures of those items to index cards. Give the cards to groups of two or three children, so they can listen for that item. When you get back, write all the sounds the children heard on a large sheet of paper. Some of the children might illustrate the paper during self-selected time in the art area.

Why do I have children do this?

- To go for a walk (large muscle).
- To listen for dogs, cats, trains (language).
- To talk about what they heard (language).

What do I need?

1. Pictures of what might be heard on the walk.
2. Index cards.
3. Large sheet of paper.
4. Markers.

What might I see children doing?

- Walking.
- Listening.
- Talking about their walk.
- Drawing what they heard.

What might I talk about with children?

1. Where do you think the blue jay went when it flew away?
2. What animals live in trees?

I LIKE TO GO TO THE BEACH
Learning Center (water play)

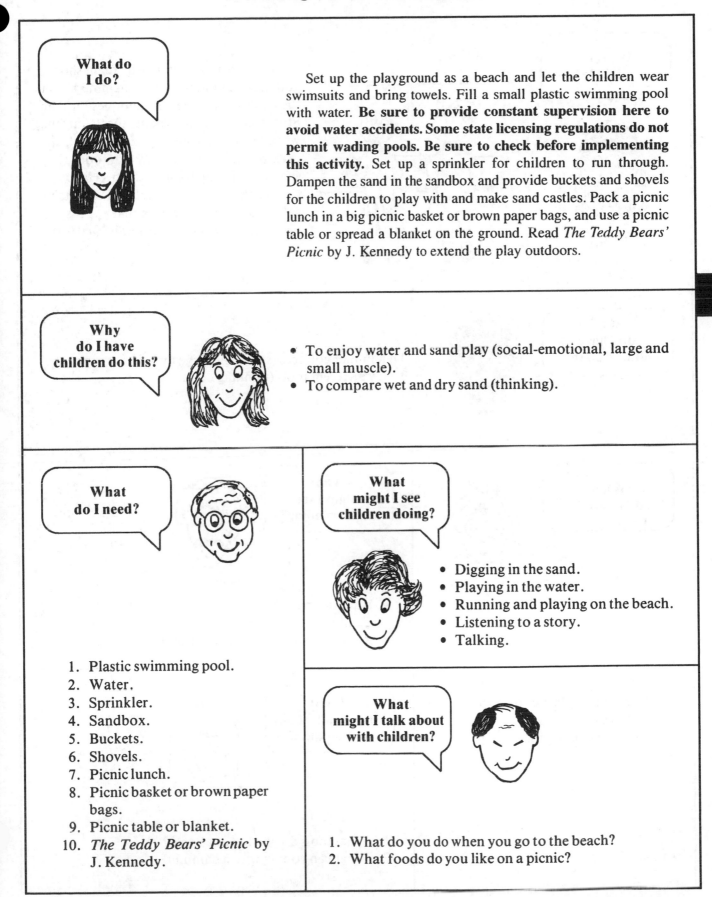

What do I do?

Set up the playground as a beach and let the children wear swimsuits and bring towels. Fill a small plastic swimming pool with water. **Be sure to provide constant supervision here to avoid water accidents. Some state licensing regulations do not permit wading pools. Be sure to check before implementing this activity.** Set up a sprinkler for children to run through. Dampen the sand in the sandbox and provide buckets and shovels for the children to play with and make sand castles. Pack a picnic lunch in a big picnic basket or brown paper bags, and use a picnic table or spread a blanket on the ground. Read *The Teddy Bears' Picnic* by J. Kennedy to extend the play outdoors.

Why do I have children do this?

- To enjoy water and sand play (social-emotional, large and small muscle).
- To compare wet and dry sand (thinking).

What do I need?

What might I see children doing?

- Digging in the sand.
- Playing in the water.
- Running and playing on the beach.
- Listening to a story.
- Talking.

1. Plastic swimming pool.
2. Water.
3. Sprinkler.
4. Sandbox.
5. Buckets.
6. Shovels.
7. Picnic lunch.
8. Picnic basket or brown paper bags.
9. Picnic table or blanket.
10. *The Teddy Bears' Picnic* by J. Kennedy.

What might I talk about with children?

1. What do you do when you go to the beach?
2. What foods do you like on a picnic?

I CAN HIT IT!
Learning Center (woodworking)

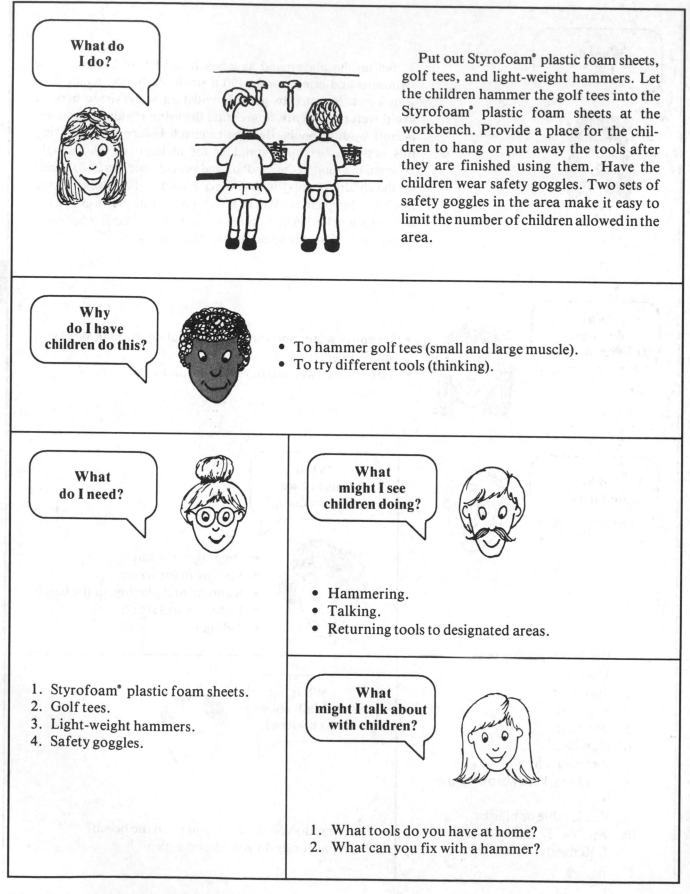

What do I do?

Put out Styrofoam® plastic foam sheets, golf tees, and light-weight hammers. Let the children hammer the golf tees into the Styrofoam® plastic foam sheets at the workbench. Provide a place for the children to hang or put away the tools after they are finished using them. Have the children wear safety goggles. Two sets of safety goggles in the area make it easy to limit the number of children allowed in the area.

Why do I have children do this?

- To hammer golf tees (small and large muscle).
- To try different tools (thinking).

What do I need?

1. Styrofoam® plastic foam sheets.
2. Golf tees.
3. Light-weight hammers.
4. Safety goggles.

What might I see children doing?

- Hammering.
- Talking.
- Returning tools to designated areas.

What might I talk about with children?

1. What tools do you have at home?
2. What can you fix with a hammer?

FOLLOW MY FEET
Outdoor Large Muscle

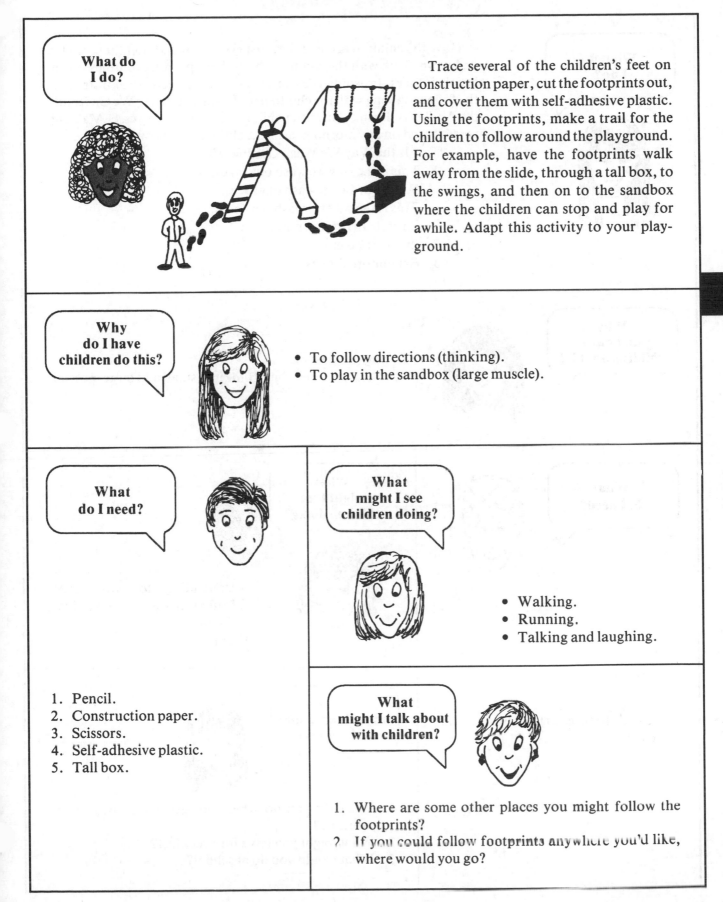

What do I do?

Trace several of the children's feet on construction paper, cut the footprints out, and cover them with self-adhesive plastic. Using the footprints, make a trail for the children to follow around the playground. For example, have the footprints walk away from the slide, through a tall box, to the swings, and then on to the sandbox where the children can stop and play for awhile. Adapt this activity to your playground.

Why do I have children do this?

- To follow directions (thinking).
- To play in the sandbox (large muscle).

What do I need?

1. Pencil.
2. Construction paper.
3. Scissors.
4. Self-adhesive plastic.
5. Tall box.

What might I see children doing?

- Walking.
- Running.
- Talking and laughing.

What might I talk about with children?

1. Where are some other places you might follow the footprints?
2. If you could follow footprints anywhere you'd like, where would you go?

THIS IS THE WAY WE WASH OUR FACES
Indoor or Outdoor Large Muscle, Group, Learning Center (music)

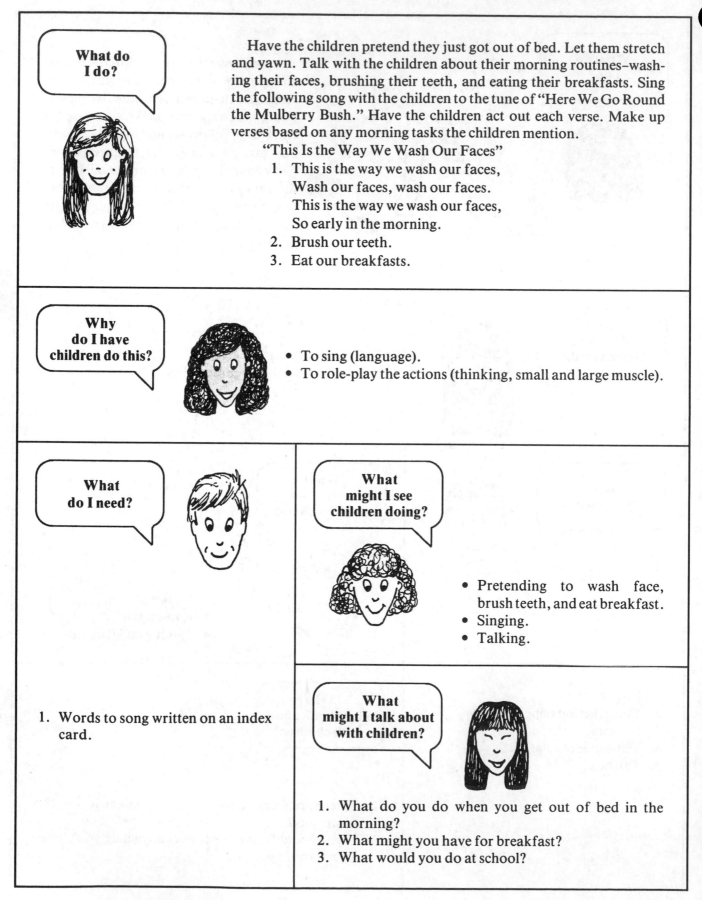

What do I do?

Have the children pretend they just got out of bed. Let them stretch and yawn. Talk with the children about their morning routines–washing their faces, brushing their teeth, and eating their breakfasts. Sing the following song with the children to the tune of "Here We Go Round the Mulberry Bush." Have the children act out each verse. Make up verses based on any morning tasks the children mention.

"This Is the Way We Wash Our Faces"

1. This is the way we wash our faces,
   Wash our faces, wash our faces.
   This is the way we wash our faces,
   So early in the morning.
2. Brush our teeth.
3. Eat our breakfasts.

Why do I have children do this?

- To sing (language).
- To role-play the actions (thinking, small and large muscle).

What do I need?

1. Words to song written on an index card.

What might I see children doing?

- Pretending to wash face, brush teeth, and eat breakfast.
- Singing.
- Talking.

What might I talk about with children?

1. What do you do when you get out of bed in the morning?
2. What might you have for breakfast?
3. What would you do at school?

MIRROR, MIRROR ME
Indoor or Outdoor Large Muscle

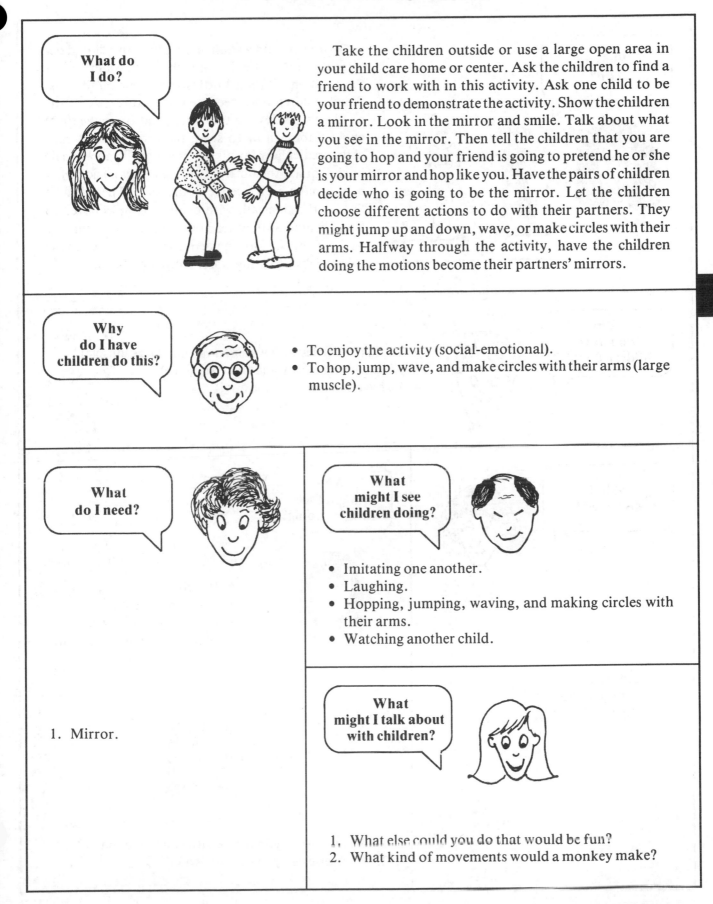

What do I do?

Take the children outside or use a large open area in your child care home or center. Ask the children to find a friend to work with in this activity. Ask one child to be your friend to demonstrate the activity. Show the children a mirror. Look in the mirror and smile. Talk about what you see in the mirror. Then tell the children that you are going to hop and your friend is going to pretend he or she is your mirror and hop like you. Have the pairs of children decide who is going to be the mirror. Let the children choose different actions to do with their partners. They might jump up and down, wave, or make circles with their arms. Halfway through the activity, have the children doing the motions become their partners' mirrors.

Why do I have children do this?

- To enjoy the activity (social-emotional).
- To hop, jump, wave, and make circles with their arms (large muscle).

What do I need?

1. Mirror.

What might I see children doing?

- Imitating one another.
- Laughing.
- Hopping, jumping, waving, and making circles with their arms.
- Watching another child.

What might I talk about with children?

1. What else could you do that would be fun?
2. What kind of movements would a monkey make?

THE BIG SQUEEZE
Outdoor Large Muscle, Learning Center (science)

What do I do?

Give each child a squirt bottle or empty liquid detergent squirt bottle. Fill a bucket with water and let the children fill their bottles and screw on the lids. Small children may need help with this task. If the children's bottles are too heavy and full, give them choices about how to solve the problem. Let each child predict how far his or her water will go when he or she squirts the bottle. Let him or her decide what might make a difference in distance. Then draw a line on the sidewalk with chalk for the children to stand behind as they see how far they can squirt the water. They can also make designs or pictures on the sidewalk by squirting water from their bottles.

Why do I have children do this?

- To fill the bottles with water (small and large muscle).
- To talk about empty and full (language).
- To have fun (social-emotional).

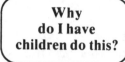

What do I need?

1. Squirt bottles or empty liquid detergent bottles.
2. Bucket.
3. Water.
4. Chalk.

What might I see children doing?

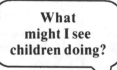

- Pouring water.
- Squirting water.
- Laughing and talking.
- Making designs and pictures.

What might I talk about with children?

1. What else can you make with your water paint?
2. What else can you do with water?

HOW BIG IS MY BODY?
Indoor or Outdoor Large Muscle

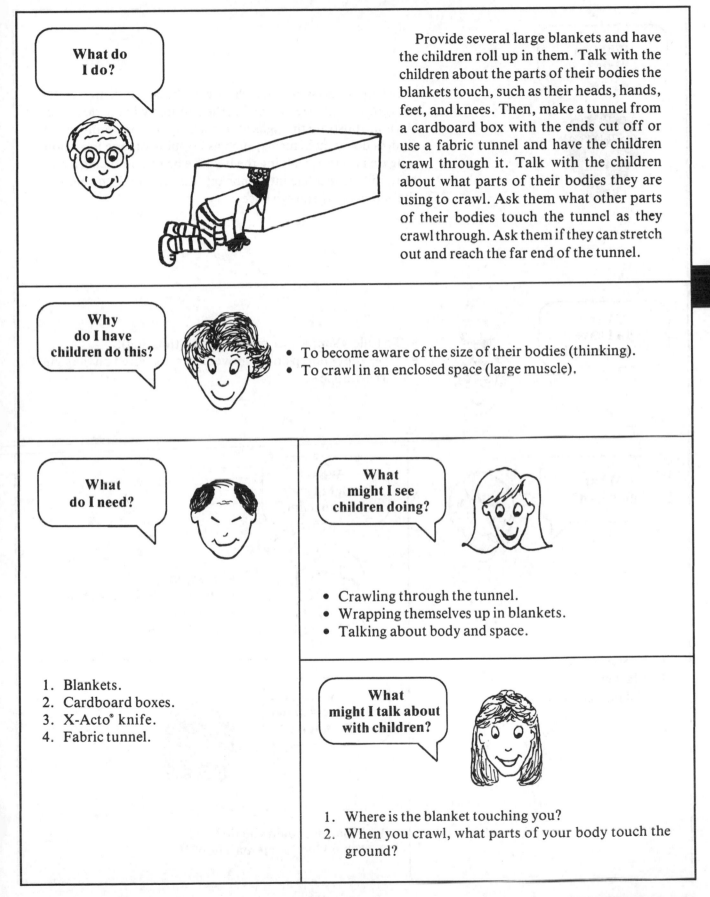

What do I do?

Provide several large blankets and have the children roll up in them. Talk with the children about the parts of their bodies the blankets touch, such as their heads, hands, feet, and knees. Then, make a tunnel from a cardboard box with the ends cut off or use a fabric tunnel and have the children crawl through it. Talk with the children about what parts of their bodies they are using to crawl. Ask them what other parts of their bodies touch the tunnel as they crawl through. Ask them if they can stretch out and reach the far end of the tunnel.

Why do I have children do this?

- To become aware of the size of their bodies (thinking).
- To crawl in an enclosed space (large muscle).

What do I need?

1. Blankets.
2. Cardboard boxes.
3. X-Acto® knife.
4. Fabric tunnel.

What might I see children doing?

- Crawling through the tunnel.
- Wrapping themselves up in blankets.
- Talking about body and space.

What might I talk about with children?

1. Where is the blanket touching you?
2. When you crawl, what parts of your body touch the ground?

LOOK WHAT I CAN DO!
Indoor or Outdoor Large Muscle

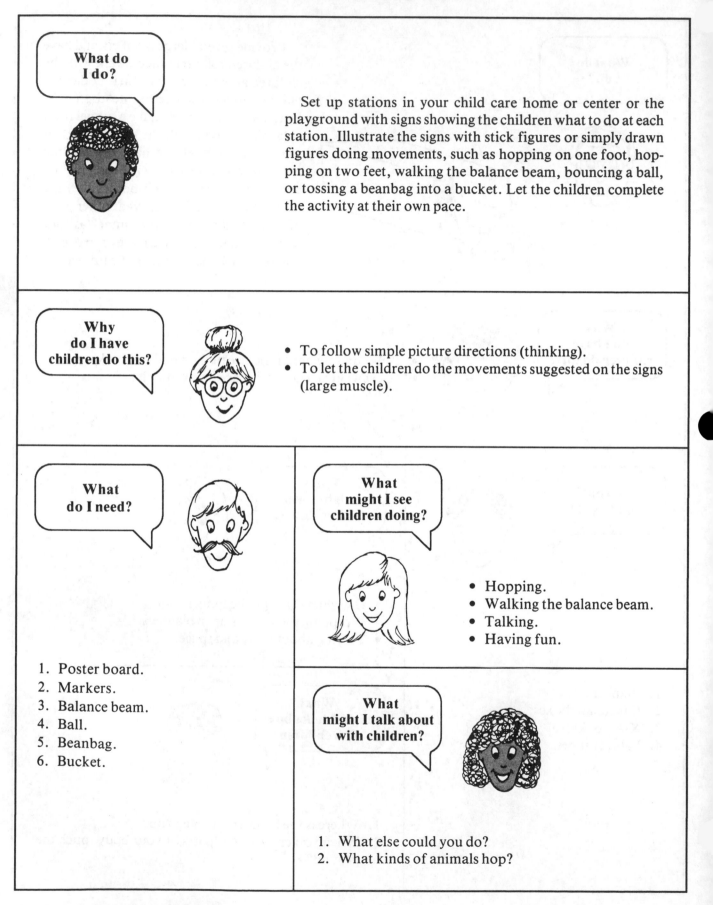

What do I do?

Set up stations in your child care home or center or the playground with signs showing the children what to do at each station. Illustrate the signs with stick figures or simply drawn figures doing movements, such as hopping on one foot, hopping on two feet, walking the balance beam, bouncing a ball, or tossing a beanbag into a bucket. Let the children complete the activity at their own pace.

Why do I have children do this?

- To follow simple picture directions (thinking).
- To let the children do the movements suggested on the signs (large muscle).

What do I need?

1. Poster board.
2. Markers.
3. Balance beam.
4. Ball.
5. Beanbag.
6. Bucket.

What might I see children doing?

- Hopping.
- Walking the balance beam.
- Talking.
- Having fun.

What might I talk about with children?

1. What else could you do?
2. What kinds of animals hop?

I LOVE A PARADE
Outdoor Large Muscle

What do I do?

Put out tricycles, wagons, doll carriages, crepe paper streamers, hats, dress-up clothes, paper, and markers. Encourage the children to decorate the riding toys with streamers and signs and to dress up in the hats and dress-up clothes. Then let them parade on the sidewalk.

Why do I have children do this?

- To have fun and use their imaginations (social-emotional).
- To pedal, push, or pull the riding toys (large muscle).

What do I need?

1. Tricycles.
2. Wagons.
3. Doll carriages.
4. Crepe paper streamers.
5. Hats.
6. Dress-up clothes.
7. Paper.
8. Markers.

What might I see children doing?

- Making signs.
- Having fun.
- Pushing and pulling.
- Laughing.
- Talking.

What might I talk about with children?

1. Where could this parade go?
2. What else could be in your parade?

A QUIET TIME FOR YOU AND ME
Outdoor Large Muscle

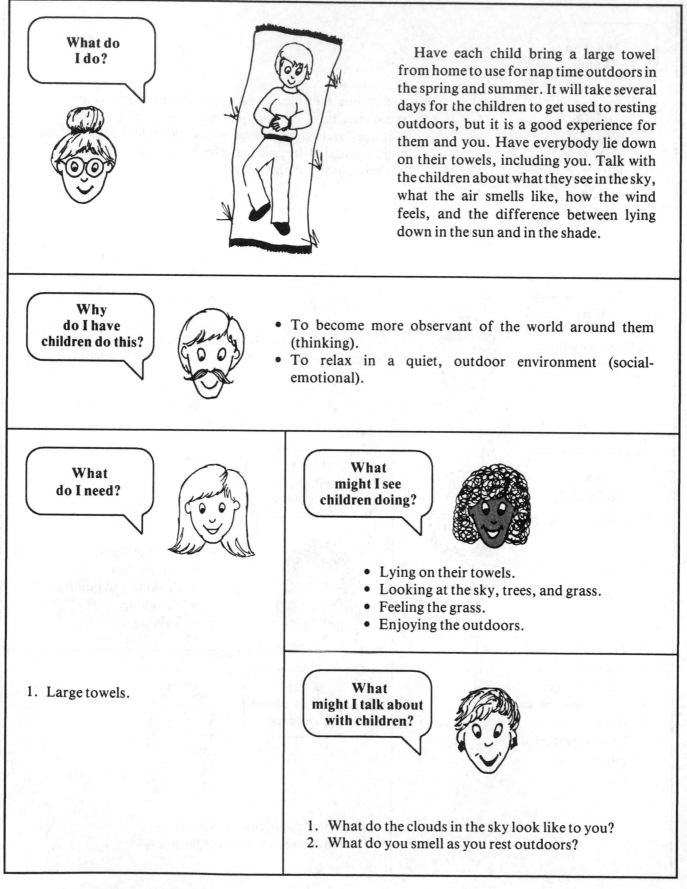

What do I do?

Have each child bring a large towel from home to use for nap time outdoors in the spring and summer. It will take several days for the children to get used to resting outdoors, but it is a good experience for them and you. Have everybody lie down on their towels, including you. Talk with the children about what they see in the sky, what the air smells like, how the wind feels, and the difference between lying down in the sun and in the shade.

Why do I have children do this?

- To become more observant of the world around them (thinking).
- To relax in a quiet, outdoor environment (social-emotional).

What do I need?

1. Large towels.

What might I see children doing?

- Lying on their towels.
- Looking at the sky, trees, and grass.
- Feeling the grass.
- Enjoying the outdoors.

What might I talk about with children?

1. What do the clouds in the sky look like to you?
2. What do you smell as you rest outdoors?

I STRETCH
Indoor or Outdoor Large Muscle

What do I do?

Give each child a sixty-inch piece of one-half-inch elastic with the ends tied together. Have the children stretch the elastic around the sides of their bodies from head to toe. Suggest different ways for the children to move in the elastic, such as jumping, pushing their arms out, or raising their arms high. Let two children use the elastic together. Give the children time to explore and try new movements on their own.

Why do I have children do this?

- To find ways to make elastic stretch with their bodies (thinking).
- To pull with their arms and legs (large and small muscles).
- To have fun (social-emotional).

What do I need?

1. Sixty-inch pieces of one-half-inch elastic.

What might I see children doing?

- Stretching elastic.
- Moving their bodies.
- Talking and having fun.

What might I talk about with children?

1. How can you stretch the elastic from your head to your toes?
2. What can you do inside your elastic?

"HOKEY POKEY"
Indoor or Outdoor Large Muscle

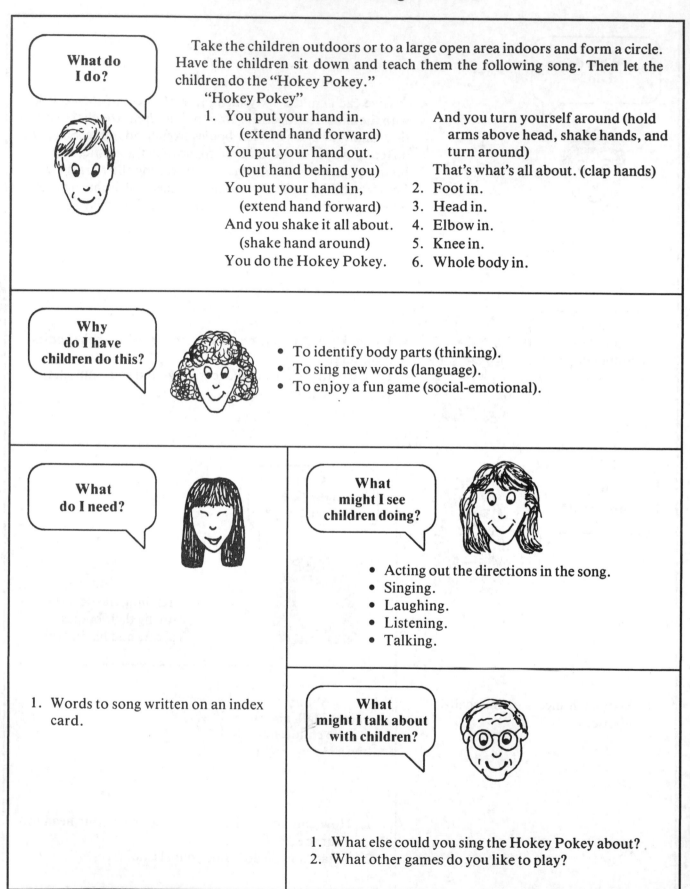

What do I do?

Take the children outdoors or to a large open area indoors and form a circle. Have the children sit down and teach them the following song. Then let the children do the "Hokey Pokey."

"Hokey Pokey"

1. You put your hand in.
   (extend hand forward)
You put your hand out.
   (put hand behind you)
You put your hand in,
   (extend hand forward)
And you shake it all about.
   (shake hand around)
You do the Hokey Pokey.

And you turn yourself around (hold arms above head, shake hands, and turn around)
That's what's all about. (clap hands)
2. Foot in.
3. Head in.
4. Elbow in.
5. Knee in.
6. Whole body in.

Why do I have children do this?

- To identify body parts (thinking).
- To sing new words (language).
- To enjoy a fun game (social-emotional).

What do I need?

1. Words to song written on an index card.

What might I see children doing?

- Acting out the directions in the song.
- Singing.
- Laughing.
- Listening.
- Talking.

What might I talk about with children?

1. What else could you sing the Hokey Pokey about?
2. What other games do you like to play?

I CAN BE ALL KINDS OF THINGS
Indoor or Outdoor Large Muscle

What do I do?

Take the children outdoors or to a large open area indoors. Talk with them about what they can pretend to be. Let them suggest what they can be and then let them role-play those things. Some examples are a ball, egg beater, kite, spider, saw cutting wood, bird, frog, elephant, and yo-yo.

Why do I have children do this?

- To crawl, roll, and jump (large muscle).
- To name what they can be (thinking).

What do I need?

No supplies are needed.

What might I see children doing?

- Rolling.
- Jumping.
- Pretending to fly.
- Laughing.
- Talking.

What might I talk about with children?

1. What else could you be?
2. If you were a kite, where would you like to fly?

SNOWY DAY TRACKS
Outdoor Large Muscle

What do I do?

If you live in an area where it snows, read *The Snowy Day* by E. J. Keats and talk about what Peter wore when he went out to play. As you and the children are getting ready to go outdoors to play in the snow, talk about zipping coats, tying hats, and putting on boots. Let the children dress themselves as much as possible. Make cardboard tracks for the children to put on their feet once you get outside. Cut out several different-shaped sets of tracks. Staple pieces of elastic to the sides of each track, so the children can wear them over their boots. Have the children compare the cardboard tracks and their footprints in the snow. Look for real rabbit, dog, or squirrel tracks.

Why do I have children do this?

- To zip and button coats and put on boots (social emotional).
- To make tracks in the snow (large muscle).
- To compare cardboard tracks and their footprints (thinking).

What do I need?

1. *The Snowy Day* by E. J. Keats.
2. Cardboard.
3. Scissors.
4. Elastic.
5. Stapler.

What might I see children doing?

- Putting on cardboard tracks.
- Looking for tracks.
- Comparing tracks.
- Talking.

What might I talk about with children?

1. Where would be a good place to look for tracks?
2. What else could you do to make marks in the snow?

"ROUND AND ROUND THE PLAYGROUND I GO"
Outdoor Large Muscle

What do I do?

Tie colored streamers on different items around the playground, such as the swings, slide, trees, bushes, and sandbox. Take the children out to the playground and stop at each streamer. Have the children form a circle and move clockwise as they sing the following song to the tune of "Pop Goes the Weasel." Have the children act out the motion in the song as they go around the circle. At each streamer, change the last line of the song. Have the children help you make up new last lines to the song.

"Round and Round the Playground I Go"

1. Round and round the playground I go.
   It is fun and easy.
   Won't you come and follow me
   On your tippie-toesies?

2. In your running shoesies?
3. With your hopping bunnies?
4. On your galloping horsie?

Why do I have children do this?

- To sing (language).
- To run, hop, and gallop (large muscle).

What do I need?

What might I see children doing?

- Singing.
- Running.
- Hopping.
- Galloping.
- Having a good time.

1. Colored streamers.
2. Words to song written on an index card.

What might I talk about with children?

1. If you could go anywhere, where would you gallop on your horse?
2. What other movements could you make?

BIBLIOGRAPHY

ME, I'M SPECIAL

Abercrombie, B. 1990. *Charlie Anderson*. New York, NY: Macmillan Children's Group Books.
A stray cat arrives to become part of Sarah and Elizabeth's family. When he doesn't return one night, they search for him and discover he has two houses and two families. The other family loves him just like they do. Good for children in stepfamilies.

Anholt, C., and Anholt, L. 1996. *What Makes Me Happy?* Cambridge, MA: Candlewick Press.
A child lists all the things that make her laugh, sad, and jealous, and ends by talking about the things that make her happy.

[3]Arbuthnot, M.H. 1968. *Time for Poetry*. Glenview, IL: ScottForesman and Company.
A collection of poetry especially for children that includes poems about people, travel, magic, wind, wisdom, and beauty.

Asch, F. 1984. *Just Like Daddy*. New York, NY: Simon and Schuster Trade.
Little bear does everything just like Daddy except when it comes to fishing. Then he catches big fish just like Mommy.

Bang, M. 1999. *When Sophie Gets Angry—Really, Really, Angry*. New York, NY: Blue Sky Press.
Everyone gets angry sometimes. For children this can be upsetting and frightening. This book helps children explore how to handle angry feelings.

Bemelmans, L. 1995. *Madeline*. New York, NY: Viking Children's Books.
A charming, memorable story about the little girls of a French school and their fearless leader, Madeline.

[3]Blanchard, A. 1988. *Sounds My Feet Make: Just Right for 2's and 3's*. New York, NY: Random House, Inc.
A child's feet make a variety of sounds while walking in a puddle, stepping on a metal grid, trudging upstairs, and wearing different types of shoes.

Bos, B. 1989. *Ollie the Elephant*. New York, NY: North-South Books.
Ollie, the elephant, wants to look like all his friends, but he realizes he is special just as he is.

Browne, A. 1989. *Willy the Wimp*. New York, NY: Alfred A. Knopf, Inc.
A young chimpanzee decides he is tired of being bullied around. He then decides to solve the problem and not be a wimp anymore.

[3]Buckley, H. 1963. *My Sister and I*. New York, NY: Lothrop, Lee, and Shepard Books.
This book details activities enjoyed by sisters, such as swinging, sharing hiding places, singing, and caring for each other when they are ill.

Carle, E. 1994. *My Apron*. New York, NY: Philomel Books.
Eric Carle recalls the apron he loved as a child. His aunt made him one to match the one worn by his Uncle Adam when he did construction work. Eric wore his apron when he helped his uncle and remembers how good it made him feel when he was asked to help.

[3]Christiansen, C.B. 1989. *My Mother's House, My Father's House*. New York, NY: Macmillan Children's Group Books.
A child describes having two different houses to live in—"my mother's house" and "my father's house"—and what it is like to travel back and forth between them.

[3]Cooney, N.E. 1981. *The Blanket That Had to Go*. New York, NY: Putnam's.
Suzi loves her blanket. She starts kindergarten soon and has to find a way to take her blanket with her.

Crowe, R. 1987. *Clyde Monster*. New York, NY: Dutton Children's Books.
Clyde is a happy monster who hates to go to bed because he is afraid a "person" is hiding in the dark to scare him. His parents help him overcome his fear of people and the dark.

Curtis, J. 1996. *Tell Me Again About the Night I Was Born*. New York, NY: Joanna Cotler Books.
A story about the night a little girl was born and the joy her parents felt when they adopted her and held her in their arms.

De Paola, T. 1981. *Now One Foot, Now the Other*. New York, NY: The Putnam Publishing Group.
The book explores the relationship between a boy and his grandfather, who has suffered a stroke. The boy reteaches his grandfather much of what his grandfather helped him learn.

Ets, M. 1965. *Just Me*. New York, NY: Viking Children's Books.
A little boy spends a day on a farm imitating various animals. However, when he is ready to go out on the pond with his father, he runs like himself. Black-and-white pictures.

Ets, M. 1976. *Play with Me*. New York, NY: Puffin Books.
A little girl loves animals and wants to play with them. She learns she must be quiet or she will frighten the animals.

Freeman, D. 1976. *Bearymore*. New York, NY: Viking Children's Books.
A circus bear has difficulty hibernating and thinking up a new act for the circus at the same time. He comes up with a successful solution.

Freeman, D. 1964. *Dandelion*. New York, NY: Viking Children's Books.
A lion decides to dress up for his friend's come-as-you-are party and is turned away because he is not recognized. He decides it is best to be himself.

Galbraith, K.O. 1990. *Laura Charlotte*. New York, NY: Philomel Books.
A mother describes her love for a toy elephant she was given as a child. She has
   now passed the gift on to her daughter.

Gould, D. 1989. *Aaron's Shirt*. New York, NY: Bradbury Press.
Aaron loves his favorite shirt and after wearing it constantly for two years, he is
   reluctant to admit he has outgrown it.

[1, 3]Green, M. 1960. *Is It Hard? Is It Easy?* New York, NY: Young Scott Books.
This fun book shows how some things are hard, some are easy, some everybody has
   trouble doing, and some we all do together.

[1, 3]Green, M. 1969. *Everybody Grows Up*. New York, NY: Franklin Watts.
The story is about growing up and how children, as well as animals, eventually do grow
   up. The book illustrates how animals and children learn new things as they grow.

Greenfield, E. 1980. *Grandma's Joy*. New York, NY: Philomel Books.
A little girl tries to cheer up her despondent grandmother by reminding her of some
   very important things.

Hoberman, M.A. 1982. *A House Is a House for Me*. New York, NY: Puffin Books.
Sing-song rhymes and detailed illustrations fill this amusing book. The story looks
   at houses for various items, such as mice, secrets, and pennies. Everything has a
   house of its own.

Hoffman, M. 1991. *Amazing Grace*. Columbus, OH: SRA McMillan/McGraw Hill.
Grace is not considered by her classmates to be right for the role of Peter Pan
   because she is a girl and is dark-skinned. However, she practices constantly and
   is encouraged by her grandmother who tells her "to do anything she imagines."

Hoffman, M. 1995. *Boundless Grace*. New York, NY: Dial Books.
Grace's father, whom she barely remembers, invites her to come to Africa to visit
   him and his new family. Nana goes to help her make the transition and to discover that love will survive great distance.

[1, 3]Howell, L., and Howell, R. 1985. *Winifred's New Bed*. New York, NY:
   Alfred A Knopf.
Winifred moves from a crib to a grownup bed, and it makes her feel lonely.
   However, she comes up with a solution that results in a colorful, cumulative tale
   that is delightful.

Keats, E.J. 1964. *Whistle for Willie*. New York, NY: Viking Children's Books.
Peter is trying to whistle so his dog, Willie, will follow him. He cannot seem to
   whistle, but he keeps on trying, and guess what?

Keats, E.J. 1967. *Peter's Chair*. New York, NY: HarperCollins Children's Books.
Peter is jealous of the new baby who sleeps in his old crib, which is now painted
   pink. In the end, he realizes he is growing and is too big for his baby chair, too.

Keats, E.J. 1976. *The Snowy Day*. New York, NY: Puffin Books.
A story about Peter and his wonderful day in the new snow.

Keats, E.J. 1987. *The Trip*. New York, NY: Mulberry Books.
Louis has just moved to a new neighborhood and is lonely. He gets out a shoebox,
   crayons, and paper and starts on an adventure.

Kennedy, J. 1989. *The Teddy Bears' Picnic*. San Marco, CA: Green Tiger Press.
The teddy bears are having a picnic and there is a big surprise at the end!

Koehler, P. 1990. *The Day We Met You*. New York, NY: Bradbury Press.
Mom and Dad recount the exciting day when they adopted their baby.

Kraus, R. 1971. *Leo the Late Bloomer*. New York, NY: HarperCollins Children's Books.
Leo couldn't do things other children were doing. His father was worried. His
    mother told him not to worry, that Leo will "bloom" in his own time. This is a
    delightful and colorfully illustrated story.

Lasker, J. 1972. *Mothers Can Do Anything*. Morton Grove, IL: Albert Whitman
    and Company.
This book discusses all the jobs mothers can do, emphasizing nontraditional roles
    such as building construction, road construction, and power and light utility jobs.

Lester, H. 1985. *It Wasn't My Fault*. Boston, MA: Houghton Mifflin.
This is a funny story about Murdley Gurdson, who is usually at fault when accidents
    happen. However, when a bird lays an egg on his head, he realizes it is nobody's
    fault. Some things just happen.

[2,3]Levitin, S. 1979. *A Sound to Remember*. New York, NY: Harcourt Brace Jovanovich.
Jacov, a child with special needs, is given the special honor of "blowing the shofar
    (ram's horn)" on the Jewish high holy day. The story illustrates that people can
    make a difference in our lives by having compassion and being concerned.

[2,3]Lexau, J. 1971. *Me Day*. New York, NY: The Dial Press.
The reader spends Rafer's birthday with him. The story takes you through Rafer's
    reaction to his parents' divorce and how important the celebration of a special
    day can be to a child.

Lindsay, J. 1996. *Do I Have a Daddy? A Story About a Single-Parent Child*. Buena
    Park, CA: Morning Glory Press.
A story that explains to a young child why his father is not present in the family as
    he is growing up. The mother explains, "Caring for a baby is a big job, and your
    daddy wasn't ready for that."

[3]Lionni, L. 1975. *Pezzettino*. New York, NY: Pantheon.
Pezzettino is so small he does not see himself as "special." A wise man helps him
    discover he is unique.

Loomans, D. 1991. *The Lovables in the Kingdom of Self-Esteem*. Tiburon, CA: H.J.
    Kramer, Inc.
Each member of the Lovables has a special gift. Each character helps the child to
    discover an avenue that leads to self-esteem.

[1]Martin, B. Jr. and Archambault, J. 1985. *Here Are My Hands*. New York, NY:
    Henry Holt and Company.
A picture book with rhyming text about body parts that invites the children to role-
    play. The illustrations offer opportunities for teaching about the similarities and
    differences in people.

[2]Martin, B. Jr. and Archambault, J. 1987. *Knots on a Counting Rope*. New York, NY:
    Henry Holt and Company.
Story of a blind Native American boy who learns to master many skills, such as
    horseback riding. This beautifully illustrated book will help children develop an
    understanding of children with disabilities.

[1]Marzollo, J. 1978. *Close Your Eyes*. New York, NY: Dial Books for Young Readers.
A wonderfully illustrated lullaby of a father's attempt to put his reluctant child to bed.

Minarik, E. 1992. *Am I Beautiful?* New York, NY: Greenwillow.
With a great deal of self-confidence and a face that only a mother could love, Young
    Hippo walks around asking, "Am I beautiful?" He receives the answer he wants
    to hear when he finds his own mother.

[3]Morris, W. 1990. *Just Listen*. New York, NY: Atheneum Children's Books.
Grandma teaches Tara how to listen to her own special song.

Munsch, R. 1986. *Love You Forever*. Buffalo, NY: Firefly Books, Ltd.
The story begins as a young mother sings "I'll love you forever" and follows the
    growth of the child to adulthood. The young man sings the same song to his
    mother when she is old and frail.

Older, E. 2000. *My Two Grandmothers*. San Diego, CA: Harcourt, Inc.
This book tells about a girl with a city grandmother and a country granny who have
    unique family and cultural traditions. Lily decides to start a "new" tradition with
    her grandmothers.

[3]Osborn, L. 1982. *My Brother Is Afraid of Just about Everything*. Niles, IL:
    Albert Whitman.
Big brother can't understand his little brother's many fears until he encounters his
    own fear.

Osofsky, A. 1992. *Dreamcatcher*. New York, NY: Orchard Books.
As a baby slumbers on his cradleboard, he is protected from bad dreams by a dream-
    catcher that was woven by his sister. The Objibway Indians of the Great Lakes
    treasured good dreams as a source of wisdom, and children were encouraged to
    remember their good dreams.

Piper, W. 1981. *The Little Engine That Could*. Cutchogue, NY: Buccaneer Books.
The story is about a little blue train that can climb the biggest mountain with some
    encouragement from friends.

Radin, R.Y. 1989. *High in the Mountains*. New York, NY: Macmillan Children's Books.
A young child describes a day spent near Grandpa's house in the mountains.

Rojany, Lisa, 1996. *Tell Me About When I Was a Baby*. New York, NY: Intervisual
    Books, Inc.
A charming pop-up book about a baby's life from birth to taking first steps.

[3]Royston, A. 1991. *What's Inside My Body?* New York, NY: Dorling Kindersley, Inc.
Designed to help young children understand the inner workings of their bodies—
    heart, lungs, and skeleton.

Simon, N. 1981. *Nobody's Perfect, Not Even My Mother*. Morton Grove, IL: Albert
    Whitman and Company.
A young child learns no one is perfect, including his mother, yet people are wonder-
    ful anyway.

[3]Solomon, D. 1990. *Oh Brother! Giggles, Gasps and Groans Growing Up Together*.
    New York, NY: Warner Juvenile Books.
Delightful story about brothers and the positive and negative things they do.

[3]Solomon, D. 1990. *Oh Sister!* New York, NY: Warner Juvenile Books.
Delightful story about sisters and the positive and negative things they do.

Viorst, J. 1989. *Alexander and the Terrible, Horrible, No Good, Very Bad Day*. New York, NY: Macmillan Children's Book Group.
Alexander's day started with gum in his hair. Everything went wrong, right down to the lima beans for supper and kissing on TV. Alexander is glad to learn some days are like that for other people, too.

Waddell, M. 1992. *Owl Babies*. Cambridge, MA: Candlewick Press.
Owl babies are shown huddling together after they wake up and realize their Mommy is not in the nest. They talk about where she might be and try to support one another as anxiety rises. The feelings of relief when she returns will be well understood by young children who need the promise that their mommies will always return.

[3]Wickstrom, S. 1989. *Mothers Can't Get Sick*. New York, NY: Crown Publishers.
Story about a mother who is planning special activities for a child when she gets sick. The children take over and show they can be very helpful.

Williams, M. 1990. *The Velveteen Rabbit*. New York, NY: David McKay Co., Inc.
Velveteen is a stuffed rabbit who wants to be real. Velveteen becomes real through the love of the little boy.

[1]Williams, V. 1990. *More More More, Said the Baby*. New York, NY: Greenwillow Books.
A toddler's energy is accentuated. Good multicultural illustrations.

Woodson, J. 2000. *Sweet, Sweet Memory*. New York, NY: Hyperion Books.
After Grandpa is gone, Sarah tries to remember what he told her about how everything and everyone goes on and on.

Yolen, J. 1987. *Owl Moon*. New York, NY: Philomel Books.
On a winter's night under a full moon, father and daughter trek into the woods to see the Great Horned Owl. The relationship between the father and daughter is heartwarming.

[3]Zindel, P. 1975. *I Love My Mother*. New York, NY: HarperCollins Children's Books.
A boy tells why he loves his mom, and at the end, how he misses his dad.

Zolotow, C. 1972. *William's Doll*. New York, NY: Harper Collins Children's Books.
William wants a doll, but his brother teases him and his father buys him other toys like a train and basketball. One day his grandmother visits; she responds to his request and gets him a doll to hug, cradle, and love so he can practice being a father.

We have marked these books if we think they are definitely more applicable to one age. Many can be used by all ages with adaptations by the teacher.

[1]Books for one-year-olds, two-year-olds, and three-year-olds.

[2]Books for five-year-olds.

[3]This book is no longer in print. However, you may be able to find it at your local library.

Unit 4

NURSERY RHYMES

CONTENTS

NURSERY RHYMES

"Nursery Rhymes" offers the children opportunities in listening, thinking, role-playing, problem-solving, creative movement, and math. It also provides opportunities for music, art, science, and language.

In this unit, you want children to learn that:

• Words in nursery rhymes, such as kittens and mittens, rhyme.
• Reading nursery rhymes and reading in general is fun.
• Listening to rhymes and stories is interesting.
• Role-playing nursery rhymes makes the nursery rhymes part of their lives and worlds.
• Nursery rhymes and fantasy are part of their heritage.

Nursery rhymes are easy to read and involve interactive language between you and the child. Many different nursery rhyme books are available. For this unit, choose your favorite version that contains a complete selection of nursery rhymes.

"HUMPTY DUMPTY"
Group

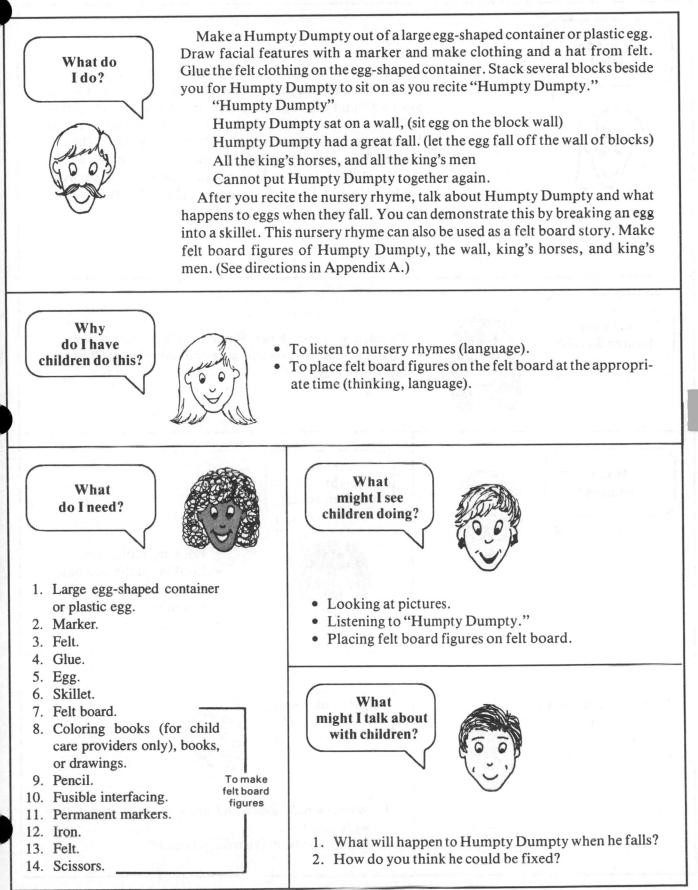

What do I do?

Make a Humpty Dumpty out of a large egg-shaped container or plastic egg. Draw facial features with a marker and make clothing and a hat from felt. Glue the felt clothing on the egg-shaped container. Stack several blocks beside you for Humpty Dumpty to sit on as you recite "Humpty Dumpty."

"Humpty Dumpty"
Humpty Dumpty sat on a wall, (sit egg on the block wall)
Humpty Dumpty had a great fall. (let the egg fall off the wall of blocks)
All the king's horses, and all the king's men
Cannot put Humpty Dumpty together again.

After you recite the nursery rhyme, talk about Humpty Dumpty and what happens to eggs when they fall. You can demonstrate this by breaking an egg into a skillet. This nursery rhyme can also be used as a felt board story. Make felt board figures of Humpty Dumpty, the wall, king's horses, and king's men. (See directions in Appendix A.)

Why do I have children do this?

- To listen to nursery rhymes (language).
- To place felt board figures on the felt board at the appropriate time (thinking, language).

What do I need?

1. Large egg-shaped container or plastic egg.
2. Marker.
3. Felt.
4. Glue.
5. Egg.
6. Skillet.
7. Felt board.
8. Coloring books (for child care providers only), books, or drawings.
9. Pencil.
10. Fusible interfacing.
11. Permanent markers.
12. Iron.
13. Felt.
14. Scissors.

To make felt board figures

What might I see children doing?

- Looking at pictures.
- Listening to "Humpty Dumpty."
- Placing felt board figures on felt board.

What might I talk about with children?

1. What will happen to Humpty Dumpty when he falls?
2. How do you think he could be fixed?

"PETER, PETER, PUMPKIN-EATER"
Group

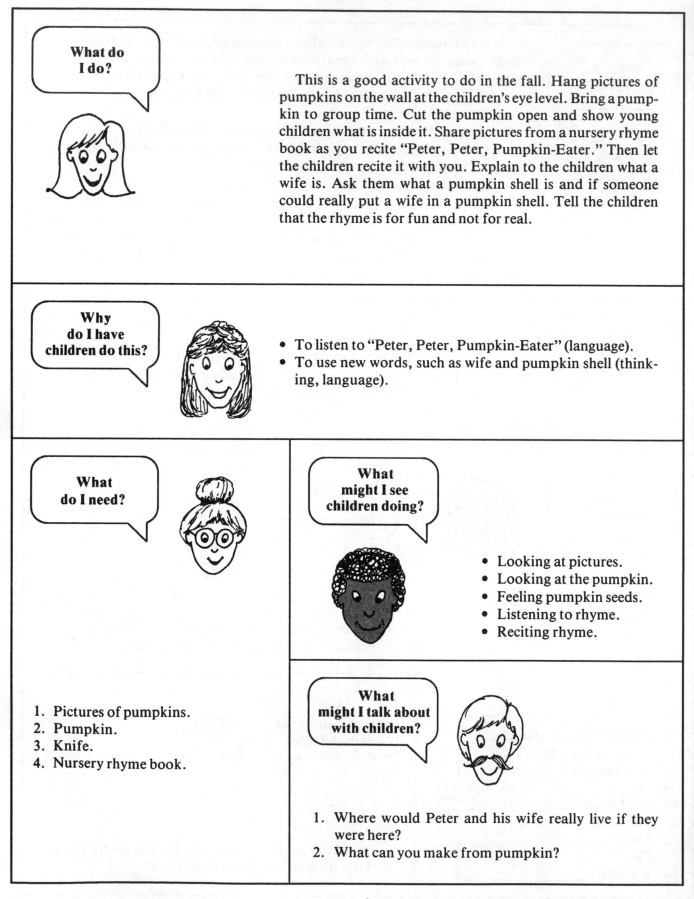

What do I do?

This is a good activity to do in the fall. Hang pictures of pumpkins on the wall at the children's eye level. Bring a pumpkin to group time. Cut the pumpkin open and show young children what is inside it. Share pictures from a nursery rhyme book as you recite "Peter, Peter, Pumpkin-Eater." Then let the children recite it with you. Explain to the children what a wife is. Ask them what a pumpkin shell is and if someone could really put a wife in a pumpkin shell. Tell the children that the rhyme is for fun and not for real.

Why do I have children do this?

- To listen to "Peter, Peter, Pumpkin-Eater" (language).
- To use new words, such as wife and pumpkin shell (thinking, language).

What do I need?

1. Pictures of pumpkins.
2. Pumpkin.
3. Knife.
4. Nursery rhyme book.

What might I see children doing?

- Looking at pictures.
- Looking at the pumpkin.
- Feeling pumpkin seeds.
- Listening to rhyme.
- Reciting rhyme.

What might I talk about with children?

1. Where would Peter and his wife really live if they were here?
2. What can you make from pumpkin?

"JACK AND JILL"
Group

What do I do?

Hang large pictures of Jack and Jill on the wall at the children's eye level. Recite the first two verses of "Jack and Jill" and share pictures from a nursery rhyme book with the children. Then let the children recite the nursery rhyme with you. Talk about the words crown (head), caper (to leap or prance about), nob (head), and vinegar. Let the children smell a small amount of vinegar. Ask them what they think about using it for medicine. Ask them what their parents use to help them when they get hurt.

Why do I have children do this?

- To listen to "Jack and Jill" (language).
- To smell the vinegar, which was used as medicine (thinking).

What do I need?

1. Pictures of Jack and Jill.
2. Nursery rhyme book.
3. Vinegar.

What might I see children doing?

- Looking at pictures.
- Listening to "Jack and Jill."
- Smelling the vinegar.
- Talking.

What might I talk about with children?

1. Where would you go if you hurt your head?
2. How would your Daddy fix your head?

"LITTLE MISS MUFFET"
Group

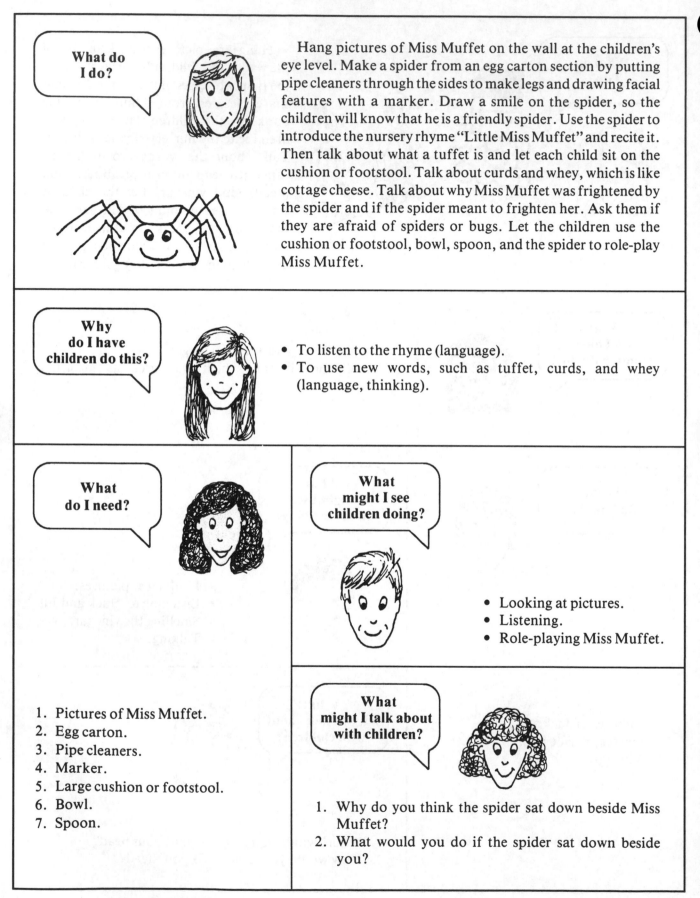

What do I do?

Hang pictures of Miss Muffet on the wall at the children's eye level. Make a spider from an egg carton section by putting pipe cleaners through the sides to make legs and drawing facial features with a marker. Draw a smile on the spider, so the children will know that he is a friendly spider. Use the spider to introduce the nursery rhyme "Little Miss Muffet" and recite it. Then talk about what a tuffet is and let each child sit on the cushion or footstool. Talk about curds and whey, which is like cottage cheese. Talk about why Miss Muffet was frightened by the spider and if the spider meant to frighten her. Ask them if they are afraid of spiders or bugs. Let the children use the cushion or footstool, bowl, spoon, and the spider to role-play Miss Muffet.

Why do I have children do this?

- To listen to the rhyme (language).
- To use new words, such as tuffet, curds, and whey (language, thinking).

What do I need?

What might I see children doing?

- Looking at pictures.
- Listening.
- Role-playing Miss Muffet.

1. Pictures of Miss Muffet.
2. Egg carton.
3. Pipe cleaners.
4. Marker.
5. Large cushion or footstool.
6. Bowl.
7. Spoon.

What might I talk about with children?

1. Why do you think the spider sat down beside Miss Muffet?
2. What would you do if the spider sat down beside you?

"THREE LITTLE KITTENS"
Group

What do I do?

Bring real kittens or stuffed kittens to the group to introduce the nursery rhyme "Three Little Kittens." (If you bring in real kittens, be sure to carefully supervise them and the children.) Then talk about kittens and what they do. Let the children tell you stories about their kittens' activities. Recite "Three Little Kittens" and share pictures from a nursery rhyme book with the children. Then repeat the nursery rhyme, letting the children make the kitten sounds.

Why do I have children do this?

- To listen to "Three Little Kittens" (language).
- To make the appropriate kitten sounds (thinking, language).

What do I need?

1. Real or stuffed kittens.
2. Nursery rhyme book.

What might I see children doing?

- Looking at kittens.
- Petting kittens.
- Talking.
- Making kitten sounds.

What might I talk about with children?

1. What do kittens like to do?
2. What would you do if you lost your mittens?

"THERE WAS AN OLD WOMAN"
Group

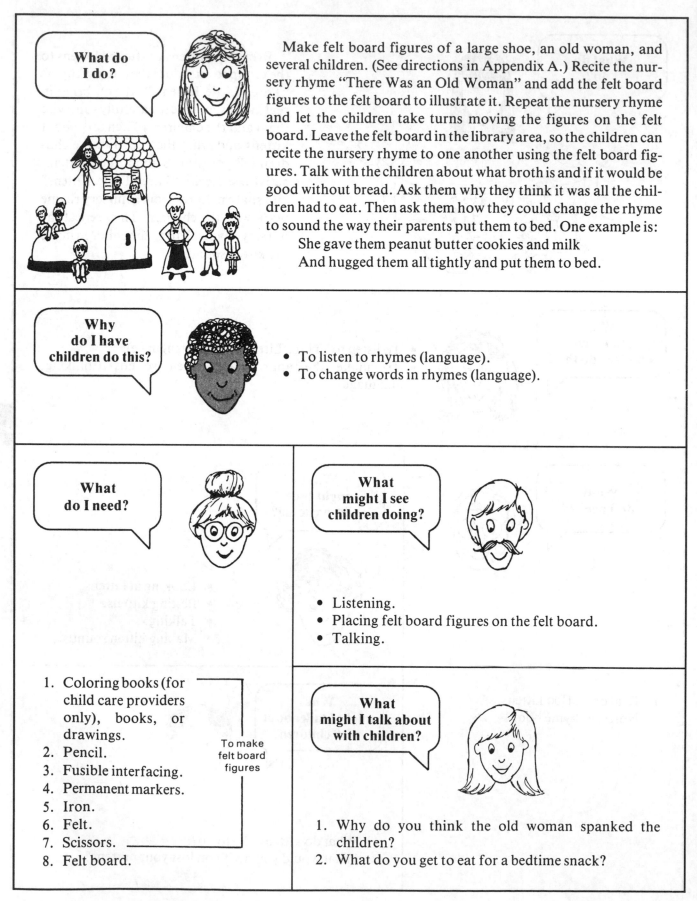

What do I do?

Make felt board figures of a large shoe, an old woman, and several children. (See directions in Appendix A.) Recite the nursery rhyme "There Was an Old Woman" and add the felt board figures to the felt board to illustrate it. Repeat the nursery rhyme and let the children take turns moving the figures on the felt board. Leave the felt board in the library area, so the children can recite the nursery rhyme to one another using the felt board figures. Talk with the children about what broth is and if it would be good without bread. Ask them why they think it was all the children had to eat. Then ask them how they could change the rhyme to sound the way their parents put them to bed. One example is:

She gave them peanut butter cookies and milk
And hugged them all tightly and put them to bed.

Why do I have children do this?

- To listen to rhymes (language).
- To change words in rhymes (language).

What do I need?

1. Coloring books (for child care providers only), books, or drawings.
2. Pencil.
3. Fusible interfacing.
4. Permanent markers.
5. Iron.
6. Felt.
7. Scissors.
8. Felt board.

To make felt board figures

What might I see children doing?

- Listening.
- Placing felt board figures on the felt board.
- Talking.

What might I talk about with children?

1. Why do you think the old woman spanked the children?
2. What do you get to eat for a bedtime snack?

"HEY, DIDDLE, DIDDLE!"
Group

What do I do?

Make felt board figures of a cat, fiddle, cow, moon, dish, spoon, and dog. (See directions in Appendix A.) Recite the nursery rhyme "Hey, Diddle, Diddle!" and add the felt board figures to the felt board to illustrate it. You can also make poster board figures and glue them to craft sticks to make puppets. Talk with the children about whether a cat can play a fiddle or a cow can jump over the moon. Ask them if a dish can really run away with a spoon. Help the children realize that this nursery rhyme is fantasy and not reality.

Why do I have children do this?

- To place the felt board figures on the felt board during the story (language, thinking).
- To distinguish between reality and fantasy in stories (thinking, social-emotional).

What do I need?

1. Coloring books (for child care providers only), books, or drawings.
2. Pencil.
3. Fusible interfacing.
4. Permanent markers.
5. Iron.
6. Felt.
7. Scissors.
8. Felt board.
9. Poster board.
10. Craft sticks.

To make felt board figures

What might I see children doing?

- Listening.
- Placing felt board figures on felt board.
- Talking.

What might I talk about with children?

1. Where do you think the spoon and the dish went?
2. Where can you find the moon?

"OLD KING COLE"
Group

What do I do?

Recite the nursery rhyme "Old King Cole." Let the children recite the rhyme, while role-playing Old King Cole and his fiddlers. Provide a box that contains a crown, a robe, a bubble pipe, a bowl, three cardboard fiddles, and a box or chair for a throne. Give each child a chance to participate.

Why do I have children do this?

- To listen to the nursery rhyme (language).
- To role-play the nursery rhyme (language, social-emotional).

What do I need?

What might I see children doing?

- Listening.
- Putting on dress-up clothes.
- Role-playing "Old King Cole."
- Talking.

1. Box.
2. Crown.
3. Robe.
4. Bubble pipe.
5. Bowl.
6. Three cardboard fiddles.
7. Box or chair for throne.

What might I talk about with children?

1. Why does Old King Cole have fiddlers?
2. What do you think Old King Cole put in his bowl?

"POLLY, PUT THE KETTLE ON"
Group

What do I do?

Share pictures from a nursery rhyme book as you recite the nursery rhyme "Polly, Put the Kettle On." Then talk about what Polly is doing–putting the kettle on the range to heat water for tea–and what Sukey is doing–taking the kettle off the range. Ask the children what else people have at tea parties. Tell them that they can have a tea party in the dramatic play activity "Polly and Sukey's Tea Party" on page 311.

Why do I have children do this?

- To listen to rhymes (language).
- To talk about what is done at a tea party (language).

What do I need?

1. Nursery rhyme book.

What might I see children doing?

- Listening to rhyme.
- Looking at pictures in nursery rhyme books.
- Talking.

What might I talk about with children?

1. What would you like at a tea party?
2. How do you make tea?

"BAA, BAA, BLACK SHEEP"
Group

What do I do?

Make felt board figures of a sheep, man, woman, little boy, and three bags of wool. (See directions in Appendix A.) Recite the nursery rhyme "Baa, Baa, Black Sheep" and add the felt board figures to the felt board to illustrate it. Repeat the nursery rhyme and let the children take turns moving the figures on the felt board. Leave the felt board in the library area, so the children can recite the nursery rhyme to one another using the felt board figures. Talk with the children about where the wool comes from and what we do with wool. Provide several pieces of wool clothing for the children to feel. Try to get a piece of natural wool from a sheared sheep.

Why do I have children do this?

- To use the felt board to tell the nursery rhyme "Baa, Baa, Black Sheep" (language, small muscle).
- To feel clothes to identify wool (thinking).

What do I need?

1. Coloring books (for child care provider only), books, or drawings.
2. Pencil.
3. Fusible interfacing.
4. Permanent markers.
5. Iron.
6. Felt.
7. Scissors.
8. Felt board.
9. Wool clothing.
10. Piece of natural wool.

To make felt board figures

What might I see children doing?

- Listening to nursery rhyme.
- Placing felt board figures on felt board.
- Reciting nursery rhyme.
- Feeling clothing.

What might I talk about with children?

1. Where do sheep live?
2. What is a lane?

KITTEN BOOK
Learning Center (art)

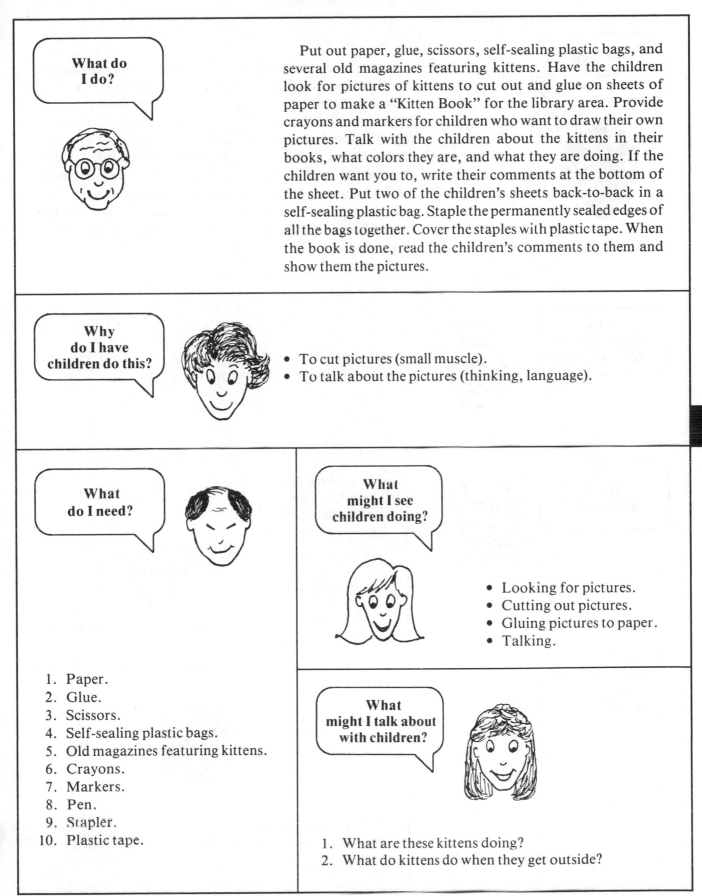

What do I do?

Put out paper, glue, scissors, self-sealing plastic bags, and several old magazines featuring kittens. Have the children look for pictures of kittens to cut out and glue on sheets of paper to make a "Kitten Book" for the library area. Provide crayons and markers for children who want to draw their own pictures. Talk with the children about the kittens in their books, what colors they are, and what they are doing. If the children want you to, write their comments at the bottom of the sheet. Put two of the children's sheets back-to-back in a self-sealing plastic bag. Staple the permanently sealed edges of all the bags together. Cover the staples with plastic tape. When the book is done, read the children's comments to them and show them the pictures.

Why do I have children do this?

- To cut pictures (small muscle).
- To talk about the pictures (thinking, language).

What do I need?

What might I see children doing?

- Looking for pictures.
- Cutting out pictures.
- Gluing pictures to paper.
- Talking.

1. Paper.
2. Glue.
3. Scissors.
4. Self-sealing plastic bags.
5. Old magazines featuring kittens.
6. Crayons.
7. Markers.
8. Pen.
9. Stapler.
10. Plastic tape.

What might I talk about with children?

1. What are these kittens doing?
2. What do kittens do when they get outside?

"HUMPTY DUMPTY" EGG DECORATING
Learning Center (art)

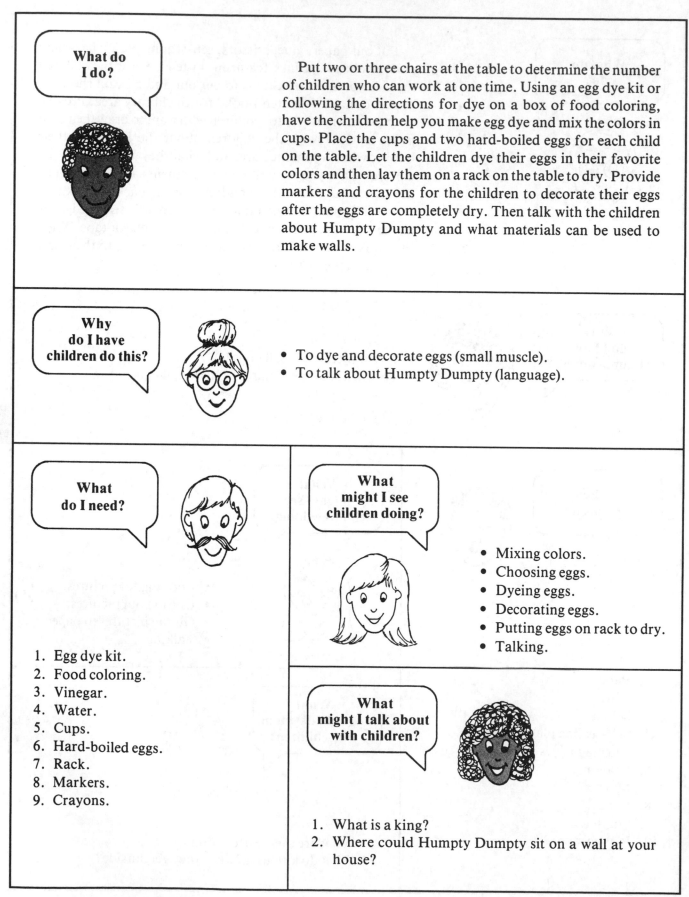

What do I do?

Put two or three chairs at the table to determine the number of children who can work at one time. Using an egg dye kit or following the directions for dye on a box of food coloring, have the children help you make egg dye and mix the colors in cups. Place the cups and two hard-boiled eggs for each child on the table. Let the children dye their eggs in their favorite colors and then lay them on a rack on the table to dry. Provide markers and crayons for the children to decorate their eggs after the eggs are completely dry. Then talk with the children about Humpty Dumpty and what materials can be used to make walls.

Why do I have children do this?

- To dye and decorate eggs (small muscle).
- To talk about Humpty Dumpty (language).

What do I need?

1. Egg dye kit.
2. Food coloring.
3. Vinegar.
4. Water.
5. Cups.
6. Hard-boiled eggs.
7. Rack.
8. Markers.
9. Crayons.

What might I see children doing?

- Mixing colors.
- Choosing eggs.
- Dyeing eggs.
- Decorating eggs.
- Putting eggs on rack to dry.
- Talking.

What might I talk about with children?

1. What is a king?
2. Where could Humpty Dumpty sit on a wall at your house?

"HUMPTY DUMPTY" COLLAGE
Learning Center (art)

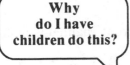

What do I do?

Hang pictures of Humpty Dumpty and the king's men on the wall at the children's eye level. Collect dyed eggshells from the decorated hard-boiled eggs in the food activity "'Humpty Dumpty Deviled Eggs'" on page 319. Make sure the eggshells have as little leftover egg on them as possible. Let the eggshells dry out for a couple of days on a tray. Then put out paper, markers, crayons, paper scraps, scissors, glue, and the dyed eggshells. Let the children experiment with the different materials. Pour the glue into small margarine tubs and let the children use cotton swabs to apply the glue to the eggshells and paper. Talk with the children about the colors, the designs they make, and how the eggshells feel.

Why do I have children do this?

- To make pictures from collage materials—eggshells, paper (small muscle, thinking).
- To enjoy working with other children (social-emotional).

What do I need?

What might I see children doing?

- Coloring with markers and crayons.
- Gluing eggshells.
- Cutting paper.
- Talking.

1. Pictures of Humpty Dumpty and the king's men.
2. Dyed eggshells.
3. Tray.
4. Paper.
5. Markers.
6. Crayons.
7. Paper scraps.
8. Glue.
9. Margarine tubs.
10. Cotton swabs.

What might I talk about with children?

1. What other Humpty Dumpty activities have you done this week?
2. What is an eggshell?

PAINTING SPIDER WEBS
Learning Center (art)

What do I do?

Take the children outdoors to look at a spider web. Then mix white tempera paint in a coffee can. Cut sheets of dark blue or black construction paper to fit in the bottom of a shallow box. Let four- and five-year-olds drop marbles into the white paint and scoop them out with a large spoon. Let the two- and three-year-olds dip pieces of heavy string into the white paint, while holding onto one end to keep it dry. Then let the children drop the paint-covered marbles or string in the shallow box on top of the dark construction paper. Let them push the marbles with a spoon, pull the string across the paper, or shake the box with the lid on it. They can also use thin paintbrushes to paint white lines on the dark construction paper or experiment with the paint as they wish. Talk with the children about what the white lines, formed by the marbles, string, or the paintbrushes, look like.

Why do I have children do this?

- To experiment with paint in a different manner (small muscle).
- To enjoy working with other children (social-emotional).

What do I need?

1. Spider web.
2. White tempera paint.
3. Coffee can.
4. Dark blue or black construction paper.
5. Shallow box with lid.
6. Marbles.
7. Heavy string.
8. Spoons.
9. Thin paintbrushes.

What might I see children doing?

- Looking at spider webs.
- Choosing paper.
- Rolling marbles.
- Painting.
- Talking.

What might I talk about with children?

1. Where do you find spider webs?
2. What else can you make with white paint?

OLD KING COLE ON TV
Learning Center (art)

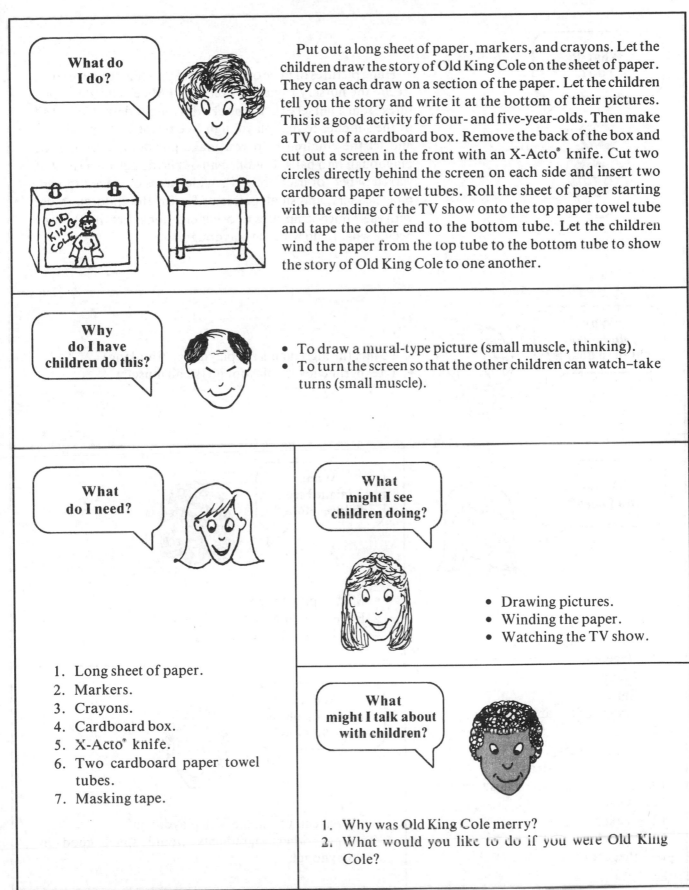

What do I do?

Put out a long sheet of paper, markers, and crayons. Let the children draw the story of Old King Cole on the sheet of paper. They can each draw on a section of the paper. Let the children tell you the story and write it at the bottom of their pictures. This is a good activity for four- and five-year-olds. Then make a TV out of a cardboard box. Remove the back of the box and cut out a screen in the front with an X-Acto® knife. Cut two circles directly behind the screen on each side and insert two cardboard paper towel tubes. Roll the sheet of paper starting with the ending of the TV show onto the top paper towel tube and tape the other end to the bottom tube. Let the children wind the paper from the top tube to the bottom tube to show the story of Old King Cole to one another.

Why do I have children do this?

- To draw a mural-type picture (small muscle, thinking).
- To turn the screen so that the other children can watch–take turns (small muscle).

What do I need?

1. Long sheet of paper.
2. Markers.
3. Crayons.
4. Cardboard box.
5. X-Acto® knife.
6. Two cardboard paper towel tubes.
7. Masking tape.

What might I see children doing?

- Drawing pictures.
- Winding the paper.
- Watching the TV show.

What might I talk about with children?

1. Why was Old King Cole merry?
2. What would you like to do if you were Old King Cole?

PLAYDOUGH MICE
Learning Center (art)

What do I do?

Hang pictures of mice on the walls at the children's eye level. Recite the nursery rhyme "Three Blind Mice" and share pictures from a nursery rhyme book with the children. Collect all of the supplies to mix playdough (see recipe in Appendix A) and let the children help you make playdough. Divide the playdough into balls. Put one ball of playdough on a sheet of waxed paper for each child. Provide pieces of waxed thread, pipe cleaners, and small pieces of fur for the children to use with their mice sculptures or other creations. Let the children decide what to do with the playdough.

Why do I have children do this?

- To mix the ingredients for playdough (thinking).
- To experiment with playdough (small muscle).

What do I need?

1. Pictures of mice.
2. Nursery rhyme book.
3. Vegetable oil. ⎤
4. Flour.
5. Salt.
6. Cream of tartar.
7. Water. ⎬ To make playdough
8. Food coloring.
9. Peppermint extract.
10. Self-sealing plastic bags. ⎦
11. Waxed paper.
12. Waxed thread.
13. Pipe cleaners.
14. Pieces of fur.

What might I see children doing?

- Mixing playdough.
- Experimenting with playdough.
- Talking to one another.

What might I talk about with children?

1. What can you make with playdough?
2. What other ingredients would smell good in playdough?

HUMPTY DUMPTY PLAYS IN THE BLOCKS
Learning Center (blocks)

What do I do?

Hang pictures of Humpty Dumpty on the wall at the children's eye level. Place several large egg-shaped containers in the block area along with crayons on a shelf. Some children may want to decorate the egg-shaped containers. Add horses and people figures to the shelves. Build a short section of a wall before the children arrive. Then, when the children come to the block area, let them use their imaginations. Talk with them about their work after they get started. Recite "Humpty Dumpty" and encourage the children to recite it with you.

Why do I have children do this?

- To build with blocks (large muscle).
- To talk about Humpty Dumpty and what happened to him (language).

What do I need?

1. Pictures of Humpty Dumpty.
2. Large egg-shaped containers.
3. Crayons.
4. Horse figures.
5. People figures.

What might I see children doing?

- Looking at pictures.
- Putting facial features on egg.
- Building a wall.
- Letting Humpty Dumpty fall.

What might I talk about with children?

1. Why do you think Humpty Dumpty sat on the wall?
2. What do you think he could see from the wall?

A BARN FOR POOR ROBIN
Learning Center (blocks)

What do I do?

Hang pictures of different types of barns on the walls at the children's eye level. Put out several different-sized blocks along with farm animal figures, tractors, and trucks on the shelves. Recite the nursery rhyme "Poor Robin" and share pictures from a nursery rhyme book with the children. Encourage the children to build a barn for the robin. When you take the children outside, look for robins. Put out birdseed and bread crumbs in a bird feeder near a window, so the children can watch the birds eat. Once you put out a bird feeder, be sure to continue to fill it, since birds will rely on it for food.

Why do I have children do this?

- To build with blocks (small and large muscle).
- To care for birds (social-emotional).

What do I need?

1. Pictures of different types of barns.
2. Different-sized blocks.
3. Farm animal figures.
4. Tractors.
5. Trucks.
6. Nursery rhyme book.
7. Birdseed.
8. Bread crumbs.
9. Bird feeder.

What might I see children doing?

- Looking at pictures.
- Building with blocks.
- Talking.
- Looking for birds.

What might I talk about with children?

1. Where do the birds live in winter?
2. What do you feed birds and animals in winter?

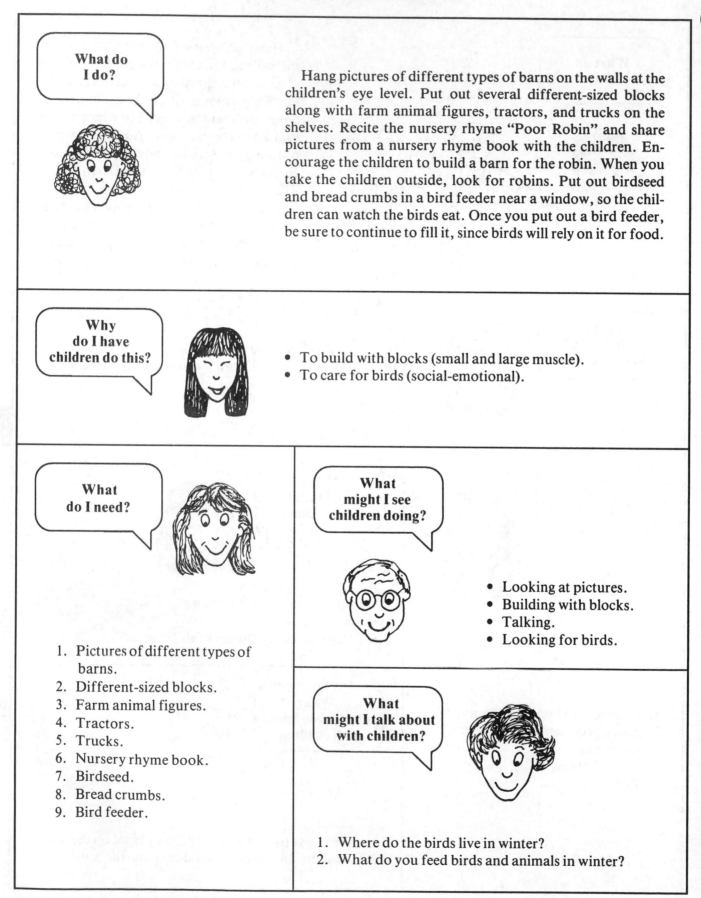

POLLY AND SUKEY'S TEA PARTY
Learning Center (dramatic play)

What do I do?

Place a tablecloth, teacups, plates, flatware, napkins, tea kettle, and play range in the dramatic play area for a tea party. Add dolls, a doll carriage, and a doll bed. Put out dress-up clothes, so the children can dress up for the tea party. Sit down and talk with the children about the special food they are preparing for the tea party. Recite the first verse of "Polly, Put the Kettle On" as the children prepare for the tea party and the second verse as they clean up and everyone leaves.

Why do I have children do this?

- To pretend to have a tea party (social-emotional).
- To care for the babies (social-emotional).

What do I need?

1. Tablecloth.
2. Teacups.
3. Plates.
4. Flatware.
5. Napkins.
6. Tea kettle.
7. Play range.
8. Dolls.
9. Doll carriage.
10. Doll bed.
11. Dress-up clothes.

What might I see children doing?

- Putting on dress-up clothes.
- Putting tea kettle on range.
- Setting table.
- Having tea.
- Caring for babies.

What might I talk about with children?

1. What kind of party have you been to?
2. What are Polly and Sukey having to eat at their tea party?

CATCH THE DISH AND SPOON TO SET THE TABLE
Learning Center (dramatic play)

What do I do?

Make four place mats from large sheets of construction paper. Glue a picture of a plate, glass, napkin, knife, fork, and spoon in the correct place on each place mat. Cover the place mats with self-adhesive plastic. Then set out plates, glasses, napkins, knives, forks, and spoons and let the children practice setting the table. Talk with the children about how to correctly set a table. Explain how they can help their parents by setting the table and getting ready for supper. Let the children set up the dramatic play area for a pretend meal. Sit down and talk with them while they pretend to eat.

Why do I have children do this?

- To set the table for a meal (thinking, social-emotional).
- To talk with others at mealtime (language).

What do I need?

What might I see children doing?

- Putting place mats on table.
- Setting table.
- Pretending to cook.
- Pretending to eat.
- Talking.

1. Construction paper.
2. Pictures of plates, glasses, napkins, knives, forks, and spoons.
3. Glue.
4. Self-adhesive plastic.
5. Plates.
6. Glasses.
7. Napkins.
8. Knives.
9. Forks.
10. Spoons.

What might I talk about with children?

1. What do you do to help your mommy?
2. What do you do to help your daddy?

THE OLD WOMAN'S SHOE STORE
Learning Center (dramatic play)

What do I do?

Collect several shoe boxes and pairs of women's, men's, and children's shoes and display them on shelves. Set up a table with a cash register, pads of paper for sales slips, pencils, and bags for the customers. Put several chairs in a row for the children to sit in as they try on shoes and a low footstool for the salesclerk to use to help customers try on shoes. Include a shoehorn for the salesclerk. You might add an unbreakable mirror at floor level, so the children can look at the shoes as they try them on. Also add a ruler to measure the length of the feet and shoes.

Why do I have children do this?

- To write sales slips (language, small muscle).
- To try on shoes (small muscle).

What do I need?

1. Shoe boxes.
2. Women's, men's, and children's shoes.
3. Cash register.
4. Pads of paper for sales slips.
5. Pencils.
6. Bags.
7. Chairs.
8. Low footstool.
9. Shoehorn.
10. Unbreakable mirror.
11. Ruler.

What might I see children doing?

- Choosing shoes.
- Trying on shoes.
- Helping customers.
- Writing sales slips.
- Talking.

What might I talk about with children?

1. What kind of shoes would you like to try?
2. What is your name and address for my sales slip?
3. Which pairs of shoes look like your size?

THE CAT AND THE FIDDLE PUPPET SHOW
Learning Center (dramatic play)

What do I do?

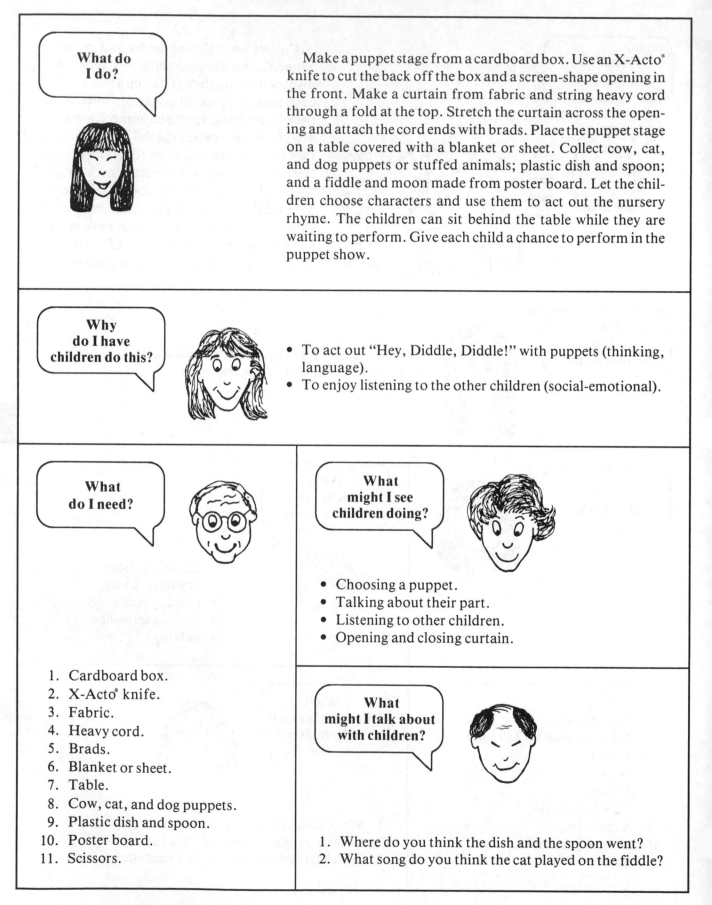

Make a puppet stage from a cardboard box. Use an X-Acto® knife to cut the back off the box and a screen-shape opening in the front. Make a curtain from fabric and string heavy cord through a fold at the top. Stretch the curtain across the opening and attach the cord ends with brads. Place the puppet stage on a table covered with a blanket or sheet. Collect cow, cat, and dog puppets or stuffed animals; plastic dish and spoon; and a fiddle and moon made from poster board. Let the children choose characters and use them to act out the nursery rhyme. The children can sit behind the table while they are waiting to perform. Give each child a chance to perform in the puppet show.

Why do I have children do this?

- To act out "Hey, Diddle, Diddle!" with puppets (thinking, language).
- To enjoy listening to the other children (social-emotional).

What do I need?

What might I see children doing?

- Choosing a puppet.
- Talking about their part.
- Listening to other children.
- Opening and closing curtain.

What might I talk about with children?

1. Cardboard box.
2. X-Acto® knife.
3. Fabric.
4. Heavy cord.
5. Brads.
6. Blanket or sheet.
7. Table.
8. Cow, cat, and dog puppets.
9. Plastic dish and spoon.
10. Poster board.
11. Scissors.

1. Where do you think the dish and the spoon went?
2. What song do you think the cat played on the fiddle?

HUMPTY DUMPTY GOES TO THE HOSPITAL
Learning Center (dramatic play)

What do I do?

Tell the children that Humpty Dumpty has fallen off the wall and needs to be put together again. Decorate a wagon as an ambulance and set up a cot and blanket in the dramatic play area. Hang a sign over the bed saying, "HUMPTY DUMPTY'S ROOM–QUIET!" Put out a nurse's cap, play medical kit, adhesive bandages, gauze, and old white dress shirts or T-shirts for lab coats. Make a crown out of poster board and cover it with aluminum foil for the king to wear. Use markers to draw cracks all over an old shirt and set it out along with an old hat, so a child can dress up like Humpty Dumpty. Set up a table for Humpty Dumpty to check into the hospital. Have a pad of paper and pencil to write down important information, such as his address, who to call when he is sick, and what his major injuries are.

Why do I have children do this?

- To bandage Humpty Dumpty (small muscle, social-emotional).
- To write the information on the pad of paper (language).

What do I need?

1. Wagon.
2. Cot.
3. Blanket.
4. "HUMPTY DUMPTY'S ROOM–QUIET" sign.
5. Nurse's cap.
6. Play medical kit.
7. Adhesive bandages.
8. Gauze.
9. Old white dress shirts or T-shirts.
10. Poster board.
11. Aluminum foil.
12. Markers.
13. Old hat.
14. Table.
15. Pad of paper.
16. Pencil.

What might I see children doing?

- Pulling Humpty Dumpty to the hospital.
- Checking him into the hospital.
- Looking at his injuries.
- Talking.

What might I talk about with children?

1. Where do you think Humpty Dumpty was hurt when he fell from the wall?
2. What do you think you can do to help him?

WASHING THE KITTENS' MITTENS
Learning Center (dramatic play), Indoor or Outdoor Large Muscle

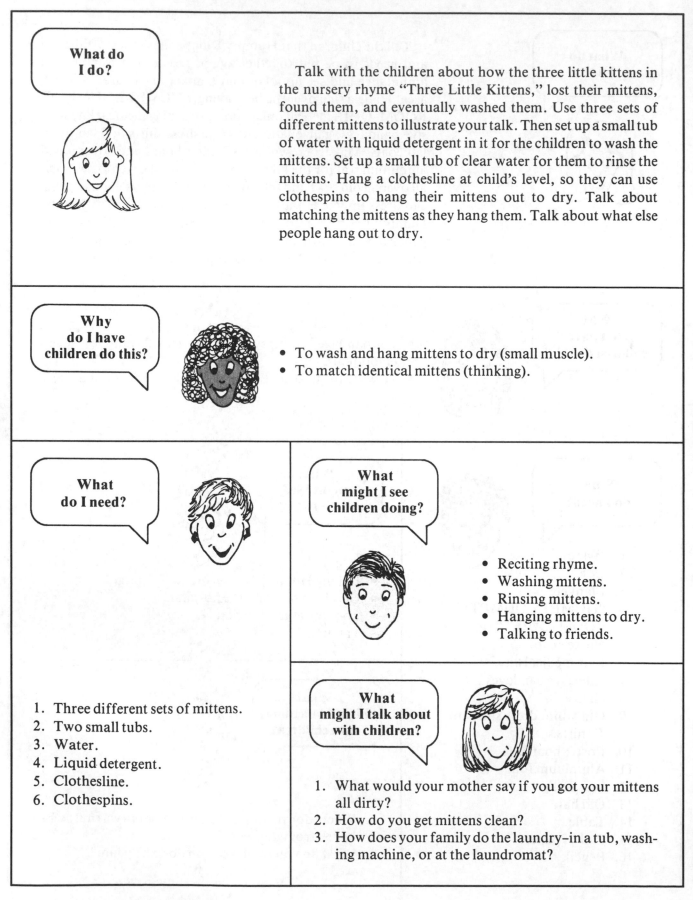

What do I do?

Talk with the children about how the three little kittens in the nursery rhyme "Three Little Kittens," lost their mittens, found them, and eventually washed them. Use three sets of different mittens to illustrate your talk. Then set up a small tub of water with liquid detergent in it for the children to wash the mittens. Set up a small tub of clear water for them to rinse the mittens. Hang a clothesline at child's level, so they can use clothespins to hang their mittens out to dry. Talk about matching the mittens as they hang them. Talk about what else people hang out to dry.

Why do I have children do this?

- To wash and hang mittens to dry (small muscle).
- To match identical mittens (thinking).

What do I need?

1. Three different sets of mittens.
2. Two small tubs.
3. Water.
4. Liquid detergent.
5. Clothesline.
6. Clothespins.

What might I see children doing?

- Reciting rhyme.
- Washing mittens.
- Rinsing mittens.
- Hanging mittens to dry.
- Talking to friends.

What might I talk about with children?

1. What would your mother say if you got your mittens all dirty?
2. How do you get mittens clean?
3. How does your family do the laundry—in a tub, washing machine, or at the laundromat?

MOTHER CAT'S PIE
Learning Center (food)

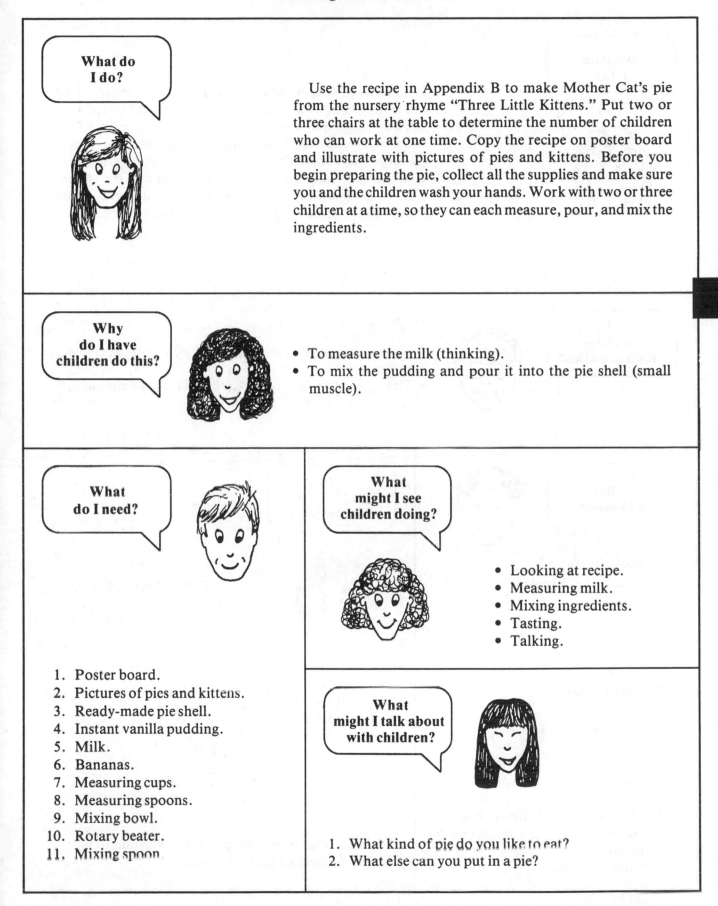

What do I do?

Use the recipe in Appendix B to make Mother Cat's pie from the nursery rhyme "Three Little Kittens." Put two or three chairs at the table to determine the number of children who can work at one time. Copy the recipe on poster board and illustrate with pictures of pies and kittens. Before you begin preparing the pie, collect all the supplies and make sure you and the children wash your hands. Work with two or three children at a time, so they can each measure, pour, and mix the ingredients.

Why do I have children do this?

- To measure the milk (thinking).
- To mix the pudding and pour it into the pie shell (small muscle).

What do I need?

What might I see children doing?

- Looking at recipe.
- Measuring milk.
- Mixing ingredients.
- Tasting.
- Talking.

1. Poster board.
2. Pictures of pies and kittens.
3. Ready-made pie shell.
4. Instant vanilla pudding.
5. Milk.
6. Bananas.
7. Measuring cups.
8. Measuring spoons.
9. Mixing bowl.
10. Rotary beater.
11. Mixing spoon.

What might I talk about with children?

1. What kind of pie do you like to eat?
2. What else can you put in a pie?

PETER, PETER, PUMPKIN-EATER'S BREAD
Learning Center (food)

What do I do?

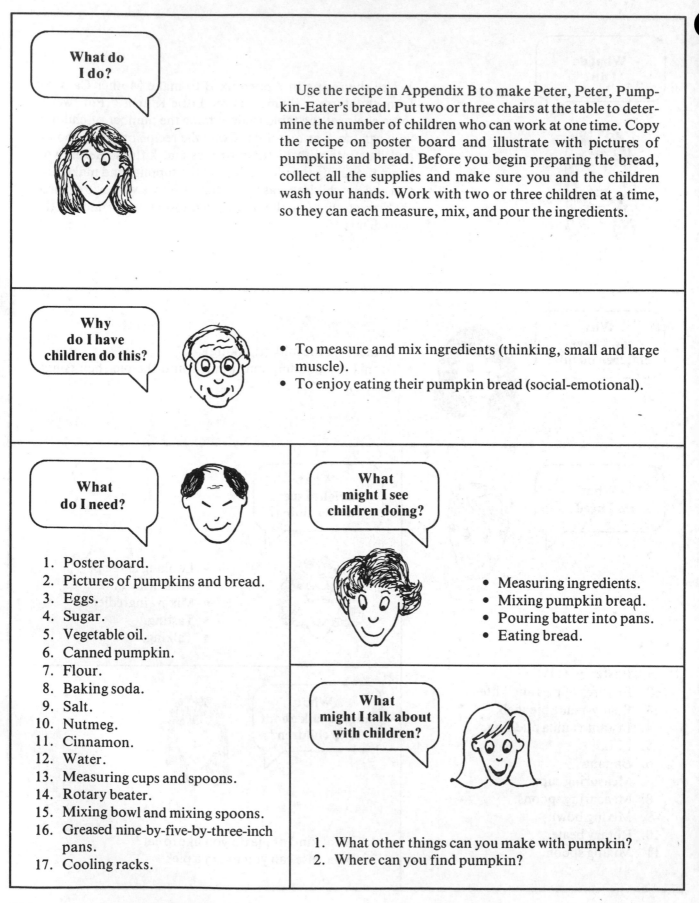

Use the recipe in Appendix B to make Peter, Peter, Pumpkin-Eater's bread. Put two or three chairs at the table to determine the number of children who can work at one time. Copy the recipe on poster board and illustrate with pictures of pumpkins and bread. Before you begin preparing the bread, collect all the supplies and make sure you and the children wash your hands. Work with two or three children at a time, so they can each measure, mix, and pour the ingredients.

Why do I have children do this?

- To measure and mix ingredients (thinking, small and large muscle).
- To enjoy eating their pumpkin bread (social-emotional).

What do I need?

1. Poster board.
2. Pictures of pumpkins and bread.
3. Eggs.
4. Sugar.
5. Vegetable oil.
6. Canned pumpkin.
7. Flour.
8. Baking soda.
9. Salt.
10. Nutmeg.
11. Cinnamon.
12. Water.
13. Measuring cups and spoons.
14. Rotary beater.
15. Mixing bowl and mixing spoons.
16. Greased nine-by-five-by-three-inch pans.
17. Cooling racks.

What might I see children doing?

- Measuring ingredients.
- Mixing pumpkin bread.
- Pouring batter into pans.
- Eating bread.

What might I talk about with children?

1. What other things can you make with pumpkin?
2. Where can you find pumpkin?

"HUMPTY DUMPTY" DEVILED EGGS
Learning Center (food)

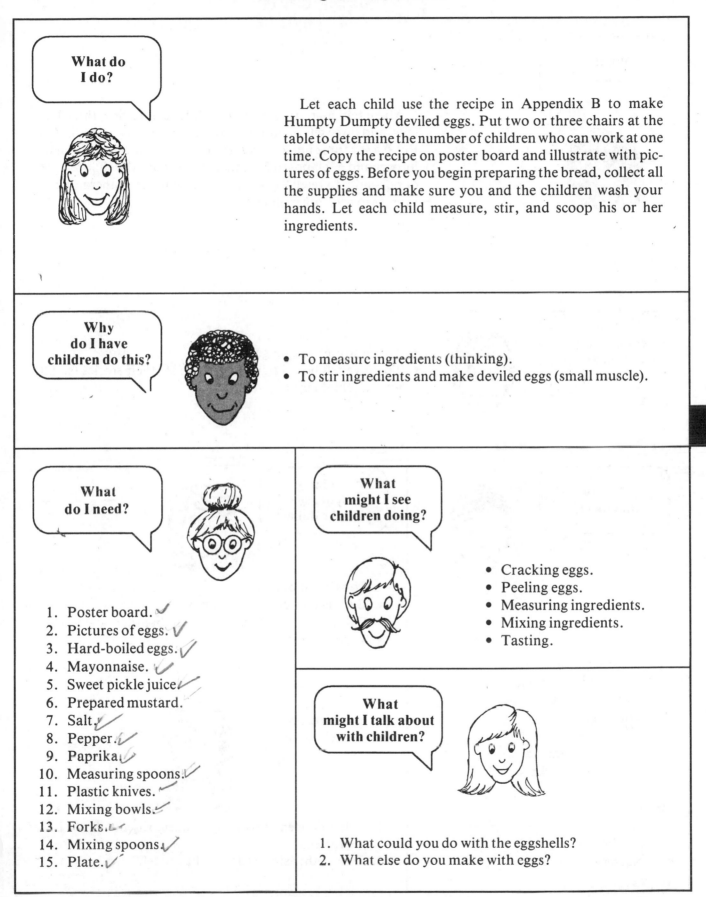

What do I do?

Let each child use the recipe in Appendix B to make Humpty Dumpty deviled eggs. Put two or three chairs at the table to determine the number of children who can work at one time. Copy the recipe on poster board and illustrate with pictures of eggs. Before you begin preparing the bread, collect all the supplies and make sure you and the children wash your hands. Let each child measure, stir, and scoop his or her ingredients.

Why do I have children do this?

- To measure ingredients (thinking).
- To stir ingredients and make deviled eggs (small muscle).

What do I need?

1. Poster board.
2. Pictures of eggs.
3. Hard-boiled eggs.
4. Mayonnaise.
5. Sweet pickle juice.
6. Prepared mustard.
7. Salt.
8. Pepper.
9. Paprika.
10. Measuring spoons.
11. Plastic knives.
12. Mixing bowls.
13. Forks.
14. Mixing spoons.
15. Plate.

What might I see children doing?

- Cracking eggs.
- Peeling eggs.
- Measuring ingredients.
- Mixing ingredients.
- Tasting.

What might I talk about with children?

1. What could you do with the eggshells?
2. What else do you make with eggs?

"THREE LITTLE KITTENS" FELT BOARD STORY
Learning Center (library)

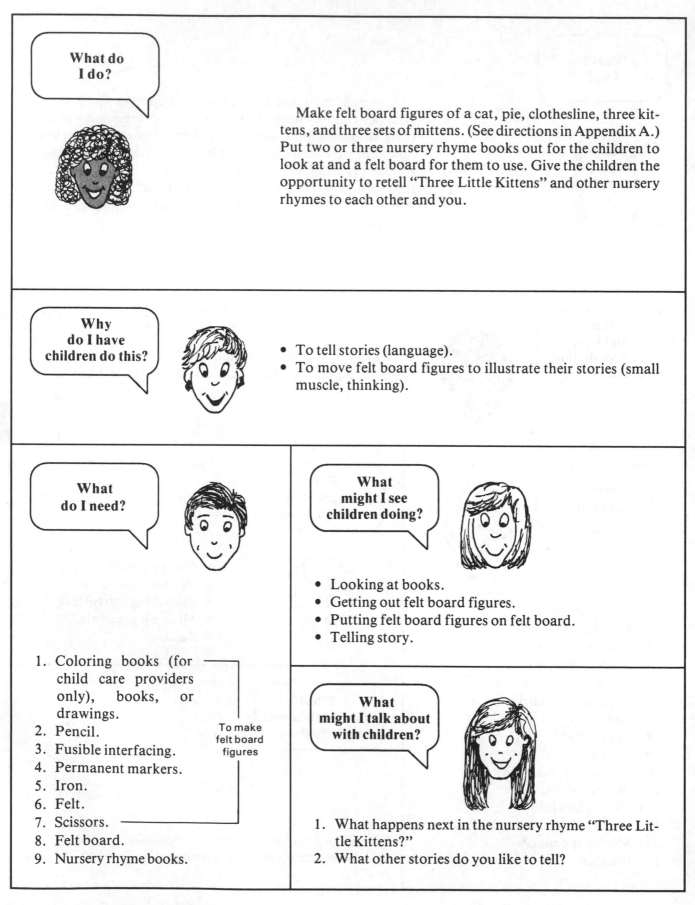

What do I do?

Make felt board figures of a cat, pie, clothesline, three kittens, and three sets of mittens. (See directions in Appendix A.) Put two or three nursery rhyme books out for the children to look at and a felt board for them to use. Give the children the opportunity to retell "Three Little Kittens" and other nursery rhymes to each other and you.

Why do I have children do this?

- To tell stories (language).
- To move felt board figures to illustrate their stories (small muscle, thinking).

What do I need?

1. Coloring books (for child care providers only), books, or drawings.
2. Pencil.
3. Fusible interfacing.
4. Permanent markers.
5. Iron.
6. Felt.
7. Scissors.
8. Felt board.
9. Nursery rhyme books.

To make felt board figures

What might I see children doing?

- Looking at books.
- Getting out felt board figures.
- Putting felt board figures on felt board.
- Telling story.

What might I talk about with children?

1. What happens next in the nursery rhyme "Three Little Kittens?"
2. What other stories do you like to tell?

NURSERY RHYME PUZZLES
Learning Center (manipulatives)

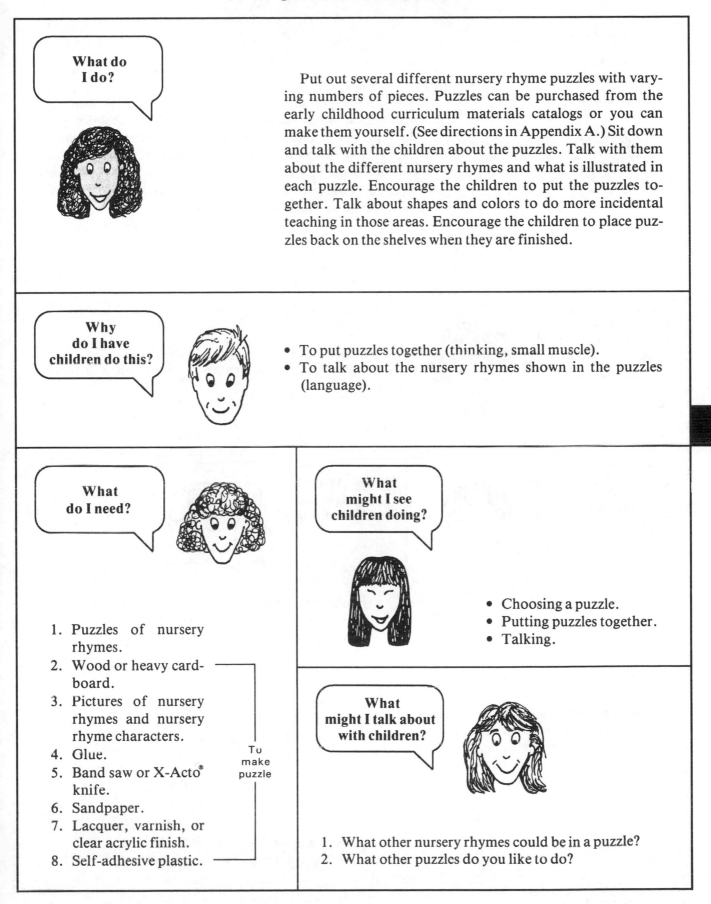

What do I do?

Put out several different nursery rhyme puzzles with varying numbers of pieces. Puzzles can be purchased from the early childhood curriculum materials catalogs or you can make them yourself. (See directions in Appendix A.) Sit down and talk with the children about the puzzles. Talk with them about the different nursery rhymes and what is illustrated in each puzzle. Encourage the children to put the puzzles together. Talk about shapes and colors to do more incidental teaching in those areas. Encourage the children to place puzzles back on the shelves when they are finished.

Why do I have children do this?

- To put puzzles together (thinking, small muscle).
- To talk about the nursery rhymes shown in the puzzles (language).

What do I need?

1. Puzzles of nursery rhymes.
2. Wood or heavy cardboard.
3. Pictures of nursery rhymes and nursery rhyme characters.
4. Glue.
5. Band saw or X-Acto® knife.
6. Sandpaper.
7. Lacquer, varnish, or clear acrylic finish.
8. Self-adhesive plastic.

To make puzzle

What might I see children doing?

- Choosing a puzzle.
- Putting puzzles together.
- Talking.

What might I talk about with children?

1. What other nursery rhymes could be in a puzzle?
2. What other puzzles do you like to do?

MATCH THE SHOES
Learning Center (manipulatives)

What do I do?

Collect several different pairs of shoes, such as sneakers, high heels, cowboy boots, baby shoes, and soccer shoes. Line them up out of order. Sit down and talk with the children about the sizes, shapes, and colors. See if they can match the pairs of shoes. Talk about where people would wear each particular pair of shoes. Ask them which pairs of shoes would fit the different members of their families.

Why do I have children do this?

- To match shoes by size, shape, and color (thinking).
- To talk about who could wear each pair of shoes (language, thinking).

What do I need?

What might I see children doing?

- Looking at the shoes.
- Matching the shoes.
- Talking about who might wear the shoes.

1. Several different pairs of shoes, such as sneakers, high heels, cowboy boots, baby shoes, and soccer shoes.

What might I talk about with children?

1. Who might wear some of these shoes?
2. How many types of these shoes have you worn?

"ONE, TWO, BUCKLE MY SHOE"
Learning Center (manipulatives)

What do I do?

Place a variety of shoes with different fasteners, such as buckles, hooks, and Velcro® hook and loop tape, on a table. Encourage the children to work with the different fasteners on the shoes. The children in kindergarten and above should also be encouraged to work with shoelaces. See if the children can match the shoes with the same fasteners. Let them put the shoes on over their own shoes and fasten them.

Why do I have children do this?

- To fasten shoes with buckles, hooks, and Velcro® hook and loop tape (small muscle).
- To match the shoes with the same fasteners (thinking).

What do I need?

What might I see children doing?

- Buckling shoes.
- Attaching Velcro® hook and loop tape.
- Matching shoes with the same fasteners.
- Trying on shoes.

1. Shoes with different fasteners, such as buckles, hooks, Velcro® hook and loop tape, and shoelaces.

What might I talk about with children?

1. Where do you find these kinds of buckles?
2. What kinds of shoes do you have at your house?

MITTEN LACING CARDS
Learning Center (manipulatives)

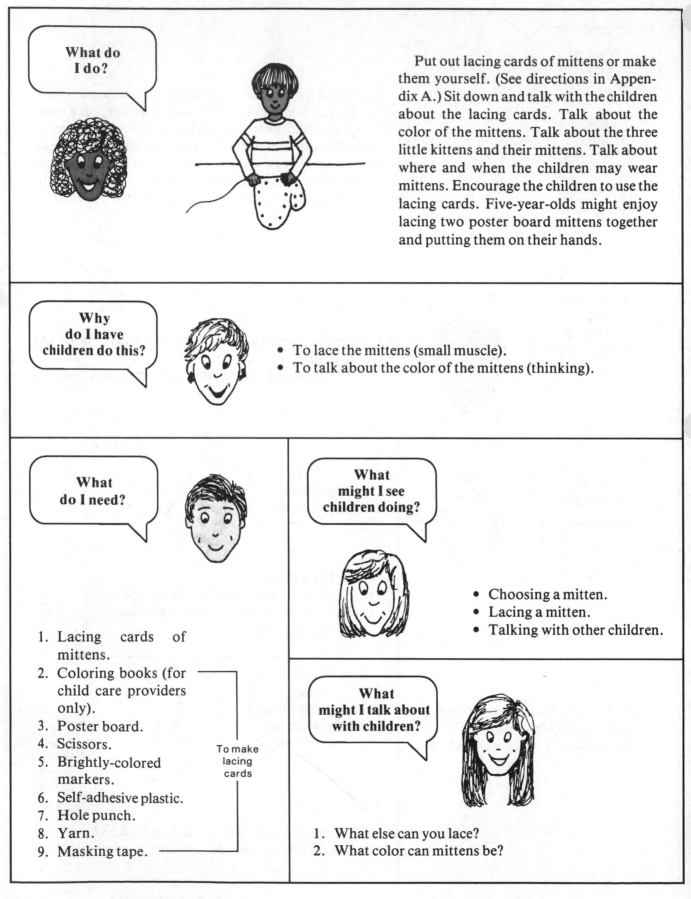

What do I do?

Put out lacing cards of mittens or make them yourself. (See directions in Appendix A.) Sit down and talk with the children about the lacing cards. Talk about the color of the mittens. Talk about the three little kittens and their mittens. Talk about where and when the children may wear mittens. Encourage the children to use the lacing cards. Five-year-olds might enjoy lacing two poster board mittens together and putting them on their hands.

Why do I have children do this?

• To lace the mittens (small muscle).
• To talk about the color of the mittens (thinking).

What do I need?

1. Lacing cards of mittens.
2. Coloring books (for child care providers only).
3. Poster board.
4. Scissors.
5. Brightly-colored markers.
6. Self-adhesive plastic.
7. Hole punch.
8. Yarn.
9. Masking tape.

To make lacing cards

What might I see children doing?

• Choosing a mitten.
• Lacing a mitten.
• Talking with other children.

What might I talk about with children?

1. What else can you lace?
2. What color can mittens be?

NURSERY RHYME DOMINOES
Learning Center (manipulatives)

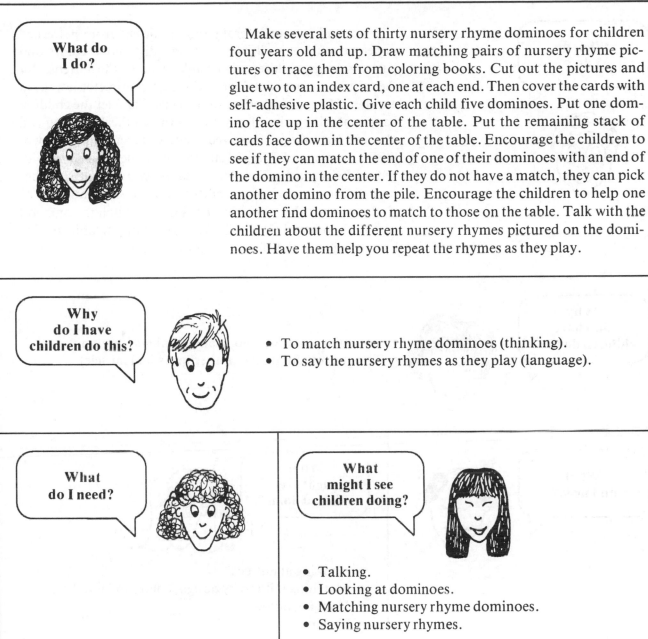

What do I do?

Make several sets of thirty nursery rhyme dominoes for children four years old and up. Draw matching pairs of nursery rhyme pictures or trace them from coloring books. Cut out the pictures and glue two to an index card, one at each end. Then cover the cards with self-adhesive plastic. Give each child five dominoes. Put one domino face up in the center of the table. Put the remaining stack of cards face down in the center of the table. Encourage the children to see if they can match the end of one of their dominoes with an end of the domino in the center. If they do not have a match, they can pick another domino from the pile. Encourage the children to help one another find dominoes to match to those on the table. Talk with the children about the different nursery rhymes pictured on the dominoes. Have them help you repeat the rhymes as they play.

Why do I have children do this?

- To match nursery rhyme dominoes (thinking).
- To say the nursery rhymes as they play (language).

What do I need?

1. Matching pairs of nursery rhyme pictures.
2. Pencil.
3. Markers.
4. Paper.
5. Coloring books (for child care providers only).
6. Scissors.
7. Glue.
8. Index cards.
9. Self-adhesive plastic.

What might I see children doing?

- Talking.
- Looking at dominoes.
- Matching nursery rhyme dominoes.
- Saying nursery rhymes.

What might I talk about with children?

1. What other nursery rhyme pictures do you see?
2. Where do you think the king's men will go when they ride off on the horses?

HELP ME FIND MY MITTENS
Learning Center (manipulatives, math)

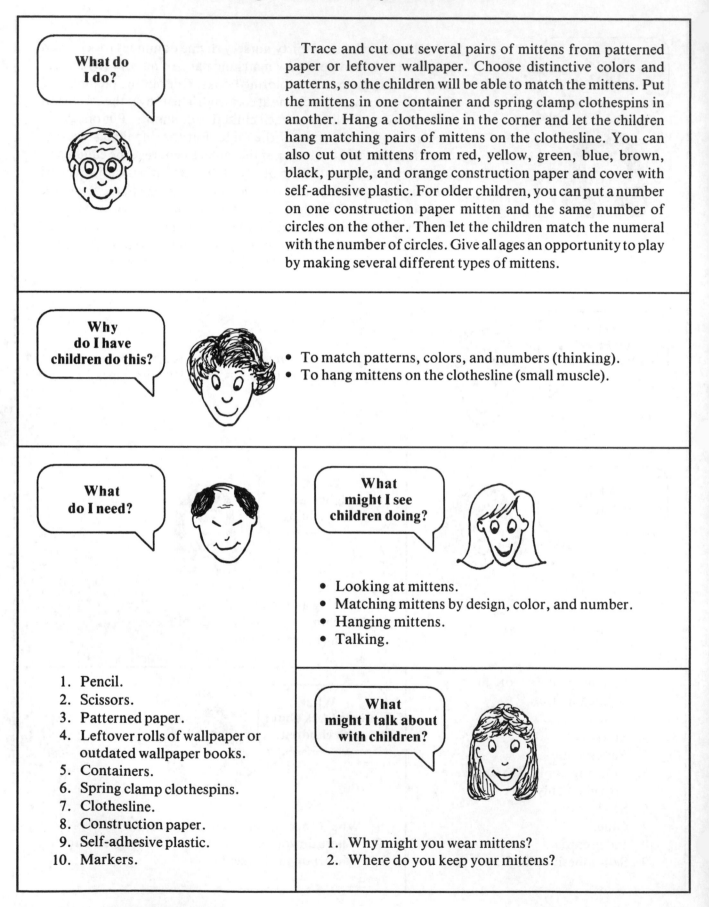

What do I do?

Trace and cut out several pairs of mittens from patterned paper or leftover wallpaper. Choose distinctive colors and patterns, so the children will be able to match the mittens. Put the mittens in one container and spring clamp clothespins in another. Hang a clothesline in the corner and let the children hang matching pairs of mittens on the clothesline. You can also cut out mittens from red, yellow, green, blue, brown, black, purple, and orange construction paper and cover with self-adhesive plastic. For older children, you can put a number on one construction paper mitten and the same number of circles on the other. Then let the children match the numeral with the number of circles. Give all ages an opportunity to play by making several different types of mittens.

Why do I have children do this?

- To match patterns, colors, and numbers (thinking).
- To hang mittens on the clothesline (small muscle).

What do I need?

What might I see children doing?

- Looking at mittens.
- Matching mittens by design, color, and number.
- Hanging mittens.
- Talking.

1. Pencil.
2. Scissors.
3. Patterned paper.
4. Leftover rolls of wallpaper or outdated wallpaper books.
5. Containers.
6. Spring clamp clothespins.
7. Clothesline.
8. Construction paper.
9. Self-adhesive plastic.
10. Markers.

What might I talk about with children?

1. Why might you wear mittens?
2. Where do you keep your mittens?

MEASURE WITH YOUR SHOE
Learning Center (math)

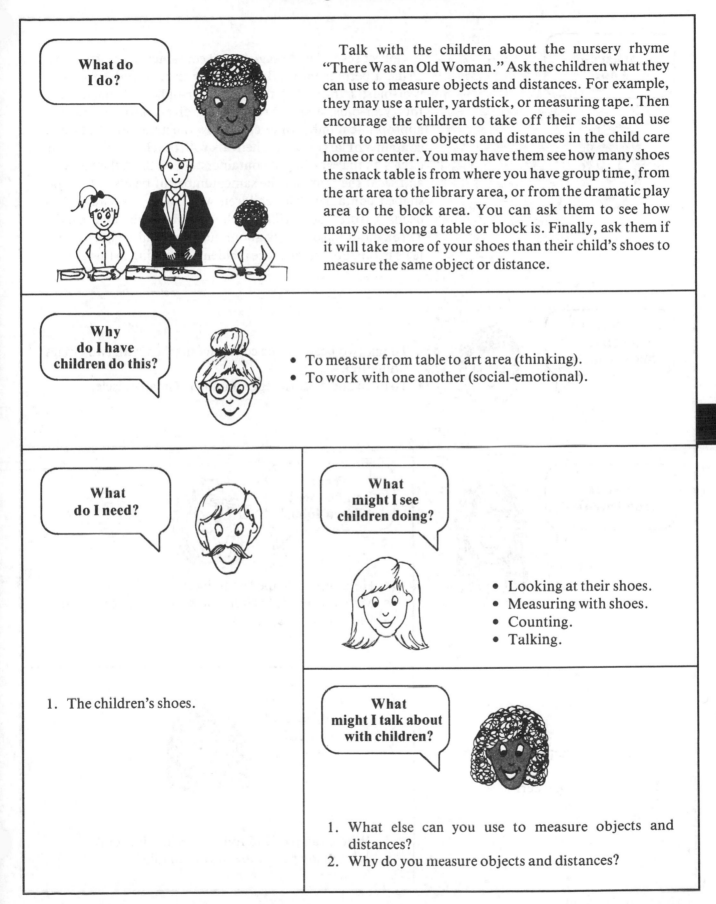

What do I do?

Talk with the children about the nursery rhyme "There Was an Old Woman." Ask the children what they can use to measure objects and distances. For example, they may use a ruler, yardstick, or measuring tape. Then encourage the children to take off their shoes and use them to measure objects and distances in the child care home or center. You may have them see how many shoes the snack table is from where you have group time, from the art area to the library area, or from the dramatic play area to the block area. You can ask them to see how many shoes long a table or block is. Finally, ask them if it will take more of your shoes than their child's shoes to measure the same object or distance.

Why do I have children do this?

- To measure from table to art area (thinking).
- To work with one another (social-emotional).

What do I need?

1. The children's shoes.

What might I see children doing?

- Looking at their shoes.
- Measuring with shoes.
- Counting.
- Talking.

What might I talk about with children?

1. What else can you use to measure objects and distances?
2. Why do you measure objects and distances?

"HUMPTY DUMPTY NUMBERS"
Learning Center (math)

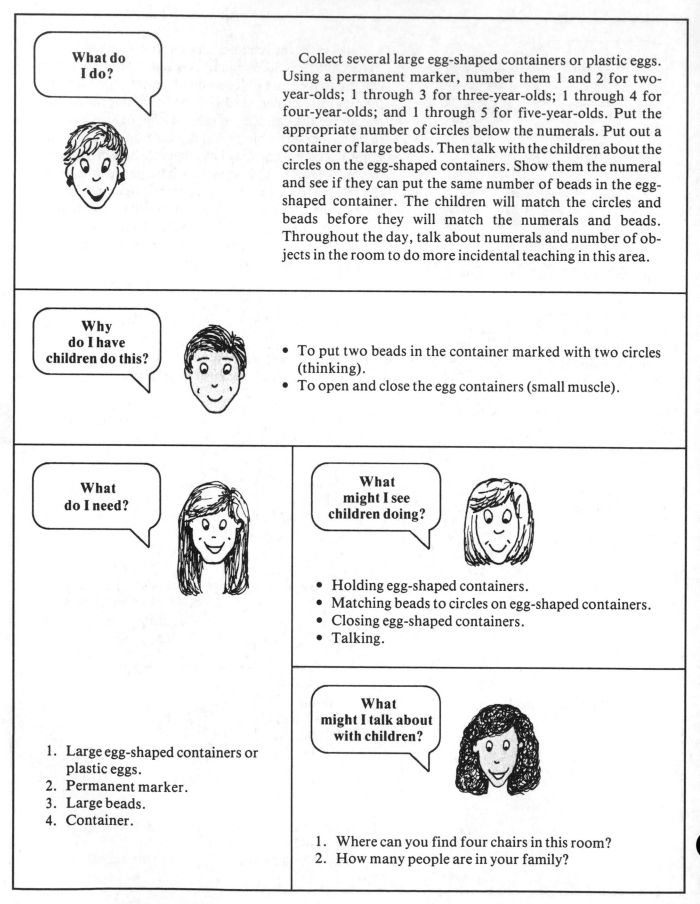

What do I do?

Collect several large egg-shaped containers or plastic eggs. Using a permanent marker, number them 1 and 2 for two-year-olds; 1 through 3 for three-year-olds; 1 through 4 for four-year-olds; and 1 through 5 for five-year-olds. Put the appropriate number of circles below the numerals. Put out a container of large beads. Then talk with the children about the circles on the egg-shaped containers. Show them the numeral and see if they can put the same number of beads in the egg-shaped container. The children will match the circles and beads before they will match the numerals and beads. Throughout the day, talk about numerals and number of objects in the room to do more incidental teaching in this area.

Why do I have children do this?

- To put two beads in the container marked with two circles (thinking).
- To open and close the egg containers (small muscle).

What do I need?

What might I see children doing?

- Holding egg-shaped containers.
- Matching beads to circles on egg-shaped containers.
- Closing egg-shaped containers.
- Talking.

1. Large egg-shaped containers or plastic eggs.
2. Permanent marker.
3. Large beads.
4. Container.

What might I talk about with children?

1. Where can you find four chairs in this room?
2. How many people are in your family?

WHAT IS A FIDDLE?
Learning Center (music)

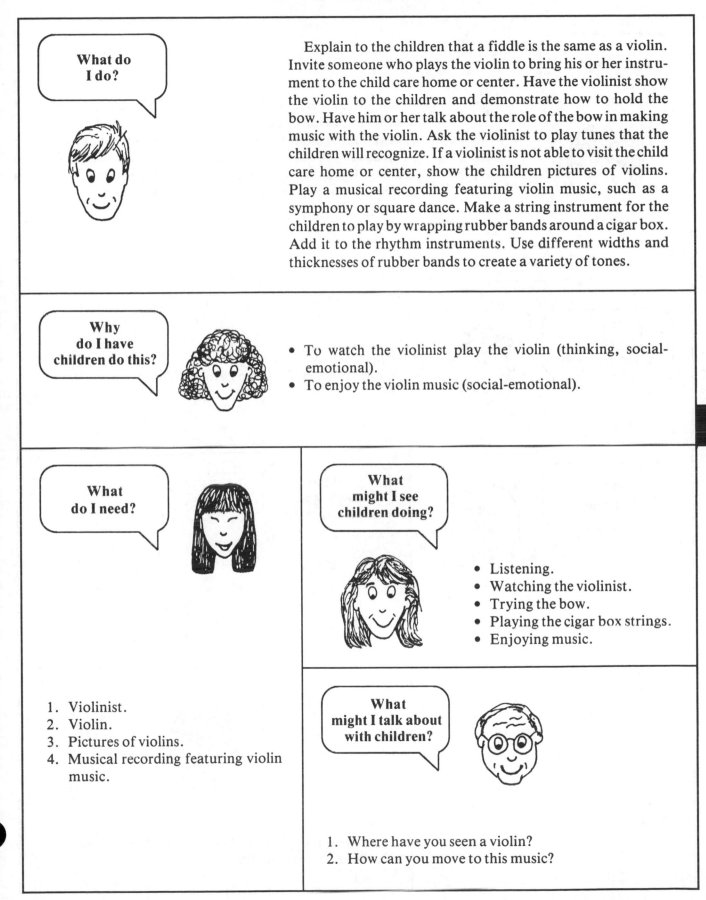

What do I do?

Explain to the children that a fiddle is the same as a violin. Invite someone who plays the violin to bring his or her instrument to the child care home or center. Have the violinist show the violin to the children and demonstrate how to hold the bow. Have him or her talk about the role of the bow in making music with the violin. Ask the violinist to play tunes that the children will recognize. If a violinist is not able to visit the child care home or center, show the children pictures of violins. Play a musical recording featuring violin music, such as a symphony or square dance. Make a string instrument for the children to play by wrapping rubber bands around a cigar box. Add it to the rhythm instruments. Use different widths and thicknesses of rubber bands to create a variety of tones.

Why do I have children do this?

- To watch the violinist play the violin (thinking, social-emotional).
- To enjoy the violin music (social-emotional).

What do I need?

1. Violinist.
2. Violin.
3. Pictures of violins.
4. Musical recording featuring violin music.

What might I see children doing?

- Listening.
- Watching the violinist.
- Trying the bow.
- Playing the cigar box strings.
- Enjoying music.

What might I talk about with children?

1. Where have you seen a violin?
2. How can you move to this music?

"MARY HAD A LITTLE LAMB"
Learning Center (music)

What do I do?

Sing all the verses to "Mary Had a Little Lamb." Use a stuffed lamb to introduce the song. You can also make a lamb by covering a box with white paper. Glue cotton balls all over it and attach felt ears, a pink felt tongue, and black felt eyes. Make the legs and tail from folded paper. Attach yarn, so the children can take turns having the lamb follow them.

Why do I have children do this?

- To listen to rhymes (language).
- To sing "Mary Had a Little Lamb" (thinking, language).

What do I need?

1. Stuffed lamb.
2. Box.
3. White paper.
4. Glue.
5. Cotton balls.
6. Felt.
7. Scissors.
8. Yarn.

What might I see children doing?

- Listening.
- Singing.
- Holding lamb.

What might I talk about with children?

1. Why was the lamb not allowed to go to school?
2. What animals do you have at home?

"EENCY, WEENCY SPIDER"
Learning Center (music)

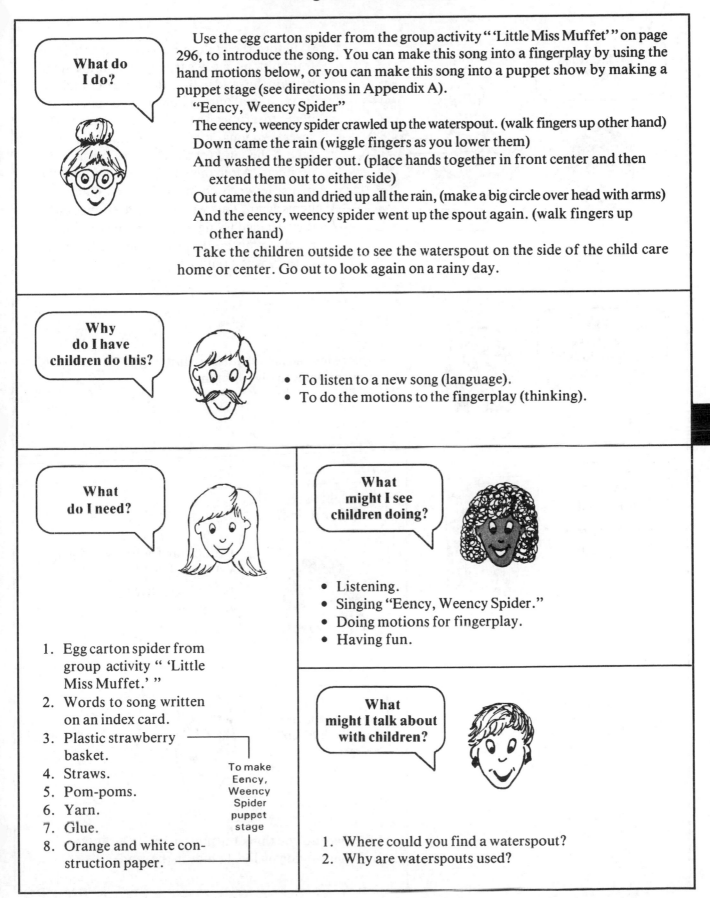

What do I do?

Use the egg carton spider from the group activity " 'Little Miss Muffet' " on page 296, to introduce the song. You can make this song into a fingerplay by using the hand motions below, or you can make this song into a puppet show by making a puppet stage (see directions in Appendix A).

"Eency, Weency Spider"

The eency, weency spider crawled up the waterspout. (walk fingers up other hand)

Down came the rain (wiggle fingers as you lower them)

And washed the spider out. (place hands together in front center and then extend them out to either side)

Out came the sun and dried up all the rain, (make a big circle over head with arms)

And the eency, weency spider went up the spout again. (walk fingers up other hand)

Take the children outside to see the waterspout on the side of the child care home or center. Go out to look again on a rainy day.

Why do I have children do this?

- To listen to a new song (language).
- To do the motions to the fingerplay (thinking).

What do I need?

1. Egg carton spider from group activity " 'Little Miss Muffet.' "
2. Words to song written on an index card.
3. Plastic strawberry basket.
4. Straws.
5. Pom-poms.
6. Yarn.
7. Glue.
8. Orange and white construction paper.

To make Eency, Weency Spider puppet stage

What might I see children doing?

- Listening.
- Singing "Eency, Weency Spider."
- Doing motions for fingerplay.
- Having fun.

What might I talk about with children?

1. Where could you find a waterspout?
2. Why are waterspouts used?

YOU LOST YOUR MITTENS!
Learning Center (sand)

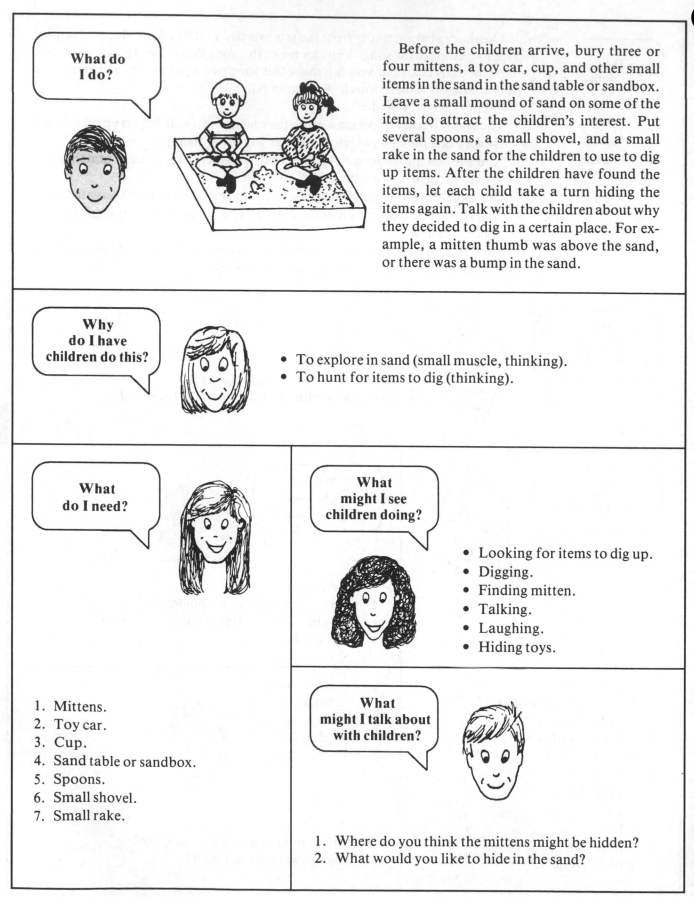

What do I do?

Before the children arrive, bury three or four mittens, a toy car, cup, and other small items in the sand in the sand table or sandbox. Leave a small mound of sand on some of the items to attract the children's interest. Put several spoons, a small shovel, and a small rake in the sand for the children to use to dig up items. After the children have found the items, let each child take a turn hiding the items again. Talk with the children about why they decided to dig in a certain place. For example, a mitten thumb was above the sand, or there was a bump in the sand.

Why do I have children do this?

- To explore in sand (small muscle, thinking).
- To hunt for items to dig (thinking).

What do I need?

1. Mittens.
2. Toy car.
3. Cup.
4. Sand table or sandbox.
5. Spoons.
6. Small shovel.
7. Small rake.

What might I see children doing?

- Looking for items to dig up.
- Digging.
- Finding mitten.
- Talking.
- Laughing.
- Hiding toys.

What might I talk about with children?

1. Where do you think the mittens might be hidden?
2. What would you like to hide in the sand?

WHAT HAPPENED TO THE EGG?
Learning Center (science, food)

What do I do?

Use the recipe in Appendix B to make scrambled eggs. Put three or four chairs at the table to determine the number of children who can work at one time. Copy the recipe on poster board. Before you begin preparing the scrambled eggs, collect all the supplies and make sure you and the children wash your hands. (To prevent salmonella, also wash hands after touching raw egg.) Work with three or four children at a time, so they can all crack, mix, and scramble eggs. Have the children eat their scrambled eggs for snack. Discuss each step as they work.

Why do I have children do this?

- To notice changes in the eggs (thinking).
- To see differences in parts of eggs (thinking).
- To taste and enjoy scrambled eggs (social-emotional).

What do I need?

What might I see children doing?

- Looking at the colors.
- Watching the eggs cook.
- Eating eggs.

1. Poster board.
2. Eggs.
3. Milk.
4. Butter or margarine.
5. Small bowls.
6. Fork.
7. Whisk.
8. Electric skillet.
9. Wooden spoon.
10. Plates.
11. Forks and spoons.

What might I talk about with children?

1. What will happen to the egg when it cooks?
2. How does the egg become scrambled?

HOW MANY LEGS DOES MISS MUFFET'S SPIDER HAVE?
Learning Center (science, math)

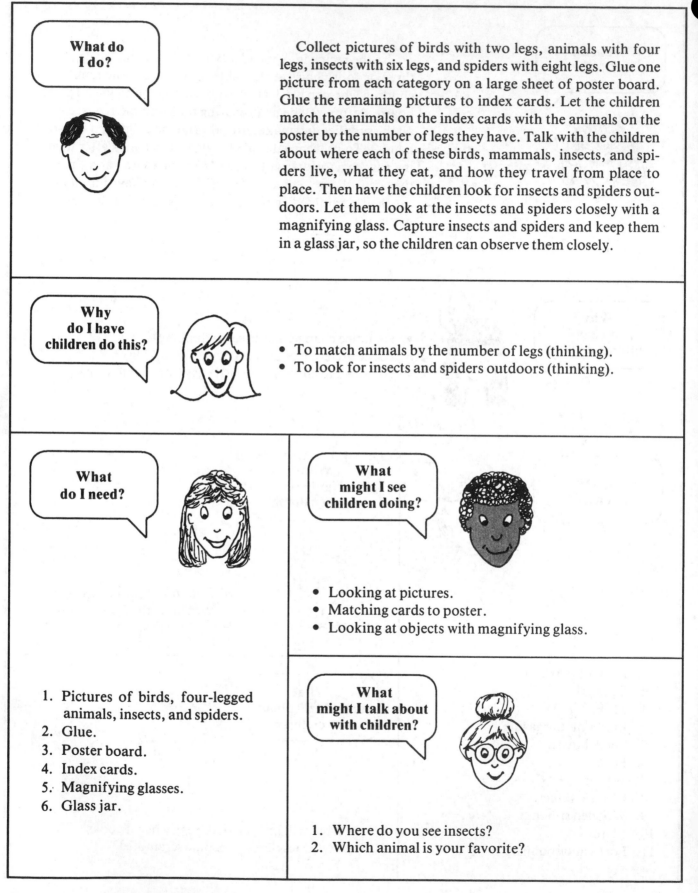

What do I do?

Collect pictures of birds with two legs, animals with four legs, insects with six legs, and spiders with eight legs. Glue one picture from each category on a large sheet of poster board. Glue the remaining pictures to index cards. Let the children match the animals on the index cards with the animals on the poster by the number of legs they have. Talk with the children about where each of these birds, mammals, insects, and spiders live, what they eat, and how they travel from place to place. Then have the children look for insects and spiders outdoors. Let them look at the insects and spiders closely with a magnifying glass. Capture insects and spiders and keep them in a glass jar, so the children can observe them closely.

Why do I have children do this?

- To match animals by the number of legs (thinking).
- To look for insects and spiders outdoors (thinking).

What do I need?

What might I see children doing?

- Looking at pictures.
- Matching cards to poster.
- Looking at objects with magnifying glass.

1. Pictures of birds, four-legged animals, insects, and spiders.
2. Glue.
3. Poster board.
4. Index cards.
5. Magnifying glasses.
6. Glass jar.

What might I talk about with children?

1. Where do you see insects?
2. Which animal is your favorite?

LOOKING FOR SPIDER WEBS
Learning Center (science)

What do I do?

Locate a spider web with a spider spinning the web. Take the children to the spider web and let them watch the spider at work. Locate another spider web that no longer has a spider in it. Let the children look at the spider web closely with magnifying glasses. Talk about how hard the spider works making its web, which is its home. Talk about how people often knock down spider webs. Talk about Miss Muffet and what happened when she saw the spider. Sing "Eency, Weency Spider."

Why do I have children do this?

- To look at spider webs with magnifying glasses (thinking).
- To say nursery rhymes (language).

What do I need?

What might I see children doing?

- Looking at spider web.
- Listening.
- Saying "Little Miss Muffet."
- Singing "Eency, Weency Spider."

1. Spider web with spider spinning web.
2. Spider web without a spider.
3. Magnifying glasses.
4. Words to "Little Miss Muffet" written on an index card.
5. Words to "Eency, Weency Spider" written on an index card.

What might I talk about with children?

1. Where have you seen spider webs before?
2. What don't you like about spiders?

JACK AND JILL GET WATER FOR THE SAND
Learning Center (water play)

What do I do?

Put a small bucket in the sandbox along with containers and small shovels and rakes. Let the children pretend to be Jack and Jill and walk up the hill to bring back water to moisten the sand. Talk about the differences between dry sand and wet sand. Ask which is easier to hold together if they want to make a building or a hill for Jack and Jill to climb. Ask them what else they could make with the wet sand.

Why do I have children do this?

- To carry small bucket of water (large muscle).
- To build with sand (small and large muscle).

What do I need?

1. Sandbox.
2. Small bucket.
3. Containers.
4. Small shovel.
5. Small rake.
6. Water.

What might I see children doing?

- Reciting "Jack and Jill."
- Carrying water.
- Building roads.
- Building houses.
- Having fun.

What might I talk about with children?

1. Where would Jack and Jill go if they went over the hill?
2. What else could they carry in the bucket?

AFTER POLLY AND SUKEY'S TEA PARTY
Learning Center (water play)

What do I do?

Extend the dramatic play activity "Polly and Sukey's Tea Party" on page 311, by putting water in the sink, so the children can wash the tea party dishes. Provide aprons for the children to wear. Be sure there are sponges for washing the dishes and dish towels for drying the dishes. Invite a child to help clean up after the guests have gone home from the party.

Why do I have children do this?

- To wash the dishes (small muscle).
- To talk about the tea party (language).
- To work together (social-emotional).

What do I need?

What might I see children doing?

- Washing dishes.
- Drying dishes.
- Putting dishes in the cupboard.
- Talking.
- Laughing.

1. Sink.
2. Water.
3. Dishes.
4. Tea cups.
5. Aprons.
6. Sponges.
7. Dish towels.

What might I talk about with children?

1. Who helps with the dishes at your house?
2. Why do dishes need to be washed?

WOODWORKING WITH A WOODCHUCK
Learning Center (woodworking)

What do I do?

Set up the woodworking area with a workbench, vise, hammers, saws, screwdrivers, nails, screws, glue, soft wood, such as pine or balsa, and other supplies that you have available. Limit the number of children in the area to two. Recite the following rhyme as you work with the children. Show them a picture of a woodchuck as you recite the rhyme. They may giggle as they listen to the woodchuck rhyme and try to repeat it.

"Woodchuck"
How much wood would a woodchuck chuck,
If a woodchuck could chuck wood?
He would chuck as much wood
As a woodchuck could
If a woodchuck could chuck wood.

Why do I have children do this?

• To listen to rhymes or tongue twisters (language).
• To saw and hammer the wood (small and large muscle).

What do I need?

What might I see children doing?

• Sawing.
• Hammering.
• Talking.
• Giggling.

What might I talk about with children?

1. Workbench.
2. Vise.
3. Hammers.
4. Screwdrivers.
5. Nails.
6. Screws.
7. Glue.
8. Pine wood.
9. Balsa wood.
10. Pictures of woodchucks.

1. Where do woodchucks live?
2. How does a woodchuck cut down trees?

OLD WOMAN'S SHOPPING LIST
Learning Center (writing)

What do I do?

After completing the group activity " 'There Was an Old Woman' " page 298, talk with the children about all the food the old woman needed to feed her children. Talk about how it helps to make a list before going to the store. Place scrap paper and pencils on the table for the children to make shopping lists. Ask the children what their parents buy when they go to the store. Set a good example for the children by writing down what you need for the child care home or center before you go shopping. Talk with the children about what you are putting on your list.

Why do I have children do this?

- To demonstrate another need for writing (small muscle, social-emotional).
- To pretend to be the old woman, parent, or teacher writing a shopping list (social-emotional).

What do I need?

1. Scrap paper.
2. Pencils.

What might I see children doing?

- Writing a list.
- Talking.
- Watching you write a list.
- Laughing.

What might I talk about with children?

1. What is on your list?
2. Why do you make a list?

A COOKBOOK FOR MISS MUFFET
Learning Center (writing)

What do I do?

Encourage the children to write down their favorite recipes for Miss Muffet, so she can choose what to have for lunch. (This is a good way for you to get ideas for lunches that the children might enjoy.) Sit down and talk with the children about the steps to prepare a recipe. Avoid telling them that their descriptions are inaccurate. Put out pencils, plain paper, crayons, markers, old food magazines, scissors, and glue for the children to use. Put out a three-ring binder that the children can add individual sheets to after they have written down their favorite recipes.

Why do I have children do this?

- To choose and write down their favorite recipes (small muscle, thinking).
- To glue food pictures on their recipes (small muscle).

What do I need?

What might I see children doing?

- Writing recipes.
- Choosing food pictures.
- Gluing pictures on the recipe pages.
- Talking to friends.

1. Pencils.
2. Plain paper.
3. Crayons.
4. Markers.
5. Old food magazines.
6. Scissors.
7. Glue.
8. Three-ring binder.

What might I talk about with children?

1. What is your favorite food for lunch?
2. Where can you find recipes?

PLANTING PUMPKIN SEEDS
Outdoor Large Muscle

What do I do?

In the late spring or early summer, dig up a section of the playground for a garden or fill an old tire with soil. Let the children rake the soil smooth. Have them help you plant the seeds, following the directions on the packet. Let them help you check the pumpkin plants each day to water them and check on their progress. The children may find it hard to wait for the pumpkins to grow unless you talk about it and watch the garden together. Make a progress chart and read it to the children often, so they can see the pumpkins' progress. Talk with the children about how long it takes seeds to sprout, plants to grow, and pumpkins to get big enough to eat. Explain to children that weeds can keep the seeds from growing. Have them help you pull weeds. Let them dig around the sprouting plants when they come up to keep the soil loose, so the plants can grow. Let the children help pick the pumpkins and eat the pumpkins they have grown. They can complete the food activity "Peter, Peter, Pumpkin-Eater's Bread" on page 318, after the pumpkin are harvested.

Why do I have children do this?

- To dig and rake the garden (large muscle).
- To watch for changes in plants as they grow (thinking).
- To pick pumpkins (large muscle).

What do I need?

1. Garden or old tire filled with soil.
2. Shovels.
3. Rakes.
4. Pumpkin seeds.
5. Water.
6. Poster board.
7. Markers.

What might I see children doing?

- Digging soil.
- Raking soil.
- Planting seeds.
- Watering plants.
- Pulling weeds.
- Talking.
- Picking pumpkins.

What might I talk about with children?

1. What else could you plant in the garden?
2. What vegetables do you have in your garden at home?

LIVING IN A PUMPKIN SHELL
Outdoor Large Muscle, Learning Center (dramatic play)

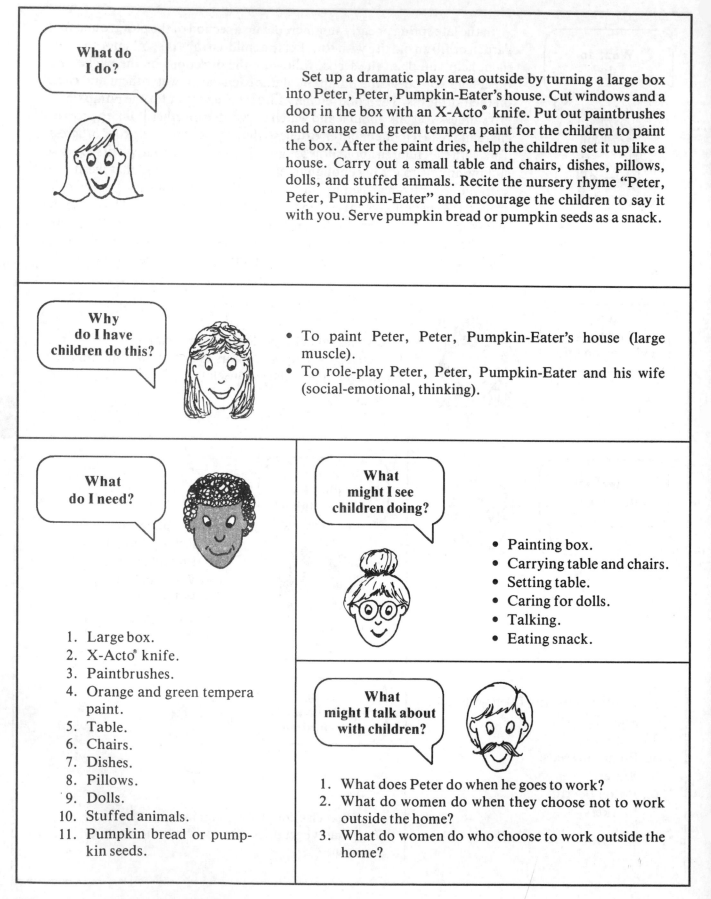

What do I do?

Set up a dramatic play area outside by turning a large box into Peter, Peter, Pumpkin-Eater's house. Cut windows and a door in the box with an X-Acto® knife. Put out paintbrushes and orange and green tempera paint for the children to paint the box. After the paint dries, help the children set it up like a house. Carry out a small table and chairs, dishes, pillows, dolls, and stuffed animals. Recite the nursery rhyme "Peter, Peter, Pumpkin-Eater" and encourage the children to say it with you. Serve pumpkin bread or pumpkin seeds as a snack.

Why do I have children do this?

- To paint Peter, Peter, Pumpkin-Eater's house (large muscle).
- To role-play Peter, Peter, Pumpkin-Eater and his wife (social-emotional, thinking).

What do I need?

1. Large box.
2. X-Acto® knife.
3. Paintbrushes.
4. Orange and green tempera paint.
5. Table.
6. Chairs.
7. Dishes.
8. Pillows.
9. Dolls.
10. Stuffed animals.
11. Pumpkin bread or pumpkin seeds.

What might I see children doing?

- Painting box.
- Carrying table and chairs.
- Setting table.
- Caring for dolls.
- Talking.
- Eating snack.

What might I talk about with children?

1. What does Peter do when he goes to work?
2. What do women do when they choose not to work outside the home?
3. What do women do who choose to work outside the home?

PUMPKIN TOSS
Outdoor Large Muscle

What do I do?

Draw an outline of a pumpkin on a large box and cut a large mouth out of the box with an X-Acto® knife. Place the box on the playground. Talk with the children about how hungry the pumpkin is and how they can feed it by throwing the beanbags at it. Make a chalk line on the ground for the children to stand on or behind as they toss the beanbags into the pumpkin's mouth. Place the line farther away for older children. Let one child stand near the pumpkin and throw the beanbags back after they are tossed at the pumpkin's mouth.

Why do I have children do this?

- To throw beanbags at the pumpkin (large muscle).
- To enjoy playing with the other children (social-emotional).

What do I need?

What might I see children doing?

- Standing on or behind the line.
- Tossing beanbags at the pumpkin.
- Throwing beanbags back to the line.

1. Large box.
2. Markers.
3. X-Acto® knife.
4. Chalk.
5. Beanbags.

What might I talk about with children?

1. What do you think a pumpkin would like to eat?
2. What else can you throw to the pumpkin to eat?

"JACK BE NIMBLE"
Indoor or Outdoor Large Muscle

What do I do?

Recite the nursery rhyme "Jack Be Nimble." Draw a candlestick with a lighted candle in it on the side of a low box or use a cylinder unit block as a candle to jump over. Make sure it is small and stable. Let the children jump over it. Talk with the children about how Jack might have gotten burned or burned his clothes if he jumped over the lighted candlestick. Talk about fire safety. Teach the children how to stop, drop, and roll if their clothes catch on fire. This will smother the flames and prevent them from spreading.

Why do I have children do this?

- To jump (large muscle).
- To talk about fire safety (thinking, language).

What do I need?

1. Markers.
2. Low box.

What might I see children doing?

- Listening.
- Jumping over candlestick.
- Laughing.
- Talking.

What might I talk about with children?

1. Where do you keep candlesticks at your house?
2. What are candlesticks used for?

THE DISH RAN AWAY WITH THE SPOON
Outdoor Large Muscle

What do I do?

Set up a path on the playground for the children to follow as they pretend to be the dish or the spoon. Have several sets of plastic plates and spoons for the children to carry as they follow the path. Draw arrows on paper plates to direct the children along the path. Starting at the door to the playground, direct them to the swings, running in and out of tires on the ground, to the climbing playground equipment, through a tunnel, and over to a table where they can eat a snack using their plates and spoons. Tie a half moon made from cardboard to a jump rope. Let the children pretend to jump over the moon with the rope on the ground. Then help two children hold the jump rope taut and raise it a little higher and let the other children jump over it. Keep raising the rope until the children can no longer jump over it.

Why do I have children do this?

- To run, swing, and crawl on the playground (large muscle).
- To jump over the rope (large muscle).

What do I need?

1. Plastic plates.
2. Plastic spoons.
3. Markers.
4. Paper plates.
5. Tape.
6. Snack.
7. Cardboard.
8. Jump rope.

What might I see children doing?

- Running to swings.
- Swinging.
- Running in and out of tires.
- Sitting at table and eating snack.

What might I talk about with children?

1. What else could you put in the path?
2. What kind of snacks do you like to eat in a bowl?

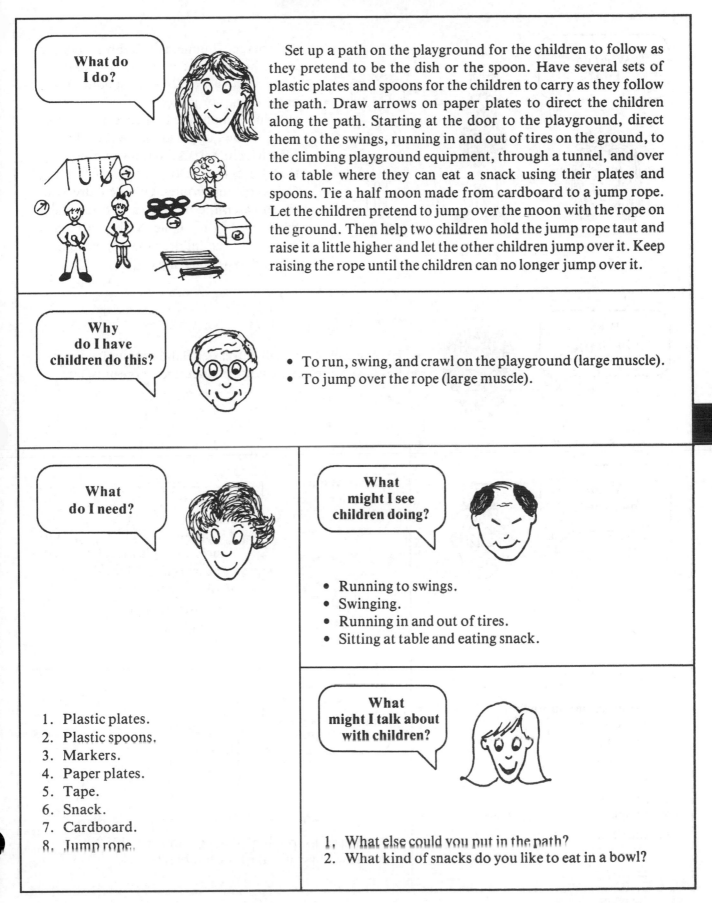

OLD KING COLE LIKES TO BLOW BUBBLES TOO!
Outdoor Large Muscle

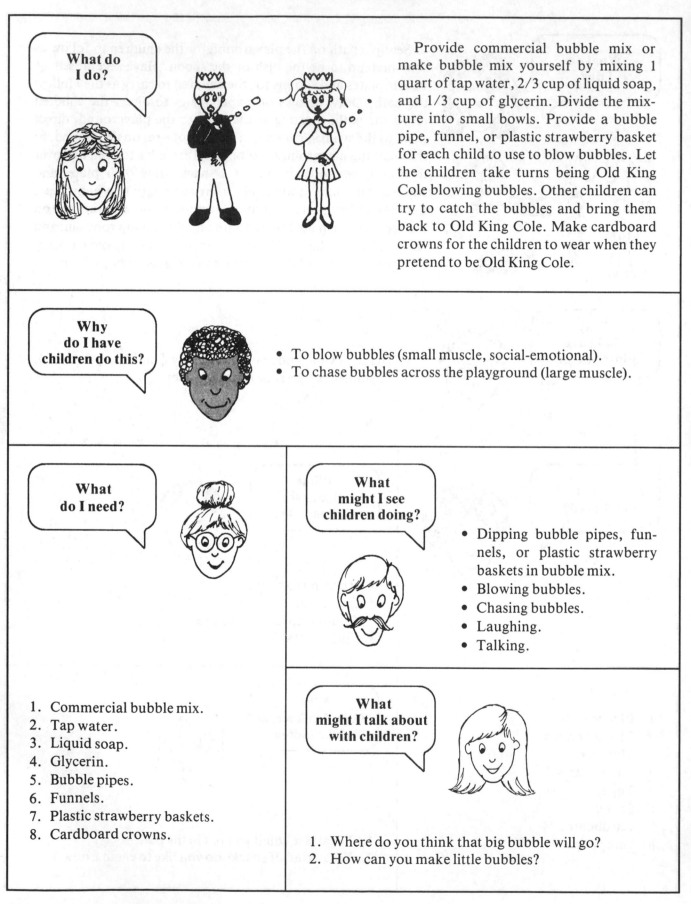

What do I do?

Provide commercial bubble mix or make bubble mix yourself by mixing 1 quart of tap water, 2/3 cup of liquid soap, and 1/3 cup of glycerin. Divide the mixture into small bowls. Provide a bubble pipe, funnel, or plastic strawberry basket for each child to use to blow bubbles. Let the children take turns being Old King Cole blowing bubbles. Other children can try to catch the bubbles and bring them back to Old King Cole. Make cardboard crowns for the children to wear when they pretend to be Old King Cole.

Why do I have children do this?

- To blow bubbles (small muscle, social-emotional).
- To chase bubbles across the playground (large muscle).

What do I need?

1. Commercial bubble mix.
2. Tap water.
3. Liquid soap.
4. Glycerin.
5. Bubble pipes.
6. Funnels.
7. Plastic strawberry baskets.
8. Cardboard crowns.

What might I see children doing?

- Dipping bubble pipes, funnels, or plastic strawberry baskets in bubble mix.
- Blowing bubbles.
- Chasing bubbles.
- Laughing.
- Talking.

What might I talk about with children?

1. Where do you think that big bubble will go?
2. How can you make little bubbles?

A CASTLE FOR A KING
Outdoor Large Muscle

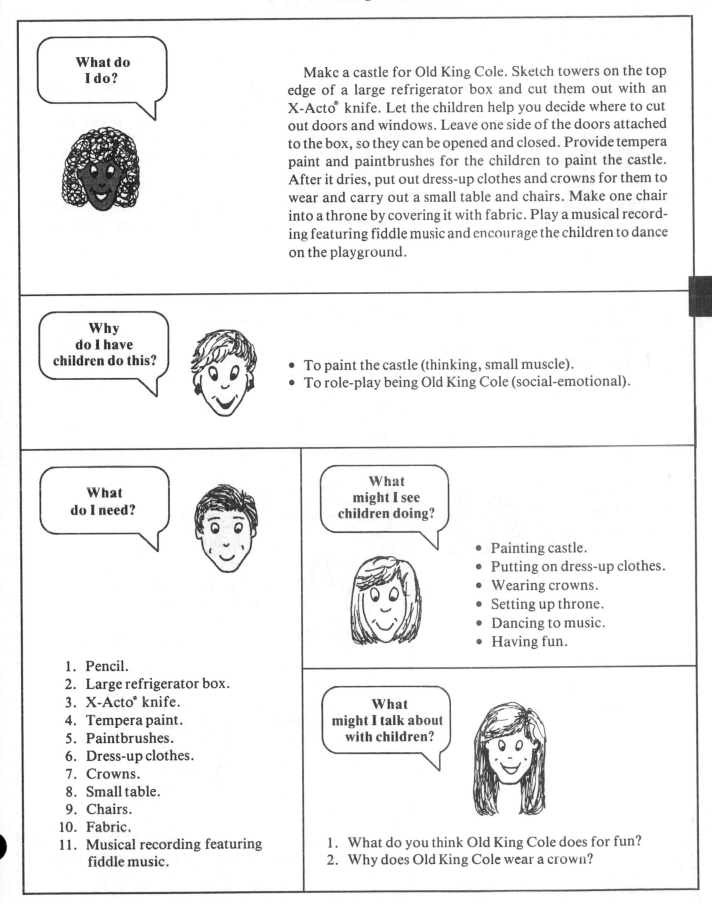

What do I do?

Make a castle for Old King Cole. Sketch towers on the top edge of a large refrigerator box and cut them out with an X-Acto® knife. Let the children help you decide where to cut out doors and windows. Leave one side of the doors attached to the box, so they can be opened and closed. Provide tempera paint and paintbrushes for the children to paint the castle. After it dries, put out dress-up clothes and crowns for them to wear and carry out a small table and chairs. Make one chair into a throne by covering it with fabric. Play a musical recording featuring fiddle music and encourage the children to dance on the playground.

Why do I have children do this?

- To paint the castle (thinking, small muscle).
- To role-play being Old King Cole (social-emotional).

What do I need?

1. Pencil.
2. Large refrigerator box.
3. X-Acto® knife.
4. Tempera paint.
5. Paintbrushes.
6. Dress-up clothes.
7. Crowns.
8. Small table.
9. Chairs.
10. Fabric.
11. Musical recording featuring fiddle music.

What might I see children doing?

- Painting castle.
- Putting on dress-up clothes.
- Wearing crowns.
- Setting up throne.
- Dancing to music.
- Having fun.

What might I talk about with children?

1. What do you think Old King Cole does for fun?
2. Why does Old King Cole wear a crown?

FIND THE SHOE
Outdoor Large Muscle

What do I do?

Collect two or three pairs of shoes. Hide them on the playground before the children go out to play. Leave the shoes partially exposed. Tell the children that there are several shoes hidden on the playground, and you are going to help them find the shoes. After all the shoes have been found, let two children hide them, so the other children can hunt for them. Do this several times, so all the children have a chance to hide the shoes. Then talk with the children about the different kinds of shoes, where you would wear them, and what colors they are.

Why do I have children do this?

- To find the shoes (large muscle, thinking).
- To hide the shoes (small muscle, thinking).

What do I need?

What might I see children doing?

- Hunting for shoes.
- Hiding shoes.
- Running.
- Talking about the shoes.

1. Two or three pairs of shoes.

What might I talk about with children?

1. Where could you hide these shoes?
2. What else could you hide on the playground?

A MOUSE FINDS THE CHEESE
Outdoor Large Muscle

What do I do?

Recite different nursery rhymes about mice, such as "Three Blind Mice" and "Hickory, Dickory, Dock." Talk about how mice like to eat cheese. Tell the children that you are hiding a yellow ball that looks like cheese and show it to them before you hide it. Let them pretend they are mice hunting for the cheese. When they find the ball, let them take turns hiding it for the other children to hunt.

Why do I have children do this?

- To hunt for the cheese (thinking).
- To run and play on the playground (large muscle).

What do I need?

1. Large yellow ball.

What might I see children doing?

- Running on the playground.
- Hunting for the cheese.
- Hiding the cheese.
- Having fun.

What might I talk about with children?

1. Where could you hide the cheese next?
2. What would you do with the ball if it really were cheese?

BIBLIOGRAPHY

NURSERY RHYMES

Arnold, T. 1990. *Mother Goose's Words of Wit and Wisdom: A Book of Months*. New York, NY: Dial Books for Young Readers.

Aylesworth, J. 1990. *The Completed Hickory Dickory Dock*. New York, NY: Atheneum.
Follow the energetic mouse through the other eleven hours of the day.

Beskow, E. 1988. *Around the Year*. United Kingdom: Floris Books.
A collection of rhymes depicting the months of the year.

[1]Butler, D. 1991. *Higgledy, Piggledy, Hobbledy, Hoy*. New York, NY: Greenwillow Books.
A rhyme that will tickle both boys and girls. Cheerful illustrations.

Chorao, K. 1977. *The Baby's Lap Book*. New York, NY: Dutton Children's Books.
Beautiful illustrations of favorite nursery rhymes.

Cole, J., and Colmenson, S. 1991. *Eentsy, Weentsy Spider*. New York, NY: Morrow Junior Books.
Selection of nursery rhymes, fingerplays, and action rhymes.

[3]De Angeli, M. 1954. *Book of Nursery Rhymes and Mother Goose Rhymes*. New York, NY: Doubleday and Company.
A rich collection of nursery rhymes and colorful illustrations.

De Paola, T. 1985. *Tomie de Paola's Mother Goose*. New York, NY: G.P. Putnam's Sons.
Colorfully illustrated collection of over two hundred Mother Goose nursery rhymes.

Father Gander Nursery Rhymes. Santa Barbara, CA: Advocacy Press. 1985.
A beautifully illustrated collection of traditional nursery rhymes that have been rewritten to stress equality, love, responsibility, appreciation of life and all things living, good nutrition, and conservation of resources.

Fuller, T. 1989. *Father Gander Rhymes*. Rock Hill, SC: Acosta and Alder.
Traditional Mother Goose Nursery rhymes rewritten for today's world.

[3]Gill, S. 1987. *Alaska Mother Goose*. Homer, AK: Paws IV Publishing.

Kirk, D. 2000. *Humpty Dumpty*. New York, NY: G.P. Putnam's Inc.
A traditional nursery rhyme with a new twist—this time Humpty Dumpty becomes a special friend of the young king.

[3]Knight, H. 1962. *Hilary Knight's Mother Goose*. New York, NY: Golden Press.
Fun illustrations fill this book.

Loomans, D., Koberg, K., and Loomans, J. 1991. *Positively Mother Goose*. Tiburon,
CA: H.J. Kramer, Inc.
Traditional nursery rhymes are rewritten to accentuate positive feelings and self-
esteem. Colorful illustrations. Alternative for those who object to the original
nursery rhymes.

[3]Maclean, M. 1989. *Mary Had a Little Lamb*. New York, NY: Doubleday.
A fanciful adaptation of the original rhyme. Colorful illustrations.

Marshall, J. 1979. *James Marshall's Mother Goose*. New York, NY: Farrar, Straus
and Giroux.
A fresh and funny look at Mother Goose.

Mother Goose: The Original Holland Edition. New York, NY: Outlet Book Co. 1985.
A classic version of Mother Goose. Beautifully illustrated.

Prelutsky, J. 1986. *Read-Aloud Rhymes for the Very Young*. New York, NY: Alfred A.
Knopf, Inc.
A splendid collection of more than two hundred sparkling verses that will open
young minds and eyes to the magic and meaning of words.

[3]Provensen, A., and Provensen, M. 1976. *The Mother Goose Book*. New York, NY:
Random House Juvenile.
A selection of traditional Mother Goose rhymes with illustrations.

The Real Mother Goose. New York, NY: Checkerboard Press. 1991.
The classic black-and-white checkerboard Mother Goose. Does not have as many
illustrations as some other collections.

Real Mother Goose Husky Books. New York, NY: Checkerboard Press.
A series of four books that are great for small hands to hold.

[3]Reed, P. 1963. *Mother Goose and Nursery Rhymes*. New York, NY: Atheneum.
Mother Goose nursery rhymes illustrated with wood engravings. The book has an
antique look. It is filled with a rich collection of rhymes.

Rifkin, J. 2001. *The Everything Mother Goose Book*. Holbrook, MA: Adams
Media Corporation.
This collection of 300 nursery rhymes includes games and will captivate children.

[3]San Souci, D. 1986. *The Mother Goose Book: A Collection of Nursery Rhymes*.
New York, NY: Julian Messner.
A beautifully illustrated collection of well-known nursery rhymes.

[3]Scarry, R. 1970. *Richard Scarry's Best Mother Goose Ever*. New York, NY:
Golden Press.
A fun book of nursery rhymes with animals as our favorite Mother Goose characters.

[3]Sutherland, Z. 1990. *The Orchard Book of Nursery Rhymes*. New York, NY:
Orchard Books.
Collection of traditional nursery rhymes that are a perfect way to introduce the
development of language skills and an interest in poetry.

[3]Thompson, B. 1989. *Catch It If You Can*. New York, NY: Viking Children's Books.
Collection of poetry written just for fun.

Trapani, I. 1993. *The Itsy Bitsy Spider*. Dallas, TX: Whispering Coyote Press.
A delightful book that follows the heroine from the waterspout and beyond into gig-
    gling adventures sure to delight young children.

Walt Disney's *Mother Goose*. 2000. New York, NY: Disney Editions.
Help children relive treasured moments of Disney magic with this book of beloved
    nursery rhymes.

We have marked these books if we think they are definitely more applicable to one age. Many can be used by all ages with adaptations by the teacher.

[1]Books for one-year-olds, two-year-olds, and three-year-olds.

[2]Books for five-year-olds.

[3]This book is no longer in print. However, you may be able to find it at your local library.

Unit 5

PETS

CONTENTS

PETS

Pets can be an integral part of children's lives. They may include dogs, cats, birds, gerbils, guinea pigs, fish, calves, horses, or lambs that have been tamed and are kept as special friends. When children have pets, they learn to differentiate between wild and domesticated animals.

"Pets" consists of activities to help children learn how to care for pets and learn what pets eat, how they sleep, where they live, and how they move. The children learn the importance of being responsible for a living creature. They will also learn that:

• Pets are living creatures that need food, water, air, and attention.
• Different pets have different physical characteristics.
• Different pets make different sounds.
• Pets live in a variety of homes, such as a doghouse, fishbowl, basket, or stall.
• Baby animals are different from their parents.

KITTEN FOR A DAY
Group

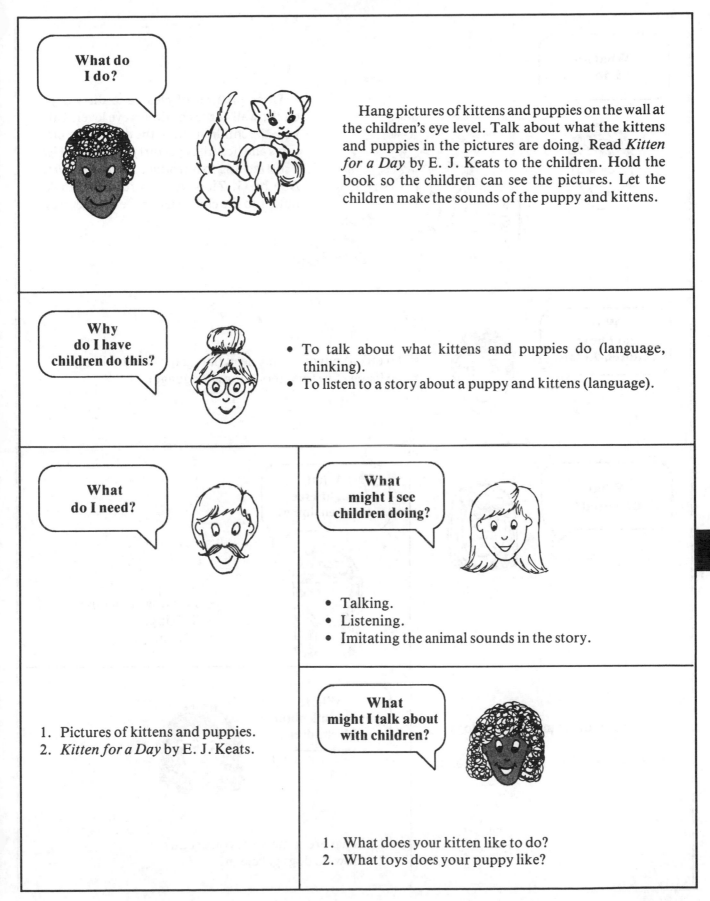

What do I do?

Hang pictures of kittens and puppies on the wall at the children's eye level. Talk about what the kittens and puppies in the pictures are doing. Read *Kitten for a Day* by E. J. Keats to the children. Hold the book so the children can see the pictures. Let the children make the sounds of the puppy and kittens.

Why do I have children do this?

- To talk about what kittens and puppies do (language, thinking).
- To listen to a story about a puppy and kittens (language).

What do I need?

1. Pictures of kittens and puppies.
2. *Kitten for a Day* by E. J. Keats.

What might I see children doing?

- Talking.
- Listening.
- Imitating the animal sounds in the story.

What might I talk about with children?

1. What does your kitten like to do?
2. What toys does your puppy like?

HARRY THE DIRTY DOG
Group

What do I do?

Hang pictures of clean and dirty dogs on the wall at the children's eye level. Talk with the children about the dogs in the pictures and how they get dirty and clean. Use a stuffed dog to introduce *Harry the Dirty Dog* by G. Zion. As you read the book, hold it so the children can see the pictures.

Why do I have children do this?

- To talk about dirty and clean (language and thinking).
- To listen to a story about dogs (language).

What do I need?

What might I see children doing?

- Looking at pictures.
- Talking.
- Listening.

1. Pictures of clean and dirty dogs.
2. Stuffed dog.
3. *Harry the Dirty Dog* by G. Zion.

What might I talk about with children?

1. What are some ways you get dirty?
2. How do dogs get clean?

BUNNY TROUBLE
Group

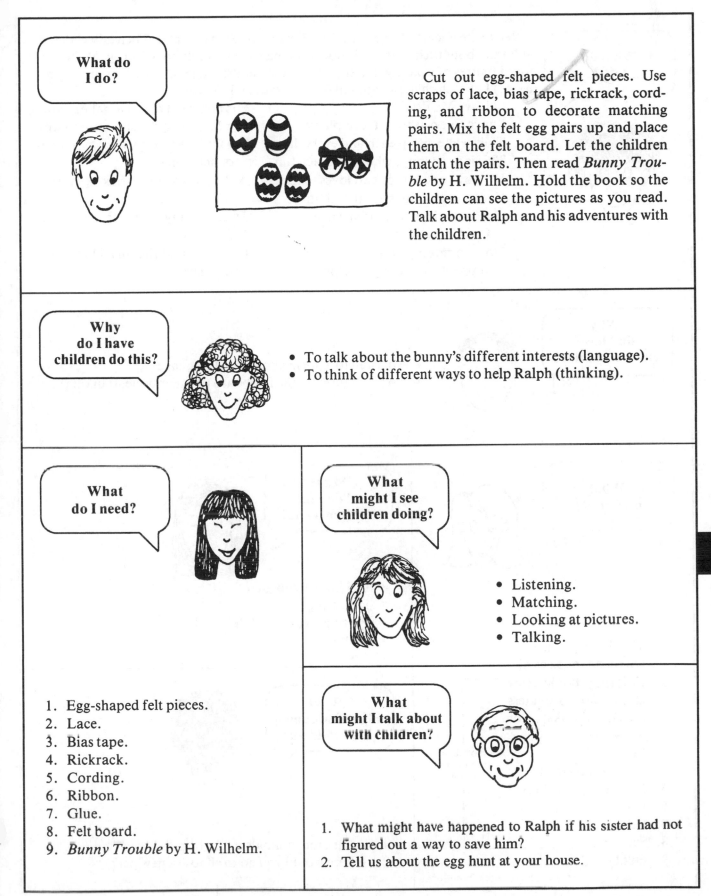

What do I do?

Cut out egg-shaped felt pieces. Use scraps of lace, bias tape, rickrack, cording, and ribbon to decorate matching pairs. Mix the felt egg pairs up and place them on the felt board. Let the children match the pairs. Then read *Bunny Trouble* by H. Wilhelm. Hold the book so the children can see the pictures as you read. Talk about Ralph and his adventures with the children.

Why do I have children do this?

- To talk about the bunny's different interests (language).
- To think of different ways to help Ralph (thinking).

What do I need?

What might I see children doing?

- Listening.
- Matching.
- Looking at pictures.
- Talking.

1. Egg-shaped felt pieces.
2. Lace.
3. Bias tape.
4. Rickrack.
5. Cording.
6. Ribbon.
7. Glue.
8. Felt board.
9. *Bunny Trouble* by H. Wilhelm.

What might I talk about with children?

1. What might have happened to Ralph if his sister had not figured out a way to save him?
2. Tell us about the egg hunt at your house.

"I LOVE MY PETS"
Group

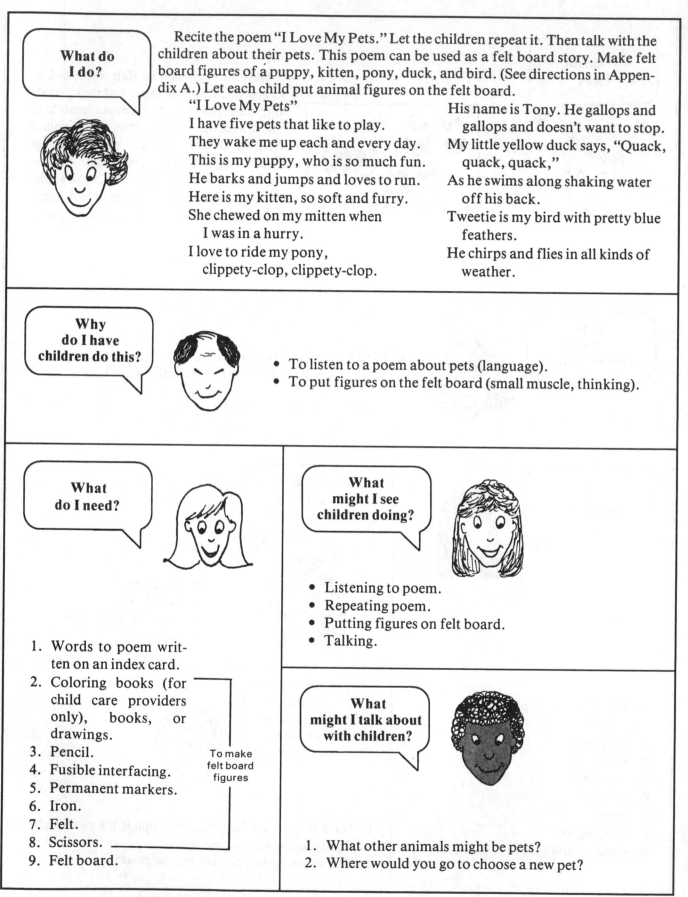

What do I do?

Recite the poem "I Love My Pets." Let the children repeat it. Then talk with the children about their pets. This poem can be used as a felt board story. Make felt board figures of a puppy, kitten, pony, duck, and bird. (See directions in Appendix A.) Let each child put animal figures on the felt board.

"I Love My Pets"

I have five pets that like to play.
They wake me up each and every day.
This is my puppy, who is so much fun.
He barks and jumps and loves to run.
Here is my kitten, so soft and furry.
She chewed on my mitten when
    I was in a hurry.
I love to ride my pony,
    clippety-clop, clippety-clop.

His name is Tony. He gallops and
    gallops and doesn't want to stop.
My little yellow duck says, "Quack,
    quack, quack,"
As he swims along shaking water
    off his back.
Tweetie is my bird with pretty blue
    feathers.
He chirps and flies in all kinds of
    weather.

Why do I have children do this?

- To listen to a poem about pets (language).
- To put figures on the felt board (small muscle, thinking).

What do I need?

1. Words to poem written on an index card.
2. Coloring books (for child care providers only), books, or drawings.
3. Pencil.
4. Fusible interfacing.
5. Permanent markers.
6. Iron.
7. Felt.
8. Scissors.
9. Felt board.

To make felt board figures

What might I see children doing?

- Listening to poem.
- Repeating poem.
- Putting figures on felt board.
- Talking.

What might I talk about with children?

1. What other animals might be pets?
2. Where would you go to choose a new pet?

"OH, WILL I HAVE A LITTLE PET?"
Group

What do I do?

Hang up pictures of pets on the walls at the children's eye level. Then sing the following song to the tune of "The Muffin Man." Let the children suggest additional verses. Expand the activity by letting the children act out the pet's actions.

"Oh, Will I Have a Little Pet?"

Oh, will I have a little pet, a little pet, a little pet?

Oh, will I have a little pet that I can choose today?

Oh, yes I have a little dog, a little dog, a little dog.

Oh, yes I have a little dog that runs and plays with me.

Why do I have children do this?

- To sing (language).
- To make up verses about pets and the pet's actions (thinking).

What do I need?

1. Pictures of pets.
2. Words to song written on an index card.

What might I see children doing?

- Singing.
- Talking.
- Suggesting other verses.
- Role-playing pets.

What might I talk about with children?

1. What pets could you sing about?
2. What tricks can a dog do?

A RABBIT COMES TO VISIT
Group

What do I do?

Have a child from the group or a person who owns a rabbit bring it to the child care home or center. (Make sure the rabbit is friendly and used to children before you let them pet it.) Provide a bowl of water and a bowl of rabbit food, so the children can watch the rabbit eat. Talk with the children about how the rabbit feels, the noises it makes, and how it moves.

Why do I have children do this?

- To watch the rabbit move, eat, and drink (social-emotional).
- To talk about rabbits (language).

What do I need?

1. Rabbits.
2. Bowl of water.
3. Bowl of rabbit food.

What might I see children doing?

- Petting rabbit.
- Feeding rabbit.
- Talking.

What might I talk about with children?

1. How do rabbits ears move?
2. What does the rabbit like to eat?

PET STORIES
Group

What do I do?

Have the children bring in photos of their pets. (If a child does not have a pet, let him or her cut out a picture of the pet he or she would like to have from an old magazine.) Attach the photos to a sheet of paper. Talk with the children about their pets. Then ask each child if you can write a story about his or her pet on the sheet of paper. Hang up the pictures and stories on the wall at the children's eye level, so the children can share their stories.

Why do I have children do this?

- To talk about their pets (language).
- To see you write their stories (language).

What do I need?

1. Paper.
2. Photos of pets.
3. Old magazines.
4. Glue.
5. Pencil.

What might I see children doing?

- Talking about their pets.
- Sharing stories of their pets.
- Listening.

What might I talk about with children?

1. Where do you play with your dog?
2. What do you think your goldfish would say if he could talk?

BAG FULL OF PUPS
Group

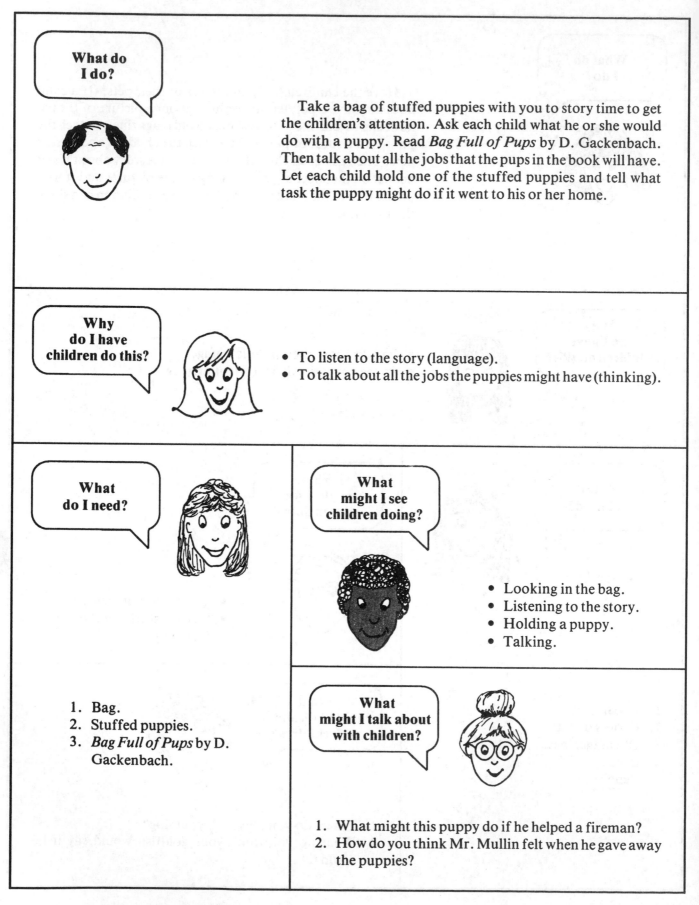

What do I do?

Take a bag of stuffed puppies with you to story time to get the children's attention. Ask each child what he or she would do with a puppy. Read *Bag Full of Pups* by D. Gackenbach. Then talk about all the jobs that the pups in the book will have. Let each child hold one of the stuffed puppies and tell what task the puppy might do if it went to his or her home.

Why do I have children do this?

- To listen to the story (language).
- To talk about all the jobs the puppies might have (thinking).

What do I need?

1. Bag.
2. Stuffed puppies.
3. *Bag Full of Pups* by D. Gackenbach.

What might I see children doing?

- Looking in the bag.
- Listening to the story.
- Holding a puppy.
- Talking.

What might I talk about with children?

1. What might this puppy do if he helped a fireman?
2. How do you think Mr. Mullin felt when he gave away the puppies?

WE LEARN ABOUT PETS
Group

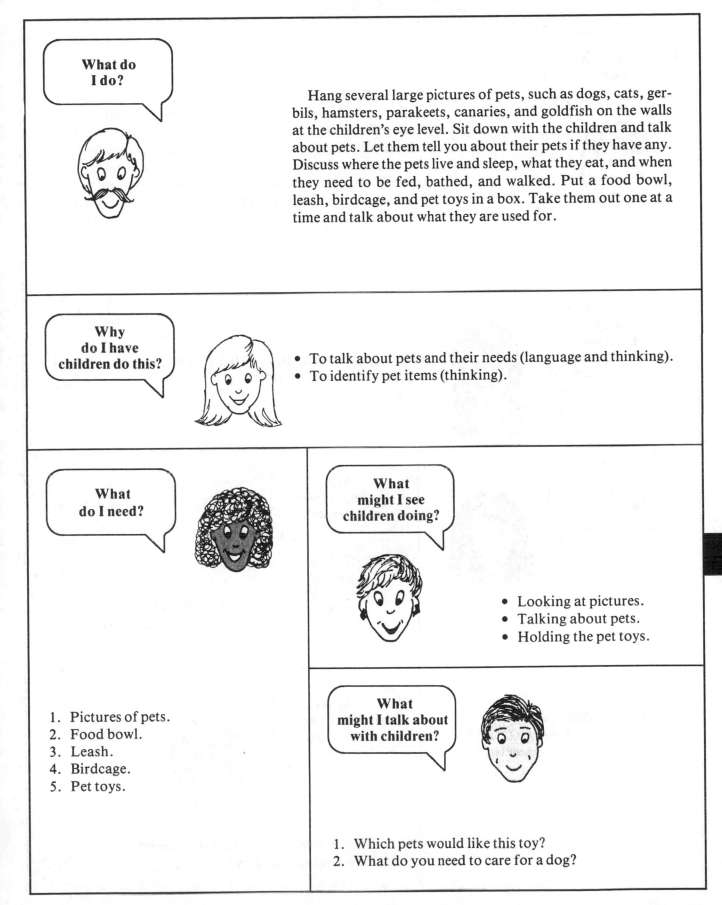

What do I do?

Hang several large pictures of pets, such as dogs, cats, gerbils, hamsters, parakeets, canaries, and goldfish on the walls at the children's eye level. Sit down with the children and talk about pets. Let them tell you about their pets if they have any. Discuss where the pets live and sleep, what they eat, and when they need to be fed, bathed, and walked. Put a food bowl, leash, birdcage, and pet toys in a box. Take them out one at a time and talk about what they are used for.

Why do I have children do this?

- To talk about pets and their needs (language and thinking).
- To identify pet items (thinking).

What do I need?

1. Pictures of pets.
2. Food bowl.
3. Leash.
4. Birdcage.
5. Pet toys.

What might I see children doing?

- Looking at pictures.
- Talking about pets.
- Holding the pet toys.

What might I talk about with children?

1. Which pets would like this toy?
2. What do you need to care for a dog?

SHAGS FINDS A KITTEN
Group, Learning Center (library)

What do I do?

Bring a real or stuffed kitten to the group to introduce *Shags Finds a Kitten* by G. Fujikawa or *Annie and the Wild Animals* by J. Brett. (If you bring in a real kitten, be sure to carefully supervise it and the children.) Talk with the children about dogs and cats. Talk about how animals get lost if we do not take good care of them, and what you sometimes need to do to find them. Then read one of the books, holding it so the children can see the pictures.

Why do I have children do this?

- To talk about dogs and cats (language).
- To share a new book (language).

What do I need?

What might I see children doing?

- Petting the kitten.
- Talking about dogs and cats.
- Listening to the story.

1. Real or stuffed kitten.
2. *Shags Finds a Kitten* by G. Fujikawa.
3. *Annie and the Wild Animals* by J. Brett.

What might I talk about with children?

1. What else can a dog do to help a friend?
2. How does a kitten play?

LISTEN TO THE PETS
Group, Learning Center (library)

What do I do?

Make felt board figures of a dog, cat, cow, and bird. (See directions in Appendix A.) Talk with the children about listening for the pet sounds. Then place the felt board where the children can reach it and play a recording of a dog barking, a cat meowing, a cow mooing, and a bird chirping. As the children hear the pet sounds, let them take turns identifying the sounds and placing the correct figure on the board. When all the pets are on the felt board, play the tape recording again. Let the children take turns taking the pet off the board.

Why do I have children do this?

- To listen to different sounds that pets make (language).
- To identify the appropriate pet when its sound is heard (thinking).

What do I need?

1. Coloring books (for child care providers only), books, or drawings.
2. Pencil.
3. Fusible interfacing.
4. Permanent markers.
5. Iron.
6. Felt.
7. Scissors.
8. Felt board.
9. Tape recorder or record player.
10. Recording of animal sounds.

To make felt board figures

What might I see children doing?

- Listening.
- Putting a pet on the felt board.
- Taking a pet off the felt board.

What might I talk about with children?

1. What are some sounds that other pets make?
2. Where could you go to make a tape recording of other pet sounds?

TAPE THE TAIL ON THE CAT
Group, Indoor or Outdoor Large Muscle

What do I do?

Draw a large picture of a cat without a tail on poster board. Cut out one tail for each child from poster board. Hang the cat on a bulletin board at the children's eye level. You can explain to the children that Bouncer, the cat, got his tail caught in the screen door and they are going to try to tape it back on the right spot. Blindfold one child at a time and place tape on his or her tail. If a child does not want to be blindfolded, do not force the issue. Let him or her walk towards the poster board cat and place the tail on the cat. This is a good activity for four- and five-year-olds.

Why do I have children do this?

- To have fun (social-emotional).
- To tape the tail on the cat (small muscle).

What do I need?

1. Poster board.
2. Marker.
3. Poster board tails.
4. Tape.

What might I see children doing?

- Taping the tail on the cat.
- Talking about Bouncer.
- Giggling.

What might I talk about with children?

1. What do you think Bouncer was trying to do when he got his tail caught in the screen door?
2. Where do you think the tail should go?

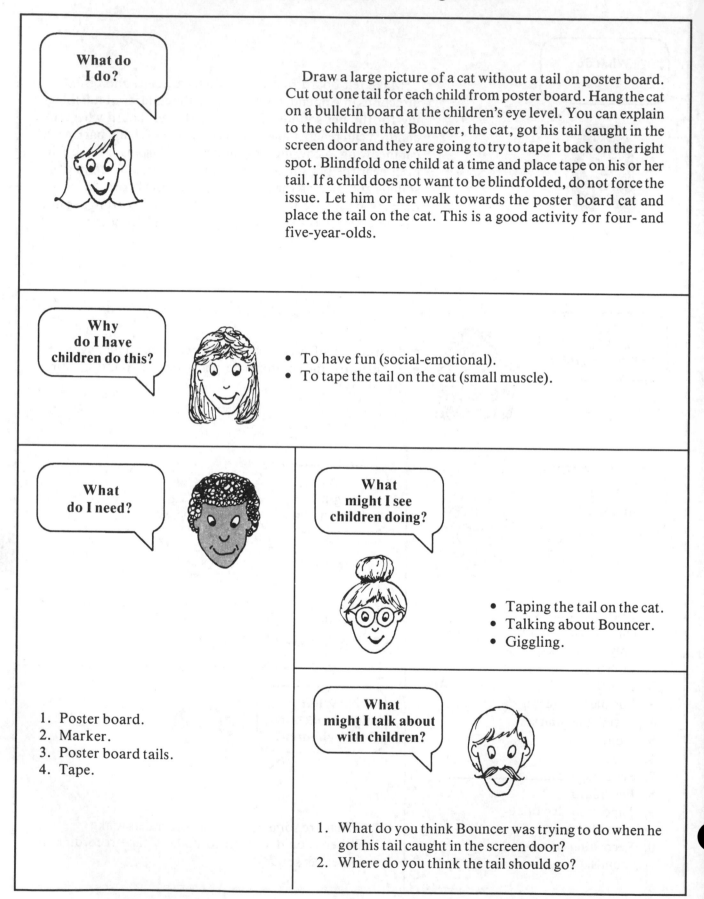

PLAYDOUGH PETS
Learning Center (art)

What do I do?

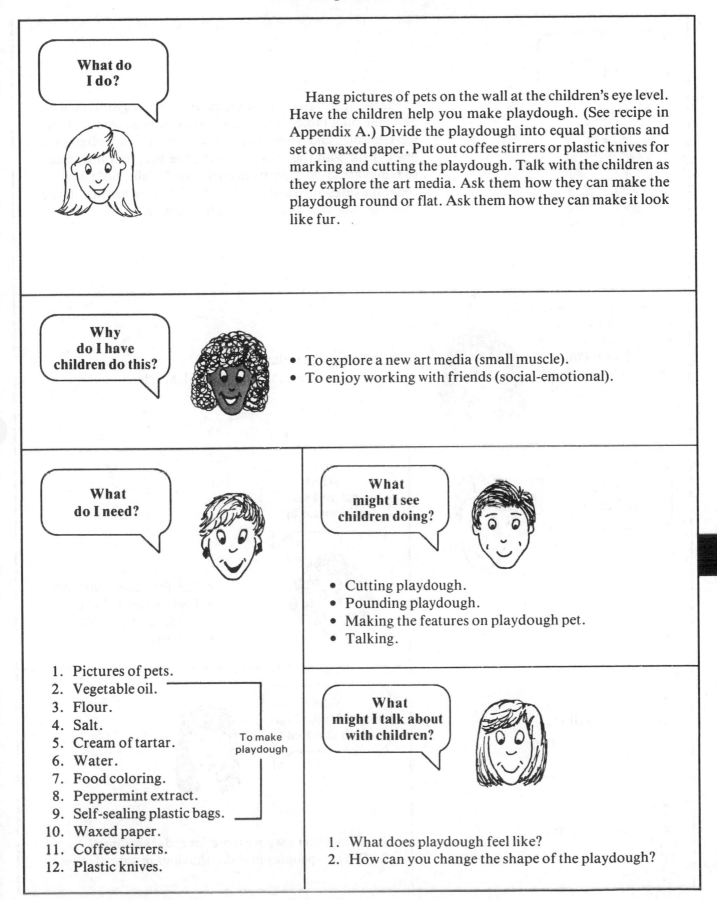

Hang pictures of pets on the wall at the children's eye level. Have the children help you make playdough. (See recipe in Appendix A.) Divide the playdough into equal portions and set on waxed paper. Put out coffee stirrers or plastic knives for marking and cutting the playdough. Talk with the children as they explore the art media. Ask them how they can make the playdough round or flat. Ask them how they can make it look like fur.

Why do I have children do this?

- To explore a new art media (small muscle).
- To enjoy working with friends (social-emotional).

What do I need?

What might I see children doing?

- Cutting playdough.
- Pounding playdough.
- Making the features on playdough pet.
- Talking.

1. Pictures of pets.
2. Vegetable oil.
3. Flour.
4. Salt.
5. Cream of tartar.
6. Water.
7. Food coloring.
8. Peppermint extract.
9. Self-sealing plastic bags.
10. Waxed paper.
11. Coffee stirrers.
12. Plastic knives.

To make playdough

What might I talk about with children?

1. What does playdough feel like?
2. How can you change the shape of the playdough?

PET SHOP PICTURES
Learning Center (art)

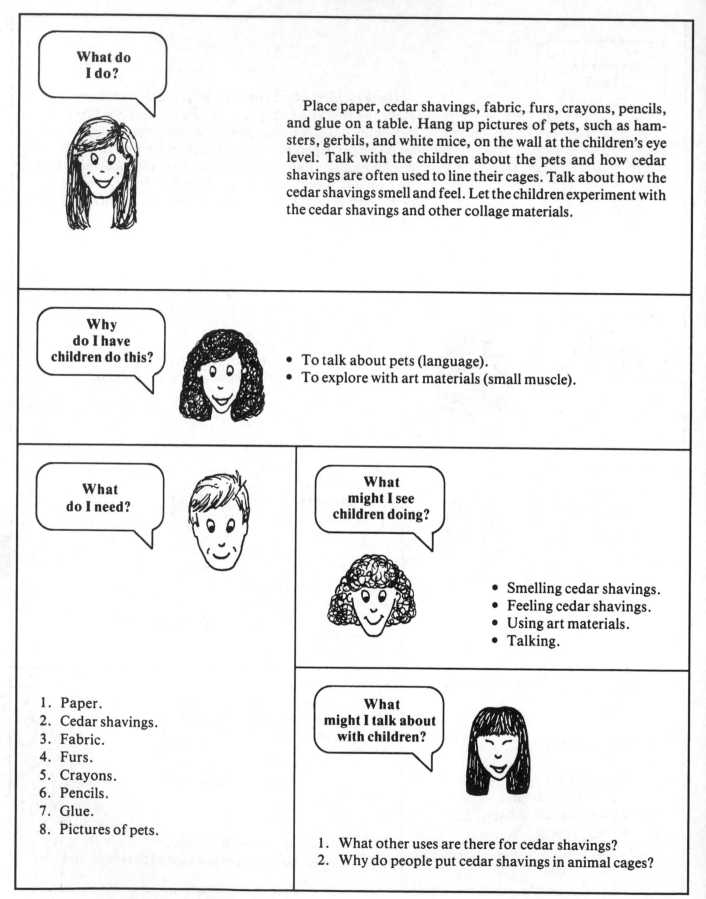

What do I do?

Place paper, cedar shavings, fabric, furs, crayons, pencils, and glue on a table. Hang up pictures of pets, such as hamsters, gerbils, and white mice, on the wall at the children's eye level. Talk with the children about the pets and how cedar shavings are often used to line their cages. Talk about how the cedar shavings smell and feel. Let the children experiment with the cedar shavings and other collage materials.

Why do I have children do this?

- To talk about pets (language).
- To explore with art materials (small muscle).

What do I need?

1. Paper.
2. Cedar shavings.
3. Fabric.
4. Furs.
5. Crayons.
6. Pencils.
7. Glue.
8. Pictures of pets.

What might I see children doing?

- Smelling cedar shavings.
- Feeling cedar shavings.
- Using art materials.
- Talking.

What might I talk about with children?

1. What other uses are there for cedar shavings?
2. Why do people put cedar shavings in animal cages?

PET COLLAGE
Learning Center (art, library)

What do I do?

Put out old magazines featuring animals, glue, tape, scissors, and a large piece of newsprint. Encourage the children to cut out pictures of pets from the magazines. Let the children glue or tape the pictures on the large piece of paper to make a pet collage.

Why do I have children do this?

- To pick out pet pictures from magazines (thinking).
- To cut and glue or tape (small muscle).

What do I need?

1. Old magazines featuring animals.
2. Glue.
3. Tape.
4. Scissors.
5. Large piece of newsprint.

What might I see children doing?

- Looking at pictures.
- Cutting.
- Gluing or taping.

What might I talk about with children?

1. Where do these pets live?
2. Which pets would you like to have live at your house?

BUNNY TROUBLE EGGS
Learning Center (art)

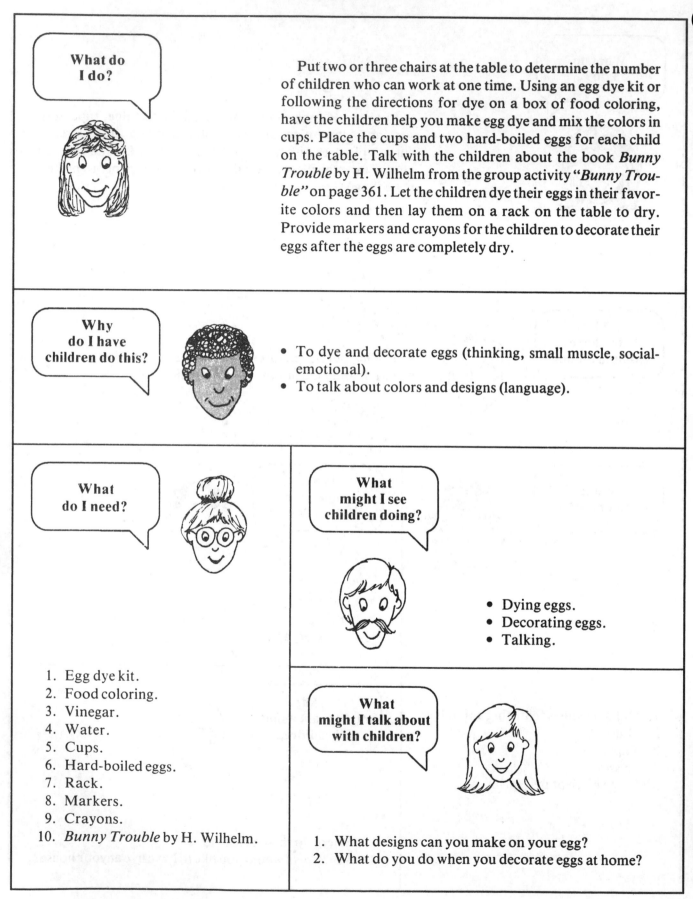

What do I do?

Put two or three chairs at the table to determine the number of children who can work at one time. Using an egg dye kit or following the directions for dye on a box of food coloring, have the children help you make egg dye and mix the colors in cups. Place the cups and two hard-boiled eggs for each child on the table. Talk with the children about the book *Bunny Trouble* by H. Wilhelm from the group activity "*Bunny Trouble*" on page 361. Let the children dye their eggs in their favorite colors and then lay them on a rack on the table to dry. Provide markers and crayons for the children to decorate their eggs after the eggs are completely dry.

Why do I have children do this?

- To dye and decorate eggs (thinking, small muscle, social-emotional).
- To talk about colors and designs (language).

What do I need?

1. Egg dye kit.
2. Food coloring.
3. Vinegar.
4. Water.
5. Cups.
6. Hard-boiled eggs.
7. Rack.
8. Markers.
9. Crayons.
10. *Bunny Trouble* by H. Wilhelm.

What might I see children doing?

- Dying eggs.
- Decorating eggs.
- Talking.

What might I talk about with children?

1. What designs can you make on your egg?
2. What do you do when you decorate eggs at home?

PET BOOK
Learning Center (art)

What do I do?

Put out paper, glue, scissors, self-sealing plastic bags, and several old magazines featuring animals. Have the children look for pictures of pets to cut out and glue on sheets of paper to make a "Pet Book" for the library area. Provide crayons and markers for children who want to draw their own pictures. Talk with the children about the pets they chose. If the children want you to, write their comments at the bottom of the sheet. Put two of the children's sheets back-to-back in a self-sealing plastic bag. Staple the permanently sealed edges of all the bags together. Cover the staples with plastic tape. When the book is done, read the children's comments to them and show them the pictures.

Why do I have children do this?

- To cut pictures (small muscle).
- To select favorite pets (thinking).
- To describe what pets are doing (language).

What do I need?

What might I see children doing?

- Choosing pictures of pets.
- Cutting.
- Gluing.
- Talking.
- Watching you write words.

1. Paper.
2. Glue.
3. Scissors.
4. Self-sealing plastic bags.
5. Old magazines featuring animals.
6. Crayons.
7. Markers.
8. Pen.
9. Stapler.
10. Plastic tape.

What might I talk about with children?

1. What are your favorite pets?
2. What kinds of food does your pet like?

EASEL PAINTING
Learning Center (art)

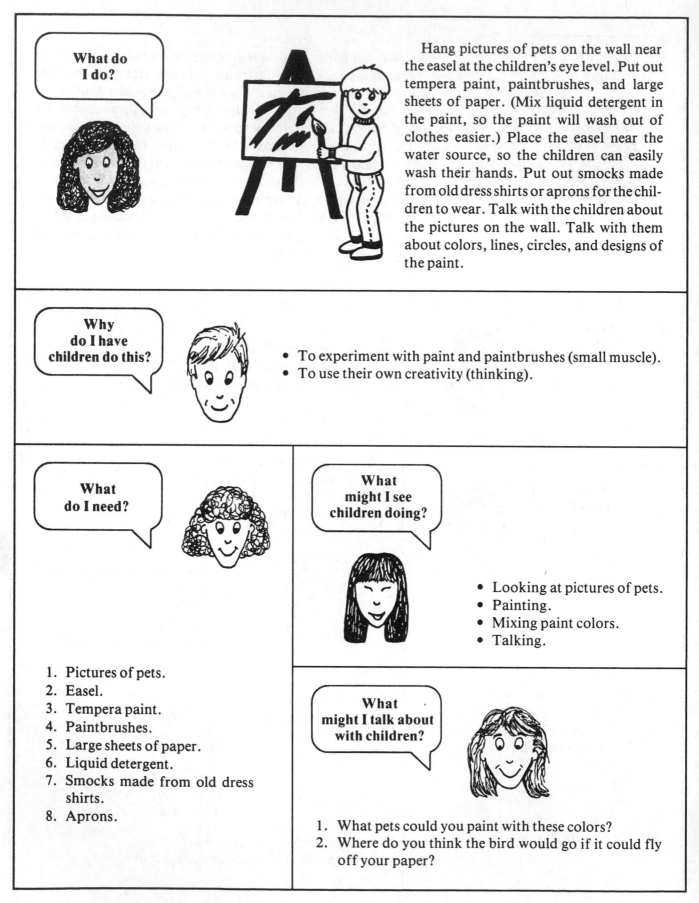

What do I do?

Hang pictures of pets on the wall near the easel at the children's eye level. Put out tempera paint, paintbrushes, and large sheets of paper. (Mix liquid detergent in the paint, so the paint will wash out of clothes easier.) Place the easel near the water source, so the children can easily wash their hands. Put out smocks made from old dress shirts or aprons for the children to wear. Talk with the children about the pictures on the wall. Talk with them about colors, lines, circles, and designs of the paint.

Why do I have children do this?

- To experiment with paint and paintbrushes (small muscle).
- To use their own creativity (thinking).

What do I need?

1. Pictures of pets.
2. Easel.
3. Tempera paint.
4. Paintbrushes.
5. Large sheets of paper.
6. Liquid detergent.
7. Smocks made from old dress shirts.
8. Aprons.

What might I see children doing?

- Looking at pictures of pets.
- Painting.
- Mixing paint colors.
- Talking.

What might I talk about with children?

1. What pets could you paint with these colors?
2. Where do you think the bird would go if it could fly off your paper?

BUNNY PUFFS
Learning Center (art)

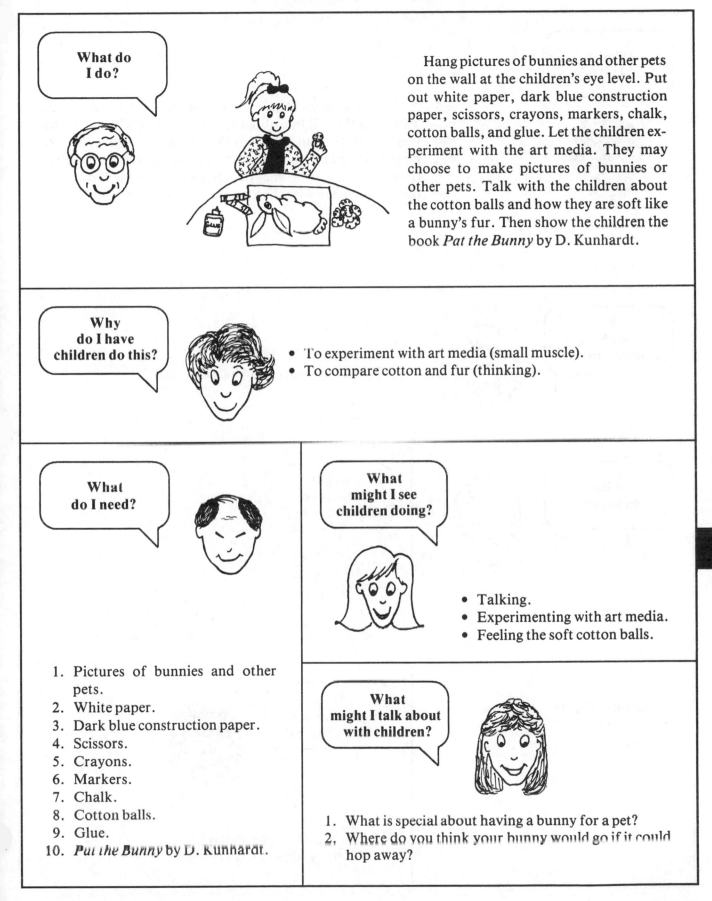

What do I do?

Hang pictures of bunnies and other pets on the wall at the children's eye level. Put out white paper, dark blue construction paper, scissors, crayons, markers, chalk, cotton balls, and glue. Let the children experiment with the art media. They may choose to make pictures of bunnies or other pets. Talk with the children about the cotton balls and how they are soft like a bunny's fur. Then show the children the book *Pat the Bunny* by D. Kunhardt.

Why do I have children do this?

- To experiment with art media (small muscle).
- To compare cotton and fur (thinking).

What do I need?

1. Pictures of bunnies and other pets.
2. White paper.
3. Dark blue construction paper.
4. Scissors.
5. Crayons.
6. Markers.
7. Chalk.
8. Cotton balls.
9. Glue.
10. *Pat the Bunny* by D. Kunhardt.

What might I see children doing?

- Talking.
- Experimenting with art media.
- Feeling the soft cotton balls.

What might I talk about with children?

1. What is special about having a bunny for a pet?
2. Where do you think your bunny would go if it could hop away?

PICTURES FOR PET STORIES
Learning Center (art)

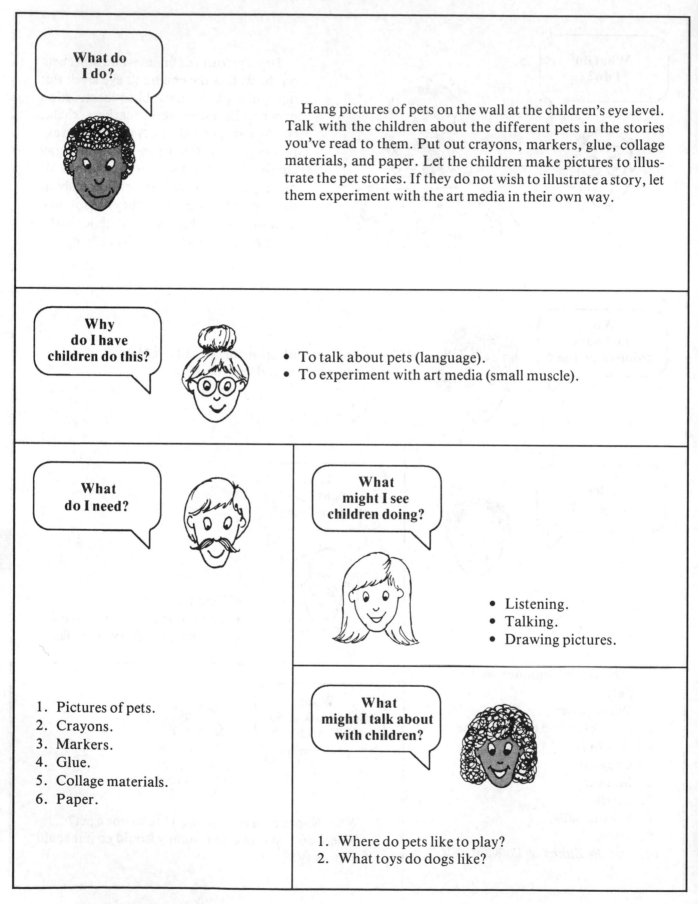

What do I do?

Hang pictures of pets on the wall at the children's eye level. Talk with the children about the different pets in the stories you've read to them. Put out crayons, markers, glue, collage materials, and paper. Let the children make pictures to illustrate the pet stories. If they do not wish to illustrate a story, let them experiment with the art media in their own way.

Why do I have children do this?

- To talk about pets (language).
- To experiment with art media (small muscle).

What do I need?

1. Pictures of pets.
2. Crayons.
3. Markers.
4. Glue.
5. Collage materials.
6. Paper.

What might I see children doing?

- Listening.
- Talking.
- Drawing pictures.

What might I talk about with children?

1. Where do pets like to play?
2. What toys do dogs like?

PET SCULPTURES
Learning Center (art)

What do I do?

Hang pictures of pets on the wall at the children's eye level. Put out a variety of curved and square Styrofoam® plastic foam pieces, different-sized Styrofoam® plastic foam balls, glue, scissors, craft sticks, yarn, felt, furry fabric, and bits of leather. Talk with the children about pets as they experiment with the art media. Let them create their own sculptures. Talk with the children about the shapes and colors of the materials, the furry fabric, and the long and short pieces of yarn.

Why do I have children do this?

- To explore a variety of art media (small muscle).
- To use new words, such as soft, furry, circles, squares (thinking).

What do I need?

1. Pictures of pets.
2. Curved and square Styrofoam® plastic foam pieces.
3. Different-sized Styrofoam® plastic foam balls.
4. Glue.
5. Scissors.
6. Craft sticks.
7. Yarn.
8. Felt.
9. Furry fabric.
10. Bits of leather.

What might I see children doing?

- Choosing materials.
- Cutting.
- Gluing.
- Talking.

What might I talk about with children?

1. What else feels like this fabric?
2. What could you use to hold these pieces together?

FUZZY CAT COLLAGE
Learning Center (art)

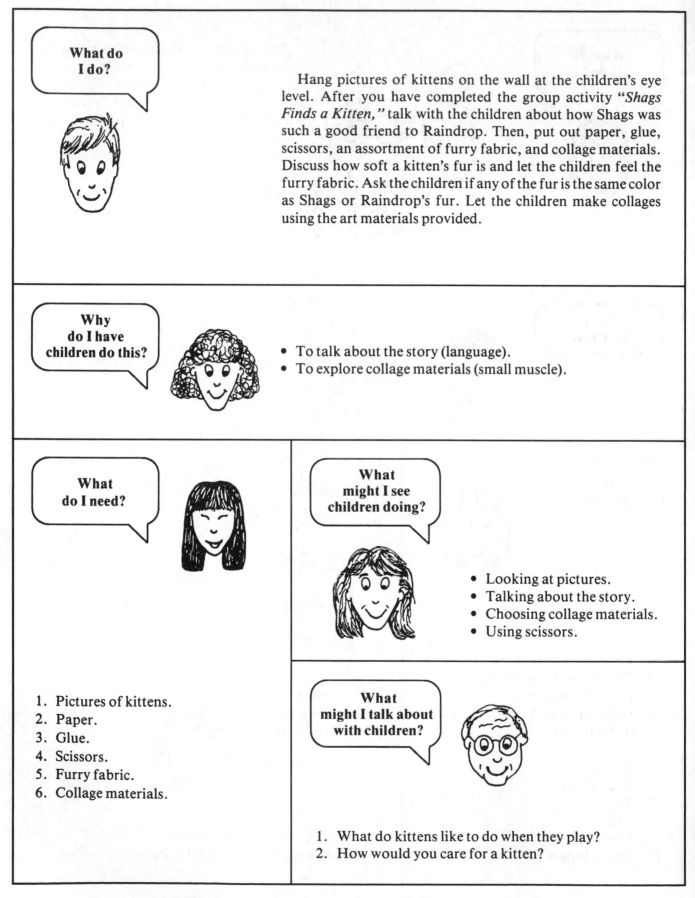

What do I do?

Hang pictures of kittens on the wall at the children's eye level. After you have completed the group activity *"Shags Finds a Kitten,"* talk with the children about how Shags was such a good friend to Raindrop. Then, put out paper, glue, scissors, an assortment of furry fabric, and collage materials. Discuss how soft a kitten's fur is and let the children feel the furry fabric. Ask the children if any of the fur is the same color as Shags or Raindrop's fur. Let the children make collages using the art materials provided.

Why do I have children do this?

- To talk about the story (language).
- To explore collage materials (small muscle).

What do I need?

What might I see children doing?

- Looking at pictures.
- Talking about the story.
- Choosing collage materials.
- Using scissors.

1. Pictures of kittens.
2. Paper.
3. Glue.
4. Scissors.
5. Furry fabric.
6. Collage materials.

What might I talk about with children?

1. What do kittens like to do when they play?
2. How would you care for a kitten?

PET STICK PUPPETS
Learning Center (art)

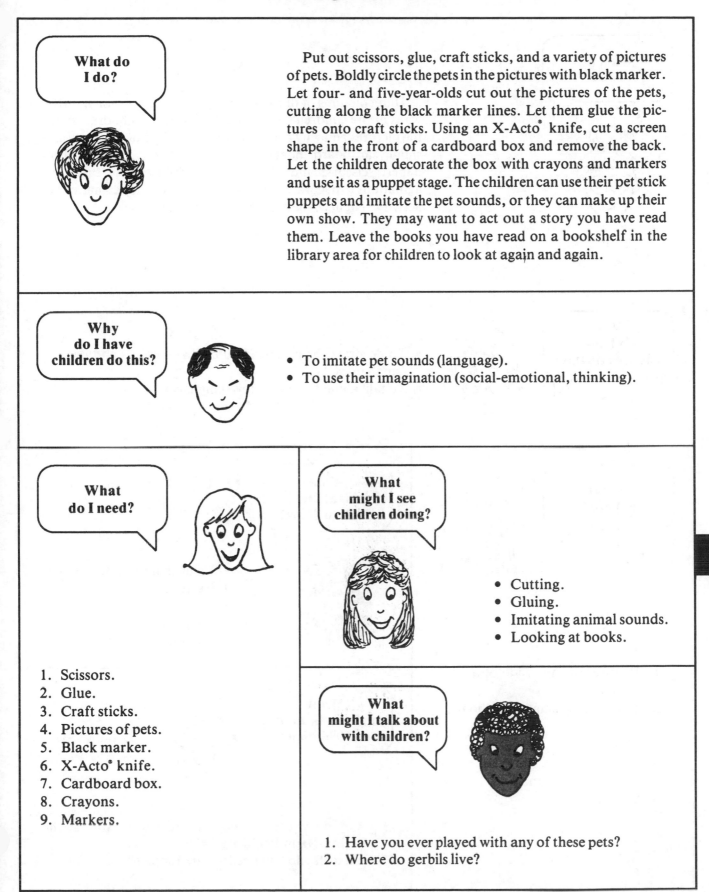

What do I do?

Put out scissors, glue, craft sticks, and a variety of pictures of pets. Boldly circle the pets in the pictures with black marker. Let four- and five-year-olds cut out the pictures of the pets, cutting along the black marker lines. Let them glue the pictures onto craft sticks. Using an X-Acto° knife, cut a screen shape in the front of a cardboard box and remove the back. Let the children decorate the box with crayons and markers and use it as a puppet stage. The children can use their pet stick puppets and imitate the pet sounds, or they can make up their own show. They may want to act out a story you have read them. Leave the books you have read on a bookshelf in the library area for children to look at again and again.

Why do I have children do this?

- To imitate pet sounds (language).
- To use their imagination (social-emotional, thinking).

What do I need?

1. Scissors.
2. Glue.
3. Craft sticks.
4. Pictures of pets.
5. Black marker.
6. X-Acto° knife.
7. Cardboard box.
8. Crayons.
9. Markers.

What might I see children doing?

- Cutting.
- Gluing.
- Imitating animal sounds.
- Looking at books.

What might I talk about with children?

1. Have you ever played with any of these pets?
2. Where do gerbils live?

DECORATING THE NIGHTY-NIGHT PET MOTEL
Learning Center (art)

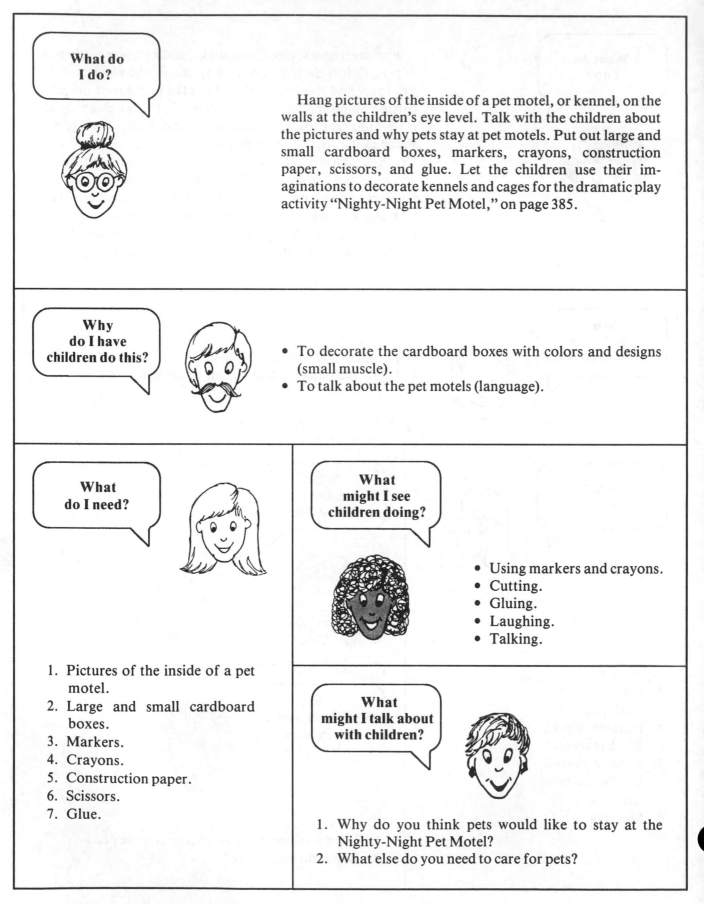

What do I do?

Hang pictures of the inside of a pet motel, or kennel, on the walls at the children's eye level. Talk with the children about the pictures and why pets stay at pet motels. Put out large and small cardboard boxes, markers, crayons, construction paper, scissors, and glue. Let the children use their imaginations to decorate kennels and cages for the dramatic play activity "Nighty-Night Pet Motel," on page 385.

Why do I have children do this?

- To decorate the cardboard boxes with colors and designs (small muscle).
- To talk about the pet motels (language).

What do I need?

1. Pictures of the inside of a pet motel.
2. Large and small cardboard boxes.
3. Markers.
4. Crayons.
5. Construction paper.
6. Scissors.
7. Glue.

What might I see children doing?

- Using markers and crayons.
- Cutting.
- Gluing.
- Laughing.
- Talking.

What might I talk about with children?

1. Why do you think pets would like to stay at the Nighty-Night Pet Motel?
2. What else do you need to care for pets?

GETTING READY FOR A PET
Learning Center (blocks, dramatic play)

What do I do?

Hang pictures of pets on the wall at the children's eye level. Talk with the children about how people must care for their pets and how they can make sure their pets are well. Talk with the children about building homes for their pets. Put out props such as blankets, leashes, stuffed animals, feeding bottles, cedar shavings, and milk carton blocks. You can make milk carton blocks by cutting the tops off two cardboard milk cartons, stuffing them with crumpled newspaper, and fitting one carton over the other. You may need to slit the corners to make them fit. Tape the cartons together with masking tape and cover with colored self-adhesive plastic. Laundry detergent boxes can also be used. Tape the lid shut before covering the box with self-adhesive plastic.

Why do I have children do this?

- To build with blocks (large muscle).
- To use new words, such as leash and pets (language).
- To role-play the actions of the animal and people (social-emotional).

What do I need?

1. Pictures of pets.
2. Blankets.
3. Leashes.
4. Stuffed animals.
5. Feeding bottles.
6. Cedar shavings.
7. Cardboard milk cartons.
8. Scissors.
9. Newspaper.
10. Masking tape.
11. Colored self-adhesive plastic.
12. Laundry detergent boxes.

What might I see children doing?

- Building a doghouse.
- Talking.
- Role-playing putting a bird in its cage.

What might I talk about with children?

1. What does a puppy do when you take it outside?
2. What might a cat do all night while you are asleep?

VETERINARIAN'S OFFICE
Learning Center (dramatic play)

What do I do?

Hang pictures of veterinarian's working with pets on the wall at the children's eye level. Set up a veterinarian's office in the dramatic play area. Provide stuffed animals, cages, blankets, white dress shirts for lab coats, adhesive bandages, gauze, tape, play medical kit, plastic syringes with needles removed, and a stethoscope for the children to use. Put a chair and table near the entrance to be a reception area. Put a notebook, pencil, and telephone on the table. The children may use the materials to role-play people and animals at the veterinarian's office.

Why do I have children do this?

- To talk about what they need to do for sick pets (language).
- To pretend to be veterinarians, pet owners, and receptionists (thinking).

What do I need?

1. Pictures of veterinarians working with pets.
2. Stuffed animals.
3. Cages.
4. Blankets.
5. White shirts for lab coats.
6. Adhesive bandages.
7. Gauze.
8. Tape.
9. Play medical kit.
10. Plastic syringes with needles removed.
11. Stethoscope.
12. Chair.
13. Table.
14. Notebook.
15. Pencil.
16. Telephone.

What might I see children doing?

- Role-playing people and animals.
- Talking.
- Helping the sick pets.

What might I talk about with children?

1. Why did your pet need to come to see the doctor?
2. What are you going to do to help this pet get better?

NIGHTY-NIGHT PET MOTEL
Learning Center (dramatic play)

What do I do?

Put out the kennels and cages the children decorated in the art activity "Decorating the Nighty-Night Pet Motel," on page 382 along with a birdcage, fishbowl, stuffed animals, food and water bowls, leashes, newspapers, and empty pet food or dry cereal containers. Provide brooms, dustpans, and small shovels for the children to use. Talk with the children about pet motels and how they are set up to care for pets when their owners go away. Put a chair and table by the entrance to be a reception area. Hang a sign that says "NIGHTY-NIGHT PET MOTEL" above the table. Put paper and pencils on the table, so the owners can register their pets. Provide a cash register and play money, so the owners can pay to have their pets taken care of. Make a sign that says "LARGE DOG $4.00, SMALL DOG $3.00, CAT $2.00, BIRD $1.00, AND FISH $1.00" and hang it up by the table.

Why do I have children do this?

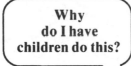

- To care for pets (social-emotional).
- To write bills for pet care at the Nighty-Night Pet Motel (thinking, language).

What do I need?

1. Kennels and cages from the art activity "Decorating the Nighty-Night Pet Motel."
2. Birdcage and fishbowl.
3. Stuffed animals.
4. Food and water bowls.
5. Leashes.
6. Newspapers.
7. Empty pet food or dry cereal containers.
8. Brooms, dustpans, and small shovels.
9. Chair and table.
10. "NIGHTY-NIGHT PET MOTEL" sign.
11. Paper and pencils.
12. Cash register and play money.
13. Price sign.

What might I see children doing?

- Talking to owners.
- Walking pets.
- Feeding pets.
- Cleaning up after pets.
- Writing bills.

What might I talk about with children?

1. What do you think you will need to care for Rover?
2. What would you do if the cat cried for its owner?

LET'S PLAY CAT
Learning Center (dramatic play)

What do I do?

Set up the dramatic play area as a house. Put out stuffed cats and furry fabric for the children to wear to pretend to be cats. Put out a box for a cat basket and bowls for food and water. Talk with the children about petting the cats softly and how cats may purr when they are petted. Ask the children what else they need to do to care for their pets.

Why do I have children do this?

- To care for a cat (social-emotional).
- To talk about pets (language).

What do I need?

1. Stuffed cats.
2. Furry fabric.
3. Box.
4. Bowls.

What might I see children doing?

- Pretending to be a cat.
- Petting cats.
- Talking.

What might I talk about with children?

1. What is the cat saying to you when it purrs?
2. What other animals are furry?

BIRD NESTS
Learning Center (food)

What do I do?

Let the children make bird nests, using the recipe in Appendix B. Put two or three chairs at the table to determine the number of children who can work at one time. Copy the recipe on poster board and illustrate with pictures of birds and nests. Before you begin preparing the bird nests, collect all the supplies and make sure you and the children wash your hands. Work with two or three children at a time, so they can each measure, mix, and mold the ingredients.

As the children are eating the bird nests at snacktime, talk about the differences between pet birds and wild birds.

Why do I have children do this?

- To measure ingredients (thinking).
- To mix ingredients (small muscle).

What do I need?

What might I see children doing?

- Measuring cereal, coconut, and peanut butter.
- Mixing ingredients.
- Molding nests.
- Tasting nests.

1. Poster board.
2. Pictures of birds and nests.
3. Wheat cereal.
4. Coconut.
5. Peanut butter.
6. Mixing bowl.
7. Wooden spoon.

What might I talk about with children?

1. What do you think makes the bird nests stick together?
2. What do you think birds use to make their nests?

PUPPY DOG PEARS
Learning Centers (food)

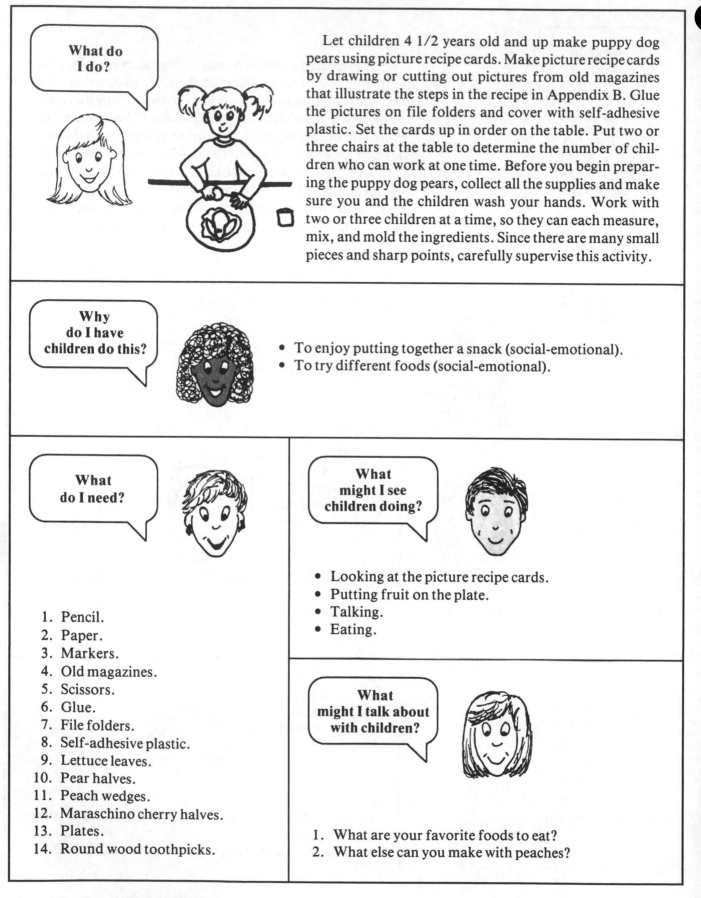

What do I do?

Let children 4 1/2 years old and up make puppy dog pears using picture recipe cards. Make picture recipe cards by drawing or cutting out pictures from old magazines that illustrate the steps in the recipe in Appendix B. Glue the pictures on file folders and cover with self-adhesive plastic. Set the cards up in order on the table. Put two or three chairs at the table to determine the number of children who can work at one time. Before you begin preparing the puppy dog pears, collect all the supplies and make sure you and the children wash your hands. Work with two or three children at a time, so they can each measure, mix, and mold the ingredients. Since there are many small pieces and sharp points, carefully supervise this activity.

Why do I have children do this?

- To enjoy putting together a snack (social-emotional).
- To try different foods (social-emotional).

What do I need?

1. Pencil.
2. Paper.
3. Markers.
4. Old magazines.
5. Scissors.
6. Glue.
7. File folders.
8. Self-adhesive plastic.
9. Lettuce leaves.
10. Pear halves.
11. Peach wedges.
12. Maraschino cherry halves.
13. Plates.
14. Round wood toothpicks.

What might I see children doing?

- Looking at the picture recipe cards.
- Putting fruit on the plate.
- Talking.
- Eating.

What might I talk about with children?

1. What are your favorite foods to eat?
2. What else can you make with peaches?

PET ROOM
Learning Center (library)

What do I do?

Hang up pictures of pets on the wall at the children's eye level. Set out books about pets, such as dogs, cats, fish, ponies, and rabbits. Cut an opening in a large cardboard box with an X-Acto® knife and decorate it as a doghouse. This can be a quiet place for the children to sit and look at books.

Why do I have children do this?

- To look at and read books (language).
- To enjoy reading in a quiet place (social-emotional).

What do I need?

What might I see children doing?

- Looking at pictures.
- Reading.
- Relaxing.

1. Pictures of pets.
2. Books about pets.
3. Large cardboard box.
4. X-Acto® knife.
5. Markers.

What might I talk about with children?

1. What pets do you have at home?
2. What do you like to do with your pet?

FEED THE DOG A BONE
Learning Center (library, manipulatives)

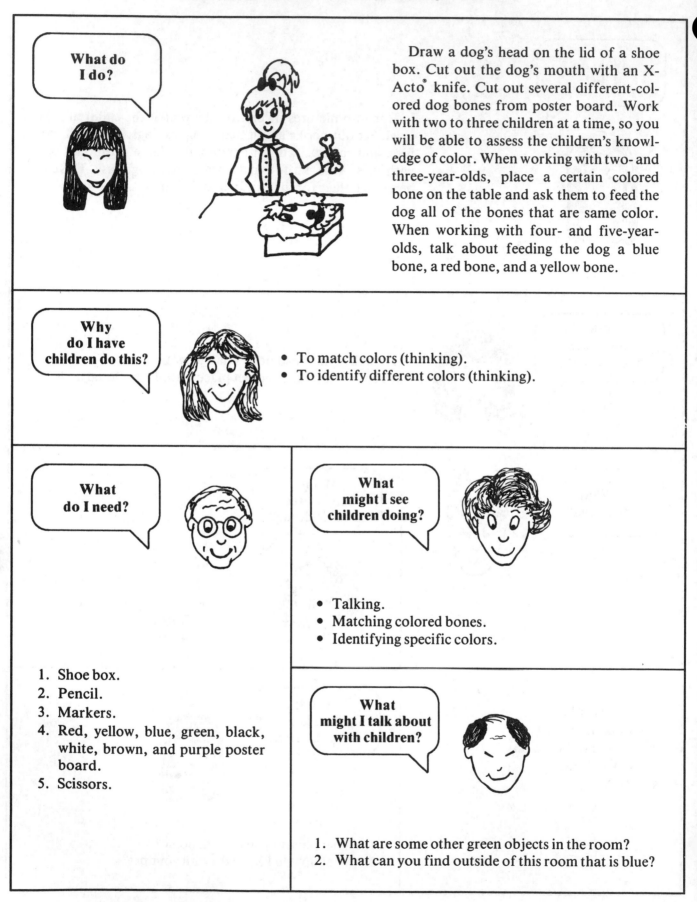

What do I do?

Draw a dog's head on the lid of a shoe box. Cut out the dog's mouth with an X-Acto® knife. Cut out several different-colored dog bones from poster board. Work with two to three children at a time, so you will be able to assess the children's knowledge of color. When working with two- and three-year-olds, place a certain colored bone on the table and ask them to feed the dog all of the bones that are same color. When working with four- and five-year-olds, talk about feeding the dog a blue bone, a red bone, and a yellow bone.

Why do I have children do this?

• To match colors (thinking).
• To identify different colors (thinking).

What do I need?

1. Shoe box.
2. Pencil.
3. Markers.
4. Red, yellow, blue, green, black, white, brown, and purple poster board.
5. Scissors.

What might I see children doing?

• Talking.
• Matching colored bones.
• Identifying specific colors.

What might I talk about with children?

1. What are some other green objects in the room?
2. What can you find outside of this room that is blue?

BUNNY MATCH
Learning Center (library, manipulatives)

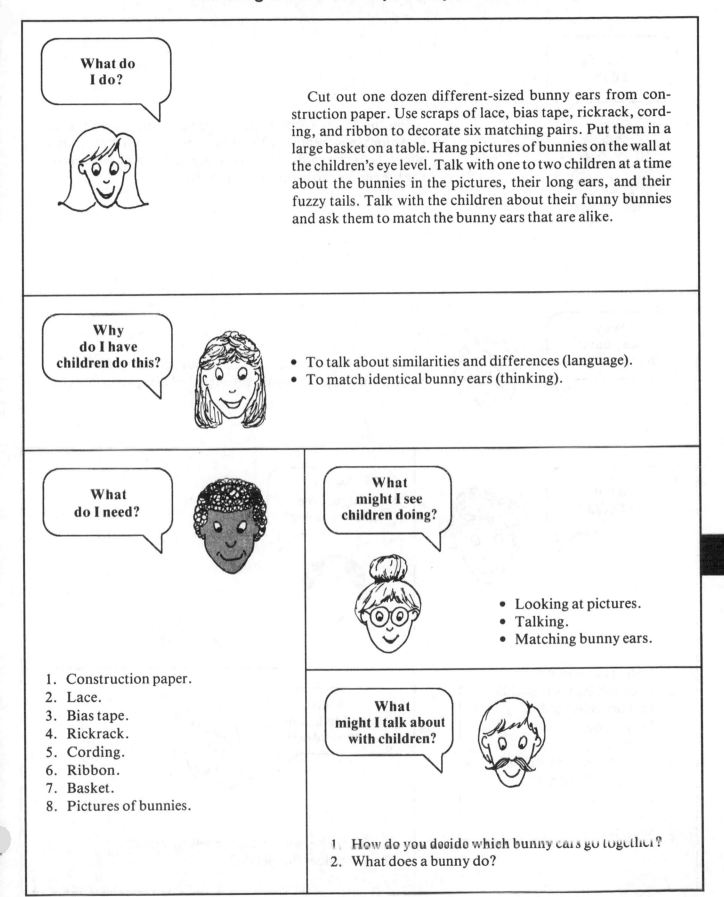

What do I do?

Cut out one dozen different-sized bunny ears from construction paper. Use scraps of lace, bias tape, rickrack, cording, and ribbon to decorate six matching pairs. Put them in a large basket on a table. Hang pictures of bunnies on the wall at the children's eye level. Talk with one to two children at a time about the bunnies in the pictures, their long ears, and their fuzzy tails. Talk with the children about their funny bunnies and ask them to match the bunny ears that are alike.

Why do I have children do this?

- To talk about similarities and differences (language).
- To match identical bunny ears (thinking).

What do I need?

1. Construction paper.
2. Lace.
3. Bias tape.
4. Rickrack.
5. Cording.
6. Ribbon.
7. Basket.
8. Pictures of bunnies.

What might I see children doing?

- Looking at pictures.
- Talking.
- Matching bunny ears.

What might I talk about with children?

1. How do you decide which bunny ears go together?
2. What does a bunny do?

PET LACING CARDS
Learning Center (manipulatives, library)

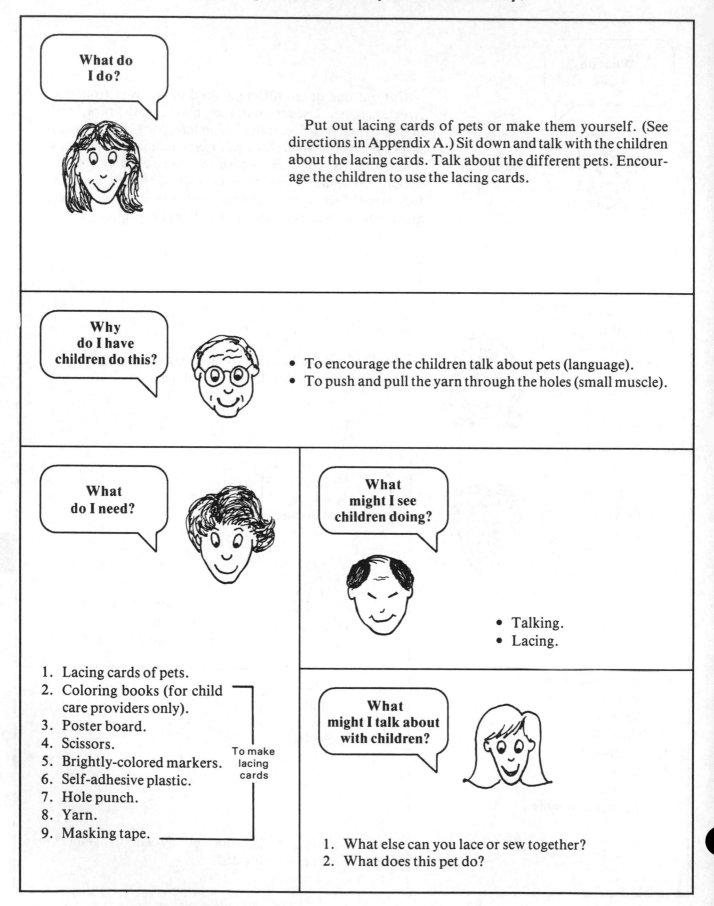

What do I do?

Put out lacing cards of pets or make them yourself. (See directions in Appendix A.) Sit down and talk with the children about the lacing cards. Talk about the different pets. Encourage the children to use the lacing cards.

Why do I have children do this?

• To encourage the children talk about pets (language).
• To push and pull the yarn through the holes (small muscle).

What do I need?

1. Lacing cards of pets.
2. Coloring books (for child care providers only).
3. Poster board.
4. Scissors.
5. Brightly-colored markers.
6. Self-adhesive plastic.
7. Hole punch.
8. Yarn.
9. Masking tape.

To make lacing cards

What might I see children doing?

• Talking.
• Lacing.

What might I talk about with children?

1. What else can you lace or sew together?
2. What does this pet do?

PET PUZZLES
Learning Center (manipulatives)

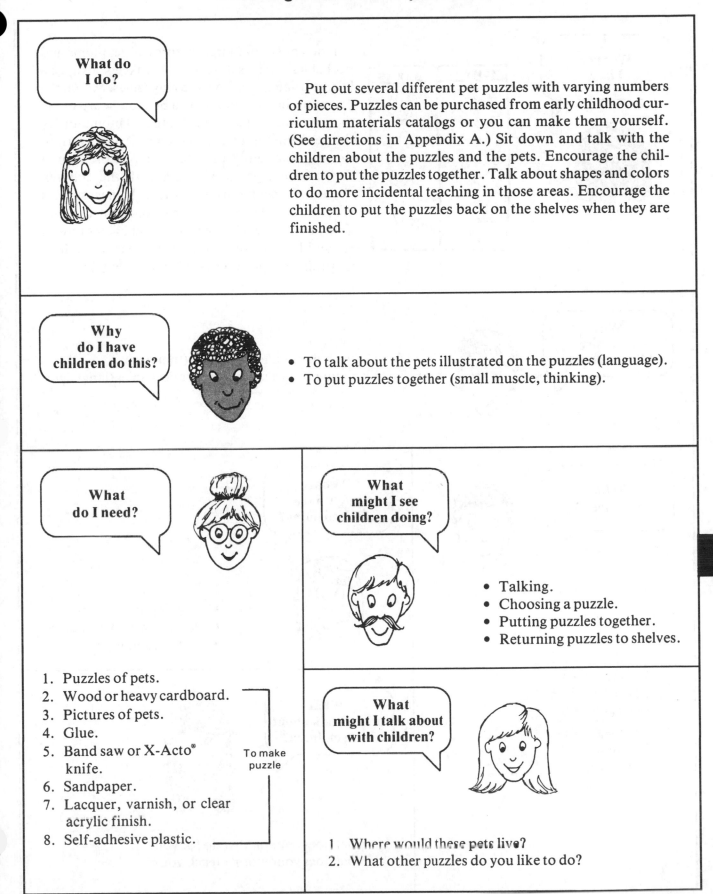

What do I do?

Put out several different pet puzzles with varying numbers of pieces. Puzzles can be purchased from early childhood curriculum materials catalogs or you can make them yourself. (See directions in Appendix A.) Sit down and talk with the children about the puzzles and the pets. Encourage the children to put the puzzles together. Talk about shapes and colors to do more incidental teaching in those areas. Encourage the children to put the puzzles back on the shelves when they are finished.

Why do I have children do this?

- To talk about the pets illustrated on the puzzles (language).
- To put puzzles together (small muscle, thinking).

What do I need?

What might I see children doing?

- Talking.
- Choosing a puzzle.
- Putting puzzles together.
- Returning puzzles to shelves.

1. Puzzles of pets.
2. Wood or heavy cardboard.
3. Pictures of pets.
4. Glue.
5. Band saw or X-Acto® knife.
6. Sandpaper.
7. Lacquer, varnish, or clear acrylic finish.
8. Self-adhesive plastic.

To make puzzle

What might I talk about with children?

1. Where would these pets live?
2. What other puzzles do you like to do?

PET MOMS AND THEIR BABIES
Learning Center (manipulatives)

What do I do?

Draw or cut out large pictures of pet moms and pet babies, such as dogs, cats, parakeets, fish, gerbils, and hamsters, from old magazines. Mount the pet moms in one column on a bulletin board or lay them out on a table in a column and mount or lay the pet babies in another column. Attach yarn to the pet moms and let the children pull the yarn to the matching pet baby. Talk with the children about what pet moms do for their babies, such as provide food, keep them warm, and protect them. Talk about how pet moms teach pet babies how to eat and how to stay warm. Ask the children how they think the pet moms carry the pet babies.

Why do I have children do this?

• To match pet moms and pet babies (thinking).
• To talk about how pet moms care for pet babies (language).

What do I need?

1. Paper.
2. Pencil.
3. Markers.
4. Old magazines.
5. Scissors.
6. Bulletin board.
7. Thumb tacks.
8. Yarn.

What might I see children doing?

• Looking at pet pictures.
• Pulling yarn to pet babies.
• Talking about pets.

What might I talk about with children?

1. What does your mother do for you?
2. What does your mother teach you?

DOG SORT
Learning Center (manipulatives)

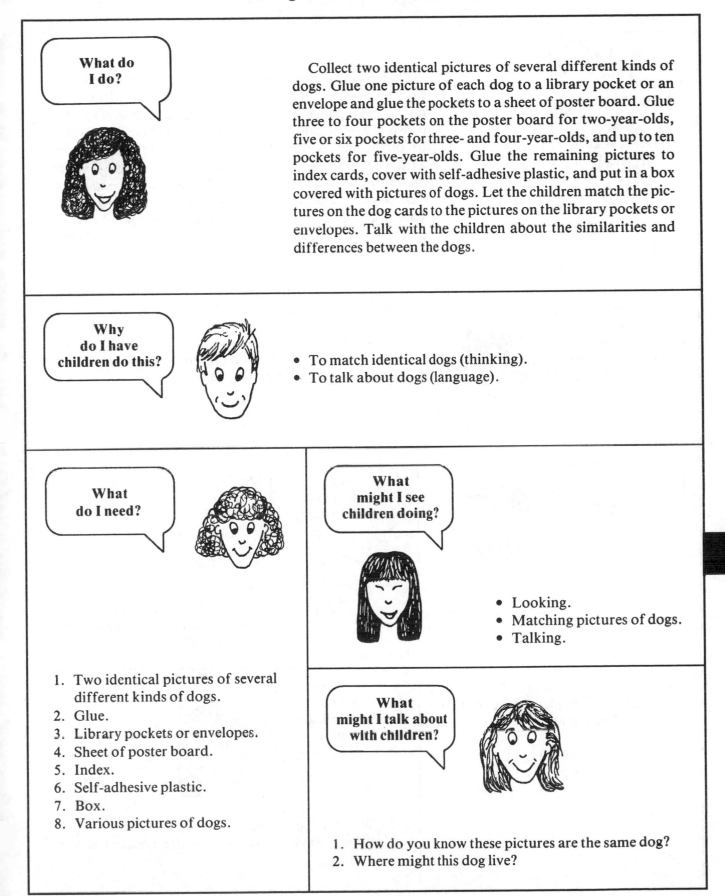

What do I do?

Collect two identical pictures of several different kinds of dogs. Glue one picture of each dog to a library pocket or an envelope and glue the pockets to a sheet of poster board. Glue three to four pockets on the poster board for two-year-olds, five or six pockets for three- and four-year-olds, and up to ten pockets for five-year-olds. Glue the remaining pictures to index cards, cover with self-adhesive plastic, and put in a box covered with pictures of dogs. Let the children match the pictures on the dog cards to the pictures on the library pockets or envelopes. Talk with the children about the similarities and differences between the dogs.

Why do I have children do this?

- To match identical dogs (thinking).
- To talk about dogs (language).

What do I need?

1. Two identical pictures of several different kinds of dogs.
2. Glue.
3. Library pockets or envelopes.
4. Sheet of poster board.
5. Index.
6. Self-adhesive plastic.
7. Box.
8. Various pictures of dogs.

What might I see children doing?

- Looking.
- Matching pictures of dogs.
- Talking.

What might I talk about with children?

1. How do you know these pictures are the same dog?
2. Where might this dog live?

PET SORT
Learning Center (manipulatives)

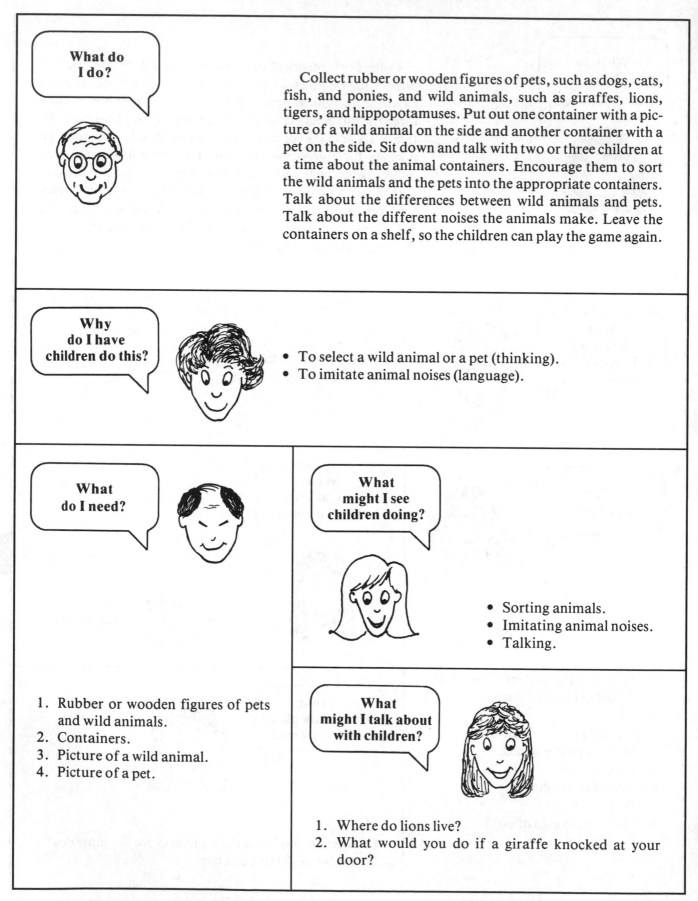

What do I do?

Collect rubber or wooden figures of pets, such as dogs, cats, fish, and ponies, and wild animals, such as giraffes, lions, tigers, and hippopotamuses. Put out one container with a picture of a wild animal on the side and another container with a pet on the side. Sit down and talk with two or three children at a time about the animal containers. Encourage them to sort the wild animals and the pets into the appropriate containers. Talk about the differences between wild animals and pets. Talk about the different noises the animals make. Leave the containers on a shelf, so the children can play the game again.

Why do I have children do this?

- To select a wild animal or a pet (thinking).
- To imitate animal noises (language).

What do I need?

1. Rubber or wooden figures of pets and wild animals.
2. Containers.
3. Picture of a wild animal.
4. Picture of a pet.

What might I see children doing?

- Sorting animals.
- Imitating animal noises.
- Talking.

What might I talk about with children?

1. Where do lions live?
2. What would you do if a giraffe knocked at your door?

MEASURE A FEATHER
Learning Center (math)

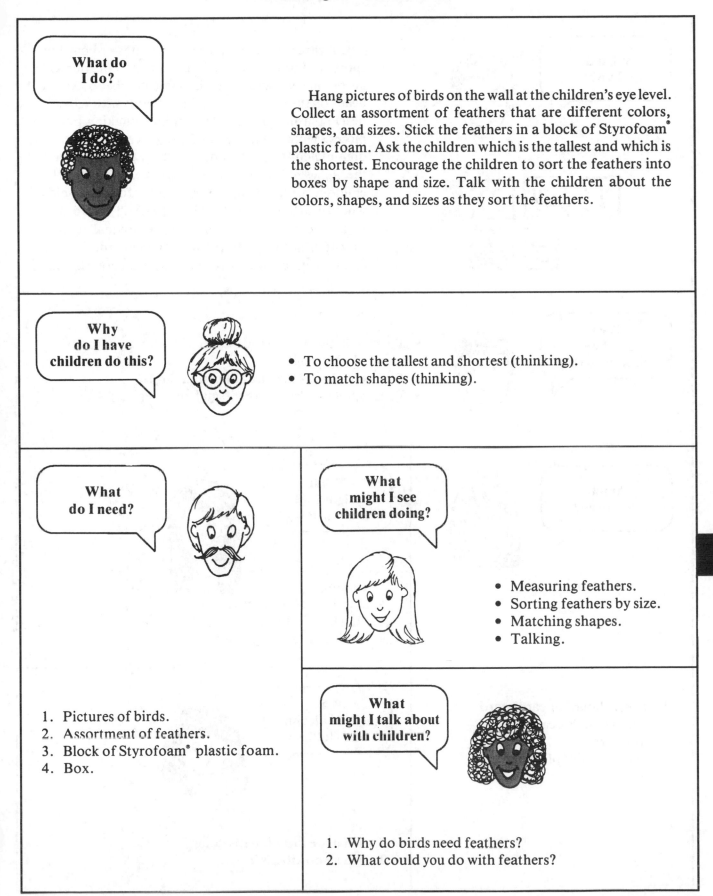

What do I do?

    Hang pictures of birds on the wall at the children's eye level. Collect an assortment of feathers that are different colors, shapes, and sizes. Stick the feathers in a block of Styrofoam® plastic foam. Ask the children which is the tallest and which is the shortest. Encourage the children to sort the feathers into boxes by shape and size. Talk with the children about the colors, shapes, and sizes as they sort the feathers.

Why do I have children do this?

- To choose the tallest and shortest (thinking).
- To match shapes (thinking).

What do I need?

What might I see children doing?

- Measuring feathers.
- Sorting feathers by size.
- Matching shapes.
- Talking.

1. Pictures of birds.
2. Assortment of feathers.
3. Block of Styrofoam® plastic foam.
4. Box.

What might I talk about with children?

1. Why do birds need feathers?
2. What could you do with feathers?

MATCH THE KITTENS
Learning Center (math)

What do I do?

Cut three-by-six-inch cards from poster board or cardboard or use unlined index cards. Write numerals on one end and draw the same number of kitten heads on the other end. Cover the cards with self-adhesive plastic and cut them in half, making puzzle pieces. Mix the puzzle pieces together. Let the children match the pieces and put them together. Have the highest numeral on the cards match the age of the children using them. For example, four-year-olds would use the number 1, 2, 3, and 4 sets. For two- and three-year-olds, make sets that have an equal number of kitten heads on both ends of the card. Let the children match pictures of one kitten and one kitten.

Why do I have children do this?

- To match the number of objects with the appropriate numeral (thinking).
- To match objects that are alike (thinking).
- To fit puzzle pieces together (small muscle).

What do I need?

1. Poster board or cardboard.
2. Unlined index cards.
3. Markers.
4. Self-adhesive plastic.
5. Scissors.

What might I see children doing?

- Talking.
- Matching objects and numerals.
- Matching kittens.
- Putting puzzles together.

What might I talk about with children?

1. What are these kittens doing?
2. Where do kittens live?

HOW MANY FEET ON THIS PET?
Learning Center (math)

What do I do?

Hang up pictures of pets on the wall at the children's eye level. Put out stuffed dogs, cats, turtles, fish, birds, and gerbils. Talk with the children about the number of feet, eyes, ears, and tails each animal has, if any. Let the children hold the stuffed animals and count.

Why do I have children do this?

- To count onc beak, two ears, four feet (thinking).
- To talk about the number of body parts each pet has (language).

What do I need?

What might I see children doing?

- Touching eyes, beaks, and feet as they count.
- Listening.
- Talking.

What might I talk about with children?

1. Pictures of pets.
2. Stuffed animals.

1. What other pets have a beak?
2. Which pets have four legs?

"OLD MACDONALD"
Learning Center (music)

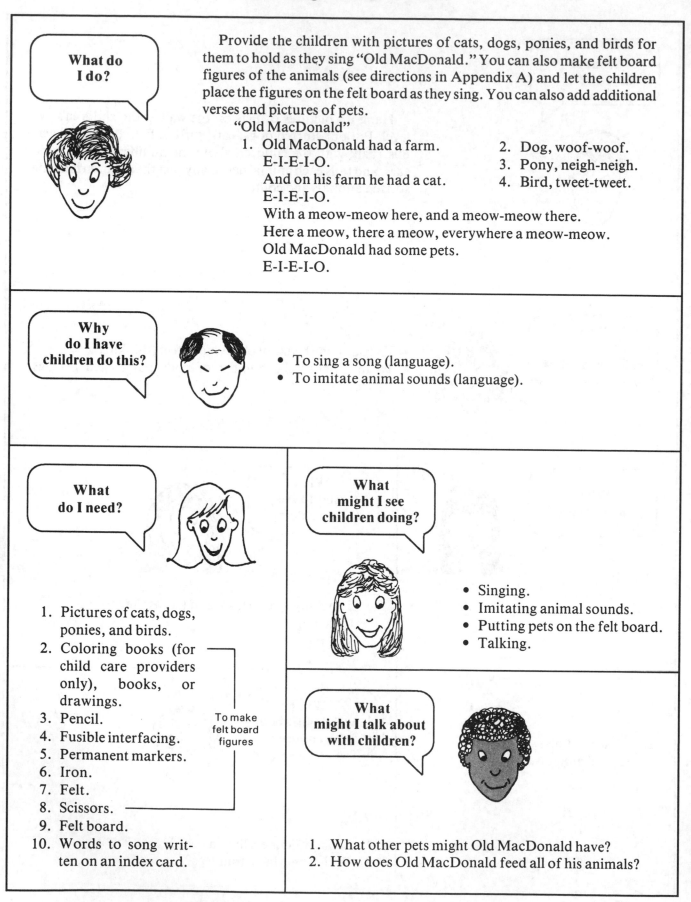

What do I do?

Provide the children with pictures of cats, dogs, ponies, and birds for them to hold as they sing "Old MacDonald." You can also make felt board figures of the animals (see directions in Appendix A) and let the children place the figures on the felt board as they sing. You can also add additional verses and pictures of pets.

"Old MacDonald"

1. Old MacDonald had a farm.
   E-I-E-I-O.
   And on his farm he had a cat.
   E-I-E-I-O.
   With a meow-meow here, and a meow-meow there.
   Here a meow, there a meow, everywhere a meow-meow.
   Old MacDonald had some pets.
   E-I-E-I-O.

2. Dog, woof-woof.
3. Pony, neigh-neigh.
4. Bird, tweet-tweet.

Why do I have children do this?

- To sing a song (language).
- To imitate animal sounds (language).

What do I need?

1. Pictures of cats, dogs, ponies, and birds.
2. Coloring books (for child care providers only), books, or drawings.
3. Pencil.
4. Fusible interfacing.
5. Permanent markers.
6. Iron.
7. Felt.
8. Scissors.
9. Felt board.
10. Words to song written on an index card.

To make felt board figures

What might I see children doing?

- Singing.
- Imitating animal sounds.
- Putting pets on the felt board.
- Talking.

What might I talk about with children?

1. What other pets might Old MacDonald have?
2. How does Old MacDonald feed all of his animals?

"BINGO"
Learning Center (music)

What do I do?

Use a stuffed dog to introduce the song "Bingo." Talk with the children about how Bingo was a friend to the child and what they may have liked to do together.

"Bingo"
There was a child who had a dog,
And Bingo was his name-o.
B-I-N-G-O
B-I-N-G-O
B-I-N-G-O
And Bingo was his name-o.

Why do I have children do this?

- To sing a song (language).
- To talk about how a dog is a friend (language).

What do I need?

What might I see children doing?

- Petting the stuffed dog.
- Singing.
- Talking.

1. Stuffed dog.
2. Words to song written on an index card.

What might I talk about with children?

1. What special activities do you think Bingo can do?
2. What are some other names for dogs?

CEDAR SHAVINGS TABLE
Learning Center (sand), Outdoor Large Muscle

What do I do?

Clean the sand out of the sand table and add a bag of cedar shavings. Hang pictures of gerbils in their cages on the wall at the children's eye level. Talk with the children about how the cedar shavings feel. Talk with the children about how cedar shavings are used in gerbil cages and why gerbils like the shavings. Explain that gerbils often like to hide under the cedar shavings. Then put out a variety of small objects, such as combs, blocks, and pencils. Let the children take turns hiding the objects and having the other children find them. Give each child a chance to hide the objects if he or she wants.

Why do I have children do this?

- To feel different textures (thinking).
- To locate objects by touch (thinking).

What do I need?

1. Sand table.
2. Bag of cedar shavings.
3. Pictures of gerbils in their cages.
4. Small objects, such as combs, blocks, and pencils.

What might I see children doing?

- Feeling the cedar shavings.
- Hunting for objects.
- Talking.

What might I talk about with children?

1. What do these cedar shavings feel like to you?
2. What are some other objects you can hide?

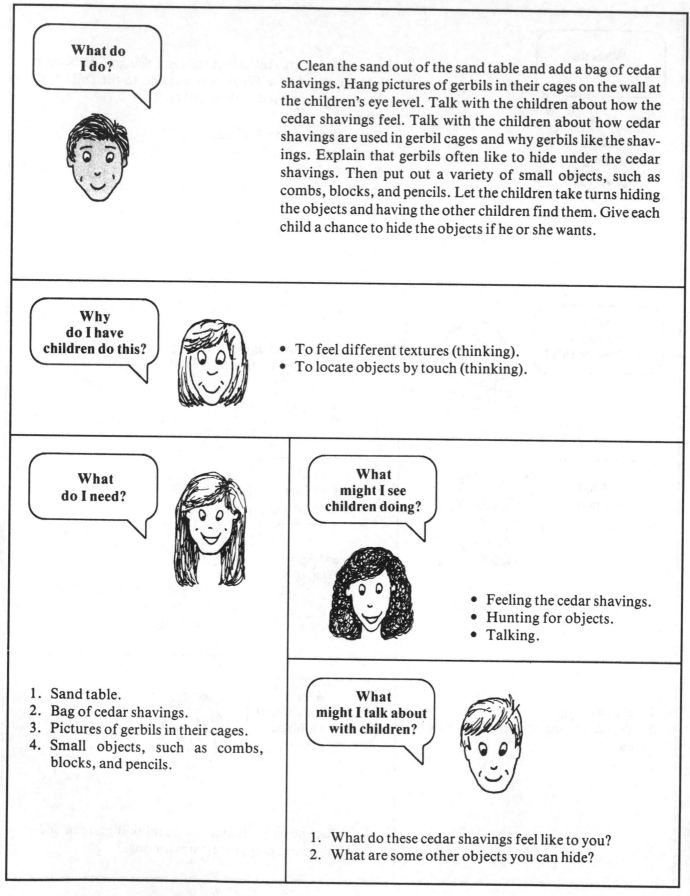

CARING FOR A GERBIL
Learning Center (science)

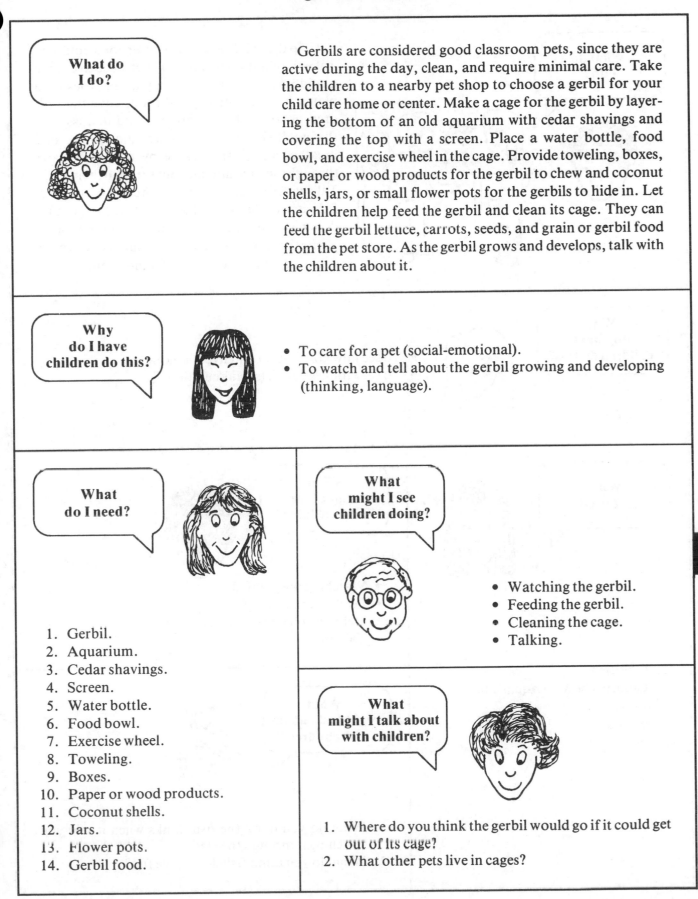

What do I do?

Gerbils are considered good classroom pets, since they are active during the day, clean, and require minimal care. Take the children to a nearby pet shop to choose a gerbil for your child care home or center. Make a cage for the gerbil by layering the bottom of an old aquarium with cedar shavings and covering the top with a screen. Place a water bottle, food bowl, and exercise wheel in the cage. Provide toweling, boxes, or paper or wood products for the gerbil to chew and coconut shells, jars, or small flower pots for the gerbils to hide in. Let the children help feed the gerbil and clean its cage. They can feed the gerbil lettuce, carrots, seeds, and grain or gerbil food from the pet store. As the gerbil grows and develops, talk with the children about it.

Why do I have children do this?

- To care for a pet (social-emotional).
- To watch and tell about the gerbil growing and developing (thinking, language).

What do I need?

1. Gerbil.
2. Aquarium.
3. Cedar shavings.
4. Screen.
5. Water bottle.
6. Food bowl.
7. Exercise wheel.
8. Toweling.
9. Boxes.
10. Paper or wood products.
11. Coconut shells.
12. Jars.
13. Flower pots.
14. Gerbil food.

What might I see children doing?

- Watching the gerbil.
- Feeding the gerbil.
- Cleaning the cage.
- Talking.

What might I talk about with children?

1. Where do you think the gerbil would go if it could get out of its cage?
2. What other pets live in cages?

MY GOLDFISH
Learning Center (science)

What do I do?

Help the children make a home for a goldfish. Take the children to a nearby pet store to choose a goldfish, goldfish bowl or aquarium, rocks and plants for the bottom, and food. Give the children opportunities to observe and discuss how the goldfish eats, moves up and down, and breathes air. (Fish breathe by taking in water through their mouths and out through their gills.) Talk with the children about the color of the goldfish, its eyes, and how its fins work. Let the children help feed the goldfish and change its water. Name the goldfish and make a chart story to hang above its bowl or aquarium telling about it.

Why do I have children do this?

- To see how goldfish eat and live (thinking).
- To care for a goldfish (social-emotional).

What do I need?

1. Goldfish.
2. Goldfish bowl or aquarium.
3. Rocks.
4. Plants.
5. Food.
6. Paper.
7. Pencil.
8. Markers.

What might I see children doing?

- Watching the goldfish.
- Feeding the goldfish.
- Helping you write the chart story.
- Talking.

What might I talk about with children?

1. What do you think the fish thinks when it sees you watching it through the glass?
2. What do you think fish do to have fun?

DOG GROOMING
Learning Centers (water play)

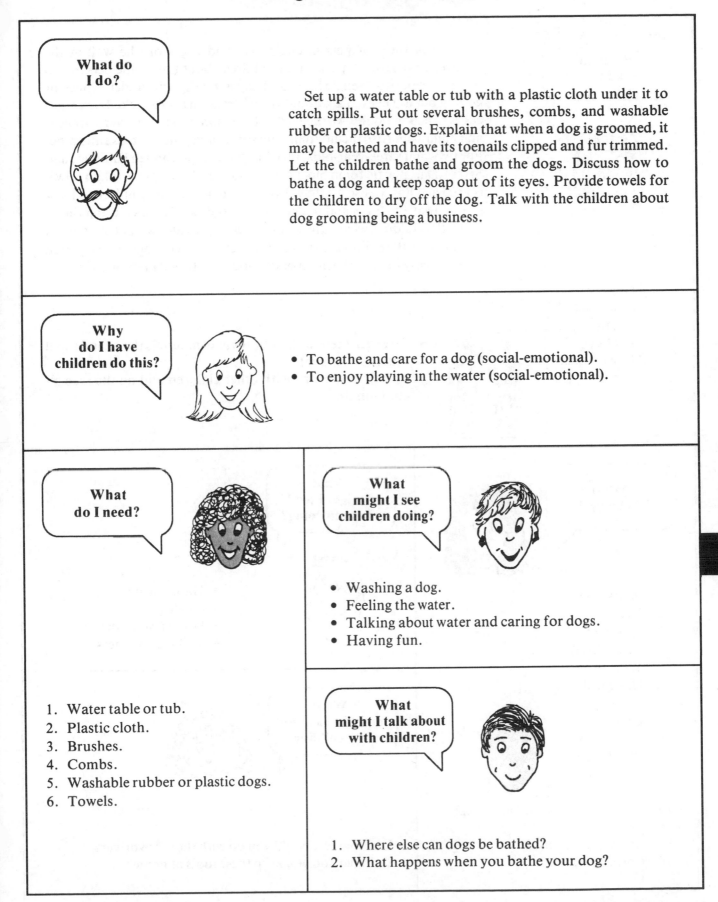

What do I do?

Set up a water table or tub with a plastic cloth under it to catch spills. Put out several brushes, combs, and washable rubber or plastic dogs. Explain that when a dog is groomed, it may be bathed and have its toenails clipped and fur trimmed. Let the children bathe and groom the dogs. Discuss how to bathe a dog and keep soap out of its eyes. Provide towels for the children to dry off the dog. Talk with the children about dog grooming being a business.

Why do I have children do this?

- To bathe and care for a dog (social-emotional).
- To enjoy playing in the water (social-emotional).

What do I need?

1. Water table or tub.
2. Plastic cloth.
3. Brushes.
4. Combs.
5. Washable rubber or plastic dogs.
6. Towels.

What might I see children doing?

- Washing a dog.
- Feeling the water.
- Talking about water and caring for dogs.
- Having fun.

What might I talk about with children?

1. Where else can dogs be bathed?
2. What happens when you bathe your dog?

MY PETS LIKE TO ESCAPE
Learning Center (woodworking)

What do I do?

Hang pictures of pets in enclosures and cages on the wall at the children's eye level. Talk with the children about how some pets like to try to escape from enclosures and cages by digging under fences or getting out of cages. Talk about the materials used to make fences and cages. Then put out a workbench, saw, hammer, screwdriver, wrench, and hand drill. Also include nails and soft woods, such as balsa and pine. For two- and three-year-olds, provide golf tees, a wooden hammer, and Styrofoam® plastic foam blocks. Introduce each tool and explain how it is used and how to use it safely. Provide a place for the children to hang or put away the tools and materials after they are finished using them. Have the children wear safety goggles and provide carpenters' aprons and hats for the children to wear. Two sets of safety goggles in the area makes it easy to limit the number of children allowed in the area.

Why do I have children do this?

- To experiment with the tools and materials (large and small muscle, thinking).
- To talk and work with other children and adults (social-emotional).

What do I need?

1. Workbench.
2. Saw.
3. Hammer.
4. Screwdriver.
5. Wrench.
6. Hand drill.
7. Nails.
8. Glue.
9. Balsa wood.
10. Pine wood.
11. Golf tees.
12. Wooden hammer.
13. Styrofoam® plastic foam blocks.
14. Safety goggles.
15. Carpenters' aprons.
16. Carpenters' hats.

What might I see children doing?

- Hammering.
- Sawing.
- Using a screwdriver.
- Talking to others.

What might I talk about with children?

1. What else could you do with the screwdriver?
2. Where do you keep these tools at home?

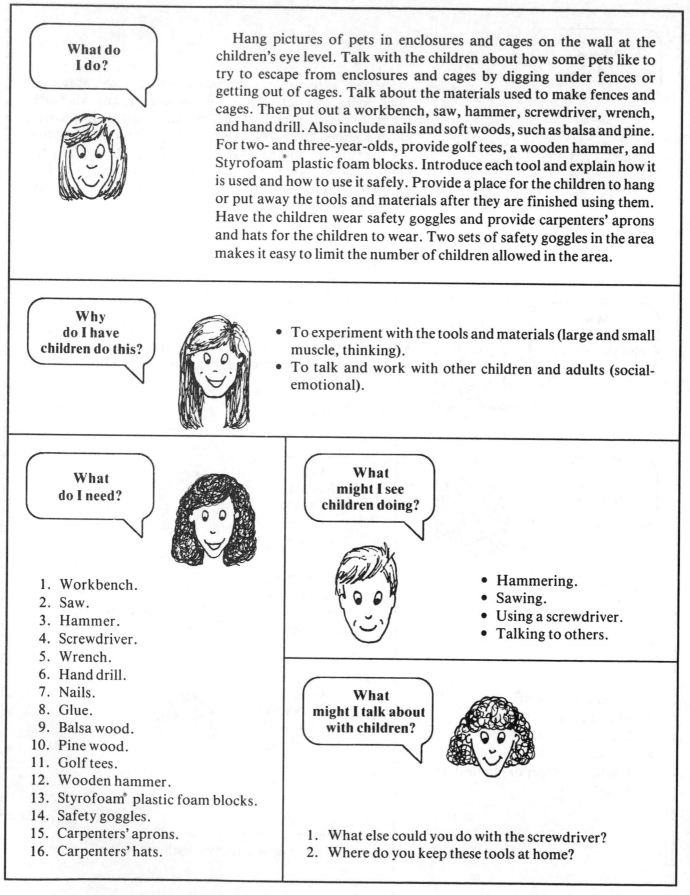

DIRECTIONS FOR THE NIGHTY-NIGHT PET MOTEL
Learning Center (writing)

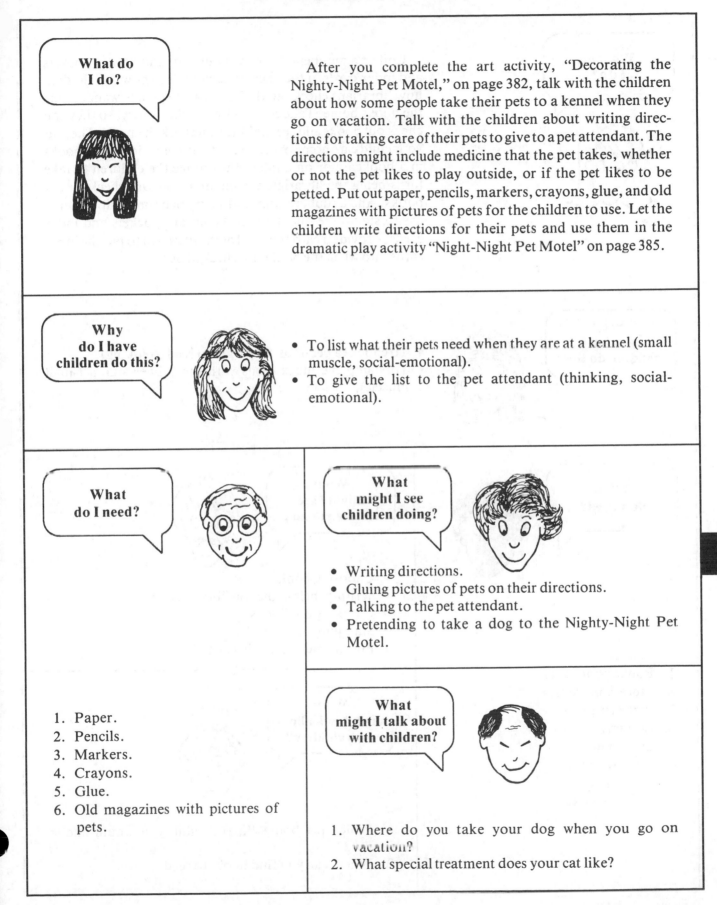

What do I do?

After you complete the art activity, "Decorating the Nighty-Night Pet Motel," on page 382, talk with the children about how some people take their pets to a kennel when they go on vacation. Talk with the children about writing directions for taking care of their pets to give to a pet attendant. The directions might include medicine that the pet takes, whether or not the pet likes to play outside, or if the pet likes to be petted. Put out paper, pencils, markers, crayons, glue, and old magazines with pictures of pets for the children to use. Let the children write directions for their pets and use them in the dramatic play activity "Night-Night Pet Motel" on page 385.

Why do I have children do this?

- To list what their pets need when they are at a kennel (small muscle, social-emotional).
- To give the list to the pet attendant (thinking, social-emotional).

What do I need?

1. Paper.
2. Pencils.
3. Markers.
4. Crayons.
5. Glue.
6. Old magazines with pictures of pets.

What might I see children doing?

- Writing directions.
- Gluing pictures of pets on their directions.
- Talking to the pet attendant.
- Pretending to take a dog to the Nighty-Night Pet Motel.

What might I talk about with children?

1. Where do you take your dog when you go on vacation?
2. What special treatment does your cat like?

CHECKING PET BOOKS OUT OF THE LIBRARY
Learning Center (writing)

What do I do?

Collect a number of books about pets. Put library pockets and index cards in the back of each book. Show the children how librarians check out the books when people want to take the books home. Take the children to the library, so they can check out books and see the librarian check them out. Then, at your child care home or center, put out a selection of pet books in a bookcase or on a table. Encourage the children to take turns being the librarian and children who are checking out books. Add a rubber stamp and stamp pad for the librarian to use to stamp the due date on the library pockets and index cards. Provide a card file box for the librarian to put the index cards into when the books are checked out.

Why do I have children do this?

- To choose a pet book they want to read (thinking).
- To stamp the index cards with the rubber stamp (small muscle).

What do I need?

1. Books about pets.
2. Library pockets.
3. Index cards.
4. Library.
5. Librarian.
6. Rubber stamp.
7. Stamp pad.
8. Card file box.

What might I see children doing?

- Choosing books.
- Writing their names on library cards.
- Checking out books.
- Stamping index cards.
- Putting index cards in card file.

What might I talk about with children?

1. Which pet books do you think you would like to read?
2. Where can you find books to read?

PET TRACKS
Outdoor Large Muscle

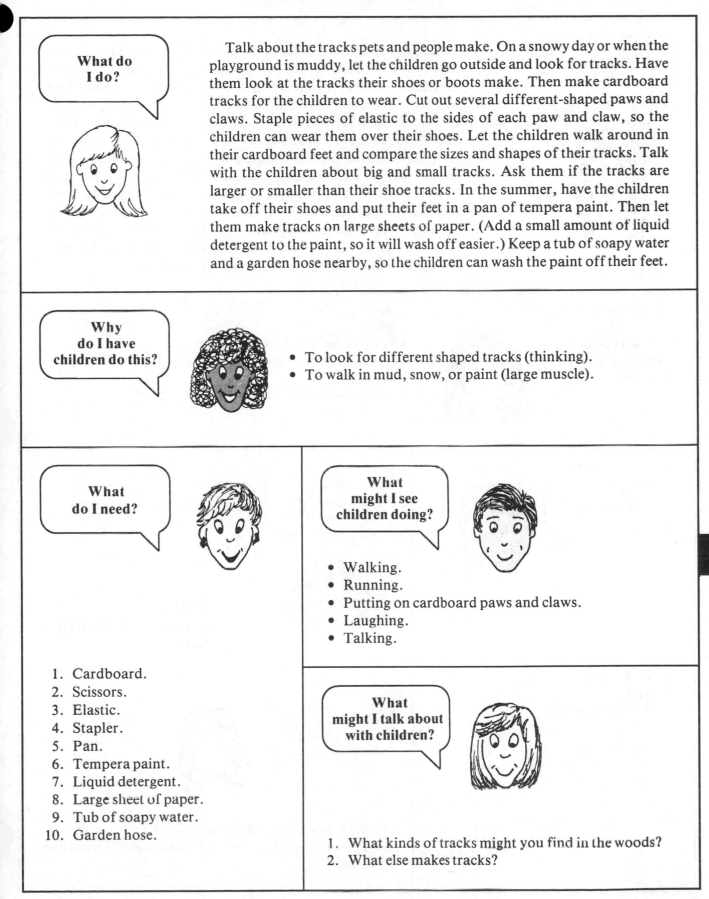

What do I do?

Talk about the tracks pets and people make. On a snowy day or when the playground is muddy, let the children go outside and look for tracks. Have them look at the tracks their shoes or boots make. Then make cardboard tracks for the children to wear. Cut out several different-shaped paws and claws. Staple pieces of elastic to the sides of each paw and claw, so the children can wear them over their shoes. Let the children walk around in their cardboard feet and compare the sizes and shapes of their tracks. Talk with the children about big and small tracks. Ask them if the tracks are larger or smaller than their shoe tracks. In the summer, have the children take off their shoes and put their feet in a pan of tempera paint. Then let them make tracks on large sheets of paper. (Add a small amount of liquid detergent to the paint, so it will wash off easier.) Keep a tub of soapy water and a garden hose nearby, so the children can wash the paint off their feet.

Why do I have children do this?

- To look for different shaped tracks (thinking).
- To walk in mud, snow, or paint (large muscle).

What do I need?

What might I see children doing?

- Walking.
- Running.
- Putting on cardboard paws and claws.
- Laughing.
- Talking.

1. Cardboard.
2. Scissors.
3. Elastic.
4. Stapler.
5. Pan.
6. Tempera paint.
7. Liquid detergent.
8. Large sheet of paper.
9. Tub of soapy water.
10. Garden hose.

What might I talk about with children?

1. What kinds of tracks might you find in the woods?
2. What else makes tracks?

LET'S GO ON A PET WALK
Outdoor Large Muscle

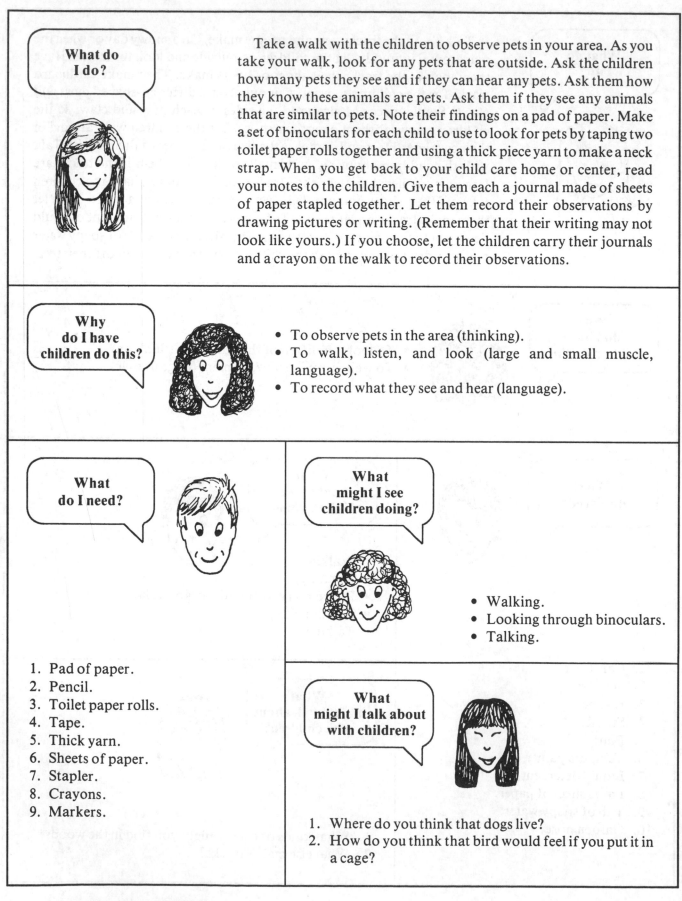

What do I do?

Take a walk with the children to observe pets in your area. As you take your walk, look for any pets that are outside. Ask the children how many pets they see and if they can hear any pets. Ask them how they know these animals are pets. Ask them if they see any animals that are similar to pets. Note their findings on a pad of paper. Make a set of binoculars for each child to use to look for pets by taping two toilet paper rolls together and using a thick piece yarn to make a neck strap. When you get back to your child care home or center, read your notes to the children. Give them each a journal made of sheets of paper stapled together. Let them record their observations by drawing pictures or writing. (Remember that their writing may not look like yours.) If you choose, let the children carry their journals and a crayon on the walk to record their observations.

Why do I have children do this?

- To observe pets in the area (thinking).
- To walk, listen, and look (large and small muscle, language).
- To record what they see and hear (language).

What do I need?

1. Pad of paper.
2. Pencil.
3. Toilet paper rolls.
4. Tape.
5. Thick yarn.
6. Sheets of paper.
7. Stapler.
8. Crayons.
9. Markers.

What might I see children doing?

- Walking.
- Looking through binoculars.
- Talking.

What might I talk about with children?

1. Where do you think that dogs live?
2. How do you think that bird would feel if you put it in a cage?

GIVE A PET A BATH
Outdoor Large Muscle

What do I do?

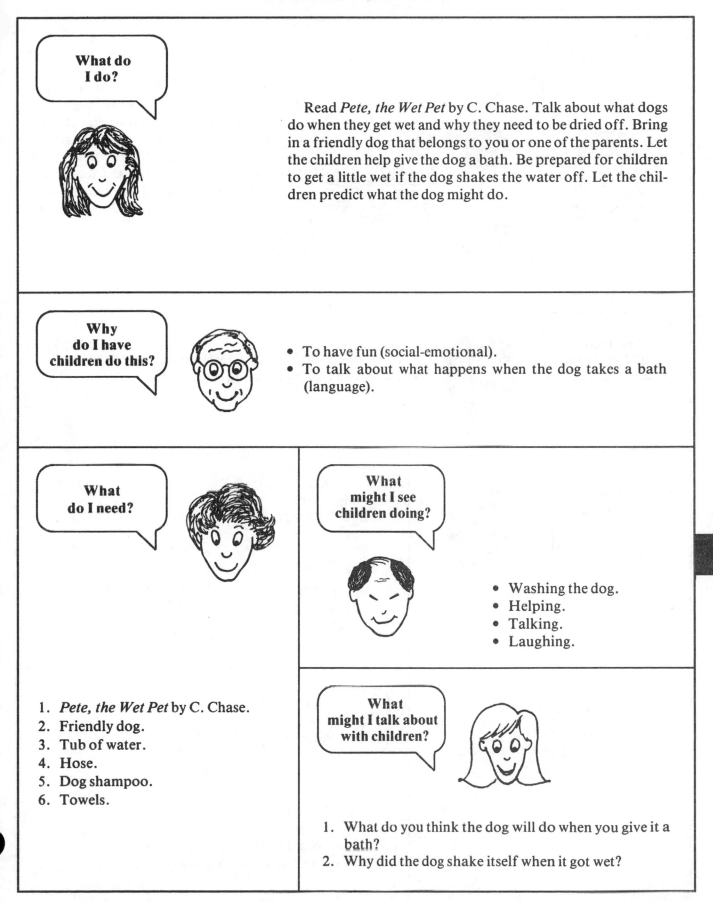

Read *Pete, the Wet Pet* by C. Chase. Talk about what dogs do when they get wet and why they need to be dried off. Bring in a friendly dog that belongs to you or one of the parents. Let the children help give the dog a bath. Be prepared for children to get a little wet if the dog shakes the water off. Let the children predict what the dog might do.

Why do I have children do this?

- To have fun (social-emotional).
- To talk about what happens when the dog takes a bath (language).

What do I need?

What might I see children doing?

- Washing the dog.
- Helping.
- Talking.
- Laughing.

1. *Pete, the Wet Pet* by C. Chase.
2. Friendly dog.
3. Tub of water.
4. Hose.
5. Dog shampoo.
6. Towels.

What might I talk about with children?

1. What do you think the dog will do when you give it a bath?
2. Why did the dog shake itself when it got wet?

PAINT THE DOGHOUSE
Outdoor Large Muscle

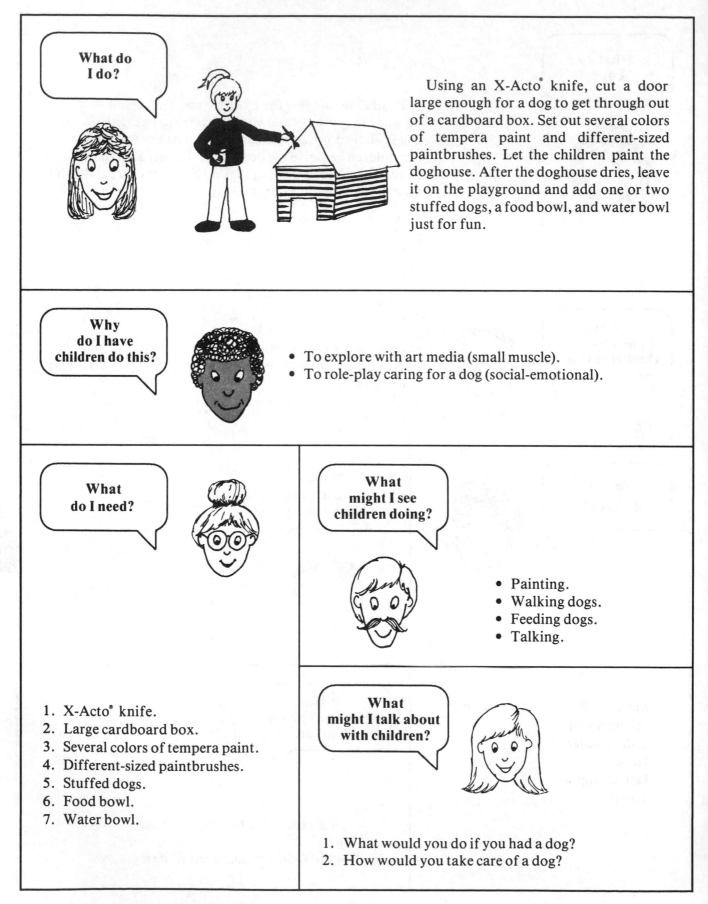

What do I do?

Using an X-Acto® knife, cut a door large enough for a dog to get through out of a cardboard box. Set out several colors of tempera paint and different-sized paintbrushes. Let the children paint the doghouse. After the doghouse dries, leave it on the playground and add one or two stuffed dogs, a food bowl, and water bowl just for fun.

Why do I have children do this?

- To explore with art media (small muscle).
- To role-play caring for a dog (social-emotional).

What do I need?

What might I see children doing?

- Painting.
- Walking dogs.
- Feeding dogs.
- Talking.

1. X-Acto® knife.
2. Large cardboard box.
3. Several colors of tempera paint.
4. Different-sized paintbrushes.
5. Stuffed dogs.
6. Food bowl.
7. Water bowl.

What might I talk about with children?

1. What would you do if you had a dog?
2. How would you take care of a dog?

FOLLOW THE PET LEADER
Outdoor Large Muscle

What do I do?

FLY LIKE A BIRD

Take several pictures of pets, such as dogs, cats, birds, gerbils, ponies, and birds, with you to the playground. Sit down and talk with the children about the pets. Talk about how the different pets move from one place to another. Then let one child at a time pretend that he or she is a pet. Have him or her lead the other children around the playground as he or she flies like a bird, gallops like a pony, or runs like a dog. Let the children make the pet sounds as they move.

Why do I have children do this?

- To imitate animal movements (large muscle).
- To have fun (social-emotional).

What do I need?

1. Pictures of pets.

What might I see children doing?

- Looking at pet pictures.
- Running.
- Galloping.
- Flying.
- Talking.
- Laughing.

What might I talk about with children?

1. Where would you fly if you were a bird?
2. How can a dog tell you it loves you?

LET'S PLAY CATCH
Outdoor Large Muscle

What do I do?

Take balls or Frisbee® flying discs outside and talk with the children about how some dogs like to catch balls or Frisbee® flying discs. Let the children choose partners and decide who will role-play the dog catching the ball or Frisbee® flying disc. Have the pairs of children choose their own space on the playground. Then encourage the children to throw and catch the balls or Frisbee® flying discs. They can cheer or bark. After a period of time, give them the chance to switch roles.

Why do I have children do this?

- To throw and catch a ball or Frisbee® flying disc (large muscle).
- To run and play (large muscle).
- To have fun (social-emotional).

What do I need?

1. Balls.
2. Frisbee® flying discs.

What might I see children doing?

- Throwing balls.
- Catching Frisbee® flying discs.
- Running.
- Barking.
- Laughing.

What might I talk about with children?

1. Where might the dog go if it runs away with the Frisbee® flying disc?
2. How many ways can you throw the ball?

FOLLOW SPOT
Outdoor Large Muscle

What do I do?

Show the children a stuffed dog. Tell them that its name is Spot, and it is hungry. Set up a path on the playground for the children to follow as they help Spot find its food. Cut several bones out of cardboard and cover them with self-adhesive plastic. Use the bones to direct the children along the path. Starting at the door to the playground, direct the children through a tunnel or large box, to the slide, through tires on the ground, to the swings, and to a ball that can be kicked and chased to Spot's dish. Provide a snack for the children at the last bone, so they can eat with Spot.

Why do I have children do this?

- To crawl, climb, slide, run, and swing (large muscle).
- To help Spot find his food (social-emotional).

What do I need?

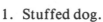

What might I see children doing?

- Running, crawling, and climbing.
- Swinging and sliding.
- Talking.
- Having fun.

1. Stuffed dog.
2. Cardboard.
3. Scissors.
4. Self-adhesive plastic.
5. Snack.

What might I talk about with children?

1. Where would you put Spot's dish?
2. What else can we do on this path?

PET MOVES
Indoor or Outdoor Large Muscle

What do I do?

Hang pictures of pets on the walls at the children's eye level or take a few pictures outdoors with you. Sit down and talk with the children about how pets move. Then let the children act out the movements. Make sure that you are in a large enough area, so the children can spread out as they move. The children may choose to run like a dog, fly like a bird, swim like a fish, or gallop like a horse. Let the children choose other pets to imitate.

Why do I have children do this?

- To talk about the different ways animals move (language, thinking).
- To imitate pet movements (large muscle).

What do I need?

1. Pictures of pets.

What might I see children doing?

- Talking.
- Running.
- Flying.
- Swimming.
- Galloping.
- Laughing.

What might I talk about with children?

1. What other animals gallop?
2. What special movements can you make?

BIBLIOGRAPHY

PETS

Bemelmans, L. 1953. *Madeline's Rescue*. New York, NY: Viking Children's Books.
A Caldecott Award winning story of a dog who saves Madeline.

[1]Boynton, S. 1984. *Doggies*. New York, NY: Simon and Schuster Trade.
A counting board book that shows dogs of all sizes.

Brett, J. 1985. *Annie and the Wild Animals*. Boston, MA: Houghton Mifflin Company.
A beautifully illustrated book about Annie's cat, Taffy, who disappears. Annie
    attempts to find Taffy by asking the animals of the woods if they know where
    Taffy is.

[1, 3]Brown, R. 1986. *Our Cat Flossie*. New York, NY: Dutton Children's Books.
Flossie lives an interesting life as a city cat. This book includes colorful pictures.

[3]Burton, J. 1991. *Kitten*. New York, NY: Lakeston Books.
A story of a kitten from birth to ten weeks that includes wonderful pictures.

Carle, E. 1996. *Have You Seen My Cat?* New York, NY: Simon and Schuster Trade,
    Little Simon Merchandise.
Little board book portraying a boy's hunt for his cat and illustrating all the cats he
    finds along the way.

[2]Carrick, C. 1979. *The Accident*. Boston, MA: Houghton Mifflin.
After his dog is hit by a truck and killed, Christopher must deal with his feelings of
    depression and guilt. This book is good to share with younger children who have
    lost a pet.

[3]Chase, C. 1981. *Pete, the Wet Pet*. New York, NY: Elservier/Nelson Books.
A little boy describes his pet dog, Pete, who loves the rain. Pete gets wet in the rain
    and the little boy dries him off.

[2]Cohen, M. 1984. *Jim's Dog Muffins*. New York, NY: Greenwillow Books.
When Jim's dog is killed, the other first graders share his natural reactions to death.

[1]Day, A. 1991. *Carl's Afternoon in the Park*. New York, NY: Farrar, Straus and Giroux.
Beautiful illustrations of Carl the dog taking care of a puppy and baby in the park.
    The book shows many animals in the children's zoo.

[1]Day, A. 1991. *Carl's Christmas*. New York, NY: Farrar, Straus and Giroux.
Carl the dog takes care of the baby on Christmas Eve, and they have a wonderful adventure. This book contains beautiful illustrations.

Day, A. 1993. *Carl Goes to Day Care*. New York, NY: Farrar, Straus and Giroux.
Colorful picture story of Carl's adventure in the day care center when the teacher gets locked out of the building.

De Regniers, B.S. 1988. *So Many Cats*. New York, NY: Ticknor and Fields.
Counting verses explain how a family ended up with a dozen cats.

Disalvo-Ryan, D. 1999. *A Dog Like Jack*. New York, NY: Holiday House.
The story of the love of a family for their dog and their sadness when Jack gets old and dies.

Dunn, J. 1980. *The Little Rabbit*. New York, NY: Random House Juvenile.
Wonderful photographs help tell the story of Sarah's Easter rabbit. Sarah and her rabbit become very close.

Ellis, A.L. 1984. *Dabble Duck*. New York, NY: HarperCollins Children's Books.
Jason and his pet duck, Dabble, are great pals. However, when Jason begins school, Dabble gets lonely. Dabble solves her problem by befriending a dog.

[3]Fujikawa, G. 1983. *Shags Finds a Kitten*. New York, NY: Grosset and Dunlap Publishers.
Sam and his dog, Shags, hear a noise one rainy night. They find a kitten outside Sam's window. Sam adopts the kitten, and Shags has to learn how to cope with the new pet. This is a fun book.

Gackenbach, D. 1989. *Bag Full of Pups*. New York, NY: Ticknor and Fields.
Mr. Mullin is giving away twelve pups. All of them find homes where they can have a special job. Most of the people want their pups to perform tasks for them. However, a little boy just wants a pet to love. Older children may enjoy counting the pups from 12 down to 0.

Gave, M. 1996. *Cats and Kittens at Your Fingertips*. New York, NY: McClanahan Book Company, Inc.
This colorful book contains lots of information about cats and kittens.

[1]Hill, E. 1980. *Where's Spot? A Lift-the-Flap Book Miniature Edition*. New York, NY: G.P. Putnam's Sons.
Spot is everywhere! Just lift the flap and there he is. The book is a peek-a-boo pop-up book.

[1]Hoban, T. 1974. *Where Is It?* New York, NY: Macmillan Children's Books.
Rhyming verse illustrated with photographs. The main character is a cuddly, white rabbit. Very simple picture book that younger children will enjoy.

Keats, E.J. 1984. *Kitten for a Day*. New York, NY: Macmillan Children's Book Group.
A puppy has a good time playing with some kittens and pretending he is one, too.

Kellogg, S. 1979. *The Mysterious Tadpole*. New York, NY: Dial Books for Young Readers.
It soon becomes clear that Louis' pet tadpole is not turning into an ordinary frog.

[1]Kunhardt, D. 1988. *Pat the Bunny*. New York, NY: Western Publishing Company, Inc.
A very small book that younger children will love to look at and carry around with them. It is a sensory book with a furry bunny the children can pat.

[1]Kunhardt, E. 1984. *Pat the Cat*. New York, NY: Western Publishing Company, Inc.
A very small book that younger children will love to play with.

[3]Leichman, S. 1973. *Shaggy Dogs and Spotty Dogs and Shaggy and Spotty Dogs*. New York, NY: Harcourt Brace Jovanovich, Publishers.
Uses rhyme and funny illustrations to describe many kinds of dogs.

L'Engle, M. 2001. *The Other Dog*. New York, NY: Sea Star Books.
The pet of the house tells a story about when another "dog" (baby) was brought home and she had to learn to cope.

[1]Lindgren, B. 1983. *Sam's Ball*. New York, NY: Morrow Junior Books.
Sam and his cat clash over who gets to play with the ball. This is a little book with cute pictures and few words.

McMillan, B. 1993. *Mouse Views: What the Class Pet Saw*. New York, NY: Holiday House.
Photographic close-ups provide a visual challenge for young children as they follow a pet mouse through the school and try to identify objects in the area.

McPhail, D. 1985. *Emma's Pet*. New York, NY: Dutton Children's Books.
Emma's search for a soft, cuddly pet has a surprising ending.

Nayer, J. 1996. *Dogs and Puppies*. New York, NY: McClanahan Book Company, Inc.
Many colorful pictures of dogs and puppies with lots of basic information about them.

[1,3]Oxenbury, H. 1984. *Our Dog*. New York, NY: E.P. Dutton, Inc.
A boy and his mother are learning to get along with their dog. The dog loves to roll in the mud among other things. This is a fun book that is full of action.

Palmer, H. 1961. *A Fish Out of Water*. New York, NY: Beginner Books.
Mr. Carp said to feed the fish only one spot of food. Watch what happens when the fish is fed the entire box.

Penney, I. 1991. *A Shop Full of Kittens*. New York, NY: G.P. Putnam's Sons.
Tabitha and her family of kittens live in the basement of a department store. The kittens prowl all the departments at night. Will Tabitha find them before the store opens?

Polushkin, M. 1988. *Who Said Meow?* New York, NY: Bradbury Press.
Puppy tries to find out which animal makes the meow sound he hears. This is a book with large print and colorful illustrations.

Rylant, C. 1988. *Henry and Mudge in the Sparkle Days: The Fifth Book of Their Adventures*. New York, NY: Bradbury Press.
In the winter Henry and his big dog, Mudge, play in the snow, share a family Christmas dinner, and gather around a crackling winter fireplace.

Smath, J. 1980. *The Housekeeper's Dog*. New York, NY: Parents Magazine Press.
A dog who likes to roll, scratch, and play with bones is quite a different dog after attending Madame De Poochio's School for Dogs.

[2, 3]Spier, P. 1981. *The Pet Store*. New York, NY: Doubleday.
This is an informational book about many different pets and the items needed to care for them.

[3]Stein, S.B. 1985. *Cat*. New York, NY: Harcourt Brace Jovanovich, Publishers.
Text and illustrations examine the physical characteristics, habits, and daily activities of a cat. Wonderful bold, colorful illustrations are used to tell the story with few words.

Thayer, J. 1958. *The Puppy Who Wanted a Boy*. New York, NY: Mulberry Books.
When Petey the puppy decides he wants a boy for Christmas, he discovers he must go out and find one on his own.

Tildes, P. 1995. *Counting on Calico*. Watertown, MA: Charlesbridge Publishing.
Learn about cats and numbers by following Calico Cat and her kittens. This is a good book to share at group time.

Waddell, M. 2001. *A Kitten Called Moonlight*. Cambridge, MA: Candlewick Press.
Charlotte's favorite story is the story of a lost little kitten all alone on a cold moonlight, winter night and the little girl and her mother that rescue him.

Wilhelm, H. 1985. *Bunny Trouble*. New York, NY: Scholastic, Inc.
Ralph is a bunny who is supposed to decorate Easter eggs, but has only one interest—soccer. The story tells of his adventures and problems.

Wilhelm, H. 1989. *I'll Always Love You*. New York, NY: Crown Publishers.
Boy and dog had always been together. Then suddenly, dog is old. A child's love for his aging and dying dog is movingly told in this tender and comforting, yet realistic story.

[3]Wirth, B. 1983. *Margie and Me*. New York, NY: Four Winds Press.
The story is about a young girl's pet, Margie. The little girl is telling of her love for her pet and how to care for it.

[3]Wong, H., and Vessel, M. 1969. *My Goldfish*. Reading, MA: Addison-Wesley Publishing Company.
Colorful book that is fun and gives scientific information about goldfish.

Zion, G. 1976. *Harry the Dirty Dog*. New York, NY: HarperCollins Children's Books.
Because Harry the dog hates taking baths, he runs away for the day.

We have marked these books if we think they are definitely more applicable to one age. Many can be used by all ages with adaptations by the teacher.

[1]Books for one-year-olds, two-year-olds, and three-year-olds.

[2]Books for five-year-olds.

[3]This book is no longer in print. However, you may be able to find it at your local library.

Unit 6

TRANSPORTATION

CONTENTS

TRANSPORTATION

Transportation refers to ways of moving people and materials. People use vehicles to get from one place to another or for recreation. Vehicles are also used to deliver food, furniture, and toys to stores and to help build structures and roads.

"Transportation" consists of activities to help children learn more about transportation. They will learn that:

- They need transportation to go to their child care center, the store, or Grandma and Grandpa's house.
- There are many different kinds of transportation, such as cars, trucks, vans, bicycles, airplanes, boats, and trains.
- Many vehicles used for transportation have wheels.
- Vehicles used for transportation can be many shapes, sizes, and colors.
- People are needed to operate the different forms of transportation.
- Tricycles and scooters are forms of transportation that they can use.

CARS
Group

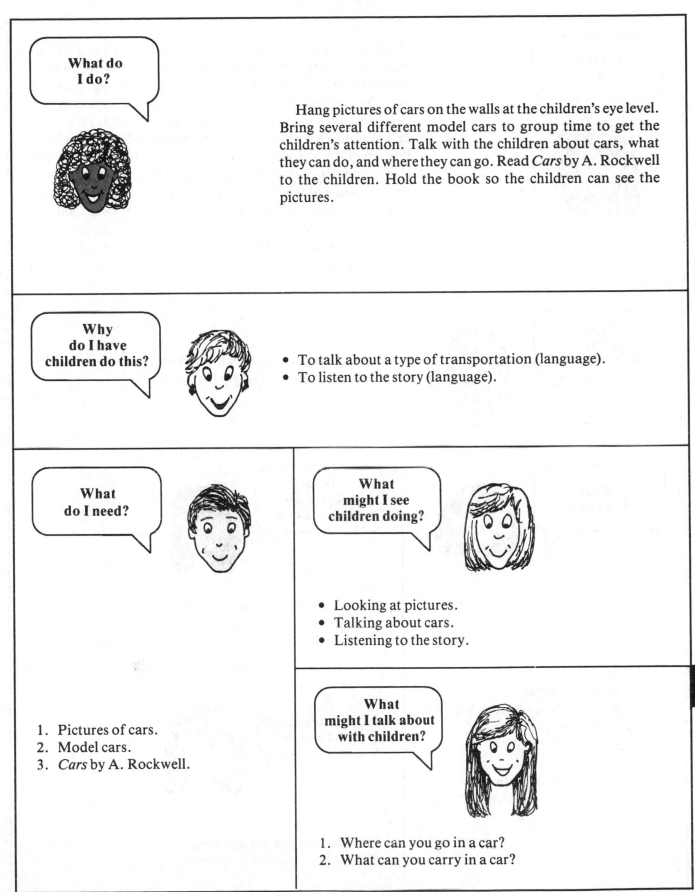

What do I do?

Hang pictures of cars on the walls at the children's eye level. Bring several different model cars to group time to get the children's attention. Talk with the children about cars, what they can do, and where they can go. Read *Cars* by A. Rockwell to the children. Hold the book so the children can see the pictures.

Why do I have children do this?

- To talk about a type of transportation (language).
- To listen to the story (language).

What do I need?

What might I see children doing?

- Looking at pictures.
- Talking about cars.
- Listening to the story.

1. Pictures of cars.
2. Model cars.
3. *Cars* by A. Rockwell.

What might I talk about with children?

1. Where can you go in a car?
2. What can you carry in a car?

BUCKLE UP FOR SAFETY
Group

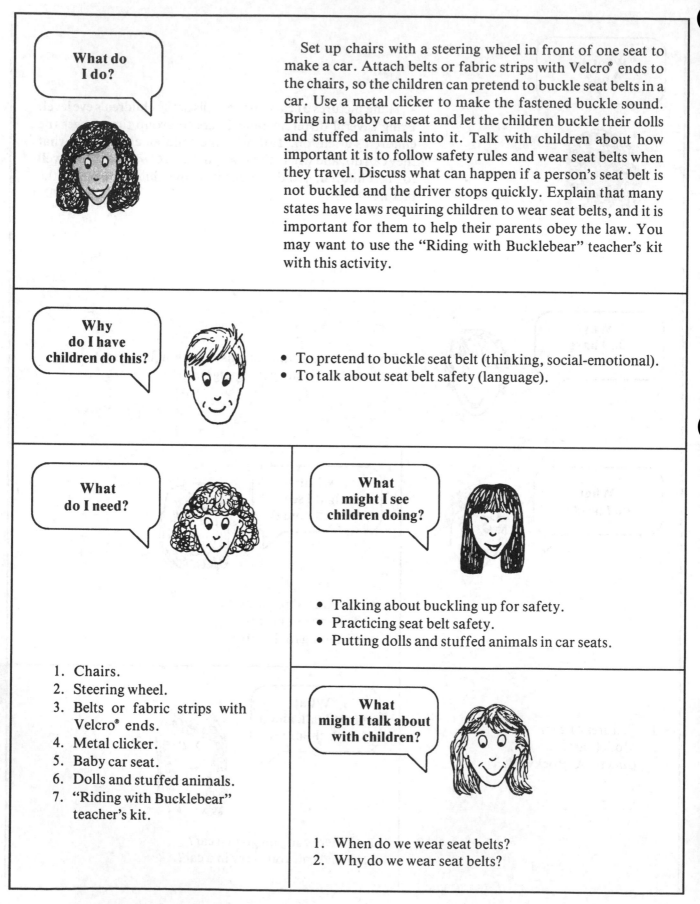

What do I do?

Set up chairs with a steering wheel in front of one seat to make a car. Attach belts or fabric strips with Velcro® ends to the chairs, so the children can pretend to buckle seat belts in a car. Use a metal clicker to make the fastened buckle sound. Bring in a baby car seat and let the children buckle their dolls and stuffed animals into it. Talk with children about how important it is to follow safety rules and wear seat belts when they travel. Discuss what can happen if a person's seat belt is not buckled and the driver stops quickly. Explain that many states have laws requiring children to wear seat belts, and it is important for them to help their parents obey the law. You may want to use the "Riding with Bucklebear" teacher's kit with this activity.

Why do I have children do this?

- To pretend to buckle seat belt (thinking, social-emotional).
- To talk about seat belt safety (language).

What do I need?

What might I see children doing?

- Talking about buckling up for safety.
- Practicing seat belt safety.
- Putting dolls and stuffed animals in car seats.

1. Chairs.
2. Steering wheel.
3. Belts or fabric strips with Velcro® ends.
4. Metal clicker.
5. Baby car seat.
6. Dolls and stuffed animals.
7. "Riding with Bucklebear" teacher's kit.

What might I talk about with children?

1. When do we wear seat belts?
2. Why do we wear seat belts?

MY LIFT-THE-FLAPS PLANE BOOK
Group

What do I do?

Hang pictures of airplanes, airports, and runways on the walls at the children's eye level. Talk with the children about places they might go on an airplane. Read *My Lift-the-Flaps Plane Book* by A. Royston. Hold the book so the children can see the pictures of an airline reservation desk, Jetway®, airplane cabin, and baggage area. Talk about how flight attendants bring people magazines and snacks and serve meals on long trips. Talk about how flight attendants help keep passengers safe. Explain that they teach people how to use their seat belts and other safety equipment. Talk about how movies are sometimes shown on long flights.

Why do I have children do this?

- To use new words, such as Jetway® and flight attendant (language).
- To talk about flying on an airplane (thinking).

What do I need?

1. Pictures of airplanes, airports, and runways.
2. *My Lift-the-Flaps Plane Book* by A. Royston.

What might I see children doing?

- Looking at pictures.
- Listening to the story.
- Talking about the airport.

What might I talk about with children?

1. What does the airline pilot do?
2. What does the flight attendant do?

PLANES
Group

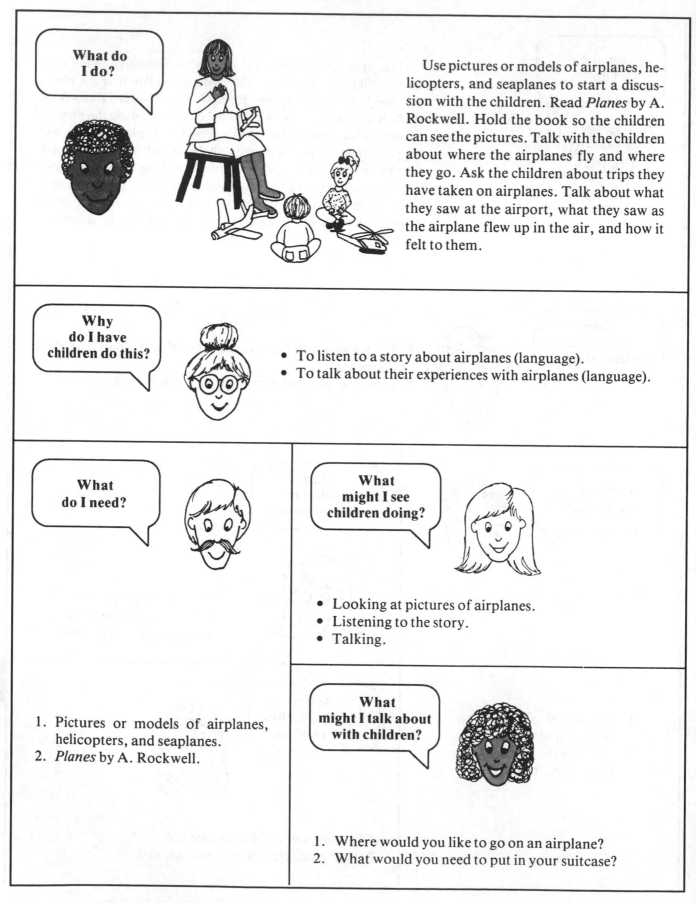

What do I do?

Use pictures or models of airplanes, helicopters, and seaplanes to start a discussion with the children. Read *Planes* by A. Rockwell. Hold the book so the children can see the pictures. Talk with the children about where the airplanes fly and where they go. Ask the children about trips they have taken on airplanes. Talk about what they saw at the airport, what they saw as the airplane flew up in the air, and how it felt to them.

Why do I have children do this?

- To listen to a story about airplanes (language).
- To talk about their experiences with airplanes (language).

What do I need?

1. Pictures or models of airplanes, helicopters, and seaplanes.
2. *Planes* by A. Rockwell.

What might I see children doing?

- Looking at pictures of airplanes.
- Listening to the story.
- Talking.

What might I talk about with children?

1. Where would you like to go on an airplane?
2. What would you need to put in your suitcase?

VISITING THE AIRPORT
Group

What do I do?

Hang pictures of airplanes and the inside and outside of an airport on the wall at the children's eye level. Talk with the children about what they can see at the airport. Then read *My Lift-the-Flaps Plane Book* by A. Royston. Talk about what a passport is and why people need one if they travel outside their country. If you have a passport, show it to the children.

Why do I have children do this?

- To use new words, such as passport, radar system, and customs (thinking, language).
- To listen to the story (language).

What do I need?

1. Pictures of airplanes and the inside and outside of airports.
2. *My Lift-the-Flaps Plane Book* by A. Royston.

What might I see children doing?

- Looking at the pictures.
- Listening to the story.
- Pretending to fly on an airplane.

What might I talk about with children?

1. What would you do if you were an airplane pilot?
2. What do you think the flight attendant does when he or she is at work?

YOU CAN MAKE IT GO!
Group

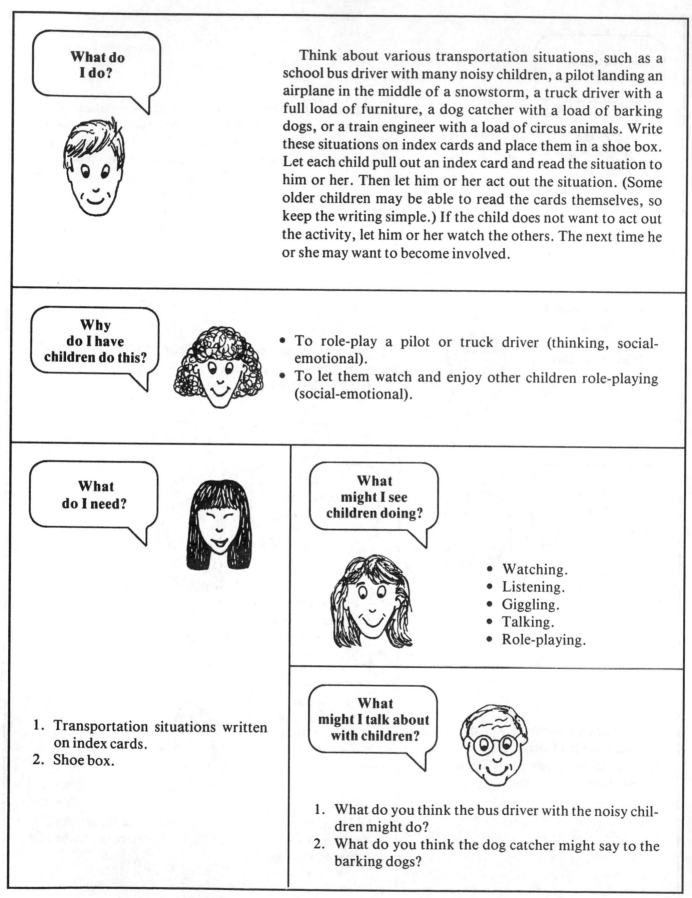

What do I do?

Think about various transportation situations, such as a school bus driver with many noisy children, a pilot landing an airplane in the middle of a snowstorm, a truck driver with a full load of furniture, a dog catcher with a load of barking dogs, or a train engineer with a load of circus animals. Write these situations on index cards and place them in a shoe box. Let each child pull out an index card and read the situation to him or her. Then let him or her act out the situation. (Some older children may be able to read the cards themselves, so keep the writing simple.) If the child does not want to act out the activity, let him or her watch the others. The next time he or she may want to become involved.

Why do I have children do this?

- To role-play a pilot or truck driver (thinking, social-emotional).
- To let them watch and enjoy other children role-playing (social-emotional).

What do I need?

1. Transportation situations written on index cards.
2. Shoe box.

What might I see children doing?

- Watching.
- Listening.
- Giggling.
- Talking.
- Role-playing.

What might I talk about with children?

1. What do you think the bus driver with the noisy children might do?
2. What do you think the dog catcher might say to the barking dogs?

"THE LITTLE RED CABOOSE"
Group, Learning Center (music)

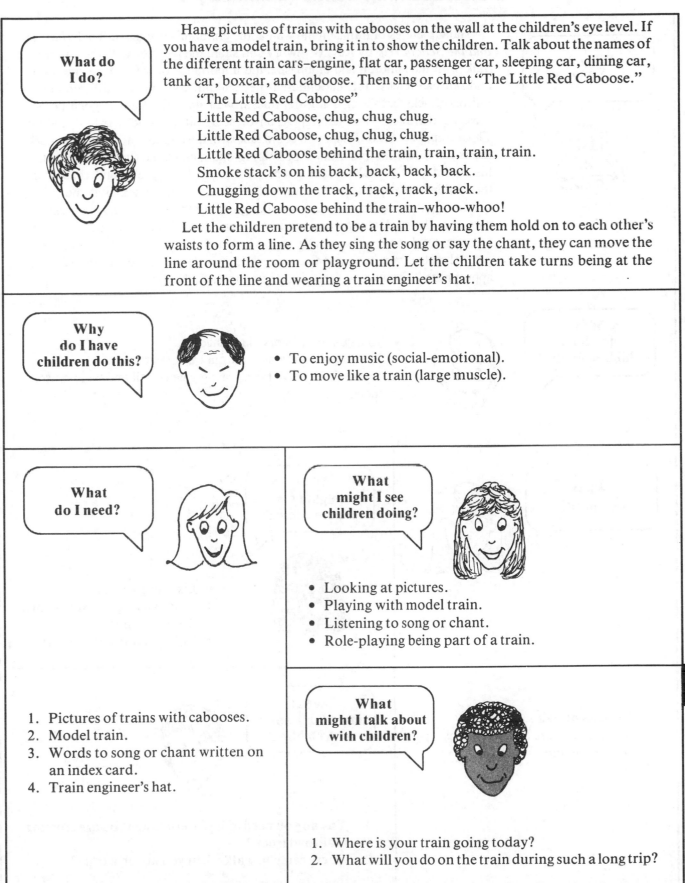

What do I do?

Hang pictures of trains with cabooses on the wall at the children's eye level. If you have a model train, bring it in to show the children. Talk about the names of the different train cars–engine, flat car, passenger car, sleeping car, dining car, tank car, boxcar, and caboose. Then sing or chant "The Little Red Caboose."

"The Little Red Caboose"
Little Red Caboose, chug, chug, chug.
Little Red Caboose, chug, chug, chug.
Little Red Caboose behind the train, train, train, train.
Smoke stack's on his back, back, back, back.
Chugging down the track, track, track, track.
Little Red Caboose behind the train–whoo-whoo!

Let the children pretend to be a train by having them hold on to each other's waists to form a line. As they sing the song or say the chant, they can move the line around the room or playground. Let the children take turns being at the front of the line and wearing a train engineer's hat.

Why do I have children do this?

- To enjoy music (social-emotional).
- To move like a train (large muscle).

What do I need?

What might I see children doing?

- Looking at pictures.
- Playing with model train.
- Listening to song or chant.
- Role-playing being part of a train.

1. Pictures of trains with cabooses.
2. Model train.
3. Words to song or chant written on an index card.
4. Train engineer's hat.

What might I talk about with children?

1. Where is your train going today?
2. What will you do on the train during such a long trip?

STOP, LOOK, AND LISTEN
Group, Learning Center (dramatic play)

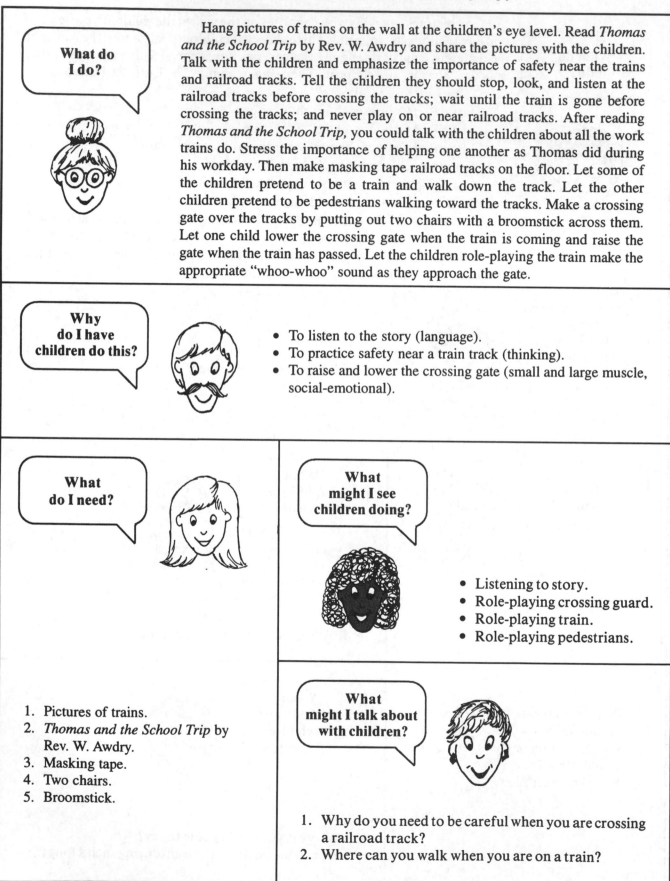

What do I do?

Hang pictures of trains on the wall at the children's eye level. Read *Thomas and the School Trip* by Rev. W. Awdry and share the pictures with the children. Talk with the children and emphasize the importance of safety near the trains and railroad tracks. Tell the children they should stop, look, and listen at the railroad tracks before crossing the tracks; wait until the train is gone before crossing the tracks; and never play on or near railroad tracks. After reading *Thomas and the School Trip,* you could talk with the children about all the work trains do. Stress the importance of helping one another as Thomas did during his workday. Then make masking tape railroad tracks on the floor. Let some of the children pretend to be a train and walk down the track. Let the other children pretend to be pedestrians walking toward the tracks. Make a crossing gate over the tracks by putting out two chairs with a broomstick across them. Let one child lower the crossing gate when the train is coming and raise the gate when the train has passed. Let the children role-playing the train make the appropriate "whoo-whoo" sound as they approach the gate.

Why do I have children do this?

- To listen to the story (language).
- To practice safety near a train track (thinking).
- To raise and lower the crossing gate (small and large muscle, social-emotional).

What do I need?

What might I see children doing?

- Listening to story.
- Role-playing crossing guard.
- Role-playing train.
- Role-playing pedestrians.

1. Pictures of trains.
2. *Thomas and the School Trip* by Rev. W. Awdry.
3. Masking tape.
4. Two chairs.
5. Broomstick.

What might I talk about with children?

1. Why do you need to be careful when you are crossing a railroad track?
2. Where can you walk when you are on a train?

RIDING OUR TRAIN
Group, Learning Center (music), Outside

What do I do?

Show the children pictures of trains and talk about how they move, the sounds they make when they move and stop, and the sounds their whistles make. Let the children form a train by holding on to each other's waists and move to music, such as "The Train Song" from *Macmillan Sing and Learn Program: Large Motor Skills* from the Macmillan Educational Company or "Train Game" from *Macmillan Sing and Learn Program: Classroom Games* from the Macmillan Educational Company. Make a train engineer hat for the child at the front of the train by forming a cylinder out of a sheet of construction paper and stapling it together to fit his or her head.

Why do I have children do this?

- To listen to music (language).
- To pretend to be a train and move to the music (social-emotional, large muscle).

What do I need?

1. Pictures of trains.
2. *Macmillan Sing and Learn Program: Large Motor Skills* from the Macmillan Educational Company.
3. Construction paper.
4. Stapler.

What might I see children doing?

- Pretending to be a train.
- Listening to the records.
- Making train noises.
- Putting on train engineer's hat.

What might I talk about with children?

1. What might you see when you look out of the train window?
2. What would you choose to eat when you go to the dining car?

BOAT BOOK
Group

What do I do?

Show the children pictures of different kinds of boats, such as rowboats, sailboats, canoes, cruise ships, freighters, and aircraft carriers, and talk about how they are used. Read *Boat Book* by G. Gibbons and share the pictures with the children. Talk with the children about the boats that they have been on. Talk about all the activities they can do on a boat, such as fish, eat, and sleep. Show the children a life jacket and talk about how they need to wear a life jacket when they are in a boat or canoe. Let the children try on the life jacket.

Why do I have children do this?

- To talk about what they can do on a boat (thinking).
- To listen to a story (language).

What do I need?

What might I see children doing?

- Looking at pictures.
- Listening to story.
- Talking and trying on life jacket.

1. Pictures of different kinds of boats.
2. *Boat Book* by G. Gibbons.
3. Life jacket.

What might I talk about with children?

1. Where can you go in a rowboat?
2. Why do you need to wear a life jacket?

GUESS WHAT I AM?
Group

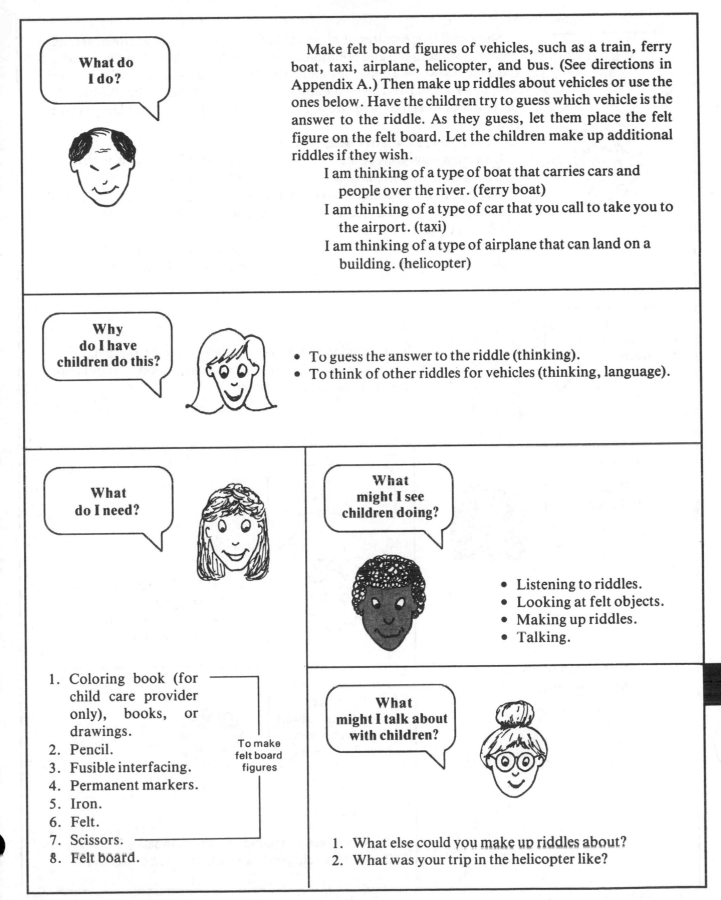

What do I do?

Make felt board figures of vehicles, such as a train, ferry boat, taxi, airplane, helicopter, and bus. (See directions in Appendix A.) Then make up riddles about vehicles or use the ones below. Have the children try to guess which vehicle is the answer to the riddle. As they guess, let them place the felt figure on the felt board. Let the children make up additional riddles if they wish.

   I am thinking of a type of boat that carries cars and people over the river. (ferry boat)

   I am thinking of a type of car that you call to take you to the airport. (taxi)

   I am thinking of a type of airplane that can land on a building. (helicopter)

Why do I have children do this?

- To guess the answer to the riddle (thinking).
- To think of other riddles for vehicles (thinking, language).

What do I need?

What might I see children doing?

- Listening to riddles.
- Looking at felt objects.
- Making up riddles.
- Talking.

1. Coloring book (for child care provider only), books, or drawings.
2. Pencil.
3. Fusible interfacing.
4. Permanent markers.
5. Iron.
6. Felt.
7. Scissors.
8. Felt board.

To make felt board figures

What might I talk about with children?

1. What else could you make up riddles about?
2. What was your trip in the helicopter like?

"ROW, ROW, ROW YOUR BOAT"
Group

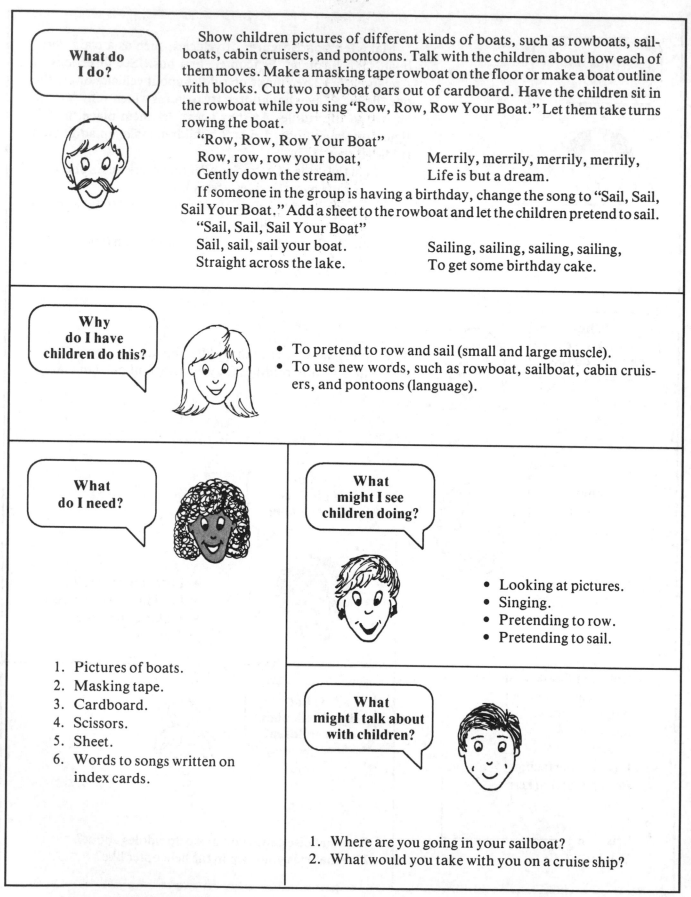

What do I do?

Show children pictures of different kinds of boats, such as rowboats, sailboats, cabin cruisers, and pontoons. Talk with the children about how each of them moves. Make a masking tape rowboat on the floor or make a boat outline with blocks. Cut two rowboat oars out of cardboard. Have the children sit in the rowboat while you sing "Row, Row, Row Your Boat." Let them take turns rowing the boat.

"Row, Row, Row Your Boat"

Row, row, row your boat,   Merrily, merrily, merrily, merrily,
Gently down the stream.   Life is but a dream.

If someone in the group is having a birthday, change the song to "Sail, Sail, Sail Your Boat." Add a sheet to the rowboat and let the children pretend to sail.

"Sail, Sail, Sail Your Boat"

Sail, sail, sail your boat.   Sailing, sailing, sailing, sailing,
Straight across the lake.   To get some birthday cake.

Why do I have children do this?

- To pretend to row and sail (small and large muscle).
- To use new words, such as rowboat, sailboat, cabin cruisers, and pontoons (language).

What do I need?

1. Pictures of boats.
2. Masking tape.
3. Cardboard.
4. Scissors.
5. Sheet.
6. Words to songs written on index cards.

What might I see children doing?

- Looking at pictures.
- Singing.
- Pretending to row.
- Pretending to sail.

What might I talk about with children?

1. Where are you going in your sailboat?
2. What would you take with you on a cruise ship?

RIDING ON A BUS
Group

What do I do?

Hang pictures of school buses, city buses, and travel buses on the walls at the children's eye level. Talk with the children about how buses are used as a form of transportation. Ask the children about bus rides they have taken. Read *Riding on a Bus* by D. Chlad and share the pictures with the children. In the corner, set up chairs in rows and put a steering wheel in front of one chair to make a bus. Let the children practice the safety rules discussed in the book. This activity can be used to reinforce bus safety before you take field trips.

Why do I have children do this?

- To demonstrate the safe way to use a bus (thinking).
- To talk about buses and why people travel on them (language, thinking).

What do I need?

What might I see children doing?

- Looking at pictures.
- Listening to the story.
- Role-playing bus safety.
- Talking.

1. Pictures of buses.
2. *Riding on a Bus* by D. Chlad.
3. Chairs.
4. Steering wheel.

What might I talk about with children?

1. Where can you go on a bus?
2. If you were going on a long trip on a bus, what would you take with you?

THE LITTLE ENGINE THAT COULD
Group

What do I do?

Hang up pictures of freight trains and passenger trains on the wall at the children's eye level. Talk about what can be shipped on freight trains and what kinds of cars are on passenger trains. Then read *The Little Engine That Could* by W. Piper and show the children the pictures. Talk with the children about the story. Explain how saying, "I think I can" may help them do something they didn't think they could do. Ask the children what they have done that they didn't think they could do at first, such as jump on one foot or ride a tricycle.

Why do I have children do this?

- To listen to a story (language).
- To talk about what they think they can't do (social-emotional).

What do I need?

What might I see children doing?

- Looking at pictures.
- Listening to the story.
- Talking about what they can do.

1. Pictures of freight trains and passenger trains.
2. *The Little Engine That Could* by W. Piper.

What might I talk about with children?

1. What can you do that you thought you couldn't do at first?
2. What did the little train have in its cars?

TRANSPORTATION MURAL
Learning Center (art, library)

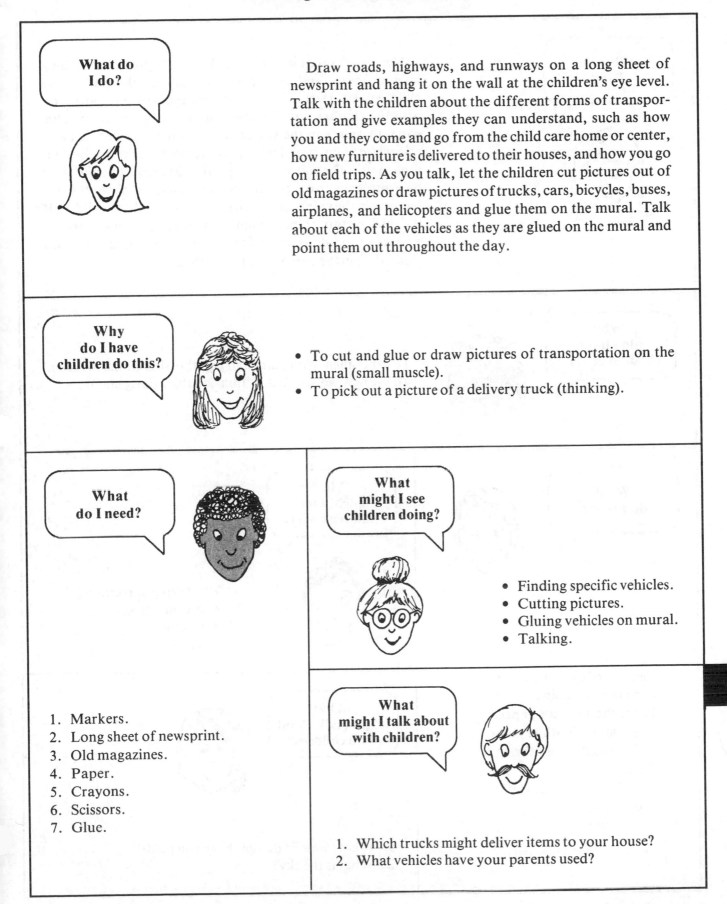

What do I do?

Draw roads, highways, and runways on a long sheet of newsprint and hang it on the wall at the children's eye level. Talk with the children about the different forms of transportation and give examples they can understand, such as how you and they come and go from the child care home or center, how new furniture is delivered to their houses, and how you go on field trips. As you talk, let the children cut pictures out of old magazines or draw pictures of trucks, cars, bicycles, buses, airplanes, and helicopters and glue them on the mural. Talk about each of the vehicles as they are glued on the mural and point them out throughout the day.

Why do I have children do this?

- To cut and glue or draw pictures of transportation on the mural (small muscle).
- To pick out a picture of a delivery truck (thinking).

What do I need?

1. Markers.
2. Long sheet of newsprint.
3. Old magazines.
4. Paper.
5. Crayons.
6. Scissors.
7. Glue.

What might I see children doing?

- Finding specific vehicles.
- Cutting pictures.
- Gluing vehicles on mural.
- Talking.

What might I talk about with children?

1. Which trucks might deliver items to your house?
2. What vehicles have your parents used?

TRANSPORTATION AT THE EASEL
Learning Center (art)

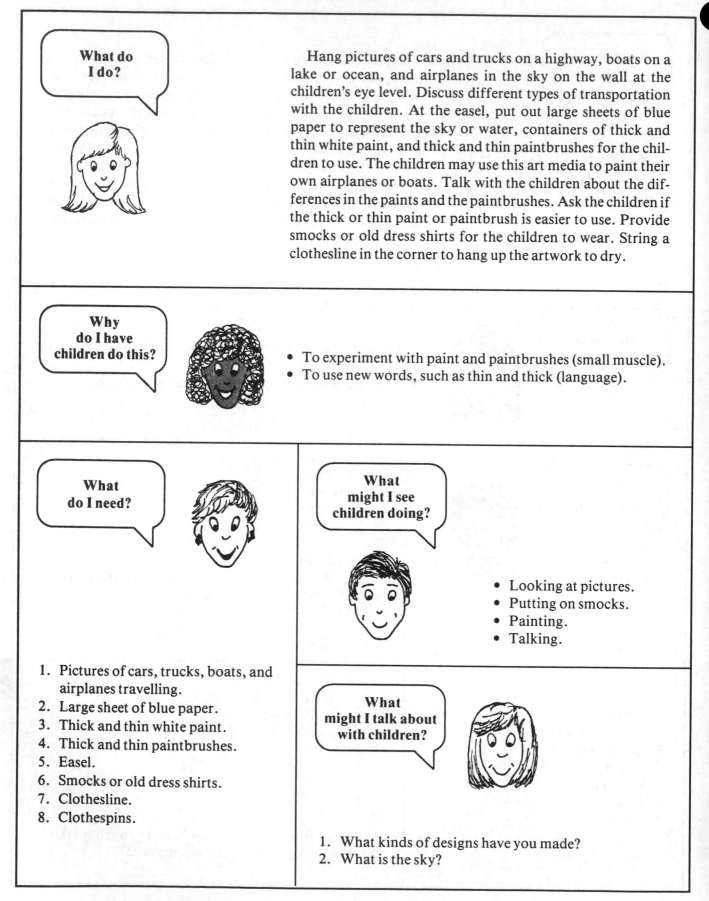

What do I do?

Hang pictures of cars and trucks on a highway, boats on a lake or ocean, and airplanes in the sky on the wall at the children's eye level. Discuss different types of transportation with the children. At the easel, put out large sheets of blue paper to represent the sky or water, containers of thick and thin white paint, and thick and thin paintbrushes for the children to use. The children may use this art media to paint their own airplanes or boats. Talk with the children about the differences in the paints and the paintbrushes. Ask the children if the thick or thin paint or paintbrush is easier to use. Provide smocks or old dress shirts for the children to wear. String a clothesline in the corner to hang up the artwork to dry.

Why do I have children do this?

- To experiment with paint and paintbrushes (small muscle).
- To use new words, such as thin and thick (language).

What do I need?

1. Pictures of cars, trucks, boats, and airplanes travelling.
2. Large sheet of blue paper.
3. Thick and thin white paint.
4. Thick and thin paintbrushes.
5. Easel.
6. Smocks or old dress shirts.
7. Clothesline.
8. Clothespins.

What might I see children doing?

- Looking at pictures.
- Putting on smocks.
- Painting.
- Talking.

What might I talk about with children?

1. What kinds of designs have you made?
2. What is the sky?

SPONGE VEHICLES
Learning Center (art)

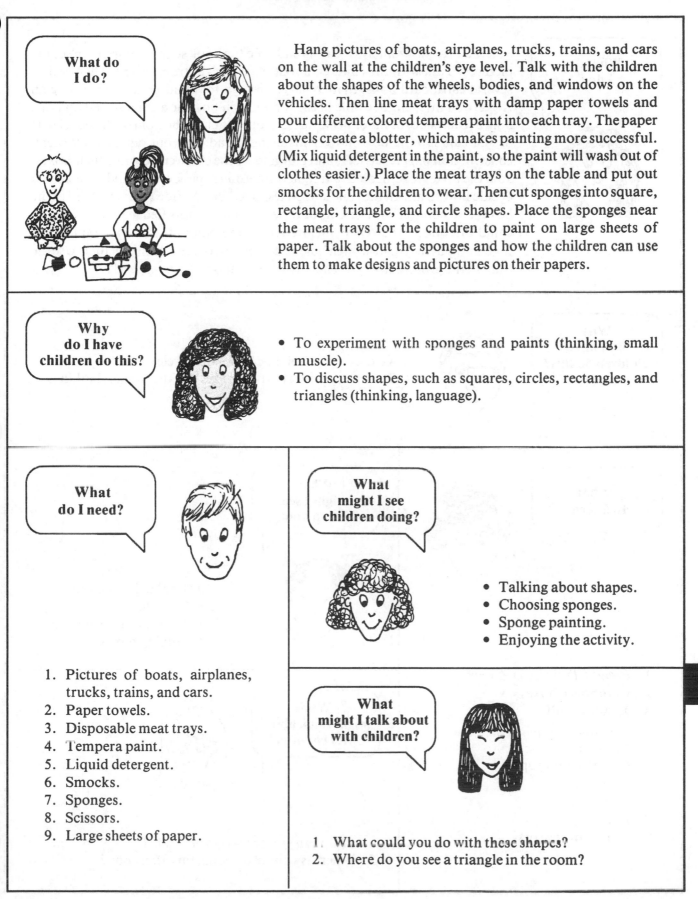

What do I do?

Hang pictures of boats, airplanes, trucks, trains, and cars on the wall at the children's eye level. Talk with the children about the shapes of the wheels, bodies, and windows on the vehicles. Then line meat trays with damp paper towels and pour different colored tempera paint into each tray. The paper towels create a blotter, which makes painting more successful. (Mix liquid detergent in the paint, so the paint will wash out of clothes easier.) Place the meat trays on the table and put out smocks for the children to wear. Then cut sponges into square, rectangle, triangle, and circle shapes. Place the sponges near the meat trays for the children to paint on large sheets of paper. Talk about the sponges and how the children can use them to make designs and pictures on their papers.

Why do I have children do this?

- To experiment with sponges and paints (thinking, small muscle).
- To discuss shapes, such as squares, circles, rectangles, and triangles (thinking, language).

What do I need?

1. Pictures of boats, airplanes, trucks, trains, and cars.
2. Paper towels.
3. Disposable meat trays.
4. Tempera paint.
5. Liquid detergent.
6. Smocks.
7. Sponges.
8. Scissors.
9. Large sheets of paper.

What might I see children doing?

- Talking about shapes.
- Choosing sponges.
- Sponge painting.
- Enjoying the activity.

What might I talk about with children?

1. What could you do with these shapes?
2. Where do you see a triangle in the room?

CARDBOARD FREIGHT TRAIN
Learning Center (art)

What do I do?

Read *Freight Train* by D. Crews and hold the book so the children can see the pictures. Talk with the children about what freight trains carry. Then collect several cardboard boxes that are large enough for children to wear. Using an X-Acto® knife, cut one hole in the top of each box for a child's head and one hole in each side for his or her arms. Cut out the entire bottom of the box, so he or she can slip the box on over his or her head. Put out crayons, markers, construction paper, scissors, and glue and let the children decorate their boxes. Join the boxes together into a freight train using rope. Let the children help you decide how to attach the rope and boxes together. One idea is to cut "Vs" in the boxes and connect with lengths of rope with large knots tied in them. Children could disconnect the "cars" themselves. Some other ideas are to staple them together, put the rope through holes in the boxes, or tape them together. Use the train in the group activity " 'The Little Red Caboose' " on page 431.

Why do I have children do this?

- To decorate a freight car (small muscle).
- To construct a train from boxes (small muscle, thinking).

What do I need?

1. *Freight Train* by D. Crews.
2. Cardboard boxes.
3. X-Acto® knife.
4. Crayons.
5. Markers.
6. Construction paper.
7. Scissors.
8. Glue.
9. Rope.
10. Stapler or scissors.

What might I see children doing?

- Looking at pictures.
- Talking about trains.
- Decorating freight cars.
- Joining boxes.

What might I talk about with children?

1. What can you carry on your train?
2. Where is your train going this afternoon?

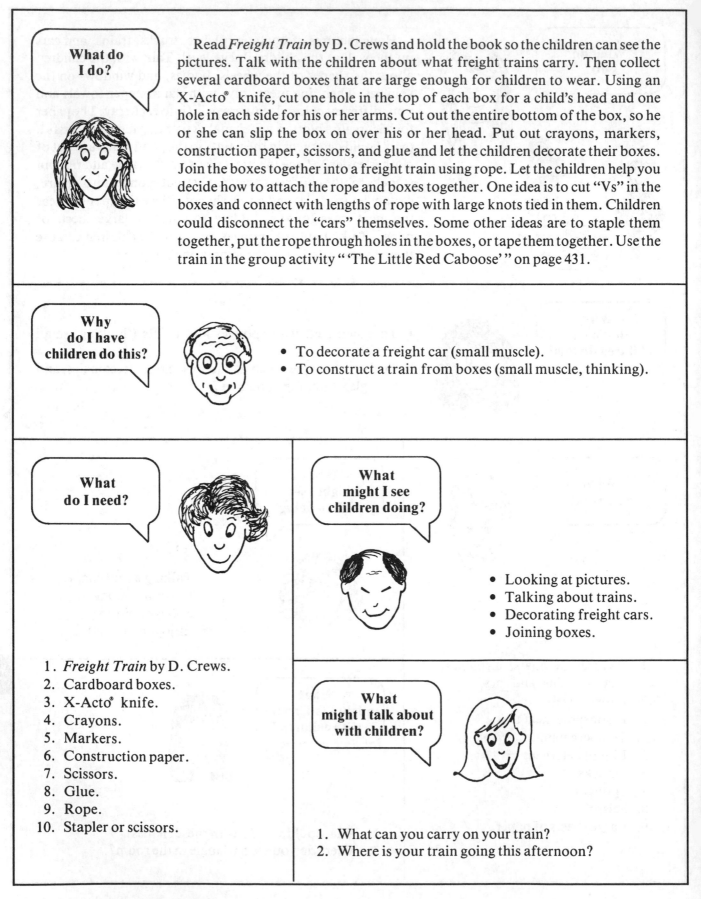

DRIVING THROUGH PAINT
Learning Center (art)

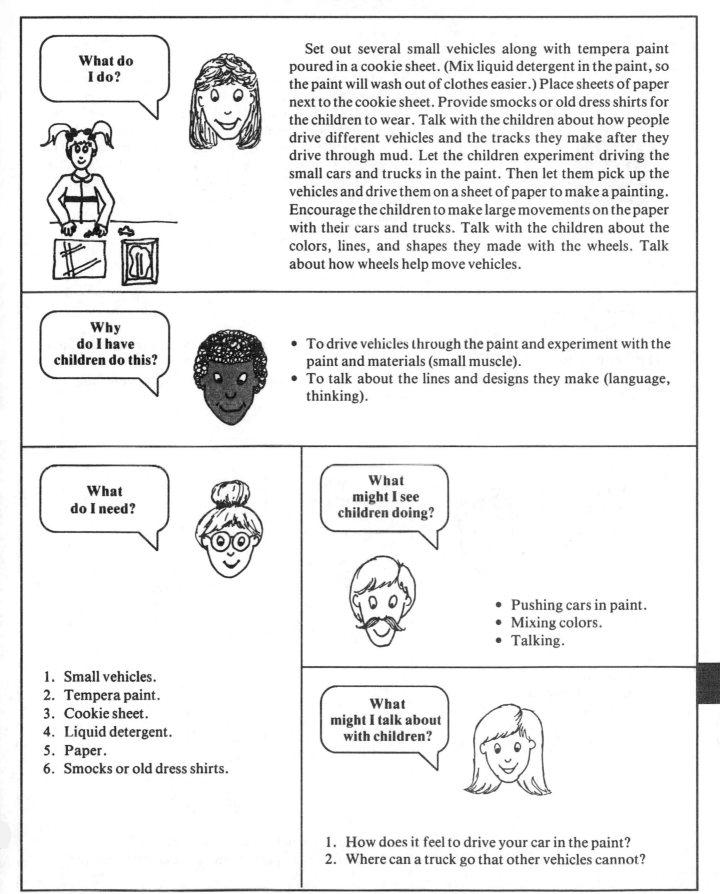

What do I do?

Set out several small vehicles along with tempera paint poured in a cookie sheet. (Mix liquid detergent in the paint, so the paint will wash out of clothes easier.) Place sheets of paper next to the cookie sheet. Provide smocks or old dress shirts for the children to wear. Talk with the children about how people drive different vehicles and the tracks they make after they drive through mud. Let the children experiment driving the small cars and trucks in the paint. Then let them pick up the vehicles and drive them on a sheet of paper to make a painting. Encourage the children to make large movements on the paper with their cars and trucks. Talk with the children about the colors, lines, and shapes they made with the wheels. Talk about how wheels help move vehicles.

Why do I have children do this?

- To drive vehicles through the paint and experiment with the paint and materials (small muscle).
- To talk about the lines and designs they make (language, thinking).

What do I need?

What might I see children doing?

- Pushing cars in paint.
- Mixing colors.
- Talking.

What might I talk about with children?

1. Small vehicles.
2. Tempera paint.
3. Cookie sheet.
4. Liquid detergent.
5. Paper.
6. Smocks or old dress shirts.

1. How does it feel to drive your car in the paint?
2. Where can a truck go that other vehicles cannot?

BUILDING FOR TRANSPORTATION
Learning Center (blocks)

What do I do?

Hang pictures of roads, bridges, docks, runways, and launching pads on the walls at the children's eye level to encourage block play. Place small wooden cars, trucks, airplanes, and people and cattle figures on the shelves in the block area. Add small blocks, twigs, pebbles, and spools that can be transported in the trucks, trains, and airplanes. Talk with the children about the pictures on the wall and what they see on the roads and streets near their homes and your child care center or home. Be available to help problem solve when the children are trying to build bridges or viaducts.

Why do I have children do this?

- To build bridges and roads with blocks (small and large muscles).
- To use new words, such as bridge, dock, launching pad (language).

What do I need?

1. Pictures of roads, bridges, docks, runways, and launching pads.
2. Small wooden cars, trucks, airplanes, and people and cattle figures.
3. Small wooden blocks.
4. Twigs.
5. Pebbles.
6. Spools.

What might I see children doing?

- Choosing blocks.
- Constructing roads.
- Looking at pictures.
- Loading trucks.
- Having fun.

What might I talk about with children?

1. What are you loading into your truck?
2. What are you going to need to make this bridge?

COMMUNITY VEHICLES
Learning Center (blocks)

What do I do?

Set out a Duplo® Community Vehicles preschool toys set in the block area. Let the children use the pieces of the set to construct cars, trucks, and trains. Supplement the Duplo® preschool toys set with other blocks, so the children can build additional roads and buildings. Talk with the children about the different types of transportation and how they are used. Explain that all forms of transportation have drivers, and they often have special names, such as pilot, captain, engineer, and astronaut. When a child is driving a Duplo® preschool toy vehicle, call him or her by the correct title. For example, when a child is driving a train, call him or her an engineer.

Why do I have children do this?

- To put Duplo® preschool toys together (small muscle).
- To use new words, such as pilot, captain, engineer, and astronaut (language).

What do I need?

1. Duplo® preschool toys Community Vehicles set.
2. Additional blocks.

What might I see children doing?

- Building with Duplo® preschool toys.
- Loading trucks and airplanes.
- Talking.

What might I talk about with children?

1. What could you carry on your train?
2. What else can you make with the Duplo® preschool toys?

BUILDING AT THE AIRPORT
Learning Center (blocks)

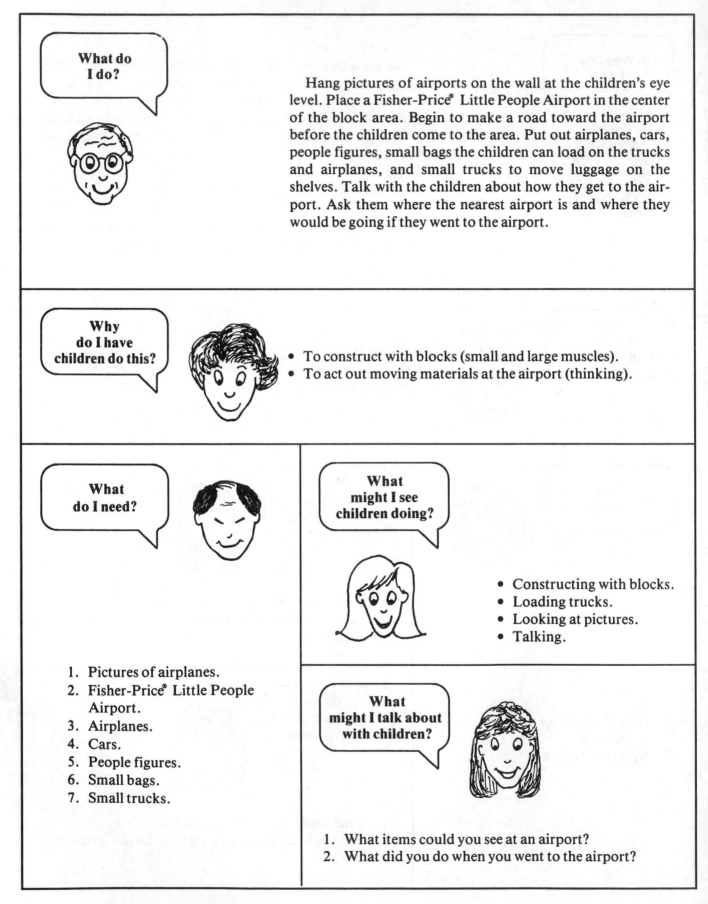

What do I do?

Hang pictures of airports on the wall at the children's eye level. Place a Fisher-Price® Little People Airport in the center of the block area. Begin to make a road toward the airport before the children come to the area. Put out airplanes, cars, people figures, small bags the children can load on the trucks and airplanes, and small trucks to move luggage on the shelves. Talk with the children about how they get to the airport. Ask them where the nearest airport is and where they would be going if they went to the airport.

Why do I have children do this?

- To construct with blocks (small and large muscles).
- To act out moving materials at the airport (thinking).

What do I need?

1. Pictures of airplanes.
2. Fisher-Price® Little People Airport.
3. Airplanes.
4. Cars.
5. People figures.
6. Small bags.
7. Small trucks.

What might I see children doing?

- Constructing with blocks.
- Loading trucks.
- Looking at pictures.
- Talking.

What might I talk about with children?

1. What items could you see at an airport?
2. What did you do when you went to the airport?

TRANSPORTING BUILDING MATERIALS
Learning Center (blocks)

What do I do?

Place Lego® plastic building blocks, people, and vehicles on the floor or table where the children can work with them. Hang pictures of vehicles, roads, rivers, and skies on the wall at the children's eye level where they can look at them as they build. As the children work, talk with them about the different structures and roads. Talk about tall and short buildings, curvy and straight roads, and deep water. Ask the children what they will need to build an airport or road. Ask them how they will get across the lake or what they can haul in the truck.

Why do I have children do this?

- To build with Lego® plastic building blocks (small muscle).
- To select blocks that will make a bridge or building (thinking).

What do I need?

What might I see children doing?

- Looking at pictures.
- Choosing blocks.
- Building structures.
- Talking.

1. Lego® plastic building blocks.
2. Lego® plastic people.
3. Lego® plastic vehicles.
4. Pictures of vehicles, rivers, roads, and skies.

What might I talk about with children?

1. What kinds of buildings can you build with these Lego® plastic building blocks?
2. Where could you go in this car?

LET'S BUILD A BOATHOUSE
Learning Center (blocks)

What do I do?

Hang pictures of boats, boathouses, and docks on the wall at the children's eye level. Add play boats and sheets for sails to the area, so the children can build boats. As the children are building, talk to them about how people dock their boats, where boat docks are located, and how people store their boats in boathouses for the winter in cold areas of the country. Talk about the shapes of the boathouses in the pictures and the shapes of the blocks. Be available to help the children find additional resources to extend their play.

Why do I have children do this?

- To use new words, such as dock and boathouse (thinking, language).
- To build with blocks (small and large muscle).

What do I need?

What might I see children doing?

- Looking at pictures.
- Building with blocks.
- Making sailboats.
- Talking.

1. Pictures of boats, boathouses, and boat docks.
2. Play boats.
3. Sheets.

What might I talk about with children?

1. Where would you like to go on your boat?
2. Where have all the boats been that are at your dock?

CYNTHIA'S SERVICE STATION AND CAR WASH
Learning Center (dramatic play)

What do I do?

Make a gas pump by standing a large cardboard box on end and writing numbers on the front to designate gallons and price. Attach a length of old garden hose to the side and make a nozzle by adding a glass cleaner bottle to the end of the hose. Make a car wash by setting a large refrigerator box on its side and cutting out an opening on either end with an X-Acto® knife. Leave a six-inch frame on the sides and top of the opening. Attach a matchbox to the side for a coin box. Hang fabric strips or yarn from the center of the inside of the box and attach a length of old garden hose to the side. Provide a spray bottle of water and rags or paper towels for cleaning windows. These items could also be used to wash tricycles and wagons outside. Strap empty two-liter plastic bottles to the vehicles to use as gas tanks that can be filled outside. Put out a table with a cash register and give each child play money to pay for the gas and car wash. Put pads of paper on the table for the service station attendant to use as a receipt book.

Why do I have children do this?

- To pretend to wash windows and clean cars (large muscle, thinking).
- To make change and write receipts (thinking, language).

What do I need?

1. Play vehicles.
2. Large cardboard box.
3. Marker.
4. Old garden hose.
5. Glass cleaner bottle.
6. Large refrigerator box.
7. X-Acto® knife.
8. Matchbox.
9. Fabric strips or yarn.
10. Spray bottle of water.
11. Rags or paper towels.
12. Two-liter plastic bottles.
13. Table.
14. Cash register.
15. Play money.
16. Pads of paper.

What might I see children doing?

- Filling cars with gas.
- Making change.
- Washing cars.
- Talking to one another.
- Writing receipts.

What might I talk about with children?

1. What type of vehicles would need to come to Cynthia's Service Station?
2. How do you think people clean big airplanes?

WE TRAVEL BY CAR
Learning Center (dramatic play)

What do I do?

Before the children arrive, lay a large refrigerator box on its side and use duct tape to attach a washing machine box to its top. Cut in a windshield and rear and side windows in the top box with an X-Acto® knife. Make doors in the bottom box by cutting the top, bottom, and one side, leaving a six-inch frame. Leave the side toward the front attached, so the door can be opened and closed. Attach a steering wheel inside the bottom box and put small chairs inside for seats. Attach cardboard pizza servers to the outside as wheels. Cut a trunk in the back to store bags of groceries or suitcases. Let the children decorate the car with markers or tempera paint when they get to the dramatic play area. (Mix liquid detergent in the paint, so the paint will wash out of clothes easier.) Place a large plastic cloth under the car and provide smocks or old dress shirts if the children are using paint. After the paint dries, hang pictures of places cars might travel on the walls at the children's eye level, so the children can see them as they drive along in the car.

Why do I have children do this?

- To paint the car (small muscle, thinking).
- To pretend to drive the car (thinking, social-emotional).

What do I need?

1. Large refrigerator box.
2. Washing machine box.
3. Duct tape.
4. X-Acto® knife.
5. Steering wheel.
6. Chairs.
7. Cardboard pizza servers.
8. Grocery bags.
9. Suitcases.
10. Markers.
11. Tempera paint.
12. Liquid detergent.
13. Paintbrushes.
14. Large plastic cloth.
15. Smocks or old dress shirts.
16. Pictures of places where cars may go.

What might I see children doing?

- Putting suitcases in the trunk.
- Driving the car.
- Talking about their trip.
- Laughing.

What might I talk about with children?

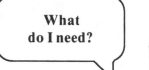

1. What are you taking on your trip?
2. When are you going on your vacation?

A RIDE ON THE SINGING BUS
Learning Center (dramatic play)

What do I do?

To extend the music activity " 'Wheels on the Bus,' " on page 467, set out suitcases, clothes, diapers, doll, and baby bottle. Make a ticket counter from a table and add tickets and a cash register for the ticket agent. Let the bus driver collect the tickets the passengers have bought. Talk with the children about how luggage is often stored in a compartment under the bus or may go under their seats. Let them put their luggage in the appropriate place. Talk with the children about where they plan to go on the bus.

Why do I have children do this?

- To pretend to ride a bus (social-emotional, thinking).
- To store their luggage in the luggage compartment (small muscle).
- To use new words, such as ticket agent and luggage compartment (language).

What do I need?

1. Suitcases.
2. Clothes.
3. Diapers.
4. Doll.
5. Baby bottle.
6. Table.
7. Tickets.
8. Cash register.

What might I see children doing?

- Buying tickets.
- Putting suitcases in luggage compartment.
- Sitting on bus.
- Singing "Wheels on the Bus."
- Enjoying the bus.

What might I talk about with children?

1. Where are you going on this bus?
2. What towns will you go through on your way to Grandma and Grandpa's?

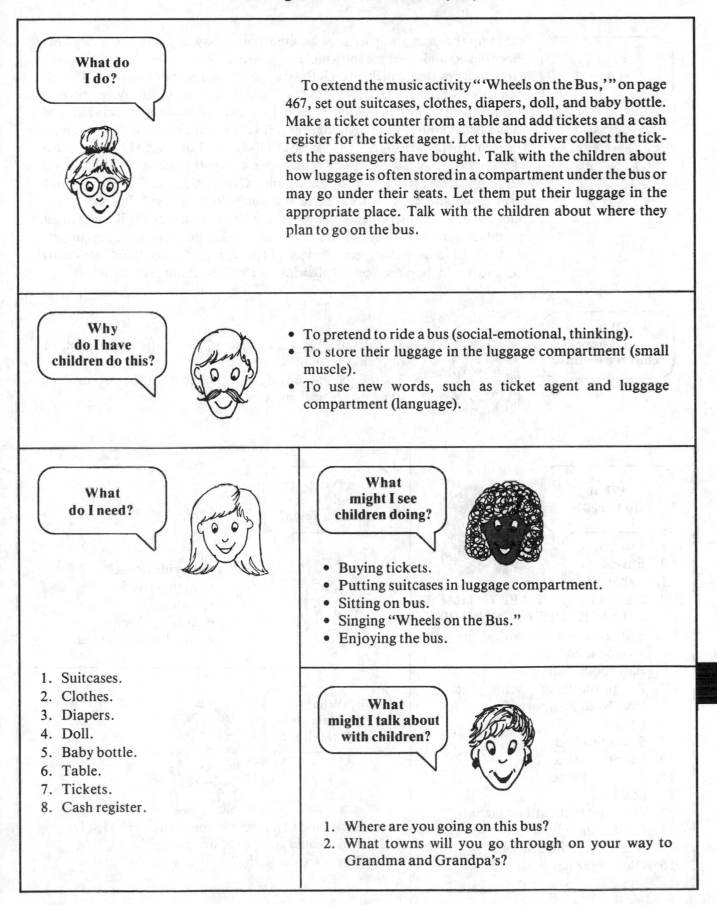

LET'S GET ON AN AIRPLANE
Learning Center (dramatic play)

What do I do?

Set up the dramatic play area as an airport lobby and adjoining airplane. Place tickets and envelopes on a table to make a ticket counter where the passengers can check in and pick up their tickets. Hang a sign saying "HAPPY TIMES AIRLINES TICKET COUNTER" above the ticket counter. Provide suitcases or boxes with string tied around them for luggage. Set out a bathroom scale next to the ticket counter to weigh luggage. Have the children bring the passports they made in the writing activity "We Need Passports" on page 477. Set up a row of chairs for the cabin of the airplane. Set up another chair in front with a steering wheel in front of it for the cockpit. Using an X-Acto® knife, cut up a large cardboard box, so it has three adjoining sides and set it in front of the pilot's seat. Draw instruments on it and cut out windows. Set out pilot and flight attendant hats. Let the flight attendants use cookie sheets to serve real or pretend snacks to the passengers. Provide old magazines for the flight attendants to hand out to the passengers. Talk with the children about these activities.

Why do I have children do this?

- To role-play being a passenger, flight attendant, pilot, or ticket agent (thinking).
- To talk about buying a ticket and riding an airplane (language, social-emotional).

What do I need?

1. Tickets.
2. Envelopes.
3. Table.
4. Sign saying "HAPPY TIMES AIRLINES TICKET COUNTER."
5. Suitcases or boxes with string tied around them.
6. Bathroom scale.
7. Passports from writing activity "We Need Passports."
8. Chairs.
9. Steering wheel.
10. Cardboard box.
11. X-Acto® knife.
12. Markers.
13. Pilot and flight attendant hats.
14. Cookie sheets.
15. Real or pretend snacks.
16. Old magazines.

What might I see children doing?

- Buying tickets.
- Eating snacks.
- Talking.
- Storing luggage.
- Reading magazines.

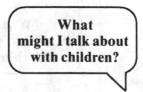

What might I talk about with children?

1. What kind of magazine would you like to read?
2. What would you like to drink?
3. Where are you going?

LET'S TAKE OFF TO OUTER SPACE
Learning Center (dramatic play)

What do I do?

Turn a large cardboard box into a spaceship by using an X-Acto® knife to cut windows in two sides and a flap window in a third side. On the remaining side, cut a door six inches from the top and sides, leaving the bottom attached and reinforcing it with duct tape. Punch holes in the flap window and door and attach yarn, so the children can open and close them. Take the box and spray paint it with silver paint. After the paint dries, bring the box back inside and draw an instrument panel on the inside of the spaceship. Make a radio transmitter by attaching a large matchbox to the instrument panel with yarn. Make oxygen packs by taping two 2-liter bottles together and attaching yarn for shoulder straps. Make vests by slitting the entire front of a grocery bag and making a circle in the bottom of the bag for the child's head and slits in the sides for his or her arms. Let the children decorate the vests with space patches or pictures. Put a cot and blanket in the spaceship. Set up a table with a radio for ground control. Have the children tell you by radio what they see, feel, and hear as they travel in space. Talk with the children about trips in space being long.

Why do I have children do this?

- To role-play being astronauts (social-emotional).
- To talk about space travel (language).

What do I need?

1. Large cardboard box.
2. X-Acto® knife.
3. Duct tape.
4. Hole punch.
5. Yarn.
6. Silver spray paint.
7. Markers.
8. Large matchbox.
9. Two-liter bottles.
10. Scissors.
11. Grocery bags.
12. Space patches or pictures.
13. Cot.
14. Blanket.
15. Table.
16. Radio.

What might I see children doing?

- Pretending to be astronauts.
- Decorating vests.
- Looking at pictures.
- Putting on space gear.

What might I talk about with children?

1. What will you need to take on a long trip in space?
2. What will you see when you are in outer space?

"AN ADVENTURE IN SPACE"
Learning Centers (dramatic play)

What do I do?

After the children have completed the dramatic play activity "Let's Take Off to Outer Space" on page 453, play the musical recording "An Adventure in Space" from *On the Move with Greg and Steve*. Talk with the children about what is happening on the musical recording. Then let the children act out a trip to space and the landing of their spacecraft while listening to the recording again. Practice the countdown 3-2-1-Blast-off! Hang pictures of outer space on the wall at the children's eye level, so they can imagine that they are flying through space. Emphasize that you need special clothes for special times, such as coats for cold weather and space suits for space travel. Discuss why people need oxygen tanks in outer space and suits to protect them from the heat and cold in outer space.

Why do I have children do this?

- To act out "An Adventure in Space" (thinking, language).
- To talk about space, space suits, and gravity (language).

What do I need?

1. Spaceship and materials from the dramatic play activity "Let's Take Off to Outer Space."
2. "An Adventure in Space" from *On the Move with Greg and Steve.*
3. Record player or cassette tape player.
4. Pictures of outer space.

What might I see children doing?

- Listening to the musical recording.
- Acting out a trip to space.
- Counting down for take-off.
- Talking.

What might I talk about with children?

1. What will you need to take on a trip to outer space?
2. What would you like to do if you could go to outer space?

TRANSPORTATION FRUIT SALAD
Learning Center (food)

What do I do?

Talk with the children about how fruit gets to the local grocery store. Bananas often come from South America on a boat, strawberries from California on an airplane, and oranges from Florida on a truck or train. The older children will understand this better. Use a globe or map to point out the locations mentioned. Most fruit in the grocery store is delivered directly to the store by truck, and then people go to the store in a car and bring it home. Talk with the children about fruit that grows in local gardens or on local farms. Then work with the children to make a fruit salad together. Before you begin preparing the fruit salad, collect all the supplies and make sure you and the children wash your hands. Set out oranges, apples, bananas, and kiwis, or another unusual fruit. Put out plates and let each child use a heavy-duty, serrated plastic knife to cut pieces of fruit to put in a large bowl. Chill the fruit salad in the refrigerator until lunch or snacktime. Let each child spoon out his or her serving onto a plate. As you eat, talk about the crisp apple, the juicy orange, the soft banana, and the cool kiwi. Talk about the colors of the orange, apple, banana, and kiwi.

Why do I have children do this?

- To cut fruit into pieces for fruit salad (small muscle).
- To use new words, such as crisp, juicy, soft, and cool (language).

What do I need?

1. Oranges.
2. Apples.
3. Bananas.
4. Kiwis.
5. Plates.
6. Heavy-duty serrated plastic knives.
7. Large bowl.
8. Large spoon.

What might I see children doing?

- Looking at fruit.
- Cutting fruit.
- Putting fruit in large bowl.
- Tasting fruit.
- Talking.

What might I talk about with children?

1. What fruit do you eat at home?
2. Where does your family get its fruit?

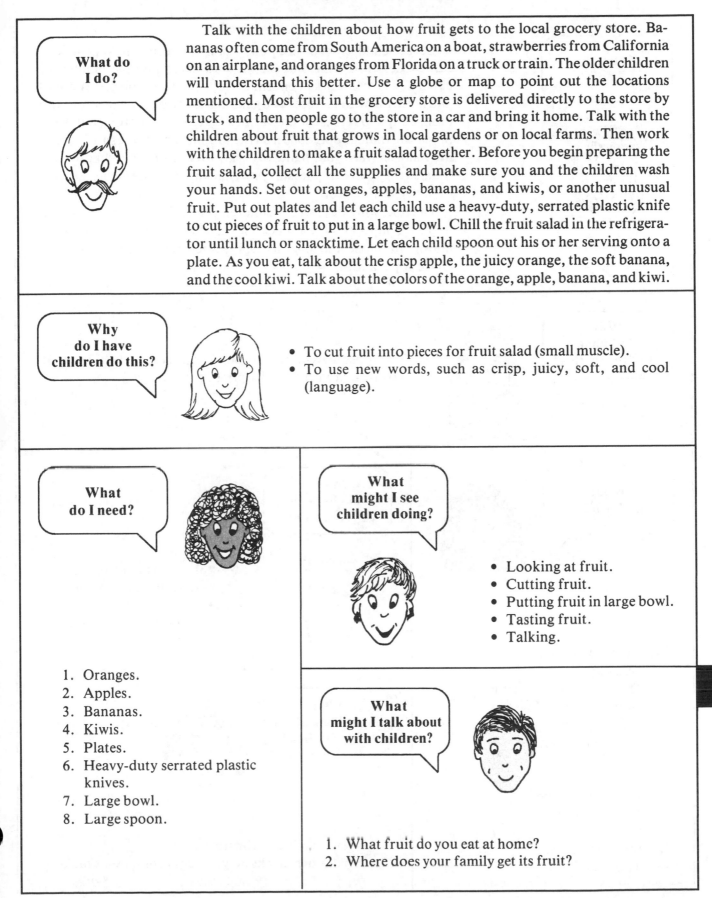

LET'S DRIVE TO THE ICE POP STAND
Learning Center (food, dramatic play)

What do I do?

Let the children make ice pops, using the recipe in Appendix B. Put two or three chairs at the table to determine the number of children who can work at one time. Copy the recipe on poster board and illustrate with pictures of a gelatin box, two clear cups, and two orange cups to represent the various ingredients. Before you begin preparing the ice pops, collect all the supplies and make sure you and the children wash your hands. Work with two or three children at a time, so they can each measure, stir, and dip the ingredients. Discuss each step as they work.

The following day, let the children pretend that they are driving to the ice pop stand for a snack. Set up chairs with a steering wheel in front of one seat to make a car. Place ice pops on a table to make an ice pop stand.

Why do I have children do this?

- To choose ingredients in order from recipe chart (thinking).
- To mix ingredients for ice pops (small muscle).

What do I need?

What might I see children doing?

- Looking at recipe.
- Opening gelatin box.
- Pouring gelatin.
- Pouring orange juice.
- Mixing ice pops.

1. Poster board.
2. Markers.
3. Orange-flavored gelatin.
4. Bowl.
5. Boiling water.
6. Wooden spoon.
7. Orange juice.
8. Ladle.
9. Five-ounce paper cups.
10. Ice pop sticks.
11. Chairs.
12. Steering wheel.
13. Table.

What might I talk about with children?

1. What is your favorite treat?
2. What other snacks do you help your parents make?

TRANSPORTATION MATCH-UP
Learning Center (library, manipulatives)

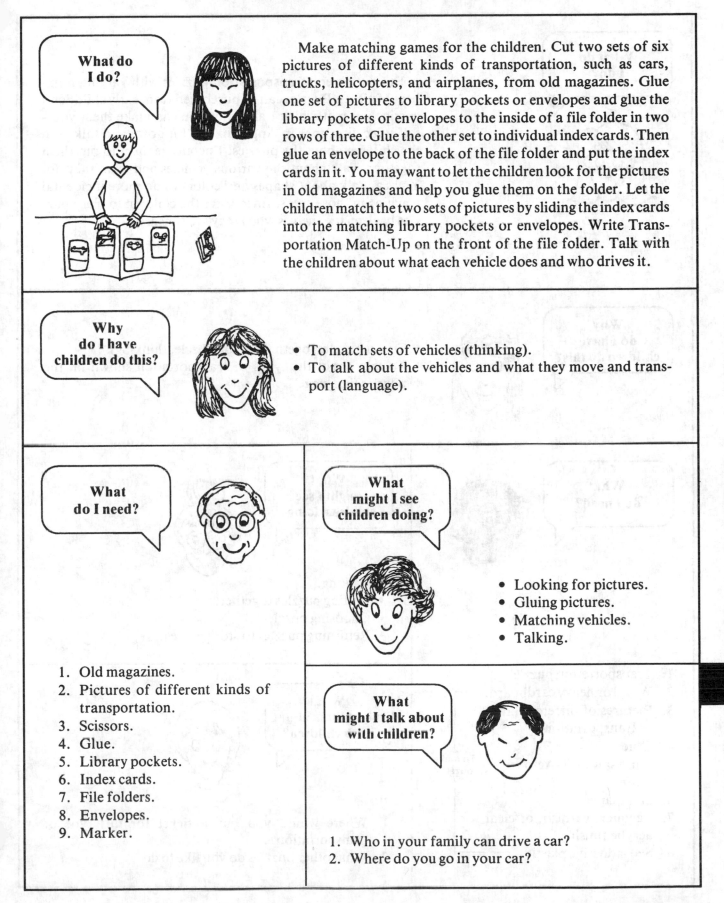

What do I do?

Make matching games for the children. Cut two sets of six pictures of different kinds of transportation, such as cars, trucks, helicopters, and airplanes, from old magazines. Glue one set of pictures to library pockets or envelopes and glue the library pockets or envelopes to the inside of a file folder in two rows of three. Glue the other set to individual index cards. Then glue an envelope to the back of the file folder and put the index cards in it. You may want to let the children look for the pictures in old magazines and help you glue them on the folder. Let the children match the two sets of pictures by sliding the index cards into the matching library pockets or envelopes. Write Transportation Match-Up on the front of the file folder. Talk with the children about what each vehicle does and who drives it.

Why do I have children do this?

- To match sets of vehicles (thinking).
- To talk about the vehicles and what they move and transport (language).

What do I need?

1. Old magazines.
2. Pictures of different kinds of transportation.
3. Scissors.
4. Glue.
5. Library pockets.
6. Index cards.
7. File folders.
8. Envelopes.
9. Marker.

What might I see children doing?

- Looking for pictures.
- Gluing pictures.
- Matching vehicles.
- Talking.

What might I talk about with children?

1. Who in your family can drive a car?
2. Where do you go in your car?

TRANSPORTATION PUZZLES
Learning Center (manipulatives)

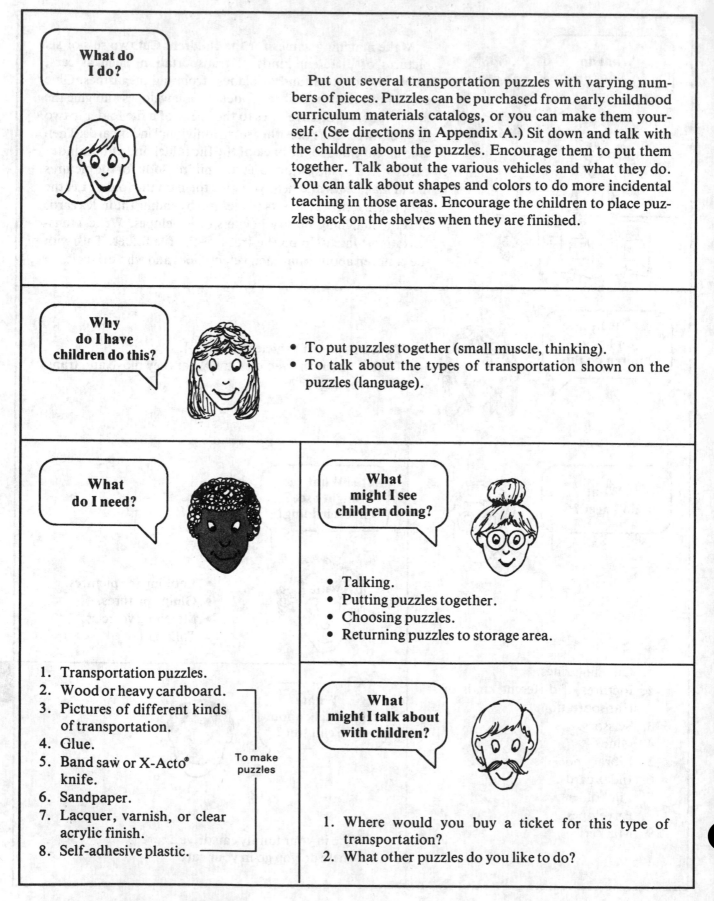

What do I do?

Put out several transportation puzzles with varying numbers of pieces. Puzzles can be purchased from early childhood curriculum materials catalogs, or you can make them yourself. (See directions in Appendix A.) Sit down and talk with the children about the puzzles. Encourage them to put them together. Talk about the various vehicles and what they do. You can talk about shapes and colors to do more incidental teaching in those areas. Encourage the children to place puzzles back on the shelves when they are finished.

Why do I have children do this?

- To put puzzles together (small muscle, thinking).
- To talk about the types of transportation shown on the puzzles (language).

What do I need?

1. Transportation puzzles.
2. Wood or heavy cardboard.
3. Pictures of different kinds of transportation.
4. Glue.
5. Band saw or X-Acto® knife.
6. Sandpaper.
7. Lacquer, varnish, or clear acrylic finish.
8. Self-adhesive plastic.

To make puzzles

What might I see children doing?

- Talking.
- Putting puzzles together.
- Choosing puzzles.
- Returning puzzles to storage area.

What might I talk about with children?

1. Where would you buy a ticket for this type of transportation?
2. What other puzzles do you like to do?

TRANSPORTATION LACING CARDS
Learning Centers (manipulatives)

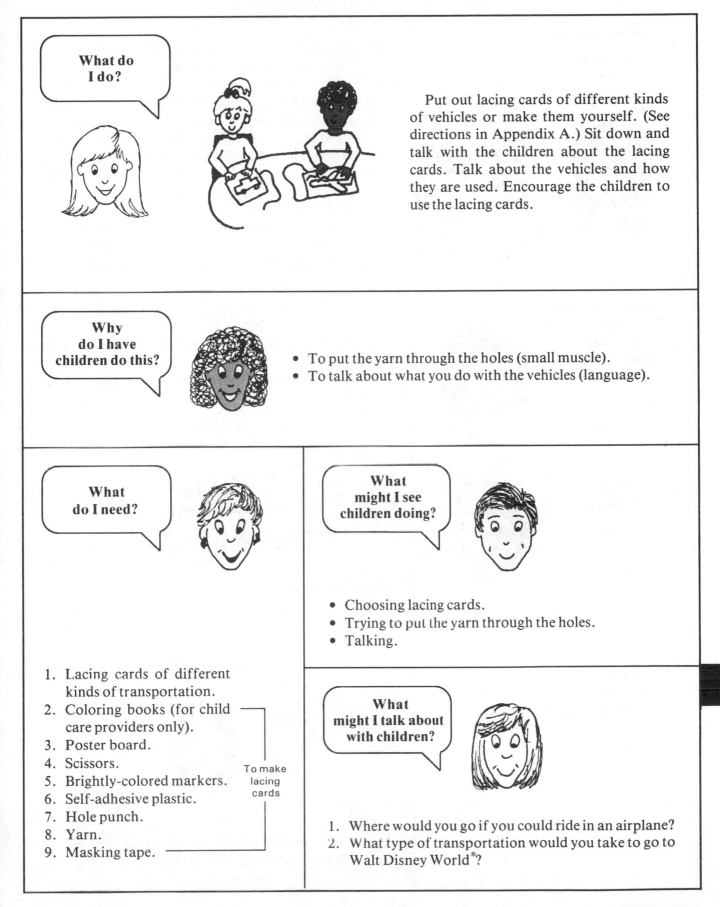

What do I do?

Put out lacing cards of different kinds of vehicles or make them yourself. (See directions in Appendix A.) Sit down and talk with the children about the lacing cards. Talk about the vehicles and how they are used. Encourage the children to use the lacing cards.

Why do I have children do this?

- To put the yarn through the holes (small muscle).
- To talk about what you do with the vehicles (language).

What do I need?

1. Lacing cards of different kinds of transportation.
2. Coloring books (for child care providers only).
3. Poster board.
4. Scissors.
5. Brightly-colored markers.
6. Self-adhesive plastic.
7. Hole punch.
8. Yarn.
9. Masking tape.

To make lacing cards

What might I see children doing?

- Choosing lacing cards.
- Trying to put the yarn through the holes.
- Talking.

What might I talk about with children?

1. Where would you go if you could ride in an airplane?
2. What type of transportation would you take to go to Walt Disney World®?

WHERE DO I BELONG—WATER, AIR, LAND, OR SPACE?
Learning Center (manipulatives)

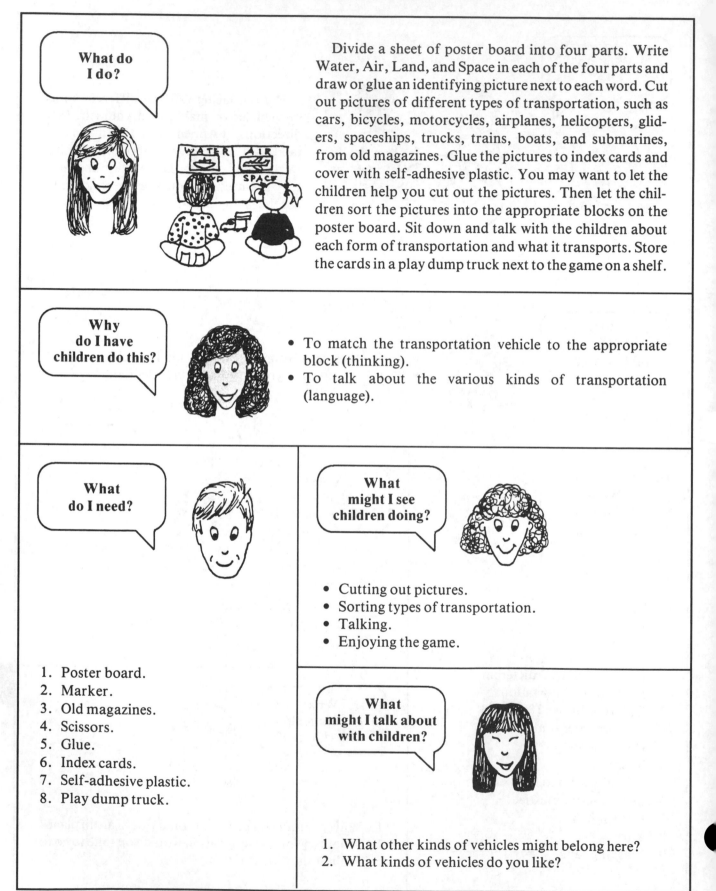

What do I do?

Divide a sheet of poster board into four parts. Write Water, Air, Land, and Space in each of the four parts and draw or glue an identifying picture next to each word. Cut out pictures of different types of transportation, such as cars, bicycles, motorcycles, airplanes, helicopters, gliders, spaceships, trucks, trains, boats, and submarines, from old magazines. Glue the pictures to index cards and cover with self-adhesive plastic. You may want to let the children help you cut out the pictures. Then let the children sort the pictures into the appropriate blocks on the poster board. Sit down and talk with the children about each form of transportation and what it transports. Store the cards in a play dump truck next to the game on a shelf.

Why do I have children do this?

- To match the transportation vehicle to the appropriate block (thinking).
- To talk about the various kinds of transportation (language).

What do I need?

1. Poster board.
2. Marker.
3. Old magazines.
4. Scissors.
5. Glue.
6. Index cards.
7. Self-adhesive plastic.
8. Play dump truck.

What might I see children doing?

- Cutting out pictures.
- Sorting types of transportation.
- Talking.
- Enjoying the game.

What might I talk about with children?

1. What other kinds of vehicles might belong here?
2. What kinds of vehicles do you like?

CAN YOU FIND THE RED GARAGE?
Learning Center (manipulatives)

What do I do?

Cover eight half-pint milk cartons with red, yellow, green, blue, brown, black, purple, and orange construction paper. Make them into garages by cutting open one side of each milk carton, leaving the bottom attached. Collect eight small cars that are the same colors as the garages. Then let the children match the cars to the garages by color. You can also ask them to put the yellow car in the yellow garage. Ask them to find other objects in the room that are the same color as the car they are holding.

Why do I have children do this?

- To match a red car and a red garage (thinking).
- To recognize other objects in the room that are the same color (thinking).

What do I need?

1. Eight half-pint milk cartons.
2. Red, yellow, green, blue, brown, black, purple, and orange construction paper.
3. Scissors.
4. Red, yellow, green, blue, brown, black, purple, and orange small cars.

What might I see children doing?

- Pushing cars.
- Matching cars to same-colored garage.
- Finding same-colored items in room.

What might I talk about with children?

1. Where would you like to go in this car if you could choose a place?
2. What colors were the cars you saw this morning?

TRANSPORTATION FELT BOARD FUN
Learning Center (manipulatives)

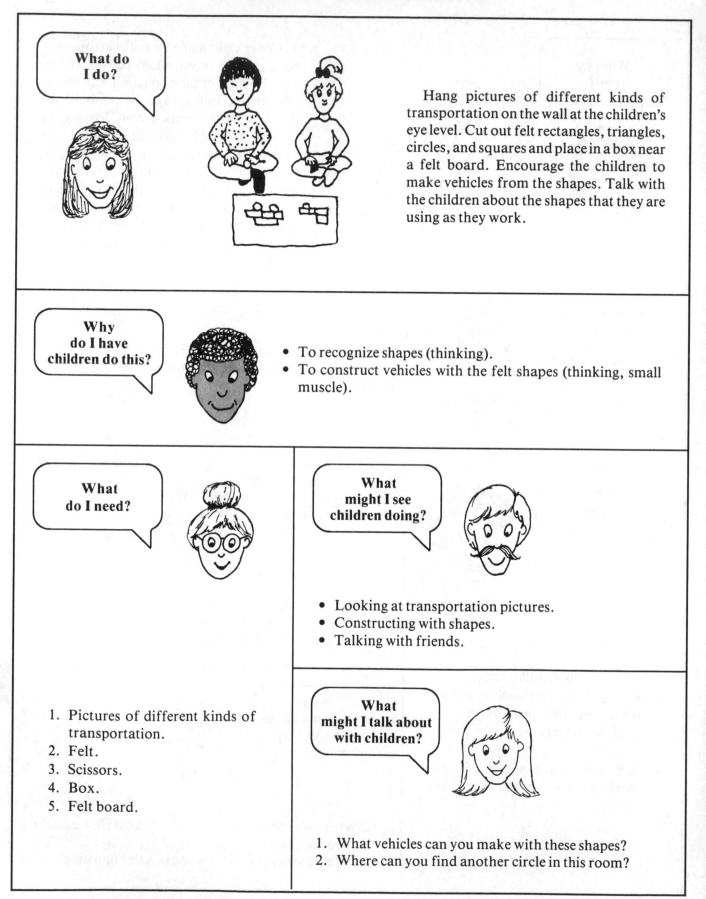

What do I do?

Hang pictures of different kinds of transportation on the wall at the children's eye level. Cut out felt rectangles, triangles, circles, and squares and place in a box near a felt board. Encourage the children to make vehicles from the shapes. Talk with the children about the shapes that they are using as they work.

Why do I have children do this?

- To recognize shapes (thinking).
- To construct vehicles with the felt shapes (thinking, small muscle).

What do I need?

1. Pictures of different kinds of transportation.
2. Felt.
3. Scissors.
4. Box.
5. Felt board.

What might I see children doing?

- Looking at transportation pictures.
- Constructing with shapes.
- Talking with friends.

What might I talk about with children?

1. What vehicles can you make with these shapes?
2. Where can you find another circle in this room?

LOADING THE TRUCKS
Learning Center (math)

What do I do?

Place a container full of cotton balls on the table with sets of ice tongs. Collect one to ten small trucks depending upon the development of the children. Start with one to five trucks for two- and three-year-olds. On index cards, draw one to five circles and tape one card to the side of each truck. For the four- and five-year-olds, write the numerals 1 to 10 on individual index cards with the corresponding number of circles. Tape one card to the side of each truck. The two- and three-year-olds can use the ice tongs to match the correct number of cotton balls to the circles on the trucks. The four- and five-year-olds can match the correct number of cotton balls to the numerals and corresponding circles on the trucks. The children will be matching the number of circles and cotton balls before they will recognize the numerals. This is appropriate for them. Talk with the children about matching the cotton balls to the circles, choosing the correct numeral, and the softness of the cotton balls.

Why do I have children do this?

- To pick up cotton balls with ice tongs (small muscle).
- To match objects with objects and objects with numerals (thinking).

What do I need?

What might I see children doing?

- Picking up cotton balls.
- Matching number of cotton balls to number of balls on truck.

1. Container.
2. Cotton balls.
3. Ice tongs.
4. Small trucks.
5. Index cards.
6. Marker.
7. Tape.

What might I talk about with children?

1. What else could you move in this truck?
2. Where will the driver take these cotton balls?

BIG TRUCKS, LITTLE TRUCKS
Learning Center (math)

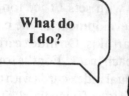

What do I do?

Place several big trucks and little trucks on the floor or table. Write the word "Big" on a copy paper box lid and "Little" on a shoe box lid and put both lids on the floor or table. Sit down and talk with the children about the different-sized trucks. Talk to them about what the driver might haul in his or her truck. See if the children can sort the big and little trucks onto the appropriate lids. Then see if they can locate a big chair and a little chair, a big book and a little book, and a big block and a little block in your child care home or center.

Why do I have children do this?

- To classify big and little items (thinking).
- To talk about what could be hauled in the different-sized trucks (thinking, language).

What do I need?

What might I see children doing?

- Sorting big and little trucks.
- Talking.
- Looking for big and little items in the room.

What might I talk about with children?

1. Big trucks.
2. Little trucks.
3. Copy paper box lid.
4. Shoe box lid.
5. Marker.

1. What does the driver haul in his or her truck?
2. What other objects in this room are big?
3. What other objects in this room are little?

LET'S GO FISHING IN MY BOAT
Learning Center (math, dramatic play)

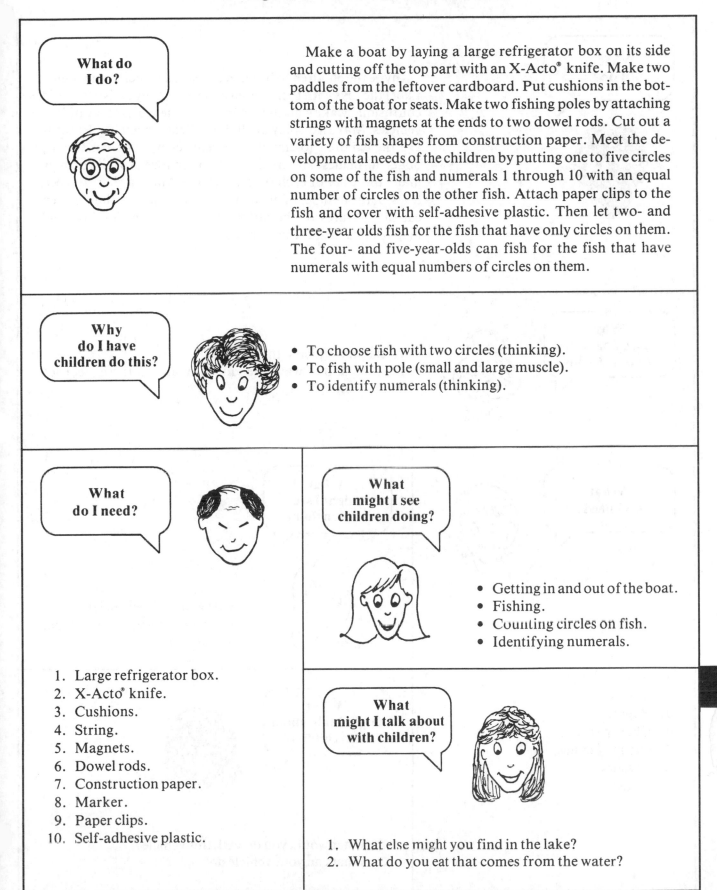

What do I do?

Make a boat by laying a large refrigerator box on its side and cutting off the top part with an X-Acto® knife. Make two paddles from the leftover cardboard. Put cushions in the bottom of the boat for seats. Make two fishing poles by attaching strings with magnets at the ends to two dowel rods. Cut out a variety of fish shapes from construction paper. Meet the developmental needs of the children by putting one to five circles on some of the fish and numerals 1 through 10 with an equal number of circles on the other fish. Attach paper clips to the fish and cover with self-adhesive plastic. Then let two- and three-year olds fish for the fish that have only circles on them. The four- and five-year-olds can fish for the fish that have numerals with equal numbers of circles on them.

Why do I have children do this?

- To choose fish with two circles (thinking).
- To fish with pole (small and large muscle).
- To identify numerals (thinking).

What do I need?

1. Large refrigerator box.
2. X-Acto® knife.
3. Cushions.
4. String.
5. Magnets.
6. Dowel rods.
7. Construction paper.
8. Marker.
9. Paper clips.
10. Self-adhesive plastic.

What might I see children doing?

- Getting in and out of the boat.
- Fishing.
- Counting circles on fish.
- Identifying numerals.

What might I talk about with children?

1. What else might you find in the lake?
2. What do you eat that comes from the water?

HOW MANY VEHICLES ARE THERE?
Learning Center (math)

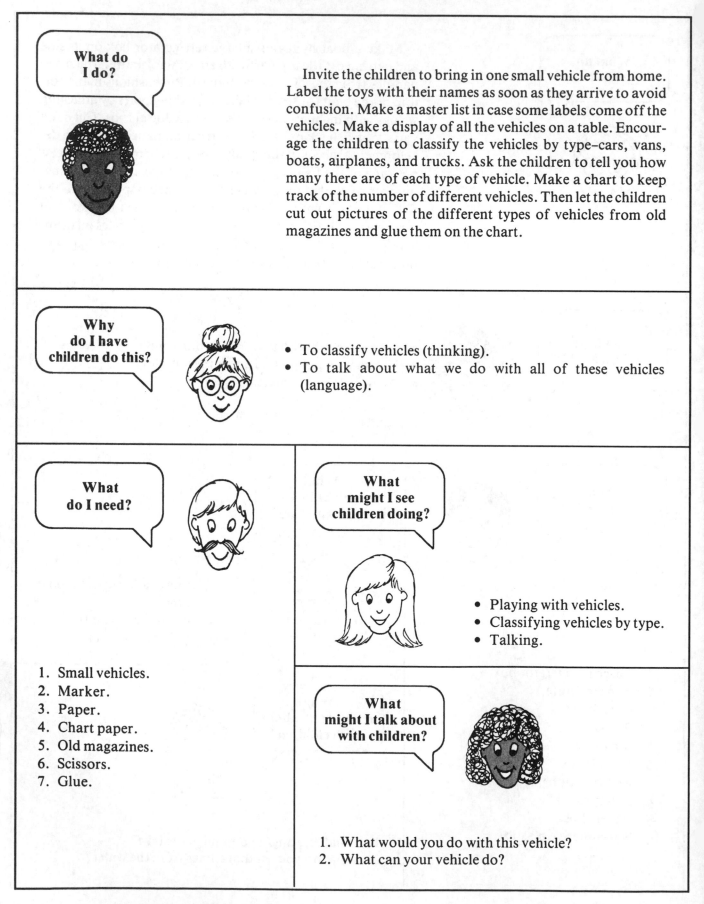

What do I do?

Invite the children to bring in one small vehicle from home. Label the toys with their names as soon as they arrive to avoid confusion. Make a master list in case some labels come off the vehicles. Make a display of all the vehicles on a table. Encourage the children to classify the vehicles by type–cars, vans, boats, airplanes, and trucks. Ask the children to tell you how many there are of each type of vehicle. Make a chart to keep track of the number of different vehicles. Then let the children cut out pictures of the different types of vehicles from old magazines and glue them on the chart.

Why do I have children do this?

- To classify vehicles (thinking).
- To talk about what we do with all of these vehicles (language).

What do I need?

1. Small vehicles.
2. Marker.
3. Paper.
4. Chart paper.
5. Old magazines.
6. Scissors.
7. Glue.

What might I see children doing?

- Playing with vehicles.
- Classifying vehicles by type.
- Talking.

What might I talk about with children?

1. What would you do with this vehicle?
2. What can your vehicle do?

"WHEELS ON THE BUS"
Learning Center (music, dramatic play)

What do I do?

Set up rows of chairs with a steering wheel in front of one seat to make a bus. Sing the following song and let the children act out the verses. Let the children suggest additional verses.

"Wheels on a Bus"

1. The wheels on the bus go round and round,
   Round and round, round and round.
   The wheels on the bus go round and round
   All through the town.
2. The driver on the bus says, "Move to the back."
3. The baby on the bus says "Wah, wah, wah."
4. The mommy on the bus says, "Look, look, look."
5. The children on the bus say, "Go, go, go."

Why do I have children do this?

- To select different actions to role-play (thinking).
- To enjoy singing (social-emotional).

What do I need?

1. Chairs.
2. Steering wheel.
3. Words to song written on an index card.

What might I see children doing?

- Singing.
- Role-playing.
- Laughing.
- Pretending to drive bus.
- Talking.

What might I talk about with children?

1. What else might people do on the bus?
2. Where could you go on the bus?

"FLY WITH US"
Learning Center (music), Group

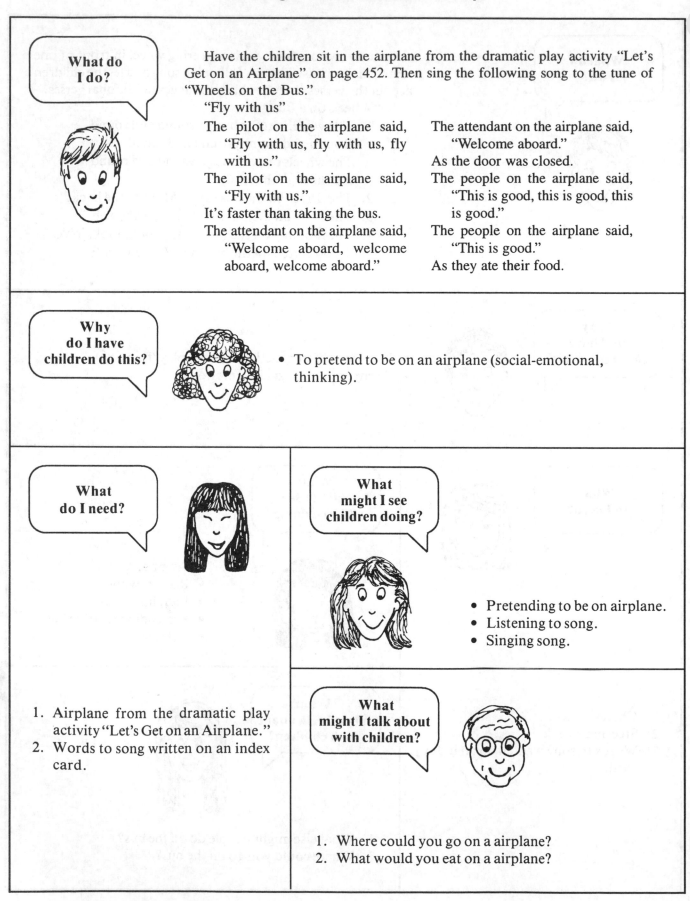

What do I do?

Have the children sit in the airplane from the dramatic play activity "Let's Get on an Airplane" on page 452. Then sing the following song to the tune of "Wheels on the Bus."

"Fly with us"

The pilot on the airplane said, "Fly with us, fly with us, fly with us."
The pilot on the airplane said, "Fly with us."
It's faster than taking the bus.
The attendant on the airplane said, "Welcome aboard, welcome aboard, welcome aboard."

The attendant on the airplane said, "Welcome aboard."
As the door was closed.
The people on the airplane said, "This is good, this is good, this is good."
The people on the airplane said, "This is good."
As they ate their food.

Why do I have children do this?

- To pretend to be on an airplane (social-emotional, thinking).

What do I need?

What might I see children doing?

- Pretending to be on airplane.
- Listening to song.
- Singing song.

1. Airplane from the dramatic play activity "Let's Get on an Airplane."
2. Words to song written on an index card.

What might I talk about with children?

1. Where could you go on a airplane?
2. What would you eat on a airplane?

MAKING ROADS
Learning Center (sand)

What do I do?

Put a steam shovel, small shovels, rakes, and buckets in the sandbox along with several kinds of small vehicles. Talk with the children about how the vehicles move and what they need to move on. Talk about the different kinds of roads, such as city streets, rural roads, turnpikes, and expressways. Talk about how airplanes use roads called runways. Encourage the children to build roads. Be available to help the children build different types of roads and structures, such as bridges and tunnels. Put out paper, markers, and short dowel rods, so the children can make traffic and direction signs, such as STOP, AIRPORT, and TAXI STAND.

Why do I have children do this?

- To dig sand to build roads and runways (small and large muscles).
- To make signs to use on their roads and buildings (language).

What do I need?

What might I see children doing?

- Digging sand.
- Making signs.
- Talking.
- Playing with vehicles.

1. Steam shovel.
2. Shovels.
3. Rakes.
4. Buckets.
5. Small vehicles.
6. Paper.
7. Markers.
8. Dowel rods.

What might I talk about with children?

1. What could you use to make a bridge?
2. How can the truck get to the airport?

TRAVEL THROUGH THE SANDBOX
Learning Center (sand)

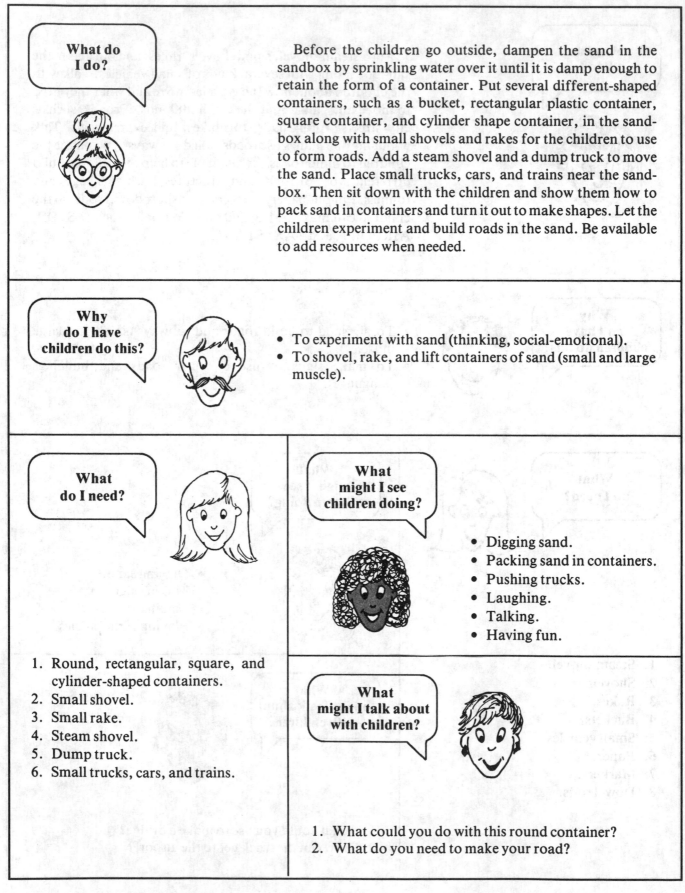

What do I do?

Before the children go outside, dampen the sand in the sandbox by sprinkling water over it until it is damp enough to retain the form of a container. Put several different-shaped containers, such as a bucket, rectangular plastic container, square container, and cylinder shape container, in the sandbox along with small shovels and rakes for the children to use to form roads. Add a steam shovel and a dump truck to move the sand. Place small trucks, cars, and trains near the sandbox. Then sit down with the children and show them how to pack sand in containers and turn it out to make shapes. Let the children experiment and build roads in the sand. Be available to add resources when needed.

Why do I have children do this?

- To experiment with sand (thinking, social-emotional).
- To shovel, rake, and lift containers of sand (small and large muscle).

What do I need?

1. Round, rectangular, square, and cylinder-shaped containers.
2. Small shovel.
3. Small rake.
4. Steam shovel.
5. Dump truck.
6. Small trucks, cars, and trains.

What might I see children doing?

- Digging sand.
- Packing sand in containers.
- Pushing trucks.
- Laughing.
- Talking.
- Having fun.

What might I talk about with children?

1. What could you do with this round container?
2. What do you need to make your road?

HAULING A LOAD UP THE MOUNTAIN
Learning Center (science)

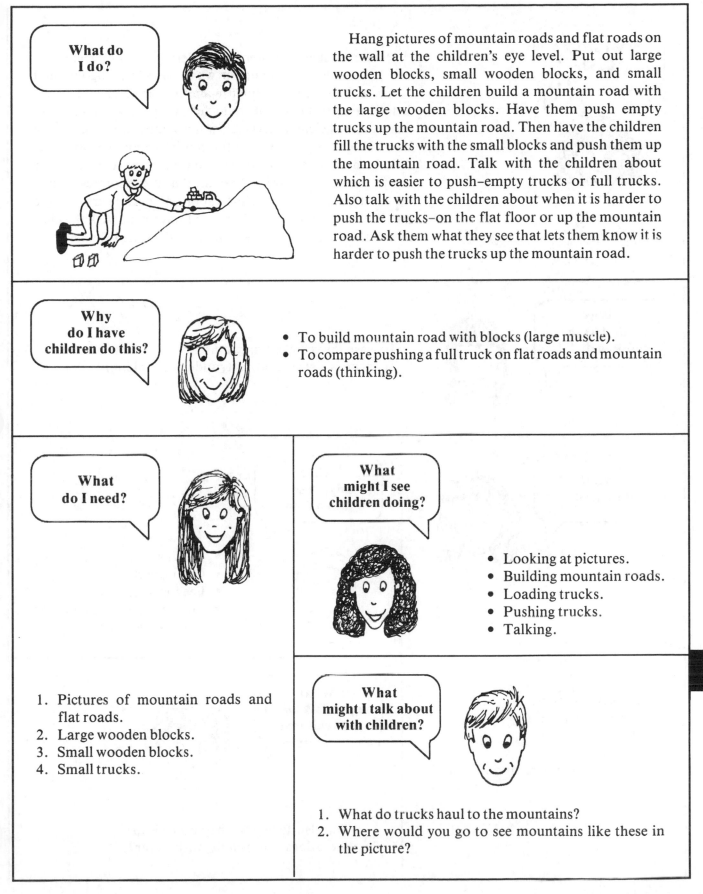

What do I do?

Hang pictures of mountain roads and flat roads on the wall at the children's eye level. Put out large wooden blocks, small wooden blocks, and small trucks. Let the children build a mountain road with the large wooden blocks. Have them push empty trucks up the mountain road. Then have the children fill the trucks with the small blocks and push them up the mountain road. Talk with the children about which is easier to push–empty trucks or full trucks. Also talk with the children about when it is harder to push the trucks–on the flat floor or up the mountain road. Ask them what they see that lets them know it is harder to push the trucks up the mountain road.

Why do I have children do this?

- To build mountain road with blocks (large muscle).
- To compare pushing a full truck on flat roads and mountain roads (thinking).

What do I need?

1. Pictures of mountain roads and flat roads.
2. Large wooden blocks.
3. Small wooden blocks.
4. Small trucks.

What might I see children doing?

- Looking at pictures.
- Building mountain roads.
- Loading trucks.
- Pushing trucks.
- Talking.

What might I talk about with children?

1. What do trucks haul to the mountains?
2. Where would you go to see mountains like these in the picture?

SCIENCE AT THE CAR WASH
Learning Center (science)

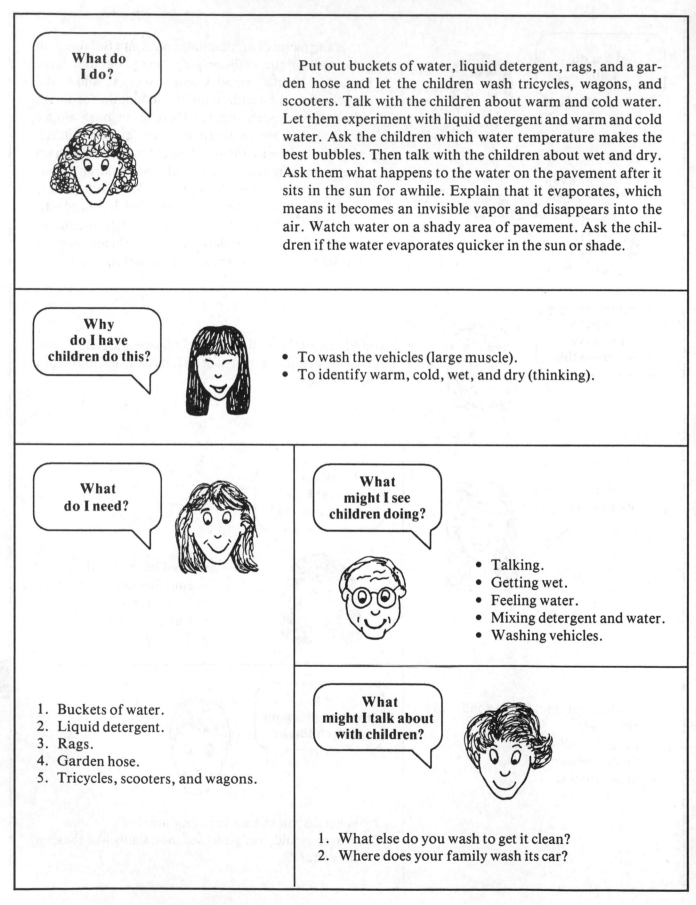

What do I do?

Put out buckets of water, liquid detergent, rags, and a garden hose and let the children wash tricycles, wagons, and scooters. Talk with the children about warm and cold water. Let them experiment with liquid detergent and warm and cold water. Ask the children which water temperature makes the best bubbles. Then talk with the children about wet and dry. Ask them what happens to the water on the pavement after it sits in the sun for awhile. Explain that it evaporates, which means it becomes an invisible vapor and disappears into the air. Watch water on a shady area of pavement. Ask the children if the water evaporates quicker in the sun or shade.

Why do I have children do this?

- To wash the vehicles (large muscle).
- To identify warm, cold, wet, and dry (thinking).

What do I need?

1. Buckets of water.
2. Liquid detergent.
3. Rags.
4. Garden hose.
5. Tricycles, scooters, and wagons.

What might I see children doing?

- Talking.
- Getting wet.
- Feeling water.
- Mixing detergent and water.
- Washing vehicles.

What might I talk about with children?

1. What else do you wash to get it clean?
2. Where does your family wash its car?

BUBBLES FLY
Learning Center (water play)

What do I do?

Provide commercial bubble mix or make bubble mix yourself by mixing 1 quart of tap water, 2/3 cup of liquid soap, and 1/3 cup of glycerin. Divide the mixture into small bowls. Provide a bubble pipe, straw, tube, funnel, or plastic strawberry basket for each child to use to blow bubbles. Let the children blow bubbles and watch them fly. Let them chase the bubbles and talk about their adventures. Then sit down with the children and talk about other items that fly, such as butterflies, birds, and airplanes.

Why do I have children do this?

- To try blowing bubbles with different equipment (thinking).
- To enjoy blowing bubbles (social-emotional).
- To chase the bubbles (large muscles).

What do I need?

What might I see children doing?

- Choosing a bubble blower.
- Dipping blower into bubble liquid.
- Watching bubbles fly.
- Laughing.
- Chasing bubbles.

1. Commercial bubble mix.
2. Tap water.
3. Liquid soap.
4. Glycerin.
5. Bubble pipes.
6. Straws.
7. Tubes.
8. Funnels.
9. Plastic strawberry baskets.

What might I talk about with children?

1. Where do you think the bubble will go?
2. Where would you like to go if you could fly like a bubble?

SAILING ACROSS THE LAKE
Learning Center (water play)

What do I do?

Fill the water table or a tub with water and add blue food coloring. Make sailboats by gluing paper triangles to straws. Then glue the straws to the sides of small margarine tubs. Put out straws, so the children can blow through them to make the sailboats move across the water. Let the children experiment with different types of toy boats, such as sailboats, rowboats, and speedboats. Put out small people figures and small items for the children to load on the boats. Talk with the children about how people can travel in boats, and how materials and equipment can be transported in boats. Talk about objects that float, such as boats, and those that sink, such as rocks. Let the children experiment with different items to see if they sink or float.

Why do I have children do this?

- To experiment with straws to make boats move (thinking, small muscle).
- To discuss how boats are used by people (thinking).
- To classify objects that float and those that sink (language).

What do I need?

1. Water table or tub of water.
2. Blue food coloring.
3. Paper triangles.
4. Straws.
5. Glue.
6. Small margarine tubs.
7. Toy boats, such as sailboats, rowboats, and speedboats.
8. People figures.
9. Small items.

What might I see children doing?

- Blowing through straws to see if boats move.
- Laughing.
- Talking about boats.
- Experimenting with items that float and items that sink.

What might I talk about with children?

1. What kinds of boats have you used for transportation?
2. How does it feel to ride in a sailboat?

NUTS AND BOLTS FOR VEHICLE REPAIRS
Learning Center (woodworking)

What do I do?

When the dramatic play activity "Cynthia's Service Station and Car Wash" on page 449, is set up, let the children three years old and up, who do not put objects in their mouths, come to the woodworking area. Put several different-sized nuts and bolts in the empty sand table or a plastic tub. (You can use real nuts and bolts or large plastic ones that are available from early childhood catalogs.) Tell the children that when vehicles don't work, nuts and bolts are often used to repair them. Let the children match same-sized nuts and bolts and twist the nut onto the bolt. Talk with the children about where else nuts and bolts are used. Ask them if they have ever helped their parents take nuts and bolts apart.

Why do I have children do this?

- To match nuts and bolts (thinking, small muscle).
- To assemble the nuts and bolts (small muscle).

What do I need?

1. Real nuts and bolts.
2. Large plastic nuts and bolts.
3. Empty sand table or plastic tub.

What might I see children doing?

- Matching nuts and bolts.
- Assembling nuts and bolts.
- Talking.

What might I talk about with children?

1. Where do you use nuts and bolts?
2. Why are nuts and bolts needed to make vehicle repairs?

TRANSPORTATION IN THE WOODWORKING AREA
Learning Center (woodworking)

What do I do?

Set out small pieces of white pine wood, wheels that you purchase or cut from dowel rods, nails, hammers, saws, sandpaper, and glue. Propellers can be made from circular plastic lids. Then let the children build vehicles if they choose. Do not expect them to make specific vehicles. Introduce each tool and explain how it is used and how to use it safely. Provide a place for the children to hang or put away the tools and materials after they are finished using them. Have the children wear safety goggles and provide carpenters' aprons and hats for them to wear. Two sets of safety goggles in the area makes it easy to limit the number of children allowed in the area.

Why do I have children do this?

- To hammer and saw the wood (small muscle).
- To enjoy using the woodworking equipment (social-emotional).

What do I need?

1. Workbench.
2. White pine wood.
3. Purchased wheels or wheel cut from dowel rods.
4. Nails.
5. Hammers.
6. Saws.
7. Sandpaper.
8. Glue.
9. Plastic lids.
10. Safety goggles.
11. Carpenters' aprons.
12. Carpenters' caps.

What might I see children doing?

- Putting on safety goggles.
- Hammering.
- Sawing.
- Gluing.
- Talking.

What might I talk about with children?

1. What can you do with this hammer?
2. Who uses these tools at your house?

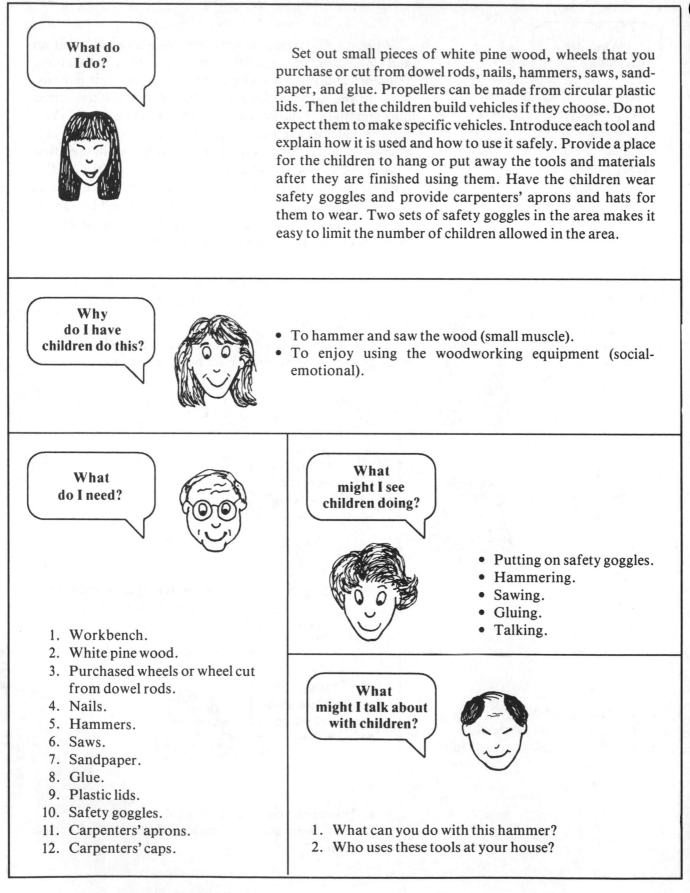

WE NEED PASSPORTS
Learning Center (writing)

What do I do?

Show the children your passport if you have one. Fold sheets of construction paper in half and give one to each child. Put out crayons, markers, and glue. Take photographs of each child and let him or her attach it to his or her passport. Let the children write their names under their pictures if they wish or you can write their names for them. Talk with the children about what a passport is and explain that when people travel outside of their countries, they need to carry passports, so other people will know what country they are from and who they are. Show the children a globe or map of the world and point out the United States, so they can become aware of where it is located. If they want to locate other countries, help them find them. Then, write each child's address under his or her name. Put U.S.A. on the front of the passport and let each child stamp his or her passport with a rubber stamp with a design on it. (This is not the official seal, but they will enjoy the process.)

Why do I have children do this?

- To talk about why people need passports (language).
- To stamp passports.

What do I need?

1. Passport.
2. Construction paper.
3. Crayons.
4. Markers.
5. Glue.
6. Camera.
7. Film.
8. Globe or map of the world.
9. Rubber stamp.
10. Stamp pad.

What might I see children doing?

- Looking at real passport.
- Writing names.
- Watching you write addresses.
- Looking at map or globe.
- Stamping passports.

What might I talk about with children?

1. Where would you like to go to use your passport?
2. Where are some other places that you need to write your name?

ROAD MAPS
Learning Center (writing)

What do I do?

Hang several road maps and a map that you've made of the playground on the wall at the children's eye level. Talk with the children about the road maps the children's parents may have in their cars. Talk with the children about why people use road maps and how road maps help people figure out how to get somewhere, such as a friend's house or Walt Disney World®. Put out newsprint, markers, crayons, and pencils on a table, so the children can make their own road maps. Add old magazines and catalogs that they can use to illustrate their road maps. This activity is more appropriate for four- and five-year-olds.

Why do I have children do this?

- To talk about using road maps to figure out how to get somewhere (language).
- To make their own road maps (thinking, small muscle).

What do I need?

What might I see children doing?

- Looking at road maps.
- Making road maps.
- Illustrating road maps.
- Talking to one another.
- Using their road maps in play.

1. Road maps.
2. Map of playground.
3. Newsprint.
4. Markers.
5. Crayons.
6. Pencils.
7. Old magazines and catalogs.

What might I talk about with children?

1. Where do your parents keep their road maps?
2. Why do you need road maps when you travel?

A TRUCK ON THE PLAYGROUND
Outdoor Large Muscle, Learning Center (dramatic play)

What do I do?

Place a wooden freight box large enough for two or three children to climb into on concrete blocks in the playground. You may need to sand the boards of the box to ensure the safety of the children and prevent splinters. Drill a few holes in the bottom of the box to let water drain out after it rains. Put a bench for the children to sit on in the box. Attach an old steering wheel to the box. On different days, put different props in the box to represent various types of trucks. For example, put in a coil of old hose to represent a fire truck, several different-sized boxes to represent a delivery truck, or a rope attached to a tricycle behind the box to represent a tow truck. Make a STOP sign and provide a police officer's hat for the children to use. Put out tricycles and scooters.

Why do I have children do this?

- To use imagination to change from fire engine to delivery truck to tow truck (thinking).
- To pedal tricycles (large muscle).

What do I need?

What might I see children doing?

- Driving truck.
- Pedaling tricycles.
- Acting like police officer.
- Having fun.

1. Large wooden freight box.
2. Concrete blocks.
3. Drill.
4. Bench.
5. Old steering wheel.
6. Old hose.
7. Different-sized boxes.
8. Rope.
9. Tricycles.
10. STOP sign.
11. Police officer's hat.
12. Scooters.

What might I talk about with children?

1. Where are you driving this delivery truck?
2. What are you delivering today?

SURVEY TEAM
Outdoor Large Muscle, Learning Center (math)

What do I do?

Talk to four- and five-year-olds about how they are going to go outside and count vehicles that go by the corner. Let them cut out pictures of a car, truck, bus, bicycle, and pedestrian from old magazines and glue them to a sheet of paper to make a chart. Walk to the corner with the children and sit in the grass as far away from the street as possible. When they see one of the types of vehicles go by, let them make a mark with a crayon beside the picture of the appropriate vehicle on their charts. Then bring the charts back inside and hang them on the wall or a bulletin board. Talk with the children about the types of vehicles that went by the corner and count the marks on the charts. Explain how street construction people also count vehicles to decide if a corner is busy enough for a STOP sign or traffic light.

Why do I have children do this?

- To observe traffic (thinking).
- To make a mark for each vehicle on chart (thinking).
- To talk about vehicles (language).

What do I need?

1. Old magazines.
2. Scissors.
3. Paper.
4. Glue.
5. Crayons.

What might I see children doing?

- Watching traffic.
- Marking charts by appropriate vehicles.
- Talking.
- Counting vehicles.

What might I talk about with children?

1. What kind of vehicles did you see on our street?
2. What do you think the trucks were hauling?

PARACHUTE PLAY
Outdoor Large Muscle

What do I do?

Talk with the children about how people sometimes jump out of airplanes and parachute to the ground. Provide a bright parachute from the early childhood catalogs or a queen- or king-sized sheet for parachute play. Have the children stand all around the parachute and lift it high over their heads and then down again. Put a ball in the center of the parachute and have the children gently move the parachute to keep the ball bouncing. Let the children lift the parachute high and have a child from each side run under it while it is up in the air. Let the children make waves with the parachute by moving it up and down slowly and then more rapidly. Have the children lift the parachute as high as they can reach and drop it. As the parachute falls, have the children fall under it, roll out from under it, and stand again. Let the children suggest other activities to do with the parachute.

Why do I have children do this?

- To lift the parachute (large muscle).
- To choose a different activity to do with the parachute (thinking).

What do I need?

1. Parachute or queen- or king-sized sheet.
2. Ball.

What might I see children doing?

- Lifting parachute.
- Bouncing ball on parachute.
- Running under parachute.
- Having fun.

What might I talk about with children?

1. What else could you do with this parachute?
2. Why are parachutes carried in some airplanes?

TRAVELING TO A PRETEND LAKE
Outdoor Large Muscle

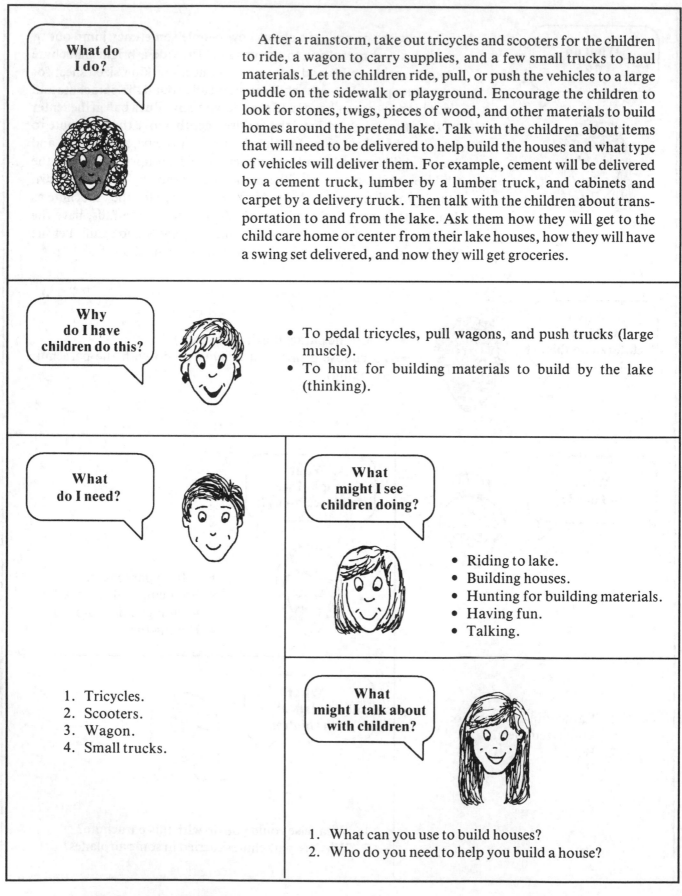

What do I do?

After a rainstorm, take out tricycles and scooters for the children to ride, a wagon to carry supplies, and a few small trucks to haul materials. Let the children ride, pull, or push the vehicles to a large puddle on the sidewalk or playground. Encourage the children to look for stones, twigs, pieces of wood, and other materials to build homes around the pretend lake. Talk with the children about items that will need to be delivered to help build the houses and what type of vehicles will deliver them. For example, cement will be delivered by a cement truck, lumber by a lumber truck, and cabinets and carpet by a delivery truck. Then talk with the children about transportation to and from the lake. Ask them how they will get to the child care home or center from their lake houses, how they will have a swing set delivered, and now they will get groceries.

Why do I have children do this?

- To pedal tricycles, pull wagons, and push trucks (large muscle).
- To hunt for building materials to build by the lake (thinking).

What do I need?

What might I see children doing?

- Riding to lake.
- Building houses.
- Hunting for building materials.
- Having fun.
- Talking.

1. Tricycles.
2. Scooters.
3. Wagon.
4. Small trucks.

What might I talk about with children?

1. What can you use to build houses?
2. Who do you need to help you build a house?

DRIVING ON AN EXPRESSWAY
Outdoor Large Muscle

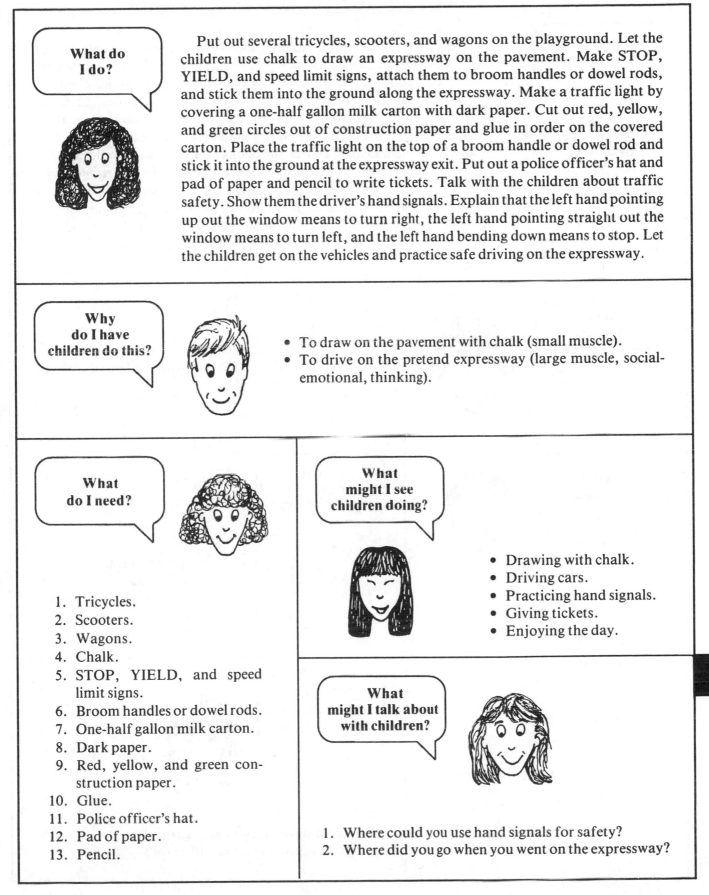

What do I do?

Put out several tricycles, scooters, and wagons on the playground. Let the children use chalk to draw an expressway on the pavement. Make STOP, YIELD, and speed limit signs, attach them to broom handles or dowel rods, and stick them into the ground along the expressway. Make a traffic light by covering a one-half gallon milk carton with dark paper. Cut out red, yellow, and green circles out of construction paper and glue in order on the covered carton. Place the traffic light on the top of a broom handle or dowel rod and stick it into the ground at the expressway exit. Put out a police officer's hat and pad of paper and pencil to write tickets. Talk with the children about traffic safety. Show them the driver's hand signals. Explain that the left hand pointing up out the window means to turn right, the left hand pointing straight out the window means to turn left, and the left hand bending down means to stop. Let the children get on the vehicles and practice safe driving on the expressway.

Why do I have children do this?

- To draw on the pavement with chalk (small muscle).
- To drive on the pretend expressway (large muscle, social-emotional, thinking).

What do I need?

1. Tricycles.
2. Scooters.
3. Wagons.
4. Chalk.
5. STOP, YIELD, and speed limit signs.
6. Broom handles or dowel rods.
7. One-half gallon milk carton.
8. Dark paper.
9. Red, yellow, and green construction paper.
10. Glue.
11. Police officer's hat.
12. Pad of paper.
13. Pencil.

What might I see children doing?

- Drawing with chalk.
- Driving cars.
- Practicing hand signals.
- Giving tickets.
- Enjoying the day.

What might I talk about with children?

1. Where could you use hand signals for safety?
2. Where did you go when you went on the expressway?

TIRE GARDENS
Outdoor Large Muscle, Learning Center (food, manipulatives, science)

What do I do?

Talk with the children about how old tires on vehicles need to be changed for safety reasons. Tell the children that they are going to plant gardens in old tires. Choose small plants or seeds, such as carrots, radishes, cherry tomatoes, peas, lettuce, and watermelon, for the children to plant. Have them help you fill the tires with soil and plant the seeds or plants. Let them help you check the plants each day to see if they need to be watered or weeded. When the vegetables are ripe, harvest them and prepare them for snacks. The children will probably eat the vegetables they harvest, although they might not usually eat them. Talk with the children about nutrition and how important vegetables are for helping them grow.

Why do I have children do this?

- To dig in the garden (large muscle).
- To choose seeds or plants that they wish to plant (thinking).

What do I need?

1. Old tires.
2. Soil.
3. Small plants or seeds.
4. Small shovels.
5. Small rakes.
6. Small hoes.
7. Watering can or garden hose.

What might I see children doing?

- Shoveling soil.
- Raking soil.
- Planting seeds or plants.
- Watering plants.
- Watching the garden.

What might I talk about with children?

1. What did you plant in your garden?
2. Which vegetables do you like best?

PAINT THE AIRPORT
Outdoor Large Muscle

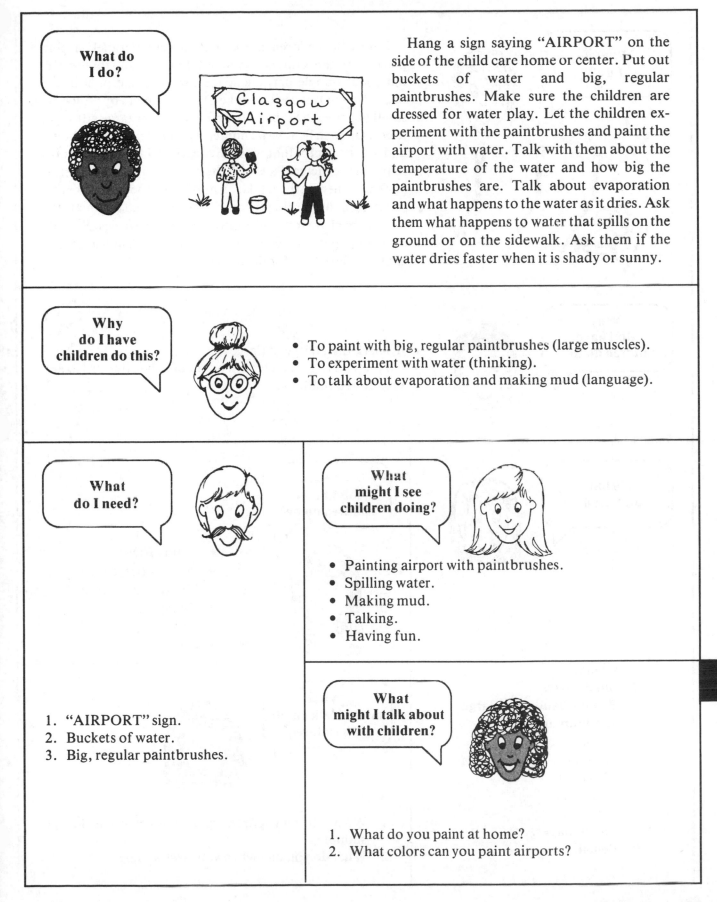

What do I do?

Hang a sign saying "AIRPORT" on the side of the child care home or center. Put out buckets of water and big, regular paintbrushes. Make sure the children are dressed for water play. Let the children experiment with the paintbrushes and paint the airport with water. Talk with them about the temperature of the water and how big the paintbrushes are. Talk about evaporation and what happens to the water as it dries. Ask them what happens to water that spills on the ground or on the sidewalk. Ask them if the water dries faster when it is shady or sunny.

Why do I have children do this?

- To paint with big, regular paintbrushes (large muscles).
- To experiment with water (thinking).
- To talk about evaporation and making mud (language).

What do I need?

1. "AIRPORT" sign.
2. Buckets of water.
3. Big, regular paintbrushes.

What might I see children doing?

- Painting airport with paintbrushes.
- Spilling water.
- Making mud.
- Talking.
- Having fun.

What might I talk about with children?

1. What do you paint at home?
2. What colors can you paint airports?

PARK YOUR VAN
Outdoor Large Muscle

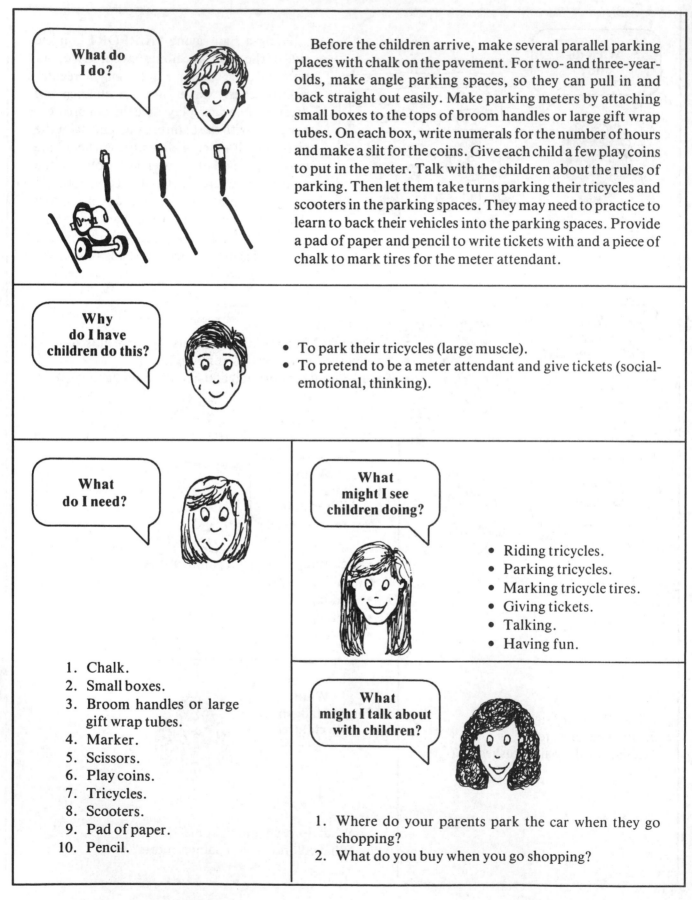

What do I do?

Before the children arrive, make several parallel parking places with chalk on the pavement. For two- and three-year-olds, make angle parking spaces, so they can pull in and back straight out easily. Make parking meters by attaching small boxes to the tops of broom handles or large gift wrap tubes. On each box, write numerals for the number of hours and make a slit for the coins. Give each child a few play coins to put in the meter. Talk with the children about the rules of parking. Then let them take turns parking their tricycles and scooters in the parking spaces. They may need to practice to learn to back their vehicles into the parking spaces. Provide a pad of paper and pencil to write tickets with and a piece of chalk to mark tires for the meter attendant.

Why do I have children do this?

- To park their tricycles (large muscle).
- To pretend to be a meter attendant and give tickets (social-emotional, thinking).

What do I need?

1. Chalk.
2. Small boxes.
3. Broom handles or large gift wrap tubes.
4. Marker.
5. Scissors.
6. Play coins.
7. Tricycles.
8. Scooters.
9. Pad of paper.
10. Pencil.

What might I see children doing?

- Riding tricycles.
- Parking tricycles.
- Marking tricycle tires.
- Giving tickets.
- Talking.
- Having fun.

What might I talk about with children?

1. Where do your parents park the car when they go shopping?
2. What do you buy when you go shopping?

TRAIN TOSS
Indoor or Outdoor Large Muscle

What do I do?

Cut the tops off eight cardboard boxes with an X-Acto® knife. Tie the boxes together with rope to make a train. Let the children paint each box a different color, using red, yellow, green, blue, brown, black, purple, and orange tempera paint. Use only red, yellow, green, and blue paint with two-year-olds and young three-year-olds. (Mix liquid detergent in the paint, so the paint will wash out of clothes easier.) Place a large plastic cloth under the boxes and provide smocks or old dress shirts for the children to wear. When the paint on the boxes is dry, put out red, yellow, green, blue, brown, black, purple, and orange beanbags. Then let the children throw beanbags into matching train cars. Ask the children to find other green objects on the playground.

Why do I have children do this?

- To match colored beanbag and train car (thinking).
- To throw a beanbag into the appropriately-colored train car (thinking, large muscle).

What do I need?

1. Eight cardboard boxes.
2. X-Acto® knife.
3. Rope.
4. Red, yellow, green, blue, brown, black, purple, and orange tempera paint.
5. Liquid detergent.
6. Paintbrushes.
7. Large plastic cloth.
8. Smocks or old dress shirts.
9. Red, yellow, green, blue, brown, black, purple, and orange beanbags.

What might I see children doing?

- Choosing beanbag.
- Throwing beanbag into matching train car.
- Looking for colors on playground.

What might I talk about with children?

1. How else can this train be used?
2. What color is your family car?

BIBLIOGRAPHY

TRANSPORTATION

[2,3]Arnold, C. 1983. *How Do We Travel?* New York, NY: Franklin Watts.
Describes the various kinds of vehicles used in the community, including bicycles, motorcycles, cars, trucks, buses, trains, boats, airplanes, and helicopters.

Awdry, Rev.W. 1993. *Thomas and the School Trip*. New York, NY: Random House.
A bright, cheery book that shows the trains getting ready for work as the children come from school to visit. Thomas hopes to get back from his work in time to take them home. It illustrates all the adventures in his day.

[3]Baker, E. 1972. *I Want to Be a Service Station Attendant*. Chicago, IL: Children's Press.
Describes the duties of a service station attendant.

[1]Barton, B. 1982. *Airport*. New York, NY: HarperCollins Children's Books.
Bold, colorful pictures and simple phrases describe what happens from the time an airplane passenger arrives at an airport to when the airplane is in the air.

Bingham, C. 2001. *Big Book of Airplanes*. New York, NY: Doolick Kindersley.
Distinctive pictures and descriptions of many airplanes.

Burton, V.L. 1988. *Choo Choo: The Story of a Little Engine Who Ran Away*. Boston, MA: Houghton Mifflin Co.
Choo Choo decides to see the world beyond its daily route.

[3]Chlad, D. 1983. *Stop, Look, and Listen for Trains*. Chicago, IL: Children's Press.
Greg briefly describes the types of cars on freight and passenger trains. He presents tips for safety at railroad tracks and crossings. Simple text and bold illustrations.

[3]Chlad, D. 1985. *Riding on a Bus*. Chicago, IL: Children's Press.
A child describes the safety precautions he and his friends take while riding on buses. Simple text and bold illustrations.

[2]Cole, J. 1987. *The Magic School Bus Inside the Earth*. New York, NY: Scholastic Inc.
Ms. Frizzle's class explores "Inside the Earth" on an imaginary school bus and learns a great deal about rocks, sod, and layers of earth.

[1]Crews, D. 1978. *Freight Train*. New York, NY: Greenwillow Books.
A brief text and colorful illustrations trace the journey of a train as it goes through tunnels, by cities, and over trestles. It also teaches about colors.

[1]Crews, D. 1982. *Harbor*. New York, NY: Greenwillow Books.
This picture book presents various kinds of boats that come and go in a busy harbor.

[1]Crews, D. 1986. *Flying*. New York, NY: Greenwillow Books.
A colorful book with few words that talks about an airplane taking off, flying, and
    landing. It also describes what an airplane might fly over, such as highways,
    rivers, and cities.

[2,3]Dupasquier, P. 1984. *The Airport*. New York, NY: Grosset and Dunlap.
Very busy illustrations depict a hectic day, from morning to night, at an airport. This
    book is full of action and excitement.

[2,3]Dupasquier, P. 1984. *The Service Station*. New York, NY: Grosset and Dunlap.
Busy illustrations depict a hectic day's activities at a service station.

[2,3]Dupasquier, P. 1984. *The Train Station*. New York, NY: Grosset and Dunlap.
Very busy illustrations depict a hectic day at a train station. This book is full of
    action and excitement.

Edwards, J. 2000. *Dumpy, The Dump Truck*. New York, NY: Hyperion Books.
An old dump truck is rebuilt for use on the farm.

[3]Fowler, R. 1986. *Mr. Little's Noisy Car*. New York, NY: Grosset and Dunlap.
Pop-up book that describes car noises. Labels parts of a car and has illustrations of
    animals.

[2]Gibbons, G. 1981. *Trucks*. New York, NY: HarperCollins Children's Books.
Detailed illustrations present a variety of trucks that work around people every day.

Gibbons, G. 1983. *Boat Book*. New York, NY: Holiday House.
Introduces many kinds of boats and ships, such as rowboats, canoes, sailboats,
    speedboats, cruise ships, submarines, tugboats, and tankers, and their uses.

Gramatky, H. 1988. *Little Toot*. New York, NY: G.P. Putnam's Sons.
Little Toot shows the other tugboats that he can work as hard as they do when he
    saves the great cruise ship.

Hoban, T. 1975. *Dig, Drill, Dump, Fill*. New York, NY: Greenwillow Books.
Photographs alone introduce heavy construction machines, such as earthmovers,
    mixers, and diggers.

[2,3]Holland, M., and Cooper, D. 1986. *A Look Around Space*. Pinellas Park, FL:
    Willowisp Press, Inc.
Discussion of outer space with information regarding space shuttles and lunar rovers.

Horenstein, H. 1989. *Sam Goes Trucking*. Boston, MA: Houghton Mifflin Company.
Description of Sam's trip with his dad in his semi. Illustrations are very informative.

Keats, E.J. 1981. *Regards to the Man in the Moon*. New York, NY: Aladdin Books.
Louis and his friends travel through space with help from his parents, scraps of junk,
    and their imaginations.

[3]Kroll, S. 1983. *Toot! Toot!* New York, NY: Holiday House.
While playing with his toy train set, Lawrence imagines he is on a visit to his grandparents' farm.

[2,3]Magee, D. 1986. *Trucks You Can Count On.* New York, NY: G.P. Putnam's Sons.
Photographs and bold text introduce the tractor-trailer truck. The book also uses counting from one to ten and one to eighteen, as the reader counts the number of parts on the truck and the number of wheels.

Macmillan Educational Company. 1988. *Macmillan Sing and Learn Program: Large Motor Skills.* Hicksville, NY.
Music that helps children do interesting movements, such as hopping, jumping, waddling, and skipping.

Macmillan Educational Company. 1989. *Macmillan Sing and Learn Program: Classroom Games.* Hicksville, NY.
Songs to use to play games with children in child care.

McPhail, D. 1977. *The Train.* Boston, MA: Little, Brown and Company.
The story is about a young boy's ride on his toy train.

Millang, S., and Scelsa, G. 1983. *On the Move with Greg and Steve.* Los Angeles, CA: Youngheart Records.
Music with a contemporary beat that invites children to move with rhythm and sing, feel, and grow.

Oxenbury, H. 1983. *The Car Trip.* New York, NY: Dial Books for Young Readers.
A funny story about a small boy's car trip. His experiences include having to go to the bathroom and getting carsick.

Peet, B. 1980. *The Caboose Who Got Loose.* Boston, MA: Houghton Mifflin Company.
Katy Caboose wishes to be free of the train, and her wish comes true. Children will enjoy the story of Katy's adventure.

[2,3]Petersen, D. 1981. *Airplanes: A New True Book.* Chicago, IL: Children's Press.
A basic introduction to many kinds of airplanes, and some of the jobs they do. Illustrated with colorful photographs.

[3]Petty, K. 1984. *On a Plane.* New York, NY: Franklin Watts, Inc.
Full-color illustrations and easy-to-read text take the reader on an airplane trip with a family. The book talks about airplanes, airports, customs procedures, baggage, pilots, flight attendants, and air traffic controllers.

Piper, W. 1981. *The Little Engine That Could.* Cuchogue, NY: Buccaneer Books.
The classic story about a little blue engine that with encouragement from friends pulled the little train over the mountain as he said, "I think I can. I think I can."

[2]Provenesen, A., and Provenesen, M. 1987. *The Glorious Flight.* New York, NY: Puffin Books.
Conveys the exciting and historic story of Mr. Louis Bleriot's flight across the English Channel.

[3]Quackenbush, R. 1981. *City Trucks*. Chicago, IL: Albert Whitman and Company.
Features the various trucks that are part of a city's maintenance and transportation
   system.

Reif, P. 1999. *Look Inside Trucks*. New York, NY: Scholastic, Inc.
The youngest truck lovers can see how a dump truck moves, how a moving van carries furniture, and how construction trucks are used.

[3]Rey, M., and Shalleck, A.J. 1987. *Curious George at the Airport*. Boston, MA:
   Houghton Mifflin Company.
Curious George goes to the airport.

[3]Rey, M., and Shalleck, A.J. 1988. *Curious George at the Railroad Station*. Boston,
   MA: Houghton Mifflin.
Curious George goes to the railroad station.

Rockwell, A. 1984. *Cars*. New York, NY: Dutton Children's Books.
A lively, colorful book about cars, what they do, and where they can go.

[1]Rockwell, A. 1984. *Trucks*. New York, NY: Dutton Children's Books.
Introduces a variety of trucks and their purposes. Includes moving vans, tow trucks,
   bookmobiles, and campers.

[1]Rockwell, A. 1985. *Boats*. New York, NY: Dutton Children's Books.
A simple look at boats and ships of varying sizes and their uses.

[1]Rockwell, A. 1989. *Things That Go*. New York, NY: Dutton Children's Books.
A picture book of things that go, such as trains, tow trucks, sailboats, buses, sleds,
   jeeps, and bicycles. They are categorized by where they can be seen: on water,
   on the road, in the air, on snow and ice, and in the city.

[1]Rockwell, A. 1989. *Planes*. New York, NY: Dutton Children's Books.
A simple text and illustrations introduce different types of airplanes and where they go.

[1,3]Rockwell, A., and Rockwell, H. 1972. *Thruway*. New York, NY: The
   Macmillan Company.
The reader travels through tollbooths, traffic lanes, cloverleafs, and drawbridges.
   Introduces children to the vocabulary of the thruway.

[3]Rogers, F. 1989. *Going on an Airplane*. New York, NY: G.P. Putnam's Sons.
Bright, colorful pictures show a modern airport facility.

[3]Ross, P., and Ross, J. 1981. *Your First Airplane Trip*. New York, NY: Lothrop, Lee
   and Shepard Books.
Takes the reader on an airplane trip with two children. It gives an account of what ordi-
   narily happens when children travel by themselves on a commercial airplane.

Royston, A. 1991. *Cars*. New York, NY: Aladdin Books.
Describes different kinds of cars, such as sports, vintage, racing, and sedan, with
   bright colorful pictures.

Royston, A. 1993. *My Lift-the-Flaps Plane Book*. New York, NY: G.P. Putnam's Sons.
Children are shown all the interesting things involved in using airplanes as transportation. The lift-the-flaps detail illustrates the answers to all the questions children ask about air travel—fuel, luggage, food, bathroom, pilots, and landing.

[3]Seaman, J. 1988. *Bucklebear Video*. Glendale, CA: Weinger-Seaman Productions.
A video that teaches seat belt safety to children. Based on the teacher's kit "Riding with Bucklebear."

[3]Seaman, J. 1982. "Riding with Bucklebear." Glendale, CA: Weiner-Seaman Productions.
A teacher's kit for seat belt safety that includes patterns for felt board figures and puppets, a guidebook with stories and plays, and a clicker to use to buckle a seat belt.

Shaw, N. 1989. *Sheep on a Ship*. Boston, MA: Houghton Mifflin Company.
Rhyming words are used to tell the story of sheep that go on a sailing trip. Pictures illustrate the dangers.

Siebert, D. 1987. *Truck Song*. New York, NY: HarperCollins Children's Books.
Over highways, through hills and valleys, the author follows a trucker and his rig across the country.

Siebert, D. 1990. *Train Song*. New York, NY: HarperCollins Children's Books.
Through cities, suburbs, and countrysides, the voyage of the train is detailed in rhyming text with illustrations that are colorful and descriptive.

Zelinsky, P. 2000. *The Wheels on the Bus*. New York, NY: Penguin Putnam Books.
This is a pop-up version of the old favorite.

We have marked these books if we think they are definitely more applicable to one age. Many can be used by all ages with adaptations by the teacher.

[1]Books for one-year-olds, two-year-olds, and three-year-olds.

[2]Books for five-year-olds.

[3]This book is no longer in print. However, you may be able to find it at your local library.

APPENDIX A

EENCY, WEENCY SPIDER PUPPET STAGE

       plastic strawberry basket
4   straws
2   pom-poms
       yarn
       glue
       orange and white construction paper
       scissors

1. Attach a straw waterspout to the side of plastic strawberry basket.
2. Glue two pom-poms together and glue on yarn legs to make a spider.
3. Cut out a sun from orange construction paper.
4. Cut out a cloud from white construction paper. Glue yarn off the sides to represent rain.
5. Attach the spider, sun, and cloud to straws, so each can be moved up and down in the basket with the action.

FELT BOARD FIGURES

       coloring books (for child care providers only), books, or drawings
       pencil
       fusible interfacing
       permanent markers
       iron
       felt
       scissors

1. Trace figures from coloring books, books, or drawings onto fusible interfacing.
2. Color figures with permanent markers.
3. Iron figures onto felt.
4. Cut out individual figures.

...er's® white glue and one part liquid starch in a mixing bowl with your
...of kneading to get rid of the moisture and achieve the correct consis-

...y and store in an airtight container when not in use.

...G CARDS

coloring books (for child care providers only)
poster board
scissors
markers
self-adhesive plastic
hole punch
yarn
masking tape

1. Trace patterns from coloring books onto poster board and cut them out.
2. Draw in the details of the pattern with brightly-colored markers and cover with self-adhesive
   plastic.
3. Punch two holes at each space for children under three years old. Punch holes along the
   edge, spacing the holes further apart for younger children.
4. Tie one end of a piece of yarn through a hole on each card and wrap masking tape tightly
   one and one-half inches from the end of the other end to make a needle.

PLAYDOUGH

    2   tablespoons vegetable oil
    1   cup flour
   1/2   cup salt
    2   teaspoons cream of tartar
    1   cup water
         food coloring
         few drops of peppermint extract

1. Turn burner on high*, pour oil in a pot, and coat all sides of pot.
2. Mix all ingredients in the pot with a large spoon.
3. Turn burner to low and cook for 3 minutes, stirring continually.
4. Let mixture cool.
5. Knead the mixture.
6. Store in self-sealing plastic bags in the refrigerator. It lasts forever. (If it gets sticky, add more flour.)

*Adults should do the cooking on the range over high heat.

PUPPET GLOVES

    coloring books (for child care providers only), books, or drawings.
    pencil
    fusible interfacing
    permanent markers
    iron
    felt
    scissors
    glove
    adhesive-backed Velcro® hook and loop tape strips

1. Trace figures from coloring books, books, or drawings onto fusible interfacing.
2. Color figures with permanent markers.
3. Iron figures onto felt.
4. Cut out individual figures.
5. Attach figures to the fingers of a glove with strips of adhesive Velcro®.

PUZZLE

(Makes 1 puzzle)
 wood or heavy cardboard
 pictures
 glue
 band saw or X-Acto® knife
 sandpaper
 lacquer, varnish, or clear acrylic finish
 self-adhesive plastic

1. Cut 2 pieces of 9 x 12" wood or heavy cardboard.
2. Glue or draw many different simple pictures on one of the 9 x 12" sections.
3. Cut the individual pictures out with a band saw on the wood or an X-Acto® knife on the cardboard.
4. Glue the frame that remains after you cut out the pieces onto the remaining 9 x 12" section.
5. Sand the edges of the puzzle, frame, and puzzle pieces until they are smooth.
6. Cover the wood puzzle and pieces with lacquer, varnish, or clear acrylic finish.
7. Cover the cardboard puzzle and pieces with self-adhesive plastic.

AGGRESSION COOKIES

(Makes 3 dozen cookies)

3	cups oatmeal
1 1/2	cups brown sugar
1 1/2	teaspoons baking powder
1 1/2	cups flour
1 1/2	cups butter

1. Mix all the ingredients together in a large bowl.
2. Then take the dough and mash it! Knead it! Pound it!
3. Roll the dough into small balls on waxed paper. Place dough balls on a lightly-greased cookie sheet about two inches apart.
4. Bake at 350°F for 10 to 12 minutes.

BIRD NESTS

(Makes four bird nests)

1	cup wheat cereal
1/2	cup coconut
1/2	cup peanut butter

1. Mix the ingredients together in a bowl with a wooden spoon.
2. Stir mixture until it sticks together. (If needed, add more peanut butter.)
3. Mold the mixture into little nests.

CHERRY PIE

(Makes one pie)

2	cups sifted flour
1	teaspoon salt
2/3	cup shortening
5 to 7	tablespoons of ice water
1	can of cherry pie filling

1. Sift flour and salt together into a mixing bowl.
2. Cut in shortening with fork.
3. Sprinkle water over the mixture and blend with a mixing spoon until moist.
4. Place the dough on a piece of waxed paper sprinkled with flour. Roll dough with a rolling pin until it is large enough to fit a nine-inch pie plate.
5. Place the rolled dough in the pie plate and fill with cherry pie filling.
6. Bake at 400°F for 40 minutes.

CHICKEN RICE SOUP

(Makes 6 to 8 small servings)

1	large can chicken broth
1	large can water
4	chicken bouillon cubes
1	small onion (chopped)
	carrots and celery stalks (chopped)
1 1/2	cups rice
	salt and pepper to taste

1. Combine all ingredients in a 4-quart soup pot.
2. Add salt and pepper to taste.
3. Cook on range until vegetables are tender, stirring occasionally.
4. Serve in cups.

HUMPTY DUMPTY DEVILED EGGS

(Makes two deviled eggs)

1	dyed hard-boiled egg
1	teaspoon mayonnaise
1/8	teaspoon sweet pickle juice
1/8	teaspoon prepared mustard
	dash salt
	dash pepper
	paprika

1. Crack the eggshell, peel off the eggshell, and save.
2. Cut egg in half lengthwise with a plastic knife.
3. Scoop yolk into bowl. Set whites aside.
4. Mash the yolk with fork.
5. Stir in mayonnaise, sweet pickle juice, prepared mustard, salt, and pepper until well blended.
6. Refill whites with yolk mixture.
7. Place on plate. Sprinkle with paprika. Chill to blend flavors.

ICE POPS

(Makes eight ice pops)

1	package orange-flavored gelatin
2	cups boiling water
2	cups orange juice

1. Open package of orange-flavored gelatin and pour it into bowl. (What does the gelatin smell like? What does it feel like?)
2. Pour boiling water into a bowl. Let the children stir as you supervise them. (Why is steam coming off the water?)
3. Add orange juice to bowl and stir. (What has happened to the liquid mixture?)
4. Dip the mixture into 5 oz. paper cups. (What can we use to move the mixture from the bowl to the cups?)
5. Put paper cups in the freezer to freeze until slushy. (What do you think will happen to the ice pops?)
6. When the ice pop mixture is slushy, put sticks in paper cups and return to freezer. (What happened to the ice pops in the freezer?)

MORTAR MIX

(Makes two cups)

- 1 carrot
- 1/2 cup raisins
- 3 oz. cream cheese
- 1/2 cup peanut butter
- 1 teaspoon honey
- graham crackers

1. Let the children grate the carrot and mix it with raisins, cream cheese, peanut butter, and honey.
2. Give the children plastic knives to spread the mortar on the graham crackers.

MOTHER CAT'S PIE

(Makes one pie)

- 1 ready-made pie shell
- 1 package of instant vanilla pudding
- 2 cups milk
- 2 bananas

1. Pour package of instant pudding in bowl.
2. Pour milk in bowl
3. Mix with a rotary beater.
4. Cut up bananas and stir into pudding.
5. Pour the mixture into pie shell.
6. Place pie in refrigerator to chill for two to three hours.

PETER, PETER, PUMPKIN-EATER'S BREAD

(Makes two small loaves of bread)

4	eggs	2	teaspoons baking soda
3	cups sugar	1 1/2	teaspoons salt
1	cup vegetable oil	1	teaspoon nutmeg
2	cups canned pumpkin	1	teaspoon cinnamon
3 1/3	cups flour	2/3	cup water

(Continued)

PETER, PETER, PUMPKIN-EATER'S BREAD (Continued)

1. Mix the eggs, sugar, vegetable oil, and pumpkin together in large mixing bowl. Use a rotary beater.
2. Add the remaining ingredients and mix well using a mixing spoon.
3. Pour into two greased nine-by-five-by-three-inch pans.
4. Bake at 350°F for 1 to 1 1/2 hours or until toothpick comes out clean.
5. Cool on racks.

PUPPY DOG PEARS

(Makes one puppy dog pear)

    lettuce leaf
    pear half
2 peach wedges
    maraschino cherry halves

1. Place a lettuce leaf on a plate.
2. Place a pear half on the lettuce leaf.
3. Place a peach wedge on each side of the pear half.
4. Make eyes, nose, and mouth by placing maraschino cherry halves on the pear with round wood toothpicks. (Make sure that the children remove the toothpicks before eating their puppy dog pears.)

SCRAMBLED EGGS

(Makes one serving)

    egg
1 tablespoon milk
2 tablespoons butter or margarine

1. Crack egg into small bowl. (What does the egg look like? What color is the yolk and the egg white?)
2. Add milk. Mix egg and milk lightly with a fork or whisk. (What is happening to the egg?)
3. Melt butter or margarine in electric skillet. Pour egg mixture into electric skillet on low heat. (What happened to the butter or margarine?)
4. Stir egg with a wooden spoon slowly as it cooks. (What is happening to the egg as you stir it?)
5. Cook egg until solid and well done. Spoon the scrambled egg on to each child's plate. (How is the cooked egg different from the raw egg?)

SMOOTHIES

(Makes eight one-half cup servings)

  1   banana
  2   cups milk
  1   tablespoon peanut butter
      dash nutmeg

1. Mix the ingredients together using a blender.
2. Pour into small glasses.

STOP, GO, BE CAREFUL COOKIES

(Makes 6 dozen cookies)

  3/4   cup shortening
1 1/2 cups sugar
   3   eggs
1 1/2 tablespoons milk
   3   cups flour
      a dash of salt
   3   teaspoons baking powder
  3/4 teaspoon vanilla flavoring
      food coloring (red, yellow, green)

1. Cream shortening, sugar, and eggs together.
2. Add milk, flour, salt, baking powder, and vanilla.
3. Divide dough into three sections and place in small bowls.
4. Add one color food coloring (red, yellow, or green) to each bowl. Mix with the dough.
5. Chill dough 20 minutes.
6. Place dough on waxed paper. Roll dough with a rolling pin.
7. Cut out red, yellow, and green circles with circle-shaped cookie cutters and place on a cookie sheet.
8. Bake at 400°F for 8 minutes.